RESEARCH HANDBOOK ON POLITICAL PROPAGANDA

Research Handbook on Political Propaganda

Edited by

Gary D. Rawnsley

Professor of Public Diplomacy, School of International Studies and Dean, Faculty of Humanities and Social Sciences, University of Nottingham Ningbo China, China

Yiben Ma

Convenor of the Preliminary Year Programme for International Communications, Centre for English Language Education, University of Nottingham Ningbo China, China

Kruakae Pothong

Visiting Research Fellow, Department of Media and Communications, London School of Economics and Political Science, UK

Edward Elgar
PUBLISHING

Cheltenham, UK • Northampton, MA, USA

© Gary D. Rawnsley, Yiben Ma and Kruakae Pothong 2021

All rights reserved. No part of this publication may be reproduced, stored in a retrieval system or transmitted in any form or by any means, electronic, mechanical or photocopying, recording, or otherwise without the prior permission of the publisher.

Published by
Edward Elgar Publishing Limited
The Lypiatts
15 Lansdown Road
Cheltenham
Glos GL50 2JA
UK

Edward Elgar Publishing, Inc.
William Pratt House
9 Dewey Court
Northampton
Massachusetts 01060
USA

A catalogue record for this book
is available from the British Library

Library of Congress Control Number: 2021947839

This book is available electronically in the **Elgar**online
Political Science and Public Policy subject collection
http://dx.doi.org/10.4337/9781789906424

Printed on elemental chlorine free (ECF)
recycled paper containing 30% Post-Consumer Waste

ISBN 978 1 78990 641 7 (cased)
ISBN 978 1 78990 642 4 (eBook)

Printed and bound in the USA

Contents

List of figures viii
List of tables ix
List of contributors x

Introduction to the *Research Handbook on Political Propaganda* 1
Gary D. Rawnsley, Yiben Ma, and Kruakae Pothong

1 World propaganda and personal insecurity: intent, content, and contentment 7
  Naren Chitty

2 Fake news, trust, and behaviour in a digital world 28
  Terry Flew

3 Cambridge Analytica 41
  David R. Carroll

4 'Believe me': political propaganda in the age of Trump 51
  Gary D. Rawnsley

5 The information war paradox 67
  Peter Pomerantsev

6 Digital propaganda as symbolic convergence: the case of Russian ads during the 2016 US presidential election 80
  Corneliu Bjola and Ilan Manor

7 Getting the message right in Xi Jinping's China: propaganda, story-telling, and the challenge of reaching people's emotions 98
  Kerry Brown

8 Political communication in the age of media convergence in China 111
  Xiaoling Zhang and Yiben Ma

9 Xi Jinping's grand strategy for digital propaganda 127
  Titus C. Chen

10 Constructing its own reality: the CCP's agenda for the Hong Kong anti-extradition bill movement 143
   Luwei Rose Luqiu

11 Sexuality and politics: 'coming out' in German and Chinese queer films 156
   Hongwei Bao

12	The compassion 'spectacle': the propaganda of piety, virtuosity, and altruism within neoliberal politics *Colin Alexander*	168
13	Political propaganda and the global struggle against Apartheid, 1948–1994 *Nicholas J. Cull*	183
14	Refugees, migration, and propaganda *Gillian McFadyen*	197
15	Brexit uncertainties: political rhetoric versus British core values in the NHS *Georgia Spiliopoulos*	211
16	The media, antisemitism, and political warfare in Jeremy Corbyn's Labour Party, 2015–2019 *James R. Vaughan*	224
17	Terrorist propaganda *Afzal Ashraf*	243
18	Propaganda through participation: counterterrorism narratives in China *Chi Zhang*	257
19	Countermeasures to extremist propaganda: a strategy for countering absolutist religious beliefs in northeast Nigeria *Jacob Udo-Udo Jacob*	270
20	Imagined minorities: making 'real' images of ethnic harmony in Chinese tourism *Melissa Shani Brown and David O'Brien*	285
21	The language of protest: slogans and the construction of tourism contestation in Barcelona *Neil Hughes*	300
22	The Mexican 2018 presidential election in the media landscape: newspaper coverage, TV spots, and Twitter interaction *Rubén Arnoldo González*	315
23	Political propaganda and memes in Mexico: the 2018 presidential election *Penélope Franco Estrada and Gary D. Rawnsley*	333
24	Political parties, rallies, and propaganda in India *Andrew Wyatt*	347
25	Media and majoritarianism in India: eroding soft power? *Daya Thussu*	359
26	Korean cultural diplomacy in Laos: soft power, propaganda, and exploitation *Mary J. Ainslie*	373

| 27 | Fact-checking false claims and propaganda in the age of post-truth politics: the Brexit referendum
Jen Birks | 390 |
| 28 | Beyond the smear word: media literacy educators tackle contemporary propaganda
Renee Hobbs | 405 |

Index 421

Figures

10.1	Posts on the Hong Kong anti-government movement by CCTV and the *People's Daily*, 1 June–10 October 2019 (N = 1195)	145
22.1	Content of the spots	326
22.2	Candidates' interaction after the first debate	327
22.3	Candidates' interaction after the second debate	327
22.4	Candidates' interaction after the third debate	328
27.1	Polling from April 2015 to June 2016 (from the Referendum Act passing to the referendum poll date)	398
27.2	Polling indicating that voters were less worried about the impact of Brexit on their own wealth or income than that of the country	399

Tables

6.1	Topical categories of African American ads	88
6.2	Fantasy theme analysis of African American ads	91
6.3	Average number of impressions by ad type	94
6.4	Average number of clicks by issue	94
9.1	Major Internet content regulations issued in 2017 by the CAC	136
10.1	Targets of criticism by CCTV and the *People's Daily*, 1 June–10 October 2019	149
10.2	Online initiatives launched by CCTV and the *People's Daily*, 1 June–10 October 2019	153
19.1	Categories of absolutist beliefs	275
20.1	Visual signifiers of 'traditionality'	292
20.2	Positive and negative valences: implicit meanings of signifiers of 'traditionality'	292
21.1	Terrorist slogans	307
22.1	Press coverage of candidates and coalitions	322
22.2	Issues covered by the newspapers during the campaign	323
22.3	Actors included in the coverage of the campaigns	323
22.4	Proposals, rational arguments, and framing of the coverage	324
22.5	Indicators of personalisation in the 2018 Mexican presidential election TV spots	325
28.1	Media literacy theory aligned with high school lessons in contemporary propaganda	417

Contributors

Mary J. Ainslie is Associate Professor in Media and Communications and Deputy Head of School at the School of International Communications, University of Nottingham Ningbo China. Her research specialises in inter-cultural links across the Asia region and she has won funding from the Korea Foundation, the Academy of Korean Studies, and the Vidal Sassoon International Center for the Study of Anti-Semitism at the Hebrew University of Jerusalem, Israel. She is the author of *Anti-Semitism in Contemporary Malaysia: Malay Nationalism, Philosemitism and Pro-Israel Expressions* (Palgrave Macmillan, 2019).

Colin Alexander is Senior Lecturer in Political Communications at Nottingham Trent University, UK. He has spent much of his academic career writing about propaganda and political communications in different historical and contemporary contexts, focusing on public diplomacy, ethics, and the role of charity within society. He is the author of *China and Taiwan in Central America: Engaging Foreign Publics in Diplomacy* (2014) and *Administering Colonialism and War* (2019). He is the editor of *The Frontiers of Public Diplomacy: Hegemony, Morality and Power in the International Sphere* (2021).

Afzal Ashraf has a diverse career background including being a senior British military officer, holding a position in the UK Foreign and Commonwealth Office, and acting as a senior Counter Terrorism Advisor to a department of the UK Home Office. He holds a PhD from St Andrews University, UK in terrorist ideology. After working for the Royal United Services Institute (RUSI) think tank on international diplomacy issues, he became an Assistant Professor of International Relations and Security at the University of Nottingham, UK.

Hongwei Bao is Associate Professor in Media Studies at the University of Nottingham, UK, where he also directs the Centre for Contemporary East Asian Cultural Studies. His research primarily focuses on queer media and culture in contemporary China. He is the author of *Queer Comrades: Gay Identity and Tongzhi Activism in Postsocialist China* (NIAS Press, 2018), *Queer China: Lesbian and Gay Literature and Visual Culture under Postsocialism* (Routledge, 2020), and *Queer Media in China* (Routledge, 2021).

Jen Birks is Associate Professor of Media in the Department of Cultural, Media and Visual Studies at the University of Nottingham, UK, and co-convener of the Political Studies Association Media and Politics Group. Her research focuses on the role of publics, civil society and experts in political media and communication. She is the author of *News and Civil Society* and *Fact-checking Journalism and Political Argumentation*.

Corneliu Bjola is Associate Professor in Diplomatic Studies at the University of Oxford, UK, and Head of the Oxford Digital Diplomacy Research Group. His research focuses on the impact of digital technology on the conduct of diplomacy with a focus on strategic communication, digital influence, and methods for countering digital propaganda. He has authored or co-edited several volumes, including *Digital Diplomacy and International Organizations: Autonomy, Legitimacy and Contestation* (with R. Zaiotti, 2020), *Countering Online Propaganda and Violent Extremism: The Dark Side of Digital Diplomacy* (with J. Pamment, 2018), and *Digital*

Diplomacy: Theory and Practice (with M. Holmes, 2015). His work has been published in journals such as the *European Journal of International Relations, Review of International Studies, Ethics and International Affairs, International Negotiation, Cambridge Review of International Affairs*, and others.

Kerry Brown is Professor of Chinese Studies and Director of the Lau China Institute at King's College London, UK. He is an Associate of the Asia Pacific Programme at Chatham House, London, UK, an adjunct of the Australia New Zealand School of Government in Melbourne, and the co-editor of the *Journal of Current Chinese Affairs*, run from the German Institute for Global Affairs in Hamburg. He is the author of over 20 books on modern China.

Melissa Shani Brown is an affiliate with East Asian Politics at Ruhr University Bochum, Germany. She is interdisciplinary in both interests and training, informing a variety of projects concerned with the articulation and representation of identities: the delimiting of national or ethnic identities in museums, tourist sites, or popular media; the representation of animals or other non/humans; the defining or disruption of sexual or gendered identities in texts and contexts. Her research interests include the conceptualisation of 'silence' in critical theory, as well as the representation of intersectional identity in media texts.

David R. Carroll is an Associate Professor of Media Design at Parsons School of Design, USA, and former director of the MFA Design and Technology graduate programme. He is well known for challenging the Cambridge Analytica companies in the UK in connection with the 2016 US presidential elections, resulting in the only criminal conviction of the companies by the Information Commissioner's Office. Featured in the Oscar short-listed and Emmy and BAFTA nominated Netflix documentary *The Great Hack* (2019).

Titus C. Chen is Associate Professor at the Institute of Political Science, National Sun Yat-sen University, Taiwan. Dr Chen specialises in international relations theory, international norms, international human rights, East Asian regionalism, Chinese politics and foreign policy, and text analytics. Dr Chen's research has been published in leading academic periodicals, including *Journal of Contemporary China* and *British Journal of Politics and International Relations*. Dr Chen is working on a book manuscript that investigates China's online propaganda in Xi Jinping's era.

Naren Chitty AM has a PhD in International Relations (American University, DC, USA). He is Inaugural Director of the Soft Power Analysis and Resource Centre, and Professor of International Communication at MCCALL, Faculty of Arts, Macquarie University, Australia. He is a co-editor of *The Routledge Handbook of Soft Power*, series editor of Anthem Studies in Soft Power and Public Diplomacy, and editor-in-chief of the *Journal of International Communication*. He was awarded the Order of Australia (AM) for services to education.

Nicholas J. Cull is Professor of Public Diplomacy at the Annenberg School for Communication and Journalism, University of Southern California, USA. Originally from the UK, he is a well-known historian of propaganda and the role of political communication in world affairs. His books include two volumes on the history of the United States Information Agency (USIA) and the survey text *Public Diplomacy: Foundations for Global Engagement in the Digital Age* (Polity, 2019). His current project is a comprehensive history of the global propaganda battle over Apartheid.

Terry Flew is Professor of Digital Communication and Culture at the University of Sydney, Australia. His books include *The Creative Industries, Culture and Policy* (SAGE, 2015), *Global Creative Industries* (Polity, 2013), *Media Economics* (Palgrave, 2015), *Understanding Global Media* (Palgrave, 2018) and *Regulating Platforms* (Polity, 2021). He was President of the International Communications Association (ICA) from 2019 to 2020 and was elected an ICA Fellow in 2019. He is a Fellow of the Australian Academy of the Humanities (FAHA), elected in 2019.

Penélope Franco Estrada started her career as a communicator, journalist, and photographer for art festivals in Mexico. In 2007, The Mexican government awarded her a scholarship to study culture and business in China. Then she began her career on language education at the University of Nottingham Ningbo China. She has been also a columnist for Mexican and Chinese magazines. Currently she is the Director of the Language Centre, and has wide experience of teaching Spanish in Asia.

Rubén Arnoldo González is a journalist and scholar. He has a PhD in Communication Studies from the University of Leeds (UK). He has been a reporter and editor of the newspaper *La Voz de Michoacán* (Morelia, Mexico). He is currently a researcher at the Institute of Government Sciences and Strategic Development (Benemérita Universidad Autónoma de Puebla, Mexico), where he chairs the Centre for Political Communication Studies. His research interests are journalism studies (mainly professionalisation and anti-press violence), political communication, and media systems in emergent democracies.

Renee Hobbs is Professor of Communication Studies and Director of the Media Education Lab at the University of Rhode Island's Harrington School of Communication and Media, USA. She is the author of 12 books and more than 150 scholarly papers on digital and media literacy education, copyright and fair use for digital learning, and other topics. She is the founding editor of the *Journal of Media Literacy Education*, the peer-reviewed journal of the National Association for Media Literacy Education. Hobbs received an EdD in Human Development from Harvard University, USA, and has other degrees in communication, film/video studies, and English literature from the University of Michigan, USA.

Neil Hughes combines the roles of Director of Modern Language Teaching and Digital Learning Director in the Faculty of Arts at the University of Nottingham, UK. His main research interests are in the area of Spanish politics, with a particular emphasis on social movement discourse. He also writes on issues related to digital learning design, primarily in the context of modern foreign language teaching. In 2020, his work in this area was recognised by the Association of Learning Technology (ALT), when he was awarded Learning Technologist of the Year.

Jacob Udo-Udo Jacob is Dean of Graduate School and Research at the American University of Nigeria. His research interest is at the intersection of strategic communication, war, and peacebuilding in contemporary society with particular reference to West, Central, and East Africa. He is a Visiting Professor in International Studies at Dickinson College and Adjunct Professor at the US Army War College, Carlisle, Pennsylvania, USA. Jacob has provided consultation and policy advice to a range of governmental and international organisations including the World Bank, the US Institute of Peace, and the UN's Office of Rule of Law and Security Institutions. A Fellow of the Royal Society of Arts, Jacob has been a two-term member of the distinguished judging panel of the Facebook Global Digital Challenge.

Luwei Rose Luqiu is Assistant Professor of Journalism at Hong Kong Baptist University. Her research interests include censorship, propaganda, and social movements in authoritarian regimes. She has been a journalist for 20 years and was a Nieman Fellow at Harvard University, USA.

Yiben Ma is the Convenor of the Preliminary Year Programme for International Communications Studies at the University of Nottingham Ningbo China. He obtained his PhD in Media and Communication from the University of Leeds, UK. He has a keen research interest in political communication, including Chinese online nationalism, propaganda, social media and democratisation, and critical discourse analysis.

Ilan Manor (PhD, Oxford University, UK) is a postdoctoral fellow at Tel Aviv University's Department of Communications, Israel, and a visiting fellow at the University of Southern California's Center on Public Diplomacy, USA. Manor's 2019 book, *The Digitalization of Public Diplomacy*, was published by Palgrave Macmillan. His co-edited volume, *Public Diplomacy and the Politics of Uncertainty*, was published by Palgrave Macmillan in 2021. Manor has contributed to numerous academic journals including *International Studies Review*, *Cambridge Review of International Affairs*, and *Media, War and Conflict*.

Gillian McFadyen is a Lecturer at the Department of International Politics, Aberystwyth University, UK. She teaches, researches, and writes in the area of British refugee politics, and has published in the *British Journal of Politics and International Relations*, *Journal of Immigrant and Refugee Studies*, and has recently published her first book, *Refugees in Britain: Practices of Hospitality and Labelling* (2020, Edinburgh University Press). Gillian is also interested in detention practices, internment, and postcolonialism, as well as interdisciplinary collaborations on political embroidery.

David O'Brien is a Lecturer in East Asian Politics at Ruhr University Bochum, Germany. His research focuses on ethnicity and politics in China, where he has lived and worked for many years. His research has explored Han and Uyghur ethnic identity in Xinjiang, commodified ethnicity in Chinese tourism, and China's Belt and Road Initiative (BRI). Before pursuing an academic career he was a newspaper journalist, and continues to contribute on matters relating to Xinjiang and China to the *Financial Times*, Reuters, *Washington Post*, *Deutsche Welle* and RTE, among others.

Peter Pomerantsev is a Senior Fellow at the SNF Agora Institute at Johns Hopkins University, USA, where he co-directs the Arena Initiative. Between 2017 and 2020 he was a Senior Fellow at the London School of Economics and Political Science, UK, where he was the director of the Arena Initiative, a research project dedicated to overcoming the challenges of digital era disinformation and polarisation. He is the author of the two award-winning books: *Nothing is True and Everything is Possible* and *This is Not Propaganda*.

Kruakae Pothong is a Researcher at 5Rights and Visiting Research Fellow in the Department of Media and Communications at the London School of Economics and Political Science, UK. Her current research focuses on child-centred design of digital services. Her research spans the areas of human–computer interaction, digital ethics, data protection, Internet, media and communication policies. She specialises in designing social-technical research, using deliberative methods to elicit people's expectations of technological advances, such as the Internet of Things (IoT) and distributed ledgers.

Gary D. Rawnsley is Dean of the Faculty of Humanities and Social Sciences and Professor of Public Diplomacy at the University of Nottingham Ningbo China. He works at the intersection of international communications and international relations, with particular expertise on propaganda, public and cultural diplomacy, soft power, and international broadcasting. He has published in *Political Communication*, *China Quarterly*, the *Historical Journal of Film, Radio and Television*, and the *Journal of International Communication*. A Fellow of the Royal Society of Arts, Rawnsley is Adjunct Professor at Asia University in Taichung (Taiwan) and the Guangdong University of Foreign Studies, China.

Georgia Spiliopoulos holds a PhD in Applied Social Science from Lancaster University, UK. Her research interests are in gender and migration; mostly migration of nurses, care and domestic workers from South and Southeast Asia to other destinations, especially in the Global North. She joined the School of International Studies, University of Nottingham Ningbo China in 2016 and has recently completed two funded projects on the effects of Brexit on the retention and recruitment of migrant nurses, and on returnee Filipino nurses.

Daya Thussu is Professor of International Communication at the Hong Kong Baptist University. He was Distinguished Visiting Professor and Inaugural Disney Chair in Global Media, 2018–2019, at Schwarzman College, Tsinghua University in Beijing, China. For many years, he was Professor of International Communication at the University of Westminster in London, UK. Founder and managing editor of the SAGE journal *Global Media and Communication*, he is the author or editor of 20 books, including *Communicating India's Soft Power: Buddha to Bollywood*.

James R. Vaughan is a Lecturer in International History in the Department of International Politics at Aberystwyth University, UK. He is the author of several articles on the evolution of British attitudes and policies towards Zionism and the Arab–Israeli dispute, and is currently working on a major book entitled *British Politics and the Question of Israel*.

Andrew Wyatt is Senior Lecturer in Politics at the University of Bristol, UK. He is the author of *Party System Change in South India* (2009) and co-author of *Contemporary India* (2010). His research interests lie in the areas of economic nationalism, political and business elites, populism, and political parties.

Chi Zhang is a British Academy Postdoctoral Fellow at the University of St Andrews, UK, and an Associate Member of the Handa Centre for the Study of Terrorism and Political Violence. Her areas of research interest fall broadly within security studies, constructivism, and Chinese political philosophy. She holds a PhD in Politics and International Studies from the University of Leeds, UK. She has published extensively in *Terrorism and Political Violence*, *Studies in Conflict and Terrorism*, *Politics and Religion*, and *Asian Security*.

Xiaoling Zhang is Professor and Head of the Department of Media and Communication in Xi'an Jiaotong-Liverpool University, Suzhou, China. She has published widely on China's media, communication, and society. In addition to the evolving policies, the development of the industries as part of China's economic development, and the wider social transformation, she also researches on their role in the nation's attempt to refresh its image and to build international soft power.

Introduction to the *Research Handbook on Political Propaganda*

Gary D. Rawnsley, Yiben Ma, and Kruakae Pothong

This book is published at a time when interest in and awareness of propaganda is escalating. Of course, we do not claim that the relevance of political propaganda is returning, because it never disappeared. To assume that it died with the Cold War is as delusional and self-defeating as thinking propaganda is only organised in the non-democratic or less mature democratic political systems (Taylor, 2002a, 2002b; Herman and Chomsky, 2010). Revelations about Cambridge Analytica and the violent extremist propaganda of Islamic State (IS) demonstrate that the practice of propaganda is not confined to states and governments, while the extraordinary political and social polarisation of the United States (US) during Donald Trump's presidency and the United Kingdom's (UK) Brexit referendumcampaign confirms that propaganda is also prevalent inside those political cultures that claim a long constitutional commitment to 'free speech'. It stands to reason that propaganda thrives in an age of 'post-truth' uncertainties and so-called 'alternative facts'. But propaganda does not just speak to the shadier side of modern politics. While communications can incite, divide, cast blame, and confuse, equally they can unite, build nations, promote mutual understanding, help manage a global pandemic, and save lives. Propaganda is still valued as an instrument for advancing all shades of political interests and agendas, and we can detect today the propaganda techniques that defined its practice throughout history (Taylor, 2003; Connelly et al., 2019: 1–12). So, is there anything new to learn?

Transformations in the global media ecology challenge our understanding of political processes, institutions, and actors at both the domestic and international levels. Concerns about the power of social media to disrupt political cultures have given rise to discussions about 'fake news', 'bots', and 'trolling', while the credibility of traditional sources of news and information across the world – the print and broadcast media – is questioned as never before. In democracies and authoritarian political systems alike, professional journalists are routinely labelled 'the enemy', and citizen journalism struggles to contextualise information in a satisfactory and accurate way. In turn, news organisations continue to challenge political authority; but also because the social media make it easier for political actors to bypass journalists, news organisations are more mindful than ever of the need to expose misleading statements and falsehoods and to 'fact check' information from political sources.

By the autumn of 2018, the *Washington Post*, the newspaper that was central to both the publication of the Pentagon Papers and the Watergate investigation in the early 1970s, had detected over 5000 such statements since President Donald Trump's inauguration in 2017, while *Time* magazine found 1950 'false claims' in 2017 alone. Together with growing uncertainty in the political space with the rebirth of far-right politics across Europe (M5S in Italy), North and South America (the election of Jair Bolsonaro in Brazil), and Asia (Narendra Modi in India, Rodrigo Duterte in the Philippines) and issues such as anti-immigration pushing a nationalist turn (for example, President Trump's so-called 'Muslim ban' and the UK's Brexit referendum campaign), the new media and information landscape is a driver of government and electoral choice. Communication platforms are now more powerful politically than at any time in the past.

This *Handbook* begins from the premise that we need to better understand modern propaganda and how political actors seek to influence each other, as well as public opinion and behaviour through strategic communications. In particular the contributors address how social and digital media platforms have moved 'influence' away from states and institutions, making the means for shaping communication and public opinion more easily accessible to a broader range of actors. While governments still use propaganda as an instrument of statecraft (for example, the weaponisation of information by the Chinese and Russian governments is well documented), new communication technologies have 'democratised' the production and distribution of political propaganda. Through their affordability, accessibility, reach, and popularity, digital platforms empower non-governmental organisations, civil society groups, private corporations, protest movements, and individual actors to engage in their own influence operations. In fact, our participation in the 'attention economy' means that even the seemingly trivial acts of 'liking' or 'sharing' content on social media makes us complicit in 'the viral spread of propaganda' (Hobbs, 2020: 69). Every time a liberal journalist or outraged voter retweeted one of Donald Trump's attacks on journalists, or CNN showed yet more footage of Majorie Taylor Greene's filmed inflammatory remarks, the original message is amplified and reaches a bigger audience. It also gives the source a level of influence and credibility that perhaps they do not deserve. Propaganda lesson #1: do not draw attention to your opponents' propaganda. However, this lesson is sometimes forgotten in the social media echo chamber.

Bringing together an international team of commentators, analysts, and scholars, this *Handbook* offers a fresh, timely, and above all an interdisciplinary perspective on political propaganda. The chapters discuss how propaganda is operationalised in various forms, application contexts, and political systems. Taking the communication perspective, our scope and definition of propaganda centre on its common attributes, namely:

- Its persuasive function.
- Audiences.
- Intentions and agendas for cultivating particular ideas or directing particular behaviours.
- Use of flawed reasoning or emotional appeal.

These attributes derive from descriptions of propaganda identified since the earliest scientific studies of propaganda were published in the 20th century (Lasswell, 1927; Institute for Propaganda Analysis, 1937; Welch, 2002; Taylor, 2003; Shabo, 2008; Stanley, 2015).

Hence, the editors acknowledge that we stand on the shoulders of giants. However, eschewing the approach of previous studies that offer a definitional and historical assessment based on an understanding of propaganda largely drawn from experience of 20th century warfare (Taylor, 2003; Welch, 2014; Connelly et al., 2019), most of the chapters in the present volume provide a contemporary perspective. This means that we are analysing a moving target. While we prepared the manuscript, we watched the Trump presidency rise and fall, the sudden eruption of a global pandemic that has transformed almost everybody's life, Brexit, a military coup in Myanmar in which the military cut all access to the Internet, continuing political turmoil in the Ukraine and war in Yemen, protests in Thailand, the Black Lives Matter movement in the US, and countless other events, big and small. All are interesting case studies of political propaganda: 'the deliberate attempt to influence public opinion through the transmission of ideas and values for a specific persuasive purpose that has been consciously devised to serve the self-interest of the propagandist, either directly or indirectly' (Welch, 2003: xv–xxi). All have something to tell us about the way modern communications disrupt or reinforce political authority. It was impossible to keep up to date with these events and to attempt to address them all in this book. However, we are confident that the case studies chosen for this volume represent the diversity of ways in which political propaganda is understood and used today.

Contributors interrogate definitions of propaganda to reshape analyses of the 21st century communication space. We are familiar with the idea that propaganda is a value neutral concept, that it is a 'process for the sowing, germination and cultivation of ideas' (Taylor, 2003: 2). Scholars reference repeatedly Pope Gregory XV's creation in 1622 of the Congregation of the Propagation of the Faith to indicate both the long history of propaganda's formal organisation and that it is not necessarily a pejorative activity. We turn to one of the most important scholars of propaganda, David Welch, to understand how this value neutral definition sits with 'misconceptions' about propaganda. In his landmark book, *The Third Reich: Politics and Propaganda*, Welch (2002) identifies a series of misconceptions about propaganda: that it is about changing opinions, when propaganda is 'more often ... concerned with reinforcing existing trends and beliefs'; that propaganda deals only in deception. 'In fact,' writes Welch, 'it operates with many different kinds of truth – the outright lie, the half truth, the truth out of context.' Welch also discusses the idea that propaganda appeals to the 'irrational instincts of man', but then notes that 'because our attitudes and behaviour are also the product of rational decisions, propaganda must appeal to the rational elements in human nature as well' (Welch, 2002: 5). This underpins Welch's research on Nazi propaganda that suggests voters were not 'mesmerised by a well functioning propaganda machine' into voting for Hitler and the NSDAP (Nazi Party). Explaining the Nazi Party's success as the result of propaganda alone assumes voters were acting irrationally, instead of accepting that 'many groups ... perceived voting for the NSDAP as being in their own interests and that Nazi propaganda served to reinforce such beliefs ... To over-emphasise the importance of propaganda', says Welch, 'would be to diminish the failure of the Weimar system to solve prevailing economic and social problems and of political opponents of the NSDAP to provide viable alternatives' (ibid.: 8). This is an important point: propaganda does not and cannot operate within a vacuum, but must be sensitive to wider social and political trends. Thus, it is essential to understand the context in which propaganda operates: social and economic problems, why people feel so alienated that they are willing to support extremist political parties offering attractive solutions, and why they are so ready to blame their problems on other groups in societies. General Erich Ludendorff's much quoted explanation of Germany's defeat in World War One – 'We were hypnotised by the enemy propaganda as a rabbit is by a snake' (Ludendorff, 1919 [1940]: 360) – is too bold a claim and attributes to propaganda an undeserving degree of power to influence, one that is separated from military and political failures.

This leads Welch to an important conclusion: the preoccupation with irrational rather than rational behaviour 'ignores the basic fact that propaganda is ethically neutral – it may be good or bad. The first task of the student of propaganda is to divest the word of its pejorative and derogatory associations' (Welch, 2002: 5).

How useful is this value neutral definition today? Is propaganda 'merely' another form of persuasion, or does recent history – Donald Trump's presidency, IS, Cambridge Analytica, virulent nationalism – suggest that this description is no longer fit for purpose? We recognise propaganda used by terrorist groups such as IS to normalise and justify extreme violence and lure new recruits with tantalising utopian portraits of the society it wishes to create; and that democratic governments also use propaganda to challenge these misleading ideas (Lieberman, 2017). For a time, British news organisations decided to preface all their reports by saying 'so-called' Islamic State – which arguably is bad journalism – thus engaging in a form of counter-propaganda. At the same time, propaganda was used to restore peace in Northern Ireland (McLaughlin and Baker, 2010), while perpetuating the sectarian divisions there (murals, parades, and so on). Propaganda is also discovered in public health campaigns. During the Covid-19 pandemic Britons were encouraged to 'Stay home, Protect the NHS, Save lives', and 'Stay alert, Control the virus, Save lives' (Waterson, 2020). Thailand adopted a more nationalist message, rolling out a slogan that translates into English as 'Control the virus for the nation', while the New Zealand government opted for 'Be kind, Stay calm' (BBC News, 2020). Meanwhile, propaganda that spread the idea that Covid-19 was the 'China virus' fed into and encouraged anti-China narratives, especially in the US where there existed a notion that the pandemic was not real. Such narratives helped rationalise resistance to control measures such as social distancing and wearing masks in public.

Perhaps the label matters less than the intention after all – Stuart Cunningham (2002: 64) has claimed that 'There is no unintentional propaganda' – and anyway, one man's public diplomacy, public relations, or healthcare warning is another man's propaganda. Whatever the intention, the label is at the behest of the audiences, not the source of the messages, and we cannot hide from the fact that however much we drive home the idea that propaganda is a value neutral form of communication, it will always resonate with sinister connotations. Why else would the Chinese Communist Party change the name – in English only – of its Propaganda Department to Publicity Department?

Today the literature on influence is dominated by studies of public diplomacy and soft power, the latter too often a universal 'catch-all' term that is used by policymakers and academics alike to describe strategic communications via attraction. Some have decided that the concept of soft power is insufficient to capture all the influence activities that governments undertake, and that yet another (quite unnecessary) label, sharp power, is required to describe many of the actions that would have been described previously as propaganda or political warfare. Some think that inventing such new terms adds clarity. It does not.

Moreover, digital diplomacy is today receiving growing attention (Bjola and Holmes, 2015; Manor, 2019), while more considered analyses of the Internet and social media recognise that the democratic vision we talked of not so long ago is in fact becoming suspect (Mozorov, 2011; Moore, 2018). Many of the chapters in this *Handbook* evaluate how the digital media contribute to modern political propaganda and disinformation, but still acknowledge that we must not ignore other, perhaps more traditional media. After all, most of what we call 'propaganda' still occurs on traditional platforms, with the broadcast and print media still the main vehicles of delivery in many parts of the world. In some societies, posters remain important. In China the increase in the number of propaganda posters on view in urban areas reflects the importance that Xi Jinping's government attaches to influence, while protest movements and non-governmental actors discover old and new ways to disseminate their propaganda. In Barcelona, for example, graffiti is still important for the Catalan movement, while the Internet 'meme' reflects the popular creation, circulation, and consumption of political messages and satire that challenge the existing political order. In the aftermath of a coup in Myanmar in 2021, the junta may have cut access to the Internet, but protestors still mobilised throughout the country, and audiences around the world were still able to see coverage of the increasingly violent clashes between the military and opponents. Political activism, like political propaganda, will always continue offline.

Again, we need to be mindful of intention. Writing on the 2011 'Arab Spring', Moore says that the mistake of democratic governments and those responsible for digital platforms:

> was to assume that their tools were inherently democratizing, when technology was simply enabling new ways of pursuing political ends. Those who say how politically powerful these platforms could be, and used digital tools to pursue their political aims, benefitted disproportionately. It did not matter if these aims were democratic, autocratic or anarchistic. (Moore, 2018: 7)

If the history of propaganda teaches us anything, it is that those who wish to exercise power over public opinion – for good or bad intentions – will always find a way to do so. New communications technologies simply make it possible for a range of messengers beyond state actors and institutions to spread ideas faster and to a more select audience. The blurring of producer, distributor, and consumer complicates our understanding of communications and makes it increasingly difficult to recognise not only propaganda but also the propagandists. The transformation of communicative practices – the often unconscious 'liking' and 'sharing' of information – also plays a part in reconfirming and reinforcing particular ideas among the same-minded in the echo chamber, leaving less room for critical assessment. Hence, Chapter 28 concludes this volume with an urgent call for greater awareness of digital literacy and the development of skills needed to navigate the new information and communication landscape:

> Our stock response to dealing with the circulation of 'fake news', or indeed views that we do not support, is to control the info-sphere further still. Our dilemma – balancing the right to freedom of expression with the need to limit our exposure to harmful views or false information – is not so very different from that of our inter-war predecessors, even though the global scope and scale of communications has changed. (Connelly et al., 2019: 3)

Digital platforms are merely the latest in a long line of communication innovations stretching far back before the 20th century that have created new opportunities for propaganda (Taylor, 2003). While this may be the logical conclusion of a technological process – there is a definite resemblance in the techniques, style, and content of propaganda we encounter today and about which we read in the history books – our exposure to more propaganda and the close analyses of the way IS, Cambridge Analytica, Donald Trump, and a host of other actors and institutions have organised their influence activities also suggests a greater opportunity to engage with and question the propaganda we encounter on a day-to-day basis. We hope that this collection of chapters will make such a contribution.

The editors wish to thank all the contributors to this volume. We appreciate your hard work, your patience, and your responses to the reviewers' feedback. Many of you joined the project at the beginning in early 2019, others towards the end near Christmas 2020. Despite lockdowns, the move to online teaching, and endless Zoom meetings disrupting our lives, we have all managed to produce a fascinating volume of chapters that make a strong contribution to our understanding of modern political propaganda. Thank you.

The editors dedicate this volume to three giants in the field of media and communications studies – the bright lights of the Institute of Communications Studies (ICS) at the University of Leeds – who inspired the editors and so many of the contributors, as well as generations of scholars and students across the world:

Professor Nicholas Pronay, founder of ICS and a pioneer in the field of historical approaches to propaganda.
Professor Philip M. Taylor, 1954–2010.
Professor Jay Blumler, 1924–2021.

Thank you all for your part in creating and shaping the field, as well as for your warm friendship. We hope you are proud of us, your 'intellectual offspring'.

REFERENCES

BBC News (2020), 'Coronavirus: How New Zealand relied on science and empathy', 20 April, available at https://www.bbc.com/news/world-asia-52344299.
Bjola, Corneliu and Marcus Holmes (2015), *Digital Diplomacy: Theory and Practice*, London: Routledge.
Connelly, Mark, Jo Fox, Stefan Goebel, and Ulf Schmidt (eds) (2019), *Propaganda and Conflict: War, Media and Shaping the Twentieth Century*, London: Bloomsbury.
Cunningham, Stuart (2002), *The Idea of Propaganda: A Reconstruction*, London: Praeger.
Herman, Edward S. and Noam Chomsky (2010), *Manufacturing Consent: The Political Economy of the Mass Media*, London: Random House.
Hobbs, Renee (2020), *Mind Over Media: Propaganda Education for a Digital Age*, New York: W.W. Norton & Company.
Institute of Propaganda Analysis (1937), 'How to Detect Propaganda', *Propaganda Analysis* 1, no. 2 (November).
Lasswell, Harold D. (1927), 'The Theory of Political Propaganda', *American Political Science Review*, 21 (3): 627–631.
Lieberman, Ariel V. (2017), 'Terrorism, the Internet, and Propaganda: A Deadly Combination', *Journal of National Security Law and Policy*, 9 (95): 95–124.
Ludendorff, Erich (1919 [1940]), *My War Memories 1914–1918*, Ann Arbor, MI: University of Michigan Library.
Manor, Ilan (2019), *The Digitalisation of Public Diplomacy*, London: Palgrave Macmillan.
McLaughlin, Greg and Stephen Baker (2010), *The Propaganda of Peace: The Role of Media and Culture in the Northern Ireland Peace Process*, Bristol: Intellect Books.
Moore, Martin (2018), *Democracy Hacked: Political Turmoil and Information Warfare in the Digital Age*, London: Oneworld.
Mozorov, Evgeny (2011), *The Net Delusion: The Dark Side of Internet Freedom*, New York: PublicAffairs.
Shabo, Magedah E. (2008), *Techniques of Propaganda and Persuasion*, Smyrna, DE: Prestwick House.
Stanley, Jason (2015), *How Propaganda Works*, Princeton, NJ: Princeton University Press.
Taylor, Philip M. (2002a), 'Perception Management and the "War" Against Terrorism', *Journal of Information Warfare*, 1 (3): 16–29.
Taylor, Philip M. (2002b), 'Strategic Communications or Democratic Propaganda?', *Journalism Studies*, 3 (3): 437–441.
Taylor, Philip M. (2003), *Munitions of the Mind: A History of Propaganda from the Ancient World to the Present Era* (3rd edn), Manchester: Manchester University Press.
Waterson, Jim (2020), 'Hands, Face, Space: Boris Johnson Unveils New Covid-19 Slogan', *Guardian*, 31 July, available at https://www.theguardian.com/uk-news/2020/jul/31/hands-face-space-boris-johnson-unveils-new-coronavirus-slogan.
Welch, David (2002), *The Third Reich: Politics and Propaganda* (2nd edn), London: Routledge.
Welch, David (2003), 'Introduction: Propaganda in Historical Perspective', in Nicholas J. Cull, David Culbert, and David Welch (eds), *Propaganda and Mass Persuasion: A Historical Encyclopedia, 1500 to the Present*, Santa Barbara, CA: ABC Clio, pp. xv–xxi.
Welch, David (ed.) (2014), *Propaganda, Power and Persuasion: From World War One to Wikileaks*, London: I.B. Taurus.

1. World propaganda and personal insecurity: intent, content, and contentment
Naren Chitty

BIG TENT PROPAGANDA

This chapter's propaganda narrative is shaped by Harold Lasswell's insight that elites constantly arise in social structures. They seek security, through ascendancy, by extracting values from and distributing values to the masses. The latter find security through receiving values. The main influence behind this search for security through ascendancy (on the part of elites) or dependency (on the part of the 'masses') is knowledge of mortality. Value-extracting elites/skill groups/influencers (Lasswell's term is 'influential', but the term 'influencer' has become popular and is used in this chapter) possess military, economic, and communication skills. Influencing opinion is important for all three types (Lasswell, 1965; Chitty, 1992: 29; Chitty, 2017b: 20). In the cognitive revolution that transpired 70 000 years ago, humans learnt to describe physical and social environments they observed, as well as things they imagined. Rhetorical skills facilitated persuasion of large numbers to join groups (Harari, 2011: 3, 41; Chitty, 2017b: 13). Narratives – hunters'/warriors' post-hunt/battle boasts; merchants' trade promotion; and shamans' tales of spirit worlds and their demands/boons – were early proto-propaganda.

Propaganda in the sense used here is all encompassing and meta-ideological, including all tangible or intangible artefacts that influence people. This is a big tent propaganda. The ancient Hindu Vedas constituted propaganda that shaped Indian social hierarchies as a Lasswellian political-economic pyramid. Sudras (service folk/non-influencers) were at the base. Vaishyas (merchants) were above them in the first influential layer. Above the Vaishyas were the Kshatriyas (warriors). Brahmins (priests) were at the apex (Chitty, 1992: 29). For Nicholas Onuf (1989: 79) this was an example of an 'Indo-European tripartite ideology'. Ideologies are in some ways propaganda clouds or bubbles, developed from words of influencers, that can be promoted and adopted as the dominant organising ideational framework of a social system. They can be propagated by states *inter alia* through educational institutions and media while being counter-propagandised by 'counter-apparatuses' such as trade unions and political parties in liberal democracies (Therborn, 1980: 87).

'Propaganda' is a powerful word. This statement has a connoted meaning that is central to this chapter. Some kinds of propaganda can have and can be intended to have powerful effects. The question whether propaganda can be other than 'powerful' will be addressed: what is propaganda if disassociated from power? The reference here is to power being 'intended' influence (Lasswell and Kaplan, 1950). Power is a type of influence in a binary based on intentionality and the lack thereof. What is power's counterpart in a 'bisected influence' remains a question; a single powerful word such as 'power' is hard to imagine. Perhaps it is fitting that a descriptor of influence *sans* power would be a term *sans* power. The collocation 'unintended influence' is used here for want of a satisfactory single word under Lasswell's dichotomisation. Inclusion of types of propaganda that are disassociated from intention or direct intention impacts upon the meaning(s) of propaganda. Others look at the terms 'power' and 'influence' differently. Reich and Lebow (2014: 6–8) distinguish between materially based power and influence. If one were to use this distinction it would be necessary to speak of intended and unintended power and intended and unintended influence. Intentionality does not figure substantially in Nye's discussion of approaches to power either. Nye undertakes a comparative analysis of literature on power but privileges preferred outcomes over unintended consequences (Nye, 2011: 7). 'Unintended soft (power)' is often a by-product of people's daily lives. However, Lasswell and Kaplan would not see 'unintended soft (power)' as a type of power, hence my bracketing of power here (Chitty, 2020). Ellul speaks of intent but only in terms of hiding or lying about one's intentions, affiliations, and values (Ellul, 1973: 57–61). Habermas (1979, 1987) and Habermas and MacCarthy (2004) develop a theory of communication action that normatively promotes dialogic rather than strategic communication. Dialogic communication has influenced theorisation of two-way interactive public relations (Grunig et al., 1995) and strategic and dialogic public diplomacy (Gregory, 2005; Chitty, 2011: 252–269; Izadi and Nelson, 2020: 391–404). As Lasswell introduces the notion of intended and unintended, his categories are selected.

DEFINITIONS OF PROPAGANDA

This section will introduce a few classical definitions of propaganda as well as a big tent view that consists of propositions, commissives, and directives (Onuf, 1989). Some of the propositions are interlaced as theory, in what Thomas Berger and Peter Luckmann (1991: 83) call 'symbolic universe'. When Berger and Luckmann see being unable to have a theory accepted by another to be 'a problem of propaganda', the connection with propaganda in their minds is revealed.

According to Lasswell (1927: 9) the term 'propaganda':

> refers to the control of opinion by significant symbols, or to speak more concretely and less accurately, by stories, rumors, reports, pictures, and other forms of social communication. Propaganda is concerned with management of opinions and attitudes by the direct manipulation of social suggestion rather than by altering other conditions in the environment or in the organism.

A further formulation crafted by the Institute of Propaganda Analysis, with which Lasswell was associated, states that '[p]ropaganda is the expression of opinions or actions carried out deliberately by individuals or groups with a view to influencing the opinions or actions of other individuals or groups for predetermined ends and through psychological manipulation' (Ellul, 1973: xii).

Ellul identifies two domains of propaganda, political and sociological. Political propaganda 'involves techniques of influence employed by a government, a party, an administration, a pressure group, with a view to changing the behaviour of the public'. On the other hand, sociological propaganda 'is the penetration of an ideology by means of its sociological context'. It consists of 'manifestations by which society seeks to integrate the maximum number of individuals into itself, to unify its members' behaviour according to a pattern, to spread its style of life abroad, and thus impose itself on other groups'. While political propaganda attempts to 'spread an ideology through the mass media of communication in order to lead the public to accept some political or economic structure or to participate in some action', in sociological propaganda 'existing economic, political, and sociological factors progressively allow an ideology to penetrate individuals or masses' (ibid.: 62–63). Propaganda facilitates social construction at the level of society.

Traditional international relations theory is propaganda either of a warrior world based on conflict, or of a trader/communicator/farmer world based on cooperation. The proponents consciously or unconsciously voice the perspectives of interest groups. Critical international relations theory is normative and reflective of various agendas: 'a heterogeneous group of theories has been labelled as critical in international relations, including feminism, poststructuralism, critical geopolitics, critical security studies, critical international political economy, postcolonialism, and international historical sociology' (Yalvaç, 2017: 1).

A CONSTRUCTIVIST WORLD PROPAGANDA

World politics is constructed through layers of social, institutional, state, and interstate behaviour that includes propaganda formation and distribution that shape the behaviour of these actors as well. Of the three salient paradigms in international relations – realism, liberalism, and constructivism (each with its variations) – constructivism sees 'mind' (through intersubjective structures) as the shaper of international politics, rather than material conditions, human nature, or domestic politics (Wendt, 1992; Chitty, 2017b: 14–15).

Theoretical positions influence policy and the behaviour of the system, constituent states, and agents. Actors and propaganda practice within international relations are considered here. The state as a system, and its agents acting both inwardly toward sub-systems and outwardly toward horizontal external systems, and the institutionalised international system itself, are actors. The international system is accessed here through international regimes: these are diffused versus specific, formal versus informal, allow evolutionary change versus revolutionary change (Puchala and Hopkins, 1983: 64–65). Here the focus is on diffused regimes associated with salient periods in recent history. A regime 'is a set of principles, norms, rules and procedures around which actors' expectations converge … diffused regimes are normative superstructures, which are reflected in functionally or geographically specific substructures or regimes' (Puchala and Hopkins, 1983: 61–64). My contention is that regimes are manifestations of propaganda under the big tent definition; they emanate propaganda and are battlegrounds for the use of instrumental policy spearheads of propaganda by competing states. Great powers have an impetus to engage in 'diffusion of policies across national jurisdictions – policy transnationalization' (Chitty et al., 2018: 1–20). Specific formal regimes have four substantive norms geared to their own issue areas such as food, health, human rights, and trade: these are non-discrimination, liberalisation, reciprocity, and safeguard (Finlayson and Zacher, 1983: 278–296). itself, are actors. The international system is accessed here through international regimes: these are diffused versus specific, formal versus informal, allow evolutionary change versus revolutionary change (Puchala and Hopkins, 1983: 64–65). Here the focus is on diffused regimes associated with salient periods in recent history. A regime 'is a set of principles, norms, rules and procedures around which actors' expectations converge … diffused regimes are normative superstructures, which are reflected in functionally or geographically specific substructures or regimes' (Puchala and Hopkins, 1983: 61–64). My contention is that regimes are manifestations of propaganda under the big tent definition; they emanate propaganda and are battlegrounds for the use of instrumental policy spearheads of propaganda by competing states. Great powers have an impetus to engage in 'diffusion of policies across national jurisdictions – policy transnationalization' (Chitty et al., 2018: 1–20). Specific formal regimes have four substantive norms geared to their own issue areas such as food, health, human rights, and trade: these are non-discrimination, liberalisation, reciprocity, and safeguard (Finlayson and Zacher, 1983: 278–296).

Impact on the meanings of propaganda is also evident. The term has been used to signify various practices by actors at different levels of analysis in several epochs. 'Propaganda' is a noun that refers to a type of communication as well as a type of content. Terms that overlap to one degree or another with propaganda include advertising, communication, cultural imperialism, hegemony, influence, information flow, persuasion, psychological warfare, public diplomacy, public relations, soft power, sharp power, and strategic communication. This is not a comprehensive list of overlaps under the big tent conception. Notably, while there is an aspect of will behind all types of human communication, the position taken here is that there can be influence *sans* intention to influence; in the case of propaganda as in the case of soft power (Chitty, 2017a: 454). Alternatively, there could be an intent not to influence, as in the case of a conscious espousal of dialogic communication in an ideal speech situation of communicative action (Habermas, 1987; Habermas and MacCarthy, 2004). In Ellul's view sociological propaganda is organic and 'not the result of deliberate propaganda action'. He gives the example of an American film producer who when he 'makes a film, he has certain definite ideas he wants to express, which are not intended to be propaganda. Rather, the propaganda element is in the American way of life with which he is permeated and which he expresses in his film without realizing it.' But though it may begin in an involuntary manner it can evolve to have the intention to be influential. The Motion Picture Association required American cinema 'to promote "the highest types of social life," "the proper conception of society," "the proper standards of life," and to avoid "any ridicule of the law (natural or human) or sympathy for those who violate the law' (Ellul, 1973: 64–67)., sharp power, and strategic communication. This is not a comprehensive list of overlaps under the big tent conception. Notably, while there is an aspect of will behind all types of human communication, the position taken here is that there can be influence *sans* intention to influence; in the case of propaganda as in the case of soft power (Chitty, 2017a: 454). Alternatively, there could be an intent not to influence, as in the case of a conscious espousal of dialogic communication in an ideal speech situation of communicative action (Habermas, 1987; Habermas and MacCarthy, 2004). In Ellul's view sociological propaganda is organic and 'not the result of deliberate propaganda action'. He gives the example of an American film producer who when he 'makes a film, he has certain definite ideas he wants to express, which are not intended to be propaganda. Rather, the propaganda element is in the American way of life with which he is permeated and which he expresses in his film without realizing it.' But though it may begin in an involuntary manner it can evolve to have the intention to be influential. The Motion Picture Association required American cinema 'to promote "the highest types of social life," "the proper conception of society," "the proper standards of life," and to avoid "any ridicule of the law (natural or human) or sympathy for those who violate the law' (Ellul, 1973: 64–67).

So far, propaganda has been cast neutrally under a big tent conception. This is not to say that there are no sub-categories; and that there would be views of the virtue or villainy inherent in the propaganda of competitors, or even one's own government or state. The way in which propaganda has been viewed has switched a few times since it was introduced into the Congregation for Propagating the Faith (*Congregatio de propaganda fide*), established by Pope Gregory XV in 1622 and 'which had jurisdiction over missionary work' (Frederick, 1993: 230). Clearly its own propaganda was seen in a positive light by the Vatican, its outposts in the far corners of the world and by the Faithful in general. While successful in the Americas, there were twin failures in the Ottoman Near East because of 'Muslim resistance to conversion ... Christian conversion to Islam' in a contest of proselytisation (Lee, 2012). Evangelisation can be viewed differently by the evangelist and rival communities of faith. There could be communities of religious or secular faith. Ideologies are the scriptures of communities of political faith. Whether propaganda is viewed negatively or not depends very much on how the source and content of propaganda are viewed. or villainy inherent in the propaganda of competitors, or even one's own government or state. The way in which propaganda has been viewed has switched a few times since it was introduced into the Congregation for Propagating the Faith (*Congregatio de propaganda fide*), established by Pope Gregory XV in 1622 and 'which had jurisdiction over missionary work' (Frederick, 1993: 230). Clearly its own propaganda was seen in a positive light by the Vatican, its outposts in the far corners of the world and by the Faithful in general. While successful in the Americas, there were twin failures in the Ottoman Near East because of 'Muslim resistance to conversion ... Christian conversion to Islam' in a contest of proselytisation (Lee, 2012). Evangelisation can be viewed differently by the evangelist and rival communities of faith. There could be communities of religious or secular faith. Ideologies are the scriptures of communities of political faith. Whether propaganda is viewed negatively or not depends very much on how the source and content of propaganda are viewed.

The social construction of world politics and the world political construction of society is a two-way process, so one could start at either end in a discussion. I will begin with larger social structures in international relations, the propaganda of which shape societies much of the time and transform them incrementally by evolution or radically by revolution. I have selected three periods and particular diffused regimes. The first is the Cold War period, where United States (US)-led Western political and economic ideologies were contested by the Soviet-led communist bloc. The second is the period of globalisation, where the contest between Western and Islamicist ideologies returned to saliency. The third is the current period, with its fractured globalisation and contestation of liberal democracy by authoritarian states such as China and Russia and their agents; an updated playback of the first period. Contesting communities of secular faith have arisen even within democracies in the 21st century. I will also discuss instigation to act and intent to act at the level of state actors, as well as analyse the content of propaganda drawing on rhetorical, propaganda, and soft power theory; and addressing the world political moment of the intersection of the ascendancy of China, the COVID-19 pandemic, and the 2020 US election. I will address propaganda in international relations, and actors' intent and propaganda content. Examining propaganda can be disassociated from power. A classificatory framework that arises out of the previous section will appear in the conclusion. period, where United States (US)-led Western political and economic ideologies were contested by the Soviet-led communist bloc. The second is the period of globalisation, where the contest between Western and Islamicist ideologies returned to saliency. The third is the current period, with its fractured globalisation and contestation of liberal democracy by authoritarian states such as China and Russia and their agents; an updated playback of the first period. Contesting communities of secular faith have arisen even within democracies in the 21st century. I will also discuss instigation to act and intent to act at the level of state actors, as well as analyse the content of propaganda drawing on rhetorical, propaganda, and soft power theory; and addressing the world political moment of the intersection of the ascendancy of China, the COVID-19 pandemic, and the 2020 US election. I will address propaganda in international relations, and actors' intent and propaganda content. Examining propaganda can be disassociated from power. A classificatory framework that arises out of the previous section will appear in the conclusion.

WORLD PROPAGANDA

In the interbellum years Harold Lasswell was preoccupied with the 'dark side' of political propaganda. The three selected postbellum periods associated with diffused regimes are the Cold War period, the period of globalisation, and the current period of fractured globalisation. In the post-war world of the 1950s Daniel Lerner focused on the 'light side' of the propagation of modernity (Chitty, 2005: 555–559). Lasswell and Lerner had been collaborators in propaganda studies at the Institute of Propaganda Analysis. Seventy years later, public diplomacy and development communication have been described as 'Two sides of the same coin' (Pamment, 2020: 430–437). My use of the terms 'dark side' and 'light side' to refer to political propaganda and propagation of modernity was shorthand, but the terms need further analysis. Some political propaganda, for example the promotion of democracy, could be seen as being on the 'light side' by liberal democrats. Liberal democrats could also see the propagation of Soviet or Maoist style economic modernisation, through collectivisation, as the 'dark side'. Contrarian views would have been entertained by agents of the Soviet or Chinese states of the postbellum period. These opposing views resulted in contests of propaganda by these states and their affiliates. was preoccupied with the 'dark side' of political propaganda. The three selected postbellum periods associated with diffused regimes are the Cold War period, the period of globalisation, and the current period of fractured globalisation. In the post-war world of the 1950s Daniel Lerner focused on the 'light side' of the propagation of modernity (Chitty, 2005: 555–559). Lasswell and Lerner had been collaborators in propaganda studies at the Institute of Propaganda Analysis. Seventy years later, public diplomacy and development communication have been described as 'Two sides of the same coin' (Pamment, 2020: 430–437). My use of the terms 'dark side' and 'light side' to refer to political propaganda and propagation of modernity was shorthand, but the terms need further analysis. Some political propaganda, for example the promotion of democracy, could be seen as being on the 'light side' by liberal democrats. Liberal democrats could also see the propagation of Soviet or Maoist style economic modernisation, through collectivisation, as the 'dark side'. Contrarian views would have been entertained by agents of the Soviet or Chinese states of the postbellum period. These opposing views resulted in contests of propaganda by these states and their affiliates.

Propaganda is easily identified with the state or organs of the state, with political propaganda being directed internally, externally, or in both directions. There is a spectrum of levels in which propaganda (as the propagation of ideas) is produced and received. I will simplify this to Waltz's three levels of analysis in international relations – international system, state, and individual – with the addition of the group (Waltz, 2001). The international system is a theatre of contestation of actors' influence. Indeed, contests of influence occur in all discourses as capillary power. Foucauldian power 'forms a dispersed capillary woven into the entire social order' (Barker, 2004a: 103; Chitty, 2017b: 10). Actors include groups of states,

states, institutionalised groups, groups of individuals, and individuals. Groups of states include the United Nations (UN) organization and sub and sister organizations. Other groups include corporations, ethnic groups, faith groups, and terrorist groups. 's three levels of analysis in international relations – international system, state, and individual – with the addition of the group (Waltz, 2001). The international system is a theatre of contestation of actors' influence. Indeed, contests of influence occur in all discourses as capillary power. Foucauldian power 'forms a dispersed capillary woven into the entire social order' (Barker, 2004a: 103; Chitty, 2017b: 10). Actors include groups of states, states, institutionalised groups, groups of individuals, and individuals. Groups of states include the United Nations (UN) organization and sub and sister organizations. Other groups include corporations, ethnic groups, faith groups, and terrorist groups.

> The UN, in its creation was a 'normative consequence' of European speech acts (and their interaction with countervailing speech acts from the soviet bloc) of three kinds identified by Onuf (1989) and applied here to a world order context – assertives (that describe world order or propose a new description of the present order without calling for transformation), directives (that lead to changes in world order or ordering) and commissives (that commit an actor to a desired world order that it projects). (Chitty, 2017b: 20)

The contests of influence mostly between states and groups of states (through geopolitics, geoeconomics, and international intercultural relations) construct widely accepted instances of normative superstructure (described immediately below), that shape the behaviour of states and other international actors either as adherents of the system or as recalcitrant actors. While backed by military, economic, and cultural assets, much of the contest is conducted through competing propaganda. The term is used here neutrally without the pejorative connotations affixed by actors when using the term on the external (and sometimes internal) messaging of their rivals.

The normative superstructures are akin to 'diffused regimes' as contrasted with 'specific regimes' in international regime theory. For instance, colonial expansion was a normative superstructure and regulated this diffused regime area (Puchala and Hopkins, 1983: 61–91). The colonial expansion diffused regime shaped different kinds of propagandist messaging. These included messaging on pseudo-scientific theories of racial superiority and a hierarchy of races; legal messaging on *terra nullius*; and economic messaging on acceptability of colonial exploitation. The normative superstructure was itself propaganda, that had the intention of justifying colonialism so that colonised races would accept their fates; and colonising states could manage competition within a balance-of-power regime., 1983: 61–91). The colonial expansion diffused regime shaped different kinds of propagandist messaging. These included messaging on pseudo-scientific theories of racial superiority and a hierarchy of races; legal messaging on *terra nullius*; and economic messaging on acceptability of colonial exploitation. The normative superstructure was itself propaganda, that had the intention of justifying colonialism so that colonised races would accept their fates; and colonising states could manage competition within a balance-of-power regime.

COLD WAR, MODERNISATION, AND PROPAGANDA

Colonialism formally ended with the evolution of a diffused regime that was geared toward managing the balance of power between the victors of the Second World War: the United Kingdom, China, France, the Soviet Union, and the United States. The Soviet Union and China (after the People's Republic of China entered the Security Council) represented the Eastern bloc, and the US, France, and Britain represented the Western bloc. The other great divide was North–South. Apart from China the other great powers were in the more economically advantaged countries, described as the North. The two partly hybrid axes (the North including the West and elements of the East) provided kindling for the Cold War. While direct conflict between the two superpowers (the US and Soviet Union) was avoided in the Cold War, competition for hearts and minds in the South through propaganda was massive. Ideologies of political modernisation and economic modernisation were contested. The superpowers possessed nuclear weapons; alliances became important for external balancing. A third category, non-alignment, surfaced. Salient propaganda themes in the security arena were alignment with the West or the East, or non-alignment.. While direct conflict between the two superpowers (the US and Soviet Union) was avoided in the Cold War, competition for hearts and minds in the South through propaganda was massive. Ideologies of political modernisation and economic modernisation were contested. The superpowers possessed nuclear weapons; alliances became important for external balancing. A third category, non-alignment, surfaced. Salient propaganda themes in the security arena were alignment with the West or the East, or non-alignment.

In the Cold War period the communist world sought to present itself in the West and the Global South with tailored propaganda. Its projected image in the West was one of industrially driven 'planned social order'; the image presented in the Global South promised 'an accelerated industrialization to come' (Morris and Watnick, 1966: 282–292). And '[w]estern propaganda held political and economic liberalisation that would lead to modern developed societies' (Lippmann, 1960: 468–486). The 'Kitchen debate' at the American International Exhibition in Moscow (in 1959), between the Soviet Premier and the US Vice President, brought into sharp and memorable focus the propaganda war between the US and the Soviet Union, with 'Nixon demonstrating the advances of American technology while Khruschev defended the merits of communism' (Sevin, 2017: 63). period the communist world sought to present itself in the West and the Global South with tailored propaganda. Its projected image in the West was one of industrially driven 'planned social order'; the image presented in the Global South promised 'an accelerated industrialization to come' (Morris and Watnick, 1966: 282–292). And '[w]estern propaganda held political and economic liberalisation that would lead to modern developed societies' (Lippmann, 1960: 468–486). The 'Kitchen debate' at the American International Exhibition in Moscow (in 1959), between the Soviet Premier and the US Vice President, brought into sharp and memorable focus the propaganda war between the US and the Soviet Union, with 'Nixon demonstrating the advances of American technology while Khruschev defended the merits of communism' (Sevin, 2017: 63).

Both sides invested heavily in propaganda directed internally, toward each other and toward countries in the Global South, many of which responded with their own position and propaganda of the Non-Aligned Movement, with its promoting of peaceful coexistence in an era beset by nuclear confrontation. The 'broad anti-colonialist movement' that sought 'world peace by exhorting the powers to avoid a nuclear holocaust' had grown to be 'the advocate of a new political and economic order on a global level' (Singham, 1977: x). Mowlana credits Colin Cherry with recognising that '[p]ropaganda can be a vital factor in human emancipation' (Mowlana, 1986: 184). Non-alignment addresses emancipation from the yoke of colonialism and lingering post-colonialism., with its promoting of peaceful coexistence in an era beset by nuclear confrontation. The 'broad anti-colonialist movement' that sought 'world peace by exhorting the powers to avoid a nuclear holocaust' had grown to be 'the advocate of a new political and economic order on a global level' (Singham, 1977: x). Mowlana credits Colin Cherry with recognising that '[p]ropaganda can be a vital factor in human emancipation' (Mowlana, 1986: 184). Non-alignment addresses emancipation from the yoke of colonialism and lingering post-colonialism.

From the 1950s through the 1970s, dependency and world system theoretic positions were among the stimulants of countervailing propaganda. World system theorist Immanuel Wallerstein recognises a single 'capitalist world economy' and 'so-called sovereign states defined by and constrained by their membership of an interstate network or system'. In this Cold War period the: positions were among the stimulants of countervailing propaganda. World system theorist Immanuel Wallerstein recognises a single 'capitalist world economy' and 'so-called sovereign states defined by and constrained by their membership of an interstate network or system'. In this Cold War period the:

> Hegemony in the system refers to that situation in which the ongoing rivalry between the so-called 'great powers' is so unbalanced that that one power is truly *primus inter pares*; that is, one power can largely impose its rules and its wishes (at the very least by effective veto power) in the economic, political, military, diplomatic, and even cultural arenas. (Wallerstein, 1991: 236–237)

Dependency theory critiqued the centre–periphery North–South relations that allowed continuation of imbalanced flows of trade and information that began in colonial times. It generated emancipatory propaganda as well as strategies for counteracting the unfavourable flows. Dependency theory's influence on diplomacy sought to improve economic opportunities for newly independent developing countries, through seeking changes to the trade regime. The discussion was conducted in the United Nations Economic and Social Council.

The late 1970s saw the rise of cultural imperialism theories and recognition by developing countries that cultural domination and distorted information flows between North and South disadvantaged developing countries. 'Cultural imperialism is said to involve the domination of one culture by another and is usually thought of as a set of processes involving the ascendancy of one nation and/or the global domination of consumer capitalism' (Barker, 2004b: 38), and its close relative postcolonial theory is '[a] critical theory that explores the conditions of post-coloniality, that is colonial relations and their aftermath' (Barker, 2004b: 148). A new international information regime was called for in the United Nations Educational, Scientific and Cultural Organization (UNESCO) in the shape of a proposed New World Information and Communication Order. theories and recognition by developing countries that cultural domination and distorted information flows between North and South disadvantaged developing countries. 'Cultural imperialism is said to involve the domination of one culture by another and is usually thought of as a set of processes involving the ascendancy of one nation and/or the global domination of consumer capitalism' (Barker, 2004b: 38), and its close relative postcolonial theory is '[a] critical theory that explores the conditions of post-coloniality, that is colonial relations and their aftermath' (Barker, 2004b: 148). A new international information regime was called for in the United Nations Educational, Scientific and Cultural Organization (UNESCO) in the shape of a proposed New World Information and Communication Order.

Communicators in the United States soon distanced themselves from propaganda. New approaches to influencing emerged such as public relations, advertising, persuasion, development communication, agenda-setting, and so on. It was not until the age of globalisation that these terms with their practices were adopted in post-communist and communist countries.

GLOBALISATION, TERRORISM, AND PROPAGANDA

With the sudden evaporation of the Union of Soviet Socialist Republics (USSR) the propaganda war between it and its fellow superpower fizzled out. Francis Fukuyama (1993) announced prematurely that history had ended; liberal democratic ideology had won: 'The totalitarian state hoped to remake Soviet man himself by changing the very structure and beliefs and values through control of the press, education, and propaganda', but '[t]he most fundamental failure of totalitarianism was its failure to control thought. Soviet citizens, as it turned out, had all along retained an ability to think for themselves. Many understood, despite years of government propaganda that their government was lying to them.' The history that had ended was that of the Soviet state's propaganda about the efficacy of the Soviet system in bringing prosperity to the developed world. The Soviet Union's leading successor state, Russia, continued within Wallerstein's Western-led capitalist world economic system. (1993) announced prematurely that history had ended; liberal democratic ideology had won: 'The totalitarian state hoped to remake Soviet man himself by changing the very structure and beliefs and values through control of the press, education, and propaganda', but '[t]he most fundamental failure of totalitarianism was its failure to control thought. Soviet citizens, as it turned out, had all along retained an ability to think for themselves. Many understood, despite years of government propaganda that their government was lying to them.' The history that had ended was that of the Soviet state's propaganda about the efficacy of the Soviet system in bringing prosperity to the developed world. The Soviet Union's leading successor state, Russia, continued within Wallerstein's Western-led capitalist world economic system.

The 1990s saw the rise of globalisation theory and the diffused regime of globalisation. Northeast and Southeast Asian countries sped forward economically. China was admitted to the World Trade Organization (WTO) at the end of 2001. There was little to propagandise on the economic front. Capitalism or movement toward capitalism was widely accepted. Globalisation as a propaganda wave and material presence all over the world kindled fires of reaction in the Muslim world. As much as there had been Muslim resistance to conversion in the time of Pope Gregory XV, the new evangelisation around globalisation made some Muslims uncomfortable; and some among these were easily radicalised by al Qaeda and later Islamic State agents through propaganda and training programmes. The principal enemy was no longer Russia. Rather, Islamist terrorist organisations and their propaganda and violence dominated the international theatre. Jihad became the rallying call pronounced by Islamist influencers to trigger militant activity. It refers to struggles both internal and external to the individual, but it is the external military struggle that generally comes to mind: the notion has been exploited by Islamicist influencers (Karim, 2004: 108–109). theory and the diffused regime of globalisation. Northeast and Southeast Asian countries sped forward economically. China was admitted to the World Trade Organization (WTO) at the end of 2001. There was little to propagandise on the economic front. Capitalism or movement toward capitalism was widely accepted. Globalisation as a propaganda wave and material presence all over the world kindled fires of reaction in the Muslim world. As much as there had been Muslim resistance to conversion in the time of Pope Gregory XV, the new evangelisation around globalisation made some Muslims uncomfortable; and some among these were easily radicalised by al Qaeda and later Islamic State agents through propaganda and training programmes. The principal enemy was no longer Russia. Rather, Islamist terrorist organisations and their propaganda and violence dominated the international theatre. Jihad became the rallying call pronounced by Islamist influencers to trigger militant activity. It refers to struggles both internal and external to the individual, but it is the external military struggle that generally comes to mind: the notion has been exploited by Islamicist influencers (Karim, 2004: 108–109).

If ideologies are the scriptures of communities of political faith, scriptures are the ideologies of faith communities. Al Qaeda propaganda drew nourishment from the normative superstructure of Islam, even if there was no desire from peace-loving Muslim communities to be associated with its militant jihad. If one of Marxist thought's attractions to academics is its political-economic-sociological provenance – that preceded the liberal slicing and dicing of political philosophy into politics, economics, and sociology – Islam's attraction to intellectuals born into that tradition is that it is a comprehensive religious ideology, that incorporates guidance on the aforesaid societal areas. It was noted earlier that ideologies are clouds of propaganda that can be adopted as the dominant organising ideational framework of a social system and be propagated by state institutions. Islam does this for Muslim societies and its '*ummah wahidah*' or community of believers. propaganda drew nourishment from the normative superstructure of Islam, even if there was no desire from peace-loving Muslim communities to be associated with its militant jihad. If one of Marxist thought's attractions to academics is its political-economic-sociological provenance – that preceded the liberal slicing and dicing of political philosophy into politics, economics, and sociology – Islam's attraction to intellectuals born into that tradition is that it is a comprehensive religious ideology, that incorporates guidance on the aforesaid societal areas. It was noted earlier that ideologies are clouds of propaganda that can be adopted as the dominant organising ideational framework of a social system and be propagated by state institutions. Islam does this for Muslim societies and its '*ummah wahidah*' or community of believers.

9/11 led to media outrage and retributive plans by the Bush administration. The media played what many outraged Americans would have seen as an essential role. It was responsible for 'forestalling of public doubt' through 'Mass mobilisation ... Vilification of culprit ... Ignoring alternative sources of culpability ... The great sell of a "wartime" president ... Neglect or manipulation of history ... Abandonment of journalistic curiosity ... Assimilating administration propaganda and compliance with controls' (Boyd-Barrett, 2003: 37–48). These actions are akin to propaganda techniques, as will be seen in the next section. How does this square with America's tradition of negatively viewing propaganda? led to media outrage and retributive plans by the Bush administration. The media played what many outraged Americans would have seen as an essential role. It was responsible for 'forestalling of public doubt' through 'Mass mobilisation ... Vilification of culprit ... Ignoring alternative sources of culpability ... The great sell of a "wartime" president ... Neglect or manipulation of history ... Abandonment of journalistic curiosity ... Assimilating administration propaganda and compliance with controls' (Boyd-Barrett, 2003: 37–48). These actions are akin to propaganda techniques, as will be seen in the next section. How does this square with America's tradition of negatively viewing propaganda?

The other feature of this period that is relevant to this chapter is the much-heralded rise of China, through its spectacular economic performance after being admitted into the WTO, the institution that embodies the world trade regime. China sagaciously moved away from terms and ways that looked like propaganda, to public relations, public diplomacy, and soft power. It sought 'to assure others of the benevolence and rectitude of its actions in international relations, actions that are associated in international relations theory with a hegemon' (Chitty et al., 2018: 3). It professed a distaste for hegemony., through its spectacular economic performance after being admitted into the WTO, the institution that embodies the world trade regime. China sagaciously moved away from terms and ways that looked like propaganda, to public relations, public diplomacy, and soft power. It sought 'to assure others of the benevolence and rectitude of its actions in international relations, actions that are associated in international relations theory with a hegemon' (Chitty et al., 2018: 3). It professed a distaste for hegemony.

FRACTURED GLOBALISATION

This section examines the fracturing of the globalisation regime in the 2020s by populist reactions to Western working-class underperformance and Chinese overperformance, heightened by the global COVID-19 pandemic.

Globalisation has been fractured through producing discontented losers and contented winners, within countries and among states. The United States and China are important to focus on here. It was its economic superiority that gave the US its strategic victory over the Soviet Union. The window was opened for the modernisation drive to amplify qualitatively and quantitatively, in order to sufficiently brand the post-Cold War epoch. The globalisation regime was born. Through astute management of its propaganda and policy transnationalisation imperatives in the United Nations systems, and particularly in the WTO, China grew rich and did so rapidly. are important to focus on here. It was its economic superiority that gave the US its strategic victory over the Soviet Union. The window was opened for the modernisation drive to amplify qualitatively and quantitatively, in order to sufficiently brand the post-Cold War epoch. The globalisation regime was born. Through astute management of its propaganda and policy transnationalisation imperatives in the United Nations systems, and particularly in the WTO, China grew rich and did so rapidly.

China's propaganda messages included the following sentiments. China experienced a century of shame that needs to be remedied. Its rise is inevitable and peaceful. It should be given its due place in the international system. China is not and never will be a hegemon. It is a developing country and needs to be treated as such in the WTO, enjoying concessions afforded to developing countries. These are items of faith among Chinese nationals, and they are believed variously by some in the rest of the world.. China is not and never will be a hegemon. It is a developing country and needs to be treated as such in the WTO, enjoying concessions afforded to developing countries. These are items of faith among Chinese nationals, and they are believed variously by some in the rest of the world.

In what Reich and Lebow (2014: 6–8) call a post-hegemonic world, an aspiring hegemon would need to shoulder three kinds of responsibilities. These are setting international agendas, managing international economic structures and processes, and sponsoring global initiatives

(Chitty, 2017b). China has followed this playbook faithfully through setting up new international forums such as BRICS (Brazil–Russia–India–China–South Africa), financing institutions such as the New Development Bank and the Asia Infrastructure Investment Bank, and the Belt and Road Initiative (BRI): an incipient hegemon's public diplomacy plexus. 'The United Nations was an incipient hegemon's security-economic-plexus (IHPDP). The Chinese IHPDP, BRI, is not of the same scale and scope of the UN system; it also inhabits and draws sustenance from parts of the UN' (Chitty et al., 2018: 5). From a big tent propaganda perspective what BRI as a Chinese IHPDP does is propaganda. The BRI propaganda effort seeks to bring more and more countries under the BRI agreement. Messaging by Chinese media such as the China Global Television Network (CGTN) is viewed as a soft power tool (Li, 2020: 21–45). China has developed its media hardware and content production that facilitates its media being latched onto BRI for propaganda purposes. A study shows that BRI messaging reflected in the newspapers of eight Indian Ocean littoral (IOR) countries (Australia, India, Indonesia, Iran, South Africa, Kenya, Singapore, and Pakistan) had been relatively effective. The 'percentage of combined positive and neutral frames that have been registered by IOR newspapers must be heart-warming to China. However, there is mixed sentiment in Quad countries and Singapore where the Indian critique of aspects of BRI finds sympathetic audiences' (Chitty et al., 2018: 17). The Quad (Quadrilateral Security Dialogue) is a strategic forum of four democracies: Australia, Japan, India, and the US. (Brazil–Russia–India–China–South Africa), financing institutions such as the New Development Bank and the Asia Infrastructure Investment Bank, and the Belt and Road Initiative (BRI): an incipient hegemon's public diplomacy plexus. 'The United Nations was an incipient hegemon's security-economic-plexus (IHPDP). The Chinese IHPDP, BRI, is not of the same scale and scope of the UN system; it also inhabits and draws sustenance from parts of the UN' (Chitty et al., 2018: 5). From a big tent propaganda perspective what BRI as a Chinese IHPDP does is propaganda. The BRI propaganda effort seeks to bring more and more countries under the BRI agreement. Messaging by Chinese media such as the China Global Television Network (CGTN) is viewed as a soft power tool (Li, 2020: 21–45). China has developed its media hardware and content production that facilitates its media being latched onto BRI for propaganda purposes. A study shows that BRI messaging reflected in the newspapers of eight Indian Ocean littoral (IOR) countries (Australia, India, Indonesia, Iran, South Africa, Kenya, Singapore, and Pakistan) had been relatively effective. The 'percentage of combined positive and neutral frames that have been registered by IOR newspapers must be heart-warming to China. However, there is mixed sentiment in Quad countries and Singapore where the Indian critique of aspects of BRI finds sympathetic audiences' (Chitty et al., 2018: 17). The Quad (Quadrilateral Security Dialogue) is a strategic forum of four democracies: Australia, Japan, India, and the US.

Globalisation had winners and losers in the United States as well. Unlike workers in declining industries, elites in the US and Europe benefit from globalisation. It follows that blue-collar workers blame elites for their misfortunes. They believe political correctness blocks a blunt addressing of problems dumped on them by globalisation and outsiders. As such, the blunt power of strongmen is attractive to these individuals. Rather than play with the potentially weak hands dealt to them, strongmen throw down their cards and demand a new game (Chitty, 2019). in the US and Europe benefit from globalisation. It follows that blue-collar workers blame elites for their misfortunes. They believe political correctness blocks a blunt addressing of problems dumped on them by globalisation and outsiders. As such, the blunt power of strongmen is attractive to these individuals. Rather than play with the potentially weak hands dealt to them, strongmen throw down their cards and demand a new game (Chitty, 2019).

The new social media became a mechanism for the organic production and dissemination of propaganda picked up and amplified by talk radio and cable television. The propaganda of the postbellum society was challenged by a new propaganda that sought to jettison political correctness, monolithic notions of truth, and political propriety. 'Blue collar individuals drift from "mainstream" media to more appealing social media influencers. Denigration of the rules of social propriety as products of "political correctness" leads to social collisions, and this erosion of civility removes gentle rule structures that avert outbreaks of hurtful behavior' (Chitty, 2019). became a mechanism for the organic production and dissemination of propaganda picked up and amplified by talk radio and cable television. The propaganda of the postbellum society was challenged by a new propaganda that sought to jettison political correctness, monolithic notions of truth, and political propriety. 'Blue collar individuals drift from "mainstream" media to more appealing social media influencers. Denigration of the rules of social propriety as products of "political correctness" leads to social collisions, and this erosion of civility removes gentle rule structures that avert outbreaks of hurtful behavior' (Chitty, 2019).

The technological developments, coupled with the natural tendency (as seen in democracies across the world) for democratic electorates to cleave into left and right halves, led to party ideologies becoming akin to faiths. Importantly there is a political-economic aspect to the cultural cleavage into ideological faiths. The ideological faiths of the right and left peopled by over 70 million voters in each wing, according to the 2020 US presidential election results, make vote and audience banks of each group for politicians and media, respectively.. The ideological faiths of the right and left peopled by over 70 million voters in each wing, according to the 2020 US presidential election results, make vote and audience banks of each group for politicians and media, respectively.

The dictum 'all is fair in love and war' has extended to politics as well. Politics is a kind of war after all. Machiavelli 'has inspired political behaviour ever since the sixteenth century, exhorting the ruler to exercise fox-like cunning and leonine strength' (Chitty, 2004: 60; Machiavelli, 1952). Politics is 'a terrain dotted with half-truths, broken promises, and white lies' (Chitty, 2004: 59). The imperative to protect vote and audience banks, associated with right and left ideological faiths, shapes the ideological stances and explanations of events, of media, and political actors on each side, who see the other side distributing false propaganda, fake news, and plain lies. Abraham Lincoln reportedly said, 'you may fool people for a time; you can fool a part of the people all the time; but you can't fool all the people all the time' (Schwartz, 2018). Some influencers are happy to fool part of the people all the time. This internally directed propaganda is of immense consequence because the US is a superpower, and one half of the US propaganda cloud may be used by influencers to promote either populism or globalisation, unilateralism or multilateralism, isolationism or engagement. 'has inspired political behaviour ever since the sixteenth century, exhorting the ruler to exercise fox-like cunning and leonine strength' (Chitty, 2004: 60; Machiavelli, 1952). Politics is 'a terrain dotted with half-truths, broken promises, and white lies' (Chitty, 2004: 59). The imperative to protect vote and audience banks, associated with right and left ideological faiths, shapes the ideological stances and explanations of events, of media, and political actors on each side, who see the other side distributing false propaganda, fake news, and plain lies. Abraham Lincoln reportedly said, 'you may fool people for a time; you can fool a part of the people all the time;

but you can't fool all the people all the time' (Schwartz, 2018). Some influencers are happy to fool part of the people all the time. This internally directed propaganda is of immense consequence because the US is a superpower, and one half of the US propaganda cloud may be used by influencers to promote either populism or globalisation, unilateralism or multilateralism, isolationism or engagement.

However, the Lasswellian top-down model does not neatly explain sociological propaganda in an age when social media has fractured the elite–mass communication hierarchy. Challenging the power of the old influencers is the power of new influencers, who generate new clouds of propaganda through their social media communication. They have alternative theories about the origins of global pandemics; different notions of good actors and bad actors among international and national health organisations, nation states, and their political leaders; conflicting views on governmental and personal strategies for curbing the spread of the virus. In the contemporary era the so-called sudras are influential too, through the use of social media. When they find a populist political leader who expresses their views, he or she becomes their voice. If elected to office, the leader is able to seek to shape policy on their behalf. in an age when social media has fractured the elite–mass communication hierarchy. Challenging the power of the old influencers is the power of new influencers, who generate new clouds of propaganda through their social media communication. They have alternative theories about the origins of global pandemics; different notions of good actors and bad actors among international and national health organisations, nation states, and their political leaders; conflicting views on governmental and personal strategies for curbing the spread of the virus. In the contemporary era the so-called sudras are influential too, through the use of social media. When they find a populist political leader who expresses their views, he or she becomes their voice. If elected to office, the leader is able to seek to shape policy on their behalf.

In contrast the Chinese party-state has used its ideological apparatus (media, the education system, party cells) to promote ideological convergence. I discussed this promotion by apex influencers of ideological convergence among lower-level influencers – such as academics and journalists – as a superimposition on technological convergence, with a Chinese academic (13 January 2020). Promotion of ideological convergence under the party-state normative structure, together with parallel strategies of shepherding opinion on social media, allow traditional influencers (party-state officials) to maintain ideological stability, at least for the time being. In communist states, 'solidarity and achievement depend on ideological unanimity, and communication provides the model with which to conform' (Yu, 1963: 259). Today, globalisation and social media have nibbled at ideological unanimity; the need to institute convergence is a response.. I discussed this promotion by apex influencers of ideological convergence among lower-level influencers – such as academics and journalists – as a superimposition on technological convergence, with a Chinese academic (13 January 2020). Promotion of ideological convergence under the party-state normative structure, together with parallel strategies of shepherding opinion on social media, allow traditional influencers (party-state officials) to maintain ideological stability, at least for the time being. In communist states, 'solidarity and achievement depend on ideological unanimity, and communication provides the model with which to conform' (Yu, 1963: 259). Today, globalisation and social media have nibbled at ideological unanimity; the need to institute convergence is a response.

INTENT, CONTENT, AND CONTENTMENT

Propaganda as intended influence is used by all states, whether liberal democracies, authoritarian, or totalitarian. Authoritarian countries have been accused of engaging in sharp power in the guise of soft power. While sharp power shares some characteristics with techniques of political propaganda (and may be accompanied by a climate of propaganda), it is not propaganda. It involves coercion or inducement and is therefore not soft power either. It makes targets act in preferred ways that are to the advantage of the influencing state. Sharp power influence is likely to be subsumed under a larger propaganda effort such as eroding faith in liberal democracy. 'The attempt at total manufacturing and control of opinion, positively through propaganda and negatively through censorship' is a 'major characteristic of totalitarianism' with the goal of turning 'the population from a potential threat into its pliant tool' (Kautsky, 1962: 95). While Kautsky's words refer to the Cold War, the following are from the 21st century:. While sharp power shares some characteristics with techniques of political propaganda (and may be accompanied by a climate of propaganda), it is not propaganda. It involves coercion or inducement and is therefore not soft power either. It makes targets act in preferred ways that are to the advantage of the influencing state. Sharp power influence is likely to be subsumed under a larger propaganda effort such as eroding faith in liberal democracy. 'The attempt at total manufacturing and control of opinion, positively through propaganda and negatively through censorship' is a 'major characteristic of totalitarianism' with the goal of turning 'the population from a potential threat into its pliant tool' (Kautsky, 1962: 95). While Kautsky's words refer to the Cold War, the following are from the 21st century:

> Authoritarian influence efforts are 'sharp' in the sense that they pierce, penetrate, or perforate the political and information environments in the targeted countries. In the ruthless new competition that is under way between autocratic and democratic states ... [t]hese regimes are not necessarily seeking to 'win hearts and minds,' the common frame of reference for soft power efforts, but they are surely seeking to manipulate their target audiences by distorting the information that reaches them. (Walker and Ludwig, 2017) efforts, but they are surely seeking to manipulate their target audiences by distorting the information that reaches them. (Walker and Ludwig, 2017)

Employing techniques of propaganda implies intent to use propaganda; this is intended influence.

Recall that sociological propaganda is organic and 'not the result of deliberate propaganda action' (Ellul, 1973: 64–67). At the other end of the propaganda interface, social media usage at the molecular level can be organic but have significant impact when molar patterns emerge. Users of social media may or may not have an intention to influence, in the form of willingness to change others' behaviour. Some may merely want to express views, react, or be noticed. However, their interactions can contribute to the generation of unintended propaganda that media, advertisers, and politicians can use in their own intended propaganda efforts. Clicking on 'like' can have an effect if something goes viral, if numbers are large enough for influencers to consider them to be of consequence. is organic and 'not the result of deliberate propaganda action' (Ellul, 1973: 64–67). At the other end of the propaganda interface, social media usage at the molecular level can be organic but have significant impact when molar patterns emerge. Users of social media may or may not have an intention to influence, in the form of willingness to change others' behaviour. Some may merely want to express views, react, or be noticed. However, their interactions can contribute to the generation of unintended propaganda that media, advertisers, and politicians can use in their own intended propaganda efforts. Clicking on 'like' can have an effect if something goes viral, if numbers are large enough for influencers to consider them to be of consequence.

Content refers to what is contained in a message whatever the medium, whether the medium is the human body and its organs, or extensions thereof. Contentment refers to consequences of message reception, whether the result is contentment or discontentment. Content maybe characterised by virtue and virtuosity. Virtue here consists of assertives, directives, and commissives that are drawn from the worldview of a propagandist, seen as such by a receiver with whom this worldview resonates (Chitty, 2017b: 20). Where there is resonance there is contentment. When the preferred worldview is politically operationalised, there can be contentment in the receiver.. Virtue here consists of assertives, directives, and commissives that are drawn from the worldview of a propagandist, seen as such by a receiver with whom this worldview resonates (Chitty, 2017b: 20). Where there is resonance there is contentment. When the preferred worldview is politically operationalised, there can be contentment in the receiver.

Virtuosity, in relation to people's tangible and intangible products, is related to excellence in crafting, signifying superlative technique. It is possible to admire the virtuosity of propaganda messages and be discontented by what a receiver may see as its lack of virtue (ibid.: 25–29). Rhetoric, as a means of crafting persuasive content, is meant to go beyond virtuosity of composition, to include 'civic commitment' (Crowley, 2003). The question is to whose civic commitment does this refer in a situation, as in the US after the 2020 election, where there are over 70 million people on two sides of an argument about what civic commitment might be.

Perceptions that prevail in a society colour views of internal and external propaganda. Propaganda was associated with German espionage and disingenuity during the First World War, but 'by 1930, propaganda was understood to include efforts by just about anyone to influence public opinion – especially the US government' (Sproule, 1984: 9). It was Sigmund Freud's nephew Edward L. Bernays who sought to sanitise propagandist public relations by recommending an ethical professional framework (ibid.: 5, 10–12). As a term, 'propaganda' fell out of favour after the communists began to use 'agitation propaganda'. But in times of war, 'the need to win increases the appeal of and acceptance of propaganda. As peace looms ahead, American suspicions of propaganda resurface with a vengeance. Propaganda again falls out of favor' (Zaharna, 2004: 222; Brown, 2008). Nancy Snow (2020: 422–429) and Louis Roth and Richard Arndt (1986: 723) have written about a 'good' American propaganda that will promote the values of the nation's republican democracy. who sought to sanitise propagandist public relations by recommending an ethical professional framework (ibid.: 5, 10–12). As a term, 'propaganda' fell out of favour after the communists began to use 'agitation propaganda'. But in times of war, 'the need to win increases the appeal of and acceptance of propaganda. As peace looms ahead, American suspicions of propaganda resurface with a vengeance. Propaganda again falls out of favor' (Zaharna, 2004: 222; Brown, 2008). Nancy Snow (2020: 422–429) and Louis Roth and Richard Arndt (1986: 723) have written about a 'good' American propaganda that will promote the values of the nation's republican democracy.

CONCLUSION

This discussion shows that sociological propaganda includes instances of 'unintended influence', but that political propaganda is generally 'intended'. The fundamental factor is influence and is constituted by power and 'unintended influence'. Where intention is at play, hard, soft, smart, and sharp power are ways in which power is exercised, in terms of how associated resources are used: through coercion, inducement, or attraction. Hard and soft power could come into play unintentionally as well. Charisma, cultural imperialism, hegemony, and propaganda are associated with normative structures linked to influence. Communication is the broad concept associated with the operationalisation of both types of influence. Development communication, international public relations, marketing, persuasion, propaganda, and strategic communication are methods of communication through which intended influence can be exercised. This is by no means the final word. This chapter can only be a prolegomenon to a comprehensive treatise on propaganda as influence. includes instances of 'unintended influence', but that political propaganda is generally 'intended'. The fundamental factor is influence and is constituted by power and 'unintended influence'. Where intention is at play, hard, soft, smart, and sharp power are ways in which power is exercised, in terms of how associated resources are used: through coercion, inducement, or attraction. Hard and soft power could come into play unintentionally as well. Charisma, cultural imperialism, hegemony, and propaganda are associated with normative structures linked to influence. Communication is the broad concept associated with the operationalisation of both types of influence. Development communication, international public relations, marketing, persuasion, propaganda, and strategic communication are methods of communication through which intended influence can be exercised. This is by no means the final word. This chapter can only be a prolegomenon to a comprehensive treatise on propaganda as influence.

Unintended sociological propaganda is an important source of influence and is the feeder for intended political propaganda. It is doubly important today in the propaganda contest between the two superpowers, the US and China. New social media allows sociological propaganda to emanate from the base of the Lasswellian pyramid in the US, and to be voiced by influencers who disregard elements of the old normative superstructure (Lasswell, 1965). The result is a society with a split normative superstructure, two broad realities, and conflicting 'truths'. The dynamic is strengthened because of political-economic advantages possessed by influencers. In China, on the other hand, the potential for the normative superstructure to be eroded by propaganda generated by social media is managed carefully. Clashing today are the normative structures of superpowers, as well as the elite-generated and mass-generated normative structures. is an important source of influence and is the feeder for intended political propaganda. It is doubly important today in the propaganda contest between the two superpowers, the US and China. New social media allows sociological propaganda to emanate from the base of the Lasswellian pyramid in the US, and to be voiced by influencers who disregard elements of the old normative superstructure (Lasswell, 1965). The result is a society with a split normative superstructure, two broad realities, and conflicting 'truths'. The dynamic is strengthened because of political-economic advantages possessed by influencers. In China, on the other hand, the potential for the normative superstructure to be eroded by propaganda generated by social media is managed carefully. Clashing today are the normative structures of superpowers, as well as the elite-generated and mass-generated normative structures.

REFERENCES

Barker, C. (2004a), *Cultural studies: theory and practice*, London: SAGE.
Barker, C. (2004b), *The SAGE dictionary of cultural studies*, London: SAGE.
Berger, P. and T. Luckmann (1991), *The social construction of reality: a treatise in the sociology of knowledge*, Garden City, NY: Anchor Books.
Boyd-Barrett, O. (2003), 'Doubt foreclosed: US mainstream media and the attacks of September 11, 2001', in N. Chitty, R. Rush, and M. Semati (eds), *Studies in terrorism: media scholarship and the enigma of terrorism*, Penang: Southbound, pp. 35–49.
Brown, J. (2008), 'Public diplomacy & propaganda: their differences', *American Public Diplomacy: Insight and Analysis from Foreign Affairs Practitioners and Scholars*, available at: http://americandiplomacy.web.unc.edu/2008/09/public-diplomacy-propaganda-their-differences/.
Chitty, N. (1992), 'Development is communication: self-reliance, self-development, and empowerment', *Telematics and Informatics*, 9(1): 21–42.
Chitty, N. (2004), 'Weapons of mass distraction: world security and personal politics', in Y. Kamalipour and N. Snow (eds), *War, media, and propaganda*, Lanham MD: Rowman & Littlefield, pp. 59–68.
Chitty, N. (2005), 'International communication: continuing into the 21st century as an academic "commons"', *Gazette: The International Journal for Communication Studies*, 67(6): 555–559.
Chitty, N. (2011), 'Public diplomacy: courting publics for short-term advantage or partnering publics for lasting peace and sustainability', in A. Fisher and S. Lucas (eds), *Trials of engagement: the future of US public diplomacy*, Leiden: Martinus Nijhoff, pp. 252–269.
Chitty, N. (2017a), 'Conclusion', in N. Chitty, L. Ji, G. Rawnsley, and C. Hayden (eds), *The Routledge Handbook of Soft Power*, London: Routledge, pp. 453–463.
Chitty, N. (2017b), 'Soft power, civic virtue and world politics', in N. Chitty, L. Ji, G. Rawnsley, and C. Hayden (eds), *The Routledge Handbook of Soft Power*, London: Routledge, pp. 9–36.
Chitty, N. (2019), 'The rise of blunt power in the strongman era', *Georgetown Journal of International Affairs*, 28 February, available at: https://www.georgetownjournalofinternationalaffairs.org/online-edition/2019/2/28/the-rise-of-blunt-power-in-the-strongman-era, accessed 21 November 2020.
Chitty, N. (2020), 'Love in a covid climate', Talk for International Cultural Relations Research Alliance conference, 28 October.
Chitty, N., D. Ahlawat, M. Li, and L. Gopal (2018), 'The Chinese Belt and Road Initiative and the Indian Ocean Region: sentiment towards economic prosperity and security implications', *Indian Journal of Politics*, 52(1–2): 1–20.
Crowley, S. (2003), 'Composition is not rhetoric', *Enculturation*, 5(1), available at: http://www.enculturation.net/5_1/crowley.html, accessed 18 November 2020.
Ellul, J. (1973), *Propaganda: the formation of men's attitudes*, New York: Vintage Books.
Finlayson, J. and M. Zacher (1983). 'The GATT and the regulation of trade barriers: regime dynamics and functions', in S. Krasner (ed.), *International regimes: lessons from inductive analysis*, London: Cornell University Press, pp. 273–314.
Frederick, H. (1993), *Global communication and international relations*, Belmont, CA: Wadsworth.
Fukuyama, F. (1993), *The end of history and the last man*, London: Penguin.
Gregory, B. (2005), 'Public diplomacy and strategic communication: cultures, firewalls, and imported norms', Paper presented at the American Political Science Association, Conference on International Communication and Conflict, George Washington University and Georgetown University, Washington, DC, available at: http://www8.georgetown.edu/cct/apsa/papers/gregory.pdf, accessed 22 November 2020.
Grunig, J., L. Grunig, K. Sriramesh, and A. Lyra (1995), 'Models of public relations in an international setting', *Journal of Public Relations Research*, 7(3): 163–186.
Habermas, J. (1979), *Communication and the evolution of society*, translated by T. McCarthy, Boston, MA: Beacon Press.
Habermas, J. (1987), *The theory of communicative action. Vol. 2: Lifeworld and system: a critique of functionalist reason*, Cambridge: Polity Press.
Habermas, J. and T. MacCarthy (2004), *The theory of communicative action. Volume 1: Reason and the rationalization of society*, Cambridge: Polity Press.
Harari, Y. (2011), *Sapiens: a brief history of mankind*, London: Vintage Books.

Izadi, F. and R. Nelson (2020), 'Ethics and social issues in public diplomacy', in N. Snow and N. Cull (eds), *Routledge handbook of public diplomacy* (2nd edn), New York: Routledge, pp. 391–404.

Karim, K. (2004), 'War, propaganda, and Islam in Muslim and western sources', in Y. Kamalipour and N. Snow (eds), *War, media, and propaganda: a global perspective*, Lanham MD: Rowman & Littlefield, pp. 1–261.

Kautsky, J. (1962), *Political change in developed countries: nationalism and communism*, New York: John Wiley & Co, pp. 3–347.

Lasswell, H. (1927), *Propaganda technique in the world war*, New York: A.A. Knopf.

Lasswell, H. (1965), *World politics and personal insecurity*, New York: Free Press.

Lasswell, H. and A. Kaplan (1950), *Power and society; a framework for political inquiry*, New Haven, CT: Yale University Press.

Lee, R. (2012), 'Theologies of failure: Islamic conversion in early modern Rome', *Essays in History*, 45, http://www.essaysinhistory.net/theologies-of-failure-islamic-conversion-in-early-modern-rome/#more-758.

Li, M. (2020), *Chinese television and soft power communication in Australia*, London: Anthem Press. *communication in Australia*, London: Anthem Press.

Lippmann, W. (1960), 'The world outside and the pictures in our heads', in W. Schramm (ed.), *Mass communications*, Urbana IL: University of Illinois Press, pp. 468–486.

Machiavelli, N. (1952), *The Prince*, translated by L. Ricci, New York: New American Library of World Literature., N. (1952), *The Prince*, translated by L. Ricci, New York: New American Library of World Literature.

Morris, B. and M. Watnick (1966), 'Current communist strategy in nonindustrialized countries', in J. Kautsky (ed.), *Political change in underdeveloped countries: nationalism and communism*, New York: John Wiley & Sons, pp. 282–292.

Mowlana, H. (1986), *Global information and world communication*, New York: Longman.

Nye, J. (2011), *The future of power*, New York: Public Affairs.

Onuf, N. (1989), *World of our making and rule in social theory and international relations*, Columbia: University of South Carolina Press.

Pamment, J. (2020), 'Public diplomacy and development communication: two sides of the same coin?', in N. Snow and N. Cull (eds), *Routledge handbook of public diplomacy* (2nd edn), New York: Routledge, pp. 430–437.

Puchala, D. and R. Hopkins (1983), 'International regimes', in S. Krasner (ed.), *International regimes: lessons from inductive analysis*, London: Cornell University Press, pp. 61–91.

Reich, S. and R. Lebow (2014), *Good-bye hegemony! Power and influence in the global system*, Princeton, NJ: Princeton University Press.

Roth, L. and R. Arndt (1986), 'Information, culture, and public diplomacy: searching for an American style of public diplomacy', in W. Brasch and D. Uloth (eds), *The press and the state: sociohistorical and contemporary interpretations*, Lanham, MD: University Press of America.

Schwartz, T. (2018), '"You can fool all of the people", Lincoln never said that', Abraham Lincoln Association, available at: https://abrahamlincolnassociation.org/you-can-fool-all-of-the-people-lincoln-never-said-that/, accessed 21 November 2020.

Sevin, E. (2017), Understanding soft power through public diplomacy', in N. Chitty, L. Ji, G. Rawnsley, and C. Hayden (eds), *The Routledge handbook of soft power*, London: Routledge, pp. 62–71. through public diplomacy', in N. Chitty, L. Ji, G. Rawnsley, and C. Hayden (eds), *The Routledge handbook of soft power*, London: Routledge, pp. 62–71.

Singham, A. (ed.) (1977), *The nonaligned movement in world politics*, Westport CT: Lawrence Hill & Co.

Snow, N. (2020), 'Exchanges as good propaganda', in N. Snow and N. Cull (eds), *Routledge handbook of public diplomacy* (2nd edn), New York: Routledge, pp. 422–429.

Sproule, M. (1984), 'The propaganda analysis movement since World War I', available at: https://files.eric.ed.gov/fulltext/ED253902.pdf, accessed 19 November 2020.

Therborn, G. (1980), *The ideology of power and the power of ideology*, London: Verso Editions & MLB.

Walker, C. and J. Ludwig (2017), 'The meaning of sharp power: how authoritarian states project influence', *Foreign Affairs*, 16 November, available at: https://www.foreignaffairs.com/articles/china/2017-11-16/meaning-sharp-power, accessed 21 November 2020.

Wallerstein, E. (1991), 'The three instances of hegemony in the history of world capitalism', in G. Crane and A. Amawi (eds), *The theoretical evolution of international political economy: a reader*, New York: Oxford University Press, pp. 236–244.

Waltz, K. (2001), *Man, the state, and war*, New York: Columbia University Press.

Wendt, A. (1992), 'Anarchy is what states make of it: the social construction of power politics', *International Organization*, 46(2): 391–425.

Yalvaç, F. (2017), 'Critical theory: international relations' engagement with the Frankfurt School and Marxism', *International Studies*, 20 November, available at: https://doi.org/10.1093/acrefore/9780190846626.013.109, accessed 18 November 2020.

Yu, F. (1963), 'Communications and politics in communist China', in L. Pye (ed.), *Communication and political development*, Princeton, NJ: Princeton University Press, pp. 259–297.

Zaharna, R. (2004), 'From propaganda to public diplomacy in the information age', in Y. Kamalipour and N. Snow (eds), *War, media, and propaganda*, Lanham, MD: Rowman & Littlefield, pp. 219–225.

2. Fake news, trust, and behaviour in a digital world
Terry Flew

INTRODUCTION: THE RISE OF 'FAKE NEWS'

> 'I'm not going to give you a question. You are fake news.'
> (Then US President-elect Donald Trump to CNN journalist Jim Acosta, 11 January 2017)

The term 'fake news' has become ubiquitous in public discourse. It was awarded the Word of the Year by the *Collins Dictionary* and the American Dialect Society in 2017, a public inquiry into 'fake news' was conducted by the United Kingdom (UK) government in 2017, and European leaders such as France's Emmanuel Macron and Germany's Angela Merkel denounced the role played by 'fake news' in their 2017 national elections (Scott and Eddy, 2017). Parliaments in Singapore, Germany, Malaysia, Algeria, and – ironically, given its perceived role in the phenomenon globally – Russia have passed anti-fake news legislation, or laws intended to limit the spread of misinformation taking the apparent form of news. United States (US) President Donald Trump persistently used the term to describe those media he deemed hostile to his presidency, including CNN, the *New York Times*, *Washington Post*, and many others. Trump's championing of the term was particularly ironic, as the uncovering of multiple fake news sites by Craig Silverman and his team at *Buzzfeed News* first drew attention to the importance of 'fake news' Facebook pages to Trump's ultimately successful presidential campaign (Gendreau, 2017; Silverman et al., 2016).

The ubiquity of the term 'fake news', and the extent to which it was weaponised by political leaders such as Trump to reject criticisms made by political opponents or in media outlets, led to a backlash against the use of the term. Claire Wardle, the co-founder of First Draft and one of the first to systematically analyse the fake news phenomenon (Wardle, 2017), proposed that the term should cease to be used. In a late 2017 paper, Wardle and co-author Hussein Derakhshan argued the need to stop using the term 'fake news' as it was too imprecise and corrupted, and to instead focus upon phenomena such as information disorder, misinformation, and disinformation (Derakhshan and Wardle, 2017). Journalists such as Margaret Sullivan at the *Washington Post* proposed that it was 'time to retire the tainted term "fake news"' (Sullivan, 2017), and the UK House of Commons Digital, Culture, Media and Sport Committee, which was tasked in early 2017 with investigating 'fake news', had concluded by 2018 that 'the term "fake news" … had taken on a variety of meanings, including a description of any statement that is not liked or agreed with by the reader' (House of Commons, 2019: 10). The UK government accepted its recommendation, and required that all official documents use the terms 'misinformation' and 'disinformation' instead of 'fake news'. Much academic and practitioner-related literature has followed this path (Benkler et al., 2018; Jack, 2017). Meanwhile, the term 'fake news' has become a kind of vernacular shorthand for rumours and other forms of information revealed to be untrue, or information which someone simply refuses to believe. Catching a taxi in New Brunswick, New Jersey in January 2020, during the peak month of bushfires in Australia, I had the driver recount to me various conspiracy theories as to who was behind the fires. When I patiently explained why these stories were incorrect, he turned to me and said, 'So it's all fake news then?'

This chapter will use the term 'fake news' in spite of the caveats that have come to surround it. I will do this for two main reasons. First, the lack of shared definition does not mean that a term is without usefulness. Benjamin Moffitt has made a similar point about another much-debated term of our times, that of 'populism' (Moffitt, 2020). Moffitt makes the point that many terms in political theory are also contested, such as freedom, democracy, and equality, and that the contestation is connected to the political forces they seek to describe. He also argues that there is a core definition of populism as a form of politics constructed around an 'elites versus the people' divide.

In a similar way, fake news can be defined as content that contains misinformation or disinformation, and is circulated through information/media platforms and potentially misleading to its audiences, in part because it takes a form that resembles traditional news. This definition is similar to the well-known definition proposed by Lazer et al. in *Science*:

> We define 'fake news' to be fabricated information that mimics news media content in form but not in organizational process or intent. Fake-news outlets, in turn, lack the news media's editorial norms and processes for ensuring the accuracy and credibility of information. Fake news overlaps with other information disorders, such as misinformation (false or misleading information) and disinformation (false information that is purposely spread to deceive people). (Lazer et al., 2018: 1094)

It is notable that analysts who use other terms, such as disinformation, propaganda, or information disorder, also make reference to fake news. In their comprehensive study of the circulation of online disinformation during the 2016 US presidential election, *Network Propaganda: Manipulation, Disinformation, and Radicalization in American Politics*, Benkler, Faris, and Roberts observe that 'echo chambers ringing with false news make democracies ungovernable', and refer to '"fake news" entrepreneurs' as one of a number of *dramatis personae* in the media ecosystem they are seeking to identify (Benkler et al., 2018: 4, 9).[1]

Not all fake news is propaganda or disinformation, and not all propaganda or disinformation takes the form of fake news. As we will note below, the drivers of fake news certainly include politically and ideologically motivated actors, but they are far from the only players in the space. In this chapter, we will approach political propaganda as taking the form of manipulated or fabricated content that takes the form of news, is explicitly designed to manipulate or deceive its audience, and is politically motivated in its production, distribution, and underlying intent. This definition differentiates 'fake news' as propaganda from genres such as news parody or satire, misleading content produced by those whose intentions were not explicitly to deceive audiences (for example, biased or opinion-driven professional journalism), and from primarily commercially driven content that takes the form of news. While there can be some overlap in these categories, this definition sets some boundaries for the consideration of 'fake news' as political propaganda.

This connects to the second feature of fake news, and why the term remains useful even if problematic, which is that it takes the form of news in a manner that makes sense to its audiences. Tandoc, Lim, and Ling make the point that 'Fake news appropriates the look and feel of real news; from how websites look; to how articles are written; to how photos include attributions. Fake news hides under a veneer of legitimacy as it takes on some form of credibility by trying to appear like real news' (Tandoc et al., 2018: 147).

It is commonly observed that the rise of fake news is intimately connected to more people accessing news from the Internet generally, and from social media sites such as Facebook and Twitter in particular (Allcott and Gentzkow, 2017). The proliferation of content on such sites, the difficulties in verifying and fact-checking multiple online sources, and the tendency of those engaged in social media practices such as liking, sharing, and commenting to form online communities with shared beliefs and world views – sometimes also referred to as echo chambers or filter bubbles (Bruns, 2019; Napoli, 2019b; Parisier, 2011) – has commonly been seen as a critical factor in the incubation and proliferation of fake news sites.

However, it is important to be aware that what we today term 'fake news' has a long history, and has been circulated as much by mainstream news organisations and journalists as it has by propagandists or fake news entrepreneurs (Schudson and Zelizer, 2017). The urgency of the debate surrounding fake news today is only partly about the technological affordances that enable a proliferation of informational content of highly variable degrees of quality, accuracy, and veracity. It is also connected to a wider crisis of trust and legitimacy facing the so-called 'mainstream' news media, which is shared in some respect with other social institutions such as governments and corporations, but which has its own dynamics in the face of various public scandals, changing business models, and challenges to traditional approaches to journalism and news reportage (Caplan et al., 2018; Flew, 2019; Waisbord, 2018).

TYPOLOGIES OF FAKE NEWS

Under the umbrella term 'fake news' sits a range of very different types of media content. Wardle identified seven forms of content that could, under varying definitions, be considered to be 'fake news', misinformation, or disinformation:

1. Satire or parody, which has no intention to cause harm but has potential to fool.
2. News content that makes false connections, such as headlines, visuals, or captions that do not support the content.
3. Misleading content.
4. Content accompanied by false contextual information.
5. Imposter content, which conflates genuine sources with false, made-up sources (for example, the infamous 'Pope Francis endorses Donald Trump' news story prior to the 2016 US presidential election).
6. Manipulated content, where genuine information or imagery is manipulated to deceive, as with a 'doctored' photo.
7. Fabricated content, where the content is '100% false, designed to deceive and do harm' (Wardle, 2017).

Satire or parody is not fake news. As developed by a range of comedians such as Stephen Colbert in the US, Jonathan Pie in the UK, and Shaun Micallef in Australia, as well as the many parody websites that have followed in the wake of the *Onion*, this is comedy that adheres closely to the forms and conventions of news journalism so as to maximise comedic effect. This genre, as well as the related 'newstainment' genre where actual news stories form the basis for humorous reinterpretation, is as much a parody of the forms of news as their content, often grounded in an implicit critique of contemporary news as failing to meet the expectations of citizens about the quality of news they are receiving (Harrington, 2013; McNair et al., 2017). News that is misleading, makes false connections, sensationalises people and events, and attracts readers on the basis of headlines that do not match the content (so-called online 'clickbait'), is also not so much 'fake news' as it is poor journalism. It is only the latter four categories identified in Wardle's taxonomy – content accompanied by false contextual information, imposter content, manipulated content, and fabricated content – that approximate 'fake news'. Such content is often motivated by economic, political, ideological intentions that come to approximate propaganda, deliberate manipulation, and the wilful spread of disinformation.

A second taxonomy of fake news has been proposed by Tandoc, Lim, and Ling (Tandoc et al., 2018). Drawing upon a systematic literature review of published studies, they identify six categories of fake news in the academic literature:

1. News satire (TV programmes such as the *Colbert Report* and *Mad As Hell*).
2. News parody (websites such as the *Onion* and *Betoota Advocate*).
3. News fabrication, often generated by partisan news sites such as Breitbart.
4. Photo and image manipulation, which now includes the growing phenomenon of 'deep-fakes' (Vaccari and Chadwick, 2020).
5. Forms of advertising and public relations content that resemble news, such as 'native advertising', or sponsored content that matches the form and function of the platform upon which it appears (Macnamara, 2020).
6. Propaganda.

Tandoc et al.'s taxonomy shares with Wardle a focus upon facticity and intention as demarking content that can be read as a critique of mainstream media, such as news satire and parody, and that which promulgates deliberately false information and/or intends to manipulate its audience. They differ from Wardle in bringing the question of audiences more explicitly to the fore. They observe that 'while news is constructed by journalists, it seems that fake news is co-constructed by the audience, for its fakeness depends a lot on whether the audience perceives the fake as real' (Tandoc et al., 2018: 148). This means that fake news needs to be considered in the context of news as a whole, while suggesting that the clear lines drawn between 'real' and 'fake' news in other definitions, such as in Lazer et al. (2018), require closer scrutiny.

A third approach to understanding fake news, focusing upon its implications for content moderation as well as regulation and public policy, has been developed by Caplan, Hanson, and Donovan at the Data and Society Institute (Caplan et al., 2018). They observe that the term 'fake news' is politicised not only because it is used by political actors or for political purposes, but also because it is 'used both to extend critiques of mainstream media and refer to the growing spread of propaganda and problematic content online' (Caplan et al., 2018: 1). They look at various attempts to identify fake news, including by:

1. Intent: did its creators seek to spread false and/or misleading information?
2. Type: the content-based approach that distinguishes hoaxes and propaganda from satire or parody.
3. Features: textual signifiers that raise doubt about the veracity of the news content.

They find that none of these indicators is fully satisfactory, and when applied in practice by digital platform companies or government regulators, they are highly likely to either 'over-block' content (that is, identify legitimate news content as 'fake news'), or 'underblock' (that is, give the appearance of controlling the spread of 'fake news', while allowing misinformation to continue to circulate). Part of the problem is that the traditional standards used to define quality news, such as objectivity or balance, have themselves been under sustained challenge from alternative voices, from the political left as well as the right,[2] and that the Internet enables critics not simply to sideline commentators on the mainstream news media, but to develop their own alternative news sources. The Internet has long been championed as a platform which enables an opening up of the public sphere to new voices – sometimes referred to as the Fifth Estate (Dutton, 2009) – and while there is a reassessment of that opening up going on in light of the dominance of digital platforms over news distribution and the circulation of disinformation and 'fake news' (Entman and Usher, 2018; Napoli, 2019a), there are no serious calls for a return to a world of mass media oligopolies of the sorts that prevailed in the latter part of the 20th century. As a result, fake news may be an unintended byproduct of greater media choice.

A final typology of fake news to be considered is from the economists Hunt Allcott and Matthew Gentzkow (Allcott and Gentzkow, 2017). Allcott and Gentzkow approach the rise of fake news during the 2016 US presidential election as a market phenomenon, arising out of the increased supply of news and consumer demand. The supply-side issues are relatively straightforward. Allcott and Gentzkow identify incentives to produce and distribute fake news as arising out of a mix of economic incentives and ideological motivations. For some, such as the Macedonian teenagers of Veres who created pro-Trump websites, the motivations were almost exclusively economic: advertiser algorithms such as Google AdSense directed advertising revenue to the most popular sites, Trump voters were heavy consumers of pro-Trump online news, and the returns from delivering a product that met their preferences were considerable. Others were motivated by ideological drivers. The Breitbart editor Steve Bannon, who became an advisor to Trump after his election, described the main enemy to conservatives in the US as being not the Democrats, but the media, which he saw as inherently opposed to a populist-nationalist political project such as that of Trump. As Bannon viewed it as impossible to change the embedded liberalism of the mainstream news media, he instead described his motivation as being to 'flood the zone with shit', or to disseminate so much misinformation that it would leave the media's capacity to sift through so much content, and to sort out truth and lies, fatally compromised (Illing, 2020).[3]

The picture is more complex on the demand side. Consumers derive psychic benefit, or utility, from news in two ways. First, they want truthful and accurate information as providing the foundations upon which they can make decisions as consumers and citizens. But, second, consumers may also derive psychological utility from news that is consistent with their already held beliefs, or what Denzau and North (1994) term their shared mental models, or pre-existing worldviews. They argue that 'consumers face a trade-off: they have a private incentive to consume precise and unbiased news, but they also receive psychological utility from confirmatory news' (ibid.: 18). In such an environment, producers of 'fake news' can identify incentives to cater to these pre-existing worldviews, even at the cost of trust in their news brand, as the costs of producing and distributing news have been lowered, and as there is lower brand awareness of news access through online or social media sites. The resulting dissemination of fake news comes at a considerable social cost, but it taps into a pre-existing scepticism about news generally, which has been consistently registered in a variety of studies showing a decline in trust in news media (Edelman, 2020; Flew, 2019; Gallup, 2018).

THE BEHAVIOURAL ECONOMICS OF 'FAKE NEWS'

The academic literature on fake news, misinformation, and disinformation has tended to have a supply-side focus. There is much attention given to what it is and how to identify it, with a mix of political, ideological, and economic motives identified as driving its distribution. The Internet generally, and social media platforms in particular, are viewed as being key incubators for the circulation of fake news, as they allow for the rapid distribution of information with very few filters or gatekeepers managing the flow of that information, other than predictive algorithms that direct flows based upon past user activities and the maximisation of views and shares. More generally, fake news appears here as a by-product of the 'attention economy' (Lanham, 2006; Williams, 2018), where information abundance generates attention scarcity, and where the preparedness to filter for truth or falsehood – whether it be by users, digital platforms, news providers, fact-checkers, or governments – is compromised by the sheer volume of information in circulation.

I would argue that this supply-side focus needs to be complemented by consideration of where the demand for fake news comes from. Allcott and Gentzkow allude to this when they discuss consumer demand for news, and identify individual preferences for both quality and unbiased news, and news from which they 'may derive psychological utility from seeing reports that are consistent with their priors'(Allcott and Gentzkow, 2017: 218). Such preferences are not stable, and would vary considerably between one person and another. Indeed, given that society as a whole benefits from news that is of a high quality standard, unbiased, and accurate, governments have an interest in investing in such provision, whether through support for public service media, press subsidies or grants to support high-quality journalism, or provision to underserved communities (which may also be provided by philanthropic foundations, as is most common in the United States) (Cairncross, 2019; Hendy, 2013). There is the added complication with news that it is what economists term a credence good, meaning that it is not only difficult to ascertain its quality prior to consumption, but remains difficult to determine after consumption (Dulleck et al., 2011; Dulleck and Kerschbamer, 2006). This is another way of framing the familiar challenge presented by fake news: namely, how can one know what is true and what is false, except through publicly available information, of which news is the most widely available source?

The political economist Jan Schnellenbach has identified three psychological factors that are relevant to considering such demand-side questions. Applying a behavioural perspective that places 'psychological biases … at the centre of discussion, rather than paradoxical patterns of behaviour that result from a strict application of rational responses to incentives' (Schnellenbach, 2017: 162), relevant psychological factors that can lie behind the propensity to consume 'fake news' include:

1. Loss aversion: the preparedness to actively seek out information that supports already held 'gut feelings', and to actively avoid information that challenges pre-existing preferences and beliefs.
2. Effects: where news is not actually false, but the information is framed in such a way as to exaggerate one side of a story; this can serve to reinforce already existing 'shared mental models' (Denzau and North, 1994).

3. Availability cascades: in an attention economy framework, the circulation of similar information by a wide variety of sources can in itself generate the perception that such information is true by virtue of being consistently restated and reinforced.

Other factors could be added to such a list, as they sit within the general category of cognitive biases, and particularly those relating to heuristics and confirmation bias (Haselton et al., 2005; Kahneman, 2011; Nickerson, 1998). From this extensive literature, we can observe that political or ideological preferences, once formed, can prove to be highly durable and resilient to contrary information, not least because there are time and resource constraints that enable heuristics, or 'rules of thumb', to continue to be applied. As Denzau and North observed:

> Ideas matter; and the way that ideas are communicated among people is crucial to theories that will enable us to deal with strong uncertainty problems at the individual level. For most of the interesting issues in political and economic markets, uncertainty, not risk, characterizes choice-making. Under conditions of uncertainty, individuals' interpretation of their environment will reflect their learning. Individuals with common cultural backgrounds and experiences will share reasonably convergent mental models, ideologies, and institutions; and individuals with different learning experiences (both cultural and environmental) will have different theories (models, ideologies) to interpret their environment. Moreover, the information feedback from their choices is not sufficient to lead to convergence of competing interpretations of reality … Mental models are shared by communication, and communication allows the creation of ideologies and institutions in a co-evolutionary process. (Denzau and North, 1994: 3–4, 20)

SOCIAL MEDIA AND POLITICAL POLARISATION AS CONTRIBUTING FACTORS

At one level, none of this is new. Propaganda, conspiracy theories, and politically motivated misinformation have a long history, as does the deliberate spread of falsehoods for economic or personal gain. Historically, news media organisations have provided a degree of inoculation in this regard. A well-established news organisation wishes to preserve a reputation for accuracy, even if there are different benchmarks applied to quality and impartiality (for example, broadsheet versus tabloid press, mainstream and partisan media). These are reinforced by external forms of regulation of news publishers, such as press councils and government regulators, as well as by professional codes of ethics, journalistic norms, and the capacity to use the courts to seek redress against misrepresentation, slander, and libel.

However, there are two distinctive factors in the 2010s and 2020s that need to be considered as changing this equation. The first is the rise of the Internet and the growing distribution of news online through social media platforms. The significance of the rise of 'social news' (Martin and Dwyer, 2019) for trust in news, news quality, and the accuracy of information has been widely debated and hotly contested. Some associate social news with so-called filter bubbles and echo chambers, arguing that the algorithms of platforms such as Google, Facebook, and Twitter promote information-sharing among small groups based upon ideological affinities, with little regard to the trust or accuracy of the information circulated (Napoli, 2019b; Parisier, 2011). Others contest the filter bubble metaphor, arguing that online news consumers in fact read more widely, and are more likely to read across partisan divides, and that social media platforms have enabled a greater diversity of news sources that is of net benefit to the public sphere (Bruns, 2019; Dubois and Blank, 2018; Dutton et al., 2017). It may be possible for both effects to be operating simultaneously, not least because online news consumers may also be increasingly prepared to subscribe to news sources they consider to be of high quality, even as they also access freely available news through Facebook and Twitter.

A second factor that may have been underestimated has been the growth in political polarisation, particularly in liberal democracies. Political polarisation is estimated to have increased in many countries, most notably the United States (Azzimonti and Fernandes, 2018). Moreover, disagreements have come to be not only about the most appropriate policies to address problems of common concern (for example, is it better to have lower taxes or higher government spending?), but about the nature of social reality itself. Stephen Coleman has observed that part of the crisis of news lies not only in whether news outlets report accurately on events, but over the nature of 'facts' themselves (Coleman, 2012). This can be seen, to take one prominent example, in the case of climate change: while the majority of people identify this as a serious concern, there is a significant minority who do not, and who view claims about climate change as part of a political or ideological agenda (Newman et al., 2020). It has been a consistent finding of US trust surveys that Republican voters distrust mainstream media more than Democrats, and that trend accelerated under Donald Trump's presidency, as he actively encouraged his supporters on Twitter and elsewhere to view the major media outlets as 'fake news'.

However, the issue of declining trust in news based on partisan politics is not confined to one side of politics. In its 2020 *Digital News Report* the Reuters Institute for the Study of Journalism (Newman et al., 2020) found that the sharpest decline in trust in news between 2015 and 2020 had been in the United Kingdom, and came from those who identified politically with the left, among whom trust in news fell from 46 per cent in 2015 to 15 per cent in 2020. By contrast, in the United States, where trust in news had been low for some time, trust among those who identified with the political right fell from 25 per cent to 13 per cent between 2015 and 2020, and was considerably lower than trust among those identifying with the left (33 per cent) (Newman et al., 2020: 15). Summarising their findings on the continuing decline in trust in news media internationally, Newman et al. observe that: 'Divided societies seem to trust the media less, not necessarily because the journalism is worse but because people are generally dissatisfied with institutions in their countries and perhaps because news outlets carry more views that people disagree with' (Newman et al., 2020: 15).

In a survey undertaken of news consumption during the UK's General Election in 2019, the Reuters Institute (Fletcher et al., 2020) observed that distrust in mainstream news media did not necessarily lead to greater demand for alternative media. It found that ten well-established mainstream news media sources accounted for at least 90 per cent of political news consumption over the election period, and that five outlets (BBC, *Daily Mail*, *Guardian*, *Sun*, and *Mirror*) accounted for 67 per cent of online political news consumption during the campaign (Fletcher et al., 2020: 11). Taking these studies together suggests that distrust of conventional news media is not necessarily leading to a migration away to online news sources. If anything, new online news providers have struggled more than the established news brands to develop sustainable business models. It does suggest, however, that distrust towards news media does relate to political polarisation and societal divides, more than is typically assumed from those approaches that take a supply-side focus upon better managing online flows of news and information.

CONCLUSION: BEYOND INFORMATION MANAGEMENT

In this chapter I have chosen to refer to 'fake news', notwithstanding the definitional issues that it raises (for example, how does it differ from news parody or satire?), the extent to which the term has been weaponised by politicians such as Donald Trump, and the degree to which the content sits in the wider context of online misinformation or disinformation. I have done so because it is more helpful to understand the content in question as news rather than simply as information. While information is pervasive online, there are still attributes that are attached to both the production and consumption of news that make it appropriate to differentiate news from information – online databases contain information, but not necessarily news – and which allow for a better understanding of what individuals and societies value in news, and what is threatened by the circulation of fake news.

I have argued that fake news cannot simply be understood as a supply-side phenomenon driven by the Internet and social media, and agents with particular political, economic, or ideological motivations. Fake news would not exist without the technologies or the motivated interests, but it would also not exist, or at least not be a significant concern, were it not for the ability of such content to tap into the expectations and desires of individuals and groups. For that reason, fake news has been approached as something more than simply 'flooding the zone with shit', to use Steve Bannon's felicitous phrase, and as a phenomenon where demand is explicable in part by behavioural economics and psychology, as it can easily (and profitably) conform to pre-existing shared mental models at a time when established news media organisations are under unprecedented political and economic pressure (Australian Competition and Consumer Commission, 2019; Cairncross, 2019; Knight Commission on Trust, Media and Democracy, 2019).

We noted that this audience focus was consistent with much academic literature on the topic. Tandoc et al. emphasised that the nature of fake news could not be determined through content analysis alone, and drew attention to the degree to which 'fake news is co-constructed by its audience, for its fakeness depends a lot on whether the audience perceives the fake as real' (Tandoc et al., 2018: 148). Caplan et al. observed that one of the difficulties arising in identifying fake news is that its rise coexists with a significant critique of traditional news media and media business models (Caplan et al., 2018). This suggests that the issue is not so much the lack of media literacy of consumers as the increasingly porous boundaries between journalism as traditionally defined and a plethora of online news and information sources that operate differently to traditional news models. Allcott and Gentzkow pointed out that consumers have a complex balance of preferences with regard to news, where the psychological utility derived from the reinforcement of one's pre-existing worldviews coexisted with a demand for unbiased and accurate news (Allcott and Gentzkow, 2017).

I would note that this audience-centred or demand-side approach is not the dominant one to fake news. The dominant approach to fake news, particularly in policy circles, treats its existence as primarily an information problem, and tends towards solutions aimed at promoting 'good' information and weeding out 'bad' information or 'fake news'. A good example of such an approach can be found with the European Commission's (EC) *Final Report of the High Level Expert Group on Fake News and Online Disinformation* (European Commission, 2018). This EC report offers a familiar list of measures to restrict the circulation of misinformation and fake news, including promoting greater digital media literacy, third-party fact-checking, providing online platform users with greater tools to check information sources, and promoting more cooperative relations between digital platforms and news publishers. Lazer et al. come to similar conclusions, while also discussing the scope for artificial intelligence to detect fake news and for major platforms such as Google and Facebook to reconfigure their algorithms to promote more trusted news sources (Lazer et al., 2018).

Such initiatives are important, and are certainly a preferable state of affairs to the relative free-for-all that was prevailing on major digital platforms in the second half of the 2010s, where platform algorithms were easily gamed by motivated online actors. At the same time, a supply-side approach to addressing the problem of 'fake news' comes up against some predictable problems when applied in practice. First, there is the problem of potential overreach: as was noted in the introduction, the association of news with facticity means that genres such as news parody and news satire can be condemned, and potentially blocked, as 'fake news'. Second, it is important to be aware that the demand for alternative news sources – some of which may well be fake news – arose in the context of significant distrust of the established news media publishers, and of professional journalism, which is likely to remain even if digital platforms make alternative sources harder to access. Third, as the roots of 'fake news' also lie in populist discontent with poltical, economic, and media elites, and a suspicion of claims to expert knowledge, simply telling people to trust in the establishment may well generate further discontent, particularly if causes of populist discontent, such as elite corruption and widening economic inequalties, remain unaddressed (Eatwell and Goodwin, 2018; Norris and Ingelhart, 2019).

Behavioural heuristics, cognitive biases, and the manifestations of social division and political polarisation in online environments continue to provide significant demand-side drivers, and hence the undergrowth in which fake news can grow and flourish. Such wider social concerns are likely to be resistant to the technical fix that is promised by simply approaching fake news as bad information, in a public sphere where the rules of the game are otherwise broadly accepted by all citizens. Fake news has flourished in times of popular discontent with the status quo; and in the absence of significant reforms to political institutions and economic relations, it is likely to remain a feature of societies with a free media and open access to the Internet. The account developed in this chapter suggests that policy solutions to fake news are prone to either overblocking, that is, blocking legitimate news content as 'fake news'; or underblocking, that is, giving the appearance of taking action while allowing misinformation to continue to circulate.

NOTES

1. Perhaps the most famous 'fake news entrepreneurs' were the teenagers of the Macedonian town of Veres, who identified that creating pro-Donald Trump websites for US online consumers generated substantial web traffic, and with that income through Google AdSense. They had very little personal investment in US politics, and had previously generated similar sites around natural health remedies (Subramanian, 2017).
2. It is worth recalling that the 'propaganda model' of new media as systematically reporting on events in an ideologically biased manner was developed by Noam Chomsky and Edward Herman through a detailed content analysis of the *New York Times*, particularly in its foreign affairs reporting (Chomsky and Herman, 1988).
3. For an account of InfoWars founder Alex Jones as an ideological entrepreneur, whose media product combines an explicit political and ideological agenda with the selling of various commercial products, see van den Bulck and Hyzen (2020).

REFERENCES

Allcott, H. and M. Gentzkow (2017), 'Social Media and Fake News in the 2016 Election', *Journal of Economic Perspectives*, 31(2): 211–236.
Australian Competition and Consumer Commission (2019), *Digital Platforms Inquiry: Final Report*, Canberra: ACCC.
Azzimonti, M. and M. Fernandes (2018), *Social Media Networks, Fake News, and Polarization* (NBER Working Paper Series Working Paper 24462), Washington, DC: National Bureau of Economic Research.
Benkler, Y., R. Faris, and H. Roberts (2018), *Network Propaganda: Manipulation, Disinformation, and Radicalization in American Politics*, New York: Oxford University Press.
Bruns, A. (2019), *Are Filter Bubbles Real?*, Cambridge: Polity.
Cairncross, F. (2019), *The Cairncross Review: A Sustainable Future for Journalism*, UK Government, available at https://www.gov.uk/government/publications/the-cairncross-review-a-sustainable-future-for-journalism.
Caplan, R., L. Hanson, and J. Donovan (2018), *Dead Reckoning: Navigating Content Moderation After "Fake News"*, Data & Society Research Institute, available at https://datasociety.net/pubs/oh/DataAndSociety_Dead_Reckoning_2018.pdf.
Chomsky, N. and E. Herman (1988), *Manfacturing Consent: The Political Economy of Mass Media*, New York: Pantheon.
Coleman, S. (2012), 'Believing the News: From Sinking Trust to Atrophied Efficacy', *European Journal of Communication*, 27(1): 35–45.
Denzau, A. and D. North (1994), 'Shared Mental Models: Ideologies and Institutions', *Kyklos*, 47(1): 3–31.
Derakhshan, H. and C. Wardle (2017), 'Information Disorder: Definitions', in Michael Schudson and Barbie Zelizer (eds), *Understanding and Addressing the Disinformation Ecosystem*, Philadelphia, PA: Annenberg School for Communication, pp. 5–12.
Dubois, E. and G. Blank (2018), 'The Echo Chamber is Overstated: The Moderating Effect of Political Interest and Diverse Media', *Information, Communication and Society*, 21(5): 729–745.
Dulleck, U. and R. Kerschbamer (2006), 'On Doctors, Mechanics and Computer Specialists – The Economics of Credence Goods', *Journal of Economic Literature*, 44: 5–42.
Dulleck, U., R. Kerschbamer, and M. Sutter (2011), 'The Economics of Credence Goods: An Experiment on the Role of Liability, Verifiability, Reputation and Competition', *American Economic Review*, 101: 525–555.
Dutton, W.H. (2009), 'The Fifth Estate Emerging Through the Network of Networks', *Prometheus*, 27(1): 1–15.
Dutton, W., B. Riesdorf, E. Dubois, and G. Blank (2017), *Search and Politics: The Uses and Impacts of Search in Britain, France, Germany, Italy, Poland, Spain, and the United States*, Quello Center Working Paper 5-1-17, available at https://papers.ssrn.com/sol3/papers.cfm?abstract_id=2960697.
Eatwell, R. and M. Goodwin (2018), *National Populism: The Revolt Against Liberal Democracy*, London: Penguin.
Edelman (2020), *20 Years of Trust*, available at https://www.edelman.com/20yearsoftrust/?fbclid=IwAR12VvWYTk8IaqQ28CihjW_Z7a8_FfSWhUfzibgnVCxLJNLbL59PejxzqK4#01-intro, accessed 13 March 2021.
Entman, R.M. and N. Usher (2018), 'Framing in a Fractured Democracy: Impacts of Digital Technology on Ideology, Power and Cascading Network Activation', *Journal of Communication*, 68(2): 298–308.
European Commission (2018), *Final Report of the High Level Expert Group on Fake News and Online Disinformation*, available at https://ec.europa.eu/digital-single-market/en/news/final-report-high-level-expert-group-fake-news-and-online-disinformation, accessed 13 March 2021.
Fletcher, R., N. Newman, and A. Schulz (2020), *A Mile Wide, an Inch Deep: Online News and Media Use in the 2019 UK General Election* (Digital News Project 2020), Oxford: Reuters Institute for the Study of Journalism.
Flew, T. (2019), 'Digital Communication, the Crisis of Trust, and the Post-global', *Communication Research and Practice*, 5(1): 4–22.

Gallup (2018), *Confidence in Institutions*, available at https://news.gallup.com/poll/1597/confidence-institutions.aspx.

Gendreau, H. (2017), 'The Internet Made "Fake News" a Thing – Then Made It Nothing', *WIRED*, 25 February, available at https://www.wired.com/2017/02/internet-made-fake-news-thing-made-nothing/.

Harrington, S. (2013), *Australian TV News: New Forms, Functions, and Futures*, Bristol: Intellect.

Haselton, M., D. Nettle, and P. Andrews (2005), 'The Evolution of Cognitive Bias', in David M. Buss (ed.), *The Handbook of Evolutionary Psychology*, Malden, MA: John Wiley & Sons, pp. 726–746.

Hendy, D. (2013), *Public Service Broadcasting*, Basingstoke: Palgrave Macmillan.

House of Commons (2019), *Disinformation and Fake News: Final Report*, available at https://publications.parliament.uk/pa/cm201719/cmselect/cmcumeds/1791/1791.pdf.

Illing, S. (2020), '"Flood the Zone with Shit": How Misinformation Overwhelmed Our Democracy', *Vox*, 6 February, available at https://www.vox.com/policy-and-politics/2020/1/16/20991816/impeachment-trial-trump-bannon-misinformation.

Jack, C. (2017), *What's Propaganda Got To Do With It?*, Data & Society: Points, available at https://points.datasociety.net/whats-propaganda-got-to-do-with-it-5b88d78c3282#.civ4bsqz8

Kahneman, D. (2011), *Thinking, Fast and Slow*, London: Penguin.

Knight Commission on Trust, Media and Democracy (2019), *Crisis in Democracy: Renewing Trust in America* (Aspen Institute), available at https://knightfoundation.org/reports/crisis-in-democracy-renewing-trust-in-america.

Lanham, R. (2006), *The Economics of Attention: Style and Substance in the Age of Information*, Chicago, IL: University of Chicago Press.

Lazer, D.M.J., M.A. Baum, Y. Benkler, A.J. Berinsky, K.M. Greenhill, et al. (2018), 'The Science of Fake News', *Science*, 359(6380): 1094–1096.

Macnamara, J. (2020), *Beyond Post-Communication: Challenging Disinformation, Deception, and Manipulation*, New York: Peter Lang.

Martin, F. and T. Dwyer (2019), *Sharing News Online: Commentary Cultures and Social Media News Ecologies*, Basingstoke: Palgrave Macmillan.

McNair, B., T. Flew, S. Harrington, and A. Swift (2017), *Politics, Media and Democracy in Australia: Public and Producer Perceptions of the Political Public Sphere*, London: Routledge.

Moffitt, B. (2020), *Populism*, Cambridge: Polity.

Napoli, P. (2019a), *Social Media and the Public Interest: Media Regulation in the Disinformation Age*, New York: Columbia University Press.

Napoli, P. (2019b), 'What If More Speech Is No Longer the Solution? First Amendment Theory Meets Fake News and the Filter Bubble', *Federal Communications Law Journal*, 70(1): 57–104.

Newman, N., R. Fletcher, A. Schulz, S. Andi, and R.K. Neilsen (2020), *Reuters Institute Digital News Report 2020*, Oxford: Reuters Institute for the Study of Journalism.

Nickerson, R. (1998), 'Confirmation Bias: A Ubiquitous Phenomenon in Many Guises', *Review of General Psychology*, 2(2): 175–220.

Norris, P. and R. Ingelhart (2019), *Cultural Backlash: Trump, Brexit, and Authoritarian Populism*, New York: Cambridge University Press.

Parisier, E. (2011), *The Filter Bubble*, London: Penguin.

Schnellenbach, J. (2017), 'On the Behavioural Political Economy of Regulating Fake News', *ORDO*, 68(1): 159–178.

Schudson, M. and B. Zelizer (2017), 'Fake News in Context', in C. Wardle (ed.), *Understanding and Addressing the Disinformation Ecosystem*, Philadelphia, PA: Annenberg School of Communication, pp. 1–4.

Scott, M. and M. Eddy (2017), 'Europe Combats a New Foe of Political Stability: Fake News', *New York Times*, 20 February, available at https://www.nytimes.com/2017/02/20/world/europe/europe-combats-a-new-foe-of-political-stability-fake-news.html?_r=0.

Silverman, C., L. Strapageil, H. Shaban, E. Hall, and J. Singer-Vine (2016), 'Hyperpartisan Facebook Pages are Publishing False and Misleading Information at an Alarming Rate', *Buzzfeed News*, 20 October, available at https://www.buzzfeednews.com/article/craigsilverman/partisan-fb-pages-analysis#.csNNjgvgbw.

Subramanian, S. (2017), 'Meet the Macedonian Teens Who Mastered Fake News and Corrupted the US Election', *WIRED*, 15 February, available at https://www.wired.com/2017/02/veles-macedonia-fake-news/.
Sullivan, M. (2017), 'It's Time to Retire the Tainted Term "Fake News"', *Washington Post*, 8 January, available at https://www.washingtonpost.com/lifestyle/style/its-time-to-retire-the-tainted-term-fake-news/2017/01/06/a5a7516c-d375-11e6-945a-76f69a399dd5_story.html.
Tandoc, E.C., Z.W. Lim, and R. Ling (2018), 'Defining "Fake News"', *Digital Journalism*, 6(2): 137–153.
Vaccari, C. and A. Chadwick (2020), 'Deepfakes and Disinformation: Exploring the Impact of Synthetic Political Video on Deception, Uncertainty, and Trust in News', *Social Media + Society*, Jan–March: 1–13.
van den Bulck, H. and A. Hyzen (2020), 'Of Lizards and Ideological Entrepreneurs: Alex Jones and Infowars in the Relationship between Populist Nationalism and the Post-Global Media Ecology', *International Communication Gazette*, 82(1): 42–59.
Waisbord, S. (2018), 'Truth is What Happens to News', *Journalism Studies*, 19(13): 1866–1878.
Wardle, C. (2017), *Fake News. It's Complicated*, available at https://medium.com/1st-draft/fake-news-its-complicated-d0f773766c79, accessed 13 March 2021.
Williams, J. (2018), *Stand out of our Light: Freedom and Resistance in the Attention Economy*, Cambridge: Cambridge University Press.

3. Cambridge Analytica
David R. Carroll

INTRODUCTION

Cambridge Analytica (CA), the notorious sub-brand of London-based Strategic Communications Laboratories (SCL) Group, launched in 2014 to bring a 'big data' approach to SCL's core business of influence campaigns and 'election management' services. Cambridge Analytica was approved for liquidation in 2019, after burning out in a flash from its catastrophically influential identity as a swashbuckling political consultancy that claimed to specialise in the fusion of addressable adtech, political campaigning, and psychological profiling. The press initially characterised the company's claims as 'snake oil', especially as partisan operatives fed reporters a narrative of salesmanship rather than efficacy. However, after whistleblowers brought forth public allegations of unlawful and unethical activities, the underlying nature of SCL as an international, military-grade pys-ops shop engaged in information warfare services for political and government clients was no longer so easily deniable. In January 2017, I began the process of using the United Kingdom (UK) Data Protection Act of 1998 (DPA 98) to research the practices of Cambridge Analytica. The ensuing legal fight illuminated the company's refusal to cooperate with authorities, resulting in a guilty plea in January 2019 to the criminal offence of ignoring an enforcement order to disclose my complete dataset while responding to key questions about data sourcing, modelling, and recipients. In April 2019, the UK Information Commissioners provided an update to the House of Commons sub-committee continuing its investigations into disinformation in the democratic process. The Deputy Information Commissioner described how the forensic analysis of SCL's servers, seized under criminal warrant in March 2018, was drawing to a close. The UK Information Commissioner's Office (ICO) would be publishing a report in the autumn of 2019 offering a narrative of how data was sourced, blended, matched, and run through several algorithms to yield voter targeting lists for the US presidential elections, in contravention to the UK DPA 98. This chapter analyses the ICO cumulative reports on the CA/SCL data forensics, among other primary sources, and explains how the data sets were likely deployed using addressable adtech to conduct voter surveillance and practice SCL's signature target audience analysis (TAA) behavioural dynamics, to potentially have significant propaganda effects on the United States (US) electorate in 2015–2016.

WHAT WENT WRONG WITH CAMBRIDGE ANALYTICA?

Regarded as an internationally significant political scandal involving the personal data of millions of people and the elections of numerous countries, the Cambridge Analytica affair erupted at a watershed moment at the intersection of politics, advertising, digital media, technology, electioneering, campaign strategy, journalism, propaganda, influence peddling, information warfare, elections interference, defence contracting, private intelligence, and cyber-espionage.

The publicly alleged and confirmed practices of the company have since been critiqued through various lenses, from neocolonialism to neoliberalism, associated with moral, ethical, and legal lapses identified concerning electoral and data protection laws, as well as bankruptcy and insolvency laws. The scandal is commonly reported as a data breach of 87 million Facebook users whose data was misappropriated, against Facebook policy, to target US voters with so-called 'psychographic' advertising.

However, investigations, penalties, and allegations against the companies document wrongdoing that far exceeds a data breach, including allegations of voter suppression, illegal campaign coordination, entrapment, and deceptive practices. In the US, as revealed in Freedom of Information Act requests, the Special Counsel Robert Mueller's investigation probed the company's relationship to Donald Trump's 2016 presidential campaign regarding its illicit data practices, micro-targeted advertising, and its ties to Wikileaks (Bensigner et al., 2020). In addition, the Senate Select Committee on Intelligence published its final volume documenting its Russia investigation and included detailed allegations against the company, but was ultimately unable to offer a conclusive response on the matter because neither key witnesses, nor UK authorities, fully cooperated with its investigation (SSCI, 2020). The Federal Trade Commission settled with key witnesses for deceptive practices (FTC, 2019), and the UK Insolvency Service banned a key executive for seven years from holding a directorship for demonstrating a lack of commercial probity, including bribery and honey trap stings, voter disengagement campaigns, and spreading information anonymously (Insolvency Service, 2020). In this momentous situation, algorithmic accountability and its regulatory and judicial oversight as used in elections and campaigning is expressed as a function of transnational data rights. As a prototypical expression of surveillance capitalism, Shoshana Zuboff, scholar of the notion, has regarded Cambridge Analytica as a 'parasite' that feasted on the 'host' of Facebook (Zuboff, 2020).

CAMBRIDGE ANALYTICA: ORGANISATION ECOLOGY

Strategic Communications Laboratories was founded in 1993 as a for-profit outgrowth of the Behavioural Dynamics Institute (BDI) founded in 1990 by Nigel John Oakes, formerly of Saatchi & Saatchi advertising agency, who joined with his brother Alexander Oakes, Roger Michael Gabb, Julian David Wheatland, and Alexander Ashburner Nix. Company literature described offerings to clients including 'psychological warfare', 'public diplomacy', and 'influence operations' (Weinberger, 2005). The company was registered and incorporated to Companies House on 20 July 2005. Initial investors included Vincent Tchenguiz (owning 23 per cent until 2015), the Iranian-born British real estate tycoon who is also known for backing the private intelligence company Black Cube (*Times of Israel*, 2018). Other notable SCL Group shareholders and/or officers included Lord Marland, Sir Geoffrey Pattie, Rear Admiral John Tolhurst, Colonel Ian Tuncliffe, Lord Ivar Mountbatten, and Catherine Nix (Brown, 2018).

According to its own website, SCL Group's work included influencing elections in Italy, Latvia, Ukraine, Albania, Romania, South Africa, Nigeria, Kenya, Mauritius, India, Indonesia, the Philippines, Thailand, Taiwan, Colombia, Antigua, St Vincent and the Grenadines, St

Kitts and Nevis, and Trinidad and Tobago (SCL Group, 2019). The company claimed to cease operating in elections in the UK after 1997 (Issenberg, 2015). The company's literature touted defence and military clients including the UK Ministry of Defence and the US State Department.

Robert Mercer, the American computer scientist, executive at hedge fund Renaissance Technologies, and major donor of conservative causes and organisations, including the presidential campaigns of Senator Ted Cruz and Donald J. Trump, made a substantial investment of $15 million into SCL Group. This would fund the establishment of Cambridge Analytica LLC to create a US-based brand and entity to extend the companies' activities into elections in the United States in support of Republican candidates and issues favoured by the Mercer family. Former employee and whistleblower Christopher Wylie testified to the House Intelligence Committee that Mercer lawyers had Vincent Tchenguiz 'removed as a shareholder' of SCL because they were 'concerned about some of his previous business dealings' (Wylie, 2018: 15).

BUSINESS OPERATION: UNFOLDING DATA EXPLOITATION

Stephen K. Bannon, a former White House strategist, campaign manager, and head of Breitbart, the right-wing digital publisher funded by the Mercer family, also led the creation of Cambridge Analytica LLC (CA) in 2013–2014, serving as its Vice President and shareholder. As described by Christopher Wylie, Bannon sought out researchers at the Cambridge University Psychometrics Centre as a basis for commercialising these techniques for political campaigning.

However, Cambridge Analytica LLC was essentially a shell company to conceal the Mercer family investment, but the UK-based SCL Elections Ltd (SCL-E) was the actual entity that performed the activities attributed to CA (Wylie, 2019: 229–244). Head researchers Michal Kosinski and David Stillwell at the Psychometrics Centre at Cambridge University were approached by SCL Elections to commercialise their research, and originally agreed to engage using their technique of collecting personality models of people using Facebook applications, but Kosinski could not agree with SCL Elections on costs (Kogan, 2018).

As an alternative approach, SCL-E chose to work with junior faculty and graduate students Aleksandr Kogan and Joseph Chancellor, who also specialised in psychometrics research methods using Facebook data (SSCI, 2018). SCL-E directed Kogan and Chancellor to form their own company in the UK, Global Science Research Ltd (GSR), as an intermediary. SCL-E then contracted with GSR to create a Facebook application that would gather data from users and their friends to build profiles on US voters with OCEAN (openness, conscientiousness, extraversion, agreeableness, neuroticism) scores to be compared to the average.

SCL-E paid for volunteers recruited on platforms such as Amazon Turk and Qualtrics to take GSR's personality quiz. Those quiz takers would unknowingly expose their Facebook 'friend' data to GSR if their Facebook privacy settings were in the default positions. On 24 July 2019, fraudulent disclosures to these original quiz takers when they inquired about their privacy were the subject of the Federal Trade Commission (FTC) settlement between Kogan and Nix (FTC, 2019).

DATA HARVESTING, DEFRAUDING FACEBOOK

In August 2014, Ambassador John Bolton's Super PAC (Political Action Committee) was CA/SCL's client and the first to benefit from GSR's Facebook data harvesting scheme. His campaign tested psychometrically targeted advertising on social media to identify voters who could be animated by messages that promoted aggressive military stances (Rosenberg, 2018). Former Cambridge Analytica employee Brittany Kaiser later disclosed documents, emails, reports, and examples of these ads (Kaiser, 2020: 25).

It is unclear exactly when Facebook executives learned of the CA/SCL/GSR data harvesting scheme which violated its own policy prohibiting the sale of user data, first reported in the *Guardian* in December 2015 (Davies, 2015). However, Facebook demanded that CA/SCL and GSR delete the data they acquired illicitly, and Alexander Nix furnished a fraudulent certification letter to Facebook that they had complied. Later reports emerged that CA/SCL had continued to use deceptively harvested data and subsequent data models long after they had claimed to destroy them. In a letter to the UK Digital Culture, Media, and Sport Committee, the UK Information Commissioner described how SCL exhibited sub-standard data security practices and struggled to verify its capacity to sanitise its data operations from the illicit Facebook data (Denham, 2020: 15). SCL did not meet legally required data protection standards as per the UK Data Protection Act of 1998, and the ICO noted that, had the company not filed for insolvency, it would have been fined for very serious breaches of the law, including unfairly creating political profiles of people without their knowledge or consent (Denham, 2018: 35

THE TRUMP CAMPAIGN AND WIKILEAKS

In support of Donald Trump's campaign for President, CA (owned by the Mercers) was hired by the Mercers to support the Make America Number 1 PAC while also working as an official vendor for the Trump campaign. US election law requires that campaigns and PACs act independently and do not share communications and strategy. Former employee Brittany Kaiser has described the so-called firewalls instantiated within CA/SCL (Kaiser, 2019: 409–411). The Make American Number 1 (MAN1) PAC was responsible for the 'Crooked Hillary' attack campaign, developed by CA. The company developed the creative advertising for MAN1, which included deliberately deceptive manipulations, micro-targeted to match specific messages to responsive voters with high-percentile OCEAN scores. For example, a video clip of Michelle Obama used for a MAN1 ad was falsely captioned that she was referring to Hillary Clinton when the original source's context reveals Obama referred to herself (Kaiser, 2019: 437). A complaint filed by the Campaign Legal Center to the Federal Election Commission alleges with evidence provided from Brittany Kaiser's email inbox that SCL knowingly failed to maintain the legally mandated firewall between the official Trump campaign and the Mercer-backed Super PAC, Make America Number 1 (Kaiser, 2020: 738).

Alexander Nix claimed to have reached out to Julian Assange of Wikileaks while CA was contracted with Trump-related campaigns in search of Hillary Clinton-related emails. CA was interested in building a search engine for any troves of improperly obtained Clinton emails and optimising them for use by the campaigns. Nix claimed to have approached Assange through his speaker's bureau, and both Assange and Nix claimed that no engagement between CA and Wikileaks occurred. However, it is notable that other CA employees had direct contact with

Assange. Brittany Kaiser had communications with Assange related to her graduate research (Cadwalladr and Kirchgaessner, 2018). Another former CA employee, Robert Murtfeld, worked under John Jones QC before he committed suicide. Jones represented Assange in his extradition case (Marlow, 2017).

Brad Parscale, the former manager of Trump's digital campaign operation, confirmed to the House Permanent Select Committee on Intelligence that data generated by Cambridge Analytica was used to create voter lists that were uploaded into Facebook using its Custom Audiences feature, to target voters individually by matching to their Facebook profile (Parscale, 2017: 94). This admission by Parscale indicates a full-circle round-trip of Facebook user data deceptively obtained from Facebook through GSR, preserved fraudulently against Facebook's deletion order, and then used to generate data to upload back into Facebook for micro-targeting as CA/SCL-E employees were embedded in the Trump digital operation in San Antonio, Texas during the summer of 2016.

SCL Group Ltd was awarded a no-bid, sole-source contract for target audience analysis (TAA) for countering violent extremism (CVE) at the Global Engagement Center (GEC), US State Department (Rebala, 2018). This contract serves as a key example of how SCL managed to gain contracts within the US government while CA served the Trump presidential election campaign. In addition, this contract demonstrates how its military-grade TAA capabilities were deployed to conduct research by measuring locus of control and need for cognition and key indicators of influence, and adapted for use to target voters on behalf of the Trump campaign and its political action committees (Dehaye, 2017).

TRANSNATIONAL INVESTIGATIONS AND RULING

The Cambridge Analytica affair triggered dozens of investigations and court cases across several legislatures, regulatory bodies, judiciaries, and law enforcement organisations, most notably in the US, UK, Canada, Ireland, Colombia, Brazil, Kenya, India, and Trinidad and Tobago.

The UK ICO was poised to offer the most definitive assessment of the activities of Cambridge Analytica relevant to US elections between approximately 2014 and 2016 (Denham, 2018). Under Commissioner Elizabeth Denham's instruction, the ICO sought and was granted a criminal warrant by the courts to raid the headquarters of SCL Group Limited (SCL) in London, seizing equipment, including on-site servers (Corfield, 2018). The ICO then began the world's largest and most complex data forensics investigation, examining 700 terabytes of data, and found 'disturbing disregard for voter privacy' (Denham, 2018). The Deputy Information Commissioner, James Dipple-Johnstone, reported to the House of Commons Select Sub-Committee on Digital, Culture, Media, and Sport (DCMS) in April 2019, confirming that US electoral data and psychometric profile data was found on the servers. The ICO's intent was to provide a 'narrative as to how the data was used' and an account of how personal data were processed by algorithms into models. The ICO stated so to the DCMS Sub-Committee when asked whether it would seek to provide me with his Cambridge Analytica data set (UK Parliament, 2019: Q48).

In lieu of issuing a final report, a subsequent DCMS committee received a letter from Commissioner Denham responding to specific questions (Denham, 2020). Around the same time, the British broadcaster Channel 4 obtained the voter database used by the Trump campaign in 2016, which revealed how Black voters in battleground districts were disproportionately targeted for 'deterrence' and were apparently micro-targeted with advertising designed to discourage them from turning out to vote. Advertisements highlighting archival clips of Hillary Clinton's statements referencing 'superpredators' targeted at voters marked for 'deterrence' proved particularly effective at demobilising Black voters in battleground districts. Channel 4's analysis of districts in Wisconsin and Florida indicated a measurable decrease of voter participation from previous elections, and because the margins were so thin, the potential for its effectiveness could not be ruled out (Blaskey et al., 2020

Prior to liquidation by Emerdata Limited, the quickly shuttered firms of SCL Group Limited (SCL) pled guilty during their administration to the criminal offence of ignoring the ICO's order to respond to an Enforcement Notice (ICO, 2019). The defied order required SCL to respond fully to questions posed by me, a claimant in the High Court as of March 2018 under the UK Data Protection Act of 1998, and complainant to the ICO as of July 2017 after a Subject Access Request (SAR) was performed in January 2017 and received from SCL Group Ltd in March 2017 on behalf of Cambridge Analytica LLC. A £10 fee was assessed for the SAR and payable to SCL Elections Ltd, the registered data controller to the ICO. This response and the subsequent letter response proved that CA was a thin façade for SCL. Concerns raised about the completeness and explanations of the SAR, as instructed by my solicitor Ravi Naik and argued by barristers Dinah Rose QC, Ben Jaffey QC, Juliane Kerr Morrison, and Nikolaus Gruebeck, were recognised by the ICO as defensible and under jurisdiction, even across territorial and citizenship considerations (High Court of Justice, 2018).

Delaware-incorporated Cambridge Analytica LLC was effectively abandoned in the New York bankruptcy court (Kary, 2018), understood to be majority-owned by hedge fund and computer science giant Robert Mercer and his family (SSCI, 2020: 665). The board terminated Alexander Ashburner Nix's appointment as a key executive of Cambridge Analytica and certain SCL companies immediately after Channel 4 broadcast its undercover operation posing as potential clients to Nix and side-man Mark Turnbull. The executives boasted of unlawful conduct on behalf of clients, including bribery, entrapment, electoral law violations, and campaign finance violations (McKee, 2018). On 14 September 2018, after being referred to the UK Insolvency Service by the UK ICO, Nix was disqualified for seven years for not disputing the statement:

> From no later than January 2013 to March 2018 I caused or permitted SCL Elections Ltd ('SCLE') or companies associated with SCLE to market themselves as offering potentially unethical services to potential clients, thereby demonstrating a lack of commercial probity including: bribery stings and honey trap stings designed to uncover corruption, voter disengagement campaigns, the obtaining of information to discredit political opponents, the anonymous spreading of information. (Insolvency Service, 2020)

The Federal Trade Commission (FTC) in the US settled with Nix under the FTC Act for his participation in a scheme to gather data deceptively from Facebook personality quiz respondents. Nix agreed with the FTC to cease making false statements about his professional practices (FTC, 2019). Nix settled with the FTC along with Cambridge University faculty member Aleksandr Kogan, who co-founded Global Science Research Ltd (GSR) along with postdoctoral researcher Joseph Chancellor to deceptively harvest Facebook 'likes' and related user profile data for SCL Elections Ltd under contract for the purposes of matching to voter registrations in certain US states. Facebook hired Chancellor from his work at GSR and later was the topic of questions issued to Facebook by the US Select Committee on Intelligence (SSCI, 2018) and the UK House of Commons Select Committee on Digital, Culture, Media, and Sport (DCMS, 2019). Kogan also settled with the FTC over deceptive practices involving false and misleading disclosures to users who inquired with GSR and SCL as how their identities would be associated to their data (FTC, 2019).

PRESS COVERAGE AND CONTROVERSY

Substantial scepticism about Cambridge Analytica persists, as there is no consensus among researchers across fields as to the efficacy or measurable impact of Cambridge Analytica on the outcome of any of the elections it has been involved with, including the election of Donald J. Trump, nor concerns about its original proposals to the UKIP and Leave.EU campaigns that may have influenced the election strategies employed toward the referendum for the United Kingdom to leave the European Union. The elaborate narrative of Cambridge Analytica and SCL assembled through press coverage began as early as 2005 in a *Slate* piece titled, 'You can't handle the truth: psy-ops propaganda goes mainstream' (Weinberger, 2005). Press coverage of Cambridge Analytica continued throughout the campaign season of 2016 and resurfaced again just prior to the 2020 US presidential election. The first pivotal reporting was Harry Davies's piece for the *Guardian* newspaper exposing the illicit data-harvesting quiz for Facebook (Davies, 2015). Hannes Grassenger and Mikael Krogerus published their English-language translation in *Vice Motherboard* in January 2017 (Grassenger and Krogerus, 2017). Mattathias Schwartz added to the reporting in the *Intercept* specifying that 30 million Facebook users had their misappropriated data matched to their US voter files (Schwartz, 2017).

However, no journalist shaped the story more than Carole Cadwalladr, a freelance features writer for the *Observer* newspaper. She earned the trust of the first self-proclaimed whistleblower from Cambridge Analytica, Christopher Wylie (Cadwalladr, 2017). She and the *Guardian* collaborated with the *New York Times* and *Channel 4 News* to bring the Cambridge Analytica whistleblowing and undercover videos to light in the spring of 2018, because she and the *Guardian* were threatened by lawyers representing SCL and Facebook, as well as Aaron Banks, bankroller of the unofficial Brexit campaign affiliated with Nigel Farage, Leave.EU.

Channel 4's coverage in the lead-up to the 2020 re-election campaign of Trump revealed the details of the databases used in 2016, and how Black voters were disproportionately marked for deterrence while Trump supporters were targeted with messages of left-wing extremism and urban unrest (Guru-Murthy, 2020). The Campaign Legal Center filed a Federal Election Commission (FEC) complaint in the lead-up to the 2020 election, alleging illegal campaign coordination (Burke, 2020). The evidence provided included internal research documenting how emails psychographically targeted to Trump voters were opened 20 per cent more frequently when fear-based messaging was directed to voters with high-percentile neuroticism scores (Kaiser, 2020: 88–89).

CONCLUSION

The Cambridge Analytica affair brought significant attention to an internationalised electioneering firm that emerged from the military industrial complex and was backed by Tory donors in the UK and Republican political donors in the US. The response to the discovery of such mass data abuse in connection with the US presidential election of 2016 triggered not only a sudden awareness of data privacy issues, but also corresponding legislative reforms strengthening protections in many countries. The SCL Group companies intentionally targeted countries with weak data protection, and were in the process of moving operations out of the UK to avoid regulatory scrutiny when the scandal erupted in the spring of 2018, as its servers were seized by the ICO. The necessity to strengthen international cooperation for the enforcement of voter data rights remains the critical lesson of the scandal, as the spectre of misuse casts a shadow over free and fair elections, given how companies can shroud themselves in mystery, exploiting business law and offshoring while conducting deceptive, unethical, and unlawful voter analytics to micro-target political propaganda and 'black-ops' campaigns

REFERENCES

Bensigner, Ken, Jason Leopold, and Anthony Cormier (2020), 'Mueller Memos: Bonus special edition! A huge trove of new details from the Mueller Investigation', *BuzzFeed News*, 30 October, available at https://www.buzzfeednews.com/article/kenbensinger/mueller-memos-bonus-special-edition-a-huge-trove-of-new.

Blaskey, Sarah, Nicolas Nehamas, C. Isaiah Smalls II, Christina Saint Louis, Ana Claudia Chacin, et al. (2020), 'How the Trump campaign used big data to deter Miami-Dade's Black communities from voting', *Miami Herald*, 1 November, available at https://www.miamiherald.com/news/politics-government/article246429000.html.

Brown, David (2018), 'SCL Group's founders were connected to royalty, the rich and powerful', *The Times*, 21 March, available at https://www.thetimes.co.uk/article/scl-group-s-founders-were-connected-to-royalty-the-rich-and-powerful-3pxhfvhlh.

Burke, Garance (2020), 'Watchdog org: Trump '16 campaign, PAC illegally coordinated', Associated Press, 16 October, available at https://apnews.com/article/election-2020-donald-trump-political-action-committees-elections-campaigns-42a5705b23bbbc780083f57b071bbcb0.

Cadwalladr, Carole (2017), 'The great British Brexit robbery: how our democracy was hijacked', *Observer*, 7 May, available at https://www.theguardian.com/technology/2017/may/07/the-great-british-brexit-robbery-hijacked-democracy.

Cadwalladr, Carole and Stephanie Kirchgaessner (2018), 'Cambridge Analytica met Assange to discuss US election', *Guardian*, 7 June, available at https://www.theguardian.com/uk-news/2018/jun/06/cambridge-analytica-brittany-kaiser-julian-assange-wikileaks.

Corfield, Gareth (2018), 'UK watchdog finally gets search warrant for Cambridge Analytica's totally not empty offices', *Register*, 23 March, available at https://www.theregister.co.uk/2018/03/23/cambridge_analytica_ico_search_warrant_approved/.

Davies, Harry (2015), 'Ted Cruz using firm that harvested data on millions of unwitting Facebook users', *Guardian*, 11 December, available at https://www.theguardian.com/us-news/2015/dec/11/senator-ted-cruz-president-campaign-facebook-user-data.

Dehaye, Paul-Olivier (2017), 'Microtargeting of low-information voters', *Medium*, 30 December, available at https://medium.com/personaldata-io/microtargeting-of-low-information-voters-6eb2520cd473.

Denham, Elizabeth (2018), 'Investigation into the use of data analytics in political campaigns', Report to Parliament, Information Commission's Office, 6 November, available at https://ico.org.uk/media/action-weve-taken/2260271/investigation-into-the-use-of-data-analytics-in-political-campaigns-final-20181105.pdf.

Denham, Elizabeth (2020), Letter to Chair of Digital, Culture, Media, and Sport Committee, Information Commissioner's Office, 2 October, available at https://ico.org.uk/media/action-weve-taken/2618383/20201002_ico-o-ed-l-rtl-0181_to-julian-knight-mp.pdf.

Dipple-Johnstone, James (2019), 'Oral evidence: the work of the Information Commissioner's Office, HC 2125', Digital, Culture, Media, and Sport Sub-Committee on Disinformation, 23 April, available at http://data.parliament.uk/writtenevidence/committeeevidence.svc/evidencedocument/dcms-subcommittee-on-disinformation/the-work-of-the-information-commisioners-office/oral/100459.html.

Federal Trade Commission (FTC) (2019), 'In the Matter of Aleksander Kogan and Alexander Nix', Case Proceedings, 18 December, available at https://www.ftc.gov/enforcement/cases-proceedings/182-3106-182-3107/aleksandr-kogan-alexander-nix.

Grassenger, Hannes and Mikael Krogerus (2017), 'The data that turned the world upside down: how Cambridge Analytica used your Facebook data to help Donald Trump campaign in the 2016 election', *Vice Motherboard*, 28 January, available at https://www.vice.com/en_us/article/mg9vvn/how-our-likes-helped-trump-win.

Guru-Murthy, Krishnan (2020), 'How Trump campaign targets millions of white voters – and activates fears over rioting', Channel 4 News, 29 September, available at https://www.channel4.com/news/how-trump-campaign-targets-millions-of-white-voters-and-activates-fears-over-rioting.

High Court of Justice, Royal Courts of Justice, Queen's Bench Division (2018), 'Claim: David Richard Carroll v. (1) Cambridge Analytica Ltd., (2) Cambridge Analytica (UK) Ltd., (3) SCL Elections Ltd., (4) SCL Group Ltd.', 16 March, available at https://www.documentcloud.org/documents/4413896-Prof-David-Carroll-UK-Legal-Claim-against.html.

Information Commissioner's Office (ICO) (2019), 'SCL Elections prosecuted for failing to comply with enforcement notice', 9 January, available at https://ico.org.uk/about-the-ico/news-and-events/news-and-blogs/2019/01/scl-elections-prosecuted-for-failing-to-comply-with-enforcement-notice.

Insolvency Service (2020), '7-year disqualification for Cambridge Analytica boss', Press release, 24 September, available at https://www.gov.uk/government/news/7-year-disqualification-for-cambridge-analytica-boss.

Issenberg, Sasha (2015), 'Cruz-connected data miner aims to get inside US voters' heads', Bloomberg, 12 November, available at https://www.bloomberg.com/news/features/2015-11-12/is-the-republican-party-s-killer-data-app-for-real-.

Kaiser, Brittany (2019), *Targeted: The Cambridge Analytica Whistleblower's Inside Story of How Big Data, Trump, and Facebook Broke Democracy and How It Can Happen Again*, New York: Harper.

Kaiser, Brittany (2020), 'Cambridge Analytica – Select 2016 Campaign-Related Documents', Internet Archive, 28 September, available at https://archive.org/details/ca-docs-with-redactions-sept-23-2020-4pm/.

Kary, Tiffany (2018), 'Facebook user can't find anyone left at Cambridge Analytica', *Bloomberg Businessweek*, 24 October, available at https://www.bloomberg.com/news/articles/2018-10-24/-houdini-act-looms-at-cambridge-analytica-as-everyone-vanishes.

Kogan, Aleksandr (2018), 'Dr Aleksander Kogan questioned by Committee', UK Parliament, Digital, Culture, Media, and Sport Committee Hearing, 24 April, available at https://old.parliament.uk/business/committees/committees-a-z/commons-select/digital-culture-media-and-sport-committee/news/fake-news-aleksandr-kogan-evidence-17-19/.

Marlow, Ann (2017), 'Another strand in the tapestry: who is behind Trump's political data analytics company?', *Tablet Magazine*, 11 January, available at https://www.tabletmag.com/sections/news/articles/another-strand-in-the-tapestry.

McKee, Ruth (2018), 'Alexander Nix, Cambridge Analytica CEO, suspended after data scandal', *Guardian*, 20 March, available at https://www.theguardian.com/uk-news/2018/mar/20/cambridge-analytica-suspends-ceo-alexander-nix.

Parscale, Brad (2017), Interview of Brad Parscale, Materials from the Committee's Investigation into Russian Active Measures, Permanent Select Committee on Intelligence, US House of Representatives, 24 October, available at https://intelligence.house.gov/uploadedfiles/bp37.pdf.

Rebala, Pratheek (2018), 'The State Department hired Cambridge Analytica's parent company to target terrorist propaganda', *Time*, 21 August, available at https://time.com/5372923/cambridge-analytica-state-department-terrorist-propaganda/.

Rosenberg, Matthew (2018), 'Bolton was early beneficiary of Cambridge Analytica's Facebook data', *New York Times*, 23 March, available at https://www.nytimes.com/2018/03/23/us/politics/bolton-cambridge-analyticas-facebook-data.html.

Schwartz, Mattathias (2017), 'Facebook failed to protect 30 million users from having their data harvested by the Trump campaign', *Intercept*, 30 March, available at https://theintercept.com/2017/03/30/facebook-failed-to-protect-30-million-users-from-having-their-data-harvested-by-trump-campaign-affiliate/.

SCL Group (2019), Wayback Machine, available at https://web.archive.org/web/20190111195059/https://sclgroup.cc/home.

Senate Select Committee on Intelligence (SSCI) (2018), Facebook Questions for the Record, 28 October, available at https://www.intelligence.senate.gov/sites/default/files/documents/Facebook%20Questions%20for%20the%20Record.pdf.

Senate Select Committee on Intelligence (SSCI) (2020), 'Report of the Select Committee on Intelligence, United States Senate on Russian active measures campaigns and interference in the 2016 U.S. Election. Vol. 5: Counterintelligence threats and vulnerabilities', available at https://www.intelligence.senate.gov/sites/default/files/documents/report_volume5.pdf.

Times of Israel (2018), 'Cambridge Analytica-linked businessman helped start Black Cube, lawsuit claims', *Times of Israel*, 23 August, available at https://www.timesofisrael.com/cambridge-analytica-linked-businessman-helped-start-black-cube-lawsuit-claims/.

UK Parliament (2019), UK Parliament, House of Commons, Digital, Culture, Media, and Sport Sub-Committee on Disinformation, Oral evidence: The Work of the Information Commissioner's Office, HC 2125, 23 April, available at http://data.parliament.uk/writtenevidence/committeeevidence.svc/evidencedocument/dcms-subcommittee-on-disinformation/the-work-of-the-information-commisioners-office/oral/100459.html.

Weinberger, Sharon (2005), 'You can't handle the truth: psy-ops propaganda goes mainstream', *Slate*, 19 September, available at https://slate.com/news-and-politics/2005/09/psy-ops-propaganda-goes-mainstream.html.

Wylie, Christopher (2018), Interview Transcript of Christopher Wylie, Materials from the Committee's Investigation into Russian Active Measures, Permanent Select Committee on Intelligence, US House of Representatives, 25 April, available at https://intelligence.house.gov/uploadedfiles/cw_58.pdf.

Wylie, Christopher (2019), *Mindf*ck: Cambridge Analytica and the Plot to Break America*, New York: Random House.

Zuboff, Shoshana (2020), 'You are now remote controlled: surveillance capitalists control the science and the scientists, the secrets and truth', *New York Times*, 24 January, available at https://nyti.ms/2sXbT2d.

4. 'Believe me': political propaganda in the age of Trump[1]

Gary D. Rawnsley

INTRODUCTION

> 'Just remember: What you're seeing and what you're reading is not what's happening.'
> (President Donald J. Trump, the Veterans of Foreign Wars National Convention, Kansas City, 25 July 2018)

Following his warning to the Veterans of Foreign Wars, President Trump's critics on Twitter quickly spotted the parallels with George Orwell's *Nineteen Eighty-Four*: 'The party told you to reject the evidence of your eyes and ears. It was their final, most essential command.'

It is surely no coincidence that since President Donald Trump's inauguration on 20 January 2017, no book has been referenced more than Orwell's famous depiction of a dystopian future, with 'alternative facts' echoing the terror of Big Brother's Newspeak. By 25 January 2017, sales of *Nineteen Eighty-Four* jumped by over 9500 per cent in the United States (US) and 20 per cent in the United Kingdom (UK) and Australia. Similarly, Sinclair Lewis's *It Can't Happen Here*, first published in 1935 (and reprinted for the first time by Penguin in 2017), about an outsider becoming President of the US by riding on a wave of populism, now seems prophetic (de Freytas-Tamura, 2017).

With daily claims of 'fake news' (first referenced by Trump in a tweet on 10 December 2016) and 'alternative facts', and the disturbing and dangerous contempt for journalists as 'enemies of the people', Donald Trump's presidency has reawakened interest in the kind of political propaganda familiar to George Orwell's readers: what it is, how to detect and recognise it, and perhaps most importantly, how to confront and challenge it.

Identifying and understanding how both President Trump's administration and their critics practise political propaganda directs us to five themes:

1. The 'weaponisation' of information and Trump's 'media war' (Happer et al., 2019; Acosta, 2019).
2. The renewed relevance of the seven propaganda devices, first categorised by the Institute of Propaganda Analysis in 1937.
3. The relationship between political, social, and economic contexts and the efficacy of propaganda.
4. The growing symbiotic relationship between journalism (especially television news journalism) and propaganda.
5. The significance of new information and communication technologies (ICTs) and social media platforms in the design, direction, and circulation of modern political propaganda.

THE ENVIRONMENT

> 'It's frankly disgusting the press is able to write whatever they want to write.'
> (Donald Trump, Twitter, 11 October 2017)

As much as we may disparage Trump's policies and rhetoric, it is essential to concede two crucial facts if we are to approach his political propaganda both objectively and accurately.

First, just as Trump did not conceive of fake news and alternative realities, his political direction did not materialise overnight. Trump did not create the populism that propelled him to the White House. Rather, he is both the product and the reflection of a specific alt-right political culture that found in Trump a favoured presidential candidate. Happer et al. (2019: Location 217) remind us that: 'Trump wasn't just the sign of a broken reality; he was the beneficiary of it. Mainstream consensual reality had shattered along time ago; it was just the shattering *hadn't gone mainstream.*' They then summarise the reasons for his election:

> His success was the result of a violent abreaction, an out-pouring and release of dispossessed discontent that had one credo: continually articulating itself against the establishment, the elite, the mainstream, the political order, the neoliberal economic order, the global order, the established way of doing things – against, that is, the entirety of the hitherto existing mainstream reality. (Ibid., Location 225)

David Runciman, writing on *How Democracy Ends*, also recognises that Trump's success in the polls indicates a wider malaise:

> His election is symptomatic of an overheated political climate that appears increasingly unstable, riven with mistrust and mutual intolerance, fuelled by wild accusations and online bullying, a dialogue of the deaf drowning each other out with noise. In many places, not just the United States, democracy is starting to look unhinged. (Runciman, 2018: Location 35)

Meanwhile, *New York Times* journalist Nicholas Kristof (2016) laments his 'shame' in how 'the media helped make Trump'. He regrets how 'we' journalists 'failed to take Trump seriously' because 'we were largely oblivious to the pain among working-class Americans and thus didn't appreciate how much his message resonated'. This is a denunciation echoed by Howard Kurtz: 'It turns out,' he notes, that the news media 'were the ones who failed to recognize what was unfolding before their eyes. It was the most catastrophic media failure in a generation' (Kurtz, 2018: 7).

Students have long known that propaganda rarely changes society, but rather reflects it. In his seminal (and still the best) theoretical study of propaganda, the French sociologist Jacques Ellul notes that: 'All propaganda must respond to a need, whether it be a concrete need (bread, peace, security, work) or a psychological need' (Ellul, 1965: 36–37). David Welch's studies of propaganda have suggested that the success of the Nazi Party can be explained by the failures of the Weimar Republic and failure of parties other than the NSDAP to offer alternatives; Nazi propaganda identified and reinforced public opinion, it did not create it (Welch, 2002). Propaganda identifies discontents, grievances, and fears, and through a systematic process of repetitive communication, amplifies them until they become an accepted version of reality with easy explanations, equally easy solutions to social problems, and specious scapegoats. Many of Trump's supporters, especially the blue-collar workers in the American heartland who had seen their jobs disappear and their communities collapse, had reason to be angry.

For them, Trump's explanations – illegal Mexican immigrants and an imbalanced trade with China, 'crooked Hillary', the Washington 'swamp', and the neoliberal vanilla status quo – made sense; and his solutions – 'Make America great again', 'America First', 'Drain the swamp', 'Lock her up', 'Build the wall' – resonated with the tired, alienated, and disaffected.

Second, we must accept that while liberal critics have observed in Fox News a clear and unapologetic source of support for President Trump, the administration's opponents have been equally guilty of engaging in their own propaganda against Trump by using many of the same techniques as Fox. Their news agendas helped build Trump's momentum by devoting to him so much airtime during the election campaign that he did not spend the amount of funds candidates usually expend to reach the White House. One study found that while on the campaign trail in 2015, Trump received 327 minutes of nightly broadcast news coverage, while Hillary Clinton received 121 minutes and Bernie Sanders just 20 minutes (Tyndall Report, 2016). During the whole campaign Trump received between $2–3 billion in free media coverage (Confessore and Yourish, 2016; Schroeder, 2016):

> More than six months before Election Day, Trump had already garnered twice the value of the most expensive presidential campaign in history – and had only spent a fraction of that sum himself. In all, Trump only spent $600 million on his campaign – barely half of what Clinton burned through on the road to defeat. (Geoghegan, 2019: Location 2442)

The MIT–Harvard Media Cloud study of the campaign shows that the liberal mainstream media devoted around four times as much coverage to Clinton's alleged scandals than to her policies, while dedicating one-and-a-half times more coverage to Trump's policies than to the scandals in which he was implicated. 'Some of this, of course,' wrote Baldwin (2018):

> was the consequence of fair-minded journalists doing their job of providing scrutiny to both candidates. It is also the case that Trump's messaging – 'Build the wall!' – was a clearer talking point for the media to pick up on than the earnest fifteen-point plans that Clinton was producing. But the disparity is so great that it is hard to escape the conclusion that much of the media, so hostile to Trump, got suckered. (Ibid.: Location 4216)

However, after his election, CNN, MSNBC, and others who positioned themselves in opposition to both Trump and Fox News continued to neglect their own news agendas to express and reflect outrage. In a sense, the President was correct to claim in a tweet on 29 July 2018 that the media 'are driven insane by their Trump Derangement Syndrome'. In this way, the Fox News model is not judged an aberration from the normal practices of broadcast journalism. Rather, CNN, MSNBC, and others, and the way they have reacted to and reported the Trump presidency, have approved the normalisation of the Fox model, even when Trump has threatened the Constitution's First Amendment, as when he told the *Los Angeles Times*: 'With all of the Fake News coming out of NBC and the Networks, at what point is it appropriate to challenge their License?' In his 2018 book, *Media Madness*, Howard Kurtz questions the media's contribution to creating not only the Trump phenomenon, but also the social polarisation that often leads to violent reactions by Trump supporters and haters. He calls out journalists on both sides for deviating from their responsibility as objective witnesses and reporters, and choosing instead inflammatory and agenda-driven language.

The alt-right's appropriation of the American media to broadcast the populist propaganda we now associate with Trump is explained in part by the decision of the Federal Communications

Commission in 1987 to overturn the so-called Fairness Doctrine that required broadcasters to maintain balance when discussing controversial subjects. After Trump's election, Charlie Sykes, a conservative Talk Radio host, reflected with remorse on the consequences of this decision:

> I was very excited back in the 1990s to realise that we were part of creating an alternative media. I was not perhaps aware that it was going to also then, at some point, morph into an alternative reality silo. And when you try to point out, OK, this is not true, this is a lie, and then you cite *The Washington Post* or *The New York Times*, their response is 'ah that's mainstream media.' So we've done such a good job at discrediting them, that there's almost no place to go to be able to fact check. (Quoted in Baldwin, 2018: Location 332)

The blurring of fact and fiction has aroused new interest in the intersection of the political and the 'post-truth' society. Theoretical and empirical discussions are now published at an astonishing rate, including O'Connor and Weatherall (2019), Baldwin (2018), Runciman (2018), D'Ancona (2017), and Ball (2017). This is far from an exhaustive bibliography and it contains none of the books published about the Trump presidency specifically: why and how he won the election, as well as the growing number of White House 'insider' accounts (represented most famously by Wolff, 2018; Woodward, 2019; Bolton, 2020; Woodward, 2020). Nor does the list include books by the White House correspondents detailing their daily battles for the truth (Acosta, 2019; Ryan, 2018); nor all the new discussions of populism that have appeared since 2016 (most notably, Tormey, 2019). Of course post- or alternative truths are not new (O'Connor and Weatherall, 2019; Kakutani, 2018). The long and sometimes sordid history of propaganda has often turned on persuading audiences to accept competing versions of reality (Taylor, 2003), while the postmodernists and post-structuralists have long argued for the existence of alternative truths or a simulcra (Baudrillard, 1995). Their claims garnered more attention and credibility in the run-up to the 2003 Iraq War, with 'alternative facts' held responsible for the UK's involvement in the conflict. In what could be dialogue from the 1997 movie *Wag the Dog* (dir. Barry Levinson), in which a Hollywood mogul is enlisted to produce for media consumption a fake war to distract attention from political scandal, a senior advisor in President George W. Bush's White House told a journalist: 'We're an empire now and we create our own reality. And while you're studying that reality … we'll act again, creating other new realities' (Suskind, 2004).

The history of presidential propaganda is as old as the Republic, and Trump was certainly not the first resident of the White House to engage in a war with the media, question the veracity of the news, spread disinformation, or engage in 'spin' (Greenberg, 2016). However, what was distinctive in the era of Trump and the new wave of global populism was the sheer volume, speed, and reach of 'alternative facts', and the unapologetic and explicit way they were created, explained, distributed, consumed, unchallenged, and spread. They were fed by both the 'listen to me' culture of Twitter and by the media across the political spectrum that report, dissect, and thereby amplify and circulate them ever further. Michiko Kakutani (2018) has provided a very personal and somewhat polemical discussion of *The Death of Truth*, but the evidence he provides is startling: 'Trump,' says Kakutani, 'the forty-fifth president of the United States, lies so prolifically and with such velocity that *The Washington Post* calculated that he'd made 2,140 false or misleading claims during his first year in office – an average of nearly 5.9 per day' (Kakutani, 2018: Location 62). Some doubt that more fact-checking will be an effective challenge: NBC's Tom Brokaw told Nicholas Kristof of the *New York Times* that

Trump's followers 'find fault with the questions' posed by journalists, 'not with his incomplete, erroneous or feeble answers' (Kristof, 2016).

The social media, and especially Twitter ('a kind of gut focus group'; Tufekci, 2016), have become echo chambers – incubators for 'ideological silos' (Ott, 2017: 64) – where all opinions are equal and whoever shouts the loudest gets most attention. Rather than providing a platform for genuine dialogue and discussion, Twitter's format encourages terse responses to news and to others' opinions, encourages users to retreat behind their own constricted beliefs, and constrains meaningful and rational political debate: I am right, you are wrong; and if you do not agree with me, then your opinion doesn't count and you are not 'one of us' (on the simplicity encouraged by Twitter, see Kapko, 2016). In confirming our biases and reaffirming our existing worldviews and prejudices, Twitter conforms to the classic propaganda model.

The problem is that the so-called 'mainstream media' (now usually shortened to MSM) exist in a symbiotic relationship with social platforms, with news broadcasters often building their stories around online posts. The Trump team observed how, at the time of the election in 2016, only 20 per cent of American voters used Twitter, but most were hearing about the candidate's tweets because the were the focus of news stories on CNN and other mainstream media. Michael Glassner, Trump's deputy campaign manager, described this situation: 'It was like owning *The New York Times* without the overheads or the debt.' Hillary Clinton's communications director, Jennifer Palmieri, mourned how every time she tried to talk about policy, the press wanted her to respond to Trump's latest tweet. Palmieri said they 'only covered her when she talked about him' (Hohmann, 2016). However, in February 2016, Les Moonves, the chief executive of CBS, was more honest: 'It may not be good for America, but it's damn good for CBS' (Bond, 2016).

THE SEVEN DEVICES

To help us better understand political propaganda in the Trump era it is worth turning our attention to the seven propaganda devices introduced by the Institute of Propaganda Analysis in 1937. Although this typology fell somewhat out of favour among propaganda scholars, the rise of populist politics in the United States and across Europe (as well as in places as far away from each other as Brazil, Turkey, and the Philippines) prompts us to reconsider their value (Pomerantsev, 2019). In 2001, J. Michael Sproule offered a useful and timely account of the history of the seven devices as well as critiques of them. Reading this article again during the Trump presidency, Sproule's conclusions are prescient indeed:

> Social ferment in the last 30 years, as focused by today's cultural turn in communication scholarship, has established a fertile ground for detecting propaganda. Accompanied at the millennium by concerns that various of democracy's underpinnings are under fire – tolerance, civility, community feelings – succeeding decades may well produce a further upsurge of interest in [the] venerable seven propaganda devices. (Sproule, 2001: 142)

Anti-Trump propaganda observed on a daily basis a decline in tolerance, civility, and community that was encouraged in part by the President's own style of political rhetoric, as well as the alt-right political culture he represented.

The seven propaganda devices are well known. They are (Institute of Propaganda Analysis, 1937: 5–7):

1. Name calling (demonising opponents).
2. Glittering generalities (using attractive, value-driven but vague statements that appeal to emotions rather than reason.
3. Transfer (associating with people and/or groups who already enjoy high levels of trust and credibility).
4. Testimonial (using 'evidence' from 'trusted' others).
5. Plainfolk (connecting with the non-elites by suggesting we are all in this together or 'I'm just the same as you').
6. Cardstacking (repeating and exaggerating one's own position and qualities).
7. Bandwagon (tapping into the natural need to conform, the need to belong to a group).

The devices rarely work in isolation from one another: 'cardstacking' may depend on 'transfer' and 'testimonials' for credibility, while 'bandwagon' methods require 'name-calling' and 'glittering generalities' to create the necessary 'us' versus 'them' worldview. Trump appropriated and applied all of the seven devices in one way or another; and while he was certainly not the first president in American history to do so – who among recent White House residents have not used such glittering generalities as freedom, democracy, security, the American way of life? – the Trump's administration's adoption of the seven devices was both brazen and undeniable.

To demonstrate how Trump has engaged with classic propaganda techniques I will highlight just a few examples from almost a decade of tweets available.[2]

Glittering generalities are most useful for use in an alt-right political climate. Both of Trump's memorable campaign slogans – 'America First' and 'Make America Great Again' – demand emotional (rather than intellectual) responses from supporters: 'To all Americans tonight, in all our cities and towns, I make this promise. We will make America strong again. We will make America proud again. We will make America safe again. And we will make America great again.'

Trump provides no details about how he intends to accomplish these goals: what does 'Great' mean and how is it measured? What are the specific policies that will make America Great Again? He may not be able to provide information on the strategy, but he is certainly very clear who is responsible for the country's decline. The problems range from the media and rebuilding war-torn Afghanistan and Iraq, to American politicians and their trade deals with China (Trump accused the Chinese government, the 'currency manipulator', of 'trying to steal our business and factories'). On 29 October 2018, Trump tweeted:

> There is great anger in our Country caused in part by inaccurate, and even fraudulent, reporting of the news. The Fake News Media, the true Enemy of the People, must stop the open & obvious hostility & report the news accurately and fairly. That will do much to put out the flame.

> When will we stop wasting our money on rebuilding Afghanistan? We must rebuild our country first. (7 October 2011)

> Tell Congress to straighten out the many problems of our country before trying to be the policeman of the world. Make America great again! (5 September 2013)

'Telling Congress', or more accurately blaming Congress, was a common theme in tweets prior to the start of Trump's official campaign for the presidency. His propaganda positions him as an outsider, hence his call to 'drain' the Washington 'swamp' on both sides of the political divide (his first tweet on this theme in August 2011 claimed 'It's easy to see why Americans are sick of career politicians and both parties'). Trump summoned the spirit of President Richard Nixon when he referred to the so-called 'Silent Majority'. Nixon first used this phrase in November 1969 to describe Americans who did not protest against the Vietnam war or challenge core American values. Like Trump, Nixon loathed the liberal media and believed that the political elite conspired against him. Nixon also referred to the political press as 'the enemy', while his Vice-President, Spiro Agnew, called the media 'hostile critics'. Also like Trump, Nixon believed that getting 'a fair hearing from the public … required discrediting the media' (Greenberg, 2016: 398). Immediately following his 'Silent Majority' speech, Nixon's approval ratings improved, rising from $c.$ 50 per cent to 81 per cent favourable (Perlstein, 2008: 444). In 2015, Trump announced at a rally in Phoenix that 'the silent majority is back, and we're going to take our country back'. He continued the theme on Twitter:

> I truly LOVE all the millions of people who are sticking with me despite so many media lies. There is a great SILENT MAJORITY LOOMING. (29 July 2015)
>
> The polls have been consistently great. The silent majority is speaking. Politicians are failing. (30 July 2015)
>
> If the working, proud and productive people of our country don't start exerting their authority and views, the U.S. as we know it is doomed! (1 May 2015)

Sometimes, the solutions to America's problems are simple: to halt Mexican immigration, build a wall; to deal with Islamic extremists, ban Muslims from entering the country. After Freddy Gray, an African American, died in police custody in April 2015, riots erupted in Baltimore: 'Baltimore had a really tough night – only great leadership can solve the many inner-city problems facing our country. Jobs, jobs, jobs!' (2 May 2015).

This echoes his campaign rhetoric that made sweeping promises: 'If I'm elected, everybody will have a job. I guarantee it.'

Then in January 2016: 'Love seeing union and non-union members alike are defecting to Trump. I will create jobs like no one else' (8 January 2016).

Such cardstacking – 'I know how to make a deal' – played alongside the generalities. Only Trump can create jobs for all Americans, though how (other than his election) is never made clear. Cardstacking is present also in his epistrophic use of the phrase, 'Believe me' to punctuate many claims about himself and his ability. A classic sales technique – who has never encountered the confident and pushy second-hand car salesman who asks us to believe him when he tells us the reasons why we should buy from him? – Trump used this particular epistrophe no less than 30 times in the 12 Republican debates (Ortiz, 2017). It asks listeners to trust him because he has the experience, the necessary business acumen, and that he can work the art of the deal: 'Believe me, I know.' In March 2016, he claimed that not only had he studied the Iran nuclear deal, he did so, 'I will say, actually, greater by far than anybody else. Believe me. Oh, believe me.' If elected he promised to destroy Islamic State: 'We will, believe me'; and generally: 'I know how to deal with trouble. And believe me, that's why I'm going to be elected, folks.'

Such generalities – Middle America, 'working people', 'the Silent Majority' – along with his obvious proclivity for cardstacking, helped Trump's formation of 'bandwagons'. His propaganda created groups that were in opposition to one another, but only by supporting Trump will Americans feel they belong. This was most evident at his rallies, especially during the campaign when he incited supporters against his opponents, including journalists reporting for the 'fake news media'. Many of the rallies turned threatening as Trump instructed his supporters to remove opponents from the room. CNN's White House correspondent, Jim Acosta, was on the frontline:

> At one 2016 rally in Las Vegas, I watched in horror as Trump all but incited a melee in the crowd. When a protestor appeared, Trump yelled out to security to 'get them out', and then remarked that he wished he could take matters into his own hands.
> 'I'd like to punch him in the face,' he said. 'In the old days [protestors would be] carried out on stretchers,' he continued, as the audience cheered. 'We're not allowed to push back anymore,' he added in a nod to his supporters' grievances. (Acosta, 2019: 254–255)

> If you see somebody getting ready to throw a tomato, knock the crap out of them, would you? Seriously, OK? Just knock the hell … I promise I will pay for the legal fees. I promise, I promise. (1 February 2016)

> Get him [a protestor] out. Try not to hurt him. If you do, I'll defend you in court. Don't worry about it. (February 2016)

The social media intensify the efficacy of bandwagoning, as the need to join a group and conform is moved from the real to the virtual world. Each post and tweet generates its own response through likes, shares, and retweets (Sundar, 2008). Research suggests that the more reactions (both negative and positive) a post attracts, it acquires more attention and is therefore 'liked' even more, thus boosting the post's credibility and legitimacy. It is therefore more likely to spread even further along the network (Thorson, 2008) especially when, as the Pew Research Center found in 2016, 62 per cent of adults in the US obtained their news from the social media (Gottfried and Shearer, 2016; see also the Reuters Institute for the Study of Journalism, 2019 for data after the 2017 election). Hence such social media platforms are convenient for circulating unverified information and propaganda (Lokot and Diakopoulos, 2016). Craig Silverman (2016) at BuzzFeed News reported that the top 20 fake news stories in the three months prior to the 2016 election were liked or shared *c.* 8.7 million times on Facebook, while Hunt Allcott and Matthew Gentzkow (2017) found fake news stories linked to both the Clinton and Trump campaigns were shared 38 million times. Rather than growing the sources of information, revealing myriad opinions, and allowing us to engage in debate and discussion with each other, the social media actually seal our networks, encourage us to preserve our biases and opinions, protect our beliefs from those who do not share them, and thus create simple social and political binaries among users. They shield users from exposure to uncomfortable truths (Pariser, 2011). This means the social media are convenient and effective for circulating propaganda. It is not surprising, therefore, that Luke O'Brien discovered that '[M]ost alt-Righters are digital natives, and they have weaponized social media' (O'Brien, 2016). David Runciman, author of *How Democracy Ends*, describes how social media nurture our cognitive biases:

> Twenty-first century advertising preys on cognitive biases, working with them to make sure we stay in the moment. Human beings have an inbuilt tendency to value immediate gratification over future

benefits; to want to hold on to what they have; to seek reinforcement of their beliefs; to overestimate how much other people are paying attention to them; to underestimate how different their future selves might be from their present ones. Social networks are set up to satisfy these impulses and so are the machines through which we access them. They are designed to be addictive. We keep checking our phones to find out what's new, so long as what's new chimes with what we would like to be true. (Runciman, 2018: Location 2089)

Meanwhile, Zeynap Tufekci of the University of North Carolina refers to the 'cascading self-affirmation' found in the 'Trump Twittersphere':

People naturally thrive by finding like-minded others, and I watch as Trump supporters affirm one another in their belief that white America is being sold out by secretly Muslim lawmakers, and that every unpleasant claim about Donald Trump is a fabrication by a cabal that includes the Republican leadership and the mass media. I watch as their networks expand, and as followers find one another as they voice ever more extreme opinion. (Tufekci, 2016)

By talking in generalities and by creating bandwagons, especially on Twitter, Trump directed the cognitive biases of both his supporters and his opponents who refuse to acknowledge anything positive about his presidency and who create their own 'in-groups' to channel their disapproval, thus forging today's extreme polarity in American politics.

Moreover, the effect of bandwagoning is amplified by the proliferation of non-human 'bots' spreading stories, via algorithms, through the social media. One-fifth of election-related tweets from 16 September to 21 October 2016 were circulated by bots and were then retweeted by human users. Their value lies in the speed at which content is generated and distributed, and because it is difficult to authenticate the original source of the information:

Trump supporting bots systematically produced overwhelmingly positive tweets in support of their candidate. Previous studies showed that this systematic bias alters public perception. Specifically, it creates the false impression that there is a grassroots, positive, sustained support for a certain candidate. (Ferrara, 2016)

Ferrara then records how many of those tweeting in Trump's support in the Nevada primary election had stereotypical Hispanic names, indicating that the bots had been working hard to appeal to Latin voters.

Trump's use of generalities and bandwagons worked alongside his predilection for name-calling. To amplify the appeal of making America great again among his core supporters, he needed to not only show the country is broken and that he is the one to fix it, but he also needed to identify the individuals and groups he held responsible for the problems. He routinely demonised critical journalists as 'enemies of the people' – 'The FAKE NEWS media (failing @nytimes, @NBCNews, @ABC, @CBS, @CNN) is not my enemy, it is the enemy of the American People!' (17 February 2017) – and disparaged and demeaned his political opponents ('crooked Hillary' Clinton, 'sleepy Joe' Biden, 'lyin' Ted' Cruz, 'little Maro' Rubio, 'low energy Jeb' Bush, and, for Senator Elizabeth Warren, the nickname 'Pocahontas'). These tags gather rhetorical power through their repetition, a classic propaganda technique. The first of more than 200 tweets of the Trump campaign referencing 'crooked Hillary' was posted on 17 April 2016 (Oborne and Roberts, 2017: Location 3090): 'Crooked Hillary Clinton is spending a fortune on ads against me. I am the one person she doesn't want to run against.

Will be such fun!' And Trump continued to use this moniker for his former opponent even after the election.

Most disturbing is that Trump's alt-right politics required invective against groups of people and even whole nations. The generalities he identified as 'the problem' necessitated easy solutions, and propaganda works best when name-calling groups who can be easy scapegoats. Hence in Trump's universe immigration, especially from Mexico, is one of the reasons for America's problems: 'It is time for DC to protect the American worker, not grant amnesty to illegals. Let's make America Great Again!' (23 April 2015). Mexicans are 'drug dealers, criminals and rapists' and parts of the developing world are 'shithole countries':

> Mexico is allowing many thousands to go thru their country & to our very stupid open door. The Mexicans are laughing at us as buses pass by. (10 July 2014)

> Druggies, drug dealers, rapists and killers are coming across the southern border. When will the U.S. get smart and stop this travesty? (19 June 2015)

> Are all illegals pouring into our country vaccinated? I don't think so. Great danger to U.S. (3 February 2015)

During his speech to announce his candidacy in June 2015, Trump said of Mexican immigrants:

> They are not our friend, believe me. But they're killing us economically. The US has become a dumping ground for everybody else's problems ...
> When Mexico sends its people, they're not sending their best ... They're bringing drugs. They're bringing crime. They're rapists. And some, I assume, are good people.
> I like Mexico. I love the spirit of Mexican people, but we must protect our borders from people, from all over, pouring into the U.S. (19 June 2015)

Mexicans are responsible for America's economic problems: 'Mexico is killing the United States economically because their leaders and negotiators are FAR smarter than ours. But nobody beats TRUMP!' (19 June 2015).

Such propaganda combines with the 'plainfolk' device, used by candidates and presidents alike to connect with ordinary Americans. From FDR's 'fireside chats' to Eisenhower's 'spot ads' in the 1950s, and Bill Clinton wearing sunglasses and playing the saxophone on NBC's Arsenio Hall show in 1992, presidents have sought support from Middle America. Trump's populist propaganda has taken this one step further by amplifying and indeed celebrating his anti-elitist credentials, from his attacks on the Washington 'swamp' to his use of 'locker room banter' to explain his explicitly sexual and misogynist comments captured on tape (the so-called 'Billy Bush affair'). From the perspective of propaganda, three issues stand out from the Billy Bush episode.[3]

First, Trump's presidency is known for creating 'alternative facts', most famously the size of the crowd at his inauguration in January 2017. In the Billy Bush episode Trump at one point denies the voice on the tape is his. The *New York Times* reported that Trump 'suggested to a senator ... that [the tape] was not authentic'. He reportedly told one Republican senator shortly before his inauguration: 'We don't think that was my voice.' Here Trump is engaging not only in disinformation (for he had already confessed to and apologised for this episode), but he was also feeding his image as the 'outsider' with reason to be fearful of conspiracies against him.

Second, he used the occasion of a public apology to launch a fresh attack on both Bill and Hillary Clinton, accusing them without evidence of abusing and bullying women. But first came the plainfolks: 'I've never said I'm a perfect person, nor pretended to be someone that I'm not. I've said and done things I regret, and the words released today on this more-than-a-decade-old video are one of them. I said it, I was wrong, and I apologize.'

Trump then uses the opportunity to frame his comments as part of his personal journey on the campaign trail, describing the people he had met who had lost their jobs and families (cardstacking): 'I've travelled the country talking about change for America, but my travels have also changed me.'

But then Trump switches to offence: 'Hillary Clinton and her kind have run our country into the ground. I've said some foolish things, but there's a big difference between the words and actions of other people. Bill Clinton has actually abused women, and Hillary has bullied, attacked, shamed and intimidated his victims' (Haberman, 2016).

Finally, it is worth noting that the Billy Bush episode did not dent Trump's popularity among his core supporters, most of whom (including many women) accepted that what he had been recorded saying was just normal 'locker room banter'. Although many prominent members of the Republican Party were very vocal in expressing their outrage at what Trump said, one poll found that 84 per cent of those who had said they would vote for him said this incident would not 'make any difference' to how they would cast their ballot in the general election (Clement and Balz, 2016).

Name-calling and plainfolks coincided again in September 2016 when Hillary Clinton delivered a misguided speech to her supporters in the LGBT community:

> We are living in a volatile political environment. You know, to just be grossly generalistic, you could put half of Trump's supporters into what I call the basket of deplorables. Right? The racist, sexist, homophobic, xenophobic, Islamaphobic – you name it. And unfortunately there are people like that. And he has lifted them up ... He tweets and retweets their offensive, hateful, mean-spirited rhetoric. Now, some of these folks – they are irredeemable, but thankfully they are not America.

Clinton had given Trump licence to attack her elitism and appeal to his base that felt alienated and discounted: 'Wow, Hillary Clinton was SO INSULTING to my supporters, millions of amazing, hard working people. I think it will cost her at the Polls!' (10 September 2016).

In *Fire and Fury*, Michael Wolff's (2018) alleged glimpse inside the Trump White House, the President's use of plainfolks is described thus:

> In the one reality, which encompassed most of Trump's supporters, his nature was understood and appreciated. He was the anti-wonk. He was the counterexpert. His was the gut call. He was the everyman. He was jazz (some, in the telling, made it rap), everybody else an earnest folk music. (Wolff, 2018: Location 868)

Trump's use of the plainfolks device also extends to encouraging supporters to be suspicious of facts, truths, and experts, especially of scientific opinion on the problems of global warming. As Cailin O'Connor and James Weatherall (2019) discuss in their study of *The Misinformation Age*, science has long been under attack by the post-truth culture. Trump was particularly dismissive of the scientific evidence for climate change and global warming: 'GLOBAL WARMING bullshit' he tweeted in December 2015, blaming the Chinese for 'hurting' American air and creating global warming to make American manufacturing 'non-competitive'.

Trump repeatedly challenged expert opinion during the Covid-19 pandemic in 2020, using the opportunity to scapegoat China as responsible for the crisis. While unverified reports circulated that the administration referred to the virus as the 'Kung Flu', Trump preferred to eschew its scientific name – coronavirus or Covid-19 – and label it instead 'the Chinese virus':

> The United States will be powerfully, supporting those industries, like Airlines and others, that are particularly affected by the Chinese Virus. We will be stronger than ever before! (16 March 2020)

> I always treated the Chinese Virus very seriously, and have done a very good job from the beginning, including my very early decision to close the "borders" from China – against the wishes of almost all. Many lives were saved. The Fake News new narrative is disgraceful & false! (18 March 2020)

These tweets appeared only days after Robert Redfield, the Director of the Center for Disease Control, confirmed at a hearing in Congress that it was 'absolutely wrong and inappropriate' to use labels like 'Chinese coronavirus'. Dr Mike Ryan, executive director of the World Health Organization's emergency programme, also condemned using such terms. But Trump defended his labelling: asked why he continued to call it the Chinese Virus, the President replied, 'It comes from China … it's not racist … I want to be accurate' (19 March 2020).

Yet despite building his authority on such anti-elite plainfolk propaganda techniques, Trump enjoyed implying his own expert status on any number of subjects (cardstacking). This was particularly evident during the Covid-19 pandemic when Trump repeatedly suggested that he knew and understood the science, contradicting the medical experts and even offering his own advice (memorably advising Americans to inject or drink bleach). On 5 March 2020, during a meeting with doctors and scientists at the Centre for Disease Control and Prevention in Atlanta, Trump said of the science: 'I like this stuff. I really get it … People are really surprised I understand this stuff. Every one of these doctors said, "How do you know so much about this?" Maybe I have a natural ability.'[4]

Distraction from mistakes made in managing America's response to the virus, ignorance of science, and pushing inconvenient expert advice to one side, scapegoating and name-calling, cardstacking, plainfolks – the Covid-19 crisis conflated Trump's propaganda techniques, simplifying a complicated problem, igniting new racial hostility towards Asian Americans, and turning state-imposed restrictions on movement, gatherings, and the mandated wearing of face masks into a new battlefront with the Democratic Party in an election year. To observers of political propaganda, such 'weaponisation' of information – often directed at targets overseas – diverts attention from problems and policy failures at home. In *Mad Men*, the American television series set in the world of advertising, the main character, Don Draper, says that his philosophy is based around a simple formula: if you don't like what they're saying, change the conversation. Watching Trump's propaganda unfold on Twitter and elsewhere, and seeing how his propaganda determines the agendas of both liberal and conservative media, one cannot help but agree that for all the criticisms directed against him, he is certainly very skilful at changing the conversation, especially during the Covid-19 crisis which unfolded during an election year. Writing in the *New York Review of Books*, David Bromwich criticised the 'grave-faced attitude' of newspapers towards Trump's tweets: 'presidential squirts and squibs' (Bromwich, 2019: 12). Perhaps Trump's approach to communication reveals that the real danger to democracy lies in this symbiotic relationship between politics and the media;

and that if they really wish to understand the role they play in shaping, distributing, and challenging modern political propaganda of the kind we have seen on a daily basis from the Trump White House, from alt-right media and on social platforms, journalists and news organisations first have to examine themselves and very carefully ask a troubling question: how much did we help to create Trump?

CONCLUSIONS

In 1974, Hannah Arendt, a writer who perhaps has provided more insight into the character of totalitarian regimes than any other, said in an interview: 'If everybody always lies to you, the consequence is not that you believe the lies, but rather that nobody believes anything any longer' (Errera, 1978). President Trump calls on his listeners to believe him, his use of this epistrophe revealing a need to emphasise his credentials and experience. Trump is President in a post-truth environment, characterised by claims of 'alternative facts' and 'fake news' circulating faster than ever before through social media networks and distributed by 'mainstream media'. These media exist in a symbiotic relationship with both the political culture and the information found on social media platforms. Ann Curry, an American TV anchor, admitted to the *New York Times* journalist Nicholas Kristof: 'The truth is, the media has needed Trump like a crack addict needs a hit' (Kristof, 2016).

With populist political movements gaining power and credibility across the world with the help of social media, we would do well to heed Hannah Arendt's warning. The danger is not that truths are questioned, scientific opinions are challenged, and journalists are labelled the enemy of the people. The problem is that it is increasingly difficult, but also increasingly essential, to evaluate the information we receive; both the message and the source. Building and maintaining trust is now the biggest challenge:

> Many of the Trump supporters whom I've been following say they no longer trust any big institutions, whether political parties or media outlets. Instead they share personal stories that support their common narrative, which mixes falsehoods and facts – often ignored by those powerful institutions they now loathe – with the policies of racial resentment. (Tufekci, 2016)

As Arendt noted, when nobody believes anything any longer, and when the population feels estranged and impatient for simple solutions to the complex problems in their lives, political propaganda thrives. Bob Schieffer was correct to tell Nicholas Kristof of the *New York Times* that, 'We are in a new world where attitude seems to count more than facts.'

NOTES

1. This chapter was completed before the 2020 presidential election and the transfer of power to the Biden administration in January 2021.
2. Unless specified otherwise, all tweets are reproduced from Oborne and Roberts (2017). Twitter permanently suspended Donald Trump's account on 8 January 2021. Thus it is difficult to verify the accuracy of the reproduction of the tweets quoted here. Most have been checked via media sources and the Trump Twitter Archive (https://www.thetrumparchive.com/) which has 56 571 tweets dating back to 4 May 2009.

3. In 2005, Trump, on an open microphone, told NBC host Billy Bush his approach to women: 'It's like a magnet. Just kiss. I don't even wait. And when you're a star they let you do it. You can do anything … Grab them by the pussy. You can do anything.' The recording surfaced in October 2016.
4. Little wonder that comedian Sarah Cooper became an internet phenomenon by posting film of herself lip-synching to Trump's speeches, highlighting the absurdity of much of what he said. While there is much to despair in Trump's presidency, the rebirth of political satire is a source of American soft power, showing that it is still possible to challenge the political establishment.

REFERENCES

Acosta, Jim (2019), *The Enemy of the People: A Dangerous Times to Tell the Truth in America*, New York: Harper.
Allcott, Hunt and Matthew Gentzkow (2017), 'Social media and fake news in the 2016 election', *Journal of Economic Perspectives*, 31(2): 211–236.
Baldwin, Tom (2018), *Ctrl Alt Delete: How Politics and the Media Crashed Our Democracy*, London: Hurst & Co.
Ball, James (2017), *Post-Truth: How Bullshit Conquered the World*, London: Biteback Publishing.
Baudrillard, Jean (1995), *The Gulf War Did Not Take Place*, Bloomington, IN: Indiana Press.
Bolton, John (2020), *The Room Where It Happened: A White House Memoir*, New York: Simon & Schuster.
Bond, Paul (2016), 'Leslie Moonves on Donald Trump: "It may not be good for America, but it's damn good for CBS"', *Hollywood Reporter*, 29 February, https://www.hollywoodreporter.com/news/leslie-moonves-donald-trump-may-871464.
Bromwich, David (2019), 'The medium is the mistake', *New York Review of Books*, 66(19): 10–12.
Clement, Scott and Dan Balz (2016) 'Washington Post–ABC News Poll: Clinton holds four-point lead in aftermath of Trump tape', *Washington Post*, 16 October, https://www.washingtonpost.com/politics/washington-post-abc-news-poll-clinton-holds-four-point-lead-in-aftermath-of-trump-tape/2016/10/15/c31969a4-9231-11e6-9c52-0b10449e33c4_story.html?utm_term=.38b558ecbe3d.
Confessore, Nicholas and Karen Yourish (2016), '$2 billion worth of free media for Donald Trump', *New York Times*, 15 March.
D'Ancona, Matthew (2017), *Post-Truth: The New War on Truth and How to Fight Back*, London: Ebury Press.
Ellul, Jacques (1965), *Propaganda: The Formation of Men's Attitudes*, Knopf: New York.
Errera, Roger (1978), 'Hannah Arendt: from an interview', *New York Review of Books*, 26 October, http://www.nybooks.com/articles/1978/10/26/hannah-arendt-from-an-interview/.
Ferrara, Emilio (2016), 'How Twitter bots affected the US presidential campaign', *Conversation*, 18 November, https://theconversation.com/how-twitter/bots-affected-the-us-presidentialcampaign-68406.
de Freytas-Tamura, Kimiko (2017), 'George Owell's "1984" is suddenly a best-seller', *New York Times*, 25 January, https://www.nytimes.com/2017/01/25/books/1984-george-orwell-donald-trump.html.
Geoghegan, Peter (2019), 'Covering Trump: reflections from the campaign trail and the challenge for journalism', in Catherine Happer, Andrew Hoskins, and William Merrin (eds), *Trump's Media War*, London: Palgrave Macmillan, Kindle edition.
Gottfried, J. and E. Shearer (2016), 'News use across social media platforms 2016', Pew Research Centre, 26 May, http://www.journalism.org/2016/05/26/news-use-across-social-media-platforms-2016/.
Greenberg, David (2016), *Republic of Spin: An Inside History of the American Presidency*, New York: W.W. Norton & Co.
Haberman, Maggie (2016), 'Donald Trump's apology that wasn't', *New York Times*, 8 October, https://www.nytimes.com/2016/10/08/us/politics/donald-trump-apology.html.
Happer, Catherine, Andrew Hoskins, and William Merrin (eds) (2019), *Trump's Media War*, London: Palgrave Macmillan, Kindle edition.

Hohmann, James (2016), 'The Daily 202: at acrimonious post-election conference, Trump and Clinton strategists agree only on anger at the media. Even then, not really', *Washington Post*, 2 December, https://www.washingtonpost.com/news/power-post/paloma/daily-202/2016/12/02/daily-202-at-acrimonious-post-election-conference-trump-and-clinton-strategists-agree-only-on-anger-at-the-media-even-then-not-utm_term=.28142aa1ae7f.

Institute of Propaganda Analyis (1937), 'How to detect propaganda', *Propaganda Analysis* 1(2) (November).

Kakutani, Michiko (2018), *The Death of Truth*, London: William Collins, Kindle version.

Kapko, M. (2016), 'Twitter's impact on 2016 presidential election is unmistakable', CIO, 3 November, http://www.cio.com/article/3137513/social-networking/twitters-impact-on-2016-presidential-election-is-unmistakable.html.

Kristof, Nicholas (2016), 'My shared shame: the media helped make Trump', *New York Times*, 26 March.

Kurtz, Howard (2018), *Media Madness: Donald Trump, The Press, and the War Over the Truth*, Washington, DC: Regeny Publishing.

Lokot, Tetyana and Nicholas Diakopoulos (2016), 'News bots automating news and information dissemination on Twitter', *Digital Journalism*, 4(6): 682–699.

Oborne, Peter and Tom Roberts (2017), *How Trump Thinks: His Tweets and the Birth of a New Political Language*, London: Head of Zeus.

O'Brien, Luke (2016), 'My journey to the center of the Alt-Right', *Huffington Post*, 2 November, http://highline.huffingtonpost.com/articles/en/alt-right.

O'Connor, Cailin and James Owen Weatherall (2019), *The Misinformation Age: How False Beliefs Spread*, New Haven, CT: Yale University Press, Kindle version.

Ortiz, Erik (2017), 'Can Trump's style of speech work in his favor to unite country in inaugural address?', NBCNews.com, 20 January, https://www.nbcnews.com/storyline/inauguration-2017/can-trump-s-style-speech-work-his-favor-unite-country-n705731.

Ott, Brian L. (2017), 'The age of Twitter: Donald J. Trump and the politics of debasement', *Critical Studies in Media Communication*, 34(1): 59–68.

Pariser, Eli (2011), *The Filter Bubble: How the New Personalized Web is Changing What We Read and How We Think*, London: Penguin.

Perlstein, Rick (2008), *Nixonland*, New York: Scribner.

Pomerantsev, Peter (2019), *This is Not Propaganda: Adventures in the War Against Reality*, London: Faber & Faber.

Reuters Institute for the Study of Journalism (2019), *Digital News Report*, http://www.digitalnewsreport.org/.

Runciman, David (2018), *How Democracy Ends*, London: Profile Books, Kindle version.

Ryan, April (2018), *Under Fire: Reporting From the Front Lines of the Trump Presidency*, Lanham, MD: Rowman & Littlefield.

Schroeder, Robert (2016), 'Trump has gotten nearly $3 billion in "free" advertising', *Market Watch*, 6 May, http://www.marketwatch.com/story/trump-has-gotten-nearly-3-billion-in-free-advertising-2016-05-06.

Silverman, Craig (2016), 'This analysis shows how viral fake election news stories outperformed real news on Facebook', *Buzzfeed News*, 16 November, https://www.buzzfeed.com/craigsilverman/viral-fake-election-news-outperformed-real-news-on-facebook.

Sproule, Michael J. (2001), 'Authorship and origins of the seven propaganda devices: a research note', *Rhetoric and Public Affairs*, 4(1): 135–143.

Sundar, S. Shyam (2008), 'The MAIN model: a heuristic approach to understanding technology effects on credibility', in Miriam J. Metzger and Andrew J. Flanagin (eds), *Digital Media, Youth and Credibility*, Cambridge: MIT Press, pp. 73–100.

Suskind, Ron (2004), *New York Times Magazine*, 17 October.

Taylor, Philip M. (2003), *Munitions of the Mind: War Propaganda from the Ancient World to the Nuclear Age* (2nd edn), Manchester: Manchester University Press.

Thorson, Emily (2008), 'Changing patterns of news consumption and participation', *Information, Communication and Society*, 11(4): 473–489.

Tormey, Simon (2019), *Populism: A Beginner's Guide*, London: OneWorld.

Tufekci, Zeynep (2016), 'Adventures in the Trump Twittersphere', *New York Times*, 31 March.
Tyndall Report (2016), *Year in Review*, http://tyndallreport.com/yearinreview2016/.
Welch, David (2002), *The Third Reich: Politics and Propaganda* (2nd edn), London: Routledge.
Wolff, Michael (2018), *Fire and Fury: Inside the Trump White House*, London: Little, Brown.
Woodward, Bob (2019), *Fear: Trump in the White House*, London: Simon & Schuster.
Woodward, Bob (2020), *Rage*, London: Simon & Schuster.

5. The information war paradox
Peter Pomerantsev

INTRODUCTION

Russian military theory defines 'information psychological war' as a range of activities to break down the enemy without waging kinetic conflict. This includes using corruption to buy politicians, cyber offensives such as distributed denial-of-service (DDOS) attacks on state infrastructure, the use of state-directed compatriots organisations, and communication strategies, such as planting covert disinformation to corrode cohesion. In this sense, Russian 'information psychological war' is perhaps best understood as 'political warfare' (Kofman, 2017). Propaganda is a subset of this, if defined as a type of communication aimed at influencing the attitudes and behaviours of target groups in ways conducive to its creators (Roetter, 1974: 12–14); it is but one type of activity, albeit one that is augmented by the possibilities of new information technologies (Thomas, 2015: 16).

However, Russian government officials, state media, and state-aligned spokespeople increasingly use the term 'information war' in another way. They describe any type of communication activity that in any way negatively impacts upon the Russian state structures, and the Russian President especially, as a product of 'information war' of Western powers against Russia. Investigative media, anti-corruption research, protest movements against the Kremlin's allies, human rights non-governmental organisations (NGOs), and so on, are all described as weapons of information war. Historically, the Soviet Union's collapse in the Cold War is recast by some Russian academics as the product of 'information warfare' from the West. Utilised this way, the very concept of information warfare becomes a form of propaganda itself that washes away all types of criticism of the Russian state, or any facts unpleasant to it, as weaponised tricks.

Such a notion of information war reduces the space for deliberative debate or evidence-based decision-making, as communication is reduced to warfare where facts are viewed as just a coincidental tactic in one side's strategy against the other. In this sense the information war frame fits into descriptions of propaganda that make critical engagement impossible (Quaranto and Stanley, 2020), even as it uses the language of critical thinking.

This chapter examines the evolution of these concepts of 'information war'. It then looks at how these play out in Russia's invasion of Ukraine, and the struggle of Ukrainian fact-checkers, government strategic communications experts, and military to expose Russian information operations while resisting the secondary frame of information war. At the same time, they attempt to build the sort of trust and respect for facts necessary for deliberative discourse and evidence-based political decision-making.

RUSSIAN INFORMATION WAR

The idea of information war as a way to understand history has long obsessed a certain breed of Russian geopolitical analyst looking to explain the failure of the Soviet Union. Secret service agents turned academics assert the Soviet Empire collapsed not because of its poor economic policies, human rights abuses, and lies, but because of 'information viruses' planted by Western security services through Trojan horse ideas such as freedom of speech (Operation Glasnost) and economic reform (Operation Perestroika) (Panarin, 2010; Yablokov, 2018). Alleged secret agents in the Soviet establishment who posed as so-called modernisers, allied with a Washington, DC-dictated fifth column of anti-Soviet dissidents, oversaw the dissemination of these 'viruses'.

For a long time such theories were not in the Russian mainstream. However, as the Kremlin searched for ways to explain the colour revolutions and the growth of discontent at home, which erupted in hundreds of thousands protesting against Vladimir Putin's rule in 2011 and 2012, this all-pervasive information war philosophy became increasingly amplified by TV spokespeople and spin doctors. Today, runs the argument, the West wages information war against Russia with the cunning use of the BBC and human rights NGOs, fact-checking organisations, and anti-corruption investigations.

One of the most outspoken public promoters of the information war is Igor Ashmanov, a frequent guest on TV talk shows and radio (*Rossijskaja Gazeta*, 2013). 'The fall of the Soviet Union, Yugoslavia, Iraq ... we've lived through many information wars,' said Ashmanov in one of his many interviews (ibid.). He has also told Russian lawmakers that Google, Facebook, and Twitter are ideological weapons aimed at Russia (@znak_com, 2018; Ashmanov, 2013).

However, Ashmanov is no crusty spook. He is one of the fathers of the Russian Internet, the former head of the country's second-largest search engine. When I visited his high-tech office in Moscow, with piles of fresh fruit, dates, and nuts on the table, I could just as easily have been in Palo Alto or Berlin. Ashmanov, in his sports clothes and wire-rimmed glasses, could fit in at any tech gathering.

Ashmanov's big idea is 'Internet sovereignty', meaning government control over what information reaches the population. This is a concept China is well on the way to achieving with its firewall and censorship, and which the West tries to undermine with talk about 'freedom of speech'. Information sovereignty cannot be achieved, he argues, without an ideology to defend your rationale for letting some streams of information through and not others (Khnar Film, 2018):

> If your ideology is imported ... as with liberalism, then you are always playing to foreign rules, which are always being changed by someone else. You can always be called guilty, breaking the rules of democracy ... Ideology should be created inside a country, like operational systems, rockets, insulin and grain. Supported and defended by information sovereignty. (*Rossijskaja Gazeta*, 2013)

In this worldview information precedes essence. First you have an information warfare aim, and then you create an ideology to fit it. Whether the ideology is right or wrong is irrelevant, it just needs to serve a tactical function. Instead of clashing ideas leading to a Cold War, here information war necessitates the creation of ideologies.

Indeed, as Ashmanov argues, it is not hard to find many instances where the United States (US) acted hypocritically when it came to support for freedom and human rights, supporting their promotion in adversaries, and ignoring their violation in allies. But maybe that Cold War 'hypocrisy' was not always a bad thing. As long as the US kept up the facade of believing in something when promoting its image abroad, it would have to at least sometimes do something about it. Meanwhile inside the Soviet Union dissidents could use the Helsinki Accords to insist that the regime 'obey their own laws', to at least try to embarrass them internationally.

These were tiny victories in the grand scheme of the horrors of the Cold War, but the notion of information war as defining history demolishes even these achievements, replaces hypocrisy not with something better but with a world where there are no values. In this vision all information becomes, as it is for military thinkers, merely a means to undermine an enemy, a tool to disrupt, delay, confuse, subvert. There is no room for arguments, and ideals are in and of themselves irrelevant.

This leaves one with a tricky situation. In *Don't Think of an Elephant* the cognitive linguist George Lakoff defines winning and losing in politics as being about framing issues in a way conducive to your aims. Defining the argument means winning it. If you tell someone not to think of an elephant, they will end up thinking of an elephant. 'When we negate a frame, we evoke the frame ... when you are arguing against the other side, do not use their language. Their language picks out a frame – and it won't be the frame you want' (Lakoff, 2014: Location 139).

The heads of Russia's international broadcasters, RT and Sputnik, indulge in the language of information war and even receive military medals for their services to the government (Medium, 2017). Then Western journalists and analysts call them out for being information war organs. However, by describing them as such, is one actually lending them a hand, framing them in the image that they need to secure more funding from a regime that wants to see everything through the frame of information war? By evoking the Kremlin's language of information war, does one end up strengthening it? Do all the endless articles, senate hearings, and think tank events with their sour coffee – I have written for and attended plenty – risk reinforcing the notion even as they try to expose it?

The long-term implications go deeper. If all information is seen as part of a war, out go any dreams of a global information space where ideas flow freely and which bolsters deliberative democracy. Instead, the best future one can hope for is an 'information peace', in which each side respects the other's 'information sovereignty': a favoured concept of both Beijing and Moscow, and essentially a cover for enforcing censorship.

However, to merely ignore the Kremlin's information operations would be foolish. At endless panels held in think tanks in Washington, DC, London, and Brussels, military theorists, journalists, and officials have tried to make sense of the Russian approach to 'war' and international conflict. Some call it 'full-spectrum warfare', others 'non-linear war', yet others 'ambiguous' and 'grey-zone warfare' (Kofman, 2017). In Eastern Europe, 'hybrid war' state research centres have sprung up, where 'hybrid' seems to be a diplomatic way of not saying 'Russian'.

There are some things that a few experts can at least occasionally agree on. Firstly, that the Russian approach smudges the borders between war and peace, resulting in a state of permanent conflict that is neither on nor off; and in this conflict information campaigns play a remarkably important role. Summarising the aims of Russian 'next-generation warfare', Janis Berzins of the Latvian Military Academy describes a shift from direct annihilation of the opponent to its inner decay; from a war with conventional forces to irregular groupings; from direct clash to contactless war; from the physical environment to the human consciousness;

from war in a defined period of time to a state of permanent war as the natural condition in national life (Berzins, 2014: 5).

This leaves us with a paradox. On the one hand, it is necessary to recognise and reveal the way the Kremlin, with a military mindset, uses information to confuse, dismay, divide, and delay. On the other, one risks reinforcing the Kremlin's worldview in the very act of responding to it.

It is in Ukraine that this paradox plays out at its most intense. This is where the Kremlin's next-generation warfare is being tried out, but also where it is trying to spread an all-encompassing worldview of information war. So how can one win an information war when the most dangerous part could be the idea of information war itself?

UKRAINE

Of all the things one might think Tetyana Matychak could ever be, a soldier is not one of them. But back in 2013, at the height of Ukraine's revolution against a pro-Moscow president, Tetyana suddenly found herself able to command life and death. Sitting in her father's apartment in her pyjamas, she had her hand over a keyboard, knowing that if she pressed one key she might send many very real people to their death, and if she pressed another the revolution and all that she, her friends, and thousands of others had fought for, might be lost.

In 2013, Tetyana ran the Facebook page Hromadske Sektor (the Civic Sector), one of the many social media groups used to organise citizens in the Ukrainian revolution against President Viktor Yanukovych and his backers in the Kremlin (Elledge, 2015: 4). She posted photos and videos showing acts of non-violent protest action: a protester playing a piano out on the street when facing a row of riot police; photos of protesters holding mirrors up to the security forces; a drawing of a cop duelling with a protester, with the cop holding a gun and the protester 'shooting' with a Facebook sign. Online activists could organise everything from medical help to legal aid, coordinating million-strong protests and raising funds from Ukrainians abroad for food and shelter. Tetyana had kept up the click-beat over many months of protests. Hromadske Sektor had 45 000 followers, and 150 000 visitors attended their protests; people who did not trust politicians but believed in volunteers like Tetyana.

Tetyana had joined Hromadske because she wanted to be part of a historical moment, something to tell her future children about. The uprising was nicknamed the Revolution of Dignity. It began when President Yanukovych, very suddenly, dropped a long-standing pledge to sign an Association Agreement with the European Union in favour of a $16 billion loan from the Kremlin. After Yanukovych's police beat protesting students, it grew to symbolise for many the desire for a government which was less corrupt, for a more just society bound up in the word 'Europe': 'Euro-Maidan' was the revolution's other nickname.

Tetyana would post on the site as she filed stories for her real job as a financial journalist. She told herself she would somehow stay above the fray. She was for democracy and human rights, sure, but she would not get dragged into disinformation, and she would not get her hands dirty.

Tetyana's shift was in the morning. She was usually based in Kiev, but today she happened to be in her home-town of Luhansk, one of the capitals in the far east of the country known as the Donbas, where most people watched state or Russian TV, which portrayed the revolution – referred to as the 'Maidan Revolution', its name taken from the square where protesters gathered – as a neo-fascist, US-orchestrated conspiracy. Out here, Tetyana never mentioned her work for Hromadske Sektor.

She had woken at 9 a.m. and switched the computer to the live feed coming from the Maidan. At first, she thought she had tuned into some action movie by mistake, as snipers mowed people down and there was blood on the streets. Then her phone rang. It was activists at the Maidan. She could hear guns going off behind them, and after a brief time lapse heard them crackle on the live stream too.

'Get people to come to the Maidan. We need everyone here.'

However, Tetyana could also see posts popping up on her Facebook feed from people in the square, warning everyone to flee and save themselves. Activists kept calling her, demanding she tell her followers to come.

'But there are people being killed,' she said.

'The snipers will stop shooting if more people come.'

'And what if they don't?'

'It's your decision.'

It was not the first time she'd found her journalistic instinct to remain above the fray clashing with her revolutionary loyalties. A few weeks previously the pagan-nationalist, balaclava-clad Pravy Sektor (the Right Sector) had started hurling burning Molotov cocktails through the snowstorms at the riot police. Few people had heard of Pravy Sektor until then. There were only a few hundred of them, but all the publicity around their violence had increased their profile wildly. Kids looking for a little ultra-violence were now signing up to join them.

Tetyana did not approve of Pravy Sektor's violence or ideology. The Maidan was full of different 'sectors', everything from neo-Cossacks to neo-anarchists and neo-fascists, all able to organise with the help of the Internet. Everyone had their own motivation. The different sectors had nothing much in common apart from being fed up with Yanukovych's corruption and casual brutality, and it did not seem right to attack people who were beaten up by the same riot police who beat you up.

Hromadske Sektor decided to ignore Pravy Sektor's violence, but Tetyana could not ignore the massacre in Maidan Square that morning. What was her role? Was she, ultimately, a propagandist? A journalist? Was she reporting on the war, or was she a soldier in it? Every time you post or tweet, or just repost or retweet, you become a little propaganda machine (Asmolov, 2019). In this new information flux, everyone has to find their own boundaries. Tetyana had reached hers. She refused to encourage crowds to come to the Maidan. She simply reported on what was going on and let people make up their own minds.

Various Hromadske Sektor leaders logged on themselves and urged crowds to come to the Maidan. One hundred and three protesters died in those few days, but the crowds did not stop coming. They kept pushing, storming the presidential palace, while in the regions protesters, many of them now armed themselves, stormed local council after local council. President Yanukovych fled to Russia. Hromadske Sektor leaders joined political parties and stood for election. Tetyana did not want to be involved in party politics, and left the movement altogether.

Then the Kremlin began exacting its revenge. Russian TV filled up with invented stories about how Pravy Sektor was coming to slaughter ethnic Russians in Crimea, where most of the population are ethnic Russians. In Sevastopol, the Crimean capital, Cossack groups, separatist parties, and Orthodox priests (all funded by the Kremlin) led crowds begging Putin to rescue them. He obliged and annexed the peninsula.

Russian TV broadcast scare stories about Pravy Sektor coming to murder Russians in East Ukraine too. The Internet, the medium through which the revolution had been empowered, was flooded with Kremlin content pumped out of the troll factory in the St Petersburg suburbs. Students were paid a few hundred dollars a day to post pictures, comments, and videos, sowing confusion, enmity, and panic in East Ukraine. (A good resource for Kremlin influence campaigns in Ukraine is https://www.stopfake.org/en/news/.)

The Kremlin's information campaign was the prelude to action. Irregular forces, local proxies of the Kremlin, seized cities in the east: Donetsk and Tetyana's home-town of Luhansk. These parodied the same visual language as the Maidan uprising, with flag-waving crowds sometimes bussed in from across the border and piles of burning tyres, which had become the symbol of events in Kiev. It was labelled the 'Russian Spring' by Kremlin-controlled media, tapping into the language of the Czechoslovak rebellion against the Soviet Union in 1968. As with previous information campaigns around colour revolutions, the Kremlin was trying to satirise the Maidan into insignificance. At the same time, it was desperately trying to reconfigure the Maidan uprising into a greater story of Ukrainians manipulated by covert American forces, all part of the American 'regime change' which had brought catastrophe in Iraq and Libya. Of course, Igor Ashmanov and Russian state media honchos pronounced the Ukrainian uprising a product of 'information war'.

If there was one aim of the Kremlin storytelling, it was this: to show that the desire for 'freedom', that hangover of Cold War logic, did not lead to peace and prosperity, but to war and devastation (a message meant, first and foremost, for its own people so they did not become overenthusiastic for the idea). To make this narrative real meant ensuring Ukraine could never achieve peace. The country had to bleed.

When the Ukrainian military attacked the separatist strongholds, the Kremlin sent in tanks and crushed them, then retreated and claimed the military had never been there in the first place. Over the following years – indeed, up to the time of writing at the end of 2020 – the conflict flowed hither and thither, neither quite a full-blown war nor peace. Towns in the Donbas are taken and then lost again. Shells go off on either side of the lines. The Russian army holds mass exercises on the border with Ukraine, and mass panics break out throughout the country.

The war has also killed innocent foreigners. In July 2014, a Russian high-tech anti-aircraft gun shot down a Malaysia Airways passenger airliner full of Dutch tourists that was flying over territory controlled by Kremlin proxies, killing 298. To deflect blame, Kremlin and Kremlin-aligned media claimed multiple alternative theories for the causes of the disaster: that the plane had been shot down by the Ukrainian military who thought it was Putin's private jet; that dead bodies had been put on the plane in advance, and the whole thing was staged; and that Ukrainian fighter jets had taken the plane down (Polygraph, 2018).

The Supreme Allied Commander of the North Atlantic Treaty Organization (NATO) had called the Russian campaign to take Crimea 'the most amazing information warfare blitzkrieg' in history. But it was ordinary Ukrainians, often abandoned by their government, who had to find ways to make sure the information blitzkrieg would not spread to the rest of the country too (Hill, 2017). One of the most intense flashpoints of the 'information war' came in Odessa. Odessa boasts 14 local TV cable channels alone, not to mention the dozens of Ukrainian and the hundreds of international ones available in most free-to-air packages. Online there are tens of local news sites and masses of social media groups.

Odessa has always been a port city, populated by Jews and Greeks, Russians, Romanians, Ukrainians, and Bulgarians. Today the port is a major international thoroughfare for goods, both legal and otherwise, coming into Europe. Many are traded at the Seventh Kilometre, which some locals claim to be the world's largest outdoor market: acres of shipping containers stacked on top of each other in a multilayered maze, each one transformed into a shop where Nigerians sell fake Nikes, fake stereos, and fake Gucci; Vietnamese trade money; Indians hang out silks and muslins. They say you can buy weapons here too, if you know who and how to ask. Not just guns, but anti-aircraft missiles too.

It was this delicate ethnic balance that the Kremlin tried to tip into civil war. In May 2014, just as Kremlin proxies were taking town after town in the Donbas, pro-Ukrainians fought with pro-Russians holed up in Odessa's Palace of All Trade Unions. A fire broke out, and even as the flames were still engulfing the building and the dead were still being counted, the rumours and lies were already fanning through the media. The first YouTube videos were blurry and horrific. Hundreds of pro-Russian activists had been hiding out in the building. Pro-Ukrainians threw Molotov cocktails and shot at them. A fire broke out. People began falling out of the windows, so quickly it looked like they were pushed to their deaths. Some of the Ukrainians cheered (Amos, 2015).

The first photos from inside showed dozens of corpses in twisted poses. One was of a pregnant woman. Interviews appeared online with eyewitnesses who claimed Pravy Sektor death squads had been hiding in the building. The unnamed witnesses claimed the Pravy Sektor had been prepared, wearing gas masks and executing people on the spot. The initial death toll put the number of victims at around 40, but stories spread that actually there had been hundreds. The story went international. Pro-Kremlin activists in Belgium and Italy campaigned to have a European square named after the 'Odessa Martyrs'.

In the days following the fire the people of Odessa, citizens of a city of ceaseless chatter, a city famous for its humour, stopped talking to each other. No one trusted anyone. The rumours began to turn the city against itself. Opinion polls showed an even split between those who wanted the city to be part of Russia and those who wanted it to be part of Ukraine. Pro-Russian bloggers began to ask Putin to save the city from chaos and invade. Later, recordings would emerge of Russian politicians talking on cellphones directly with gangs of thugs in Odessa, giving them orders on when to provoke more fights.

A group of 13 Odessans, both pro-Russian and pro-Ukrainian, decided to take it upon themselves to launch a public investigation. They felt Odessans needed to know what happened in the fire if the city was to be whole again. It was clear that no official investigation would be forthcoming: too many bureaucrats would have to take too much blame for all the casualties.

The civic investigation pieced together the events of the day from video and multiple witness statements, autopsies, and photographs. The trouble had started earlier in the day. It was found that both sides threw Molotovs and fired shots; that the barricades around the building had lit up accidentally; that the autopsies showed 34 deaths, all from asphyxiation, none by mysterious execution. The 'pregnant' woman had been over 50 and had died from the fumes, falling back into a position that made her stomach look swollen. The eight people who had fallen to their deaths had lost consciousness and tumbled out, none had been pushed.

The public investigation had managed to establish the essential truth about what happened during the fire, but when the results were presented, few were interested. 'There's no unity here,' Tatyana Gerasimova, one of the instigators of the public investigation, told me as we sat in a cafe by the opera house. 'Everyone lives in their own reality, everyone has their own truth, there is no reconciliation. We created the investigation to show that there is a difference between truth and lies. In that sense we failed.'

I would hear similar sentiments from students at the university, where I was giving a lecture about information war. The students' friends and relatives just chose the story of the fire that fitted better their worldview. As they sat and discussed it in their social media groups, pro-Ukrainians saw it one way, pro-Russians another. Faced with wildly conflicting versions of reality, people selected the one that suited them.

However, despite this fracturing of shared reality, Odessa had not toppled into civil war. The week I visited, summer was in full swing. The bars and discotheques were full. The opera was sold out. 'The city needs to feel alive again, after it looked death in the face,' said Gerasimova. But this had not been achieved purely spontaneously. While the civic investigation had tried one way of unifying the city, other Odessans had taken a different approach. Zoya Kazanzhy was running government information campaigns when the threat of civil war was at its highest. She felt she knew something about her home town that Putin did not. Yes, Odessa is as fractured as any globalised city, but its different communities had something deeper in common. Apart from a few fanatics, most saw Odessa as a wealthy, open trading port, a city of markets and merchants. They would go with the force that could guarantee their security, whether Russian or Ukrainian, the European Union or NATO. So instead of playing on the ethnic tension, as the Kremlin might have wanted, instead of looking to divide the city further between patriots and traitors, Kazanzhy and her colleagues decided to target what all sides had in common. They put up posters across Odessa with pictures of the wrecked cities of the neighbouring Donbas, where the separatism had led to a destructive war. No one in Odessa wanted that sort of future, despite their differences. No one wanted physical destruction. The most potent manoeuvre in the information war was to jettison the idea of 'information war' altogether and show what real war led to. As I headed into the zone of actual military conflict, I would soon find that even if the shooting and shelling was real enough, at the same time every action, including military action, was taken with its impact on the information conflict in mind.

HOW TO FIGHT A WAR THAT MAY NOT EXIST

Dzerzhinsk is a mining town at the very edge of the territory held by Ukrainian forces. Separatist positions are a couple of kilometres away. There was a summer storm brewing when I arrived, thunder mixing with the sound of heavy artillery. A few days earlier a shell had hit the local lake. Fish had flown out onto the cracked paths or floated dead to the surface. The people of Dzerzhinsk ate the fish, but there were still a few drying on the paths and many more were floating belly up in the lake. The smell was strong.

I travelled with a small crew from an Internet TV station in Kiev, one of the few Ukrainian media organisations not in the pocket of an oligarch. Driving through town we passed along roads with coffin-sized craters, saw empty factories with their walls ripped out. A young boy leading his drunk mother down the lanes; local men with scabs on their faces. I stopped to photograph a concrete coal store with a gaping hole in its walls. I assumed it had been shelled, but it turned out it had been taken apart long before the war by locals looking for scrap metal.

Dzerzhinsk is named after Felix Dzerzhinsky, the man responsible for the first Soviet secret police force, the notorious Cheka. When I asked a local teenage girl whether she knew who he was, she told me she had 'heard of him at school but couldn't remember'. This wasn't unusual. A few weeks earlier a TV channel had done a joke report about how young people in Dzerzhinsk had no idea whom the town was named after. Later that year it was renamed Toretsk, in accordance with the laws against Soviet names. There were no great protests.

The mineshafts were dark against the thundery skyline. Some of the mines were now disused. Others were rusty, but functional.

The local administration of Dzerzhinsk has weathered every revolution. In April 2014 they welcomed the separatists with open arms. The two local newspapers supported the Donetsk People's Republic (DPR). When the Ukrainian army retook the town a few months later, they shelled the town hall. The administration quickly cut a deal with them. However, although the town was now officially in Ukrainian territory, you still could not get Ukrainian TV unless you had a cable package. Russian and DPR TV stations are still available everywhere. Dzerzhinsk may be in Ukrainian territory, but it is still under the Kremlin's informational sovereignty.

The pro-Ukrainian activists were jumpy. There was Oleg, an older man with a grey moustache and a cap. He had been one of the miners who helped bring down the Soviet Union in the great strike of 1989, blocking the roads with broken glass to stop the Kremlin's tanks. Volodya was younger, with big arms and a boy-band fringe. He was a miner too but had worked in Sweden for several years. He knew things did not have to be this way.

Volodya and Oleg were sure the administration wanted the activists, with their annoying anti-corruption rallies, out of town. They were worried Kiev was ready to abandon them.

'If there's no mention of us on TV, then it won't be a big deal if the town is lost,' said Volodya. 'We're being erased.' In the front of his van was a stack of leaflets:

7 TO 12 YEARS PUNISHMENT FOR EVERYDAY SEPARATISM: CALL THIS NUMBER IF YOU SPOT AN EVERYDAY SEPARATIST!
HOW TO SPOT AN EVERYDAY SEPARATIST?
– CALLS FOR RUSSIA TO INVADE
– INSULTS UKRAINIAN VALUES
– SPREADS LIES
– PLANTS DEFEATIST FEELINGS

I asked Volodya where he had obtained the leaflets. He told me with no little pride that he had made them himself. I asked whether that was such a good idea.

'The telephone numbers on them aren't even real,' he said. 'They're just to intimidate people. We're all alone here. We need to do something.'

We arrived at a Soviet block of flats, rising above an area of wooden shacks, several of which had been blown apart. The Ukrainian army base was 500 metres away and this area was hit frequently. Oleg showed us the shrapnel holes in the metal door of the apartment block. Some women were on a bench outside the front door. They were angry that the Ukrainians had put their base near here. There had been no fighting when the town had been part of the Donetsk People's Republic. The Ukrainian army had brought the war with them. One woman told me how a shell had exploded through her balcony. Oleg got angry: 'Our mayor is a separatist. That's why the army is here. He should be in prison.'

'I worked all my life for pennies, and what's my reward?' said a woman going past in a sunflower-patterned dress. 'Bombs!'

'They came from over there – those are Ukrainian positions! That's not DPR,' shouted one of the women. Later, she showed me a crater in the ground. A tree had collapsed into it. 'Look,' she said, 'it's clear it came from the Ukrainian position.'

It did not seem clear at all. I thought it unlikely the Ukrainians could shell themselves from 500 metres away. But this was not about piecing together evidence. Journalists who had travelled the region had warned me about this phenomenon: people would rearrange the evidence to fit the worldview they saw on television, however little sense it made.

'The Ukrainians are bombing each other!' said someone else. 'The Pravy Sektor wants to march on Kiev and they're fighting each other.'

'It's the Americans. They've come here to take our gas. I heard there are wounded American soldiers in the local hospitals.'

Oleg was becoming increasingly irate, shouting at the women that they were traitors. They started shooing him away. He took off his shirt and showed them a bullet wound, saying the Russians had shot at him when he was delivering food to the front lines. He said Putin was in Ukraine because he was afraid that Russia would fall apart. The women said Putin was not afraid of anything.

Oleg went to the car and came back with the leaflets and started handing them out.

'Ha – you think we're afraid of this?' The women laughed and threw the papers in the bin.

Then they turned to the cameraman and me and started shouting at us.

'You'll re-edit what we say anyway. Why should we trust you? Nobody wants to hear the Donbas!'

That phrase again, repeated here like a mantra: nobody hears the Donbas. It reminded me of a prayer, a religious lamentation for a lost God, the recurring theme of the Psalms crying out to a vanished God, the Yom Kippur prayers that beg God to hear the people.

'O God who answered Abraham, Jacob and Isaac, O God who answered us in Sinai, Hear, Hear, Hear the Donbas!'

INFORMATION WAR WITH REAL BULLETS

I woke up in the billiards room. It was still dark, and I nearly collided with some soldiers who were slumped, fully clothed, on sofas. One soldier was sleeping with his head on the floor, propping up his fat torso. He was so exhausted that he did not notice he was sleeping in a half-headstand. Outside, the rose garden and tennis court were just becoming visible in the dawn light. The roses had wilted and the tennis net was missing. I could hear rhythmic splashing as a soldier was doing the breaststroke in the outdoor pool. The light was coming on fast, revealing summer houses and garages, high-security fences, the hills beyond, and the dark green, almost black pine forests of the Luhanschina. We were north-east of Dzerzhinsk, on the edge of the territory held by Ukraine, where it bordered the Luhansk People's Republic.

We were bivouacked on the country estate of a deposed local minigarch, formerly the head of the Luhansk Court of Appeal. He was now lying low in Kiev, waiting to see which side would win. There was a hyperrealist portrait of his wife in the billiards room: a plump, grinning blonde lying in a summer field with a garland of red poppies over her head. In a cottage near the pool an officer was making breakfast: chopped cabbage and corned-beef meatballs. The TV was bursting with war propaganda. The Ukrainian president was in military fatigues, inspecting well-equipped troops. There were slow-motion clips of proud wives waving soldiers off to war or meeting them by the train with tears of joy. It was the sort of war propaganda that was used to build national morale and spur mobilisation everywhere throughout the twentieth century.

However, there was something strange: for all the war visuals it was never defined rhetorically as a war. On TV the president spoke of an 'Anti-Terrorist Operation', an ATO. 'What the hell is an ATO?' cursed the officer as he chopped more cabbage. One of the clever twists of the Kremlin's approach was that it waged war without ever openly declaring it, undermining the narrative of fighting a clear enemy.

Later, the soldiers took us to the front line. Every vehicle was a different make. I sat in the back of a small Nissan jeep and was told to look out the window to watch for separatist snipers. The window had been shattered in a previous gunfight and was held together with Scotch tape. You could not see a single thing through it. We stopped on the edge of a bluff opposite the separatist positions on the other side of the river. You could just about see them with the naked eye. 'If they start shooting, jump away from the cars,' said the commander, known as 'the ComBrig'. 'They will aim for that,' the ComBrig added.

The ComBrig ordered heavy artillery to spread out along the bluff in a show of strength. Then he timed how long it took the separatists to get their people into position, a ruse to get the other side to reveal where they had hidden their forces on the far side of the bluff. The story was that new Russian units had recently arrived.

From there we drove to the village of Lobachevo, a collection of single-storey wooden houses at skewed angles. A cow stood on the road, staring at an outhouse. Three elderly men in dusty string vests, flip-flops on dirty feet, sat drinking and smoking on some logs outside. One of them, known as Uncle Kolya, had no teeth. He claimed a separatist had knocked them out after he refused to sing the Luhansk People's Republic anthem. The soldiers suspected he had concocted the story just for them, and that the second their backs were turned he would curse Ukraine. 'We spent a long time winning their trust,' said the ComBrig. 'At first they thought we were all Pravy Sektor monsters from the Russian propaganda machine.'

Across the riverbank you could see the separatists with rifles slung over their shoulders, pacing up and down by the old ferry station. The ferry had been blown up during the fighting. Families who lived on different sides of the river had been split. The school was on one side and the shops were on the other. Local women crossed in a tiny rowing boat with a tiny motor. They complained that if they carried more than one bag of potatoes, they could be done for smuggling contraband. They did not care about Ukraine, Russia, or the Luhansk People's Republic. They cared about their village and their potatoes.

We drove out from Lobachevo, past abandoned churches and blown-up bridges that had collapsed into the green river, past women walking with goats. There was no obvious profit to be made from any of this land. Kiev had done nothing to develop it in 20 years of independence, but the Kremlin had little need for it either. If you looked closely, both sides were prepared to lose Luhanschina. The Kremlin wanted to hand it back to Ukraine while maintaining covert political control. Kiev made noises about 'unity', but many people, from top brass to academics, argued that the best outcome was a frozen territory the Kremlin had to fund and feed.

War used to be about capturing territory and planting flags, but something different was at play out here. Moscow needed to create a narrative about how pro-democracy revolutions like the Maidan led to chaos and civil war. Kiev needed to show that separatism leads to misery. What actually happened on the ground was almost irrelevant; the two governments just needed enough footage to back their respective stories. Propaganda has always accompanied war, usually as a handmaiden to the actual fighting. But the information age means that this equation has been flipped: military operations are now handmaidens to the more important information effect. It would be like a heavily scripted reality-TV show if it were not for the very real deaths. On 3 November 2015, a few months after my visit, the Kharkiv 92nd was caught up in a firefight by Lobachevo. The ComBrig was wounded but survived.

CONCLUSION

The challenge that faces Ukrainian journalists, activists, and military is how to expose Russia's frequent 'information war' operations, while not falling into the 'information war' framing that risks eating away at a democratic public sphere based on evidence-based policymaking, where facts have an intrinsic worth and not all communication is perceived as weaponised. This challenge is in turn part of Ukraine's broader challenge of needing to simultaneously fight the Russian invasion while developing its democracy. Its challenge cannot be dealt with purely through top-down actions by senior government officials, or purely by decisions taken by senior editorial staff in traditional media. The preponderance and widespread use of digital communications means Ukrainians at every level of society and in different sectors need to take responsibility for their own role as producers of information effects: from citizens considering small actions like sharing a post on social media, through to soldiers making rapid decisions about the information effects of a military action without waiting for orders issued by senior commanders.

REFERENCES

Amos, H. (2015), '"There was heroism and cruelty on both sides": the truth behind one of Ukraine's deadliest days', *Guardian*, 30 April, available at https://www.theguardian.com/world/2015/apr/30/there-was-heroism-and-cruelty-on-both-sides-the-truth-behind-one-of-ukraines-deadliest-days, accessed 13 February 2021.

Ashmanov, I. (2013), 'Freedom of speech is an illusion that is part of the information war', 5 June, available at http://z-filez.info/story/igor-ashmanov-%E2%80%9Csvoboda-slova-%E2%80%93-eto-takaya-illyuziya-kotoraya-yavlyaetsya-chastyu-informatsionn, accessed 13 February 2021.

Asmolov, G. (2019), 'The effects of participatory propaganda: from socialization to internalization of conflicts', available at https://jods.mitpress.mit.edu/pub/jyzg7j6x/release/2, accessed 13 February 2021.

Berzins, J. (2014), 'Russia's new generation warfare in Ukraine: implications for Latvian defense policy', policy paper, National Defence Academy of Latvia Center for Security and Strategic Research, April, available at https://sldinfo.com/wp-content/uploads/2014/05/New-Generation-Warfare.pdf, accessed 13 February 2021.

Elledge, K. (2015), 'Ukraine: dissident capabilities in the Cyber Age', in Legatum Institute (ed.), *Cyber Propaganda: From How to Start a Revolution to How to Beat ISIS*, available at https://www.lse.ac.uk/iga/assets/documents/arena/archives/cyber-propaganda-2015-final-pdf.pdf, accessed 13 February 2021.

Hill, T.M. (2017), 'Is the U.S. serious about countering Russia's information war on democracies?', 21 November, available at https://www.brookings.edu/blog/order-from-chaos/2017/11/21/is-the-u-s-serious-about-countering-russias-information-war-on-democracies/, accessed 13 February 2021.

Khnar Film (2018), 'И Ашманов Свобода слова как инструмент', *YouTube*, 25 December, available at https://www.youtube.com/watch?v=cb6fqc02vt0, accessed 13 February 2021.

Kofman, M. (2017), 'The Moscow School of Hard Knocks: key pillars of Russian strategy', *War on the Rocks*, 17 January, available at https://warontherocks.com/2017/01/the-moscow-school-of-hard-knocks-key-pillars-of-russian-strategy/, accessed 13 February 2021.

Lakoff, G. (2014), *Don't Think of an Elephant*, Chelsea, VT: Chelsea Green Publishing Company.

Medium (2017), 'Question that: RT's military mission', 8 January, available at https://medium.com/dfrlab/question-that-rts-military-mission-4c4bd9f72c88, accessed 13 February 2021.

Panarin, I. (2010), *The First Information World War: Collapse of the USSR*, Moscow: Piter.

Polygraph (2018), 'Disinfo news: the Kremlin's many versions of the MH17 story', 29 May, available at https://www.stopfake.org/en/disinfo-news-the-kremlin-s-many-versions-of-the-mh17-story/, accessed 13 February 2021.

Quaranto, A. and J. Stanley (2020), 'Propaganda', in J. Khoo and R. Sterken (eds), *The Routledge Handbook of Social and Political Philosophy of Language*, Abingdon: Routledge, pp. 5–9.

Roetter, C. (1974), *The Art of Psychological Warfare, 1914–1945*, New York: Stein & Day.

Rossijskaja Gazeta (2013), 'I packed my gun with data', interview with Igor Ashmanov, 23 May, available at https://rg.ru/2013/05/23/ashmanov.html, accessed 13 February 2021.

Thomas, T. (2015), 'Psycho viruses and reflexive control: Russian theories of information-psychological war', in Legatum Institute (ed.), *Information at War: From China's Three Warfares to NATO's Narratives*, available at https://li.com/reports/information-at-war-from-chinas-three-warfares-to-natos-narratives/, accessed 13 February 2021.

Yablokov, I. (2018), *Fortress Russia: Conspiracy Theories in the Post-Soviet World*, Cambridge: Polity.

6. Digital propaganda as symbolic convergence: the case of Russian ads during the 2016 US presidential election

Corneliu Bjola and Ilan Manor

INTRODUCTION

In his classic essay on the theory of propaganda, Harold Lasswell insisted that collective attitudes were amenable to many modes of alteration, including violent intimidation, or economic coercion. However, he argued, 'their arrangement and rearrangement occurs [*sic*] principally under the impetus of significant symbols; and the technique of using significant symbols for this purpose is propaganda' (Lasswell, 1927: 628). In other words, symbols make propaganda great, as only they have the power to transform collective attitudes most effectively and enduringly. It is this insight that informs the central premise of this study, namely that in the digital age, symbols are more powerful than ever. If we are to truly understand how propaganda works and how to counter it, then we need to unpack the role of social media and new digital technologies in 'arranging and rearranging' the symbolic universe of texts, visuals, and emotions that inform people's political behaviour.

The starting point of our analysis is the symbolically generative role of echo chambers (ECs), which along with trolling, online hate, and fake news, have developed a pervasive presence in the online medium. For ministries of foreign affairs (MFAs) and embassies, this has become a critical issue, as ECs deform the online space in which digital diplomats operate, encourage disinformation and hate, and occasionally lead to offline violence. From a diplomatic perspective, the issue has gained additional relevance in the context of the digital disinformation campaigns that entities affiliated with the Russian government pursued against the United States (US) and Europe. These campaigns have shown that ECs do not necessarily develop organically, but they can also be strategically designed and deployed as a form of 'sharp power' to 'pierce, penetrate or perforate' the political and information environments of the opponents (Walker and Ludwig, 2017). While online anonymity, opinion validation bias and political polarisation are generally seen as conducive factors for the formation and development of online echo chambers, little attention has been paid to understanding the internal dynamic of ECs, that is, of the contextual elements that draw and keep people inside echo chambers. This omission needs to be addressed as it holds the conceptual key to designing tools and methods by which ECs could eventually be fractured or even dismantled.

Building on Lasswell's insight and drawing on Bormann's theory of symbolic convergence, this chapter argues that what makes ECs particularly powerful are the symbolic fantasies and rhetorical visions that allow EC members to achieve group consciousness by sharing emotions, experiences, and stories. Symbolic fantasies refer to 'the creative and imaginative shared interpretations of events that fulfil a group psychological or rhetorical need' (Bormann, 1985: 130). When members of ECs share a fantasy, they may arrive at symbolic convergence in terms of common understandings, emotions, and purposes, which might be able to develop even further into rhetorical visions (that is, composite dramas that catch up with large groups of people into a symbolic reality). Applied to ECs, symbolic convergence theory allows us to advance some important hypotheses about the formation and development of online echo chambers, as well as about their possible impact and dissolution.

In order to test the empirical validity of the symbolic convergence model, this chapter focuses on the strategically designed and deployed ECs by agencies affiliated with the Russian government during the US elections in 2016. Drawing on a dataset of 107 advertisements dealing with African American issues published by Russian bodies on Facebook or Instagram between January and March of 2016, the study empirically probes three hypotheses: (1) whether messages capable of forming coherent fantasy themes dominate the disinformation campaign; (2) whether the most popular posts provide the ingredients for a possible rhetorical vision; and (3) whether chains of participation are enabled by ads that addressed issues of major concern or psychological anxiety. Following the results of the empirical analysis, the chapter concludes with a brief discussion of two symbolic divergent strategies that can expand the gaps in the symbolic reality that the ECs seek to induce.

UNDERSTANDING ECHO CHAMBERS

According to Tucker et al. (2018: 16), the prevailing narrative regarding echo chambers is that of online disinformation being amplified within communities of like-minded individuals. Disinformation goes unchallenged within these communities due to algorithmic tailoring which filters out opposing voices and contradictory information (Pariser, 2011; del Vicario et al., 2016). In this chapter we adopt Tucker et al.'s (2018: 3) definition of disinformation as 'types of information that one could encounter online that could possibly lead to misperceptions about the actual state of the world'.

Concerns over the existence of echo chambers and 'filter bubbles' grew after the 2016 US elections, for three reasons. First, the elections saw an abundance of disinformation and 'fake news' reaching large numbers of citizens (ibid.: 15). Second, some of this disinformation is believed to have been disseminated by the Russian government (Garrett, 2017). Third, disinformation is believed to increase political polarisation. Tucker et al. (2018: 3) postulate that political polarisation may make people more susceptible to disinformation, while increased disinformation leads to further polarisation. Similarly, Cass Sunstein (2017) has argued that echo chambers are breeding grounds for 'fake news' and conspiracy theories that further polarise society.

Many have argued that echo chambers are especially problematic within the context of social media platforms as these are based on filtering algorithms that expose users to information that conforms to their political affiliation and worldview. Given that between 40 and 60 per cent of adults in the developed world access news through social media sites (Shearer and Gottfried, 2017), disinformation disseminated on Facebook and Twitter goes unchallenged, which in turn may lead to mass ignorance and to people basing their political stance on lies, half-truths, and fabrications.

Strategic Use of Echo Chambers

Recent studies have found that Russia strategically uses social media and fake news sites to plant false and distorted stories with the goal of influencing Western public opinion (Ziegler, 2017; Maréchal, 2017). Such is the case with disinformation campaigns meant to promote authoritarianism in Europe and counter the promotion of democracy (Vanderhill, 2013; Way, 2015). While Russia had initially focused attention on its neighbours (for example, Ukraine and Georgia), it later deployed similar tactics for spreading disinformation and sowing discord during the 2016 US presidential election (Maréchal, 2017; Tucker et al., 2018: 27).

According to Nothhaft et al. (2019: 40), the fragmentation of the media landscape in Western democracies increases their vulnerability to hostile narratives promoted online by hybrid media channels comprised of 'old' media (newspapers, TV, radio) and 'new' (social) media. Through online narratives, authoritarian regimes such as Russia manipulate perceptions of key issues as they make it increasingly difficult to distinguish between factual and 'fake' news (Tucker et al., 2018: 28; Diamond et al., 2016; Richey, 2017).

Recent reports attest to the influence on the US elections of Russian 'fake news'. Studies and journalistic reports have found that Facebook engagement was higher for fake content than for news originating from traditional media (Higgins et al., 2016; Rogers and Bromwich, 2016; Timberg, 2016). As such, the online environment saw equal exposure to disinformation and factual news (Tucker et al., 2018). An additional tool used by Russia to spread disinformation is trolling, which refers to a specific type of malicious online behaviour intended to disrupt interactions, aggravate interactional partners and lure them into fruitless argumentation (Coles and West, 2016: 233). Unlike narratives that are spread by state-run media or posted on fake news sites, trolls post inflammatory messages to sow discord and elicit strong emotional reactions as a means towards influence and political polarisation (Phillips, 2015). Trolls often spread conspiracy theories, present oversimplified information in a misleading context, or promote false information from supposedly credible sources. A report prepared by the North Atlantic Treaty Organization (NATO) Strategic Communications Centre of Excellence (NATO StratCom COE, 2017) revealed that Russian trolls have been active on news sites in Ukraine, Poland, Finland, and the US.

In 2017, the Office of the Director of National Intelligence concluded that once Russia was assured of Hillary Clinton's victory in the 2016 elections, it undertook a strategic campaign to undermine faith in American democracy and its institutions, by calling into question Clinton's integrity, and harming her chances of winning. This campaign included covert and overt actions such as disseminating disinformation through state-run media channels, third-party interlocutors, social media sites, and Internet trolls (Tucker et al., 2018: 28; Garrett, 2017).

These studies suggest that Russia uses social media and news sites as a strategic tool to advance its foreign policy objectives, be it to undermine a democratic regime or a presidential candidate. The fact that online echo chambers may increase the resonance and influence of Russian narratives has become a major source of concern for Western governments and their intelligence services.

Questioning the Validity of Social Media Echo Chambers

The assumption that social media ECs exist implies that actors looking to counter the influence of disinformation and falsehoods must 'fracture' echo chambers, or 'burst' filter bubbles, to expose members of gated communities to new information. Yet recent studies have called into question the very existence of echo chambers.

Flaxman et al. (2016) conducted a three-month study of 50 000 news consumers in the US. The study found that most people had a diverse news diet online and that the most popular online news outlets attracted both liberals and conservatives, while new outlets that appealed only to political extremes attracted little attention. Another study (Gentzkow and Shapiro, 2011) found that people's offline interactions were more likely to be politically filtered than their online news consumption. Similarly, a study of 10 million Facebook users found that the social network's removal of oppositional news stories was quite small. Algorithmic tailoring removed 5 per cent of oppositional stories for conservatives and 8 per cent for liberals (Bakshy et al., 2015). Moreover, news consumers often seek out information that does not conform to their political affiliation. As algorithms track users' online behaviour, searching for diverse news stories also diversifies one's online information environment (Garrett, 2017: 371).

Bakshy et al. (2015) found that Facebook and Twitter users were regularly exposed to a 'surprisingly' high level of diverse political views, while in a study conducted by the Pew Research Center, most social media users reported being exposed to diverse political viewpoints (Duggan and Smith, 2016). Wojcieszak and Mutz (2009) found that online discussion spaces often saw diverse political exchanges. Intriguingly, people are willing to be exposed to news stories that contradict their beliefs so long as the news items in question acknowledge the validity of their political perspective (Carnahan et al., 2016; Knobloch-Westerwick and Kleinman, 2011). Garrett postulates that the term 'echo chamber' may be relevant for engagement with social media content, rather than exposure to content. For instance, someone who has searched for oppositional news stories online is unlikely to endorse and 'like' such stories of Facebook given fear of social sanctioning. Moreover, social media users are less likely to substantially engage with news stories that have been criticised by users with similar political affiliations (Stroud et al., 2013; Anderson et al., 2014). Comments, likes, and shares posted by one's online community can thus strengthen one's worldview, even if that view is based on disinformation.

In summary, there is empirical evidence to suggest that people encounter a broad range of opinions when consuming news on social media. Thus, the rhetoric of echo chambers and 'filter bubbles' cannot fully account for how disinformation operates and with what effect. Furthermore, these studies suggest that it is not enough to correct misperceptions. Rather, one must find a way to undermine beliefs that persist even after the introduction of new and contrary evidence (Garrett, 2017: 370). One theory that may explain how disinformation spreads online and becomes influential is the symbolic convergence theory.

SYMBOLIC CONVERGENCE THEORY

The symbolic convergence theory explores human communication through the stories humans tell or the fantasies and narratives they share. It focuses on socially shared narratives which give rise to a group consciousness that is accompanied by shared emotions, motives, and meaning. The strength of the theory stems from the fact that humans instinctively interpret events in terms of dramatic performances, with actors taking actions with subsequent ramifications (Bormann, 1985: 134). The theory is symbolic as it deals with the human tendency to interpret signs and objects and give them meaning. The symbolic convergence theory therefore analyses the shared group consciousness of a symbol and compares that shared consciousness with the reality surrounding the group.

Symbolic convergence relates to the way in which two or more private symbolic worlds incline towards each other, grow closer to one another, and even overlap. If the symbolic worlds of many individuals come to overlap as a result of symbolic convergence, they have a new basis for communicating with one another, discussing experiences, and creating a community. People experience symbolic convergence through the dynamic process of sharing group fantasies that may facilitate the formation of group consciousness (Bormann, 1985: 129).

A fantasy theme consists of a dramatised message in which characters enact an incident or a series of incidents. Fantasy themes are usually narratives about living people, historical figures, or an envisioned future, and they account for people's experiences, hopes, and fears (Bormann, 1985: 134). A fantasy enables a group to share an experience, understand it, and turn it into knowledge. Fantasies are important because they fulfil people's psychological need to reduce anxiety and confusion by providing a cognitive template for understanding past or unfolding events (Bormann, 1985: 130). They provide the means through which communities create their social reality and employ meaning.

Once symbolic convergence has occurred, and emotions and common meanings have arisen, they may be set off by an agreed-upon cryptic or symbolic cue. Such is the case with an inside joke that evokes emotion and meaning only among those who have shared a given fantasy. Other cryptic cues include code words, phrases, slogans, certain names, and even geographic locations (Bormann, 1985: 131). Scholars have noted that some fantasies have the ability to engross group members much like a novel or film. Others tend to fall flat. The psychological process of being engrossed in a fantasy stems from an altercation between good and bad characters throughout a sequence of events. If one of the characters is attractive to group members, the result is arousal, sympathy, and even empathy. An emotional investment in a character paves the way to involvement in the storyline and a dislike for those who stand in the way of the protagonist. When there is doubt regarding the protagonist's victory, the result is a feeling of suspense. Importantly, when audiences of mass media share a fantasy, they jointly experience certain emotions, celebrate certain actions, and interpret experiences in the same way. This enables them to reach symbolic convergence about their common experience (Bormann, 1985: 131).

A rhetorical vision brings together various shared scripts and provides a broad view of a group's social reality. The rhetorical vision rests on a master analogy that pulls various elements into a coherent whole, and consists of five elements. The first is the dramatis personae, who are the actors, the heroes, and the villains in the vision. The second element is the plotline or sequence of events. Visions can have diverse plotlines ranging from conspiring plotlines to romantic ones. The third element, scene, is the location of the action taking place, while the fourth element is a sanctioning agent that legitimises the vision. Sanctioning agents can include God or a courtroom. The fifth element is the master analogue that is the structure into which the vision is embedded (Endres, 1994: 295).

Cragan and Shields (1992) argue that there are three master analogue structures: righteous, which is concerned with issues of right and wrong, moral and immoral, just and unjust; social, which deals with issues such as friendship, caring, family, community, and responsibility; and pragmatic, which is concerned with issues of effectiveness or efficacy. A rhetorical community consists of the people who participate in a rhetorical vision. Symbolic convergence thus facilitates the formation of a coherent view of social reality and, in so doing, creates a social reality.

According to Bormann, an important question is: Why do some fantasy themes spark a chain of participation and sharing, while others do not? While some of the reasons are socially and culturally dependent (Bormann et al., 1997), others appear to have deep psychosocial undertones. Bales (1970: 55) suggested that group members would likely share fantasies that tended to mirror their current concerns or problems, be they internal to the group or external. However, the more disturbing the problem, the less likely group members would be to partake in an open conversation, and the more likely they would be to repress the problem. But a fantasy that mirrors this problem could spark a chain of participation, as the fantasy is a symbolic way to deal with the problem, as opposed to direct conformation. Issues such as power, sexism, social rejection, and social attraction are all deeply disturbing social anxieties, and fantasies mirroring these problems are therefore more likely to spark a chain of participation.

SYMBOLIC CONVERGENCE THEORY AND DISINFORMATION

The symbolic convergence theory suggests that content which includes disinformation may become influential if it results in the formation of a rhetorical vision that is shared by a group, and that arouses a group consciousness. To do so, the content in question would need to form coherent fantasy themes, while also including cryptic cues that can set off symbolic convergence. Importantly, the content would also have to focus on issues of major concern and psychological anxiety, so as to instigate a chain of participation and increase the content's reach and impact.

In this study, we examine whether social media advertisements, paid for by groups affiliated with the Russian government, could have instigated rhetorical fantasies and thus triggered a process of symbolic convergence. Using quantitative and qualitative methods we investigate the issues addressed in Russian ads, the fantasy themes they relate to, and the extent to which social media users shared them.

The research questions is: Does symbolic convergence theory account for the distribution of Russian disinformation during the 2016 elections? Based on the concepts of the symbolic convergence theory we hypothesise that disinformation messages do not portray casual events, but they replicate coherent fantasy themes. We also predict that the more integrated the symbolic cues and fantasy themes in Russian ads, the greater the likelihood of a rhetorical vision emerging. Finally, drawing on Bales's work we assume that ads which address issues of major concern or psychological anxiety will enable chains of participation.

The hypotheses are:

H1: Ads that inform coherent fantasy themes dominate the disinformation campaign.

H2: Ads that lead to rhetorical visions will have higher impression rates.

H3: Ads that deal with issues of major concern and psychological anxiety will have a higher number of clicks.

Methodology

Our methodology rested on a mixed-methods approach combining qualitative and quantitative research methods. During the first phase of analysis, we reviewed 251 ads published by Russian bodies on Facebook or Instagram between January and March of 2016. All ads were accessed via the US House of Representatives' Permanent Select Committee on Intelligence (2018). This revealed that Russian ads dealt with six issues: African American issues (for example, police brutality, discrimination against Blacks); law and order (for example, support for the police, need to secure America's borders); ads attacking Hillary Clinton; ads supporting the lesbian, gay, bisexual, and trans (LGBT) community; ads supporting American Muslims; and ads advocating the secession of Texas from the Union. Given space limitations and the fact that most ads focused on African American issues (107 out of 251), we decided to use this topic as the reference case study.

During the next phase of analysis, we analysed the 107 ads dealing with Africa American issues and categorised them into topical themes. This phase employed thematic analysis that Braun and Clarke defined as a method of identifying, analysing, and reporting on patterns, or themes, within a research corpus (Braun and Clarke, 2016). For instance, many ads focused on discrimination against African Americans in present-day America. Thus, a category named 'Discrimination in America' was created (fantasy theme 1). Similarly, a substantial number of ads focused on Police brutality towards African Americans, leading to the formulation of the 'Police Brutality' category (fantasy theme 2). During the analysis, four additional categories emerged (see below) covering distinct themes about the daily life of African Americans in the United States.

Once all African American ads were categorised, we used quantitative analysis to identify the five ads that gained the highest number of impressions based on the data provided for each ad in the documents made available online by the House Select Committee. We then proceeded to analyse these ads to identify possible ingredients for a broader rhetorical vision. We did this on the basis of the assumption that ads which elicit a rhetorical vision would have a higher number of impressions than ads which failed to do so. Following Bormann et al. (1982), the rhetorical vision analysis included the identification of fantasy themes (that is, dramatised messages) and symbolic cues (that is, inside references). We then reviewed these elements to check the extent to which they might have contributed to the formation of a broader rhetorical vision. When analysing the plotline of Russian ads, we relied on the work of Christopher Booker (2004), who identified seven basic plots in people's stories including defeating a monster or great enemy, the quest, and tragedy.

Once we analysed the five ads that gained the highest number of impressions, we used quantitative analysis to identify topics or issues in ads that elicited the highest number of clicks. This analysis stemmed from our assumption that ads which mirror issues of great concern and/or psychological distress would obtain the highest number of clicks, possibly leading to a chain of participation.

CASE STUDY: AFRICAN AMERICAN ISSUES

Thematic Analysis

The thematic analysis of the 107 African American-related ads resulted in the identification of six topical categories (see Table 6.1). The first was 'Discrimination in America'. Ads in this category highlighted contemporary acts of discrimination in America including the activities of the Kuk Klux Klan (KKK), historical analogies between contemporary hate in America and that which was prevalent in the 1960s, attempts to whitewash American history by failing to recognise the contribution of African Americans to American history and culture, and the fact that the Black community was not fully accepted as an equal member of American society. The second fantasy theme, 'Police Brutality', focused on police harassment of innocent African Americans and attempts by the police to hide instances of mistreatment of African Americans.

The third category, 'Fatal Shootings', focused specifically on young Black males killed by the police. Notably, Trayvon Martin, who was shot in 2012 by a neighbourhood watch volunteer, was mentioned in several of these ads. The fourth fantasy theme was 'Celebrating Black Individuals and Culture', referencing icons such as Beyoncé Knowles and Serena Williams. The fifth category, 'News from within the Black Community' shared links to news sites supposedly operated by African Americans, while the final category simply included links to external website or social media profiles.

Of the 107 ads analysed, 54 included links to external websites or social media accounts, 24 dealt with discrimination, 21 with police brutality and fatal shootings, 5 with celebrating African American culture, and 3 included links to news websites. As a result, our first hypothesis is only partially validated, as the ads informing coherent fantasy themes ('Discrimination in America', 'Police Brutality', 'Fatal Shootings', and 'Black Individuals and Culture') account for only 46 per cent of the messages, with the first three categories largely dominating the dataset. The finding could be explained by the lack of experience of those involved in the disinformation campaign, but it offers very limited insight regarding the effectiveness of the campaign, without corroboration from the other two hypotheses.

However, it is important to note that these ads were published while Black Lives Matter protests were taking place throughout the US, as were additional incidents of police officers killing young Black men. It also worthy to mention that most of these ads suggested that African Americans' lives did not improve under the tenure of Barack Obama. In so doing, these ads aimed to amplify feelings of disillusionment with politics within the African American community, and to instigate loss of faith in American institutions.

Rhetorical Vision Analysis

When analysing ads that dealt with African American issues, we assumed that those which offer ingredients for a coherent rhetorical vision would have the highest impression rates. Table 6.2 includes an analysis of the four ads with the highest impression rates.

The fantasy theme analysis presented above offers good empirical support to our research hypotheses. First, it demonstrated that the Russian ads did not portray events in a completely random fashion, with no thematic connection between them. On the contrary, 46 per cent of the messages promoted coherent fantasy themes dealing with issues of police brutality,

88 *Research handbook on political propaganda*

Table 6.1   Topical categories of African American ads

Topical category	Example	Ad text
Discrimination in America		Join us to learn more! Why aren't white hoods and white supremacist propaganda illegal here in America? Why are Germans ashamed of their bigotry, while America is proud of it? Black America @black Blacklivessss
Police Brutality		Black Community! We finally made a website! News about black racial and social issues. This happened yesterday, Feb. 2, at a dry-cleaning shop in a black neighbourhood, when this black guy went for his clothes he had already sent for laundry. 'What do you mean by you people?' The black guy asked. There was a murmur from inside the shop; the dry cleaner answered 'those who are arguing m ... Black Matters The Police should protect not Brutalize Ideally Black Women ... S. F. Police Vow To Eradicate Racism Plans to fight racism in the ranks. Black History Month The event grew out of 'Negro History Week,' the brainchild Black Matters

Digital propaganda as symbolic convergence   89

Topical category	Example	Ad text
Fatal Shootings		Trayvon Martin's lawyers wearing hoodies. Wearing hoodie doesn't make me a criminal. Click Learn more! Black America (@black Blacklivessss
Celebrating Black Individuals and Culture		Hi my people! Many of you write to me asking, why most of my videos are so negative and depressive. And that's true, I used to talk about really sad things. But today I'm gonna have some fun.

Topical category	Example	Ad text
News from within the Black Community		Get breaking news and analysis on the life of African American community in the US. Black Matters Blacklive
Links to External Websites/Profiles		No text

Digital propaganda as symbolic convergence 91

Table 6.2 Fantasy theme analysis of African American ads

Ad	Message	Fantasy theme	Symbolic cue	Rhetorical vision (ingredients)
[Image of Blacktivist Facebook ad depicting Christina Jenkins with #BlackHistoryMonth post] Impressions: 127,370	This ad depicts Christina Jenkins who invented the 'sew in weave' technique for braiding hair. The ad states that while viewers may have heard of Marilyn Monroe, it is unlikely that they have heard of Christina Jenkins. The ad was posted during Black History Month.	This ad corresponds to the fantasy theme of 'White Washing American History' and the presumed denial of the contribution of African Americans to American history and culture.	Slogan: Black History Month The hashtag Black History Month was created for the very reason that Black individuals were not celebrated in America.	*Dramatis Personae*: The hero of this ad is Christina Jenkins. *Plotline*: A quest for recognition by African Americans. *Scene*: The scene is that of the 1960s as is evident from the black and white picture, Jenkins's hair style and the reference to Marilyn Monroe. As such, the image summons the past to make sense of African Americans' present and indicates that not much has changed since the 1960s. *Sanctioning Agent*: The sanctioning agent is Marilyn Monroe, whose status as a cultural icon legitimises the critique of American culture as a whole. *Master Analogy*: Righteous type; dealing with right and wrong and the attempt to disregard African American cultural icons.

Ad	Message	Fantasy theme	Symbolic cue	Rhetorical vision (ingredients)
Impressions: 95,140	This ad consists of two images. In the top image two KKK members are conversing, or plotting, while in the bottom a young black man wears a hood. The young man is Trayvon Martin who was killed in February 2012. The ad states that 'white hoods' and white propaganda should be illegal in America and that unlike Germans, Americans are not ashamed of their bigotry but are proud of it.	This ad corresponds to the fantasy theme of 'Enduring Racial Violence' in America. By summoning the legacy of the KKK, and contrasting it with the image of Trayvon Martin, the ad suggests that racial violence remains prevalent in America.	Images of hoods The ad includes two cryptic cues that are contrasted. The white hoods of the KKK, which invokes the tragic history of white hate, and the hood of Trayvon Martin, which relates to present-day hatred.	*Dramatis Personae:* The hero of this ad is Trayvon Martin while the villains are the KKK. *Plotline:* Continued tragedy and racial violence. *Scene:* The scene is that of state-sanctioned racial violence in contemporary America. While America fears innocent young black men, it does not fear the KKK, nor has it dealt with the KKK's legacy of hate. *Sanctioning Agent:* The principle of social justice legitimises the critique of a contemporary and bigoted America. *Master Analogy:* Righteous type; dealing with right and wrong and the fear of black men over white bigots.
Impressions: 57,249	This ad depicts a large gathering of Black and White individuals. The ad is for a demonstration outside the United Nations headquarters (UN HQ) calling for an end to the genocide of Black people in America. The ad states that so long as the Black community is not 'completely eradicated' it will strive to obtain justice from its oppressors by using its voice.	This ad corresponds with the fantasy theme of the 'Civil Rights Movement'. The ad seems to depict a protest from the 1960s and thus relates to the enduring battle for African Americans' rights in America.	Name: The UN The location of the protest, the UN, is a cryptic cue as civil rights leaders called on the UN to pressure America to ending racial discrimination and segregation. Wording: The term 'genocide', and the words 'completely eradicate', foster a sense of urgency and fear of increased violence towards Black people.	*Dramatis Personae:* The heroes of the image are the forbearers of Black activism in America, those who fought for civil rights in the 1960s. The villains are those looking to 'eradicate' African Americans. *Plotline:* Tragedy as the Black community faces 'genocide'. *Scene:* The scene is that of UN HQ as a symbol of the broader international community. *Sanctioning Agent:* The global community is called upon to assist Black Americans in defending their human rights. *Master Analogy:* Social type; call to arms for closing ranks and renewing relationships of comradeship and brotherhood.

Digital propaganda as symbolic convergence

Ad	Message	Fantasy theme	Symbolic cue	Rhetorical vision (ingredients)
[Instagram ad image] Impressions: 55,413	This ad consists of two images. The image on the left depicts a statue of a Black woman holding a lantern. The image on the rights is that of the Statue of Liberty. The ad states that the real Statue of Liberty was of a black woman and that a Black woman was used as a model for the statue in New York. Moreover, the ad states that the Statue of Liberty was a gift from France to commemorate Black soldiers who fought in the Civil War.	This corresponds to the fantasy theme of 'White Washing American History' and culture and refusing to acknowledge the contribution of African Americans to American history, in this case the Civil War.	Slogan: 'Lady Liberty', referring to the Statue of Liberty and its supposed symbolism of American freedom.	*Dramatis Personae*: The hero of this vision is the Black Lady of Liberty while the villain is the white-washed Lady of Liberty. *Plotline*: A quest for recognition by African Americans. *Scene*: The scene is historical: the founding of the country as a beacon of liberty at the end of the independence war. *Sanctioning Agent*: Lady Liberty. The image of the statue serves as evidence of the claim that American history is whitewashed. *Master Analogy*: Righteous type; dealing with right and wrong and the attempt to disregard African American history.

Table 6.3   Average number of impressions by ad type

Ad type	Average number of impressions
Fantasy theme (n = 64)	16 762
Links to Website/Profile (n = 66)	3 726

Table 6.4   Average number of clicks by issue

Topical category	Average number of clicks
Police Brutality + Fatal Shootings (n = 21)	412
Discrimination in America (n = 24)	212
Police Brutality + Discrimination in America (n = 43)	306
Links to Websites/Profile (n = 66)	130

enduring racial violence, and the alleged whitewashing of American history. Notably, these fantasy themes revisited powerful sagas of African Americans (the Civil Rights movement, the Civil War). In so doing, they came together to form an emergent rhetorical vision describing African Americans as second-class citizens in the American society, despite President Obama's promise in 2008 of 'Hope and Change', which supposedly remained unfulfilled.

Second, the main ingredients of the rhetorical vision were indeed based on the most popular posts. To test our hypothesis, we calculated the average number of impressions gained by ads informing the emerging rhetorical vision and ads that simple had a link to external websites or social media profiles. As can be seen in Table 6.3, the gap between the two averages is substantial. This finding validates the assumption that coherent fantasy themes are more likely to assist the process of symbolic convergence by drawing people in the online conversation and facilitating the formation of group consciousness (as evidenced by the use of symbolic cues) around an emerging rhetorical vision. In other words, had the number of impressions to external websites been similar to that of the ads encapsulating rhetorical vision elements, then our hypothesis would have been invalidated. It would have implied that people reacted to the fantasy themes neutrally, with little concern for how these themes were connected to form a specific rhetorical vision. That was obviously not the case. It was the surplus of thematic and emotional appeal generated by the elements of the rhetorical vision that attracted the attention of the users to these ads.

Third, we analysed the average number of clicks gained by ads based on their topical categories. The ads made available by the House Select Committee did not include data about the profile of the users and therefore we could not comment on the socio-demographic background of the users reached by these ads. We therefore focused on issues evoking psychosocial strain and examined the extent to which they resonated with the online public. Our assumption is that ads evoking psychosocial strain would obtain larger numbers of clicks, thus instigating a possible chain of participation. In the absence of comments, clicks serve as a useful non-verbal indicator of users' participation in the drama. As can be seen in Table 6.4, the topical category to elicit the highest average number of clicks was that of 'Police Brutality' + 'Fatal Shootings', followed by 'Discrimination in America'. Links to external websites elicited a much lower average. Given the differences in sample sizes between the categories, we also grouped the 'Police Brutality' + 'Discrimination in America' groups and compared them to external links. Here again, we found a sizable difference in average number of clicks.

Due to the small number of ads dealing with 'Celebrating Black Individuals and Culture' (3) and 'News from within the Black Community' (5), these categories were not included in the analysis. Notably, ads 'Celebrating Black Individuals and Culture' had an average of 808 clicks. This was the highest average obtained by any topical category. This high average may stem from the fact that these ads included information and images on Black cultural icons such as Serena Williams and Beyoncé Knowles.

CONCLUSIONS

A prevalent argument in the academic literature is that echo chambers and 'filter bubbles', which social media platforms have encouraged to form through their operating algorithms, carry much of the blame for the pervasiveness of digital disinformation. In this chapter, we have challenged this assumption, by arguing that while echo chambers still retain analytical currency for explaining why and how social media helps amplify the exposure of disinformation messages within certain communities of individuals, closer attention needs to be paid to the process by which disinformation helps actually create such communities in the first place through symbolic appropriation. The distinction is subtle, but critically important. It suggests that the current focus on the causal connections between echo chambers and disinformation is epistemically unreliable, due to the amorphousness of the echo chamber concept. It has therefore been suggested that a more productive analytical avenue would be to unpack the constitutive role of digital propaganda in transforming certain segments of the online public into willing and active distributors of disinformation. By addressing the second question, we should be able to learn better how to contain, isolate, and eventually neutralise the toxic effects of digital propaganda in the public sphere.

Drawing on Bormann's theory of symbolic convergence, we have argued that the effectiveness of disinformation lies with its ability to craft a powerful rhetorical vision that is actively shared by the online public and capable of arousing group consciousness. The results presented in this chapter lend credence to our three assumptions. First, most Russian ads focusing on African American issues promoted fairly coherent fantasy themes of great social relevance for the target group, although less effectively than one would may expect from a symbolic convergence perspective. Second, ads that included ingredients of a possible rhetorical vision had a substantially higher number of impressions than ads that did not. Third, ads that dealt with issues of major concern and psychological anxiety favoured the formation of chains of participation. The analysis also revealed the presence of an embryonic form of group consciousness as evidenced by the use and sharing of symbolic cues, but its scope and depth could only be further confirmed through an in-depth anthropological investigation.

As an exploratory study, our theory of digital propaganda as symbolic convergence requires further empirical testing, but two possible strategies can already be envisaged about how to combat disinformation. First, if disinformation effectiveness is linked to the formation of a powerful rhetorical vision, as we argue, then it stands to reason that counter-disinformation measures should then aim at preventing this from happening. This would imply, for instance, a vigorous debunking of the messages that have the potential to form coherent fantasy themes, and a proactive exposure of the likely contradictions between the promoted fantasy themes so as to prevent them from coalescing into a rhetorical vision. Second, it is important to bear in mind that reactive measures are not enough, as they would likely require significant resources to keep up with the amount of disinformation that is made available online. Therefore, truth-based rhetorical visions would be crucial to develop and proactively promote, alongside reactive measures, as a way to enhance informational resilience to potential disinformation campaigns.

REFERENCES

Anderson, A., A.D. Brossard, D.A. Scheufele, M.A. Xenos, and P. Ladwig (2014), 'The "nasty effect": Online incivility and risk perceptions of emerging technologies', *Journal of Computer-Mediated Communication*, 19(3): 373–387.

Bakshy, E., S. Messing, and L. Adamic (2015), 'Exposure to ideologically diverse news and opinion on Facebook', *Science*, 348(6239): 1130–1132.

Bales, R.F. (1970), *Personality and interpersonal relations*, New York: Holt, Rinehart & Winston.

Booker, C. (2004), *The seven basic plots: Why we tell stories*, London: A&C Black.

Bormann, E.G. (1985), 'Symbolic convergence theory: A communication formulation', *Journal of Communication*, 35(4): 128–138.

Bormann, E.G., W.S. Howell, R.G. Nichols, and G.L. Shapiro (1982), *Interpersonal communication in the modern organization* (2nd edn), Englewood Cliffs, NJ: Prentice-Hall.

Bormann, Ernest G., Roxann L. Knutson, and Karen Musolf (1997), 'Why do people share fantasies? An empirical investigation of a basic tenet of the symbolic convergence communication theory', *Communication Studies*, 48(3): 254–76.

Braun, V., and Clarke, V. (2016), '(Mis)conceptualising themes, thematic analysis, and other problems with Fugard and Potts' (2015) sample-size tool for thematic analysis', *International Journal of Social Research Methodology*, 19(6): 739–743

Carnahan, D., R.K Garrett, and E. Lynch (2016), 'Candidate vulnerability and exposure to counter-attitudinal information: Evidence from two U.S. presidential elections', *Human Communication Research*, 42(4): 577–598.

Coles, B.A., and M. West (2016), 'Trolling the trolls: Online forum users constructions of the nature and properties of trolling', *Computers in Human Behavior*, 60: 233–244.

Cragan, J.F., and D.C. Shields (1992), 'The Use of Symbolic Convergence Theory in Corporate Strategic Planning: A Case Study', *Journal of Applied Communication Research*, 20(2): 199–218.

del Vicario, Michela, Alessandro Bessi, Fabiana Zollo, Fabio Petroni, Antonio Scala, et al. (2016), 'The spreading of misinformation online', *Proceedings of the National Academy of Sciences*, 113(3): 554–559.

Diamond, Larry, Marc F. Plattner, and Christopher Walker (2016), *Authoritarianism Goes Global: the Challenge to Democracy*, Baltimore, MD: Johns Hopkins University Press.

Duggan, Maeve, and Aaron Smith (2016), 'The political environment on social media', *Pew Research Center*, 25 October, available at https://assets.pewresearch.org/wp-content/uploads/sites/14/2016/10/24160747/PI_2016.10.25_Politics-and-Social-Media_FINAL.pdf.

Endres, Thomas G. (1994), 'Co-existing master analogues in symbolic convergence theory: The knights of Columbus quincentennial campaign', *Communication Studies*, 45(3–4): 294–308.

Flaxman, S., Goel, S., and J.M. Rao (2016), 'Filter bubbles, echo chambers, and online news consumption', *Public Opinion Quarterly*, 80(1): 298–320.

Garrett, R.K. (2017), 'The "echo chamber" distraction: Disinformation campaigns are the problem, not audience fragmentation', *Journal of Applied Research in Memory and Cognition*, 6(4): 370–376.

Gentzkow, M., and J.M. Shapiro (2011), 'Ideological segregation online and offline', *Quarterly Journal of Economics*, 126(4): 1799–1839.

Higgins, Andrew, Mike McIntire, and G.J. Dance (2016), 'Inside a fake news sausage factory: "This is all about income"', *New York Times*, 25 November.

Knobloch-Westerwick, S., and S. Kleinman (2011), 'Pre-election selective exposure: Confirmation bias versus informational utility', *Communication Research*, 39(2): 170–193.

Lasswell, H. (1927), 'The theory of political propaganda', *American Political Science Review*, 21(3): 627–631.

Maréchal, Nathalie (2017), 'Networked authoritarianism and the geopolitics of information: Understanding Russian internet policy', *Media and Communication*, 5(1): 29–41.

NATO Strategic Communications Centre of Excellence (NATO StratCom COE) (2017), *Internet Trolling as a Tool of Hybrid Warfare: The Case of Latvia*, 10 October, available at https://issuu.com/natostratcomcoe/docs/full_report_trolling_25012016.

Nothhaft, Howard, James Pamment, Henrik Agardh-Twetman, and Alicia Fjällhed (2019), 'Information influence in Western democracies: A model of systemic vulnerabilities', in Corneliu Bjola and James Pamment (eds), *Countering Online Propaganda and Extremism: The Dark Side of Digital Diplomacy*, London: Routledge, pp. 28–43.

Office of the Director of National Intelligence (2017), 'Intelligence community assessment: Assessing Russian activities and intentions in recent US elections', 6 January, available at https://www.dni.gov/files/documents/ICA_2017_01.pdf.

Pariser, Eli (2011), *The filter bubble: What the Internet is hiding from you*, London: Penguin.

Phillips, Whitney (2015), *This is why we can't have nice things: Mapping the relationship between online trolling and mainstream culture*, Cambridge, MA: MIT Press.

Richey, Mason (2017), 'Contemporary Russian revisionism: Understanding the Kremlin's hybrid warfare and the strategic and tactical deployment of disinformation', *Asia Europe Journal*, 15(54): 1–13.

Rogers, Katie, and Jonah Engel Bromwich (2016), 'The hoaxes, fake news, and misinformation we saw on election day', *New York Times*, 8 November.

Shearer, E., and J. Gottfried (2017), 'News use across social media platforms 2017', Pew Research Center, available at https://www.journalism.org/2017/09/07/news-use-across-social-media-platforms-2017/.

Stroud, N.J., A. Muddiman, and J.M. Scacco (2013), *Engagingnews project: Social media buttons in comment sections*, Austin, TX: Annette Strauss Institute for Civic Life, available at http://engagingnewsproject.org/enp prod/wp-content/uploads/2014/04/ENP Buttons Report.pdf.

Sunstein, Cass R. (2017), *#Republic: Divided democracy in the age of social media*, Princeton, NJ: Princeton University Press.

Timberg, Craig (2016), 'Russian propaganda effort helped spread "fake news" during election, experts say', *Washington Post*, 24 November.

Tucker, J.A., A. Guess, C. Barberá, A. Siegel, S. Sanovich, and B. Nyhan (2018), 'Social media, political polarization, and political disinformation: A review of the scientific literature', Report for the Hewlett Foundation, available at https://www.hewlett.org/wp-content/uploads/2018/03/Social-Media-Political-Polarization-and-Political-Disinformation-Literature-Review.pdf.

US House of Representatives' Permanent Select Committee on Intelligence (2018), *Social media advertisements*, available at https://democrats-intelligence.house.gov/facebook-ads/social-media-advertisements.htm.

Vanderhill, Rachel, (2013), *Promoting authoritarianism abroad*, Boulder, CO: Lynne Rienner Publishers.

Walker, Christopher, and Jessica Ludwig (2017), 'The meaning of sharp power', *Foreign Affairs*, https://www.foreignaffairs.com/articles/china/2017-11-16/meaning-sharp-power?cid=int-fls&pgtype=hpg.

Way, Lucan (2015), 'The limits of autocracy promotion: The case of Russia in the "near abroad"', *European Journal of Political Research*, 54(4): 691–706.

Wojcieszak, Magdalena E., and Diana C. Mutz (2009), 'Online groups and political discourse: Do online discussion spaces facilitate exposure to political disagreement?', *Journal of Communication*, 59(1): 40–56.

Ziegler, Charles E. (2017), 'International dimensions of electoral processes: Russia, the USA, and the 2016 elections', *International Politics*, 55: 557–574.

7. Getting the message right in Xi Jinping's China: propaganda, story-telling, and the challenge of reaching people's emotions

Kerry Brown

INTRODUCTION

As it celebrates the centenary of the foundation of the Communist Party in 2021, the People's Republic of China (PRC) is a place that is dominated by a particular story. This can be broadly described as that of the country's renaissance and rejuvenation. This is not a new story. The tale of China's resurrection from the ashes of war and revolution in the early 20th century to be a modern power has been told since the end of the Qing Dynasty in the period up to 1911. The difference is the urgency and intensity with which this story is now being recounted, and the amount of institutional and political effort being used to promote it domestically, and abroad. One feels as though this grand saga that has been a long time in the telling is now reaching its culmination. In particular, 'rejuvenation' (*fuxing*) is a word that Xi Jinping, the key leader since 2012, head of the Communist Party and President, has used exhaustively almost from the moment he came to power. It captures the aspirations and hopes of the country as it converts its rising economic prowess and importance for the outside world into more geopolitical forms of power. But there are ways in which this story, despite being derived from the same nationalist source, has been split between an internal and an external iteration, and shaped by the diverse and very different audiences it is aimed at. This is also a story that is clearly aimed at achieving, for the Party at least, an appeal not just to people's self-interest, but also to their emotional needs.

This chapter looks at the ways in which one can see the promotion of a narrative of rejuvenation and its associated vocabularies by examining the narratives promoted by Xi Jinping over the era from 2012, especially the China Dream and the Belt and Road Initiative (BRI), and the ways they differ from those preceding them. No one could dispute that since the time of Mao Zedong, the PRC has invested enormous amounts of effort on controlling information and embedding particular core ideological and political beliefs. Political propaganda has been one of the core tasks of the Party and one of the greatest sources of its power. Since 1978 economic reform has resulted in a more complex society, and this has made the task of political propaganda more difficult. The commitment to the nationalistic themes of the Xi era can be seen as an attempt to address some of these challenges. They seek to appeal not just to Chinese people's material interests, but also to their spiritual ones. This is one of the core developments of the Xi era.

SCIENTIFIC DEVELOPMENT IN THE HU ERA, AND THE CHINA DREAM UNDER XI

The development of propaganda in 21st century China can be mapped by looking at the two very different core leaders. Technocrats dominated the Hu Jintao leadership era from 2002 to 2012 in a way that is not the case with Xi (Brown, 2012). Hu was an engineer. His Premier, Wen Jiabao, was a geologist. Almost all those on the Standing Committee, the summit of Party power in the country, had similar backgrounds. In contrast, in Xi's two Politburo Standing Committees from 2012 there were a mixture of historians (Vice-President Wang Qishan), international relations experts (ideology supremo Wang Huning), and legal students (Premier Li Keqiang). The technocratic background of elite leaders in the Hu era is reflected in their language. They were comfortable with listing long lines of statistics and using a language of almost robotic quality, where everything was tangible, measurable, and data-driven. An example is from Hu's peroration at the 17th Party Congress during his keynote speech in 2007:

> Economic strength increased substantially. The economy sustained steady and rapid growth. The GDP [gross domestic product] expanded by an annual average of over 10%. Economic performance improved significantly, national revenue rose markedly year by year, and prices were basically stable. Efforts to build a new socialist countryside yielded solid results, and development among regions became more balanced. The endeavour to make China an innovative nation registered good progress, with considerable improvement in the country's capacity for independent innovation. Notable achievements were scored in the construction of infrastructure including energy, transport and telecommunications facilities and other key projects. Manned spaceflights were successfully conducted. Fresh progress was registered in energy, resources, ecological and environmental conservation. The Tenth Five-Year Plan (2001–05) was fulfilled successfully and implementation of the eleventh is in smooth progress. (Hu, 2007)

Such speeches typified a leadership style of almost faceless anonymity. This was supplemented by the abstract and emotionally almost unengaging core ideology and the supporting slogan used over this period: 'scientific development'. Such an idea, while it conveyed a sense of reassuring rationality and order, typified the often remote sound of official language at this time and symbolised the disconnect between wider society and the Party. The problem was that this kind of leadership discourse was occurring when the country was undergoing one of the most dramatic and expansive explosions of growth ever experienced by any society. The Hu years were the boom years, with rocketing growth, output, exports, imports, and every other kind of statistics. The societal impacts of this were massive. It was clear that China had an amazing story, but one it was unwilling to tell with any great drama or clarity.

Perhaps one of the factors causing this reticence was the tradition of propaganda in the Party itself, which had a smothering effect and resisted radical change. Even attempts to rename the Party propaganda department the publicity department were seen as cosmetic. The fact was that from the Maoist period the Party had privileged work on propaganda and invested enormous political capital in it. A vast apparatus had grown up, with figures such as an early editor of the official newspaper of the Party, *People's Daily*, Hu Qiaomu in the 1970s and 1980s, and chief propaganda leader in the Politburo, Ding Guangen in the 1990s, reaching the most senior levels of leadership despite their having only worked in propaganda areas (Schoenhals, 1992). Ding's successor, Liu Yunshan, in the Hu and Xi first period to 2017 belonged to this tradition, sitting in the Politburo with the remit to control propaganda (Brown, 2014: 176–183). The philosophy of propaganda underpinning this institutional structure was clear too: a way of rigging the message so that, in the words of Jowett and O'Donnell, it worked for the party telling the story and delivering the message, but it did not work for those hearing it. 'The purpose of propaganda', they state, 'is to promote a partisan or competitive cause in the best interests of the propagandist but not necessarily in the best interests of the recipient' (Jowett and O'Donnell, 1992: 20). This typified the very asymmetrical Party–society relations in terms of information dissemination and control over much of the period to 1978, and then from 1978 into the 1990s. But with the Internet, and social transformation and development, this task of Party control and propaganda work became more challenging. People could either ignore the messages being promoted to them, or simply chose which ones they wanted to hear (Stockmann, 2013). Indifference was perhaps the greatest threat. Chinese leaders had to urgently address the increasing gap between the messages and the ways in which they were promoting these messages, along with their language and society, where radical change was occurring and where much of what leaders such as Hu said sounded remote and unengaging, almost to the point of irrelevance.

Xi's leadership therefore occurs in this context of a need to urgently revivify the Party's political propaganda, and to do this by reasserting control of the main narratives that dominate society. In 2013, he instructed his Politburo colleagues to 'tell the China story'. He told the diplomats of the Ministry of Foreign Affairs to be more proactive in the way they spoke to the world, and how they conveyed China's values and its unique vision. China has become many things under Xi – a place undergoing a complex economic transition to a more service sector-orientated economic model, one where a rising middle class living in cities is becoming increasingly important, a place of aspiration and often of profound divisions – but it is also a place dominated by the new story-telling prowess of the Communist Party. To understand this, one needs to know the audiences, the modes of telling to these audiences, and the ways to achieve a balance between the rational and the emotional. These issues will now be addressed.

TO WHOM IS XI TELLING THE CHINA STORY?

Understanding the question of who the key audience for this story might be is key. One of the principal influences on a story is not only who is telling it, but to whom they are speaking. That is a fundamental of any communication theory. However, in the case of China today, the audience for Xi Jinping's story-telling is not a straightforward one. There are multiple target groups within and outside the country, and they are all listening for different things, alert and sensitive to different elements of the messages they are hearing. This marks a definite departure from the relative simplicity of the Mao era.

The domestic audience comprises broadly four groups. The first are Xi's fellow elite, the 3000 or so holding high-level official positions in the Party-state nationally and provincially. After all, these are the infantry for the telling of this story Xi said needed to be told, and they have to be united behind it. For this group, a unified China story is also a principal source of gathering public support and is a base of their legitimacy. It is their main resource, a common script that means they can sell and promote policy positions to the public they are meant to be serving. Therefore their commitment to a unified story in order to do this is critical, whatever they may feel about it in their private lives. This issue of giving the Party a new source of legitimacy will be discussed later.

Beyond this group is the emerging middle class. Aspirational, urban-living, mostly working in services, and living lives increasingly like their counterparts in Europe or America, this cohort is the most important audience, at least domestically. They are uninterested in the ideology of Marxism–Leninism, but willing to accept the Party while it is delivering a better standard of living and greater status in the world. When the government speaks to this group it has to appeal to their sense of patriotism and to their desire to be respected. The 'China Dream', language which Xi used in 2013, promoted the kind of aspirational message about where Chinese people were going and how they had the right, like any others, to a good standard of living, their own property, their own businesses, and the right to make greater and greater amounts of wealth (Xi, 2014).

The middle classes are a critical group, but there is a more problematic group: those who feel that they have been left behind or been neglected during the great enrichment from 2001 onwards. This is the third group. These are perhaps migrant workers still struggling to make ends meet, or farmers for whom the Xi era has been less attentive or generous than under Hu, when the burden of taxes was lifted from them in 2007. It might be those who have a grievance over the way they have been treated by officials, and are protesting. This group are not openly disloyal to the Party, but they have the capacity to cause it huge problems if dissatisfaction spreads among them. So a story that can at least sell to them the idea that in the long term things will come right, and that tomorrow will be better than today, is one of the main means of the Party controlling this set of risks.

Then there is the final audience. These are the small, much maligned group of dissidents, rights lawyers, and others, who have been targeted by increasingly fierce campaigns during the Xi era. Harassed, imprisoned, or intimidated into silence, these figure as opponents against the realisation of any story the Xi leadership needs to tell. In Xi's China, they are seen as those who wish to rewrite or redirect its narrative thrust and plunge China back into the dark past. For this group, the story has to be a rebuttal, a refutation, something they are presented as opposing and seeking to undermine.

Xi and his leaders have to create something, at least for the first three audience groups, that all of them can comprehend and to which they can all relate. It must also serve to exclude and suppress the final group. It is unsurprising that the notion of a great Chinese nation, with its great, long history, and its rich culture and heritage, along with the feelings of patriotism and nationalism that flow from this, has been the main foundation of this plotline. Something akin to a state religion based on the potency and importance of the country has been established. But while this tactic has worked domestically, creating pride and nationalistic fervour and commitment that the Party can then gain support and benefit from, it also generates problems for the second general audience the leadership are addressing: the outside world.

Here, a strongly nationalistic story proclaiming the dominance and prowess of Chinese power and influence would antagonise many of those who are distrustful of China, or do not understand what China is and what it wants. Within its own region, China's neighbours are mostly highly cautious about the impact their newly resurgent neighbour might want to have. Vietnam, India, and even, though in different ways, Russia and North Korea, have different kinds of histories with China, and different worries about where its powers will eventually take it. In terms of maritime neighbours, things are even more complex. Japan, South Korea, and Malaysia: these are all wary and careful with China, and in some cases actively in dispute with it over the South and East China Sea territorial issues. Chinese nationalism is an unknown quantity in modern history, largely because of the marginalised and weak position of the country since the middle of the 19th century. A strong China is a very new concept, and one that nobody quite knows what to make of. This has resulted in increasing claims since 2010 that China is assertive, aggressive, and a threat.

In the outside world the Xi leadership talks to three audiences: the friendly, the pragmatic, and the opponents. For the friendly, Pakistan is a good example. Pakistan has enjoyed very good relations with China for the last seven decades and constantly states that the two are closer than 'lips and teeth'. Xi visited Pakistan in 2015, making commitments to a massive US$46 billion of aid and investment. Access to the Gwadar port and infrastructure around this has been key. Pakistan nurtures close relations with its huge neighbour to counterbalance the problems it experiences with India. In a tough neighbourhood, for Pakistan a friend like China is a very useful one. Its acceptance of China's Belt and Road Initiative (BRI) and other foreign policy narratives has been enthusiastic and committed. Into this group also fall countries such as Zimbabwe in Africa, Russia under Putin, and Italy. In these cases, the closeness of the relationship depends sometimes on leaders who come and go, bringing with them new and more intense commitments to Beijing. Like Pakistan, North Korea is 'friendly', though in a very particular way: it is concerned more with self-preservation than affinity with China.

Falling into the pragmatic category are countries such as Vietnam, Indonesia, Germany, Saudi Arabia, and Brazil. For these places, there is a current consensus that China offers great economic potential, and that whatever its choice over its own political model, that should be regarded as China's own business, rather than being the concern of the outside world. Some have had long histories and rich experience of dealing with China that guide and inform their current posture. For self-interested reasons, they want China to be a stable country, even if they do not feel the need to enthusiastically validate and confirm its status and influence. Those whose relations with China date to more recent times carry no historic baggage, and simply see the country as offering a set of practical opportunities: aid, technology, cheap goods. Those that criticise the posture of these places say they are acting naively and are unaware of the stealthily controlling nature of Chinese power. Witness the ways China has been accused of activities of a political nature in Sri Lanka when it took back control of a port project in 2017. Pragmatists include much of Europe, Australia, and Latin America, though there are significant groups within these countries that regard China more negatively.

The best example of an opponent is the United States (US) under Donald Trump. The US–China relationship was always complex and inherently unstable because of the competitive and contrasting natures of their ambitions, political values, and worldviews. But progressively under Presidents George W. Bush, then Obama, and then overtly under Trump, it has become a relationship with many signs of sharp conflict. China is seen as opposing American intentions, values, and primacy. It was also true that America was never comfortable and never could be comfortable with a non-democratic country growing so prominent economically. However, in the past this posture was softened by the possibility that through engagement China's governance model would change. Under Xi Jinping, that has turned out resolutely not to be the case. With the unequivocal end of this phase of engagement, the two are now involved in a fight of attrition in the trade space at the time of writing (August 2019), but this is very likely to spread to other areas as their struggle intensifies.

WHAT IS XI'S CHINA STORY? CHINA'S DREAM AND THE BELT AND ROAD

It is not surprising that in view of the complex audiences within the country and externally, with their radically different attitudes and postures towards China, it was hard in the Hu and the early part of the Xi period to pin down what China's own message to this hybrid group might be without appearing to be speaking in different ways to different people, and collapsing into incoherence. In the end two interrelated but separate core stories have been crafted, aimed at the national and international groups, and linked by a commitment to support a great nation undergoing renaissance, albeit expressed in different ways and embracing different audiences.

For the home audience, the 'China Dream' has been the main tale in this new tactical approach. Xi first referred to this idea in December 2012, when he spoke at an exhibition about the Road to Rejuvenation held in Beijing. In March the next year, he stated that 'the Chinese Dream is, in the final analysis, the dream of the people'. It was about making China 'prosperous and strong' and 'bringing happiness to the Chinese people' (Xi, 2014: 41–43). In May 2013, he stated that the dream was about 'the great renewal of the Chinese nation' and that it would involve a better environment, higher living standards, beautiful cities, and high levels of satisfaction (Xi, 2014: 53). This dream was one that was available to everyone as long as they worked hard, and believed in the Party and its mission. 'China Dream' became a slogan exhaustively used across the country, and appeared in the speeches made by leaders at home.

This was accompanied by the external-facing narrative: that of the New Silk Road, which after its first appearance in 2013 became by 2015 the Belt and Road Initiative (BRI). The BRI at least offers some flexibility and has been able to appeal to these different kinds of audience outside of the country that are involved, willingly or not, in its global reach (Xi, 2017: 543–569). The idea has many guises in order to adequately address this audience. It can be presented as just an economic network largely led by self-interest, or made into something more cohesive and powerful, depending on how the partner feels about China. It is not prescriptive and therefore can defend itself against accusations that it is the same kind of normative concept which the US promoted after the Second World War in order to regularise global governance systems. It helps in creating markets for China's new technologies in places where there are less impediments than in those developed countries which once mattered to it more for its exports, namely Europe and the US. Now, it can see emerging consumers for Huawei and BYD cars and other Chinese companies in Indonesia, Malaysia, Latin America, and elsewhere. The BRI diversifies China's supply routes, meaning it can enjoy energy and raw material supplies from land routes via Central Asia, rather than from the coasts and the maritime routes so heavily influenced by the presence of US naval power. Most importantly, it addresses the need referenced by Xi to tell the China story to as wide an audience as possible, and at least supply a counternarrative to those that are already dominant; and largely set in place by the US and its allies, and tending to be more negative towards Beijing. In Chinese accounts the BRI is principally about connectivity, and while a lot of this has been in material infrastructure, soft infrastructure has also been important. This means the growth of people-to-people links and a great zone of learning where the world can become more familiar with China.

THE ROLE OF EMOTION IN THE NEW CHINA STORY

In terms of the modes of telling these core stories, along with their link to the one overall master narrative of supporting the idea of a rejuvenated strong China, the communication strategy in the Xi era has been shaped predominantly to address one challenge that has been growing in the decades since reforms started in 1978: how to shift from a narrative dominated almost wholly by stressing economic and material benefits for people, to one which alludes to something more spiritual and emotionally appealing.

Strangely, the Xi approach harks back to an earlier period and often gets inspiration from it, despite the vast changes between these two eras. In the Maoist period, the principal basis of Party legitimacy was more about the emotions that were derived from nationalism: about being part of the victorious side in winning the Sino-Japanese War up to 1945, and then unifying the country through the Civil War from 1946 to 1949 against the Nationalists and creating a country with self-autonomy and pride again. The Maoist leadership from 1949, after the Communists were victorious and the People's Republic was founded, presented itself as bringing modernity to a place humiliated and victimised at the hands of European and other countries over the last 100 years. The new government's strategy was to use rapid industrialisation, urbanisation, and a complete repudiation of China's feudal past to get out of this history into the new one. However, they supported this through the introduction of the dynamic Marxist–Leninist scientific view of history that served as their chief ideology, that saw progress as perpetual and assured as long as its political programme was followed. Mao Zedong as the key leader also subscribed to a strong belief in the need for class struggle. Chinese society, in his view, was disunited. Exploitative classes such as landlords and the urban bourgeoisie ruled over a vast mass of workers and peasants in the countryside. He inspired a number of mass campaigns in order to cleanse society of these divisions. Amongst the most epic was the Cultural Revolution from 1966, when the Party directed its energy towards cleansing Chinese society from what were perceived as inequalities, and ridding it of the malign influence of enemies within and from the outside world who were trying to return China back to the hell of the past. This notion of positive, perpetual historic development is something that has been reasserted and maintained in the Xi era. Therefore one could characterise this period as one of high emotions, and the deployment of these within political life.

However, the main problem with the Maoist practices and the implementation of its grand vision was the catastrophic social consequences that flowed from them. Events such as the great famines from 1959 to 1962, which resulted in the largest number of people dying from malnutrition and lack of food in any society, the Cultural Revolution and what the writer Ba Jin called the 'spiritual holocaust' it brought upon people, and the poor levels of economic performance and development by 1976 when Mao died, were profound (Ba, 1984: xv). Despite immense efforts to industrialise and develop the country, the turbulence from these various events meant that by 1978 China was still impoverished and backward. The failure of the Maoist vision meant that the post-Mao leadership witnessed a strategic shift by the Party so that it embraced, rather than downplayed, the crucial importance of bringing about tangible practical economic gains for people and improvements in their material well-being. It committed an act of huge simplification. The emotionally powerful grand goals of the Maoist era were jettisoned. Instead, economic, measurable, tangible outcomes were prioritised above all else. That meant permission being granted to policies such as the establishment of the Household Responsibility System, which promoted modest marketisation by letting farmers sell surplus crops back to the state for a profit; and Special Economic Zones, which allowed foreign capital and methods to enter the country in designated areas; or Joint Ventures with foreign enterprises, which would once have been regarded as wholly heretical. They were now justified in facing the core challenge, namely making China and the Chinese people better off and wealthier. The impact of this could be seen in rising GDP levels, and people's living standards.

From 1978 to the 2000s, economic success was the prime indicator for the Party's performance and legitimacy. This shift was opposed by figures such as Deng Liqun, a veteran member of the Party propaganda and ideological apparatus, and one of the key leftists in the 1980s who was vociferous in his criticism of the new market-friendly policies (Brown and van Nieuwenhuizen, 2016: 60–89). It also received a significant setback in 1989 during the Tiananmen Square massacre. But with the Southern Tour by paramount leader Deng Xiaoping in 1992, when he travelled to some of the areas his government had set up to see how they were faring, economic success was reasserted by him and those around him as the only path the country could take. It was the dominant outlook for all of this period.

For all their extraordinary material success, the reform policies created an extended crisis of faith for the ruling Communist Party as it clearly marked a significant disjuncture from the Maoist era, in particular the collectivist ethos of Marxism-Leninism, the command to practise class struggle, and to strive for Utopian ideals. In the more liberal, individualistic 1980s and into the 1990s and 2000s, Chinese society was beset by immense, rapid, and profound changes that fragmented the unified belief system of the Mao era; saw the rise again of religions including Buddhism, Christianity, and Islam after their suppression under Mao; and witnessed a new generation growing up whose memory of the Maoist era of disciplined and relative wide belief in the Mao message was faint to non-existent. Competition to the unified belief system of the Party became stronger. Emotional fidelity to it weakened. This was clearly a major challenge.

This only intensified after China's entry to the World Trade Organization (WTO) in 2001. China was becoming wealthier, materially better off, and more modern by the day, but the Party message with its insistence on continuing to subscribe to Sinified Marxism–Leninism seemed to be remote from the lives of most people. The country was considered capitalist in action and socialist in word, which was at best seen as disorientating, and at worst incoherent and irrational, for those both inside and outside. The strategy initially used in trying to deal with these contradictions was a purely rhetorical one: adding the catch-all 'with Chinese characteristics' after ideological phrases and terms, implying that China was unique and could therefore think and do things other places could not because of this. Increasingly, China was the world's great exceptionalist. But such moves often came across as obfuscation, never spelling out with any great clarity what precisely this unique ingredient 'with Chinese characteristics' was.

A focus on the economic in Party messaging at the expense of everything else was rational. Party propagandists and those that shaped the key messages and ideological formulations had to accept an indisputable fact: while the prospect of economic success and capitalist style traits such as owning nice homes, cars, having holidays abroad, and being able to buy things clearly did capture the emotions of most Chinese people, notions such as constructing the primary stage of socialism, Party building, and observing the laws of dialectics in terms of historic development did not. At most, the public largely tolerated this kind of language from the Party and its mouthpieces because in the area that mattered publicly – raising living standards – the Party could present itself as largely a success. From 2001 to 2012, the Chinese economy quadrupled in size; poverty plunged from 200 million living under $1 a day at the start of this era to less than 50 million by the end. Xi Jinping promised that absolute poverty will be wholly eliminated by 2021. For a country that had widespread famines that may have led to over 35 million dying only six decades previously, this is a massive achievement. But it was achieved by a political organisation demanding a monopoly on power, presiding over a society of almost daily dynamic change, and one that had a discourse exemplified by Hu Jintao's lack of human appeal, and a commitment to uniform ideology which was alien even to many of its own members.

WHAT THE CHINA STORY IS REALLY ABOUT: GREAT, POWERFUL, STRONG CHINA

As raw GDP growth has fallen to 6.5 per cent under Xi, and as China enters a much tougher era where it is no longer simply pulling people out of relative poverty, but trying to create a more balanced, service sector-orientated, urbanised, middle-class economic model, and where the simple appeal to economic interests is insufficient, the need to create a more compelling justifying narrative from the Party, and one that embraces more emotions, has intensified. Part of this is necessitated by the Party needing to see off the threat of political competition. If there was marketisation and broadening of choice in the economy, and more and more frequently in social space, why cannot similar changes occur in the political space? The Xi leadership also had to improve the way the Party made itself seem irreplaceable and necessary for the development of the country. Just praising its own achievements in producing GDP growth was not enough. What it needed to do was to find a more emotionally appealing storyline, one that was more ambitious and extensive than simply saying it existed to make people better off. Reverting to the more emotional tropes of the Mao era, though in very different ways, and with the means of very different platforms and technologies, makes sense. This is what we have seen.

This is because of what lies at the heart of the China story today. The principal function of the parallel narratives of the China Dream and the BRI, referred to above, and the idea of Centennial Goals that map the future in this account, are instruments to deliver one thing: a powerful, strong China liberated from its dark past of victimisation and exploitation, the place which was also aimed at by the founding Maoist era leaders (Xi, 2017: 73). The China story from 1949 to 1978, and the one afterwards, are part of the same plotline, despite being very different in their content and design. They are markedly different in terms of the institutions by which they are delivered and the technology used to disseminate them. In all these areas there has been the introduction of greater and greater complexity. But crucially they are part of the same story, separate chapters from one book, rather than wholly different volumes.

DELIVERANCE OF THE CHINA STORY UNDER XI: THE LAWS OF HISTORY

In order to achieve this rejuvenation of their legitimacy through creating a powerful story about a strong, great country, the Xi leadership have been able to find the solution to their problem within their own intellectual history. This was the idea of strict laws of historic development mentioned above. Maoism created a hybrid, indigenous form of Marxism in China, one where agrarian rather than urban revolution was prioritised, and which, through its very success, had rewritten some of the laws of Marx. But one principle of Marxism that Mao and his successors in China did subscribe to was the notion that history was not circular but teleological, and that it was guided by scientific rules, ones which meant that there was perpetual development and, for those who adopted the practices of Marxist development, an inevitable outcome. Dialectics guided this, with the phenomenon of thesis and antithesis leading to synthesis. Xi Jinping is no different from those who have preceded him in subscribing to this tradition. The path of history leads to inevitable outcomes, particularly when they come to the country's rise and the conclusion of its path of modernisation (Brown, 2017).

Mao and other like reformists through the period from the fall of the Qing in the early 20th century to the 21st, has one core aim: the ambition was to create a rich, strong, powerful country. Leading thinkers and political figures in the development of Chinese reform such as the founder of the Nationalists Sun Yatsen, intellectuals such as Kang Youwei and Liang Qichao, the President of Republican China Chiang Kai-shek, early Marxist Chen Duxiu, and Mao himself, had very different philosophies and came from different backgrounds. They were united in one characteristic: they were all nationalists. They believed in a thing called 'the Chinese nation' and that it needed to be reinvigorated and resurrected. The laws of Marxist historic development aided this because, in distinction to others, Mao and his colleagues could say that being Communists, they not only hoped to see a China resurrected from the ashes, but also knew that it would be, if certain measures were adopted.

Chinese nationalism with this long pedigree, and with this particular Communist approach, exists as a resource to which the current administration can appeal and claim they are serving its deliverance. As those who currently govern China, they are also the ones who are custodians of the mission – as Xi and Hu called it, the 'historic mission' – to achieve this dream of national resurrection and the construction of a great, powerful country. The route they have taken, of socialism with Chinese characteristics, as the means to do this is justified in their eyes because it delivers certainty over achieving the critical outcome: the creation of a great restored China. China within this discourse exists as a semi-religious entity, a source of spiritual and emotional power. It is something that has grown from deep and complex historic strands, and has immense cultural and symbolic power. Appealing to this idea of the great Chinese nation as something they can and will see the achievement of, Xi and the Party are therefore finally able to meet the challenge of how to balance the practical and the emotional. They have something that is able to transcend the limits of the economically pragmatic and functional which was so prominent in their appeals in previous phases of the Reform era from 1978. They may be materialists, but they can posit something which figures as a spiritual objective. Therefore the mission of the Party is not just about helping people get rich and feeding and clothing them, but also about tending to their souls through the religions of nationalism.

THE MORAL NECESSITY OF THE CHINA STORY

This also works on the moral plane. As China became wealthier from the 1990s, efforts did go into developing patriotism in school campaigns and through slogans and other methods. Over this period, commitment to an official historiography deepened. In its modern history, China had not just been unfortunate in its experiences of Western colonisation and exploitation and then Japanese imperial brutality during the War: more terrible than this, it had been treated unjustly. It had been a great culture brought low by the indecent and exploitative actions of others. China as innocent victim meant the Communists could make their dialectic narrative of history more bespoke. China's rise again after the era of economic development from 1978 was not just inevitable because of the working out of Marxist rules of history, but was also morally justified. The country had a right to this moment of national rejuvenation because of what it had suffered before. It was owed this by the outside world. If they contested it, they were acting unjustly.

When the Xi leadership speak about the China Dream and about the mission of national rejuvenation, as they have frequently since 2013, they are therefore speaking in not just a Marxist historical framework, nor a nationalist one, but a moral one; moral in the sense that because of the former suffering of their country and people, they are owed this moment of rectification and justice. It corrects previous injustices done to China. They are also speaking in a way that addresses their urgent need for a compelling message that has emotional – not just intellectual – purchase on their core audience, namely the Chinese people. For this vast domestic group in this context, the choice is to either support the Party in its moral mission of national restoration, or to oppose this and lose their patriotic credibility. This explains why the fourth group mentioned above, of those who are regarded as disloyal, have been treated with such fierceness under Xi. They are not just opponents of the Party. In Xi's eyes, they are traitors to the national cause.

All of this is used to shape a narrative of the future that is controlling, and shows things happening which are almost predetermined, not only because they will happen, but also because they ought to. It is morally correct that they occur, and their non-occurrence will violate not only the rational laws of historic development, but also its underlying moral narrative. Things do not just happen: they have to happen in the right and just way. China's failure to rejuvenate will be a huge injustice, leaving the tragedy of the past unredeemed and unaddressed. The Centennial Goals best encapsulate this, merging a sense of events occurring in the future through the inevitable working out of historic development, but also that of its moral direction. In 2021 the Party celebrates its 100th anniversary. At this point, too, China will reach a per capita GDP of US$12 000. It will rank as a middle-income country. This will translate into a place that is dominated more by services, consumption, and the rise of a middle class. It will also offer a moment for this leadership to announce that they have shown modernity with Chinese characteristics is viable, and has resulted in a nation which is now wealthy, strong, and on the way to becoming a fully developed one. A second date, 2049, will be when the People's Republic of China can celebrate its 100 years in existence. The official line for this is the creation of democracy with Chinese characteristics. The mission now is to ensure that this history of the future gets written, and that its phases are implemented efficiently.

CONCLUSION: A BRIGHT FUTURE

Moral narratives of great nation-building, constructed in ways which appeal to ideas of both inevitable scientific identity but also emotionally powerful ones of building a rejuvenated, renewed China, are a principal source of power for the Party under Xi. While he himself has been compared to Mao in terms of the reach of his power and its completeness, in many ways it can be argued that he is simply in receipt of the huge capital that flows from a story where China has now accrued enough influence and impact on world events to be more than just a big economy. The power in China now resides in the national story being told and the emotional authority that is derived from this. The Party has said that it alone has the right to tell this story on behalf of the Chinese people. It has used a mixture of pragmatic appeal ('if not us, no one else has the unity and purpose to be able to achieve the outcome of this story: great nation status'), and sheer coercion ('if you don't support us, you don't support our nationalist mission, and you are traitors'), sometimes even verging on violent silencing of those who dissent.

Telling a story in this way has many virtues for China under Xi. It finds a new basis of legitimacy. It marries rational and emotional sources of appeal. It shapes the future in ways that at least give the impression of being manageable, and supplies some level of certainty. For the Party, contemplating a period of more complex choices over which direction to take the country in terms of reforming and changing it as it grows more developed, a unified story at least makes this more manageable. It gives a potentially highly complex and fragmented society a common point of reference. While people the Party speaks to might be divided in terms of their relative socio-economic status and their political attitudes, appeals to patriotism can be wide and inclusive. They are one of the few common areas when so much else has been hived off or compartmentalised.

There is a particular set of words and values that have been associated with this story. One of the most heavily and frequently used is 'renaissance' (*fuxing*). Used in the Hu era by figures such as Zheng Bijian, a retired official at the Central Party School, it achieves a number of aims (Zheng, 2005). The first is to stress the continuity of Chinese cultural and national identity. The ancestry of the current entity called since 1949 the People's Republic of China is complex and often varied, reaching through a dynastic history which was often divergent and multiple. China can be said to have had histories, not a history. But in the contemporary discourse of 'renaissance', a China is unproblematically posited which has a strong, stable, and consistent identity and which reaches back 5000 years. Its longevity is presented implicitly as a source of reassurance and stability. The second is to make clear that China's current opportunities in terms of its return to global prominence and centrality are a restoration of something that was the case before, and which was disrupted and interrupted by modern history. Now, therefore, China is simply coming back to being the great power it once was, and has the right to be again. This status is therefore not novel, but affirms an order which was true up to the early 19th century, and which can now continue: China as a great country at the centre of the world. That aspect of the narrative, too, is presented unproblematically.

In the coming years, particularly as China navigates the 2021 first centenary goal, this use of a particular story and the emotions and nationalistic language and behaviour associated with it are likely to be maintained, and to figure as a central feature of the armoury of the Chinese leadership. There have been plenty of forensic and powerful critiques of this commitment to and exploitation of nationalism by the Communist Party, by figures such as the Nobel laureate the late Liu Xiaobo. But it is too compelling and useful for the Party not to deploy this kind of approach, particularly because its own ideological resources mean that it has nothing else by which to replace this. For all the power and influence the Party leadership under Xi accrue from the story they are telling, they are no less immune than others in being servants of it.

REFERENCES

Ba, Jin (1984), *Random Thoughts*, trans. G. Barme, Hong Kong: Joint Publishing Company.
Brown, K. (2012), *China's Silent Ruler: Hu Jintao*, Singapore: World Scientific.
Brown, K. (2014), *The New Emperors: Power and the Princelings in China*, London and New York: I.B. Tauris.
Brown, K. (2017), *China's Dreams: The Culture of the Communist Party of China and Its Secret Sources of Power*, Cambridge: Polity.
Brown, K. and S. van Nieuwenhuizen (2016), *China and the New Maoists*, London: Zed Books.
Hu, Jintao (2007), 'Full Text of Hu Jintao Speech at 17th Party Congress' (last updated 24 October 2007), available at www.chinadaily.com.cn/china/2007-10/24/content_6204564_2.htm, accessed 7 August 2019.
Jowett, G.S. and V. O'Donnell (1992), *Propaganda and Persuasion* (2nd edn), London: SAGE.
Schoenhals, M. (1992), *Doing Things with Words in Chinese Politics: Five Studies*, Berkeley, CA: University of California Press.
Stockmann, D. (2013), *Media Commercialisation and Authoritarian Rule in China*, Cambridge: Cambridge University Press.
Xi, Jinping (2014), *The Governance of China*, Beijing: Foreign Languages Press.
Xi, Jinping (2017), *The Governance of China, Volume Two*, Beijing: Foreign Languages Press.
Zheng, Bijian (2005), 'China's "peaceful rise" to Great Power status', *Foreign Affairs*, September/October, available at https://www.foreignaffairs.com/articles/asia/2005-09-01/chinas-peaceful-rise-great-power-status, accessed 27 November 2019.

8. Political communication in the age of media convergence in China
Xiaoling Zhang and Yiben Ma

INTRODUCTION

This chapter portrays media convergence in China as an operationalisation of political propaganda. Convergence in media and communications is often depicted as a convolution of technological advances, neoliberal ideology, globalisation, waves of policy, and regulatory changes that shape the media and communications market operation (Winston, 1998; Golding, 2000; Lax, 2009; Iosifidis, 2011). However, we argue that in China convergence, particularly at the level of media content, forms, and ideology, has a strong country-specific undercurrent. Thus, it needs to be understood in China's own media landscape, characterised by the evolving relationship and tension between the political, commercial, and technological forces. As such, the chapter starts with a brief review of the media transformation since China's economic reform in the 1970s, thus connecting it with broader processes that have shaped the trajectory of media convergence. This is followed by a more detailed examination and analysis of the overlapping and interrelated factors contributing to the convergence of the traditional media with new media technologies.

Our study is based on a review of theoretical literature on media convergence as well as empirical literature with a focus on the central state media the *People's Daily*, and analysis of official documents either from websites or from our informants. This chapter also benefits from interviews with staff members of the Key Lab for Publishing Integration Development in Zhejiang Province in 2019, which serve to contextualise our findings. Our study demonstrates that in spite of the tensions and contradictions in the process of the top-down media convergence in China, the party-state has been proactive in managing the unwanted political consequences from the development of new media technologies, and has so far harnessed them for propaganda to mobilise the public to support its own cause.

DEFINING MEDIA CONVERGENCE

Although 'media convergence' is frequently used and discussed among academics and media practitioners, it is difficult to agree on a unified definition. Quinn (2005: 30) has summarised the challenge by saying: 'convergence probably has as many definitions as the number of people who attempt to define it'. In fact it is hard even to trace who first came up with the term. Jenkins (2006a: 10) believes that Ithiel de Sola Pool is the 'prophet of convergence', who foresaw this development as early as in 1983. In his book *Technologies of Freedom*, Pool (1983: 23–24) used 'the convergence of the modes' to describe the blurring boundary between different media, and the growth of conglomerates operating across various media sectors.

Media convergence has been celebrated as a buzzword that marks a prevalent trend in the contemporary world of media industry, but it is not a novel phenomenon and has a longer history than many would think (see Lax, 2009). The combination of telecommunications and information technology companies to provide new products and services during the 1970s in the United States (US) and Europe has been commonly recognised as a starting point in the history of media convergence. The accelerated pace of media convergence, however, is largely attributed to digitisation, which removed the technological barriers between previously distinct media, thus enabling them to share resources and interact with one another (Iosifidis, 2011). Radio programmes, for instance, not only broadcast to a radio receiver, but are made accessible and downloadable via mobile phone apps, websites, and smart TVs.

The blurring boundaries between different media sectors also led to the convergence processes taking place at a structural level in the form of acquisitions and mergers. Traditional media not only actively embraced the latest technologies to establish their online presence, they also looked for strategic alliances with other new media companies through horizontal and/or vertical integration. The case of Time Warner serves a good example here. Its merger with America Online (AOL) back in 2000 supposedly gave the company direct access to the emerging online market through the main Internet service provider. The more recent merger between Time Warner and AT&T also demonstrates the attempt of these media giants to secure their advantaged positions in the increasingly converged media market by combining their respective strengths in content production and distribution. Similar cases of structural and organisational changes are common in the media and communications industries, and many concur that the economic consideration is the drive behind this form of media convergence as a way to promote partnership between industries in the production and marketing of media content (Gordon, 2003; Kolodzy, 2009).

The convergence of cultural industries and telecommunications companies has made it possible for them to reach and distribute goods and services to a global audience. Such business expansion certainly benefits from globalisation. However, the pace of media convergence is also attributed to the processes of deregulation. The prevalence of neoliberal ideology that promotes marketisation and liberalisation prompted governments not only to minimise direct state intervention into the communications and media businesses as a way to recognise the role of the market force in regulating the economy, but also to introduce new policies to encourage free market competition by dismantling former regulations that limited convergence operations and activities (Golding, 2000; Hesmondhalgh, 2007; Lax, 2009; Iosifidis, 2011). While deregulation has been celebrated for facilitating the emergence of convergent media, there is also a call for a regulatory convergence to adapt to the general industrial transition from analogue to Internet-based digital media systems (Dwyer, 2010). Iosifidis (2011: 184) echoes the need for policymakers to keep pace with the technological and structural transformations taking place in the media industry, because contents are increasingly being produced, circulated, and consumed on various platforms and networks which were regulated by separate legal regimes.

Much of the existing literature also provides extensive discussion about the ways in which convergence has brought changes to multiple media practices, especially in journalism. Here the term has been used to refer not only to the adoption of digital tools in the production, dissemination, and provision of news content, but also to a range of organisational, managerial, and professional transformations in the newsroom, including restructuring departments for better coordination and resources sharing, setting up a central hub for dealing with breaking news and processing user-generated content, and providing journalists regular training on data mining, digital story-telling, and social media (Zhang, 2009, 2012; García-Avilés et al., 2014; Li, 2018; Wang and Sparks, 2020).

However, convergence is not just a technologically oriented term used for the infrastructural merging of old and new media technologies, platforms, and industries. It also refers to an evolving process during which changing perceptions, practices, forms, and structures occur (Meikle and Young, 2012). Indeed, it is so multifaceted that Jenkins (2006a: 3) has rightly called it a term that 'manages to describe technological, industrial, cultural, and social changes depending on who's speaking and what they think they are talking about'. Most importantly, Jenkins (2006a) also reminds us of another important actor in this important shift: that is, consumers who have become increasingly involved in the creation and distribution of media content. Thanks to advances in digital technology, the boundary between media producers and consumers is increasingly blurred. This leads to what Marshall McLuhan and Barrington Nevitt (1972) call a new generation of 'prosumers', who have turned from being end consumers to producers of content. Jenkins (2006b) calls it participatory culture, in which average people are able to 'archive, annotate, appropriate, and recirculate media content in powerful new ways'.

This study takes media convergence as multidimensional and will discuss the ongoing media convergence in China from social, economic, technological, and political perspectives. As a consequence of a number of overlapping and interrelated factors and forces, media convergence has become another important terrain where the Party tries to manage and circumvent the unwanted consequences.

THE CHANGING MEDIA LANDSCAPE IN CHINA

The development of the media in China after 1978 can be divided into four stages – known as marketisation, conglomeration, capitalisation, and media convergence – each reflecting the party-state's efforts at maintaining control of the reform process and dealing proactively with unintended consequences.

When Deng Xiaoping started economic reform in 1978, the media were tasked with defining the objectives and philosophy of The Communist Party of China (CPC) and the government (Zhang, 2015). The flow of information was decidedly top-down, and the CPC used the media to the greatest possible extent to create a 'total institution' and to impose ideological hegemony on society (Lee, 1990).

The economic reforms created a radically changed media landscape shaped by an unprecedented proliferation of media outlets, diversification of media sources, and the rapid development of technological advances (television in the 1980s, and the Internet from 1994). Marketisation also redefined the political role of the media (Zhang, 2011). While retaining ultimate control over politically sensitive information, the CPC wanted the media to play a major role in the promotion of a market economy, consumerism, and the nationalist project of building a 'wealthy and powerful' nation (ibid.). Economic reforms during this period resulted in a more pluralised, commercialised, and liberalised China. That is to say, while marketisation of the media launched by the party-state led to the transformation of the whole media landscape, it also brought about unintended consequences.

Despite the reforms, the CPC leaders inherited from Mao a clear understanding of the political importance of the media. Therefore it is not surprising that as the CPC struggled to manage all aspects of the reforms, it also invested high stakes in the media and gradually developed more refined and sophisticated management, including strengthening structures to enhance regulating capacities. The second stage from the mid-1990s to 2002 saw the party-state not only deepen the market logic, but also determined to maintain control of the commercialised media industry.

CONGLOMERATION FOR OPTIMAL INTEGRATION

From the mid-1990s the government started to encourage the formation of media groups for optimal integration between control and business, by matching enterprising media outlets with its own regulating organs (Zhang, 2015). The 40 press groups formed were a blend of media outlets and government regulators (ibid.). However, media conglomerates were not commercially successful, largely due to the fact that they were designed more for the maximisation of ideological control over media than for the maximisation of profits. Although they were financially independent and were expected to rationalise production and take advantage of economies of scale, the groups were not officially incorporated as independent businesses, nor were they registered with the government's industry and trade bureau. Rather, they were affiliated with the Departments of Propaganda at different levels, with publishers and editors-in-chief appointed by and accountable to their affiliated CPC committees (ibid.). In 2003 a new reform programme called capitalisation was launched to differentiate substantively the concept of public cultural institutions, including the media, from commercial cultural enterprises, and to attribute to each clear-cut missions, and different means and ends of development.

CAPITALISATION

This policy encourages culture to become a strategic site for the development of cultural or 'soft' power in a competitive global context. Further, this move reconceptualises culture including the media as a commercial industry, a new site of economic growth. More importantly, media reform became part of China's economic reforms, effectively displacing it as a key component of political reform within the broad agenda of cultural system reform (ibid.). Following this new policy, different organisations in the media sector separated into two sub-sectors: the public service sector and the commercial sector. All of the mainstream state-owned media entities such as the CPC organs, be they press groups, broadcasting groups, or publishers, are public service units and provide political information. Other entities such as advertisers, printers, distributers, and transmitters are open to non-state investment and ownership. This move shows the state's determination to maintain control over the political information, but at the same time to allow the commercial sector to flourish. This move also authorises state capital to monopolise media heavyweights, but to exit gradually from medium-sized and small ones through asset sales and transfers, mergers, and bankruptcy. To ensure that the medium-sized or small media companies keep their 'socialist' nature, they are not fully left to (domestic or foreign) private capital. A further distinction is thus made between the editorial and business operations of these organisations. The operational sectors may be split from the editorial sectors and restructured into shareholding or limited commercial companies, which can open up the service-related value chains such as printing and publishing, retail, information transmission and distribution to investment from non-media state-owned enterprises. On the other hand, the editorial sectors must remain state monopolies, preventing overseas and private investment.

To summarise, China's economic reforms and opening up have resulted in pluralisation within the media. China observers are divided in their assessment of the political and social impact of all the changes (Zhang, 2006). For instance, marketisation in the 1980s and 1990s led some to predict that severance of state subsidies to the media would unleash media practitioners' energy to meet intense market competition. To satisfy the preference of an ever more demanding public and to compete with one another to win sizable market shares, different media outlets would have to distribute content that attracts the media publics advertisers want. However, other scholars believed that marketisation actually helped the government reach the public faster and in greater numbers as the media tried to deliver the largest number of media publics to advertisers. They believed that commercialisation of the media was a double-edged sword: the media had not only gone from delivering mass propaganda to mass entertainment, but had also continued to operate within the orbit of the party-state. Both sides had ample empirical evidence to support their arguments. However, it is noticeable that all these changes are happening in the context of the Chinese Communist Party wanting to manage and control the whole process and to stay ahead of the unwanted consequences of the reform (Zhang, 2015).

MEDIA CONVERGENCE: ANOTHER APPROACH TO PROPAGANDA?

Media convergence in China encompasses three stages, each of which is characterised by the efforts of the Chinese traditional media to adapt and integrate with digital technologies, in response to both the market need for content distribution and user engagement as well as the government call to use the Internet for economic modernisation (Zhang, 2018). The initial stage was from the mid- to late 1990s when the Internet was first introduced to China. This stage was characterised by the efforts of the Chinese media to incorporate computer and Internet technologies into their work and get online. The second stage from around 2000 to 2006 involved continued engagement of the Chinese media with the Internet by extending their online services through new forms of online media such as news portals, mobile newspapers and mobile TV. The third stage starting from 2006 onwards came along with the advent of Web 2.0. It witnessed the active involvement of the social media forms of communication, delivering and promoting content and services via such platforms as blogging, micro-blogging (weibo), Wechat (*weixin*, the Chinese instant messaging service), and mobile apps. The *People's Daily* took the lead in every stage of the media convergence in China. It established its website, *People's Daily Online* in 1997, followed by creating websites for both PC and mobile users; it started its social media accounts on microblog platforms and Wechat respectively in 2012 and 2013, and launched its official news app in 2014.

AN ECONOMIC RESPONSE

The convergence of traditional media with new media technologies is first of all an economic response from the media industry. As of February 2008, 14 years after China was connected to the Internet, the number of Chinese users became the largest in the world. According to the China Internet Network Information Center (CNNIC, 2019), the country had 854 million Internet users by June 2019, which accounted for 61.2 per cent of the overall Chinese population. The increasing Internet penetration rate and access to mobile devices mean that many Chinese use online media as the main source for information and entertainment. In addition, once passive consumers of information, they are now empowered to look for content they like amongst a plethora of official and non-official media outlets competing for their attention. The fact that the increasing number of Internet users are predominantly young, with those aged 20–29 being the largest user group, and that the majority live in cities (CNNIC, 2019), means that this demographic will remain the main customers for such popular online activities as news reading, shopping, instant messaging, and video-sharing. These changing consumption patterns have resulted in a shift of both readers and therefore advertisers from print to online, leading to the decline in traditional media's circulation and revenues (Sparks et al., 2016).

With the number of online news users climbing to 685.87 million (CNNIC, 2019), the state media have continued to provide online news. Take for example their engagement with the increasingly popular commercial short-video social networking apps. A current prominent development feature on the Internet is the growing popularity of short-video social networking apps, exemplified by Douyin, which allow users to upload videos of up to 15 seconds. By mid-2019, this prosumer (producer + consumer) number of short videos reached 648 million (ibid.). To compete for an audience, Chinese mainstream media have published content on short-video platforms. For example, of the more than 1340 media accounts on Douyin, flagship state media such as the *People's Daily* and Central China Television (CCTV) News have set up accounts attracting over 10 million and 5 million followers, respectively (People.cn, 2019).

POLITICAL REQUIREMENTS: 'WE GO WHERE THE PUBLIC GOES'

China's media convergence is top-down and driven by state policies rather than market forces. Following marketisation, conglomeration, and capitalisation, media convergence can be said to be another approach devised by the CPC to help cope with challenges it faces in the domain of propaganda and public opinion guidance on the Internet.

From the very beginning the Internet was said to have the potential to overcome authoritarian restrictions on the flow of information. It was even believed that the Internet-based new media forms such as the 'blog-sphere' make the debate over state control or interference irrelevant, as bloggers find other ways to get their news and information (Zhang, 2015). It is therefore not surprising that the Party has placed great emphasis on the ideological control of the online sphere, especially on realising that traditional media are losing popularity among their audience. However, the Chinese government also recognises the importance of the Internet: China must integrate into the global economy in order to strengthen itself for competition, and integration requires not only economic and administrative reform, but also the absorption of advanced technologies, including the potentially subversive Internet. Therefore, while Chinese leaders have taken care to manage the undesirable political consequences of the free flow of information facilitated by the Internet, they have also treated the Internet as an engine for economic and social growth, and have adopted a proactive policy to develop the Internet. 'The authoritarian state is hardly obsolete in the era of the Internet' (Kalathil and Boas, 2003: 136), because the party-state plays a crucial role in charting the development of the Internet and in conditioning the ways different actors use it.

Furthermore, the party-state also employs the technology for propaganda and to mobilise social support for its own cause. For example, the outbreak of COVID-19 has actually provided a good opportunity for online propaganda, enabling the Party to promote a favourable image by responding quickly, though selectively, to people's concerns (Repnikova, 2020).

Being interactive and reciprocal in its nature of communication, the Internet is also used to constrain negative consequences resulting from the traditional one-way communication between the state and society. For instance, numerous netizens, the urban youth in particular, prefer to express opinions, exchange ideas, and share information with their peers on the Internet. With few other ways of assessing the public mood, the Internet actually serves as a barometer to monitor online public opinion. Based on data analysis shared by Sina Weibo, Renmin Net (the affiliated website of the *People's Daily*) can construct posts on Weibo to guide online opinion about certain issues in a direction favoured by the website (Stockmann and Luo, 2017). In fact, Renmin Net established its own Public Opinion Monitoring Centre in 2008 (later renamed the Public Opinion Data Centre) to mine and gauge public sentiments on the Internet, and to provide intelligence to government officials (Denyer, 2013; Creemers, 2017).

Increasingly the Internet has become a site for contentious politics, and cases of netizens using online media to mobilise social activism (Sullivan and Xie, 2009; Yang, 2009, 2013), expose governmental corruption and official wrongdoings (Hassid, 2012), and ridicule the official ideologies through the use of satire and parody (Esarey and Xiao, 2008; Li, 2011) are well documented; and yet again, studies have shown that the CPC has developed a range of digital means for managing public opinion, ranging from overt means of censorship and blocking information undesired by the authorities, to more subtle approaches to persuasion and manipulation (MacKinnon, 2011; King et al., 2013; Han, 2015; Repnikova and Fang, 2018). Take the employment of the popular cartoon for propaganda as an example. The increasingly fragmented audience on the Internet means that traditional ways of propaganda will have little appeal to Internet users, especially the young, who are generally indifferent to politics. To attract the young, fun-loving Internet users, the CPC has shifted its propaganda approach from paternalistic and unidirectional preaching of political norms to less ideologically driven but more entertaining forms of persuasion. Soon after Xi Jinping became President, a cartoon video entitled 'How Leaders are Made' was released online, introducing Xi's rise from a community-level official to the presidency. Narrated in plain language and with amusing background music, the cartoon video compares different leadership selection processes in the US, United Kingdom, and China. It suggests that China has its own unique system that suits itself, and as long as people are satisfied and the country develops, it is working. Similarly, another cartoon, 'Where has President Xi's Time Gone?', which went viral online in 2014, depicts the President as an approachable and hard-working leader who has devoted most of his time to serving his country.

With continuous upgrades in the digital tools that emphasise interactive and participative modes of communication, the Party has been implementing new techniques of what Repnikova and Fang (2018) define as 'authoritarian participatory persuasion 2.0', which treats targets of propaganda not so much as passive recipients, but as active collaborators who can help recreate and promote pro-party discourses on the Internet. Repnikova and Fang (2018) have identified a number of means to invite the online public to join various initiatives spearheaded by the state. These range from explicitly calling for public participation in the form of sharing and retweeting messages posted by official media accounts on Weibo, and inviting netizens to upload photos or essays for officially orchestrated events, to creating interactive social media accounts and apps which allow ordinary netizens to digitally accompany President Xi on his journeys. Despite netizens' varied tastes for online content, there are topics that can constantly draw collective attention and invite public participation. Nationalism is one such topic (Qiu, 2006; Wu, 2007; Reilly, 2010; Ma, 2018). Official media outlets are keen to set up accounts on Douyin, a short-video sharing platform popular among young people, and promote 'playful nationalism' which combines dominant party ideologies with light-hearted and cheerful elements (Chen et al., 2020).

An example of this can be found in the commemoration of the 90th anniversary of the People's Liberation Army (PLA) in 2017, when the *People's Daily* launched on its official app an interactive program that allows netizens to create pictures of themselves in PLA uniforms. They only had to scan the QR code, upload a selfie, choose the period in which they would like to serve in the military, and select their gender, before receiving an artificial intelligence (AI)-generated image that they could share and circulate on Wechat and other social media. This form of 'playful nationalism' echoes Lagerkvist's (2008: 123) idea of 'ideotainment', an online propaganda technique that incorporates the use of interactive media technologies, elements of online popular culture which young people find cool, with 'subtle ideological constructs, symbols, and nationalistically inclined messages of persuasion'. The PLA uniform interactive program which amuses young netizens while being patriotic may appear innovative, but it is not totally new. A similar example dates back to 2008, when a fatal earthquake struck Sichuan Province. Due to their quick response and efficiency in the earthquake relief, the then President Hu Jintao and Premier Wen Jiabao enjoyed support from Chinese netizens who called themselves fans of the Hu–Wen leadership. To take advantage of this favourable online public opinion, the *People's Daily* set up an online fan club where netizens could sign up and obtain an electronic certificate that approved their official status as fans of the leadership (Rawnsley and Ma, 2017).

Although the 2017 PLA uniform interactive program was to some extent similar to the online fan club almost a decade ago, the former exceeded the latter in terms of popularity and influence. This is because in 2008, social media such as Weibo and Wechat, which let netizens immediately share, like, and reproduce such playful though ideologically laden content, did not even exist. The interactive program attracted more than a billion clicks within ten days of its launch, and has been considered a role model of propaganda work in the era of media convergence. Describing it as a 'phenomenal convergent media product', Yu (2018) summarises that the success of the PLA uniform program requires innovation, content, and technology, and more importantly, user awareness; that is to say, understanding what content and services users want. In this case, the PLA uniform program meets not only the users' needs for socialising and entertainment (sharing fun images with friends and commenting on social media), but also their emotional needs for expressing patriotism, a prevailing mood that many Chinese netizens share. Users, in a sense, are transformed from being the recipients, at the point of which information normally ends, to 'prosumers' who have become an essential part of what Repnikova and Fang (2018) call 'authoritarian participatory persuasion 2.0', engaging in the process of appropriating, reproducing, and recirculating media content desired by the Party, and thus cascading such content to a larger target audience.

A NATIONAL STRATEGY IN XI'S ERA

Media convergence started in the late 1990s, but it did not become a national strategy till Xi's era, characterised by a visible strengthening of the mechanisms of control within the Party (Bader, 2016). Its importance is evident in President Xi's speech to the 2013 National Conference on Propaganda and Ideological Work, during which he emphasised the urgent need to take back control of the ideological battlefield in cyberspace through media convergence. He said, 'We must treat online public opinion work as the topmost priority. Propaganda is the work that deals with people, thus the focus should be placed on where the people are' (People.cn, 2014).

On 18 August 2015, the Central Leading Group for Comprehensively Deepening Reform, chaired by President Xi, approved the 'Guiding Opinion for Promoting the Convergent Development of Traditional Media and New Media'. Media convergence was then formally elevated as a national strategy to tackle the declining influence of official media and to effectively rein in the online society that has allegedly threatened the Party's ideological dominance. With President Xi's blueprint for media convergence, state media have taken the lead in developing new communication platforms to reach out and strengthen influence among netizens. In February 2016, the *People's Daily* launched its state-of-the-art hub (referred to in Chinese as 'central kitchen') for multimedia content production that can be shared and distributed across various digital channels. This 'central kitchen' is described as a 'completely convergent system'. It not only breaks boundaries between departments, thus allowing staff from different media platforms to collaborate, but also serves as a one-stop resource centre providing support in finance, technology, content promotion, operations, and management (Xinhua, 2017). Such a convergent media system is highly centralised, with the Chief Editor Control Centre as the top decision-making body, overseeing the whole production chain including the overall planning of propaganda work, setting the news agenda, and directing human resources for information-gathering and editing (ibid.). In addition, all the content created is stored in a centralised database and can either be published straight away or used as raw material for reprocessing.

The *People's Daily* opens its 'central kitchen' to other state media outlets at provincial and local levels for content co-production, resource-sharing, and technological innovation, inviting them not only to purchase its products, but also to upload and contribute content to the database (Wang, 2016; Xinhua, 2017). Bandurski (2019) argues that this 'centralised content production strategy for an otherwise decentralised digital media landscape' gives central media such as the *People's Daily* enormous control over the flow of information in the digital sphere. The move to converging content on a single database also gives the CPC dominant discursive power, because by limiting the supply side it allows only a limited number of officially trusted content databases to produce information. As a convergent platform for content, distribution channels, and management, the system also serves as a propaganda management and control platform. This gives propaganda departments permission to oversee the comments and news content published via the system and, when necessary, to completely withdraw 'problematic content' (that is, information that contradicts or challenges the Party's authority) by one click.

BIG DATA AS A NEW FORM OF POWER

The possession of data is a new form of power in this increasingly networked society. The convergence of media not only brings together different media platforms but, more importantly, big data about the users. The Party considers the Internet as a way of connecting with the people and of listening to their opinions. Now assisted by data-driven technologies, they are also able to learn about and predict users' online behaviour through their real identities.

Firstly, the advancement of the latest networking technologies, such as algorithms, automation, and big data, allows propaganda to be devised and delivered in a way that was previously unimaginable in terms of scale, scope, and precision. Researchers have demonstrated that a growing number of governments and political parties have been experimenting with what is now termed 'computational propaganda' (Woolley and Howard, 2016; Bradshaw and Howard, 2019). What makes computational propaganda new is the use of data-driven techniques and software tools, for example automated bots and cyber troops, to amplify online certain content favoured by propagandists, or to precisely target specific groups with disinformation or trolling (Bradshaw and Howard, 2019; Woolley and Howard, 2019). Bradshaw and Howard's (2019) research suggests China's growing capacity to involve computational propaganda in targeting audiences on domestic social media platforms.

On many occasions President Xi has emphasised the importance of integrating modern technologies in media convergence for effective propaganda. For instance, during his visit to the *People's Daily* on 25 January 2019, Xi stated:

> We must heighten our sense of urgency and sense of mission, push forward continuous breakthroughs in the ... innovation of key and core technologies, explore the uses of artificial intelligence in the collection, production, distribution, reception and feedback of news ... harness 'algorithms', and comprehensively enhance the ability of guiding public opinion. (Xi, 2019)

Liu Qibao (2014), the then head of the Central Committee's Propaganda Department, described the convergence of media as a 'great strategic plan' to consolidate the Party's discursive power and expand mainstream ideology. In order to achieve this goal, he encouraged the media to 'sufficiently adopt new technologies and applications, and innovate media communication methods', in particular, big data and cloud computing technologies (ibid.).

Secondly, the CPC has realised the importance of using data-driven technologies to ensure its discursive dominance by closely monitoring the developments and trends of online public opinion, identifying criticism and grievances, and taking actions – either by suppressing these critical voices or by selectively responding to them – before they become organised protests that may move offline. For instance, by closely monitoring online discussions about the COVID-19 pandemic and analysing the big data sourced from a range of social media platforms, the authorities knew the general trends in online public opinion, and therefore could quickly refute rumours, redress misinformation, and suppress unwanted information that may jeopardise social stability. In handling the online outrage sparked by the death of Dr Li Wenliang, the whistleblower who was reprimanded by the Wuhan Police for 'spreading rumours' and who later died from the coronavirus, the Party changed from first censoring online discussion to sending the National Supervisory Commission to formally investigate the case. To appease the angry public, Wuhan police issued an official apology to Li's family and disciplined the relevant police officers for mishandling the case.

Under the guidance of the Central Propaganda Department, China's Ministry of Technology and Science approved the establishment of four national key labs to further promote media convergence, one of which is constructed and operated by the *People's Daily*. The National Key Laboratory of Communication Content Cognition under the *People's Daily* researches the application of AI and computational science in the management of online space, ensuring that content conforms to the mainstream values, and is precisely delivered and 'enters deeply into people's hearts' (People.cn, 2020).

MEDIA CONVERGENCE: TENSIONS AND CHALLENGES

Media convergence was conceived by the CPC's political will to consolidate its control of the media and strengthen its discursive dominance on the Internet. In Bandurski's (2016) words, China's media convergence is a move for 'convergent control'. Instead of being a business strategy to cope with the decline of revenue and readership facing the global media industry, media convergence in China is mainly a top-down political campaign that puts ideological concerns over economic imperatives. Consequently, the Chinese version of media convergence can easily find itself at the centre of contradictions between the Party and the market.

Firstly, while a few central media outlets such as the *People's Daily* and Xinhua continuously receive large amounts of governmental funding and subsidies that allow them to speed up convergence, the financial support for the vast numbers of lower-level media is limited. President Xi's initiative requires media across China to undertake media convergence not only at national and provincial levels, but also at county levels. This mandate is primarily a call for county-level media to enhance their communication strength and influence among the vast local population (Yin, 2019). Media such as TV, newspaper, and radio, which were once key means through which the Party's directives and voices were broadcast to the local public, have fallen into obsolescence. Fuchs (2018: 78) argues that communication power in the time of social media and big data has shifted from 'the control of production towards the control of attention and visibility'. Indeed, local-level media have to compete for attention with the popular commercial apps such as Wechat, Weibo, Douyin, and commercial news aggregators such as Tencent, Today's Headlines (*jinri toutiao*), and Sohu that were developed and are owned by major private Internet companies. However, media convergence is an expensive undertaking. Local media have to expand their presence on domestic social media platforms, and many of them set up their own 'central kitchens' after the one developed by the *People's Daily*. However, lacking subsequent funding for technical maintenance and qualified media professionals, the 'central kitchens' developed by local media outlets cannot be fully integrated into the daily practice of media production and management. Thus they become projects that only showcase the compliance of local media towards the Party (Yin and Liu, 2014; Xiong and Zhang, 2018). Worse still, many of them stop at having established accounts on social media platforms. Those social media accounts are poorly maintained, since they lack the capacity to update content on a regular basis, or simply repost news from other media outlets. As a consequence, social media accounts of this kind simply turn into 'zombie accounts' or 'content removers', which can hardly regain contact with the local audience and thus exert influence on them (Huang, 2020).

Secondly, technologies help to disseminate propaganda, but, for it to work, the content must strike a chord with the audience. Striking a balance between approved content and audience appeal is no easy task. One example is the emergence, rise, and decline of investigative journalism in China. Journalists may still choose to toe the red line to appeal to the audience, but tightening media control means investigative journalism occupies less space (Tong, 2019).

Thirdly, making a profit by selling news is difficult, not only because most Chinese Internet users are not accustomed to paying for online news content (Li, 2018), but also because the online news market has been primarily dominated by commercial news aggregators that provide free, though homogenised, content. There are few business strategies for covering the cost of media convergence. High-level state media still rely heavily on state funding. Many local and commercial newspapers tend to avoid critical reporting that may cause them problems, and have shifted from being content providers towards being service providers. The provision of governmental services – such as making appointments with hospitals and paying traffic fines, and community services such as household goods, education, and tourism – has become a business strategy for survival (Wang and Sparks, 2019).

Finally, official media rely heavily on popular and privately owned social media platforms, such as Tencent and Sina, to expand their online presence and reach out to the young, the main target of propaganda. Yet because of the nature of these companies, the CPC does not have the same grip over their policies, personnel, and content as it does with newspapers and television (Wang and Sparks, 2019). Although these commercial companies need to conform to the government, it is not surprising to know that these companies are often involved extensively in media convergence projects. The collaboration appears to benefit both sides: the official media have a channel to reach the target audience, while the private companies get access to the lucrative and fast-growing Internet market. For example, Alibaba helped develop a popular government propaganda app, Xuexi Qiangguo (literally, 'Study to Make China Strong'), which includes news stories, short videos, quizzes, and commentaries that promote President Xi's thoughts (Li and Cadell, 2019). Tencent also provides technical support on cloud computing to the *People's Daily* and helps the latter construct a major system of media convergence (People.cn, 2016). However, despite the collaboration there is also competition and tension between the state media that strive to take back control of the online discursive fields, and the commercial Internet companies who already dominate the online communicative platforms where content, technologies, and user data converge. This prompts the government to urge the key state media to construct their own independent platforms, but Lu (2020: 135–136) has warned that, 'when traditional mainstream media organisations concentrate their own capital on new platforms, they are essentially using their weaknesses to fight against the others' strengths', and this will inevitably lead to the reduction of their investments in news content production.

CONCLUSION

This chapter has shown that the current technological, economic, and political developments taking place in China are shaping the overall media landscape and convergence. Media convergence, as a top-down government strategy, demonstrates the Party's efforts to extend its propaganda operation to online platforms where various stakeholders, with diverse interests, compete for audience attention. Earlier developments in the media sphere, including commercialisation, conglomeration, and capitalisation, were the result of economic reform since the late 1970s. President Xi's government has orchestrated convergence to ensure the media continue their propaganda function to mobilise public support online and offline. In the continuing media convergence process, tensions and challenges exist. The conflict of interests between the prosumers, the official media and private companies, and the Party, will continue for the foreseeable future, and media convergence will remain a terrain where each force fights for space and control. This will occur until any of the stakeholders and any of the economic and political factors change the balance of power.

REFERENCES

Bader, J.A. (2016), *How Xi Jinping Sees the World ... and Why*, Washington, DC: Brookings Institution Press.
Bandurski, D. (2016), 'Convergent control', accessed 4 August 2020 at http://chinamediaproject.org/2016/08/25/convergent-control/.
Bandurski, D. (2019), 'China's top brass converge for media convergence, as the Party seeks to dominate the digital sphere', accessed 20 July 2020 at https://hongkongfp.com/2019/02/03/chinas-top-brass-converge-media-convergence-party-seeks-dominate-digital-sphere/.
Bradshaw, S. and P.N. Howard (2019), 'The Global Disinformation Order: 2019 Global Inventory of Organised Social Media Manipulation', accessed 25 July 2020 at https://comprop.oii.ox.ac.uk/wp-content/uploads/sites/93/2019/09/CyberTroop-Report19.pdf.
Chen, X., D.B.V. Kaye, and J. Zeng (2020), '#PositiveEnergy Douyin: constructing "playful patriotism" in a Chinese short-video application', *Chinese Journal of Communication*, 1–21. DOI: 10.1080/17544750.2020.1761848.
China Internet Network Information Center (CNNIC) (2019), 'Statistical Report on Internet Development in China', accessed 15 July 2020 at http://cnnic.com.cn/IDR/ReportDownloads/201911/P020191112539794960687.pdf.
Creemers, R. (2017), 'Cyber China: upgrading propaganda, public opinion work and social management for the twenty-first century', *Journal of Contemporary China* 26 (103): 85–100.
Denyer, S. (2013), 'In China, Communist Party takes unprecedented step: it is listening', accessed 31 July 2020 at https://www.washingtonpost.com/world/in-china-government-mines-public-opinion/2013/08/02/33358026-f2b5-11e2-ae43-b31dc363c3bf_story.html.
Dwyer, T. (2010), *Media Convergence*, Maidenhead: Open University Press.
Esarey, A. and Q. Xiao (2008), 'Political expression in the Chinese blogosphere: below the radar', *Asian Survey*, 48 (5): 752–772.
Fuchs, C. (2018). 'Propaganda 2.0: Herman and Chomsky's propaganda model in the age of the internet, big data and social media', in J. Pedro-Carañana, D. Broudy, and J. Klaehn (eds), *The Propaganda Model Today: Filtering Perception and Awareness*, London: University of Westminster Press, pp. 71–92.
García-Avilés, J.A., A. Kaltenbrunner, and K. Meier (2014), 'Media convergence revisited', *Journalism Practice*, 8 (5): 573–584.
Golding, P. (2000), 'Forthcoming features: information and communications technologies and the sociology of the future', *Sociology*, 34 (1): 165–184.
Gordon, R. (2003), 'The meanings and implications of convergence', in K. Kawamoto (ed.), *Digital Journalism*, Lanham, MD: Rowman & Littlefield, pp. 57–73.
Han, R. (2015), 'Manufacturing consent in cyberspace: China's "fifty-cent army"', *Journal of Current Chinese Affairs*, 44 (2): 105–134.
Hassid, J. (2012), 'Safety valve or pressure cooker? Blogs in Chinese political life', *Journal of Communication*, 62 (2): 212–230.
Hesmondhalgh, D. (2007), *The Cultural Industries* (2nd edn), London: SAGE.

Huang, C. (2020), 'The state, problems and trends of the current media convergence in our country' (*Dangqian woguo meiti ronghe fazhan zhuangkuang cunzai wenti ji qushi*), accessed 10 August 2020 at http://yuqing.people.com.cn/n1/2020/0724/c209043-31796941.html.

Iosifidis, P. (2011), *Global Media and Communication Policy*, New York: Palgrave Macmillan.

Jenkins, H. (2006a), *Convergence Culture: Where Old and New Media Collide*, New York: New York University Press.

Jenkins, H. (2006b), 'Confronting the challenges of participatory culture: media education for the 21st century (part one)', accessed 20 March 2020 at http://henryjenkins.org/blog/2006/10/confronting_the_challenges_of.html.

Kalathil, S. and T. Boas (2003), *Open Networks, Closed Regimes: The Impact of the Internet on Authoritarian Rule*, Washington, DC: Carnegie Endowment for International Peace.

King, G.J. Pan, and M.E. Roberts (2013), 'How censorship in China allows government criticism but silences collective expression', *American Political Science Review*, 107 (2): 326–343.

Kolodzy, J. (2009), 'Convergence explained', in A. Grant and J. Wilkinson (eds), *Understanding Media Convergence*, Oxford: Oxford University Press, pp. 31–51.

Lagerkvist, J. (2008), 'Internet ideotainment in the PRC: national responses to cultural globalization', *Journal of Contemporary China*, 17 (54): 121–140.

Lax, S. (2009), *Media and Communications Technologies: A Critical Introduction*, Basingstoke: Palgrave Macmillan.

Lee, C. (1990), 'Mass media: of China, about China', in C. Lee (ed.), *Voices of China: The Interplay of Politics and Journalism*, New York: Guildford Press, pp. 3–29.

Li, H. (2011), 'Parody and resistance on the Chinese internet', in D.K. Herold and P. Marolt (eds), *Online Society in China: Creating, Celebrating, and Instrumentalising the Online Carnival*, London: Routledge, pp. 71–88.

Li, K. (2018), 'Convergence and de-convergence of Chinese journalistic practice in the digital age', *Journalism*, 19 (9–10): 1380–1396.

Li, P. and C. Cadell (2019), 'Alibaba is the force behind hit Chinese Communist Party app: Sources', accessed 30 August 2020 at https://www.reuters.com/article/us-china-alibaba-government/alibaba-is-the-force-behind-hit-chinese-communist-party-app-sources-idUSKCN1Q70Y7.

Liu, Q. (2014), 'Accelerate the promotion of the convergent development of traditional media and new media' (*Jiakuai tuidong chuantong meiti he xinxing meiti ronghe*), accessed 30 July 2020 at http://politics.people.com.cn/n/2014/0423/c1001-24930310.html.

Lu, X. (2020), 'Lessons from Weibo: media convergence and contemporary Chinese politics', *Javnost – The Public*, 27 (2): 126–139.

Ma, Y. (2018), 'Online Chinese nationalism: a competing discourse? A discourse analysis of Chinese media texts relating to the Beijing Olympic torch relay in Paris', *Journal of International Communication*, 24(2): 305–325.

MacKinnon, R. (2011), 'China's "networked authoritarianism"', *Journal of Democracy*, 22 (2): 32–46.

McLuhan, M. and B. Nevitt (1972), *Take Today: The Executive as Drop-Out*, New York: Harcourt Brace Jovanovich.

Meikle, G. and S. Young (2012), *Media Convergence: Networked Digital Media in Everyday Life*, London: Palgrave Macmillan.

People.cn (2014), 'Compilation of Xi Jinping's brilliant quotes on "propaganda and ideological work" since 18th National Congress' (*Xi Jinping shibada yilai guanyu 'xuanchuan sixiang gongzuo' jingcai lunshu zhaibian*), accessed 20 July 2020 at http://cpc.people.com.cn/n/2014/0819/c164113-25493994.html.

People.cn (2016), 'People's Daily signs agreement with Tencent to promote media convergence', accessed 30 August 2020 at http://en.people.cn/n3/2016/0616/c98649-9073235.html.

People.cn (2019), '2018 report on Chinese media convergence index has published' (*2018 Zhongguo meiti ronghe chuangbo zhishu baogao fabu*), accessed 16 July 2020 at http://media.people.com.cn/n1/2019/0326/c120837-30994743.html.

People.cn (2020), 'What new influences will the four convergent laboratories bring' (*Sige ronghe shiyanshi, xindongzuo jiang dailai naxie xin yingxiang*), accessed 31 July 2020 at http://media.people.com.cn/n1/2020/0612/c40606-31743888.html.

Pool, I. (1983), *Technologies of Freedom*, Cambridge, MA: Harvard University Press.

Qiu, J.L. (2006), 'The changing web of Chinese nationalism', *Global Media and Communication*, 2 (1): 125–128.
Quinn, S. (2005), 'Convergence's fundamental question', *Journalism Studies*, 6 (1): 29–38.
Rawnsley, G.D. and Y. Ma (2017), 'New media and democratisation in East Asia', in T.J. Cheng and Y. Chu (eds), *Routledge Handbook of Democratization in East Asia*, New York: Routledge, pp. 314–326.
Reilly, J. (2010), 'China's online nationalism toward Japan', in S. Shen and S. Breslin (eds), *Online Chinese Nationalism and China's Bilateral Relations*, Lanham, MD: Lexington Books, pp. 45–72.
Repnikova, M. (2020), 'Does China's propaganda work?', accessed 10 August 2020 at https://www.nytimes.com/2020/04/16/opinion/china-coronavirus-propaganda.html.
Repnikova, M. and K. Fang (2018), 'Authoritarian persuasion 2.0: netizens as thought work collaborators in China', *Journal of Contemporary China*, 27(113): 763–779.
Sparks, C., H. Wang, Y. Huang, Y. Zhao, N. Lü, and D. Wang (2016), 'The impact of digital media on newspapers: comparing responses in China and the United States', *Global Media and China*, 1 (3): 186–207.
Stockmann, D. and T. Luo (2017), 'Which social media facilitate online public opinion in China', *Problems of Post-Communism*, 64 (3): 189–202.
Sullivan, J. and L. Xie (2009), 'Environmental activism, social networks and the internet', *China Quarterly*, 198 (1): 422–432.
Tong, J. (2019), 'The taming of critical journalism in China', *Journalism Studies*, 20 (1): 79–96.
Wang, D. (2016), 'Behind China's media convergence campaign', accessed 20 July 2020 at https://blogs.nottingham.ac.uk/chinesestudies/2016/12/01/behind-chinas-media-convergence-campaign/.
Wang, D. and C. Sparks (2020), 'Smartphones, Wechat and paid content: journalists and sources in a Chinese newspaper', *Journalism Studies*, 21 (1): 37–53.
Wang, H. and C. Sparks (2019), 'Chinese newspaper groups in the digital era: the resurgence of the party press', *Journal of Communication*, 69 (1): 94–119.
Winston, B. (1998), *Media technology and society: a history: from the telegraph to the Internet*, New York: Routledge.
Woolley, S.C. and P.N. Howard (2016), 'Political communication, computational propaganda and autonomous agents', *International Journal of Communication*, 10 (9): 4882–4890.
Woolley, S.C. and P.N. Howard (2019), 'Introduction: computational propaganda worldwide', in S.C. Woolley and P.N. Howard (eds), *Computational Propaganda: Political Parties, Politicians, and Political Manipulation on Social Media*, New York: Oxford University Press, pp. 3–20.
Wu, Xi (2007), *Chinese Cyber Nationalism: Evolution, Characteristics, and Implications*, Lanham, MD: Lexington Books.
Xi, J. (2019), 'Accelerate the promotion of media convergent development, construct full-media communicative structure' (*Jiakuai tuidong meiti ronghe fazhan, goujian quanmeiti chuanbo geju*), accessed 30 July 2020 at http://www.qstheory.cn/dukan/qs/2019-03/15/c_1124239254.htm.
Xinhua (2017), 'What is different about the "central kitchen" of the People's Daily (*Renmin ribao 'zhongyang chufang' you shenme bu yiyang*), accessed 20 July 2020 at http://www.xinhuanet.com/newmedia/2017-02/23/c_136078802.htm.
Xiong, H. and J. Zhang (2018), 'How local journalists interpret and evaluate media convergence: an empirical study of journalists from four press groups in Fujian', *International Communication Gazette*, 80(1): 87–115.
Yang, G. (2009), *The Power of the Internet in China: Citizen Activism Online*, New York: Columbia University Press.
Yang, G. (2013). 'Contesting food safety in Chinese media, between hegemony and counter hegemony', *China Quarterly*, 214 (June): 337–335.
Yin, L. and X. Liu (2014), 'A gesture of compliance: media convergence in China', *Media, Culture and Society*, 36 (5): 561–577.
Yin, Y. (2019), 'The significance of constructing convergent media centres at county level' (*Xianji Rongmeiti Zhognxin Jianshe de Zhongyao Yiyi*), accessed 30 August 2020 at http://www.qstheory.cn/zdwz/2019-09/23/c_1125026371.htm.
Yu, R. (2018), 'Obsession with the military uniform and fission communication – the People's Daily reveals why the "military uniform pictures" H5 becomes so popular' (*Junzhuang Qingjie yu liebian*

chuanbo – Renmin Ribao kehuduan jiemi 'junzhuang zhao' H5 weihe 'shuaping'), accessed 4 August 2020 at http://www.cac.gov.cn/2018-12/25/c_1123902380.htm.

Zhang, S. (2009), 'Newsroom convergence models of China's Beijing Youth Daily and Denmark's Nordjyske', *Chinese Journal of Communication*, 2 (3): 330–347.

Zhang, S. (2012), 'The newsroom of the future', *Journalism Practice*, 6(5–6): 776–787.

Zhang, X. (2006), 'Reading between the headlines: SARS, Focus and TV current affairs programs in China', *Media, Culture and Society*, 28(5): 715–737.

Zhang, X. (2011), *The Transformation of Political Communication in China: From Propaganda to Hegemony*, Singapore: World Scientific Publishing.

Zhang, X. (2015), 'The mass media', in X. Zang (ed.), *Understanding Chinese Society* (2nd edn), Abingdon: Routledge, pp. 165–178.

Zhang, Y. (2018), 'From media convergence to "Internet plus"', in X. Wu, H. Zheng and X. Wu (eds), *New Media and Transformation of Social Life in China*, New Delhi: SAGE, pp. 17–56.

9. Xi Jinping's grand strategy for digital propaganda
Titus C. Chen

INTRODUCTION

This chapter examines how the Chinese state under Xi Jinping's rule has conceptualised, constructed, and implemented his strategy of digital propaganda, an under-studied effort of social-political engineering to which Xi has attached great importance.

The chapter proceeds in four sections. I first review the dynamic relationship between the Chinese government and social media at the beginning of the Xi Jinping era. The rise of social media – online communication platforms designed for users to generate content, share information, and form interactive social networks – has turned out to be an enabling factor for citizens' pursuit of social justice and policy changes. Government control over social media content had been frustrated by overlapping jurisdictions and fragmented administration. Social media networks had eroded not only the power of state censorship but also the influence of regime propaganda.

I then trace major conceptual developments of Xi Jinping's digital propaganda strategy during the first year of his rule. I bring to light the key concepts regarding propaganda and thought work that Xi unveiled in policy speeches and party documents. Attention is drawn to Xi's ideas bearing upon online mass influence, such as the notions of positive propaganda, online social management, and 'cultural innovation'.

The third section sketches how the Xi administration converted his digital propaganda strategy into policy initiatives and institutional framework in 2014. I emphasise the institution-building process in which a cyberspace affairs system was established, and the policy-deliberating process in which Xi Jinping's initiative of 'media convergence' (discussed at length by Zhang and Ma, Chapter 8 in this volume) was exulted and formally adopted by the party-state bureaucracy. The two policy-engineering processes have reinforced each other, handing sweeping powers to cyberspace administration to regulate and influence online public opinion.

The last section examines the regulatory environment that took shape as a direct result of the policy-engineering processes mentioned above. A tilted regulatory environment was constructed, consisting of an expanding body of legislations, administrative decrees, and executive ordinances that were designed with the aim of restraining non-governmental voices while maximising the reach and impact of pro-regime content on the Web. Stringent Internet regulations have empowered cyberspace administrators to not only effectively discipline social media actors, but also privilege the party press, propaganda wings, and their commercial collaborators to monopolise the online news market to Beijing's advantage.

STATE–MEDIA RELATIONSHIP IN THE AGE OF SOCIAL MEDIA: CHALLENGES CONFRONTING BEIJING IN CYBERSPACE

The Internet has fundamentally changed Chinese society, and social media have revolutionised the Chinese Internet. By July 2018, official statistics recorded 802 million registered Internet users in China (CNNIC, 2018). It means that 57.7 per cent of People's Republic of China (PRC) citizens are active on the Internet for at least one hour per day. The mobile Internet population increased at an even faster pace, ballooning from 50.4 million in 2007 (24 per cent of the total Internet population) to 788 million in July 2018, which was 98.3 per cent of the total Internet population (CNNIC, 2018).

From early on, the party-state noticed and grew concerned about the subversive potential of online media (Morozov, 2011; MacKinnon, 2012; Mo, 2014a). State ownership and monopolistic control of telecommunications networks have guaranteed the Chinese government uncontested power over the Internet (Harwit, 2008: 85–86; MacKinnon, 2008, 2009; Herold, 2011: 2–4; Negro, 2017: 28–30). Government surveillance and censorship have effectively denied Chinese citizens access to a multitude of online content that was deemed offensive to the party-state (Wright, 2014; Pan, 2017; King et al., 2014; Mo, 2014b; PEN America, 2018: 33–38; Xiao, 2019).

In contrast to the first-generation online media (news portals/websites and bulletin boards), social media – such as Facebook, Twitter, Weblog, QQ, Weibo, and WeChat – that substantialised the concept of Web 2.0 were initially less regulated and restricted (Xiao, 2011: 204–205; Blank and Reisdorf, 2012; Negro, 2017: 144–146). Social media actors, colloquially referred to as the self-media (*zimeiti*), have proliferated and become convenient channels of mass communication for citizens to amplify their public agenda, air their grievances, identify and bond with like-minded netizens, and even to organise cross-regional social movements (Esarey and Xiao, 2008; Meng, 2010; Lei, 2011; Xiao, 2012; Huang and Sun, 2014; Wang, 2015). Social media had been hailed as a liberation technology that enabled and empowered citizen activists to pursue social justice and policy changes, hence challenging authoritarian rule (Niekerk et al., 2011; Weber, 2011; Wilson and Dunn, 2011; Diamond, 2012; Bellin, 2012; Hassanpour, 2014; Shen, 2015; Svensson, 2016).[1]

Before long, the Chinese Communist Party (CCP) propaganda system and the PRC internal security apparatus took note of social media's political impact. Online surveillance and censorship programmes were upgraded and deployed to prevent anti-hegemonic expression from spreading through social media. Since 2009, the Chinese government has banned foreign social media services from running in the Chinese Internet domain. Furthermore, Beijing has endeavoured to hold domestic Internet service providers (ISPs) and Internet content providers (ICPs) accountable for the content of messages posted on their online services platforms (Creemers, 2016; Gallagher and Miller, 2019; Xiao, 2019). Hence, ISPs and ICPs were obliged to carry out self-policing and self-censorship functions, detecting and filtering out anti-regime content from their services platforms (Cheung, 2016; Pan, 2017; Roberts, 2018; Han, 2018).

Overlapping jurisdictions and fragmented administration have frustrated government control over social media content (Creemers, 2016; Tsai, 2016; Creemers, 2017; Miller, 2018a). The central government did not establish a single Internet management authority until May 2011 (as a direct response to meet potential challenges presented by the Arab Spring), when the State Internet Information Office (SIIO) was created to be a subordinate agency under the State Council Information Office, or SCIO (Creemers, 2016: 97–99). Despite its creation, the SIIO had failed to address the intractable issue of cross-cutting jurisdictions, which had led to incomplete and porous censorship on the Chinese social media (Mo, 2014b; Wright, 2014; Negro, 2017: 32–33; Creemers, 2017; Miller, 2018a). Moreover, Chinese netizens had developed evasion techniques and adaptive strategies to circumvent censorship mechanisms (Xiao, 2011; Ma, 2015: 209–210; PEN America, 2018).

For the party-state, what was even more disconcerting was the decaying of the regime's will and capacity to guide and mould online public opinion. The CCP leadership was concerned that the regime had yielded online discourse power to autonomous opinion leaders (Cheung, 2016; Gries et al., 2016). Propaganda departments, government employees, and hired Internet commentators (which were mockingly termed the 'Fifty Cent Party' for the amount of payment they allegedly received for every pro-regime comment they posted online) had endeavoured to sway online public opinion by flooding social media with narratives that were either supportive of or sympathetic to the CCP government (Han, 2015a, 2015b; Tsai, 2016; King et al., 2017; Roberts, 2018; Miller, 2018b).

Social media networks had eroded not only the power of state censorship but also the influence of regime propaganda (Tsai, 2016). The golden days for social media users in China were in the period 2009 (the year Weibo was officially released) to early 2013, as outmoded censorship and unappealing propaganda had afforded Chinese civil society and citizen journalism some precious breathing room in the social media environment (Shi and Yang, 2016; Deluca et al., 2016). Autonomous social leaders – rights movement leaders, media professionals, cause lawyers, and liberal intellectuals – acted as trendsetters and opinion shapers on social media platforms, and the propaganda apparatus had been pushed to the margins (Svensson, 2015; Yang, 2016; Gallagher and Miller, 2019).

CONCEPTUAL DEVELOPMENTS OF XI JINPING'S DIGITAL PROPAGANDA STRATEGY

In China, the national leadership employ propaganda work to mould the ideological frame of reference of targeted audiences in ways that are conducive to the legitimation of ruling incumbents (Flew, 2016). When Xi assumed power in November 2012, he inherited from Hu Jintao, his predecessor, an increasingly diversifying ideological landscape. Of particular note were the liberalising narratives of autonomous opinion leaders that had influenced public opinion and challenged regime discourse via social media networks. Instead of yielding to the liberalising trend, Xi was determined to reclaim ideological control in China. On 19 August 2013, Xi Jinping unveiled his ideological and propaganda principles to the quinquennial National Conference of Propaganda and Thought Work.

Xi began his speech with a bold preface: 'While economic construction is central to the Party, ideological work is extremely important to the Party' (Xu and Hua, 2013). Xi emphasised that propaganda and thought work had to be faithful to the 'Party spirit', and further contended that party newspapers should bear the party's name and had to defend the party's integrity (*People's Daily*, 2013). Xi pointed out that propaganda narratives should highlight unison, stability, inspiration, and positivity. Propaganda officials were reminded to amplify the party-approved *leitmotif* and spread 'positive energy', that is, favourable portrayals of government performance (and also positive social aspects) (*People's Daily*, 2013). Xi Jinping urged them to greatly improve the work quality and enhance the appeal of propaganda materials

(Han, 2018: 150). Xi further brought up the idea of 'Grand Propaganda', whereby every party cadre is expected to engage in propaganda and thought work, and party secretaries at every administrative level were to bear political and leadership responsibilities for the quality and impact of their propaganda work.

To date, the new party centre remains unclear as to how to evaluate the quality of propaganda materials and measure their political impact. However, senior party cadres are already sensing Xi's dissatisfaction with the performance of the CCP propaganda and thought work system. Also, party committees were required to mobilise and integrate organisational, administrative, and material resources for propaganda work (*People's Daily*, 2013).

In addition to positive propaganda and integrative propaganda, Xi Jinping admonished propaganda officials not to ignore the 'public opinion struggle'. If left unaddressed, Xi maintained, liberal forces were bound to destabilise society, jeopardise the party centre's authority, and endanger China's national security. He reiterated the Maoist principle that the party had to take charge of mass media (*People's Daily*, 2013). It was at this juncture that Xi Jinping revealed his deep-seated belief in the political imperative of controlling the Internet.

Xi prioritised the Internet over all the other media outlets, arguing that 'the Internet has become the main battlefield for public opinion struggle' (CAC, 2014a). He believed that the security of the party's ideology and regime all hinged on an online public opinion shaping mechanism. Guiding online public opinion had to be a task of utmost importance for the propaganda system, Xi insisted, because people – young netizens in particular – now received public information almost exclusively from the Internet (CAC, 2014a; Lu, 2013). Accordingly, Xi urged officials and cadres to perform the role of gatekeepers and guardians on the Internet: improving the quality of online propaganda content, tightening 'social management' on the Web, promoting with great fanfare a healthy and upbeat Internet culture, and seeing to it that the 'correct' thoughts occupy the leading position on the Internet (CAC, 2014a; Lu, 2013). Accomplishing these tasks required party media organs to explore innovative approaches of mass influence and apply new techniques of mass persuasion (CAC, 2014a; Lu, 2013).

On 12 November 2013, the Third Plenum of 18th CCP Central Committee (hereafter: the Third Plenum Resolution) approved Xi's request to establish the Central National Security Commission (CNSC, or the *Guoanwei*) and the Central Leading Group for Comprehensively Deepening Reform (CLGCDR, or the *Shengaizu*) (Xinhua, 2013a). Xi succeeded in centralising political power by creating and leading ad hoc decision-making bodies. During his speech to the Third Plenum, Xi conceded that the government's Internet management left much room for improvement. He attributed the flawed conditions to cross-cutting jurisdictions and overlapping responsibilities of Internet management bureaucracies (Xinhua, 2013b). Xi specified that the government had been ill-prepared for the technological advances and social impact of social media (Xinhua, 2013b). It was supremely important, Xi insisted, that an adequate legal framework of Internet management be established, and that online public opinion be closely monitored and directed by the government (Xinhua, 2013b).

On the other hand, the Third Plenum Resolution declared the advance of innovation in cultural affairs. The idea of 'cultural innovation' referred to Xi's ambitious agenda of incubating and then mobilising pro-regime 'cultural forces', such as entrepreneurs of the cultural industry, practitioners of the fashion industry, and opinion leaders on social media platforms. Given this grand scheme, the notion of 'cultural innovation' entailed bold efforts of thought engineering; that is, steering online public opinion toward a 'correct' pathway (Xinhua, 2013a; Han, 2018: 150). Practically, Xi proposed a regulatory framework of online influence operations that integrated positive propaganda and fear-based Internet management. He further disclosed that the propaganda system was about to push for the integration of conventional party media and new types of media channels (that is, social media) (Xinhua, 2013a).

CONSTRUCTING A CYBERSPACE AFFAIRS SYSTEM AND THE 'MEDIA CONVERGENCE' INITIATIVE

It took only three months for Xi Jinping to put into effect his call for a bureaucratic overhaul of the Internet management system. The CCP Central Leading Group for Cyber Security and Informatization (CLGCSI) was created in February 2014 to centralise the power of Internet governance, absorbing the existing State Informatization Group and State Network and Information Security Coordination Group (Lindsay, 2015: 9). Xi assumed the chairmanship of the Leading Group, the title reflecting Xi's supreme authority, empowering him to coordinate and make key decisions.

On 27 February 2014, Xi declared that national security would be in jeopardy if cyber-security is in danger, and China's modernisation is contingent on the progress made in the infrastructure of telecommunications technology (which is called 'informatisation', or *xinxihua*, in China's official terminology) (Xinhua, 2014a). In this context, cyber-security refers to the party-state's control over online discourses. It is imperative to clarify what the leadership of the Chinese party-state means by 'cyber security' (*wangluo anquan*). Beijing has adopted a conception of cyber-security that is much broader than that of Western governments. Both Chinese and Western conceptions of cyber-security bear on the technical threats to Internet infrastructure and services (in military and civilian sectors) and the socio-legal risks of online exploitative communication (abusive language, financial crimes, industrial espionage, or terrorism). In that regard, cyber-security policy involves mainly institutional arrangements, preventive measures, and law enforcement efforts designed to protect the integrity of the Internet industry and to deal with abusive content and criminal activities on the Internet. Apart from the widely shared understanding of cyber-security, the Chinese party-state has further added political and ideological dimensions into the official understanding of cyber security. Following the Leninist–Maoist principles of rule, Beijing has insisted that cyber-security entails the protection of regime security from hostile political challenges, and the protection of ideological security from ideational contestations on the Internet. Consequently, cyber-security in the Chinese context encompasses Internet infrastructure, online law enforcement, online censorship, and online propaganda, as the website of the Cyberspace Administration of China (CAC; the Chinese government's official watchdog on the Internet) clearly demonstrates.

Xi reaffirmed the political importance he had hitherto attached to digital propaganda on the Internet when he repeatedly ordered propaganda cadres to improve the appeal of online propaganda materials, adapt to the patterns of Internet communication, and spread positive stories about government performance online (Xinhua, 2014a). Xi envisioned the Leading Group to be a unified, joint command structure with him sitting at the top. Hence, the Leading Group was mandated to coordinate the making of macro-level policy planning, long-term development strategies for the telecommunications industry, and short-term policy solutions for the digital industry and online propaganda (Xinhua, 2014a).

Beginning in April 2014, the Xi Jinping administration shifted the focus of online media control from 'social management' (that is, online censorship) to 'cultural innovation' (that is, online propaganda and thought work). On 15 April 2014, the CCP Central Propaganda Minister, Liu Qibao, published a long policy essay in the *People's Daily*. Entitled 'Accelerate the integrative development of traditional media and new media', the policy statement unveiled the party's management strategy targeting social media. Liu argued that while autonomous opinion leaders and active users exercised agenda-setting and issue-framing powers on social media, propaganda functions of conventional Party media – shaping and guiding public opinion – had consequently fallen by the wayside. Liu insisted that to avoid an existential crisis, it was critical that the conventional Party media regained vitality and influence by adopting bold reforms in their communication models.

Structural reforms of party media became an essential task for the protection of ideological security and regime security on the Chinese Internet. Liu's policy prescription for the conventional Party media was what he termed 'media convergence', which means that print and broadcast media controlled by the party-state were encouraged to cross over to online platforms, executing propaganda operations on various social media platforms, including Weibo, WeChat, and mobile apps (Liu, 2014). Here the Chinese party-state's notion of 'media convergence' refers to the mass influence strategy envisioned and employed by propaganda organs that synchronise pro-regime media content across various communication platforms, in order to maximise the exposure and susceptibility of targeted audiences to propaganda materials. Liu urged conventional Party media to quickly adapt to business models of Web-based media market, such as the interactive nature of online communication (rather than one-way delivery of media content and passive reception by audiences), diversified demands of media content, and the popular penchant for breaking news (Liu, 2014). Also, Liu Qibao instructed party media organs to reconceptualise and reorient their online operations. They were requested to develop online marketing strategies, strengthen online advertising capabilities, and enhance the appeal of their online cultural content. More pointedly, Liu directed party media organs to study and take advantage of social media platforms. He ordered party media directors to activate official accounts (OAs) on the Sina Weibo and the Tencent WeChat (Liu, 2014).

Administrators and editors running these regime-affiliated OAs were expected to enhance cultural influence and social impact of propaganda work by maximising the volume of subscription and viewership. Accordingly, Liu further revealed that the Party media's social network accounts had to showcase stimulating content: breaking news reports, short sentimental stories, authoritative commentaries, lively narrative styles, and a positive (that is, pro-regime and upbeat) tone (Liu, 2014). In particular, Liu pointed out that party media's news stories had to be redesigned to meet diverse popular demands on social media platforms (Liu, 2014).

On 18 August 2014, the CCP central leadership adopted the Guiding Opinion on Advancing the Convergent Development of Conventional Media and New Media (hereafter: the 2014 Guiding Opinion declaring to push forward the 'convergent development' of legacy media and new media, applying advanced techniques of mass communication, and providing mass-appeal content for the online news market (Xinhua, 2014c). The 2014 Guiding Opinion not only set in motion the regime-initiated synchronisation of mass influence operations across multiple media platforms, but the document also declared the construction of a couple of competitive, authoritative, politically trustworthy, and socially influential media enterprises that are to dominate the social media market, unreservedly carrying out the mouthpiece functions for the party-state on the Chinese Internet domain (Xinhua, 2014c).

Bureaucratic overhauls and regulatory build-ups soon followed to convert Xi's cyber propaganda strategy into incentive policy plans. The first step was to streamline the meandering cyberspace affairs system (Han, 2018: 150). In less than three weeks after Xi's August 2014 remarks, on 26 August the State Council issued Notice No. 33 about Internet management reform. The notice revealed that the SIIO had recently been reorganised (CAC, 2014b). Indeed, in April 2014 the SIIO was chosen to be the administrative office for the Central Leading Group for Cyber Security and Informatisation, shouldering the Leading Group's routine administrative and policy-drafting functions (Guanchazhe, 2014). Moreover, the State Council notice further unveiled that the SIIO was authorised to regulate the content of the Internet, and to oversee law enforcement operations in cyberspace.

Soon the SIIO adopted a new English title, that is, the Cyberspace Administration of China (CAC). The office secured a separate line of budget and personnel, and was uplifted to the ministerial level in the government hierarchy, which was parallel to the SCIO (Creemers, 2017: 94). An online media control system took shape, with the CLGCSI as the strategy-making and policy-coordinating body at the top, and the CAC as the central bureaucracy serving the dual functions of policy executor and supervisor in the field of Internet management.

CONSTRUCTING A REGULATORY ENVIRONMENT FACILITATING THE REGIME'S SYNCHRONISED MASS INFLUENCE STRATEGY

Following the announcement of the media convergence initiative, the upgraded CAC issued the ten-article Interim Regulations on the Development and Management of Public Information Services by Instant Messaging Tools (hereafter: the 2014 Interim Regulations) in August 2014. Chinese netizens soon realised that the 2014 Interim Regulations were designed to restrict activities on social media platforms. Article 6 lays down the administrative and legal basis of the 'real-name registration': users of online instant messaging services have to submit authentic information of personal identity to online services providers for identity verification (CAC, 2014c). The same article further obliges users of instant messaging services to sign a code-of-conduct agreement, which commits them to abiding by the 'seven bottom lines' (as outlined and promoted by Lu Wei, then SIIO Director, in August 2013).[2]

The 2014 Interim Regulations create a regulatory environment that is preferential for social media activities of party media, propaganda organs, and government agencies. Article 7 specifies that news media organisations and licensed online news portals may generate, circulate, or repost news stories of current affairs on social media platforms. The non-news media organisations which have obtained the government-issued accreditation for online news information services may also repost – but not generate – current affairs news stories on social media platforms. However, without prior approval from the CAC, all the other social media actors may not generate, circulate, or repost current affairs news on social media platforms (CAC, 2014c).

Article 7 goes so far as to encourage party organs, government agencies, public sector enterprises, and CCP-supervised civil associations to activate and run official accounts on social media platforms in order to amplify pro-regime narratives in cyberspace. Hence, the 2014 Interim Regulations were meant to create a market of online news services that unequivocally tilts toward party-state organisations, with formidable entry barriers curtailing social media engagement of private actors such as citizen journalists. By the end of 2014, the CAC planned that the number of WeChat official accounts created and operated by party-state organs would grow tenfold from 6000 to 60 000 (CAC, 2014d). The CAC further announced that it would build a comprehensive network of government-run social media sites by the end of 2015 (CAC, 2014e). Setting up social media accounts and filling them with regime-sanctioned content soon became a key indicator of performance for government agencies at all levels.

The digital propaganda campaign was carried out enthusiastically, along with unceasing and intensifying censorship operations that cracked down on social media opinion leaders posting offensive or illicit content. Synchronised online operations by propaganda and censorship departments crowded out independent and liberal voices, resulting in an increasingly 'sanitised' Chinese social media space. CCP media were emboldened to claim in December 2014 that the government had successfully reclaimed online discourse power and regained momentum in public opinion battles (Renminwang, 2014a). By the end of 2014, CCP media boasted that the Chinese Internet had taken a turn for the better, because the CAC had effectively clamped down on key opinion leaders' social influence, online public opinion had hence been 'cleared up gradually', and the 'mainstream values' (that is, 'positive energy') once again thrived on social media (Xinhua, 2014b; Renminwang, 2014b).

SCREENING AND POLICING SOCIAL MEDIA CONTENT

Throughout 2014, the Xi Jinping administration was busy with laying down policy guidelines and administrative regulations for the institutional framework of the media convergence initiative. However, in 2015–2016, Beijing shifted work priorities, directing more online regulatory efforts to the dimension of social management. In other words, in 2015 and 2016 the CAC pressed on with the unfinished business of formalising and enforcing its restrictive Internet policies. That the social management dimension reclaimed central attention came on the heels of, and may be attributed to, the Fourth Plenum Communique, which was adopted by the 18th CCP Central Committee on 23 October 2014. The Communique declared it would pursue a law-based model of governance in China. On 4 February 2015, the CAC released the Regulations on the Management of Internet User Account Names (hereafter: the Account Names Regulations), which reaffirm and formalise the requirement of real-name registration imposed on social media providers (CAC, 2015a). On 28 April 2015, the CAC further issued the Regulations on the Work of Interrogating Internet News Information Service Providers (hereafter: the Interrogation Regulations), which entrust the CAC and its sub-national departments with sweeping powers to monitor and discipline social networking providers (CAC, 2015b; Xiao, 2019).

On 3 July 2016, the CAC 2016 released the Notice on Further Strengthening the Management and Prevention of False News (hereafter: the False News Notice), which urges online news content platforms (mobile news applications, in particular) to further regularise news-gathering and editorial processes, and explicitly forbids news websites and news portals from reposting unverified news information from social media sites (CAC, 2016). Also, two sets of CAC Regulations went into effect in August 2016, namely the Regulations on the Management of Internet Information Search Services and the Regulations on the Management of Information Services by Mobile Internet Applications. These further obligated Internet service providers to collect, keep, and when necessary turn in personal data of online services users to law enforcement authorities.

AMPLIFYING DIGITAL PROPAGANDA

By the end of 2016, the Chinese government had constructed a sprawling regulatory framework for digital censorship that empowered the CAC to place the Chinese social media under a multilayered and increasingly sophisticated surveillance system (Creemers, 2017: 88). Beginning in 2017, regime attention once again shifted back to digital propaganda, which represented the dimension of cultural management in Xi Jinping's digital strategy. When jointly enforced, online censorship laws and digital propaganda regulations were expected to reinforce each other, turning the Chinese social media into a tightly regulated, closely watched public space that facilitated regime operations of mass persuasion and indoctrination.

One major approach of Beijing's digital propaganda is to co-opt and police online intermediaries (Miller, 2018a). 'Intermediaries' refers to individuals or entities that are business stakeholders of online media, such as Internet service providers (ISPs), Internet content providers (ICPs), news portal editors, online forum and chatroom administrators, and social media companies. On 2 May 2017, the new CAC Director, Xu Lin, announced the Regulations on the Management of Internet News Information Services (hereafter: the Internet News Regulations), which took effect on 1 June (CAC, 2017). Having been considered as the most stringent set of online news rules yet, the Internet News Regulations sweepingly define news information as any news reports and commentaries about current affairs involving politics, the national economy, military affairs, foreign relations, and social emergencies. Article 5 and Article 9 oblige every online news media entity to apply for a three-year permit for online news information services from the CAC (or its sub-national offices). Online news information services are defined as including news-producing services (the collection, processing, and circulation of news stories and commentaries) and news-reposting services. However, Article 6 further regulates that only legal persons registered in the PRC may apply for the CAC online news permit. Moreover, Article 6 states that responsible persons or editors-in-chief of online news media must be of PRC nationality.

Also, Article 6 and Article 27 further rule that only party-state media organisations and propaganda departments are eligible for a CAC-issued permit of online news-producing services. Apart from the CAC permit, online news media organisations are required to apply for an additional licence of telecommunications services from the Ministry of Industry and Information Technology (MIIT). While Article 7 of the Internet News Regulations prohibits any forms of foreign capital from entering the Chinese online news market, Article 8 further precludes non-state capital from investing in the business of online news-producing services. The statute literally turns the production of online news information into an exclusive business opportunity for the Party media. Moreover, Article 11 stipulates that journalists employed by online news media must be certified by the State Administration of Press, Publication, Radio, Film and Television (SAPPRFT) and therefore hold the SAPPRFT-issued press card.

In addition, Article 11 holds editors-in-chief of online news media accountable for the content of news information. Article 15 regulates that online news services providers may repost news information only from lawful and verifiable sources, that is, government-sponsored websites, government-validated news portals, or government-run social media accounts. In sum, the Internet News Regulations were tailor-made for the implementation of Xi Jinping's online propaganda strategy. The ordinances facilitate the domination of Party media in the online news market, meanwhile creating a prohibitive regulatory environment imperilling the development of citizen journalism and independent news media.

Table 9.1 *Major Internet content regulations issued in 2017 by the CAC*

Title	Date issued
Regulations on the Management of Internet News Information Services	2 May
Regulations on the Administrative Procedure of Law Enforcement in Internet Information Content Management	2 May
Enforcement Rules on the Management of Internet News Information Services Permits	22 May
Regulations on the Management of Internet Forum Community Services	25 August
Regulations on the Management of Internet Discussion Thread Services	25 August
Regulations on the Management of Internet Chat Group Information Services	7 September
Regulations on the Management of Internet User Official Account Information Services	7 September
Regulations on the Management of Content Administrators of Internet News Information Services Entities	30 October

The CAC and its provincial subordinates enforced the Internet News Regulations by accepting and reviewing applications for the permit of online news information services. By 31 December 2018, there were 761 news media (almost all of which are Party media entities) or government propaganda agencies that have been officially approved to provide online news information services. Together these privileged news organisations run 3765 online news information interfaces, including 743 news portals, 563 news information apps, 119 online news forums, and 2285 WeChat/Weibo subscription accounts (CAC, 2018). These certified online news outlets constitute an expanding List of Internet News Information Sources (the 'White List') (Xiangfa, 2019). All the other online media may cite or repost news stories and commentaries only from these certified news outlets. What this regulatory development entails is that these 761 media/propaganda organisations and their online news outlets are the only lawful sources of online news content. All the other uncertified – thus, politically untrustworthy – online news outlets (including the self-media) risk being arbitrarily labelled by law enforcement agencies as rumour mills, hence facing ominous prospects of administrative punishment or even criminal prosecution by state authorities.

In addition to screening online intermediaries for their political and professional qualifications, the other approach of digital propaganda that the CAC has employed is to hold an intermediary accountable for the content of postings on the social media platforms run by that intermediary. Beijing has delegated partial supervisory powers to the trusted intermediaries in an attempt to reduce the government's administrative burdens and law enforcement costs in cyberspace (Han, 2018; Miller, 2018a; Gallagher and Miller, 2019). Article 13 of the Internet News Regulations once again places the obligations of real-name registration and identity authentication on the providers of online news information services. Furthermore, what came along with the Internet News Regulations was a flurry of bylaws (listed in Table 9.1) that constitute an extensive legal framework for Xi Jinping's cultural management (propaganda and thought work) operations in cyberspace. These supplementary rules were designed to hold intermediaries liable for dissenting voices spreading via their social media services (Bloomberg, 2017; Reuters, 2017).

CONCLUSION: POLITICISATION OF CHINESE SOCIAL MEDIA MARKET

This *Handbook* begins from the premise that the time is ripe to revisit the matter of modern propaganda and how political actors conduct mass influence through strategic communications in the new communication space. In particular, we seek to address how social and digital media have diversified agents and channels of political propaganda for effective mass influence. New information and communications technologies have 'democratised' the production and distribution of propaganda materials. The activities of Cambridge Analytica have demonstrated how the private sector has gained access and acquired capabilities to manipulate public discourse and information for desired political ends. At the same time, however, governments still employ propaganda as an instrument of statecraft and social control. The Chinese case, as detailed in this chapter, exemplifies the persistent relevancy of state actors in contemporary propaganda.

This chapter has reviewed how the Chinese party-state in the Xi era has conceptualised, constructed, and implemented his digital propaganda strategy for media control and mass influence. I first traced initial acts of online censorship and offline repression in 2013 that effectively intimidated Chinese netizens. I then reviewed the key components of Xi Jinping's digital propaganda strategy and the corresponding policy initiative of 'media convergence'. I further discussed the creation of a bureaucratic system and regulatory framework that came along as the institutional groundwork for implementing Xi Jinping's media convergence initiative. Sweeping powers were granted to a centralised and unified cyberspace affairs system to integrate, coordinate, and execute the party-state's online censorship and propaganda operations. Stringent online news market regulations (for example, 'real-name' registration, the prohibitive licence approval requirements) and draconian stipulations of political responsibility (targeting business intermediaries of online news services and social networking services) were imposed to screen and police social media activities. Consequently, a disproportionately favourable opportunity structure was created for party-state authorities (mainly the Party press and propaganda organs) and their commercial collaborators to dominate the Chinese social media, thereby maximising the impact of mass influence and shaping online public opinion.

Xi Jinping's administration has neither sought to dismantle the Chinese online media market nor undertaken to derail the process of media marketisation. Rather, it has sought the permeation and domination of pro-regime narratives in the Chinese online news market (including the online news services market and social networking market). The central leadership was intent on learning and eventually mastering, rather than discrediting, the market logic of competition. However, attaining viewership and social influence in China's competitive online media market required party media organs to adapt to marketised business models; that is, catering their cultural products and communication styles to popular preferences. In other words, party media organs have had to go through a learning process of marketisation before they may regain social trust and ideological influence. By nurturing party media organs into ostensibly trustworthy outlets of online information, the Xi administration may politicise the Chinese social media, crowding out autonomous, critical, and dissenting voices. The 'mainstreaming' of pro-regime content in the Chinese social media – the politicisation of the Chinese social media market – was believed to hinge mainly on the marketisation of regime propaganda organs.

NOTES

1. For arguments sceptical of the liberalising effect of Chinese social media, see Leibold (2011), Bondes and Schucher (2014), Zhou (2015), and Galler (2015).
2. In August 2013, the SIIO convened a high-profile Internet forum wherein Lu Wei, then SIIO Director, exhorted online opinion leaders and social media celebrities to be aware of their social responsibility and to keep the 'seven bottom lines' (*qitiao dixian*), which referred to: (1) the law and government regulations; (2) the socialist institution; (3) the national interest; (4) lawful rights and interests of citizens; (5) public order of society; (6) the moral and ethical codes; and (7) the truthfulness of online information (Renminwang, 2013a). A propaganda campaign soon followed that promoted and enforced the 'seven bottom lines' movement and paved the way for the online censorship operations targeting autonomous online opinion leaders (Renminwang, 2013b).

REFERENCES

Bellin, Eva (2012), 'Reconsidering the Robustness of Authoritarianism in the Middle East: Lessons from the Arab Spring', *Comparative Politics*, 44(2): 127–149.
Blank, Grant and Bianca C. Reisdorf (2012), 'The Participatory Web', *Information, Communication and Society*, 15(4): 537–554.
Bloomberg (2017), 'WeChat Users Censoring Content Amid China Crackdown on Social Media', 12 September, available at www.scmp.com/news/china/policies-politics/article/2110806/wechat-users-censoring-content-amid-china-crackdown, accessed 20 September 2019.
Bondes, Maria and Günter Schucher (2014), 'Derailed Emotion: The Transformative of Claims and Targets during the Wenzhou Online Incident', *Information, Communication and Society*, 17(1): 45–65.
Cheung, Anne S.Y. (2016), 'Microbloggers' Battle for Legal Justice in China', in Jacques deLisle, Avery Goldstein, and Guobin Yang (eds), *The Internet, Social Media and a Changing China*, Philadelphia, PA: University of Pennsylvania Press, pp. 129–149.
China Internet Network Information Center (CNNIC) (2018), 'Di 42 ci Zhongguo hulian wangluo fazhan zhuangkuang tongji baogao' ('The 42nd China Statistical Report on Internet Development'), July 2018, available at www.cac.gov.cn/sjfw/hysj/A091601index_1.htm, accessed 30 September 2019.
Creemers, Rogier (2016), 'The Privilege of Speech and New Media: Conceptualizing China's Communications Law in the Internet Age', in Jacques deLisle, Avery Goldstein, and Guobin Yang (eds.), *The Internet, Social Media and a Changing China*, Philadelphia, PA: University of Pennsylvania Press, pp. 86–105.
Creemers, Rogier (2017), 'Cyber China: Upgrading Propaganda, Public Opinion Work and Social management for the Twenty-First China', *Journal of Contemporary China*, 26(103): 85–100.
Cyberspace Administration of China (CAC) (2014a), 'Xi Jinping zai quanguo xuanchuan sixiang gongzuo huiyi shang de jianghua' ('Xi Jinping's speech at the National Conference on Propaganda and Ideological Work'), 9 August, available at www.cac.gov.cn/2014-08/09/c_1115324460.htm, accessed 30 September 2019.
Cyberspace Administration of China (CAC) (2014b), 'Guowuyuan guanyu shouquan guojia hulianwang xinxi bangongshi fuze hulianwang xinxi neirong guanli gongzuo de tongzhi' ('Notice of State Council on authorizing SIIO to be responsible for Internet information content management'), 28 August, available at www.cac.gov.cn/2014-08/28/c_1112264158.htm, accessed 30 September 2019.
Cyberspace Administration of China (CAC) (2014c), 'Jishi tongxin gongju gongzhong xinxi fuwu fazhan guanli zhanxing guiding' ('Interim Provisions on the Development Management of Public Information Services for Instant Messaging Tools'), 7 August, available at www.cac.gov.cn/2014-08/07/c_1111983456.htm, accessed 30 September 2019.
Cyberspace Administration of China (CAC) (2014d), 'Guojia wangxinban: xiaban nian quanmian tuidong zhengwu weixin gonggong zhanghao sheli' ('SIIO ready to promote the activation of government WeChat accounts in the second half of the year'), 9 August, available at www.cac.gov.cn/2014-08/09/c_1112015682.htm, accessed 30 September 2019.

Cyberspace Administration of China (CAC) (2014e), 'Guojia wangxinban: dali tuidong jishi tongxin gongju zhengwu gongzhong zhanghao fazhan' ('SIIO to vigorously promote the development of government public accounts of instant communication tools'), 11 September, available at www.cac.gov.cn/2014-09/11/c_1112433310.htm, accessed 30 September 2019.

Cyberspace Administration of China (CAC) (2015a), 'Hulianwang yonghu zhanghao mingcheng guanli guiding' ('Regulations on the Management of Internet User Account Names'), promulgated on 4 February, available at www.cac.gov.cn/2015-02/04/c_1114246561.htm, accessed 30 September 2019.

Cyberspace Administration of China (CAC) (2015b), 'Hulianwang xinwen xinxi fuwu danwei yuetan gongzuo guiding' ('Regulations on the Work of Interrogating Internet News Information Services Providers'), promulgated on 28 April, available at www.cac.gov.cn/2015-04/28/c_1115112600.htm, accessed 30 September 2019.

Cyberspace Administration of China (CAC) (2016), 'Guojia wangxinban jiada lidu zhengzhi wangluo xujia xinwen' ('Cyberspace Administration of China steps up efforts to deal with online false news'), 3 July, available at http://www.cac.gov.cn/2016-07/03/c_1119155494.htm, accessed 30 September 2019.

Cyberspace Administration of China (CAC) (2017), 'Hulianwang xinwen xinxi fuwu guanli guiding' ('Regulations on the Management of Internet News Information Services'), promulgated on 2 May, available at www.cac.gov.cn/2017-05/02/c_1120902760.htm, accessed 30 September 2019.

Cyberspace Administration of China (CAC) (2018), 'Hulianwang xinwen xinxi fuwu danwei xuke xinxi' ('Information concerning organizations holding the Internet news information services permit'), 11 January, available at www.cac.gov.cn/2019-01/11/c_1122842142.htm, accessed 30 September 2019.

Deluca, Kevin Michael, Elizabeth Brunner, and Ye Sun (2016), 'Weibo, WeChat, and the Transformative Events of Environmental Activism on China's Wild Public Screens', *International Journal of Communication*, 10: 321–339.

Diamond, Larry (2012), 'Liberation Technology', in Larry Diamond and Marc F. Plattner (eds), *Liberation Technology: Social Media and the Struggle for Democracy*, Baltimore, MD: Johns Hopkins University Press, pp. 3–17.

Esarey, Ashley and Xiao, Qiang (2008), 'Political Expression in the Chinese Blogosphere: Below the Radar', *Asian Survey*, 48(5): 752–772.

Flew, Terry (2016), 'Entertainment Media, Cultural Power, and Post-Globalization: The Case of China's International Media Expansion and the Discourse of Soft Power', *Global Media and China*, 1(4): 278–294.

Gallagher, Mary E. and Blake Miller (2019), 'Who Not What: The Logic of China's Information Control Strategy', available at http://blakeapm.com, accessed 30 September 2019.

Galler, Samuel (2015), 'The Unintended Consequences of Deliberative Discourse: A Democratic Attempt of HIV NGOs in China', in Wenhong Chen and Stephen D. Reese (eds), *Networked China: Global Dynamics of Digital Media and Civic Engagement*, London: Routledge, pp. 136–152.

Gries, Peter, Derek Steiger, and Wang Tao (2016), 'Social Media, Nationalist Protests, and China's Japan Policy: the Diaoyu Islands Controversy, 2012–3', in Jacques deLisle, Avery Goldstein, and Guobin Yang (eds), *The Internet, Social Media and a Changing China*, Philadelphia, PA: University of Pennsylvania Press, pp. 161–179.

Guanchazhe (2014), 'Guojia wangxinban zhongzu guowu yuan shouquan qi fuze hulianwang neirong guanli zhifa' ('SIIO reorganized as State Council authorized it to be responsible for Internet content management enforcement'), 28 August, available at www.guancha.cn/politics/2014_08_28_261572.shtml, accessed 30 September 2019.

Han, Rongbin (2015a), 'Manufacturing Consent in Cyberspace: China's "Fifty-Cent Army"', *Journal of Current Chinese Affairs*, 44(2): 105–134.

Han, Rongbin (2015b), 'Defending the Authoritarian Regime Online: China's "Voluntary Fifty-Cent Army"', *China Quarterly*, 224: 1006–1025.

Han, Rongbin (2018), *Contesting Cyberspace in China: Online Expression and Authoritarian Resilience*, New York: Columbia University Press.

Harwit, Eric (2008), *China's Telecommunications Revolution*, Oxford: Oxford University Press.

Hassanpour, Navid (2014), 'Media Disruption and Revolutionary Unrest: Evidence from Mubarak's Quasi-Experiment', *Political Communication*, 31(1): 1–24.

Herold, David K. (2011), 'Introduction: Noise, Spectacle, Politics: Carnival in Chinese Cyberspace', in David K. Herold and Peter Marolt (eds), *Online Society in China: Creating, Celebrating, and Instrumentalising the Online Carnival*, London: Routledge, pp. 1–19.

Huang, Ronggui and Sun, Xiaoyi (2014), 'Weibo Network, Information Diffusion and Implications for Collective Action in China', *Information, Communication and Society*, 17(1): 86–104.

King, Gary, Jennifer Pan, and Margaret E. Roberts (2014), 'Reverse-Engineering Censorship in China: Randomized Experimentation and Participant Observation', *Science*, 345(6199): 1–10.

King, Gary, Jennifer Pan and Margaret E. Roberts (2017), 'How the Chinese Government Fabricates Social Media Posts for Strategic Distraction, not Engaged Argument', *American Political Science Review*, 111(3): 484–501.

Lei, Ya-wen (2011), 'The Political Consequences of the Rise of the Internet: Political Beliefs and Practices of Chinese Netizens', *Political Communication*, 28(3): 291–322.

Leibold, James (2011), 'Blogging Alone: China, the Internet, and the Democratic Illusion?', *Journal of Asian Studies*, 70(4): 1023–1041.

Lindsay, Jon R. (2015), 'Introduction – China and Cybersecurity: Controversy and Context', in Jon R. Lindsay, Tai Ming Cheung, and Derek S. Reveron (eds), *China and Cybersecurity: Espionage, Strategy and Politics in the Digital Domain*, Oxford: Oxford University Press, pp. 1–26.

Liu, Qibao (2014), 'Jiakuai tuidong chuantong meiti he xinxing meiti ronghe fazhan' ('Accelerate the integrative development of traditional media and new media'), *Renmin Ribao* (*People's Daily*), 15 April, available at http://politics.people.com.cn/n/2014/0423/c1001-24930310.html, accessed 30 September 2019.

Lu, Wei (2013), 'Ba wang shang yulun gongzuo zuo wei xuanchuan sixiang gongzuo de zhong zhong zhi zhong' ('Taking online public opinion work as the top priority of propaganda and ideological work'), 17 September, *Renmin Ribao* (*People's Daily*), p. 16.

Ma, Yiben (2015), 'Online Chinese Nationalism and Its Nationalist Discourses', in Gary D. Rawnsley and Ming-yeh T. Rawnsley (eds), *Routledge Handbook of Chinese Media*, London: Routledge, pp. 203–216.

MacKinnon, Rebecca (2008), 'Flatter World and Thicker Walls? Blogs, Censorship and Civic Discourse in China', *Public Choice*, 134(1–2): 31–46.

MacKinnon, Rebecca (2009), 'China's Censorship 2.0: How Companies Censor Bloggers', *First Monday*, 14(2), available at https://firstmonday.org/article/view/2378/2089, accessed 30 September 2019.

MacKinnon, Rebecca (2012), *Consent of the Networked: The Worldwide Struggle for Internet Freedom*, New York: Basic Books.

Meng, Bingchun (2010), 'Moving Beyond Democratization: A Thought Piece on the China Internet Research Agenda,' *International Journal of Communication*, 4: 501–508.

Miller, Blake (2018a), 'The Limits of Commercialized Censorship in China', available at http://blakeapm.com, accessed 30 September 2019.

Miller, Blake (2018b), 'Automated Detection of Chinese Government Astroturfers Using Network and Social Metadata', available at http://blakeapm.com accessed, 30 September 2019.

Mo, Zhixu (2014a), 'Guojia juyuwang de jianglin' ('A national Intranet has descended'), 18 June, available at hk.on.cc/cn/bkn/cnt/commentary/20140618/bkncn-20140618000317342-0618_05411_001_cn.html, accessed 30 September 2019.

Mo, Zhixu (2014b), 'Zhongguo wangluo ziyou de xianzhuang yu weilai' ('The current state and prospects of Internet freedom in China'), *Deutsche Welle*, available at www.dw.com/zh/中国网络自由的现状与未来/a-17407726, accessed 30 September 2019.

Morozov, Evgeny (2011), *The Net Delusion: The Dark Side of Internet Freedom*, New York: Public Affairs.

Negro, Gianluigi (2017), *The Internet in China: From Infrastructure to a Nascent Civil Society*, London: Palgrave Macmillan.

Niekerk, Brett Van, Kiru Pillay, and Manoj Maharaj (2011), 'Analyzing the Role of ICTs in the Tunisian and Egyptian Unrest from an Information Warfare Perspective', *International Journal of Communication*, 5: 1406–1416.

Pan, Jennifer (2017), 'How Market Dynamics of Domestic and Foreign Social Media Firms Shape Strategies of Internet Censorship', *Problems of Post-Communism*, 64(3–4): 167–188.

PEN America (2018), *Forbidden Feeds: Government Controls on Social Media in China*, available at pen.org/research-resources/forbidden-feeds/, accessed 30 September 2019.
People's Daily (2013), 'Gonggu zhuangda zhuliusi xiang yulun de kexue zhinan' ('A scientific guide to consolidate and strengthen the mainstream of public opinion'), 30 August, available at http://theory.people.com.cn/n/2013/0830/c40531-22744657.html, accessed 30 September 2013.
Renminwang (2013a), '*Renmin ribao*: Zhongguo hulianwang dahui changyi gongsho "qitiao dixian"' ('*People's Daily*: China Internet Conference urged the observance of "seven bottom lines"'), 16 August 2013, available at http://opinion.people.com.cn/n/2013/0816/c368024-22588798.html, accessed 24 November 2019.
Renminwang (2013b), 'Gongsho "qitiao dixian" zhuzao jiankang wangluo huanjing' ('Keeping the "seven bottom lines", creating a healthy online environment'), August–September, available at http://opinion.people.com.cn/GB/8213/368023/368412/index.html, accessed 24 November 2019.
Renminwang (2014a), '2014 niandu yuqing baogao: zhengfu zhuoli huajie hulianwang xinxing shehui fengxian' ('2014 annual public opinion report: government is working to resolve the new social risks on the Internet'), 31 December, available at http://yuqing.people.com.cn/n/2014/1231/c354318-26305896.html, accessed 30 September 2019.
Renminwang (2014b), 'Renminwang fabu 2014 nian Zhongguo hulianwang yuqing fenxi baogao' ('People's Net released the 2014 China Internet public opinion analysis report'), available at http://yuqing.people.com.cn/GB/392071/392072/index.html, accessed 30 September 2019.
Reuters (2017), 'China tightens control of chat groups ahead of Party Congress', 7 September, available at www.reuters.com/article/us-china-internet/china-tightens-control-of-chat-groups-ahead-of-party-congress-idUSKCN1BI1PC, accessed 20 September 2019.
Roberts, Margaret E. (2018), *Censored: Distraction and Diversion Inside China's Great Firewall*, Princeton, NJ: Princeton University Press.
Shen, Fei (2015), 'Campaigning on Weibo: Independent Candidates' Use of Social Media in Local People's Congress Elections in China', in Wenhong Chen and Stephen D. Reese (eds), *Networked China: Global Dynamics of Digital Media and Civic Engagement*, London: Routledge, pp. 114–135.
Shi, Zengzhi and Yang Guobin (2016), 'New Media Empowerment and State-Society Relations in China', in Jacques deLisle, Avery Goldstein, and Guobin Yang (eds), *The Internet, Social Media and a Changing China*, Philadelphia, PA: University of Pennsylvania Press, pp. 71–85.
Svensson, Marina (2015), 'Voice, Power and Connectivity in China's Microblogsphere: Digital Divide on Sina Weibo', in Guobin Yang (ed.), *China's Contested Internet*, Copenhagen: NIAS Press, pp. 227–256.
Svensson, Marina (2016), 'Connectivity, Engagement, and Witnessing on China's Weibo', in Jacques deLisle, Avery Goldstein, and Guobin Yang (eds), *The Internet, Social Media and a Changing China*, Philadelphia, PA: University of Pennsylvania Press, pp. 49–70.
Tsai, Wen-Hsuen (2016), 'How "Networked Authoritarianism" was Operationalized in China: Methods and Procedures of Public Opinion Control', *Journal of Contemporary China*, 25(101): 731–744.
Wang, Rong (2015), 'Engaging Government for Environmental Collective Action: Political Implications of ICTs in Rural China', in Wenhong Chen and Stephen D. Reese (eds), *Networked China: Global Dynamics of Digital Media and Civic Engagement*, London: Routledge, pp. 78–96.
Weber, Rolf H. (2011), 'Politics Through Social Networks and Politics by Government Blocking: Do We Need New Rules?', *International Journal of Communication*, 5: 1186–1194.
Wilson, Christopher and Alexandra Dunn (2011), 'Digital Media in the Egyptian Revolution: Descriptive Analysis from the Tahrir Data Set', *International Journal of Communication*, 5: 1248–1272.
Wright, Joss (2014), 'Regional Variation in Chinese Internet Filtering', *Information, Communication and Society*, 17(1): 121–141.
Xiangfa (2019), 'Mei jin "Baimingdan" zhe, xiuxiang renxing fabu hulianwang xinwen' ('Don't even think about releasing Internet news information without being included in the "White List"'), available at http://zhuanlan.zhihu.com/p/33521762, accessed 30 September 2019.
Xiao, Qiang (2011), 'The Battle for the Chinese Internet', *Journal of Democracy*, 22(2): 204–205.
Xiao, Qiang (2012), 'The Battle for the Chinese Internet', in Larry Diamond and Marc F. Plattner (eds), *Liberation Technology: Social Media and the Struggle for Democracy*, Baltimore, MD: Johns Hopkins University Press, pp. 63–77.
Xiao, Qiang (2019), 'President Xi's Surveillance State', *Journal of Democracy*, 30(1): 53–67.

Xinhua News Agency (Xinhua) (2013a), 'Zhonggong zhongyang guan yu quanmian shenhua gaige ruo gan zhongda wenti de jueding' ('Decision of the CCP Central Committee on several major issues concerning comprehensively deepening reform'), 15 November, available at www.gov.cn/jrzg/2013-11/15/content_2528179.htm, accessed 30 September 2019.

Xinhua News Agency (Xinhua) (2013b), 'Xi jinping: guanyu "Zhonggong zhongyang guan yu quanmian shenhua gaige ruo gan zhongda wenti de jueding" de shuoming' ('Xi Jinping: An explanation on "Decision of the CCP Central Committee on several major issues concerning comprehensively deepening reform"'), 15 November, available at www.xinhuanet.com/politics/2013-11/15/c_118164294.htm, accessed 30 September 2019.

Xinhua News Agency (Xinhua) (2014a), 'Xi Jinping zhuchi zhaokai zhongyang wangluo anquan he xinxihua lingdao xiaozu di yi ci huiyi' ('Xi Jinping presided over the first meeting of the Central Leading Group for Cyber Security and Informatization'), 27 February, available at http://cpc.people.com.cn/n/2014/0227/c64094-24486402.html, accessed 30 September 2019.

Xinhua News Agency (Xinhua) (2014b), 'Guan min heli gongqiu qinglang wangluo kongjian – 2013 nian 8 yue yilai wangluo zhili yuqing zongshu' ('Government and the people work together to seek a clean cyberspace – a review of Internet public opinion governance since August 2013'), 30 December, available at www.cac.gov.cn/2014-12/30/c_1113832880.htm, accessed 30 September 2019.

Xinhua News Agency (Xinhua) (2014c), 'Tuidong zhuliu meiti zai ronghe fazhan zhi lu shang zou wen zou kuai zou hao' ('Pushing forward the mainstream media to going steady on the road of integrative development'), 21 August, available at http://theory.people.com.cn/n/2014/0821/c49157-25512077.html, accessed 30 September 2019.

Xu, Jinyao and Chunyu Hua (2013), 'Xi Jinping: Yishi xingtai gongzuo shi dang de yi xiang jiduan zhongyao de gongzuo' ('Xi Jinping: Ideological work matters supremely to the Party'), *Renminwang (People's Net)*, 20 August, available at http://politics.people.com.cn/n/2013/0820/c1024-22634056.html, accessed 30 September 2019.

Yang, Yunkang (2016), 'How Large-Scale Protests Succeed in China: The Story of Issue Opportunity Structure, Social Media, and Violence', *International Journal of Communication*, 10: 2895–2914.

Zhou, Baohua (2015), 'Internet Use, Socio-Geographic Context, and Citizenship Engagement: A Multilevel Model on the Democratizing Effects of the Internet in China', in Wenhong Chen and Stephen D. Reese (eds), *Networked China: Global Dynamics of Digital Media and Civic Engagement*, London: Routledge, pp. 19–36.

10. Constructing its own reality: the CCP's agenda for the Hong Kong anti-extradition bill movement

Luwei Rose Luqiu

INTRODUCTION

The Chinese Communist Party (CCP) has waged an information war in opposition to protests in Hong Kong against a bill, proposed in February 2019, that would facilitate the extradition of citizens to the mainland. Thus, the party's propaganda outlets worked to discredit the protests by characterising them as violent and a product of foreign intervention. The propaganda effort in China worked to limit the anti-government movement's influence and potential to spread to the mainland. When the protests against the extradition bill began, Chinese state media outlets at first ignored them, reporting only the government's official response to domestic audiences. However, as the conflict continued to intensify in mid-August 2019, authorities abandoned the passive approach and adopted a decidedly proactive one.

The mainland state and provincial media outlets organised by the Publicity Department of the Central Committee of the Communist Party of China (CCPPD) have long created and disseminated one-sided and even fictitious stories through the selective release of information. The CCPPD has also deployed sensationalist nationalist rhetoric that in some ways recalls the Maoist language of class struggle used during the Cultural Revolution as a means to dehumanise protesters and opposition figures and depict them as enemies of the state. In order to explore the kinds of messages that have been crafted for domestic audiences and how they are framed, two official state media accounts on Weibo – the Chinese equivalent of Twitter – are analysed here: those of the *People's Daily* and of Chinese Central Television (CCTV). Agenda-building theory serves as the theoretical framework for this analysis.

THE CCP'S ATTEMPTS AT AGENDA BUILDING

Agenda building is an extension of agenda-setting theory that posits reciprocity between the media and other sources in building the public and policy agenda (Cobb and Elder, 1972). Indeed, the study of agenda setting has often focused on the relationship between the media and the public (McCombs and Shaw, 1972; McCombs et al., 1981). These outside forces may include political leaders, governments, foreign countries, and corporations (Kiousis et al., 2007; Lancendorfer and Lee, 2010; Manheim and Albritton, 1984; Zhang and Cameron, 2003). Generally speaking, agenda-building research has focused on interactions among policymakers, the mass media, and the mass public (Denham, 2010). The focus of this study is on issues and attributes that are particularly salient to the CCP's efforts to influence domestic Chinese audiences by using social media as part of its propaganda efforts.

The CCP uses its complete control of media coverage to highlight certain issues, and propagandist rhetoric has been used to rationalise the centrality of the party-state (Song and Chang, 2012). The political and ideological nature of this propaganda system is manifested in its agenda and content, and in projects that support the regime (Brady, 2009). Following the government's crushing of the Tiananmen Square students' movement in 1989, collectivism and socialism have been reinterpreted in a manner that is both consistent with China's economic reform policies and explicitly patriotic (Zhao, 2004). Since the mid-1990s, the CCP has preferred a strategy of macro-managing the production of media content, except in times of crisis, when it focuses more on the setting of norms. The CCP controls news media content through government-arranged press release and pre-editorial examination. Thus the party has learned that one effective approach to controlling information flow is to build a news agenda expressed in an authorised political terminology (Schoenhals, 1992).

The Chinese state began marketising the country's news media in the 1980s, thereby diversifying the media environment (Stockmann and Gallagher, 2011). While there was no fundamental change in the communist political system, market forces and journalists were able to transform the internal tension in Chinese news outlets into a means to alter journalistic practices, thus creating the unique dynamic of the present party press system (Pan, 2000). At the same time, this transformation eroded Mao's model of propaganda with a conceptual shift from the highly politicised term 'masses' to the less politicised 'audiences' (Yong, 2000). However, through the court system and labour market the CCP not only maintained but also strengthened its control over information during the marketisation of Chinese media outlets (Lin, 2012). Since coming to power in 2012, President Xi Jinping has consistently stressed the importance of propaganda and ideological work and has revived Maoist rhetoric, while the CCP has made use of both overt and covert mechanisms to control the media, including the limitation of opportunities for reporting and the taming of critical and investigative journalism (Tong, 2019).

Cobb and Elder (1971) described the agenda-building process in terms of three steps, namely issue creation, issue expansion, and agenda entrance. For them, agenda building concerns 'how issues are created and why some controversies or incipient issues come to command the attention and concern of decision makers, while others fail' (Cobb and Elder, 1971: 905). Successful agenda building, according to the six-step model of Lang and Lang (1983), involves both highlighting certain issues in media coverage so that audiences perceive their relevance, and framing their general sense and core meanings. From this perspective, effective media stories use language that affects audiences' interpretations and, for the purpose of issue expansion, involve well-known individuals and link issues of concern to secondary symbols, symbols within the symbols, to bear upon the underlying pattern of experience. This chapter demonstrates the agenda building process and model applied by the CCP by examining the 2019 Hong Kong protests.

METHOD AND DATASET

Data for this study included Weibo posts gathered from the official accounts of CCTV News and the *People's Daily* from 1 June 2019 to 10 October 2019 (N = 1195). The first large-scale anti-extradition bill protests occurred on 9 June, and on 4 October the government of the Hong Kong Special Administrative Region (HKSAR) invoked the Emergency Regulations

Ordinance to implement an anti-mask law. CCTV and the *People's Daily* are directly under CCPPD control and they channel the propaganda strategies of the CCP in part through the use of hashtags on social media (Shambaugh, 2017). The sample included all of the posts related to the anti-extradition bill movement in Hong Kong, whether in the form of news reports, opinion pieces, editorials, or online initiatives. The posts were contextualised through thematic analysis to reveal the CCP's propaganda strategies. Further, a grounded textual analysis of the posts also elucidated the party's representation of the anti-extradition bill movement to users of social media in mainland China.

FINDINGS: THREE STAGES OF AGENDA BUILDING

As Figure 10.1 shows, the development of the anti-government movement resolves naturally into three stages based on the number of posts on the two official accounts relating to the Hong Kong anti-extradition bill.

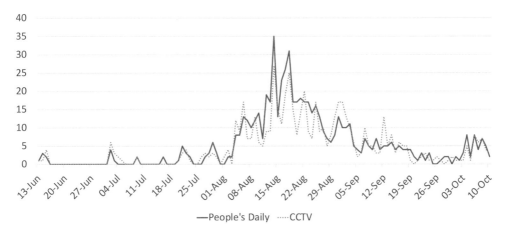

Figure 10.1   Posts on the Hong Kong anti-government movement by CCTV and the People's Daily, 1 June–10 October 2019 (N = 1195)

Stage 1: Passive Response to the Issue (13 June–3 August 2019)

The coverage of the protests by Chinese media began on 13 June when both CCTV and the *People's Daily* posted the full statement by Geng Shuang, the Chinese Foreign Ministry's spokesman, in a regular press conference:

> The Chief Executive and relevant officials of the HKSAR made statements on the latest situation, pointing out that what happened in Admiralty [part of the city's central business district] was not a peaceful assembly but an undisguised, organised riot. Any move that undermines Hong Kong's prosperity and stability is opposed by mainstream public opinion there. No civilised society ruled by law can tolerate behaviour that interrupts the peace and tranquillity, and defies the law. The central government of China strongly condemns all forms of violence and supports the HKSAR in handling them in accordance with the law. (FMPRC, 2019)

Although the protests continued, the coverage during this initial stage remained limited to official statements and reports issued at press conferences staged by the Chinese Foreign Ministry, the SAR government, the Liaison Office of the Central People's Government, and the Hong Kong and Macau Offices. On 21 July, a little over a month after its first post on the topic, the *People's Daily* published its first editorial in which it praised the 'Protect Hong Kong' demonstration organised the previous day by pro-Beijing lawmaker Junius Ho Kwan-yiu, just before that day's rally in Admiralty organised by the Civil Human Rights Front. The latter group had previously shown its ability to mobilise millions of protesters. The editorial, titled 'Fight against violence, cherish the rule of law' (*People's Daily*, 2019a), insisted that the rule of law is Hong Kong's core value. It asked: since dissidents are tempted to pursue their 'justice' by means of illegal violence, will Hong Kong become utterly lawless and experience no more days of peace? Hong Kong cannot remain in this chaotic state. In a harmonious family, there will be prosperity for all. In comparison with other such editorials, the tone of this one was moderate, more inclined to persuasion than to blame.

On the night of 21 July, protesters marched to Hong Kong's Beijing Liaison Office and defaced a national emblem of People's Republic of China, and riot police responded with tear gas and rubber bullets. At almost the same time, in Yuen Long, in the north of the city, a mob armed with batons attacked citizens in the metro station. In this case, police only appeared 39 minutes after the attack began, and the delayed response gave rise to accusations that the police officers were cooperating with local gangs (Regan et al., 2019). The following day, the *People's Daily* issued a second editorial on the movement, this time explicitly condemning the protesters for storming the Liaison Office, with the title 'It is absolutely intolerable to challenge the authority of the central government openly and undermine the principle of "one country, two systems"' (*People's Daily*, 2019b).

This editorial spoke of 'radical protesters' (*ji jin shi wei zhe*) and 'radicals' (*ji duan fen zi*). Compared with the previous editorial, then, the tone had shifted from cajoling to accusatory, with the demonstration now being characterised as an attempt to destroy the 'one country, two systems' arrangement.

Also on 22 July, CCTV reported for the first time on the anti-extradition bill during its flagship newscast *Xinwen Lianbo*, which airs simultaneously on all local TV stations in mainland China and is another key propaganda tool for the CCP (Zhang and Boukes, 2019). In this case, the issue was raised in a commentary in which the term 'troublemaker' (*luan gang fen zi*) was used for the first time by state media to describe the protesters.

In these cases, neither the *People's Daily* nor CCTV provided any details about the protests, such as their size or the protestors' demands. Rather, these opinion pieces condemned the violence witnessed at the Hong Kong demonstrations and represented it as a challenge to the central government. The overall number of relevant posts and their content suggest that, at this stage, the CCP still classified the movement as an internal matter for Hong Kong, and that its tactics for agenda building were very simple: to respond passively and minimise coverage. The clear message of these first three official responses, muted as they were, was a warning to the Hong Kong protesters, as well as the mainland public and SAR government, that the authority of the central government was not to be challenged.

Stage 2: Active Engagement with the Issue (4 August–4 September 2019)

The propaganda strategy changed dramatically after 4 August, when four protesters threw the national flag into Victoria Harbour and raised in its place the black flag of the Hong Kong SAR. It was at this point that the state media began active agenda building, as indicated by the fact that the number of posts increased significantly. Hong Kong was also discussed on *Xinwen Lianbo* again and, from 5 to 11 August, the *People's Daily* published a series of seven editorials commenting on the situation and communicating the CCP's view of the movement and how it should be dealt with. Again, the message was loud and clear: there would be no tolerance when it came to those who challenged the authority of Beijing.

The news reporting during this second stage continued to reinforce the official narrative: the scale of protests is small; the government has the situation under control; the root cause of the unrest is foreign interference; the solution to the problem is economic development. Thus, news reports focused on any violence associated with the demonstrations, while at the same time commentaries ascribed the violence to a very few radical extremists, 'a tiny minority'. On the one hand, these stories and editorials sent the signal that the movement was unpopular; on the other, they sought to divide the protesters.

Further, the party-run media framed the Hong Kong police as heroes in the pursuit of law and order, thereby hinting that Beijing wanted the Hong Kong government to arrest the protesters in order to prevent further demonstrations. This tightly controlled narrative constructed the protesters as a group of young people dissatisfied with reality, and who were being prompted and funded by foreign forces, especially the United States. Again, the message presented improving the economy as the solution to social unrest.

The CCP also demonstrated the ability to use agenda-building skills to transform seeming setbacks into patriotic lessons for its domestic audiences. Specifically, the party made use of well-known individuals, worked to make issues relevant to the audiences of its propaganda, employed emotive language, and linked key issues to secondary symbols: protests are tantamount to unpatriotic.

To begin with, on 4 August, CCTV and the *People's Daily* launched two online initiatives on Weibo with the hashtags #1.4billionNationalflagguards and #supportHongKongPolice. These posts condemned the protesters for defacing China's national flag, asserted that the Hong Kong police had been brutally attacked by protesters, and closed with a call for retweeting:

> Recently, in the violent clashes in Hong Kong, the Hong Kong police faced a serious attack by militia forces in which they received bites, broken fingers, and, in one case, a crushed skull as the result of a kick to the head. Their family members have also been bullied … They are under tremendous pressure, but they still observe their duty fearlessly and never back down! #Five-starred Red Flag has 1.4 billion national flag guards#; support HK police! Retweet!

Through sensational words and biased facts, this post sought to create the impression that the demonstrators were demanding Hong Kong's independence, and thus invoked rhetoric of national dignity and sovereignty that has long appealed to Chinese citizens' patriotism. The hashtag #1.4billionNationalflagguards appealed to a collective identity for these citizens, an identity from which the protesters were excluded as an out-group unwilling to accept what it means to be Chinese. This is the familiar narrative of the Chinese as the victims of a 'century of humiliation' in terms of which the CCP has justified its rule (Gries et al., 2011). The 'century of humiliation' refers to China's defeats in the First Opium Wars with the British, ending with the Qing government signing the 'unequal treaty'. This treaty conceded Hong Kong to British control, a 'humiliation' the Chinese have never forgotten (Schell and Delury, 2014). Stories of the violent mistreatment of mainlander protesters have also exacerbated the sense of grievance among domestic audiences by reinforcing the notion that the Hong Kong anti-government movement is fundamentally about a denial of Chinese identity.

The CCP has also enlisted celebrities in its initiatives to attract public awareness and international coverage. Thus, CCTV invited the world-renowned martial arts and movie star Jackie Chan to talk on air about what it meant to him to be Chinese, and to express the hope that peace would return to his native Hong Kong. In practical terms, Chan's appearance on the network was intended to convince mainland Chinese that most citizens of Hong Kong opposed the protests and supported the central government, and that doing so was a mark of their pride in their Chinese identity. The campaign also successfully mobilised mainland netizens to engage in a form of witch-hunting, as artists from Hong Kong who did not repost the flag guard post or express support for the police were targeted in online attacks and denounced as secessionists. Importantly, these attacks were not launched by government-organised trolls, but were rather the spontaneous actions of Chinese netizens.

The state media have also mobilised these ostensibly spontaneous actions among young Chinese in a display of the CCP's confidence in utilising nationalism. *Diba*, a long-running nationalist online forum, and the so-called 'fandom girls', a pro-government online community that engages in mass postings to boost the profiles and popularity of various celebrities, along with overseas students and rappers, have all taken their cause from the Internet into the streets by disrupting pro-Hong Kong rallies around the world. Thus it is not surprising that the appearances of representatives of both *Diba* and the fandom girls on *Xinwen Lianbo* to defend the CCP received a great deal of attention on other official media. In these media reports, the young pro-government activists were used as evidence in support of the proposition that the 'silence of the majority is a rejection of violence and an expression of the desire to guard Hong Kong through action'.

In 2016, the Chinese state media downplayed attacks by *Diba* on Tsai Ing-wen, the President of Taiwan, in an apparent effort to hold expressions of nationalism in check and avoid further damage to cross-strait relations (Zhang and Chen, 2019). In order to expand its social media audience among the young, who tend not to view *Xinwen Lianbo* or to consume television in general, CCTV started posting short videos of the sort that are popular on Chinese social media, featuring its well-known *Xinwen Lianbo* anchors using colloquial language and a casual approach to commentaries on various issues, including Hong Kong.

Although the central government does not seem to interfere directly or publicly in the domestic affairs of Hong Kong, state media have served to exert the party's cultural influence and social pressure. Private and public organisations have been called out in this forum, as well as individual business people and activists. Thus, for example, Cathay Pacific, an airline owned by the British multinational Swire Pacific, fired dozens of employees who had expressed support or sympathy for the movement, and two top managers resigned after being criticised by name by CCTV and the *People's Daily*. Also, Hong Kong's MTR rail system closed stations along protest routes for the first time after CCTV accused its officials of having 'arranged special trains for rioters to escape' (Branigan and Hale, 2019).

As Table 10.1 shows, state media have targeted various sectors of Hong Kong society, from business to education, with accusations of supporting protests and generally being insufficiently patriotic. Conversely, state media have also at the same time created positive role

Table 10.1 Targets of criticism by CCTV and the People's Daily, 1 June–10 October 2019

Sector	Target	Accusation
Private	Cathay Pacific	Employees participating in protests; media report of a pilot charged with rioting
	Journalists	Biased reporting, e.g., only showing police engaged in acts of brutality
	Hong Kong Journalist Association	Issuing press cards so that rioters can pass as journalists
	Taipan Bread and Cakes	Leading official and son of the founder of Hong Kong-based firm supporting protests
Public	Hospitals	Allowing employees to stage sit-ins at their places of work
	Expatriate judge	Foreign influence has compromised commitment to public interest and the rule of law after jailing of mainland tourist for defacing United States consulate
	MRT rail system	Conspiring with rioters by providing additional trains to help protesters leave protest sites
	General education	Causing students to act in radical ways
	Alvin Tai (liberal studies educator)	Posting controversial anti-police comments, promoting a political agenda in the classroom, and radicalising protesters
Politicians	Anson Chan, Martin Lee, Jimmy Lai, Albert Ho ('Gang of Four' leading pro-democracy figures)	Colluding with Western forces to instigate unrest and undermine Hong Kong
	Claudia Mo (pro-democratic Hong Kong legislator)	Inciting young people to protest while son lives in comfort in the United States
	Cheng Chung-tai, Jeremy Tam, Au Nok-hin (Hong Kong legislators arrested by police)	Supporting protests
Activists	Joshua Wong, Andy Chan, Nathan Law, Alex Chow (leader and other members of Umbrella movement)	Troublemakers destroying Hong Kong
	Agnes Chow (social activist arrested at home by police)	Supporting protests
	Denise Ho (pro-democracy singer and activist)	Fleeing Hong Kong for fear of military crackdown (in fact, Denise Ho attended a panel of the Antidote Festival hosted by Sydney Opera House in Australia)

models in the form of patriotic policemen and businessmen, who are controversial in Hong Kong. Such actions indicate that the CCP is unconcerned about mainstream public opinion in Hong Kong, but rather is targeting the city's elites and broader mainland audiences, in the expectation that they will communicate the party's messages through unofficial but nevertheless authoritative channels in order to mobilise these people.

In its attacks on perceived enemies of the state the CCP has deployed sensationalist and dehumanising nationalist rhetoric that in some ways recalls that of Mao's Cultural Revolution. An obvious example is the use of the phrase 'Gang of Four' to describe four high-profile individuals – a former senior official, two former Hong Kong lawmakers, and a local entrepreneur – whom the party accused of colluding with foreign governments and inciting young people to violence. The 'Gang of Four' was of course Mao's term for a group of senior party members, including his wife, who were charged with treason during the Cultural Revolution and were given lengthy prison sentences after Mao's death (Harding, 1980). Similarly loaded is the phrase 'a tiny minority' (*shaoshuren*), which has been frequently used to refer to protesters considered radical, and was used by Mao to describe 'non-people' or 'counter-revolutionary enemies' who were to be eliminated so that the class struggle could succeed (Marinelli, 2009).

The return of Maoist rhetoric is nothing new in the era of Xi Jinping. Already in 2013, during a speech at the National Propaganda and Ideology Work Conference, Xi had asserted that 'ideological work is an extremely important part of the party's work', and he told Chinese citizens, 'Dare to grasp, to wield, and to bare the sword; focus on uniting and working on behalf of the absolute majority; marshal public opinion in a rational, beneficial, and proper manner; help the cadres and the masses to draw clear boundaries between right and wrong and clarify fuzzy impressions' (Xinhua, 2013). In a 2018 speech, Xi used similarly hardline language: 'We must adhere to the truth and express it with clarity, firmly refuting falsehoods'; in the context of the 'public opinion struggle' he also praised highly the propaganda and ideological efforts of officials on the front lines, which reinforced the rhetoric of his 2013 speech (Qian, 2018). It is because of such statements by Xi that state media 'dare to bare their swords' to target 'a tiny minority' and mobilise the 'majority' to 'have the public opinion high ground' (Lam, 2017).

Stage 3: Conclusion of the Issue (5 September–10 October 2019)

Beginning on 5 September, the day after Hong Kong's Chief Executive Carrie Lam announced that the extradition bill would officially be withdrawn, the extent of news coverage of the issue and the number of related posts dropped significantly. The stories that did appear focused on individuals voicing support for the 'one country, two systems' policy, and their tone became softer. Thus there were reports of citizens singing the national anthem at shopping malls and of volunteers cleaning up the debris left by the demonstrations. Such stories gave the impression that both the SAR and Beijing had shown effective governance by maintaining law and order in Hong Kong, where society was returning to normal and the majority of the citizens were satisfied with their leadership.

With the approach of the National Day celebrations of the 70th anniversary of the founding of the People's Republic of China, it was hardly surprising that state media changed their tone regarding Hong Kong in this way. In past propaganda efforts, the state media likewise sought to limit reporting on such negative stories as accidents and natural disasters, and focused instead on scenes of celebration. So also in the context of the 70th anniversary celebrations, coverage concentrated on patriotic actions that showed the CCP to be popular, and Hong Kong was no exception. As in other Chinese provinces and cities, Hong Kong media are expected to show locals from all sectors of society displaying, in apparently spontaneous acts of patriotism, the national flag and singing songs that express love for China.

Unlike during the first and second stages of agenda building, during this third stage, press conferences and official responses ceased to serve as the main sources for state media outlets. Thus the official withdrawal of the extradition bill was mentioned only once in a brief story, the comments on which have been censored. Compared with comments under posts that mentioned the withdrawal decision, comments on CCTV and *People's Daily* stories all had the same tone of support for Hong Kong's government and police. Some angry comments criticised Carrie Lam's administration for being too lenient in its treatment of the rioters and Beijing for not using military force to crack down on the protesters. Other comments criticised

Beijing for being unfair: it should side with the majority of the citizens of Hong Kong and people on the mainland, rather than with protesters, citing the saying that 'the crying baby gets the milk', the equivalent to the saying in English that 'the squeaky wheel gets the grease'. The state media outlets seem to have worked to avoid stoking anger and dissatisfaction among mainlanders, and to contain expressions of patriotism that could prove difficult to control and could have unforeseen negative consequences.

Within its limited coverage of Hong Kong, state media have continued to support the Hong Kong police by casting them as heroes and associating them with such positive emotions as gratitude and hope. From a psychological perspective, heroes can motivate, inspire, improve morale, and guide others (Kinsella et al., 2015). In this stage, individual interviews, sensational music videos, posters, and slogans were frequently used. On the one hand, this coverage signals Beijing's continued support for the use of harsh measures by the Hong Kong police to crack down on the protests, and for large-scale arrests. On the other, it encourages domestic audiences to support the police and accept state violence as the norm.

Apart from the police, state media have continued to mobilise Hong Kong citizens who the party considers patriotic to counter the protesters in the streets, and even physical attacks on protesters have been described as heroic. Thus, suspected members of the Fujian Triad (a Chinese organized crime syndicate) who attacked protesters have been praised by state media, as have efforts by pro-establishment groups to clear messages posted on 'Lennon Walls' (walls with messages written on Post-it notes and paper expressing support for the movement) around Hong Kong in support of the anti-government movement, despite the fact that they have resulted in several violent clashes among citizens. The message to pro-government forces in Hong Kong is clear: the protesters are rioters, internal enemies must be suppressed by violent means, and doing so is a show of patriotism and love for Hong Kong. Thus, an 8 August editorial in the *People's Daily* named 'four who deserve absolute support': the chief executive, the HKSAR, the Hong Kong police, and the 'patriotic people of Hong Kong who defend the rule of law and social order' (*People's Daily*, 2019c).

The third stage, then, differed markedly from the second stage, when Hong Kong citizens who supported the government's attempts to quell the protests were portrayed as a silent majority seeking to express themselves through public assembly or state media. In contrast, in the latter stage, state media depicted pro-government partisans as brave soldiers taking to the streets to confront the demonstrators. The shift in the coverage indicated that Beijing had lost its patience with its attempts at persuasion, and was hopeful that harsh repression of the protesters by the police and radical pro-government elements would compel anti-government activists to abandon their efforts.

DISCUSSION

The coverage of the Hong Kong anti-government movement demonstrates the skill with which state media are able to build an agenda. In conjunction with censorship, the party-controlled outlets effectively construct the CCP's version of events and engineer its general acceptance by the public. This is the logic behind the description of the anti-government protesters in Hong Kong as 'a tiny minority' of young people who were swayed by 'hostile foreign forces' in order to undermine the 'one country, two systems' arrangement. Conversely, the crackdown on the protesters has been depicted as the work of a brave and dedicated police force in cooperation with the majority of Hong Kong citizens who are patriotic; which is to say, more proud of being Chinese and more loving of their country than the protesters. The social unrest in Hong Kong has also been used to teach the lesson to mainlanders that protests bring only chaos, and that they should trust the government to maintain a peaceful and stable society.

Moreover, during the movement against the extradition bill, the CCP experimented with a new style of propaganda meant to capture the attention of Chinese youth through patriotic hip-hop music and anime programmes, and with more general agenda-building efforts. An example of the party's anime is the appearance on both CCTV and the *People's Daily* of a poster hailing a Hong Kong police officer who shot beanbag rounds at anti-government protesters as a hero, even as he was being widely criticised elsewhere for using excessive force. In addition, a CCTV anchor's video praising the officer went viral. This evidence suggests that in fact new digital media have further empowered state news media, increasing their influence, in particular among young people, and generally extending the reach of the CCP's messages.

The *People's Daily* and CCTV have often been perceived as representative of the opinions of the CCP leadership, and as one of its means of signalling to the public. That is, these outlets afford the party the time and space to send up trial balloons and to adjust its strategies before making decisions, by gauging the reactions to its signals across various sectors, within the party and without, among elites and the general populace, domestically and internationally. So also in the state's response to the anti-government movement in Hong Kong, where these media outlets have frequently played a role in agenda building. Thus, while having no direct administrative power over Hong Kong's private or public sectors under the 'one country, two systems' arrangement, and only limited influence over its citizens, Beijing frequently issues warnings to the leaders of private and public institutions alike through news commentaries and editorials. The online responses to the protests among mainlanders have added to the pressure from government officials to corporations that have business interests in China and Hong Kong. The mass arrests and excessive force used against the protesters, whose actions have been causing increasing anger within Hong Kong society at large, appear to represent responses to these signals in the form of demonstrations of loyalty and obedience to Beijing. That is, some of the pro-government forces in Hong Kong have seized a political opportunity to strengthen their ties to Beijing by implementing increasingly aggressive measures to counter the anti-government movement, further polarizing and creating chaos within Hong Kong society. Table 10.2 shows how various sectors have reacted to online initiatives launched by state media, and how the CCP has used state media to influence Hong Kong's economic and cultural sectors.

The CCP's use of state media and ministerial-level governing bodies to comment on the movement has also been a source of inconsistency in the official tone of statements regarding the anti-government movement. In a press conference on 15 August 2019 involving the Hong Kong and Macau offices, the CCP's top propagandist compared the Hong Kong anti-government movement with the 'colour revolutions' in Eastern Europe, and attributed it to 'a tiny minority' of anti-China activists who were supposedly trying to destroy Hong Kong. However, the term 'colour revolution' has not since appeared in official discussions of the topic, and the protesters have been regularly described as 'rioters' and 'radicals'. By reducing the extent of coverage, altering its framing of the anti-government movement, and creating a kind of happy ending for the domestic population, the CCP is trying to cause the movement to fade away. Thus, while 1 October, China's National Day, was the most violent and bloody day in the months-long series of protests in Hong Kong, state media made no mention of the

Table 10.2 Online initiatives launched by CCTV and the People's Daily, 1 June–10 October 2019

Online initiative	Target audience in Hong Kong	Response(s)
Support Hong Kong police	Police	Use of heavy-handed tactics against protesters; denial of any wrong-doing
Guard Chinese national flag	Celebrities, such as singers and actors	Retweeting to show support; denunciation of those who kept silent by mainland netizens for alleged tacit support of independence for Hong Kong
'Hong Kong is part of China'	Celebrities, such as singers and actors	Retweeting to show support; denunciation of those who kept silent by mainland netizens for alleged tacit support of independence for Hong Kong
Anti-violence; guarding Hong Kong's peace	Pro-Beijing population	Counter-protests to support police; 'Clean-up Hong Kong' (clearing of Lennon Walls); flash mobs singing Chinese national anthem in shopping malls; violent confrontations with protesters
Support for pro-Beijing figures	Elites	Business leaders publicly condemning chaos and violence associated with the anti-government protests
'Take off the mask'	Pro-Beijing population	Urging enactment of anti-mask law; on 4 October Hong Kong's chief executive, Carrie Lam, used a colonial-era emergency law to ban face masks

conflicts. Instead, state media provided huge coverage to the invitations to Hong Kong police to Beijing for the National Day ceremony. These police representatives expressed their pride and gratitude for being recognised by the state and the people. The publicity demonstrated that Beijing gave full support to the heavy-handed tactics that the police had begun to use in combatting the protestors.

CONCLUSIONS

The news media in China are part of the political machine of the ruling party, and as such serve as government agents. The agenda-building strategies of these media reflect the CCP's realisation that the anti-government movement in Hong Kong may last longer than had initially been expected. If the state media continue their current trend – stage 3 of the events described above – of limited and harshly critical reporting on the movement, and expressing the hope that the movement will dissipate, their coverage may as a side effect lead more mainlanders to fault the government for being too lenient in its response to the unrest, and even to question the government's authority. The reporting on Hong Kong during the third stage also shows the CCP's shift back toward limiting information about the anti-government movement, hiding it from the people on the mainland, and avoiding the uncomfortable fact that the resistance in Hong Kong is still going to reduce the impact of the protests on mainland society. Based on the online comments, at least, this agenda-building strategy would seem to have been effective, since many mainlanders have said that they have lost interest in Hong Kong. However, since such online comments are heavily censored, they are not a reliable measure of the effect of the CCP's propaganda. On at least one of the party's points, though, state media were indeed successful: they were able, through agenda building, to link the demonstrations with the issue of

Hong Kong's secession from China. As a consequence, citizens on the mainland have grown reluctant to talk about or even try to understand the movement.

The analysis of CCTV's and the *People's Daily*'s agenda building in relation to the anti-extradition bill movement in Hong Kong presented here is but one example of the CCP's use of state media to manipulate facts and public opinion, send signals to target audiences, and mobilise domestic sympathisers as well as interest groups overseas. Thanks to their experience with marketisation in the 1980s, China's state media know how to perform journalistic work, to harness information technology, and to blend news and propaganda. In any case, the party's recent recentralisation of control over the news media, and the hostility of its leadership toward Western journalism, make any reform of China's news media unlikely in the near and possibly even the long term.

REFERENCES

Brady, Anne-Marie (2009), *Marketing dictatorship: Propaganda and thought work in contemporary China*, Lanham, MD: Rowman & Littlefield Publishers.
Branigan, Tania and Erin Hale (2019), 'Cathay denounced for firing Hong Kong staff after pressure from China', *Guardian*, available at theguardian.com/world/2019/aug/28/cathay-pacific-denounced-for-firing-hong-kong-staff-on-china-orders.
Cobb, Roger W. and Charles D. Elder (1971), 'The politics of agenda-building: An alternative perspective for modern democratic theory', *Journal of Politics* 33(4): 892–915.
Cobb, Roger W. and Charles D. Elder (1972), 'The dynamics of agenda-building', *Classics of Public Policy* 1972: 128–136.
Denham, Bryan E. (2010), 'Toward conceptual consistency in studies of agenda-building processes: A scholarly review', *Review of Communication* 10(4): 306–323.
FMPRC (2019), 'Foreign ministry spokesperson Geng Shuang's regular press conference on June 13, 2019', *Foreign Affairs Ministry of the People's Republic of China*, available at fmprc.gov.cn/mfa_eng/xwfw_665399/s2510_665401/2511_665403/t1672069.shtml.
Gries, Peter Hays, Qingmin Zhang, H. Michael Crowson, and Huajian Cai (2011), 'Patriotism, nationalism and China's US policy: Structures and consequences of Chinese national identity', *China Quarterly* 205: 1–17.
Harding, Harry (1980), 'Reappraising the Cultural Revolution', *Wilson Quarterly* 4(4): 132–141.
Kinsella, Elaine L., Timothy D. Ritchie, and Eric R. Igou (2015), 'Lay perspectives on the social and psychological functions of heroes', *Frontiers in Psychology* (6): 130.
Kiousis, Spiro, Cristina Popescu, and Michael Mitrook (2007), 'Understanding influence on corporate reputation: An examination of public relations efforts, media coverage, public opinion, and financial performance from an agenda-building and agenda-setting perspective', *Journal of Public Relations Research* 19(2): 147–165.
Lam, Willy Wo-Lap (ed.) (2017), *Routledge handbook of the Chinese Communist Party*, London: Routledge.
Lancendorfer, Karen M. and Byoungkwan Lee (2010), 'Who influences whom? The agenda-building relationship between political candidates and the media in the 2002 Michigan governor's race', *Journal of Political Marketing* 9(3): 186–206.
Lang, Gladys Engel and Kurt Lang (1983), *The battle for public opinion: The president, the press, and the polls during Watergate*, New York: Columbia University Press.
Lin, Fen (2012), 'Information differentiation, commercialization and legal reform: The rise of a three-dimensional state–media regime in China', *Journalism Studies* 13(3): 418–432.
Manheim, Jarol B. and Robert B. Albritton (1984), 'Changing national images: International public relations and media agenda setting', *American Political Science Review* 78(3): 641–657.

Marinelli, Maurizio (2009), 'Names and reality in Mao Zedong's political discourse on intellectuals', *Transtext(e)s Transcultures. Journal of Global Cultural Studies* 5(5), available at http://transtexts.revues.org/index268.html.
McCombs, Maxwell, D.A. Graber, and David H. Weaver (1981), *Media agenda-setting in the presidential election*, New York: Praeger.
McCombs, M.E. and D.L. Shaw (1972), 'The agenda-setting function of mass media', *Public Opinion Quarterly* 36(2), 176–187.
Pan, Zhongdang (2000), 'Spatial configuration in institutional change: A case of China's journalism reforms', *Journalism* 1(3): 253–281.
People's Daily (2019a), 'Fight against violence, cherish the rule of law', *People's Daily*, July 21, available at http://opinion.people.com.cn/BIG5/n1/2019/0721/c1003-31246298.html.
People's Daily (2019b), 'It is absolutely intolerable to challenge the authority of the central government openly and undermine the principle of "one country, two systems"', *People's Daily*, July 22, available at http://opinion.people.com.cn/BIG5/n1/2019/0722/c1003-31246818.html.
People's Daily (2019c), 'The mainstream society of Hong Kong is patriotic and loves Hong Kong', August 8, available at http://opinion.people.com.cn/BIG5/n1/2019/0808/c1003-31282189.html.
Qian, Gang (2018), 'Signals from Xi's speech on ideology', *China Media Project*, available at chinamediaproject.org/2018/08/23/signals-from-xis-speech-on-ideology/.
Regan, Helen, Chermaine Lee, Eric Cheung, and Anna Coren (2019), 'Hong Kong protests: Night of violence shocks city after seventh week of mass marches', *CNN*, available at edition.cnn.com/2019/07/21/asia/hong-kong-protest-july-21-intl-hnk/index.html.
Schell, Orville and John Delury (2014), *Wealth and power: China's long march to the twenty-first century*, New York: Random House Trade Paperbacks.
Schoenhals, Michael (1992), *Doing things with words in Chinese politics: Five studies*, Berkeley, CA: Institute of East Asian Studies, University of California, Berkeley.
Shambaugh, David (2017), 'China's propaganda system: Institutions, processes and efficacy', *Critical Readings on Communist Party of China* 4: 713–751.
Song, Yunya and Tsan-Kuo Chang (2012), 'Legitimizing ruptures of development trajectories: Party press discourse on rural society in transitional China, 1997–2006', *International Journal of Press/Politics* 17(3): 316–340.
Stockmann, Daniela and Mary E. Gallagher (2011), 'Remote control: How the media sustain authoritarian rule in China', *Comparative Political Studies* 44(4): 436–467.
Tong, Jingrong (2019), 'The taming of critical journalism in China: A combination of political, economic and technological forces', *Journalism Studies* 20(1): 79–96.
Xinhua (2013), 'Xi Jinping: Ideology work is extremely important', available at news.ifeng.com/mainland/special/yishixingtai/content-3/detail_2013_08/20/28828185_0.shtml.
Yong, Zhang (2000), 'From masses to audience: Changing media ideologies and practices in reform China', *Journalism Studies* 1(4): 617–635.
Zhang, Guoliang, Guosong Shao, and Nicholas David Bowman (2012), 'What is most important for my country is not most important for me: Agenda-setting effects in China', *Communication Research* 39(5): 662–678.
Zhang, Juyan and Glen T. Cameron (2003), 'China's agenda building and image polishing in the US: Assessing an international public relations campaign', *Public Relations Review* 29(1): 13–28.
Zhang, Phoebe and Laurie Chen (2019), 'The emergence and evolution of China's internet warriors going to battle over Hong Kong protests', *South China Morning Post*, available at scmp.com/news/china/society/article/3024223/emergence-and-evolution-chinas-internet-warriors.
Zhang, Xiaodong and Mark Boukes (2019), 'How China's flagship news program frames "the West": Foreign news coverage of CCTV's Xinwen Lianbo before and during Xi Jinping's presidency', *Chinese Journal of Communication* 12(4): 414–430.
Zhao, Suisheng (2004), *A nation-state by construction: Dynamics of modern Chinese nationalism*, Palo Alto, CA: Stanford University Press.

11. Sexuality and politics: 'coming out' in German and Chinese queer films
Hongwei Bao

INTRODUCTION

When thinking of non-normative sexualities and politics, most people have in mind the term 'queer politics', that is, how lesbian, gay, bisexual, transgender, and queer (LGBTQ) people devise strategies to fight for gender and sexual equality as well as social justice. The relationship between queer and government-led mainstream politics (sometimes known as 'the politics') is often under-examined, apart from the occasional mention of a few LGBTQ-identified, friendly, or hostile politicians' names. Similarly, the term 'political propaganda' is often placed outside the realm of sexuality, except when the term is used negatively and against LGBTQ people. For example, during World War II, Nazi propaganda portrayed homosexuals and other social groups as being 'degenerate' and thus deserving extermination (Plant, 2011); and in Vladimir Putin's Russia, the 'gay propaganda law' is used to prosecute sexual minorities on the grounds of child protection and heterosexual family values (Mole, 2019). In other words, political propaganda seems un-queer and anti-queer: it is everything that queer is not.

Such a narrow understanding of the relationship between sexuality and politics is understandable, as we bear in mind the long history of stigmatisation and persecution of sexual minorities, together with the long and arduous struggle for gender and sexual equality and justice worldwide. However, this chapter takes a different approach to sexuality and mainstream politics. I suggest that we should also think about the complicity of queerness with mainstream politics in order to yield a more nuanced understanding of the relationship between sexuality and power. After all, sexuality is not outside politics; and politics often relies on gender and sexuality to function more effectively. For example, the United States government has used Islam's intolerance of homosexuality to justify its military intervention in the Middle East. This is often labelled as 'homonationalism', a sense of national pride based on the assumed tolerance of sexual minorities in a country to such an extent that such pride justifies the sacrifice of other nations (Puar, 2007). Another example: the Israeli government has been sending queer-friendly messages to the world to shift international attention from its military occupation of land in Palestine, and this is often known as 'pink washing' (Puar, 2013). These examples reveal the successful incorporation of sexual minorities in national or transnational political imaginaries and in mainstream politics. The relationship between queer and mainstream politics is thus complicated and requires critical reflection.

In this chapter I examine the vexed relationship between queerness and post-Cold War politics by looking at two queer films, one from the German Democratic Republic (GDR), otherwise known as the former East Germany, and the other from the People's Republic of China (PRC), often referred to as China. Seeing both films as situated in complex geopolitical contexts, and thus politically and ideologically complex, I hope to reveal the 'political unconscious' (Jameson, 1981) embedded within these cultural productions. I suggest that both films, along with the non-normative sexualities they represent, have participated in shaping a post-Cold War world order dominated by liberal and neoliberal values. As I identify possible queer complicities in neoliberal capitalism represented in the two films, I also unravel latent socialist impulses and queer resistances to queer liberalism and neoliberal globalisation. I argue that, by exploring the possibility of queer existence under socialism and by challenging queer complicity with neoliberalism, these two films contest the dominant ideologies and political propaganda that only capitalism can liberate sexual minorities.

POSTSOCIALISM AND CULTURAL POLITICS

The world has changed dramatically since the end of the Cold War, and this change has had a tremendous impact on people's subjectivities, desires, and lived experiences. Individual and collective experiences are often intertwined with national and even global histories; and personal desires and intimate spheres frequently reflect political and social upheavals. Against this historical backdrop, gender, sexuality, and desire are often cited as perfect examples that testify to the change. After all, if we were to ask sexual minorities around the world about their lives before and after 1989, there is nothing better than their own testimony to demonstrate which world they would prefer to live in, and which political system is superior to the other, as gay man and ex-GDR citizen Mario Röllig in German filmmaker Jochen Hick's 2016 documentary *The GDR Complex* (*Der Ost-Komplex*) would testify. In this sense, gay identity has become a 'postsocialist allegory of modernity' (Rofel, 1999) that attests to the inevitability of socialism's demise and capitalism's triumph.

The term 'postsocialism' is key to understanding the historical experience of China and many other countries in the world. Scholars disagree on the political and ideological nature of contemporary China. Some see it as 'socialism from afar' (Zhang and Ong, 2008) and others diagnose it as 'neoliberalism with Chinese characteristics' (Harvey, 2005). 'Postsocialism' represents one of the most popular – albeit also with great controversy – understandings of China's historical condition among scholars working in Western academia (Dirlik, 1989; Rofel, 1999, 2007; Litzinger, 2002; Lu, 2007; Kipnis, 2008; McGrath, 2008; Zhang, 2008; Rojas and Litzinger, 2016). The term 'postsocialism' offers valuable insights into the understanding of contemporary Chinese society. According to Arif Dirlik (1989), postsocialism describes:

> a historical situation where (a) socialism has lost its coherence as a metahistory of politics because of the attenuation of the socialist vision in its historical unfolding ... (b) the articulation of socialism to capitalism is conditioned by the structure of 'actually existing socialism' in any given historical context which is the historical premise of all such articulations; and (c) this premise stands guard over the process of articulation to ensure that it does not result in the restoration of capitalism. Postsocialism is of necessity also postcapitalist, not in the classical Marxist sense of socialism as a phase in historical development that is anterior to capitalism, but in the sense of a socialism that represents a response to the experience of capitalism and an attempt to overcome the deficiencies of capitalist development. Its own deficiencies and efforts to correct them by resorting to capitalist methods of development are conditioned by this awareness of the deficiencies of capitalism in history.

For Dirlik, postsocialism represents an alternative to capitalism. It is a global condition in late modernity and is thus not unique to China. From today's perspective his view seems over-optimistic, especially when the incorporation of China into global neoliberal capitalism does not seem to represent a genuine alternative. However, if we recognise the continuing existence of socialist ideas, experiences, and aspirations in contemporary Chinese society, China can still be seen as neither entirely socialist nor capitalist; rather, it is characterised by the simultaneous non-contemporaneity of hybrid economies and politics which can be described as 'postsocialist'. Indeed, although China has adopted state-led capitalism, and neoliberalism has exerted a powerful influence on Chinese society, the state still owns a large part of its major industries and infrastructures, which still nominally fall under the ownership of all the people in China. What is more, socialist histories, memories, and experiences still linger on in today's China and they structure people's lives, embodiments, and emotions in significant ways. They provide legitimacy and support for citizens' rights and grassroots activism. After all, socialist modes of 'comrade' subjectivity and politics still inspire postsocialist queer identity formation and LGBTQ social movements (Bao, 2018a). Therefore it is important to recognise the socialist traces, memories, and aspirations in the postsocialist era to articulate modes of resistance to global neoliberalism.

Culture is an important arena for ideas and ideologies to function in a society and to establish their own hegemony. Neoliberalism has taken a strong hold worldwide precisely because of its close links to media and popular culture. It has also produced its unique understanding of gender and sexuality, primarily based on a heightened sense of individualism and consumerism as well as a competitive and meritocratic mode of self-actualisation (Ong, 2006; Rofel, 2007; Lewis et al., 2016). Lisa Duggan argues for the importance of cultural politics in contesting the contemporary neoliberal hegemony:

> Neoliberalism was constructed in and through cultural and identity politics and cannot be undone by a movement without constituencies and analyses that respond directly to that fact. Nor will it be possible to build a new social movement that might be strong, creative, and diverse enough to engage the work of reinventing global politics for the new millennium as long as cultural and identity issues are separated, analytically and organisationally, from the political economy in which they are embedded. (Duggan, 2003: 3)

It is therefore crucial to look at cultural productions, including film, literature and art, in a society at a particular time to tease out the ideologies and discourses embedded within, and to discover their internal contradictions and ambivalences, as well as possible ways of contestation. The purpose of such a cultural analysis is to open up alternative political imaginaries beyond the current neoliberal hegemony.

BERLIN AND BEIJING: NARRATIVES OF 'COMING OUT' IN 1989

Having lived in Beijing and Berlin myself, two cities that have witnessed dramatic transformations in the aftermath of the Cold War, I have learned to appreciate a transnational perspective in queer historiography and the concept of postsocialism. There are many reasons to compare and contrast queer lives and representations in the two cities. Despite their obvious geographical and cultural differences, both cities have a socialist history; and their cityscapes are inevitably marked by distinct imaginations of modernity, from imperial to socialist, and from modernist to postmodernist (Dutton, 2010; Ladd, 2018). To a great extent, the contemporary skylines of the two cities were shaped by 1989, a year that symbolically marked the end of the Cold War and the division between socialism and postsocialism. Francis Fukuyama (1992) celebrates the 'end of history'. In his writing, 1989 marked the triumph of liberal democracy as the ultimate form of government for all nations, and for Fukuyama there can be no progression from liberal democracy to an alternative system. In advocating free market liberalism, which morphed into neoliberalism since the 1980s, Fukuyama essentially defends capitalism against other social formations and imaginaries. Fukuyama's 'end of history' thesis is characterised by Mark Fisher as 'capitalist realism'; that is, 'the widespread sense that not only is capitalism the only viable political and economic system, but also that it is now impossible even to imagine a coherent alternative to it' (Fisher, 2009: 2). Is an alternative possible?

Films are often seen as representations of society, meaning that they record and reflect historical events and social lives. What if we also see them as polysemic, ambivalent, and ideologically loaded in the messages they convey? What if they also take part in historical processes and shape societies in which they are situated? Here I use two queer films, one from the GDR and the other one from China, to demonstrate how visual cultures document and shape history, and articulate postsocialist 'structures of feeling' (Williams, 1961).

In the history of world cinema, two queer films are closely associated with 1989: *Coming Out* (dir. Heiner Carow, GDR, 1989) and *Lan Yu* (dir. Stanley Kwan, China, 2001). Both feature 'coming out' – short for 'coming out of the closet' – narratives; that is, gay people come to terms with their own sexual identities and subsequently disclose their identities to others. The 'coming out' narrative is one of the most common narratives in queer cinema and for queer life. Coming out used to be associated with shame, and now increasingly with pride. It requires the construction of alternative narratives that run contrary to the negative stereotypes circulating in mainstream society (Coon, 2018). Coming out suggests possibilities of hope, but also conjures up feelings of insecurity and vulnerability. While one may expect to enter into a 'brave new world' with endless possibilities following the act of coming out, many are faced with a world of precariousness, discrimination, and risk. When, where, and how one should come out is a question fraught with politics, especially when it overlaps or coincides with national and transnational histories. Coming out also presumes the coherence and authenticity of the self. It creates a sense of temporary coherence and authenticity out of fragmented, contradictory, and transient identities (Pullen, 2009). Ken Plummer identifies different levels over which 'coming out' stories evolve, moving from the personal to the cultural and historical, which concerns 'the moment at which a story enters public discourse – the moment of public reception' (Plummer, 1995: 35). In other words, coming out is not simply an individual and personal experience. It can be mediated and even intertwined with national and transnational experiences, thus assuming a historical significance. Notably, the 'coming out' moments in both films are associated with dramatic, and traumatic, historical changes in 1989, thus making coming out a political act. Sexual identities, in this context, cease to exist as individual identities and intimate practices; they become national and even transnational 'allegories' (Jameson, 1986) that remind people of the continuities and ruptures in history, national identity, and political ideologies.

This chapter primarily focuses on film texts, but it also pays attention to the intertextuality between cinematic representations and the contexts of the films. While looking at cinematic representations, I also examine film scripts and sometimes a novel on which a film is based, to interrogate what gets represented on screen and why this is the case. Moreover, I situate the films in their historical, social, cultural, and industry contexts, considering how they are framed by filmmakers, interpreted by the audience, and at the same time shaped by multiple discourses circulating in a society at a particular time. Reading the films 'conjuncturally'

(Hall, 1988) – that is, in their historical and social contexts – I aim to highlight the ideological ambivalences, as well as openness, of the films in order to contest dominant ideologies and political propaganda of neoliberalism. If neoliberalism sees socialism as passé and even antithetic to gay identities and queer desires, these two films suggest otherwise, as they explore the possibilities of queer spaces within a socialist imaginary.

REIMAGINING SOCIALISM IN *COMING OUT*

Coming Out is a 1989 film directed by German film director and screenwriter Heiner Carow (1929–1997) and produced by the GDR's state film studio DEFA in its final years. The film centres on a high school teacher's 'coming out' experience in the GDR. The lead character, handsome Philipp Klarmann (Matthias Freihof), tries to reconcile his own sexuality while he is mediating his relationships with his girlfriend, Tanja (Dagmar Manzel), and his gay male lover, Matthias (Dirk Kummer). Despite being named Klarmann (literally 'a clear man'), Philipp is not clear about his own sexuality at all. Because of his indecision, he eventually hurts both people. Matthias and Tanja leave Philipp one after the other. At the end of the film, when the school headmaster calls '*Kollege Klarmann*' (colleague Klarmann) during an unexpected class visit, he answers '*Ja*' (Yes), symbolising his eventual acceptance of the gay self.

According to Kyle Frackman (2018), this ambiguous 'coming out' scene at the end of the film was a significantly cut version from its original script, which features Philipp's speech in front of his students and the colleagues sitting at the back of the classroom. The deleted words are:

> Ich habe in den letzten Monaten und Wochen begriffen, daß ich homosexuell bin. Ich habe deshalb ein Leben voll von Lügen ... Verstecken und ... und Angst gelebt ... Ich weiß, es ist ein Risiko, daß ich [das] alles zu Ihnen sage. Aber es gibt für mich keinen Ausweg. Ich bin also schwul, wie man so sagt. Ich kann anders nicht leben und ich will es auch nicht. (Cited in Frackman, 2018: 470)

> In recent months and weeks, I have realised that I am homosexual. That is to say, I have been leading a life full of lies ... concealment ... and fear ... I know it's a risk to tell you about everything, but I have no way out. So I'm gay, as they say. I can't live differently and I don't want to do this either. (Author's translation)

Despite the removal of this speech in the final cut of the film, Philipp's answer '*Ja*' can still be seen as a confirmation of his gay identity, something that he has been denying and hiding throughout the film until the last minute.

However, it is the film's debut that inscribed *Coming Out* firmly into German history. The film was premiered at the Kino International on Karl-Marx-Allee in East Berlin on the night of 9 November 1989, the night when the Berlin Wall fell. Jim Morton described the event as follows:

> By the end of the evening, the borders of East Berlin were swarming with people trying to visit the West. The border guards frantically called every official they could find but the people who could actually make a decision seemed to be in short supply that night. According to folklore, the reason none of these officials could be found that night is because they were all at a screening of Heiner Carow's controversial new movie, *Coming Out*, which just happened to be premiering the same night as the wall fell. (Morton, 2011)

Regardless of what exactly happened during the film screening that night, the fact that the premiere of GDR's allegedly first – and also last – gay film coincided with the fall of the Berlin Wall gives the film a historical significance. It also lends the film an allegorical reading: the late GDR government's recognition of its sexual minorities, and by extension the liberal values this represents, brought the socialist state to its demise.

However, the relationship between gay identity and state socialism is far more complicated than the above liberal reading would allow. Katrin Sieg (2007) sees the film as reflecting different ways of life in the GDR society at the time. Some people endorsed heteronormative lifestyles and values; others experimented with different ways of living and thinking. In other words, there was a great sense of openness in terms of lifestyles and political imaginaries at the time; Sexuality lay at the centre of these different imaginations of society and good life. 'Sexuality became a central site for the articulation of a critique of a "real existent" socialism ... a site from which the gap between revolutionary theory and praxis became painfully visible' (Sieg, 1995: 98). David Dennis (2012) sees this film as representing an effort by GDR cultural workers, including the director Heiner Carow and the script writer Wolfram Witt, to look for the 'third way' between capitalist individualism and socialist ideals. Dennis points out that *Coming Out* should be seen as a part of, and representing a particular strand in, the lesbian and gay movement in the GDR:

> [B]oth *Coming Out* and the movement shared a common vision of *Schwulsein* [being gay] in the GDR as a 'third way' between political commitment to socialism and the individual self-determination. Carow was interested in a socialist humanism that did not give up notions of 'class struggle' but rather complicated them, equating class oppression with sexual and racial oppressions. (Dennis, 2012: 69)

It is important to note that the protagonist Philipp is committed to socialism and anti-fascist struggles in the context that the GDR gained its political legitimacy through the discourse of socialism and anti-fascism. The film anchors fascism in the country's Nazi past and attributes anti-Semitism, racism, and homophobia to the lingering effect of Nazism in a socialist society. In the film, Philipp and Tanja attend an anti-fascist concert in an unnamed Jewish ghetto where Philipp's gay student sings a 'song from the ghetto' to express solidarity. On their way home, when three neo-Nazi skinheads attack a black person in a train carriage, Philipp leads his students to drive the skinheads out of the train at the next station. The train station happens to be named 'Marx-Engels Platz', symbolising the power of Marx and Engels's ideas in uniting oppressed people against social evils and injustices. In both scenes, gay and straight people form an alliance to fight against fascistic practices such as anti-Semitism and racism.

After losing both Matthias and Tanja, Philipp goes back to the gay bar where he first met Matthias. Walter, an old gay man and a regular customer at the bar, tries to calm him down when Philipp makes trouble and risks being thrown out of the bar. Walter tells Philipp of his own life story of being persecuted as a homosexual in a Nazi concentration camp, and later becoming a committed communist after World War II. Walter reiterates his socialist beliefs and remarks on the current situation in the GDR: 'We worked like crazy. We stopped mankind's exploitation by mankind, now it does not matter if the person you work with is a Jew or whatever. Except the gays. We forget them somehow.' These comments effectively serve as a critique of the GDR's Socialist Unity Party (SED) policies that turned a blind eye to the rights of sexual minorities and therefore failed to deliver its democratic and egalitarian promises to all people. However, this critique should be seen as an internal and constructive critique, aimed at improving the socialist state instead of dismantling it. As Kyle Frackman glosses the scene: 'Walter's monologue continues the film's project of gesturing towards a potential future while deploying elements of the past and present' (Frackman, 2018: 469); and this future is a socialist one in which sexual minorities play a part.

The film's history of reception among GDR intellectuals also illustrates the moderate and constructive attitude in its critique of state socialism and its imagination of solidarity among oppressed groups. As Dennis points out:

> During the years of the *Wende* ['the turning point', referring to the historical period around German reunification in 1989] and beyond, *Coming Out* became part of the broader conversation about *Lesben-und Schwulsein* [being lesbian and gay] in the GDR as activists sought to record their memories of the movement and scholars began to reconsider the significance of East German lesbian and gay life and politics. Almost invariably, activists cite the film as an important moment in the movement's history. (Dennis, 2012: 75)

In this sense, *Coming Out* ceases to be merely a work of artistic representation. It participates in the formation of gay and lesbian identities, communities, and politics under and in the aftermath of socialism. It reimagines the relationship between queer sexualities and socialism, seeing them as compatible instead of mutually exclusive. Seen in this light, Philipp's positive answer '*Ja*' to the school headmaster's interpellation can be read as an affirmation of his socialist identity and belief, to which gay people can also lay claim. In other words, as the moment epitomises Philipp's coming out as a gay man, it also symbolically marks the lesbian and gay movement's claim to legitimacy and demands for recognition under GDR's state socialism. It imagines a utopian future for sexual minorities under socialism. Indeed, gay identity is not antithetic to socialism. It should be seen as a part of the newly configured and imagined socialist imaginary, in which gender, sexuality, race, and other intersected identities all constitute part of the socialist struggle for equality and social justice.

ARTICULATING SOCIALIST ASPIRATION IN *LAN YU*

Adapted from a popular gay romance published online in the early 1990s, and directed by the renowned Hong Kong queer director Stanley Kwan (1957–), *Lan Yu* tells one of the best-known queer stories in the Chinese-speaking world. The film narrates the ten-year love story between Lan Yu (Liu Ye) and Chen Handong (Hu Jun). At the beginning of the story Lan Yu, a poor student from a working-class background, arrives in Beijing to attend university where he meets Handong, a rich businessman from a well-connected communist cadre family. Their one-night stand soon evolves into a more regular sexual relationship, although Handong still sees other men and women at the same time. It is not until the Tian'anmen incident on the early morning of 4 June 1989 that Handong begins to acknowledge his feeling for Lan Yu as true love, thus coming out as gay himself. As Handong narrates in the story:

> With the fear of death behind us, our bodies came together, each man taking the other's flesh as proof that he was alive. I loved Lan Yu's body. I loved holding him, feeling him next to me, his warmth. He was so full of life. I pressed my lips against his neck and held my cheek against his chest and listened to his heartbeat. He was mine! He was there! …
> 'I love you!' My heart pounded in my chest ... I couldn't believe I said it, but at the same time it felt so natural coming out. It was the only thing I felt at the moment, the only thing I could think of to say.

I love you, I had said. And it was love. It wasn't just sex. Whatever other people might have thought, whoever other people thought we were, I knew we were in love. (Bei, 2016: 121)

This juxtaposition of sex and love marks the boundary between sexual behaviour and sexual identity in the Foucauldian (1998) sense. Having sex with men does not necessarily constitute gay identities, whereas loving men certainly does in contemporary society. In the novel's cinematic adaptation, this explicit sex scene and passionate moment of sex and confession are turned into Lan Yu's crying in the middle of the night, as if to recover from the unspeakable shock, followed by the fragment of a radio broadcast reminding the audience of the time of the historical moment. In this way, Handong comes out to himself as gay on the same night as the government crackdown of protests takes place. In other words, gay identity becomes a consequence – and an overcoming – of contemporary China's historical trauma.

There are numerous accounts of Tian'anmen in 1989, most of which are informed by a liberalist interpretative framework, seeing student protests as requesting the end of China's socialism and the start of a Western type of liberal democracy. However, according to historian Wang (2009), demonstrating students at Tian'anmen were in fact demanding the state to address problems brought about by global capitalism, including corruption, profiteering, economic-centrism, class disparity, as well as other forms of social inequality and injustice. Seen in this light, the student protests were in effect demands for reforms within the framework of state socialism, and demands for the state to genuinely deliver its socialist promises of egalitarianism, democracy, and social justice. Wang makes distinctions between two types of socialism: the 'socialism' of old state ideology, characterised by the system of state monopoly; and the socialism for movements for social security, social democracy, and against monopoly. This distinction is unfortunately lost in most commentaries about Tian'anmen:

In the post-Cold War global context, and in the context of re-evaluating socialist practice, the 1989 movement for social security – with its deeply concealed internal social contradictions, its opposition to monopoly and special privileges, and its intention to promote democracy – remains poorly understood. (Wang, 2009: 22)

Bearing in mind the over-determined meanings of Tian'anmen, the story of *Lan Yu* can be read in multiple ways. Howard Chiang (2014) reads the story as reflecting the complex relationship between China and the Sinophone world in queer cultural formation. Drawing on Lisa Rofel's (2007) 'desiring China' thesis, David Eng (2010) reads the story as an allegory of the postsocialist Chinese modernity where neoliberalism produces entrepreneurial citizenship with desires. Michael Berry (2008) reads the story allegorically, with Lan Yu symbolising socialism and Handong representing capitalism. Their political and ideological confrontation is even manifested in their choice of means of transport: Lan Yu insists on taking the public bus instead of taxis and private cars, because the bus represents socialist values. Glossing Lan Yu's death in a car accident when he eventually takes a taxi at the end of the story, Berry comments:

Lan Yu's struggle against so much of what Chen Handong stands for takes on new meaning as he dies not amid the violence of Tian'anmen Square but years later, amid the rampant development overtaking China. Implied sacrifice for *democratic* freedom is transmuted, devolving into a random consequence of taking advantage of new forms of *capitalist* freedom. But was this not precisely the unspoken deal that the Chinese leadership made with its people in the wake of the crackdown, trading the people's political agency for new economic opportunity and capitalist freedoms? (Berry, 2008: 318)

Such ideological struggles are often played out dramatically in the story. The author of the story and the film director seem to stand on Lan Yu's side. In the film, Lan Yu refuses to be corrupted by money and bribed by material gains; and he believes in true and non-materialistic love without conditions. Lan Yu strikes a strong contrast to Lin Jingping (Su Jin), Handong's wife, a selfish, greedy, and materialistic woman. Gay love is thus juxtaposed with heterosexual love and is imagined as pure, unconditional, and non-materialistic. As Handong reflects:

> And that, I think, is the difference between men and women. When a woman has sex with you, it's because of something you have – genius, money, or whatever – or because they want to find someone who will let them be a parasite forever. After they get what they want, they use sex as a way of rewarding men. But when men have sex there's no rhyme or reason. They're just satisfying a primitive need. (Bei, 2016: 70)

As Petrus Liu aptly points out, this story 'articulates a cultural fantasy about the separability of love and money in human relations' (Liu, 2016: 375). Situated at the historical juncture of the 1980s, and during China's transition from a socialist society to a capitalistic society, such a cultural fantasy articulates a socialist longing against the reification of social relations under capitalism. This sentiment is best manifested in Lan Yu's account of his family story. The family lived a happy, albeit poor life under socialism in the early years of the Reform Era (1978–present). With China's economic reform, the father went into business and made a lot of money. Wealth changed him into a different person; he subsequently had an extramarital affair and deserted his family. The mother committed suicide out of despair. Lan Yu recalls: 'Before she did it, she wrote a long letter to me and my dad. She said she hated money – that money can make people cold, selfish, unfeeling. She said the truly precious things in life weren't silver or gold, but passion, conviction' (Bei, 2016: 105).

It was this personal experience, in the context of China's social transformation from socialism to capitalism, that shaped Lan Yu's attitude towards money and capitalism. The protagonists in the story often express a strong longing for socialism. The song they sing, 'The Internationale', reminds people of a bygone era, forgotten and marginalised in contemporary historiography. If Lan Yu's name, literally 'blue universe', conjures up a sense of internationalism and cosmopolitanism, Handong's name (literally 'defending the Mao Zedong thought') points to the cultural specificity of China's socialism. By conjuring up the 'spectres of Marx' (Derrida, 1994; Rojas and Litzinger, 2016) and by highlighting the issue of class in shaping Chinese society in the postsocialist era, gay identities in China will be constantly haunted by these historical memories and utopian longings (Bao, 2018b).

CONCLUSION

Although both films centre their 'coming out' narratives around 1989, *Coming Out* and *Lan Yu* tell different stories. In *Coming Out*, Philipp has always been gay, and he even had homoerotic encounters in his school days. It only takes an emotional entanglement with a man and a woman at the same time to force him out and to be clear about his own sexuality and socialist beliefs. For the director Heiner Carow and other like-minded cultural workers in the GDR, homosexuality has always been, and should always be, a part of socialism. The state should recognise gay people's rights, and gay people should also have faith in a reformed and more humanistic state socialism. It was the historical contingency on the night of 9 November 1989 that changed the trajectory of history, but this should not change gay people's belief in and commitment to the socialist cause.

Lan Yu faced different historical and cultural circumstances altogether. Written in the early 1990s and made into a film in 2001, the story was narrated at a historical juncture when socialism was slowly giving way to capitalism, and China was gradually adopting neoliberal market principles in many areas of the political, economic, and social life. The year 1989 becomes a watershed moment for China and for the protagonists in *Lan Yu*. Admittedly, neither Lan Yu nor Handong are gay-identified at the beginning of the story; they have sex out of financial necessity and physical pleasure. They only become gay later on, when they start to make distinctions between sex and love. They seem aware of China's homoerotic traditions. They also acknowledge the compatibility between Chinese culture and homosexuality, as the story makes references to literary tropes of homoeroticism in premodern China. However, it is the egalitarian, non-materialistic, and utopian nature of the love between men that renders homosexuality compatible with socialist values. A story about 'becoming gay' is thus heavily imbued with socialist longings.

Contrary to the popular belief that globalisation brings gay identities across the world, and only neoliberal capitalism can provide spaces for queer existence (Altman, 1996), both *Coming Out* and *Lan Yu* seem to suggest that being gay is compatible with socialism, and socialist ideals are things that queer people should adhere to instead of rejecting altogether. After all, as the Chinese term for queer – *tongzhi* (literally 'comrade') – suggests, comrades can be queer, and queer can also be comrades (Bao, 2018a).

In summary, this chapter has conducted a transcultural and comparative analysis of the 'coming out' narratives in two queer films, *Coming Out* and *Lan Yu*. Reading the two films conjuncturally in the post-Cold War context, this chapter recovers an optimistic historical moment in which queer identities were articulated with a socialist imagination of society, and queer people's coming out marked a less dogmatic and more liberal version of state socialism without rejecting core socialist values. This moment was temporary, fleeting and contingent. With the accelerated expansion of neoliberalism worldwide, such a moment soon dissipated in the 'end of history' choruses. Reassessing these two films in our own times helps us appreciate the historical moment and re-access its embedded socialist legacies and aspirations. It also serves as a timely reminder of the ambivalent political ideologies and imaginaries surrounding sexual identities and practices, as well as the complex relationship between sexuality, power, and political propaganda.

REFERENCES

Altman, Dennis (1996), 'On global queering', *Australian Humanities Review*, 2, accessed 1 October 2019 at http://australianhumanitiesreview.org/1996/07/01/on-global-queering/.

Bao, Hongwei (2018a), *Queer Comrades: Gay Identity and Tongzhi Activism in Postsocialist China*, Copenhagen: NIAS Press.

Bao, Hongwei (2018b), 'Haunted gay identity: sexuality, masculinity and class in *Beijing Story*', in Derek Hird and Geng Song (eds), *The Cosmopolitan Dream: Transnational Chinese Masculinities in a Global Age*, Hong Kong: Hong Kong University Press, pp. 73–86.

Bei, Tong (2016), *Beijing Comrades*, trans. Scott E. Myers, New York: Feminist Press.

Berry, Michael (2008), *A History of Pain: Trauma in Modern Chinese Literature and Film*, New York: Columbia University Press.

Chiang, Howard (2014), 'Deprovincialising China: queer historicism and Sinophone postcolonial critique', in Howard Chiang and Ari Larissa Heinrich (eds), *Queer Sinophone Cultures*, New York: Routledge, pp. 19–51.
Coon, David R. (2018), *Turning the Page: Storytelling as Activism in Queer Film and Media*, Brunswick, NJ: Rutgers University Press.
Dennis, David Brandon (2012), '*Coming Out* into socialism: Heiner Carow's Third Way', in Terri Ginsberg and Andrea Mensch (eds), *A Companion to German Cinema*, Oxford: Blackwell, pp. 55–81.
Derrida, Jacques (1994), *Spectres of Marx*, London: Routledge.
Dirlik, Arif (1989), 'Postsocialism? Reflections on "Socialism with Chinese characteristics"', in Arif Dirlik and Maurice Meisner (eds), *Marxism and the Chinese Experience*, Armonk, NY: M.E. Sharpe, pp. 362–384.
Duggan, Lisa (2003), *The Twilight of Equality: Neoliberalism, Cultural Politics, and the Attack on Democracy*, New York: Beacon Press.
Dutton, Michael (2010), *Beijing Time*, Cambridge, MA: Harvard University Press.
Eng, David L. (2010), 'The queer space of China: expressive desire in Stanley Kwan's *Lan Yu*', *Positions*, 18(2): 459–487.
Fisher, Mark (2009), *Capitalist Realism: Is There No Alternative?*, Winchester: Zero Books.
Foucault, Michel (1998), *The History of Sexuality*, Vol. I, London: Penguin.
Frackman, Kyle (2018), 'The East German film: *Coming Out* as melancholic reflection and hopeful projection', *German Life and Letters*, 71(4): 452–472.
Fukuyama, Francis (1992), *The End of History and the Last Man*, New York: Free Press.
Hall, Stuart (1988), *The Hard Road to Renewal: Thatcherism and the Crisis of the Left*, London: Verso.
Harvey, David (2005), *A Brief History of Neoliberalism*, Oxford: Oxford University Press.
Jameson, Fredric (1981), *The Political Unconscious: Narrative as a Social Symbolic Act*, London: Methuen.
Jameson, Fredric (1986), 'Third-World literature in an era of multinational capitalism', *Social Text* 15(Autumn): 65–88.
Kipnis, Andrew (2008), *China and Postsocialist Anthropology: Theorising Power and Society After Communism*, Manchester: Camphor Press.
Ladd, Brian (2018), *The Ghosts of Berlin: Confronting German History in the Urban Landscape*, Chicago, IL: University of Illinois Press.
Lewis, Tania, Fran Martin, and Wanning Sun (2016), *Telemodernities: Television and Transforming Lives in Asia*, Durham, NC: Duke University Press.
Litzinger, Ralph (2002), 'Theorising postsocialism: reflections on the politics of marginality in contemporary China', *South Atlantic Quarterly*, 101(1): 33–55.
Liu, Petrus (2016), 'From identity to social protest: the cultural politics of *Beijing Comrades*', in Bei Tong, *Beijing Comrades*, trans. Scott E. Myers, New York: Feminist Press, pp. 372–381.
Lu, Sheldon H. (2007), *Chinese Modernity and Global Geopolitics: Studies in Literature and Visual Culture*, Honululu, HI: University of Hawai'i Press.
McGrath, Jason (2008), *Postsocialist Modernity: Chinese Cinema, Literature, and Criticism in the Market Age*, Stanford, CA: Stanford University Press.
Mole, Richard C.M. (2019), *Soviet and Post-Soviet Sexualities*, New York: Routledge.
Morton, Jim (2011), 'Coming Out', *East German Cinema Blog*, accessed 1 October 2019 at https://eastgermancinema.com/2011/06/09/coming-out/.
Ong, Aihwa (2006), *Neoliberalism as Exception: Mutations in Citizenship and Sovereignty*, Durham, NC: Duke University Press.
Plant, Richard (2011), *The Pink Triangle: The Nazi War Against Homosexuals*, New York: Henty Holt & Company.
Plummer, Ken (1995), *Telling Sexual Stories: Power, Change and Social Worlds*, New York: Routledge.
Puar, Jasbir (2007), *Terrorist Assemblages: Homonationalism in Queer Times*, Durham, NC: Duke University Press.
Puar, Jasbir (2013), 'Rethinking homonationalism', *International Journal of Middle East Studies*, 45(2): 336–339.
Pullen, Christopher (2009), *Gay Identity, New Storytelling and the Media*, Basingstoke: Palgrave Macmillan.

Rofel, Lisa (1999), *Other Modernities: Gendered Yearnings in China After Socialism*, Berkeley, CA: University of California Press.
Rofel, Lisa (2007), *Desiring China*, Durham, NC: Duke University Press.
Rojas, Carlos and Ralph A. Litzinger (eds) (2016), *Ghost Protocol: Development and Displacement in Global China*, Durham, NC: Duke University Press.
Sieg, Katrin (1995), 'Deviance and dissidence: sexual subjects of the Cold War', in Sue-Ellen Case, Susan Leigh Foster, and Philip Brett (eds), *Cruising the Performative: Interventions into the Representation of Ethnicity, Nationality, and Sexuality*, Bloomington, IN: Indiana University Press, pp. 93–111.
Sieg, Katrin (2007), 'Homosexualität und Dissidenz: Zur Freiheit der Liebe in Heiner Carows *Coming Out*' ('Homosexuality and dissidence: toward freedom of love in Heiner Carow's *Coming Out*'), in Bettina Mathes (ed.), *Die imaginierte Nation: Identität, Körper und Geschlecht in DEFA-Filmen (The Imagined Nation: Identities, Bodies and Gender in DEFA Films)*, Berlin: DEFA-Stiftung, pp. 284–308.
Wang, Hui (2009), *China's New Order: Society, Politics and Economy in Transition*, Cambridge, MA: Harvard University Press.
Williams, Raymond (1961), *The Long Revolution*, London: Chatto & Windus.
Zhang, Li and Aihwa Ong (2008), *Privatising China: Socialism from Afar*, Ithaca, NY: Cornell University Press.
Zhang, Xudong (2008), *Postsocialism and Cultural Politics: China in the Last Decade of the Twentieth Century*, Durham, NC: Duke University Press.

12. The compassion 'spectacle': the propaganda of piety, virtuosity, and altruism within neoliberal politics
Colin Alexander

INTRODUCTION

Compassion waxes and wanes in politics, as does the call for leaders to be compassionate. Swayed by society's opinion leaders, at certain times publics appear to clamour for a 'nice guy' or 'girl' to provide modesty or to reassert some sense of decency that, it is claimed, has been eroded. Perhaps the request is also that he or she creates a more caring and fairer society where people are not as exposed to the forces of the market, the moral bankruptcy of kleptocrats, or the whims of the ruthless. However, at other times the public can request a 'strong man' or 'strong woman' who will be ruthless, decisive, and ready to make tough and sometimes brutal decisions without much concern for the fallout. To this end, there is a distinct fluidity in the prestige bestowed upon compassion within politics. Sometimes it is an asset that can deliver a politician or party to the very top; at other times it can lead to the end of a political career or be the stumbling block to a career not gaining momentum in the first place.

This chapter argues for the existence of a compassion 'spectacle' within modern neoliberal politics where pious, virtuous, and altruistic rhetoric obscures the reality of gross self-interest. Thus, as part of attempts to manufacture favourable political landscapes, much of the compassion that transpires within politics today is part of a façade wherein politicians, somewhat at the behest of their strategists and advisors, employ communications strategies as an accompanying veneer to their ambitions. Following an introduction that explains what is meant by the 'spectacle', the chapter discusses the extent to which humans are capable of genuine compassion, and the limits thereof, while also considering the works of psychoanalysts and ethical philosophers including the 19th century German writer Arthur Schopenhauer, whose treatise on morality and the role of compassion within the human psyche remains a seminal text on the subject. This discussion lays important groundwork for a more intensive consideration of compassion within politics under neoliberalism. The chapter will then profile former United States (US) President Jimmy Carter, whose incumbency in the White House (1977–1981) at the beginning of the neoliberal age has many of the hallmarks of compassionate propaganda that his contemporaries would go on to 'perfect'. Carter is a fascinating character who, sandwiched between the more flamboyant and controversial presidencies of Richard Nixon and Ronald Reagan, has been somewhat overlooked. However, despite being well into his nineties, but still alive at the time of writing in September 2021, Carter continues to manufacture successfully a dominant narrative of his own compassionate persona, and most likely believes it himself. Nevertheless, many of his major political decisions while in office, while being propagated as acts motivated by compassion and a firm personal sense of right and wrong, can be critically analysed as being underpinned by self-interested power politics.

Propaganda, strategic communication intended to instil values and opinions within its recipients that conform to the interests of the source, has been used to manoeuvre political thinking within mass groups for millennia (see Taylor, 2003). However, what Gerald Sussman (2011) calls the 'propaganda society' has developed in this age of prevailing neoliberal ideology. Sussman explains the propaganda society as a scenario wherein individuals are systematically saturated with subtly emotive messages that deprive alternative narratives of credibility, and encourage the masses to take the position that anyone who proposes alternative positions is delusional. For example, this can be seen in the field of charity, where someone arguing that charity should not be thought a blanket 'good cause' is likely to be discredited as a misanthropist. This is despite such an argument being a prominent social critique during the early 19th century as Western Europe adjusted to the Industrial Revolution.[1]

The development of the propaganda society has occurred alongside our understanding of the complexity of the human mind, the development of psychological research, and a growing percentage of our overall communications being filtered through electronic media platforms. These messages often exist in a paradox of attempting to reduce the free will of the recipient through subconscious stimulation, in a bid to guarantee certain outcomes that may or may not be in the individual's interests. According to Shoshana Zuboff (2018) this trade in human futures occurs under the guise of a diversionary claim that the motive is to empower and emancipate the individual. To this end, it can be of little coincidence that the major manufacturers of the media platforms that many rely upon for social interactions refer to us as 'users', the same terminology that medical professionals use for those with substance addiction issues.

Compassion narratives within the propaganda society are thus used as a form of seduction, distraction, and suppression; an overwhelming of the senses that results in the public not being able to determine what is genuine and what is fake, and consequently becoming apathetic to activities of the powerful. Within the political realm Martin Jenkins (2012: 10) argues that much of the impetus for these modern propaganda strategies comes from a desire to manufacture the false claim that politics and the economy are separate, disguising the market as the primary focus of much of the political elite, with many politicians sponsored into their roles to facilitate the exploitation of the public and the natural world. Similarly, Gerald Sussman has discussed the inverse ratio between the state's actual interest in protecting its citizens and its attempts to persuade the public of that interest. This it does as part of efforts to distract them from recognising its systematic ulterior motive: 'The maintenance of the corporate state requires an intensification of public persuasion through various forms of promotional speech and text in order to divert citizens from the cognitive dissonance that follows the unwillingness of the neoliberal state to protect public interests' (Sussman, 2012: 42).

Such a scenario serves the key theoretical framework of this chapter and what the French philosopher Guy Debord called 'the spectacle':

> In societies dominated by modern conditions of production, life is presented as an immense accumulation of spectacles. Everything that was directly lived has receded into a representation. The images detached from every aspect of life merge into a common stream in which the unity of that life can no longer be recovered. Fragmented views of reality regroup themselves into a new unity as a separate pseudo-world that can only be looked at. The specialisation of images of the world evolves into a world of autonomised images where even the deceivers are deceived. The spectacle is a concrete inversion of life, an autonomous movement of the non-living. The spectacle presents itself simultaneously as society itself, as a part of society, and as a means of unification. As a part of society, it is the focal point of all vision and all consciousness. But due to the very fact that this sector is separate,

it is, in reality, the domain of delusion and false consciousness; the unification it achieves is nothing but an official language of universal separation. (Debord, 2012: 32)

For Debord, then, the display of compassion by the politician forms a part of the spectacle as it is performed for public consumption. Compassion within this environment thus occurs as part of Debord's 'fragmented reality'. What is more, sat within the domain of façade and 'false consciousness', the political simulation of compassion encourages wider society to engage in similar behaviour, and has in many respects sabotaged what is now viewed as amounting to compassionate behaviour. In other words, a neoliberal process of narcissistic public image building revolves around false piety, virtuosity, and altruism. Debord continues:

> The task of the various branches of knowledge that are in the process of developing spectacular thought is to justify an unjustifiable society and to establish a general science of false consciousness. This thought is totally conditioned by the fact that it cannot recognize, and does not want to recognize, its own material dependence on the spectacular system. (Debord, 2012: 193)

Much like the wider 'spectacle' itself, the cover provided by false compassion can reach far into the political consciousness of politician and voter alike, the sense of obfuscation being enhanced by the solipsistic reality that no one can be certain of another individual's motive. Nevertheless, what is easily deduced by the trained eye as being false compassion has become commonplace under neoliberalism, with political propaganda in many ways echoing, but perhaps also leading, rhetorical trends found in charity campaigns, charitable giving, foreign aid, and so-called cultural and philanthro-capitalism. Indeed, if it is to be upheld as the prevailing doctrine, neoliberalism is dependent upon the circulation of compassion narratives among the public, false or otherwise. These encourage the availability of feel-good factors and the development of the feel-good or affective industries, which assist the justification of the system as they allow those teetering with concern to pay a penance rather than consider the upheaval of the system itself. However, compassion under such circumstances becomes a means to an individual end and is thus ultimately a falsehood. Nevertheless, because false compassion has become so commonplace, for many it has usurped how compassion ought to be, to the point that true and false sentiments cannot be distinguished in oneself or in others. Indeed, many find real compassion uncomfortable when it does occur.

THE FRAGILITY OF GENUINE COMPASSION

'Compassion' is a familiar word within the English language with most people knowing roughly what it means or insinuates. However, it finds itself squeezed among other similar terms that are erroneously used to mean the same thing, even in peer-reviewed academic publications. For example, in her work on charity and ribbon culture, Susan Moore (2008) makes continual reference to 'acts of compassion'. This refers to a moment when compassion is an intention rather than an act in and of itself. Compassion, empathy, altruism, philanthropy, sympathy, pity, and several other terms each have their own distinct definitions, but it is not the purpose of this chapter to delineate each of the terms from the others. 'Compassion' and 'empathy' are often used interchangeably, though, and so deserve some discussion here. Empathy, or the ability to empathise, involves interpreting accurately the emotional state of another living being by placing one's imagined self in that position, or by recalling positional and/or emotive knowledge to make an empathetic conclusion. Usually this involves the empathising individual having reference points from their own experiences or current positions that can be used in the development of empathetic feelings towards another. Empathy is thus a feeling based on the consideration of the imagined self. It surrounds the ability to think 'I would like/dislike to be in that position' and involves the internalising of the feelings of another within oneself. For example, feeling empathy for a homeless person is not necessarily the result of time spent homeless oneself, but can be based upon an appreciation of the known warmth and comfort of a bed or a good night's rest, the security that a home provides, or the knowledge of the harshness of the local weather or climate. Empathy is thus a feeling that comes and goes, as most feelings do, through circumstantial stimulation.

On the other hand, compassion is related to pro-social selflessness and should be viewed as a psychological ability that almost all humans have the capacity to obtain, but which is more rare than most think. While empathy is a feeling that revolves around an internalised accurate reading of the emotional situation of others, compassion has no such prerequisite and is a personality trait held at a much deeper level. It is a disposition or core personality trait, rather than a feeling subject to fluctuation, wherein the compassionate individual genuinely wants to see others gain fulfilment. The 18th century German philosopher Arthur Schopenhauer wrote that ego, compassion, and malice underpin all human activities, with the psychoanalyst and philosopher Erich Fromm later adding 'love' as a factor in its own right (rather than love as a manifestation of ego). Out of his three motives the egoistic incentive is, for Schopenhauer (1995: 131), the most important when determining human action, and he argues that it is only when egotistical motives have been thoroughly discounted (or when intent is clearly malicious) that we should turn to compassion as an ulterior. Schopenhauer (ibid.: 145) also argued that for an act to be considered 'moral', compassion should be the dominant motive. Indeed, no matter the public perception of an act, no action can be of moral worth if it is primarily motivated by egoism (let alone malice). This argument forsakes a wider discussion about inaction as a form of compassion, or where acts motivated by compassion are misguided or vacuous. To this end, Schopenhauer argued that compassion is much more rare than society might like to tell itself. Even though an action may seem or claim to have an outward moral worth and be propagated as such, an individual's choice of action (and thus dismissal of other potential courses of action that could be more helpful) regularly ensure that it also benefits the self in terms of well-being or esteem.

However, the ethicist Patrick Nowell-Smith (1954) thought differently. For Nowell-Smith, the argument made by the likes of Schopenhauer is predicated on the acceptance that the human mind always engages rationally with clarity of thought and, in the case of altruistic acts, as a witting conspirator in all matters. This is plainly not the case. Instead, Nowell-Smith suggests that the literature on 'hedonism' should also contribute to the debate. Hedonism is impulsive, like 'scratching an itch' to remove a sense of discomfort (Nowell-Smith, 1954: 134). However, hedonism is not always 'gluttonous' towards individual self-interest and, while it occurs irregularly and often in consequence to other emotional stimulations, can also enter the realm of pro-social behaviour (Nowell-Smith, 1954: 137). Nowell-Smith thus makes an important contribution to this discussion around the mindfulness behind human activities, but nevertheless the frivolity of hedonism contributes little to the discussion of compassion as a core personality trait. Nowell-Smith is right that hedonism is not always self-interested, but there can be little doubt that a significant proportion of it is. Moreover, hedonism revolves around instant gratification impulses, and that gratification is always self-centred, with the outcome varying between destruction and expedience.

Writing on altruism within the natural sciences, Samir Okasha notes that:

> an organism is said to behave altruistically when its behaviour benefits other organisms, at a cost to itself. The costs and benefits are measured in terms of reproductive fitness or expected number of offspring. So by behaving altruistically, an organism reduces the number of offspring it is likely to produce itself, but boosts the number that other organisms are likely to produce. (Okasha, 2013: 63)

The ability to think selflessly, or for the good of others despite self-interests lying elsewhere, is thus a clear prerequisite when considering human acts of compassion.[2] Furthermore, what emerges from Okasha's work is that a key part of the criteria from which compassionate responses emerge (or not) involves a consideration of the likely consequences upon the individual in terms of their reproductive fitness, potential for mating, or quality of prospective mates that they are likely to attract. This is as apparent in humans as it is other species, and links to Sigmund Freud's work on the id, ego, and superego. In 1923 Freud (2010) made the profound argument that genuine compassion was rare within humans, because any outwardly altruistic actions essentially originated from a fear of one's own castration rather than any more pro-social inclinations.[3] To this end, we can often see people feeling urges to 'give back' in later life after having raised children and secured their own genealogical legacy, or once they have secured their own economic and/or social status. However, the extent to which actions like these can claim a compassionate motive is contestable, given the minimal likelihood of it negatively impacting upon reproductive fitness.[4] Moreover, in the case of wealthy people donating large sums of money to charities and other voluntary organisations (philanthro-capitalists), while these may at first appear to be grandiose acts of generosity that garner the celebratory attention of media, such endowments tend to add to the 'good image' of the donor and likely cause little financial impact upon their sizable portfolios. Instead, when determining the compassion of the individual in their philanthropic outputs there ought to be more focus on the impact of these actions on their own economic and/or social status, as sometimes the smallest provisions provide as much, if not more, indication of compassionate inclination.

One of the most formidable groups of people to be studied by those interested in the occurrences of human compassion comprises those who helped save Jews from the Holocaust. These individuals, equally male and female, came from across the social classes within European nations during the 1930s and 1940s, and offer fascinating insight into why someone would go out of their way to shelter sometimes multiple families from persecution at significant risk to themselves and their own loved ones, and when the prevailing propaganda within their countries at the time claimed that Jewish people were beyond contempt. However, rather than immediately celebrate these acts as blanket examples of the capacity of humans to evoke compassion (which they were not), it ought first to be highlighted that very few people actually offered a helping hand to the Jews. The psychoanalyst Eva Fogelman puts the situation in stark terms when discussing the post-war commemoration of such rescues: 'by highlighting the courageous acts of a relative handful of individuals [it obscured] the essential fact that six million Jews were murdered. Two-thirds of the Jewish population of Eastern Europe was wiped out, and most people had done nothing about it' (Fogelman, 1995: xvii).

This is not to say that all those who did not help Jews had personas dominated by ego or malice. Similarly, some compassionate individuals who sat favourably towards the issue likely did not rescue Jews from the Holocaust out of fear, intimidation, lack of self-confidence, denial, a sense of their own powerlessness, or a lack of critical application towards the propaganda messages obscuring the genocide. Moreover, not all rescuers were motivated by compassion. Indeed, when Fogelman (1995: 163) categorised the predominant motive among those she interviewed, she found that compassion for the victims had the fewest responses, as most were more inclined to acknowledge ideological reasons (a political stance that opposed fascism) or religious reasons (belief in the teachings of the gospels or sense of their own divine purpose and impending judgement before God) ahead of more compassionate personal characteristics. Nevertheless, what Fogelman found when she analysed those more compassionate rescuers was that the attribute originated from within a core set of values that had been nurtured since childhood and which found expression during the Holocaust (ibid.: xviii). Those people, however, were few and far between even within the small community of rescuers.

In contrast to empathy, which is more of a feeling that can come and go, genuine compassion is a relatively stable personality characteristic. However, its manifestation into altruistic outward behaviour is determined by a combination of what Philip Zimbardo (2007) calls 'dispositional', 'situational', and 'systemic' factors. The adult temperament of an individual is thus heavily weighted towards their experiences in childhood, wherein a compassionate adult is likely one who received and witnessed the compassionate outputs of authority figures and caregivers in childhood. The adult was also encouraged to develop a sense of their own autonomous morality (as opposed to remaining heteronomous) through interactions with those caregivers and their childhood peers, and was all the while being nurtured within a social environment that disincentivises maliciousness and acute egoism, and which places value on the development of mindfulness, harmony, and peer-to-peer consideration. Compassion is thus something that, while almost all of us have the potential to develop it, has to be learned, honed, and sustained by the individual, facilitated in situ, and encouraged and valued by immediate others if it is to become a reliable disposition. Compassion is also a practice that requires discipline, concentration, and the overcoming of one's own narcissism if one is to avoid the temptations of the ease of residing within egoism. To this end, compassion is more difficult to hone than ego, which is in turn more expansive and accommodating, and has the potential to trick the human mind into believing that it is more compassionate than it actually is.

What, then, of those in political leadership positions? Very few leaders have arrived at their position unwittingly. Indeed, most are highly driven towards their own success and seek positive recognition by others for the legacy that they aim to create. Many have clambered over their peers in the pursuit of their ambitions, and others are sponsored sometimes into public administration roles by covert corporate power interests. For some, their position forms part of attempts to ensure continued government support for the exploitation of other humans, or a harnessing, and sometimes destruction, of the natural world for short-term human-centric purposes. Such evidence tempts the conclusion that there is a disproportionate dearth of compassion among those individuals who seek political power in comparison to the already small amount that exists within any given public.

The spectacle seeks to discredit or destroy anything that might contest its primacy. It demands allegiance from those who desire a place within its upper circle, and with that pledge comes the marginalisation of any compassionate virtues that the politician may have had that do not align with the spectacle's own egocentricity. Such a dynamic within a public body that must claim to work for the interests of its public leads unsurprisingly to an outpouring of compassion propaganda towards external audiences. These external communications are partly built upon internal narratives from within the spectacle as to its own righteous purpose; narratives that conveniently provide a distraction from the spectacle's self-interested reality, or even delusion. However, by the same measure these narratives are also indicative of compensation to the subconscious anxiety of those within the spectacle, an uncomfortable sense of disquiet perhaps, that compassionate shortcomings abound.

COMPASSION UNDER NEOLIBERALISM

There is an expanse between the circulation of compassion propaganda and the reality of society's actual compassion. This is the case in all societies regardless of the ideological persuasion. However, under neoliberalism, compassion – false compassion – forms part of the ideology's justification of itself. Thus most neoliberal ideologues live in a compassion delusion that has at least partly originated from propaganda that encourages a congruent, but ultimately distorted, sense of righteousness befitting the ideology's consolidation. In short, the false compassion displayed under neoliberalism is encouraged because it corresponds to the ideology's worldview and thus helps it to retain prominence. Neoliberalism can be defined as the intensification of market principles into the individual and collective consciousness. While it is conceptually an economic theory associated with 20th century economists such as Milton Friedman (1962), its principles have become the prevailing agenda of a growing number of business leaders and governments around the world since the 1970s. Despite it being primarily a theory of socio-economic organisation set amongst other theories pertaining to the same end, the advocates of neoliberal pivots have sought to present it as an inclusive ideology, simple 'common sense', or even the natural state of man. Regardless of the angle or vehemence of the endorsement, all of its advocates have intended to marginalise alternatives by making them appear unworkable, unrealistic, unnatural, or inhumane. In political terms this subtle, and sometimes subliminal, strangulation of other possibilities has resulted in the narrowing of electoral optionality to what market interests deem acceptable. As such, even those politicians who strongly oppose neoliberalism's inclinations have found it difficult to articulate coherent alternatives when up against its relentless, multidimensional, and saturating propaganda.

Beyond this, neoliberalism also propagates itself as pious, virtuous, altruistic, and compassionate. It does this despite it favouring the deregulation of commercial industries, reductions to international trade tariffs, and the privatisation and marketisation within public services. Such preferences have resulted in the intensification of human destitution around the world; tribal, indigenous, and smallholding communities being expelled from their traditional lands; unrivalled global pollution; human population growth; cultural imperialism; deforestation, soil deterioration, and desertification; global warming, climate change, and species decline. Each of these have been criticised for being diminutive, merciless, or callous, and ego- rather than eco-centric policy. However, at the top level, neoliberalism's hegemonic status remains largely unchallenged, and some of the explanation for this must be down not only to its ability to detach itself from collective responsibility for the acceleration of these global issues, but also to its claims to conscience and compassion.

Nevertheless, these narratives are essentially a mass exercise in distorted piety. Under neoliberalism, politicians, business leaders, citizens, and consumers alike feed into a witting or unwitting collective deception. The deception is the result of the conscious or subconscious guilt that these actors have for their contribution to the destitution of others and the destruction of the planet – the feeling that they should do more – and results in a compassion charade which under critical analysis shows little evidence of anything beyond ego, and is more akin to a penance for one's destructive actions than mindful abstinence, self-control, or behavioural corrections. However, to speak of false piety is a step too far. Many of the individuals who participate in the compassion spectacle most likely believe sincerely that they are assisting the resolution of social issues, and want these resolutions to occur. However, such responses exist within a neoliberal prism that confines thought and behaviour to avenues that offer little in the way of fundamental challenge to a market system that is the root of most human and environmental destitution.

Perhaps nowhere has seen the permeation of neoliberal values been seen more than in the charity industry. Modern philanthropic and anthro-zoological appeals – whether in the form of champagne and canapé-fuelled fundraising events, violin-backed 'tearjerker' videos showing the sad faces of suffering people or animals (but which tell the viewer nothing about the source of the problem and the issues behind it), telethons begging the audience to be a 'hero' and donate, or charity songs featuring a favourite pop star – are all intentionally developed transaction formats fixated on the massaging of the ego of the human donor and the individual's sense of righteousness and empowerment. To this, Eikenberry and Mirabella (2018: 46) highlight that 'people with the resources to give' are given the opportunity to play God through the 'authority to decide who benefits [from their actions] and to prescribe the mechanisms by which effectiveness is judged and implemented'. Rather than transform people's lives or address inequalities and injustices, this type of charity forms part of neoliberalism's justification of itself. As Raddon (2008: 28) argues, such charity under neoliberalism merely consolidates the existing system by providing a useful narrative to its advocates regarding their own moral validation. Moreover, it legitimises the levels of local and global social inequality, and encourages the restricting of the welfare state (in particular, the relinquishing of services formerly run by the state to the voluntary sector) and promotes a narrow ideal of one's community responsibility as that which is practised through charitable endeavour rather than peer-to-peer relations. To this end, in order to survive in the highly competitive marketplace, even charities that may be uncomfortable with the adoption of neoliberalism have had to alter their fundraising approaches to fit the model if they are to compete for monies.

As such, people in positions of power are often the facilitators of the social injustices that they claim to want to alleviate. Alternatively, they are willing participants in the production of the conditions and circumstances that optimise the potential for social injustices to occur. This is not new to the neoliberal age. Writing in 1844, Friedrich Engels accused the bourgeoisie of 'social murder' – death as a result of the squalor of one's existence within the industrial system – and critiqued the bourgeoisie's compassion pretence towards the poor:

> Let no one believe, however, that the 'cultivated' Englishman openly brags with his egotism. On the contrary, he conceals it under the vilest hypocrisy. What? The wealthy English fail to remember the poor? They who have founded philanthropic institutions, such as no other country can boast of! Philanthropic institutions forsooth! As though you rendered the proletarians a service in first sucking out their very life-blood and then practising your self-complacent, Pharisaic philanthropy upon them, placing yourselves before the world as mighty benefactors of humanity when you give back to the plundered victims the hundredth part of what belongs to them! ... charity which treads the down-trodden still deeper in the dust, which demands that the degraded, the pariah cast out by society, shall first surrender the last that remains to him, his very claim to manhood, shall first beg for mercy before your mercy deigns to press, in the shape of an alms, the brand of degradation upon his brow. (Engels, 1993: 283)

So, what is clear is that charitable activities are relational to capitalist exploitation. Indeed, many of the great philanthropic enterprises of the 19th century originated from growing awareness that the Industrial Revolution, which had begun during the latter 18th century across parts of Western Europe, degraded and devalued its workers and their families to the point of destitution. To this end, the growth of a charitable or voluntary sector serving a community of whatever kind or size sits at an inverse ratio to the exploitation of that community, wherein the actions elsewhere of those who claim to offer salvation are often contributors to that community's reliance upon donations.

Such is the extent of charitable giving as an unquestioned pillar of good conduct within many neoliberal societies, that there can be little doubt that some of the more critical-thinking democratically elected politicians around the world, despite personal misgivings, view charity endorsement as part of the propaganda accompanying their popularity optimisation strategy. Alternatively the politician, like most of the rest of society that they represent, thinks within a neoliberal prism and genuinely holds the work of all charity (bar a few instances of blatant corruption) in high regard. He or she has given little or no thought to more critical positions regarding when it is appropriate for the charity sector to operate, and when its presence allows other organisations and individuals to avoid their social and sometimes legal responsibility, which is therefore counterproductive to meaningful social change. Such validations demonstrate collusion between the market, the state, and opinion leaders that is unlikely to do anything other than consolidate the status of neoliberal policies, and encourages a distorted portrayal of human compassion.

Perhaps nowhere is compassion propaganda stronger for neoliberal governments than in the realm of the political communications that works alongside their foreign aid activities. The foreign aid industry, government-led project work to tackle extreme poverty and deprivation in the Global South, emerged as part of the post-World War II Truman Doctrine and quickly became part of the normative international behaviour of powerful states. One of foreign aid's fiercest academic critics has been the Colombian anthropologist Arturo Escobar who, using Michel Foucault's work on the dynamics of discourse and power in the representation of social reality, has discussed how the narrative surrounding foreign aid has been 'colonised' by neoliberal modes of being that marginalise the validity of alternatives. On the role of development assistance during the latter part of the 20th century he has written the following:

> Indeed, it seemed impossible to conceptualize social reality in other terms. Wherever one looked, one found the repetitive and omnipresent reality of development: governments designing and implementing ambitious development plans, institutions carrying out development programs in city and countryside alike, experts of all kinds studying underdevelopment and producing theories *ad nauseam*. The fact that most people's conditions not only did not improve but deteriorated with the passing of time did not seem to bother most experts. Reality, in sum, had been colonized by the development discourse, and those who were dissatisfied with this state of affairs had to struggle for bits and pieces of freedom within it, in the hope that in the process a different reality could be constructed. (Escobar, 1995: 5)

A critique of the foreign aid industry emerged during the 1960s and 1970s, and today it is mainly confined to small academic circles. This is because much of the public debate has been overwhelmed by the power of neoliberal propaganda to justify a world system befitting itself regardless of whether foreign aid has actually assisted in making the world a more egalitarian place as it so claims is its purpose. With the growth of neoliberal policies within mainstream politics during the 1970s and 1980s came an intensification of political communications regarding foreign aid's worthiness. Emotive rather than technical messaging was used, and projects were frequently accompanied by celebrity endorsement as part of a wider culture trend that has epitomised neoliberalism (see Brockington, 2014; Richey, 2016). Perhaps nobody puts the role of propaganda and self-delusion within the foreign aid and international charity neoliberal spectacle better than the sociologist Stanley Cohen, and it is with his unreserved words that this section ends:

> The public outpouring of emotion, the concerts, the spectacle – even the money raised – deepened the critics' misgivings. For them, [the] Live Aid [concerts in 1985] had undone the educational victories of the seventies … The African subjects of these campaigns had been objectified and then transformed into consumer items. Compassion through consumption: people could buy the paraphernalia that denoted they cared and watch pictures of themselves, or millions like them, caring. This allowed hedonism with self-delusion, while global television let them witness, and hence 'consume', the suffering and dying of the poor – and weave a message of self-congratulations about their generosity. Post-modern altruism: the reality of famine turned into a spectacle, image-driven and self-referential. (Cohen, 2001: 179)

NEOLIBERALISM AND JIMMY CARTER'S COMPASSION PROPAGANDA

In November 1976 the US elected someone who, at least until the middle of the Democrat Party's primaries, had been a little-known Georgian Senator – Jimmy Carter – to be its 39th President. Most literature on neoliberalism discusses Ronald Reagan's presidency of the US and Margaret Thatcher's incumbency as Prime Minister of the United Kingdom as watersheds in the advance of that ideology into mainstream politics. In the US, Reagan's fiscal policies, nicknamed 'Reaganomics', are the oft-touted primary evidence of his ideological doctrine. However, while the Reagan administration was certainly (and explicitly) neoliberal, there is some contention as to whether he was the first such president. Indeed, his predecessor in the White House, Jimmy Carter, laid many of the ideological seeds that would blossom once Reagan came to power. What is of particular interest to this chapter on propaganda and compassion is Carter's moral narrative that accompanied, and in many ways provided a justification for, the pivots and power interests that his administration pursued at the start of the neoliberal age.

Carter signed several deregulation Acts across different industries, tightened government expenditure, reduced the role of the state in the provision of services, and advocated for society to play a larger role in overcoming social issues (see Fink and Graham, 1998; Smith, 1986), all of which can be identified as key traits of a regime's neoliberal preference. During his 1978 and 1979 State of the Union addresses Carter made several statements that were indicative of his neoliberal ideology. The following two quotations are examples of his stance on small governance, deregulation of industry, and the primacy of society, rather than the state, in fixing social ills.

> Government cannot solve our problems … It cannot eliminate poverty, or provide a bountiful economy, or reduce inflation, or save our cities, or cure illiteracy, or provide energy. (Carter, 1978)

> America has the greatest economic system in the world. Let's reduce government interference and give it a chance to work. (Carter, 1979)

Carter's presidential campaign and subsequent time in the White House was dominated by propaganda highlighting his team's moral imperative for action rather than any explicit acknowledgement of self-interest. This approach formed part of an attempt to align with trends in perceived US public opinion at the time that felt the country had lost its way after the embarrassment of the Vietnam War, the revelations of the Pentagon Papers (1971), the Watergate scandal (1972), and the resignation of President Richard Nixon (1974). The American electorate deemed Carter, a practising Southern Baptist with a family farming background, the most suitable person to return the country to the noble and 'exceptional' course that forms much of its domestic and international propaganda, and to rearticulate what the concept of 'America' stood for around the world. The historian John Hellman summed up the impact of the American experience of the mid-1970s well when he wrote that:

> Americans entered Vietnam with certain expectations that a story, a distinctly American story, would unfold. When the story of America in Vietnam turned into something unexpected, the true nature of the larger story of America itself became the subject of intense cultural dispute. On the deepest level, the legacy of Vietnam is the disruption of our story, of our explanation of the past and vision of the future. (Hellman, 1986: x)

During his presidency Carter prioritised two pivots in American foreign policy, both of which, he argued, were motivated by an assertion of the US's moral leadership. The first was the transfer of control of the Panama Canal to the government of the Republic of Panama, and the second was the formal diplomatic recognition of the People's Republic of China ahead of the Republic of China in Taiwan. Both were framed as having moral imperative, and the former of the two will now be discussed in more detail.

At the signing of the Panama Canal treaties on 7 September 1977, Carter stated that he had pursued these negotiations out of compassion for those disenfranchised by the US imperialist policies of the past towards Latin America: 'In the peaceful process of negotiating the treaties we have shown the world a spirit which recognises and respects the rights of others and seeks to help all people to fulfil their legitimate aspirations with confidence and dignity' (Balmer, 2014: 83).

In response, the President of Panama, Omar Torrijos Herrera, referred to Carter as 'a man of great morality fully dedicated to the cause of the weak' (ibid.). According to Carter's (2010) memoirs, he believed that for too long the United States, a country founded on the principles of the Enlightenment, had preached the values of democracy, individualism, and the guarantee of civil liberties to the world, and yet it had spent much of its international effort defending its international capital interests and in the process contradicting those very principles in its relations with foreign publics. However, despite what even Carter himself may have believed were his intentions, his regime had no greater moral imperative than any other US administration. Indeed, tucked away in a sentence towards the end of his memoirs, he admits that rather than any more righteous intent, much of his administration's international propaganda surrounding the promotion of human rights was a strategic 'counterbalance' to the Soviet propaganda of the day (Carter, 2010: 264).

As such, it can be deduced with some certainty that Carter and his communications strategists, Hamilton Jordan in particular, astutely recognised the domestic and international mood surrounding the US and manufactured a bold narrative of morality, compassion, and power redistribution that they hoped would first of all deliver a Democrat to power and then sustain his credibility once in office. To this end, Carter claimed that the Panama Canal Zone (PCZ) ought to be relinquished, as the occupation of the territory was rhetorical hypocrisy that was resented by Latin Americans as a symbol of US imperialism. However, from my own research into the Carter administration, it is clear that the relinquishing of the PCZ was in fact a neoliberal pivot that formed part of an effort to promote Panama as an emerging tax haven and regional hub for international finance, conveniently located at one of the conduits of world shipping. The development and increased use of tax havens by wealthy individuals and organisations has been a feature of the neoliberal pivots since the 1970s.

Emulating the Virgin Islands and Cayman Islands in the Caribbean, or Jersey, Guernsey, and the Isle of Man in Europe, after 1978 Panama would grow its status as a tax haven for wealthy individuals, kleptocratic heads of state, and corporations looking to hide money or to protect or launder finances received from corrupt practices (see Obermayer and Obermaier, 2017; Shaxson, 2011; Zucman, 2015). Perhaps most indicative of the true focus of the Panama negotiations was Carter's appointment of Sol Linowitz to lead the US negotiating team. Linowitz was a former US ambassador to the Organization of American States, and was on the executive boards of both Pan Am airlines (whose Latin American headquarters were already in Panama) and Marine Midland bank, which alongside Bank of America, Bankers Trust, Chase Manhattan, the First National Bank of Chicago, First National City Bank, and about 60 other US banks, moved hundreds of billions of dollars of assets out of the US to Panama in the years after the 1978 treaties. Linowitz was also the Chairman of the Commission on United States–Latin American Relations. This group had been set up in 1974 and was one of the most prolific organisations for the promotion of pro-treaty propaganda. The Commission was largely funded by corporate money, including the Ford Foundation and the Rockefeller family (David Rockefeller was Chairman of Chase Manhattan bank at this time). Other members of the Commission included: W. Michael Blumenthal, who was Jimmy Carter's first Secretary of the Treasury; Samuel Huntington, an academic and aide to the National Security Council; Peter Peterson, chairman of Lehman Brothers; and Elliot Richardson, Carter's Attorney General. Thus, Wall Street banks and some of the US's largest corporations held considerable influence over the direction of the Panama negotiations, while Carter, in the role of neoliberal facilitator, provided the diversionary moralist propaganda of international treaty-making on 'good neighbour' grounds. Indeed, such has been the success of his diversion that the numerous biographies and academic publications that discuss the Carter administration (including those who profusely disliked him) make little, if anything, of his interactions with major US corporations. For example, in Fink and Graham's (1998) edited volume, which is sold as a comprehensive critical analysis of Carter policy, there is not a single reference to his administration's interactions with Wall Street firms.

At the time of writing, Carter is the oldest living former US President, and in his post-White House years he has sought to affirm his apparent disposition towards compassion and to develop his personal image as a moral standard bearer. His publications include *Keeping Faith* (1982), *Talking Peace: A Vision for the Next Generation* (1993), *An Hour Before Daylight* (2001) (which discusses his rural Southern Baptist values), and *A Call to Action: Women, Religion, Violence and Power* (2014), all of which focus on quandaries surrounding the poor, weak, or suppressed. Carter's supporters reciprocated his efforts. When he appeared on *The Late Show with Stephen Colbert* in March 2018, aged 93, he had the audience in raptures with his critique of Donald Trump's moral bankruptcy and was lauded by the show's host for his moral attainment. To this end, Fink and Graham (1998: 1) have labelled him the US's greatest former President, and someone who has made more contribution since leaving office than when he was the incumbent.

CONCLUSION

One of the problems with analysing propaganda and compassion is that we cannot be absolutely certain what the motivation of any individual is, even if they were to declare it and even if they believe themselves to be accurate. This is because compassion is especially vulnerable to the human capacity for denial, which may or may not be partially conscious, and can occur when the ego deceives the mind into believing that compassion is the primary motivator behind an action as part of efforts to preserve the individual's sense of righteousness. To this end, when it comes to matters of the self, or matters concerning Jimmy Carter or any other politician, our conclusions are the result of critical analysis more than anything else. As such, this chapter has provided evidence of the contestability of Carter's claim that compassion was the imperative behind his foreign policy pivots. However, whether Carter believed what he was saying cannot be proven.

More broadly, though, this age of neoliberalism is also the age of systematic propaganda that utilises compassion as a strategic tool for self-interested ends. This is not to say that compassion cannot or does not occur under such conditions, for it surely does, but that the instances of compassion as the primary motive for behaviour are far less than the levels of propaganda that claim it to be so. Therefore, such is the exploitation of the natural world and the levels of inequality between humans under neoliberalism, that its ideologues must present a consistent and comprehensive propaganda experience that saturates public consciousness, limits the space for critique, and makes change appear fanciful rather than achievable. Compassion, sincere or false, becomes a convenient vehicle through which neoliberalism's ideologues can articulate their righteousness while simultaneously consolidating the exploitative structures that are the superstructure's reality.

Neoliberalism thus encourages modern politics to exist within a spectacle. For its continuation, the spectacle relies upon the perceived virtuosity of its advocates, and this creates congruence between allegiance to the spectacle and the propagation of a misguided or deceitful compassion narrative that supports the interests of the powerful rather than greater agency for the weak. However, compassion is no mainstay. Despite his questionable compassion motives, Jimmy Carter was still defeated in the 1980 presidential election by the Republican Party candidate Ronald Reagan, who won in 44 of the US's 50 states. Carter's compassionate narration frame, regardless of his actual motivations, left him vulnerable to his political rivals who felt that whatever penance the US ought to have paid for its actions in the previous decade – very little, being the Reagan argument – it was now time for a reassertion of egoism and self-interest. However, this debate existed within the falsehood of the emerging neoliberal spectacle, because Reagan knew, likely as much as Carter did, that compassion was of lesser significance to the decision-making than the propaganda suggested.

NOTES

1. This argument was approached from several ideological positions with the likes of Thomas Carlyle, Charles Dickens, Friedrich Engels, and Henry David Thoreau all making contributions to the field.
2. This is one of the main areas of contestation over what constitutes altruism. Members of the popular school of philosophy writing about effective altruism argue that it can be delivered without expense to the self. William Macaskill (2015: 15), for example, writes that, 'altruism simply means improving the lives of others. Many people believe that altruism should necessarily denote sacrifice, but if you can do good while maintaining a comfortable living for yourself, that's a bonus, and I'm very happy to call that altruism.' However, Macaskill's argument, and those of others engaged in this field of study such as Peter Singer (2000), is under-theorised because the compassionate individual would not perceive their actions as being sacrificial, given their original inclination towards compassion and the sanctity with which they hold their values. The identification of 'sacrifice' within the action is thus the perception of an observer less inclined towards pro-social behaviour. This analogy sits at the very heart of what it means to be compassionate, but also the misconceptions that surround it.
3. Contemporaries of Freud have expanded or developed his original thesis. Eli Sagan (1985), for example, believed that the origins of compassion are found in the love received as a child, wherein compassion in adulthood could be framed as a desire to return the love received in childhood. Such an argument helps to explain compassion towards those who we find semblance in (memories of childhood caregivers), but runs into problems when trying to explain compassion for the natural world or for humans who are unlike us or who we are told are somehow 'different'.
4. See Macaskill's argument in note 2.

REFERENCES

Balmer, R. (2014), *Redeemer: The Life of Jimmy Carter*, New York: Basic Books.
Brockington, D. (2014), *Celebrity Advocacy and International Development*, Abingdon: Routledge.
Carter, J. (1978), 'State of the Union Address: 19th January 1978', available at https://millercenter.org/the-presidency/presidential-speeches/january-19-1978-state-union-address, accessed 4 October 2019.
Carter, J. (1979), 'State of the Union Address: 23rd January 1979', available at https://millercenter.org/the-presidency/presidential-speeches/january-23-1979-state-union-address, accessed 4 October 2019.
Carter, J. (1982), *Keeping Faith: Memoirs of a President*, New York: Bantam Books.
Carter, J. (1993), *Talking Peace: A Vision for the Next Generation*, New York: Dutton.
Carter, J. (2001), *An Hour Before Daylight*, New York: Simon & Schuster.
Carter, J. (2010), *White House Diary*, New York: Farrar, Straus & Giroux.
Carter, J. (2014), *A Call to Action: Women, Religion, Violence and Power*, New York: Simon & Schuster.
Cohen, S. (2001), *State of Denial: Knowing About Atrocities and Suffering*, Cambridge: Polity Press.
Debord, G. (2012), *Society of the Spectacle*, Eastbourne: Soul Bay Press.
Eikenberry, A. and R. Mirabella (2018), 'Extreme Philanthropy: Philanthrocapitalism, Effective Altruism, and the Discourse of Neoliberalism', *Journal of Political Science and Politics*, 51(1): 43–47.
Engels, F. (1993), *The Condition of the Working Class in England*, Oxford: Oxford University Press.
Escobar, A. (1995), *Encountering Development: The Making and Unmaking of the Third World*, Princeton, NJ: Princeton University Press.
Fink, G.M. and H.D. Graham (eds) (1998), *The Carter Presidency: Policy Choices in the Post-New Deal Era*, Lawrence, KS: University of Kansas Press.
Fogelman, E. (1995), *Conscience and Courage: Rescuers of Jews during the Holocaust*, London: Cassell.
Freud, S. (2010), *The Ego and the Id*, Los Angeles, CA: Pacific Publishing Studio.
Friedman, M. (1962), *Capitalism and Freedom*, Chicago, IL: University of Chicago Press.
Hellman, J. (1986), *American Myth and the Legacy of Vietnam*, New York: Columbia University Press.
Jenkins, M. (2012) 'Introduction', in G. Debord, *Society of the Spectacle*, Eastbourne: Soul Bay Press.
Macaskill, W. (2015), *Doing Good Better: Effective Altruism and a Radical New Way to Make a Difference*, London: Guardian Books.

Moore, S. (2008), *Ribbon Culture: Charity, Compassion and Public Awareness*, Basingstoke: Palgrave Macmillan.
Nowell-Smith, P.H. (1954), *Ethics*, London: Penguin.
Obermeyer, B., and F. Obermaier (2017), *The Panama Papers: Breaking the Story of How the Rich and Powerful Hide Their Money*, London: Oneworld.
Okasha, S. (2013), 'Biological Altruism', in M. Moody and B. Breeze (eds), *The Philanthropy Reader*, London: Routledge, pp. 62–66.
Raddon, M. (2008), 'Neoliberal Legacies: Planned Giving and the New Philanthropy', *Studies in Political Economy*, 81(1): 27–48.
Richey, L.A. (ed.) (2016), *Celebrity Humanitarianism and North-South Relations: Politics, Place and Power*, London: Routledge.
Sagan E. (1985), *At the Dawn of Tyranny: The Origins of Individualism, Political Oppression and the State*, New York: Alfred A. Knopf.
Schopenhauer, A. (1995), *On the Basis of Morality*, Cambridge: Hackett Publishing.
Shaxson, N. (2011), *Treasure Islands: Tax Havens and the Men Who Stole the World*, London: Vintage Books.
Singer, P. (2000), *Writings on an Ethical Life*, New York: Harper Collins.
Smith, G. (1986), *Morality, Reason and Power: American Diplomacy in the Carter Years*, New York: Hill & Wang.
Sussman, G. (2011), *The Propaganda Society: Promotional Culture and Politics in Global Context*, New York: Peter Lang.
Sussman, G. (2012), 'Systemic Propaganda and State Branding in Post-Soviet Eastern Europe', in N. Kaneva (ed.), *Branding Post-Communist Nations: Marketizing National Identities in the 'New' Europe*, London: Routledge, pp. 23–49.
Taylor, P. (2003), *Munitions of the Mind: A History of Propaganda from the Ancient World to the Present Era*, Manchester: Manchester University Press.
Zimbardo, P. (2007), *The Lucifer Effect: How Good People Turn Evil*, London: Rider
Zuboff, S. (2018), *The Age of Surveillance Capitalism: The Fight for a Human Future at the New Frontier of Power*, London: Profile Books.
Zucman, G. (2015), *The Hidden Wealth of Nations: The Scourge of Tax Havens*, Chicago, IL: University of Chicago Press.

13. Political propaganda and the global struggle against Apartheid, 1948–1994

Nicholas J. Cull

INTRODUCTION

Writing in 1903, W.E.B. Du Bois, the great African-American intellectual and propagandist for racial equality, observed: 'The problem of the Twentieth Century is the problem of the color line' (DuBois, 1903). His words were prophetic, but especially in the history of South Africa where the entire second half of the century was dominated by a struggle for racial justice. The associated propaganda battle transcended the boundaries of that one state and was fought by an international network of activists on one side and a desperate but resource-rich minority government on the other, for the prize of global public opinion. The struggle is revealing in the techniques and tactics used but also in the underlying processes. The conflict and the messages shaped each other. In time the messages opened opportunities for the ultimate compromise and the emergence of a new South Africa. This chapter is a synthesis of a decade of study in the role of communication around Apartheid which has included extensive work in the archives of the African National Congress (ANC), the United Kingdom's (UK) Anti-Apartheid Movement, the United Nations, and interviews with representatives of all sides. Its objective is to identify the elements of that story which are especially relevant for the wider study of propaganda, which for these purposes is defined as a process of mass political persuasion rather than something necessarily malicious or untruthful, though as will be seen, one of my conclusions is that even exaggerations made with the best motives can have negative consequences.

The propaganda battle over Apartheid passed through four distinct phases, each of which will be addressed below. A conscience-raising phase in the 1950s, dominated by a liberal perspective in which South Africans and sympathetic members of the international community appealed to international values old and new. A retrenchment phase of the 1960s, when the liberation movement was on the defensive, during which the South African government sought to legitimise its position in the world while repressing and demonising dissent. A radical phase in the 1970s, during which the liberation movement assumed full direction of the campaign and argued for a revolutionary solution. And a final phase in the 1980s, when the sides in the struggle clashed and ultimately found their way to compromise. But before that story can be told it is necessary first to remind readers of the origins of the issue.

BACKGROUND: BRITAIN'S UNSTABLE DOMINION

While it approached the middle of the 20th century constitutionally equivalent to Australia and Canada as a Dominion of the British Empire, the Union of South Africa was a profoundly unstable entity. The state was a fragile compromise of minority white interests – cobbled together to reconcile communities of British and Dutch origin in the aftermath of the South African War of 1899–1902 – but its government also had to manage the presence of a black majority, whose labour was essential to prosperity but regulated through a system of unjust laws. The state also included sizeable minorities of Indian and mixed-race origin who had become part of the nation's story during its two centuries of development, whose role and rights were politically moot. During the course of the 1930s, the Afrikaner community swung into greater militancy (some leaders openly sympathised with the Nazis), and as the war ended the community, as embodied in the National Party, called for radical solutions to secure their future. More than this, it seemed clear that the values embedded in the post-war international system of the United Nations, with its emphasis on self-determination, were not the values of the Union of South Africa. The first flashpoint was the state of South West Africa administered by South Africa as a trustee since the defeat of Germany in the Great War. South Africa did not wish to hand this territory back. Then, in 1948, the National Party (NP) won the general election and, under the leadership of Prime Minister D.F. Malan, began the process of passing a package of laws to safeguard the privilege of South Africans of European origin. The approach was called 'Apartheid', from the Afrikaans word for 'separateness' (Higginson, 2014; Dubow, 1989; Moodie, 1975).

Propaganda and censorship are two sides of the same coin, and both were part of the promotion of Apartheid.[1] The NP government argued for its system using a rhetoric of Afrikaner exceptionalism, religious duty, and associating the stability of their state with the Cold War interests of the Western world. Dissidents were branded as Communists and the phrase *Rooi Gevaar* (Red Peril) was as ubiquitous as *Swart Gevaar* (Black Peril). In terms of censorship the NP enacted the Suppression of Communism Act in 1950, which empowered the government to close radical publications and 'ban' individuals from writing or speaking in public. It fell to activists within the country and beyond to respond (for an overview of censorship under Apartheid, see Merrett, 1994).

THE LIBERAL PHASE: CONSCIENCE-RAISING

Apartheid found a pre-existing set of internal opposition organisations. While the African National Congress (established in 1912) was the best-known, there were other actors in the struggle with their own approaches and/or constituencies including a multiracial Communist Party of South Africa, operating underground as the South African Communist Party (SACP) from 1950, the South African Indian Congress (SAIC) movement, trade unions, and a Liberal Party, established in 1953. Key activities included the Defiance Campaign of 1952, a programme of civil disobedience coordinated between the ANC and Indian Congress, and the collective creation of a Freedom Charter in 1955, by which the coalition of anti-Apartheid groups within South Africa asserted a common agenda. The propaganda techniques on display included a playbook of non-violent activism borrowed from the Indian independence movement. Activists understood that in a repressive environment such as South Africa the symbolic act of defiance could be a potent messenger: propaganda of the deed. The Defiance Campaign brought many new members to the ANC (for a history by one of the ANC's lead communicators, see Meli, 1989).

Internationally, the anti-Apartheid message depended on the existence of transnational networks. Three initially loomed large: the United Nations (UN), the Anglican Church, and

English-language publishing networks whereby both news stories and fiction from South Africa were available in the UK. The three key voices were a South African novelist, Alan Paton, whose novel *Cry the Beloved Country* (1948) about a rural black preacher's search for his son in the squalor and injustice of Johannesburg won a global audience,[2] and two English priests based in South Africa: Michael Scott and Trevor Huddleston, who both cultivated links with the media. Scott had worked with the Indian community in the mid-1940s, and was invited by the Herero people of Namibia to speak in defence of their rights at the UN, where diplomats from the newly independent India were already leading demands for the UN to respond to injustice in South Africa as a whole. As Apartheid progressed to include the destruction of ethnically mixed neighbourhoods, Huddleston documented the brutal realities. He attracted the attention of the Anglo-American media, and in 1956 his observations appeared in a widely read non-fiction book called *Naught for Your Comfort*. All three men parlayed the attention that they received into organisations. Paton founded the Liberal Party within South Africa. Scott converted David Astor (proprietor of the UK'S *Observer* newspaper) into an anti-Apartheid position. Astor not only fought for the cause in print, but he also bankrolled an institution called the Africa Bureau, headed by Scott, which served as both a pressure group and a think tank for the entire African decolonisation process, and a resource for media coverage. Huddleston campaigned to press the South African government to reform through the pressure of a boycott, and even suggested that the boycott could apply in the cultural sphere. Other British activities included yet another churchman, Cannon John Collins, founder of Christian Action, who raised money to pay legal costs for those anti-Apartheid activists put on trial for treason within South Africa, and used celebrity contacts within the UK to draw attention to the cause (Yates and Chester, 2006; Denniston, 1999; Herbstein, 2004; Skinner, 2010).

Considered in retrospect, these early campaigns are remarkable for their emphasis on religious values and the social implications of faith, which also propelled the contemporaneous Campaign for Nuclear Disarmament. Many figures, including Cannon Collins and philosopher Bertrand Russell, were engaged in both movements. Activists used culture as a mechanism to appeal to donors and new recruits, but tended to work with sympathetic figures in the existing jazz or growing folk scene to produce 'benefit' events rather than working with South African musical forms. South African music, and the opportunity to discuss politics, made some inroads into Western consciousness with the export of a musical called *King Kong*, which reached London in 1961. For many audiences, especially those in France, their point of entry into understanding South Africa was an independent drama-documentary created by American director Lionel Rogosin in partnership with two young black south African writers, Bloke Modisane and Lewis Nkosi. The film was shot in secret, using amateurs, with a vibrant musical soundtrack taken straight from the community-based musicians of the townships. It introduced the singer Miriam Makeba to the world quite literally as Rogosin paid for her to leave the country. She became the embodiment not just of her country and its creativity but of her continent, for the next decade and beyond.[3]

The liberal, non-violent activism of the 1950s did not bring about the desired change. For all the salience of the campaign in British life the South African people became increasingly frustrated with restraint. The ANCsplit, losing a chunk of members to a breakaway Pan Africanist Congress (PAC), while the South African government ratcheted up repression, and prepared to introduce a state made in their preferred image to the world (Pogrund, 2006).

RETRENCHMENT

For the South African government, international propaganda drove ever more extreme reactions. The state voted to become a republic and severed its links with the British Commonwealth. In March 1960 police opened fire on a PAC-inspired crowd at Sharpeville, and by killing 69 protestors created one of the defining moments of Apartheid (for a contemporaneous account commissioned by the UN for publicity, see Reeves, 1966 [1992]).

A new Minister of Justice, John Vorster, increased censorship and banning, and hunted down radical leaders. Meanwhile the liberation movement without South Africa looked for more energetic models. Leaders connected with the Communist bloc and with post-colonial governments in Algeria, Egypt, and Ghana. The Nobel Institute in Oslo also gave the cause a boost when it awarded the Nobel Peace Prize to the ANC's President-General Albert Luthuli, but a new generation of leaders was emerging.[4]

In 1961, the ANC formed a military wing called *uMkhonto we Sizwe* (meaning Spear of the Nation and usually abbreviated as MK) and pledged a campaign of sabotage unless the government of South Africa reformed. MK's leader, Nelson Mandela, swiftly captured international attention for his ability to dodge capture. Nicknamed 'the Black Pimpernel', Mandela knew the value of granting an exclusive interview with a well-chosen foreign reporter at an 'undisclosed location'. One of the few opportunities for leaders of the opposition to speak publicly within the country was during trials, which Mandela himself did to great effect at the climax of the Rivonia trial in 1964, declaring:

> During my lifetime I have dedicated myself to this struggle of the African people. I have fought against white domination, and I have fought against black domination. I have cherished the ideal of a democratic and free society in which all persons live together in harmony and with equal opportunities. It is an ideal which I hope to live for and to achieve. But if needs be, it is an ideal for which I am prepared to die.[5]

The genre of the speech from the dock was already established in radical circles, with precedents including the famous 'history will absolve me' speech of Fidel Castro from 1953. Features of the media battle over MK activity included a clash over frames and terminology. The South African government spoke of terrorism. The MK spoke of themselves as freedom fighters, fighting racists to establish democracy and majority rule.

The Pretoria government sought to soften its image overseas by spending on advertising and public relations in Western publications in a great campaign of what would now be termed 'nation branding'. Glossy photographs of idyllic beaches and rolling vineyards were the order of the day. Tax incentives meant that it became a bargain to film a motion picture in South Africa. At least one film with a Wild West setting was rewritten to take place on the Veld. Assets for the South African government included scientific research. Dr Christiaan Barnard's completion of the first heart transplant in December 1967 was much celebrated. For a season it seemed that the Republic of South Africa might prevail. Economic difficulties in Western Europe meant that centre-left governments, which might ordinarily have been unsympathetic, were obliged to maintain arms sales and business links with South Africa for economic reasons. However, such success drove a still greater anti-reaction. (On South African government propaganda, see Nixon, 2016; Laurence, 1968).[6]

RADICAL PHASE: 1970S

By the end of the 1960s, the South African government faced a better-organised foe. At the United Nations the decade of horror at the excesses of Sharpeville had been channelled not simply into resolutions censuring South Africa, but also the creation of a dedicated infrastructure to work on South African issues. In time this included a publicity unit which created materials under the UN imprint, but no less importantly the UN Centre Against Apartheid, managed by Indian diplomat E.S. Reddy, operated as a funder and resource for the civil anti-Apartheid movement around the world. The political support for this came from newly independent nations across Africa, the countries of the Soviet Bloc, and the Nordic countries, which also provided the funds for the UN to redistribute as needed. For the decolonised countries of Africa, the issue of Apartheid was an obvious shared project and a test case for the promises of the post-war order. As each nation stepped into independence the persistence of minority regimes in places such as South Africa, Rhodesia, and Angola seemed ever more outrageous. The UN developed a calendar of events to keep South Africa in the consciousness of the world, including memorialisation of Sharpeville each March. In March 1978 the UN began the commemoration of an entire Anti-Apartheid Year of UN-sanctioned activity.[7]

The ANC had survived the repressions of the 1960s and successfully reconstituted itself in exile. The organisation was close to the Eastern Bloc, welcoming training and funding from Moscow and East Berlin, and aligning with socialist prescriptions for the future government of South Africa. The mischaracterisation of the ANC during early years of Apartheid now seemed increasingly accurate. Such British and American officials who wanted a change in South Africa looked elsewhere for their 'horse to back'. The UK's Foreign Office had high hopes of the PAC and its jailed leader Robert Sobukwe. The US had its fingers crossed for an internal leader emerging from the trade union or student movements. The ANC saw the danger and worked to remain in the imagination of South African people. From bases in Zambia, they tried occasional guerilla raids into South Africa. They also smuggled anti-Apartheid propaganda materials into the urban centres, working with sympathetic flight crew of international airlines and British students (the so-called London recruits). Outside South Africa its most effective work was building awareness of and sympathy for the anti-Apartheid cause. Foot soldiers of the campaign included a generation of left and liberal students from across South Africa's ethnic spectrum who had left the country. Many countries around the world developed anti-Apartheid movements along the same lines as the UK. Movements in the Netherlands, Germany, and Sweden were especially active. In the UK one of the first markers of the reassertion of anti-Apartheid was the movement to disrupt a tour of South Africa's rugby team and prevent a cricket tour in 1970 (Konieczna and Skinner, 2019; Brown and Høgsbjerg, 2020).

The European civil society anti-Apartheid movements in the 1970s continued to work through boycotts. They not only refused to purchase South African exports such as Cape brand apples or Outspan brand oranges, but also selected corporations with prominent interests in South Africa for boycott. Barclays Bank and Shell Oil attracted particular attention. The campaign made it easy for people to feel connected to the struggle. Simple, everyday consumption decisions were highlighted as having consequences. It was a form of participatory propaganda, and while it sent a signal to South Africa, it was also about performing or signalling virtue to one's peers, or even conforming to the mores of one's generation. The UN took the lesson and extended the economic boycott to the cultural realm, keeping a blacklist of sports people and cultural figures who visited South Africa. The sporting boycott bit especially deeply within South Africa. White South Africans were inordinately proud of their national rugby and cricket teams, and to be excluded from international competition was to be denied a stage to symbolically prove the country's strength, and to be confronted by its international pariah status.

Propaganda gambits in this period of the campaign included upgrading the visual presentation of the Anti-Apartheid Movement (AAM), thanks to the pro bono services of a team from one of the UK's top advertising agencies, DDB. Their first contribution was a poster to support the sport protest. It showed a blow-up of a particularly brutal shot from a demonstration at Cato Manor near Durban in 1959, of a policeman with his baton raised high over a protestor, coupled with the slogan devised by copywriter Malcolm Gluck: 'If you could see their national sport you might be less keen to see their cricket.' Another version had rugby. The DDB team also created covers for *Anti-Apartheid News.* These were often photo-montages in the tradition of the left-wing propaganda of the Weimar Republic: images of British politicians edited into Nazi uniform standing beside leaders from Rhodesia, or of Africans with immense burdens. The visual debt to Weimar spoke to the extent to which the Anti-Apartheid Movement lined up with memories of the Second World War. It was not a difficult leap to make when senior Afrikaner politicians had been Nazi sympathisers and the rhetoric of the Pretoria government relied on racial concepts.[8]

Every now and again events within South Africa threw new images into the visual lexicon of the struggle: images of new martyrs such as the Black Consciousness leader Steve Biko, and of new atrocities. The single news photograph, taken by a local photographer called Sam Nzima, of the dying Soweto boy Hector Pieterson being carried by a classmate after police opened fire on a demonstration in June 1976, was especially powerful (Marinovich and Silva, 2000: 10).

Children had an inherent rhetorical value as symbols of innocence, and Nzima's picture of Hector Pieterson was destined to take its place alongside the surrendering Warsaw Ghetto boy (1943) and Napalm Girl in the Vietnam War (1972) as an enduring image of the cruelty of the century. State censorship made it difficult for moving images to play much of a role in the struggle, but there were notable exceptions. A secret camera team affiliated with the PAC successfully filmed and smuggled out sufficient footage to create two impressive documentaries, *Phelandaba/End of the Dialogue* (1970) and *Last Grave at Dimbaza* (1974). Both aired on BBC television.[9]

One surprising absence from anti-Apartheid propaganda in the 1960s and early 1970s was the image of Nelson Mandela. Being jailed, there were few recent images of him, but more than this the approach of the ANCemphasised the collective challenge of a generation of political prisoners. The personality at the heart of the movement and its face was the President of the ANC in exile, Oliver Tambo. Mandela became more significant only in 1978 when a recently released ANC prisoner, Mac Maharaj, mentioned to the UN's E.S. Reddy that the year would be Mandela's 60th birthday. Reddy saw an opportunity to mount a campaign about the plight of a single political prisoner. It is testament to Mandela's lack of centrality at that point that it took some inquiries to establish exactly when his birthday was, and to the ANC's reluctance to elevate even him above his comrades, that they insisted on the campaign being Free Nelson Mandela and all Political Prisoners. Reddy's instincts were sound. Global audiences found it hard to comprehend the plight of a nation or even a section of that nation in jail, but readily identified with the story of one man. From 1978, Mandela grew in symbolic significance within the movement.[10]

The 1970s saw a surge in cultural content in anti-Apartheid propaganda. The ANC structure welcomed cultural activity as an area of endeavour for refugees joining its structure in exile. The movement organised poetry events, and in time created its own musical troupe who toured performing songs associated with the struggle, raising both consciousness and funds. ANC cultural workers also created graphic designs for use in posters. In terms of content the leadership were eager to find a winning message, and went as far as to ask senior figures in Vietnam for advice, wondering if perhaps their recent victory over the United States might provide valuable content. The Vietnamese advice was wise: for South Africans to look at their own history and consider what might inspire audiences at home. The ANC leadership noted the approaching centenary of the Zulu victory over British troops at the Battle of Isandlwana in January 1879, and built its annual theme around that, dubbing 1979 the 'Year of the Spear'.[11]

Cultural outreach coordinated by the movement was supplemented by the ongoing cultural output of writers based in South Africa. Theatre was an especially significant medium. Within South Africa, writers such as Athol Fugard and Barney Simon, and novelists such as Nadine Gordimer, drew attention to social injustice. South African plays such as the multi-award winning *Woza Albert!* toured internationally. The South African government attempted to disrupt this by trying to promote apolitical South African culture such as that seen in the stage musical *Ipi Tombi*, and picketing theatres with South African productions or performers unapproved by the ANC became a feature of British 'theatreland'.[12]

Perhaps the clearest indication of the success of this radical phase of the campaign was the reaction of the South African government. External pressure propelled the Pretoria government to fight on. In November 1977, having secured a landslide endorsement in the general election, Prime Minister Vorster defiantly declared: 'Let the world know, let it know tomorrow, let it know for all future time to come, small as we are, situated as we are, we will fight to the end with what we have got.' Letting the world know proved an expensive business. By the mid-1970s the regime was devoting immense sums of money to domestic and foreign propaganda. The Department of Information strayed into covert activity. At home the Department secretly funded the launch of a new English-language newspaper in Johannesburg called *The Citizen* to take a pro-government position; overseas it attempted to buy the *Washington Star*, and while that attempt failed, resources cascaded into attempts to sway news agency coverage of Apartheid and similar projects. Exposure of this activity and of attempts to conceal it after the fact became known as the Muldergate Scandal (after the Minister of Information, Connie Mulder). It resulted in the resignation of Vorster. Other South African government propaganda projects included international broadcasting over Radio South Africa and much work through lobbyists, advertising, and public relations agencies. South African diplomats were expected to engage with foreign media and demand equal time to tell their side of the story. They failed to prevent South Africa from becoming a pariah for the many, but succeeded in securing the friendship of the well-placed few, permitting large-scale business links between South Africa and the West well into the next decade (Rees and Day, 1980).

THE RECKONING

By the 1980s the ability of the South African government to respond to pressure from the liberation movements had become a key element in domestic legitimacy. South African president P.W. Botha declared that in the face of a Communist-inspired 'total onslaught' his government would launch a 'total strategy' to secure the country. This included invading immediate neighbour states to insulate the homeland. In his external propaganda, Botha pointed to the patchwork of internally created puppet governments in nominally independent black homelands such as Ciskei and Transkei as evidence of his support for the self-determination of blacks in their 'own' places. The South African government also covertly supported and armed a Zulu nationalist movement called Inkatha, which split from the ANC in 1979 and contested its claim to speak for all South Africans. The split boiled over into black-on-black violence between supporters of the respective groups. Hoping to relieve pressure at home and abroad, the regime conceded constitutional reform, allowing citizens of Indian and 'coloured' origin to have their own parliamentary chambers from 1984. But internal unrest continued in the form of an alliance of opposition grounds called the United Democratic Front, whose leaders included Rev. Allan Boesak. Other important voices for justice from inside South Africa included Archbishop Desmond Tutu (Allen, 2006).

The struggle became increasingly violent. In 1982 the regime used a letter bomb to assassinate one of the ANC's leading lights, Ruth First, and sent commandos to attack an ANC camp in Maseru, Lesotho. The ANC struck back by hitting 'soft targets' inside South Africa, accepting civilian casualties. The attacks complicated the presentation of their cause, as did the spectacle of black-on-black violence. The murder of a boy called Stompie Moeketsi in 1989 by youths associated with Mandela's wife Winnie Mandela did particular damage to the image of the ANC, and greatly undermined her status as an international icon.

The escalation of violence within South Africa and on its borders fuelled international pressure for change. As the 1980s progressed the anti-Apartheid cause became ever more visible. It fitted the mood of the time among young people in the Global North. It was the antithesis of the Conservatism embodied by Reagan and Thatcher. In the UK, cities with left-of-centre local governments such as Glasgow, Leeds, and London variously memorialised Mandela and the movement with freedom of the city, memorial gardens, and a statue. A mainly African concert for Mandela's 65th birthday inspired musician Jerry Dammers of Special AKA to record his single 'Free Nelson Mandela'. In the United States students demonstrated to force their universities to divest from South Africa, and musicians organised by Steven Van Zandt of the E Street Band worked together to protest against American artists performing at the South Africa Sun City resort. The movement saw the potential for mass demonstrations, and organised a series of combined concerts and demonstrations, reaching a climax in 1988 with a concert for Mandela's 70th birthday held in London's Wembley Stadium. That event saw the peak of Anti-Apartheid Movement membership.

However, the anti-Apartheid camp did not have everything their own way. The branding of the ANC and other liberation movement as 'terrorists' was a challenge in the Western media. Some in conservative and military circles worked to associate the ANC with terrorists closer to home in more than just a rhetorical sense. They argued that there was a secret alliance between the ANC and the Provisional Irish Republican Army, which was then engaged in a terrorist campaign on the UK mainland. Even once a consensus of leaders agreed that something needed to change in South Africa, there was a discussion over the best way forward, with people such as Margaret Thatcher and Ronald Reagan arguing that the best way forward was 'constructive engagement' with the regime and not sanctions. There was even an argument that sanctions were bad for black people as they would be hurt by the damage to the South African economy. There were newspapers on both sides of the debate, and even some extreme contrarians who actively campaigned in support of the South African position. In 1983 the

Federation of Conservative Students in the UK produced T-shirts and badges with the caption, 'Hang Nelson Mandela', on the grounds that he was a terrorist.[13]

Mainstream motion pictures, which tackled many of the most significant issues in the period, largely avoided the situation in South Africa, which could be commercially divisive. Paton's *Cry the Beloved Country* was adapted as a motion picture as early as 1952. Other films dealing loosely with Apartheid include *The Wilby Conspiracy* (1975), which the South African government successful limited through pressure on distributors. It was a sign of the international consensus over Apartheid that by the late 1980s it was possible to centre a big-budget motion picture on Apartheid South Africa with Richard Attenborough's *Cry Freedom* (1987), yet as critics noted at the time, it was weakened by focusing on the 'white saviour' character – journalist Donald Woods – rather than the black African character at the heart of the story, Steve Biko (Davis, 1996).

There was more bite in satire, as it turned its attention to South Africa. Apartheid was ridiculed in two novels by Tom Sharpe: *Riotous Assembly* (1971) and *Indecent Exposure* (1973). The former included the following observation: 'there didn't seem to be any significant difference between life in the mental hospital and life in South Africa as a whole. Black madmen did all the work, while white lunatics lounged around imagining they were God.' Satire thrives on stereotype, and cartoons in *Anti-Apartheid News* and other political publications could sometimes seem to surrender to a simple inversion of the race hatred which Afrikaners visited upon their non-white compatriots, by stereotyping and hating them back (for an anthology of cartoons, see Various, 1985). A clear example of this was the representation of white South Africans in the satirical British puppet show *Spitting Image*, which included a song from 1986: 'I've never met a nice South African.' As a limited export market, South Africa was a convenient source of villains for US film and television, with the best-known examples being the arms dealers and murderous diplomats in *Lethal Weapon 2* (1989). South Africa had its own satirists working within the world of censorship and banning orders. Celebrated comedians included Pieter-Dirk Uys, who developed a character of an outrageously strident Afrikaner woman diplomat named Evita Bezuidenhout, who served the Botha regime as ambassador to the imaginary Bantustan of Bapetikosweti. Evita's diatribes revealed the attitudes underpinning Apartheid and its ruling elite, so largely devoid of humour. Evita performed in the UK where she took care to thank the British people for their contribution to the origins of South Africa's situation.[14]

The anti-Apartheid movement itself had its political quirks. The sprint of the 1950s and 1960s had become an organisational marathon, and the leadership of the movement increasingly drew on people with the deepest convictions, who came disproportionately from the far left. The Communist Party of Great Britain always did what it could to support the UK Anti-Apartheid Movement (AAM). Propaganda materials created by the Anti-Apartheid Movement borrowed from the heyday of Soviet constructivist graphic design as often as the visual styles of ANC's refugee camps. The poster formats used to summon people to demonstrations were designed by David King, Britain's leading collector of Soviet posters, who also created materials for the contemporaneous Anti-Nazi League and Rock Against Racism campaign (Grimes, 2016).

Businesses linked to the Soviet bloc bought advertising space in *Anti-Apartheid News* and offered prizes for AAM events. A 'Freedom Run' in 1989 to support freeing Mandela included a chance to win a ski holiday in Bulgaria, which at the time was not without repression, and notorious for mistreating its people of Turkish origin.[15] The ANC lost no sleep over this as it fitted their own worldview. The executive committee, however, was concerned that the ordinary people coming to concerts might not be seriously politically committed and could simply be having a good time. During a debate over this issue in the run up to the 'Mandela Freedom at 70' concert, ANC communication chief Pallo Jordan pointed out that while they could be sure that some of the concert-goers were only there for fun, Pretoria would never know how many, and the scale of the event would terrify them. And so it proved.[16]

The scale of the challenge from global public opinion in the 1980s compelled South Africa to react. As pressure within the United States forced trade sanctions – despite President Reagan's veto – South African business began to explore negotiations with the ANC. The South African government attempted to step up its external propaganda, but the diplomats commissioned to deliver the message signalled back to headquarters that the South African case had become unsellable, and it was time to talk.[17]

Ironically, the key to the final phase of the struggle against Apartheid was the political change in Eastern Europe and the Soviet Union. That geopolitical shift provided the essential context for the negotiations between the Pretoria government and the ANC. For Pretoria the fall of the Soviet Union removed the threat they had always seen behind the local demands of the ANC. It enabled leaders such as F.W. de Klerk to speak in terms of a kind of 'mission accomplished'. White South Africa had held the line long enough, and now it was safe to compromise. For the ANC the decline of the Eastern Bloc and ascendency of the West meant an end to a significant stream of support. They also went into negotiations feeling that they had much to lose, and that without compromise on their part they could be shut out of a post-Apartheid South Africa (Esterhuyse, 2012).

The peace talks had their own theatre and lexicon of political images. Mandela's iconic status, built by the UN and civil society movements during the second half of his imprisonment, made his role essential. He understood this, and bravely refused to renounce violence as a condition of release in 1985. His eventual release in 1990 was one of the iconic media events of the final decades of the century. Mandela himself, first as ANC Vice President and then, following Oliver Tambo's illness, President, threw his weight into compromise where many of his peers would have preferred loyalty to the geopolitical bloc which had supported them in the years of struggle. He saw no alternative to working with the West.[18] A generation later it is not hard to find young South Africans who feel he may have conceded too much.

In 1993, Mandela and the Republic of South Africa's (RSA) President F.W. DeKlerk were jointly awarded the Nobel Peace Prize. In 1994 Mandela became the first democratically elected President of South Africa. The era of Apartheid was over, and roles changed. Some of the perpetrators of Apartheid reinvented themselves as supporters of the ruling ANC, including the Foreign Minister, Pik Botha. Some of the opponents of the old regime continued to speak out against injustice in the new. Evita Bezuidenhout also joined the ANC, explaining: '"Do you have cash?" they asked. I said yes. "Okay, you're in"' (Bezuidenhout, 2016). Evita's creator Pieter-Dirk Uys created a garden in which to deposit relics of Apartheid such as the segregation signage, which he called *Boerassic Park*. He soon added objects satirising the post-Apartheid government, including a sculpture of Winnie Mandela in the bath.[19]

CONCLUSION

Looking across the whole sweep of the struggle against Apartheid the story becomes a mirror for the wider world. From the end point of 1994, the world of the 1950s seems very different. The shared religious culture which enabled Scott and Huddleston to connect with international audiences, and to which Paton appealed in many aspects of his novel, was much diminished by the 1990s; and hardly less ironically, the radical culture of the 1970s and 1980s which took its place, in which the Eastern Bloc was a valued ally and terms such as 'comrade' and 'cadre' were exchanged proudly, also seemed to be disappearing. Canon Collins and Michael Scott did not live to see the end of Apartheid, but Huddleston did: President of the UK Anti-Apartheid Movement until it disbanded, or rather was reconstituted in 1994 as ACTSA, Action for South Africa, an organisation to channel support to the democratic state.[20]

It is fascinating to see how choices made in the communication realm, such as building up Mandela or portraying Apartheid as a necessity of the Cold War, had an impact on the actual playing out of the politics. While the leadership of the ANC built their post-Apartheid legitimacy on their achievement in fighting for liberation from exile, the sustained struggle in communication on the ground should also be credited to the civil society sympathisers around the world, and to the Eastern Bloc which sustained the fight in the darkest days. For Eastern Europeans who were aware of the flaws of their own system, assisting the liberation of South Africa gave them the exhilarating chance to be undisputedly on the right side of history. The success in South Africa was the success of a communication network, and like any network it needed structure. That structure was provided and maintained by the United Nations. It was appropriate that at the gala party winding up the international campaign against Apartheid in 1991, Tambo singled out the UN for special thanks.

It is notable how seamlessly culture was integrated into the struggle. From the 1950s through to the 1980s the culture was used to rally supporters and raise funds for the movement, and cultural figures were prominent spokesmen for the cause. It was sometimes true that the authentic culture of South Africa could be sidelined or forgotten as existing tastes of outsiders prevailed – some felt this was the case with the Mandela concert – and sometimes events drifted into collateral issues. An anti-Apartheid concert at London's Albert Hall in 1968 sparked controversy for organisers when the musician Keith Emerson of The Nice (later part of Emerson, Lake and Palmer) stabbed and burnt a United States flag (Hanson, 2008). The Amandla Festival concert in Boston in 1979, at which Bob Marley famously performed, included a number of speeches off-topic from the ANC's point of view, including Dick Gregory on conspiracy theory and Marley on the legalisation of marijuana. Commerce added another complication.[21] Whitney Houston appeared in the 1988 concert only on condition that Mandela's image be blacked out during her performance, as Fox Records forbade her from being associated with the image of a 'terrorist'.[22] The fragility of the cultural network against Apartheid was made clear in 1986 when the American singer-songwriter Paul Simon released the album *Graceland*, recorded partially in South Africa in violation of ANC/UN rules. There was much confusion over rules: whether or not Simon had broken them, and whether he had been granted permission, put the entire cultural boycott in jeopardy at a critical moment. It took considerable effort and organisation on the part of the UN and ANC to reinstate it.[23]

The use of a kind of negative cultural propaganda, excluding South Africa and any who visited from international sports, for example, was a notable feature of the campaign. In both sports and culture an essential element to the boycott was simply to maintain a register of violators at the UN and to make those who maintained contact with South Africa accountable for their choice. The prominence of sports within Afrikaner culture presented Mandela with a ready forum to use for the symbolic reintegration of the country after the transition to democracy. The high point of his presidency of South Africa was probably the moment when his ethnically diverse South African team won the 1995 Rugby World Cup, dramatised in the 2009 Hollywood film *Invictus*, in which Morgan Freeman portrayed Mandela (Carlin, 2008).

Cultures remember things and people which have ongoing relevance. In the years since the end of Apartheid the world has been encouraged to remember Mandela especially as an icon of tolerance, perseverance, reconciliation, and the struggle against racism. Part of Mandela's global presence was the codification of his legacy into his memoir, *Long Walk to Freedom*, which appeared in 1995. It is fascinating to see how a book which began as smuggled prison notes first written in 1974 developed into the polished final thoughts of a world leader, destined to be read for generations. Yet the icon of South Africa and the anti-Apartheid miracle belies the many disturbing realities of the struggle, including the complicity of most Western governments with the Apartheid regime, and serious mistakes made by the movement in its attempt to maintain the security of and authority over its forces in exile. In Mandela the world has a man to love. In the Apartheid regime the world has an array of villains to hate, comparable in their cruelty to the Nazis. And yet by elevating Mandela to iconic status and demonising the Afrikaners into monsters, the world risks avoiding the extent to which ordinary people were complicit in the operation of Apartheid and ordinary people were the soul of its destruction. Racism today is not so bold as to insist on 'European Only' signs and may be all the harder to detect and expose for that fact. Yet Apartheid remains a rhetorical touchstone. When today's statesmen or citizens accuse a state of 'Apartheid', that state may be expected to devote immense energy to rebuffing the term and heading off the application of the very same methods of boycott, divestment, and sanctions which pulled South Africa to the negotiating table in the 1980s.

It is a rule of propaganda that every successful distortion of the truth has a consequence, from an outright lie to a well-meaning exaggeration. In the case of post-Apartheid South Africa, the degree to which the country had solved its problems was certainly exaggerated. This in turn created a reputational bump when underlying problems showed through in the 21st century (Bundy, 2015). Seventy years on from the launch of the campaign, elements in the story of the struggle against Apartheid remain among the most potent political symbols of the 20th century – most especially the person of Nelson Mandela – but the sad truth is that the underlying problems of inequality remain largely undiminished, for the rising generation to address. More than this the newsworthiness of South Africa apparently rested on the open defiance of global mores of a regime that claimed that racism was good and needed to be protected by law and the violence of the state. Without the outrageous Pretoria regime at work, the problems of South Africa became simply too similar to the problems of so many other places. The attention of the world moved on.

NOTES

1. This observation has been made many times. For one version and articulation, see Welch (2003: 70).
2. The novel was written while Paton travelled abroad, and was submitted to an editor in New York in the first instance rather than being published through South African channels.

3. *Come Back, Africa* (1959, dir. Lionel Rogosin), as restored by Cineteca di Bologna in 2005 is currently distributed by Milestone films. For background, see Davis (2004); and on Makeba, see Feldstein (2013).
4. Luthuli's Nobel Prize was for 1960 but awarded in 1961. For a modern biography, see Vinson (2018). For his Nobel Prize acceptance speech, see https://www.nobelprize.org/prizes/peace/1960/lutuli/lecture/l.
5. 'I am prepared to die', The Nelson Mandela Foundation, 20 April 2011, available at: https://www.nelsonmandela.org/news/entry/i-am-prepared-to-die.
6. The case of the western converted to a South African setting – *The Naked Prey* (1965) – is told in Chapman and Cull (2009: 113–135).
7. Author interview: E.S. Reddy, 23 February 2014.
8. Author interviews: Malcolm Gluck, DDB advertising, 22 March 2019; Cristabel Gurney, *Anti-Apartheid News*, 10 April 2014.
9. *Phelandaba/End of the Dialogue* (1970, dirs Antonia Caccia and Simon Louvish, Morena Films) and *Last Grave at Dimbaza* (1974, dirs Chris Curling and Pascoe Macfarlane, Morena Films) can both be obtained from Icarus Films. The relevant files at the BBC Written Archives Centre are BBC WAC T64/311/1 and T64/95/1, and for correspondence with the South African embassy, R78/2, 312/1.
10. Author interview: E.S. Reddy, 23 February 2014; Author interview: Mac Maharaj, 24 August 2021 (via zoom).
11. Author interview: Pallo Jordan, ANC, 17 April 2014.
12. Author interview: Nic Kent, Tricycle Theatre, London, 15 June 2012.
13. In 1983 the anti-Fascist magazine *Searchlight* reported that some Federation of Conservative Students members were wearing this slogan at a conference; see 'National Front support scorned by PM,' Stephen Cook, *Guardian*, 1 June 1983, p. 2; also Stephen Cook, 29 May 1985, 'Diary', *Guardian*, p. 21.
14. Author interview: Pieter-Dirk Uys, 22 August 2020.
15. The poster is archived at Bodleian Library, MSS AAM 2512/1/72, 'Freedom Run', 11 June 1989.
16. Author interview: Pallo Jordan, ANC, 17 April 2014; for documentary see *One Humanity* (2014, dir. Mikey Madoda Dube).
17. Author interview: Gerrit Oliver, Foreign Ministry of South Africa, 3 July 2012.
18. Author interview: Abdul Minty, UK Anti-Apartheid Movement/South African Department of International Relations and Development, 23 June 2014.
19. Boerassic Park is located in Darling, Western Cape, where Pieter-Dirk Uys has built a theatre and still performs. Author interview: Uys.
20. Author interview: Cristabel Gurney, ACTSA, 10 April 2014.
21. The Amandla festival may be viewed at https://www.bobmarley.com/amandla-festival-of-unity-1979/.
22. Dali Tambo, ANC/Producer, Mandela Concert, 14 November 2014.
23. Pallo Jordan, ANC, 17 April 2014.

REFERENCES

Allen, John (2006), *Rabble-Rouser for Peace*, New York: Free Press.
Bezuidenhout, Evita (2016), 'Hi, my name is Evita and I'm a racist', *Guardian*, 4 March, available at https://www.theguardian.com/world/2016/mar/04/south-africa-racist-evita-bezuidenhout.
Brown, Geoff and Christian Høgsbjerg (2020), *Apartheid is not a Game: Remembering the Stop the Seventy Tour Campaign*, London: Redwords.
Bundy, Colin (2015), *Short Changed: South Africa since Apartheid*, Athens, OH: Ohio University Press.
Carlin, John (2008), *Playing the Enemy: Mandela and the Game that Made a Nation*, London: Penguin, 2008.
Chapman, James and Nicholas J. Cull (2009), *Projecting Empire: Imperialism and Popular Cinema*, London: I.B. Tauris.

Davis, Peter (1996), *In Darkest Hollywood: Exploring the Jungles of Cinema's South Africa*, Athens, OH: Ohio University Press.
Davis, Peter (2004), *Come Back Africa: Lionel Rogosin, A Man Possessed*, Johannesburg: STE.
Denniston, Robin (1999), *Trevor Huddleston: A Life*, London: Macmillan.
Du Bois, W.E.B (1903), *The Souls of Black Folk*, Chicago, IL: McClurg.
Dubow, Saul (1989), *Racial Segregation and the Origins of Apartheid in South Africa, 1919–36*, New York: St Martins Press.
Esterhuyse, Willie (2012), *Endgame: Secret Talks and the End of Apartheid*, Johannesberg: Tafelberg.
Feldstein, Ruth (2013), 'Screening antiapartheid: Miriam Makeba, "Come Back, Africa", and the transnational circulation of Black culture and politics', *Feminist Studies*, 39(1): 12–39.
Grimes, William (2016), 'David King, 73, a graphic designer with an eye for Soviet poster art', New York Times, 20 May, p. A23.
Hanson, Martyn (2008), *Hang on to a Dream: The Story of The Nice*, London: Helter Skelter.
Herbstein, Denis (2004), *White Lies: Cannon Collins and the Secret War Against Apartheid*, Oxford: James Currey.
Higginson, John (2014), *Collective Violence and the Agrarian Origins of South African Apartheid, 1900–1948*, Cambridge: Cambridge University Press.
Huddleston, Trevor (1956), *Naught for your Comfort*, New York: Doubleday.
Konieczna, Anna and Rob Skinner (eds) (2019), *A Global History of Anti-Apartheid: 'Forward to Freedom' in South Africa*, London: Palgrave.
Laurence, John (1968), *The Seeds of Disaster: A Guide to the Realities, Race Policies and Worldwide Propaganda Campaigns of the Republic of South Africa*, London: Gollancz.
Marinovich, Greg and João Silva (2000), *The Bang-Bang Club: Snapshots from a Hidden War*, New York: Basic Books.
Meli, Francis (1989), *South Africa Belongs to Us: A History of the ANC*, London: James Currey.
Merrett, Christopher (1994), *A Culture of Censorship: Secrecy and Intellectual Repression in South Africa*, Cape Town: David Philip.
Moodie, T. Dunbar (1975), *The Rise of Afrikanerdom: Power, Apartheid, and the Afrikaner Civil Religion*, Berkeley, CA: University of California Press.
Nixon, Ron (2016), *Selling Apartheid: South Africa's Global Propaganda War*, London: Pluto
Paton, Alan (1948), *Cry the Beloved Country*, New York: Scribner; London: Jonathan Cape.
Pogrund, Benjamin (2006), *Robert Sobukwe: How Can Man Die Better*, Johannesburg: Jonathan Ball.
Rees, Mervyn and Chris Day (1980), *Muldergate: The Story of the Info Scandal*, Johannesburg: Macmillan.
Reeves, Bishop Ambrose (1966 [1992]), 'The Sharpeville Massacre: A Watershed in South Africa', in E.S. Reddy (ed.), *The Struggle for Liberation in South Africa and International Solidarity: A Selection of Papers Published by the United Nations Centre Against Apartheid*, New York: Facet Books International, pp. 97–110.
Skinner, Rob (2010), *The Foundations of Anti-Apartheid: Liberal Humanitarians and Transnational Activists in Britain and the United States, c.1919–64*, London: Palgrave.
Various (1985), *Drawing the Line: Cartoonists Against Apartheid*, London: Anti-Apartheid Movement.
Vinson, Robert Trent (2018), *Albert Luthuli*, Athens, OH: Ohio University Press.
Welch, David (2003), 'Censorship', in Nicholas J. Cull, David Culbert, and David Welch (eds), *Propaganda and Mass Persuasion: A Historical Encyclopedia, 1500 to the Present*, Santa Barbara: ABC-Clio, p. 70.
Yates, Anne and Lewis Chester (2006), *The Troublemaker: Michael Scott and his Lonely Struggle Against Injustice*, London: Aurum.

14. Refugees, migration, and propaganda
Gillian McFadyen

INTRODUCTION

The Syrian crisis has been an ongoing and mounting conflict since 2011 when pro-democracy forces challenged the dominance of Bashar al-Assad's state authority. Since the conflict began, over 6 million Syrians have fled the country to Lebanon, Jordan, and Turkey, as well as onwards to Europe, seeking safety. A further 7 million are recognised as internally displaced, meaning they have fled their homes but have not crossed over an international border (UNHCR, 2019). The crisis has been described by Filippo Grandi, United Nations High Commissioner for Refugees, as the 'biggest humanitarian and refugee crisis of our time, a continuing cause of suffering for millions which should be garnering a groundswell of support around the world' (cited in UNHCR, 2019). In defining those who have fled the crisis, states are able to draw upon Article I.A(2) of the 1951 Convention and Protocol Relating to the Status of Refugees (UNHCR, 1951). Article I.A(2) states that a refugee is an individual who can apply for asylum 'owing to a well-founded fear of being persecuted for reasons of race, religion, nationality, membership of a particular social group, or political opinion' and who is seeking to attain refugee status (UNHCR, 2019). The Refugee Convention affirms who is or who is not a refugee, as well as the relevant rights and entitlements that are connected to the label of a refugee. Only those individuals who have crossed over an international border can be applicable for the Refugee Convention, for they are then missing, or have been denied, protection from their country of origin and are seeking alternative means of protection. The Syrian crisis had been escalating since 2011, but by 2015 the crisis was framed as a European migrant crisis, as over 1 million people sought to cross the Mediterranean Sea from the conflict in Syria, with a hot spot emerging in the Aegean Sea, between Turkey and Greece. This movement of people has led to mass tragedies unfurling in the Mediterranean, whilst the European Union and states such as the United Kingdom (UK) have struggled to grapple with the scale and enormity of the situation on their doorstep. The focus instead has been on implementing policies of border control and focusing on so-called 'pull-factors' (Mediterranean Migration Research Project, n.d.), as well as reframing the crisis as one of migration, rather than refuge, in order to diminish responsibility for a European humanitarian crisis.

Accordingly, this chapter is an examination of linguistic propaganda through the politics of labelling that the UK government have employed to frame the European crisis as one of migration, rather than refuge. The chapter begins by introducing the framework of linguistic propaganda, derived from Rhonda Zaharna (2004), to examine how language and labelling are effective techniques of power that help to control, develop, and maintain narratives, especially of the other; for labelling and language carry 'powerful emotional overtones' (Marlin, 2013: 101). The chapter then examines specifically the politics of labelling, an approach that discusses the value, identification, and power behind labels, in order to develop and strengthen the linguistic propaganda framework that is so embedded in labels, words, name-calling. For labels are inherently political, and through an examination of the refugee label we can see the various values and entitlements bestowed upon labels, as well as the exclusionary politics that emerges through language.

The chapter then examines the various labels employed within the European refugee crisis, analysing the dominance of the migrant label, and how labels have become fractured and ever further removed from the refugee label, revealing 'the many different kinds of truth, from the outright lie, the half-truth, to the truth out of context' that surround the politics of refugeehood (Welch, 2015: 7). The chapter then concludes by drawing upon the case example of the 2018 Christmas Day Channel crossing arrivals, and how the UK government drew upon the politics of labelling to reframe and fracture the label of refugee in order to successfully deflect British responsibility. In doing so, the chapter examines how the politics of labelling and linguistic propaganda have successfully been able to shape British responsibility to refugees, but also fracture the label of refugee, creating a hierarchy of refugeehood, with the refugee label becoming a highly privileged as well geographically politicised prize, for which a small minority are deemed eligible.

LINGUISTIC PROPAGANDA AND LABELLING

In developing this chapter, I first want to introduce the practice of propaganda and how it operates within the framework of refugee politics. We can understand the process of propaganda as 'deliberate and intentional' (Cunningham, 2002: 64). At its core, propaganda is a process of manipulation: 'it is a deliberate and systematic attempt to share perceptions, manipulate cognitions, and direct behaviour to achieve a response that serves the desired intent of the propagandist' (O'Shaughnessy, 2004: 19). In this aspect, I want to highlight the similarities between linguistic propaganda specifically, as identified below, and the politics language, examining the acts of power wielded by the state though linguistic labelling against the refugee, to frame, distort, and disguise the humanitarian crisis at play. For refugees can be presented as a paradox for the state, whereby they are presented as the external threatening other (Clemens and Pettman, 2004: 175). The figure who inhabits life outside of the state territory is perceived, as Sara Ahmed writes (Ahmed, 2000: 36), as the ultimate violent stranger, the outsiders of the nation space 'whose behaviours seem unpredictable and beyond control'.

In developing my approach to propaganda, I draw on the linguistic understanding of propaganda derived from Rhonda Zaharna (2004: 223), who argues that 'information control and deception' are key factors to effective propaganda. The shaping of perception and ideas is facilitated by our language and labelling that 'enables us to interpret, judge and conceptualise our perceptions' (Jowett and O'Donnell, 2006: 9). When analysing propaganda, Zaharna (2004: 223) argues that the practice of linguistic propaganda deliberately manipulates the communication through a variety of techniques so that some aspect is hidden from the audience and so that the audience feels compelled to accept the message. Indeed, propaganda as defined by Pratkins and Turner (cited in Jowett and O'Donnell, 2006: 6) can be understood as 'attempts to move a recipient to a predetermined point of view by using simple images and slogans that truncate thought by playing on prejudices and emotions', for it is the cultural distinctions that exacerbate feelings of otherness and danger (Ahmed, 2000: 37). In this regard, we can see the power of language and the exclusionary politics that linguistic propaganda can entail, in what Richard Jackson (2005: 178) has referred to as 'an exercise of power through the deployment of language'.

Zaharna (2004: 223) argues that that there are multiple tools, or techniques, for performing the process of linguistic propaganda, such as 'name-calling, labelling, bandwagon'. Indeed, linguistic propaganda entails a variety of 'symbols, words and language to influence audiences ... selective word choices; slanted language ... euphemism, epithets, and dehumanising descriptors, metaphors and weasel words' (Cunningham, 2002: 73). Within linguistic propaganda, particularly the use of labels (what Zaharna is addressing, which will be discussed later), 'they can be damning or they can be laudatory, but an ideology or perspective is inscribed within them' (O'Shaughnessy, 2004: 72). These techniques of language, Zaharna (2004: 223) asserts, are used to control and manipulate information, and also draw on features such as 'secrecy, deception, and coercion ... allowing the communicator to retain control over information and manipulate the element of surprise'. In this capacity we can perceive linguistic propaganda as the 'art to make the label enter common parlance so that every time it is used it becomes an unconscious act of propaganda'. As O'Shaughnessy (2004: 73) argues, 'words describe, but they also judge'. In this aspect, linguistic propaganda is similar to the approach advocated by David Welch (2015), that propaganda is concerned with reinforcing existing trends and beliefs to sharpen and focus them.

In following this approach to propaganda, we can see how it operates 'quite explicitly, forging explicit prejudicial associations and biases ... so as to protect its content from rational scrutiny and to create obstacles for critique' (Medina, 2018: 52). As such, 'otherness can arise easily through arbitrarily acquired labels' (O'Shaughnessy, 2004: 123). For as Randal Martin (2013: 101) observed, 'name calling in general is a powerful force for influencing opinion because names are easily remembered ... they carry powerful emotional overtones, but they also cause perceptions of the individual so named to be warped'. It is on this line of engagement that I focus in this chapter: understanding linguistic propaganda as the use of labelling as a means of miscommunication to control and present a particular narrative of humanitarianism and security. The rhetoric emerging from the UK government regarding the crisis is not focusing on the European refugee crisis, but rather framing it as a crisis of economic migrants seeking a better way of life. In creating this narrative, the government are using highly fractured as well as symbolic language to engage, as well as to minimise the humanitarian crisis. In doing so they are engaging in the linguistic propaganda techniques of labelling and name calling that Zaharna, O'Shaughnessy and Martin speak of, in order to shape and distort the humanitarian routes of the crisis.

Having set out the linguistic propaganda framework, the chapter will now turn to expanding on the concept of labelling, specifically in connection to the refugee, in order to strengthen and enhance the understanding of linguistic propaganda that is so grounded in language, labelling, and the framing of the other. The chapter will then examine how the politics of labelling operates within the British refugee system before concluding with a detailed focus on the Christmas Day arrivals of 2018, and the linguistic propaganda framing by the government, specifically through the use of labelling in order to reframe the crisis as one of security and deterrence rather than a humanitarian crisis.

THE POLITICS OF LABELLING

When it comes to refugees, words and labels are central political tools that determine not only their position, but also the level of entitlement and responsibility conferred on them. For labelling, both the construction and the application are inherently a political process, as labels do not emerge from a political void. Indeed it is better to understand labelling as a political act, for labels both include and exclude through their framing of the other (Retzlaff, 2005: 609). Once we begin to understand the power and politics behind labelling, particularly in regard to the refugee label, we can then begin to focus on exposing the 'socio-political motivations for constructing this label, and the consequential impacts and opportunities it produces' (Vigil and Abidi, 2018: 54). As Jean-Jacques Weber (2015: 6) notes, 'even the smallest linguistic details can help with the continual (re)production of ... a sense of otherness'.

Labelling is a political act by the dominant group within society that frames and categorises, as well as normalises, certain behaviours, creating divisions in behaviour and individuals, that normally disadvantages those who have been labelled, in what Geof Wood (1985) refers to as 'the act of politics involving conflict as well as authority'. To requote Jackson (2005: 178), it is 'an exercise of power through the deployment of language'. Particularly, the language and labelling employed within the field of refugee politics is not innocent (Turton, 2003). The language of politics towards refugees can be understood as a 'relationship of power, asymmetrical and one-sided' (Wood, 1985). Gayatri Spivak (1994) referred to it as the 'epistemic violence of othering'. In the unequal relationship between the refugee and the host, it is the state that is doing the labelling, for the labeller is in a position of power, determining who is to be included or excluded.

In understanding the politics of labelling, Roger Zetter is the key theorist who developed the study of labelling particularly in response to the refugee subject. For Zetter (1998: 1), the term 'refugee' 'constitutes one of the most powerful labels in the repertoire of humanitarian, national, and international public policy and social differentiation'. Zetter (1991) argues that the label of refugee is created and recreated as well as distorted within the field of refugee politics, particularly since he argues that it is distinctly a bureaucratic process. Zetter (1991: 59) stresses that it is crucial to examine and understand the politics of labelling, not only because it is central to refugee policy and the language of refugee politics, but that a 'non-labelled way out cannot exist' within the field of refugee policy. He argues that what has defined the current era of refugees is the distinct proliferation of new labels that are at best a vague interpretation, or at worst a relentless discriminatory term that disconnects individuals from the central characteristics that equate them to being a refugee, that is, a 'stereotyped identity' (Zetter, 2007: 176). It is this process of labelling that Zetter argues has been increasingly utilised and wielded to marginalise, discriminate, and undermine humanitarian responsibility.

In this process of labelling, 'far from clarifying an identity, the label conveys, instead, an extremely complex set of values and judgements which are more than just definitional' (Zetter, 1991: 40). Indeed, when labels are applied, 'patterns of social and cultural norms ... are mediated, impacted and ultimately controlled and reformulated by institutional agency'. In this aspect, we can view the significance of labelling as a stereotype 'involving the disaggregation, standardization, and the formulation of clear cut categories' (Zetter, 1991: 44). What we are witnessing within UK refugee policy is what Zetter refers to as the 'fragmentation', or what can be understood as fracturing, of the refugee label into ever more inferior labels of sanctuary and accompanying rights and entitlements that remove the individual from the label of refugee. Zetter (2000: 353) asserts that 'new meanings are being impacted to old identities. New labels are being used, not only to recognize the complexity of forced migration, but more as instruments of control, restrictionism and disengagement'. The outcome of the fracturing of the refugee label is the weakening of the master label, 'refugee', which Zetter (2000: 353) argues has led to 'a label which less and less fits the reality and experience of forced displacement. Compromised humanitarianism is the outcome.' Indeed, what can occur is that the label serves the needs of the labeller more than the labelled group, thereby revealing a considerable discrepancy between the two. Through this process of fragmentation, or what we could term fracturing, the new labels that are established from the fracture ultimately only 'impoverish' the original label by 'placing the initial meaning and form at a distance' (Zetter, 2000). Zetter argues that through the process of labelling, governments have been able to categorise and create labels of identity that can be assumed, adopted, and identified, with varying levels of power attributed to each label. The label of refugee in the end 'reveals much more the nature of bureaucratic and administrative action where process of differentiation, routines, categorizations of needs as cases are quite distinct from how the group so labelled may actually perceive its own needs' (Zetter, 1985: 437). As there is an inbuilt differentiation to labels, then there is a clear connection with resources distribution that Zetter (1985: 443) warns has strong associations with 'eligibility, exclusion … perhaps even stigma'. It is important to remember that the language and vocabulary that surrounds the figure of the asylum seeker does vary in its range, but is 'singular in its intention – to convey an image of marginality, dishonesty, a threat, unwelcomed' (Zetter, 2007: 184). As O'Shaughnessy (2004: 123) stresses, 'propagandists invent their enemies', for otherness is acquired easily through the application of labels. In this aspect, we remember that 'every source of propaganda is at its source deliberate and intentional … There is no unintentional propagandist' (Cunningham, 2002: 64). Through the framework of the politics of labelling, the approach highlights how linguistic propaganda, as a form of 'deliberate manipulation', is able to inform, alter, and reframe the language surrounding refugees, to the state's interest. In this sense, we can view the politics of labelling as a technique of linguistic propaganda.

LABELLING AND THE REFUGEE

There has been a subconscious focus on the labelling and language employed in order to frame the Mediterranean crisis. The labels of migrant and refugee have often been used interchangeably by the UK government, with the migrant label, particularly that of the economic migrant, taking precedence within the government. Indeed, the crisis has often been referred to as the 'migrant crisis', inferring that it is a crisis of economic migration, but the labels are remarkably different. There is a crucial distinction between what people given these labels are entitled to, with different levels of assistance and protection under national and international law. As the United Nations High Commissioner for Refugees (UNHCR) argues, the blurring of the labels takes attention away from the specific legal protection requirements of refugees, with 'confused and confusing terminology became an important focal point' of the Mediterranean crisis. Indeed, the UNHCR argued that specifically politicians and journalists had, through their use of labelling, 'arguably legitimated anti-migrant hostility and ethnic prejudice' through threatening language and imagery which evokes war and disease, or the negative labelling of immigrants, with terms such as 'illegal', 'bogus', and 'clandestine' (Berry et al., 2015). In this regard, we can see the practice of labelling as a technique of linguistic propaganda to 'deliberately attempt to persuade people to think and behave in a desired way' towards the refugee (O'Shaughnessy, 2004: 20).

Indeed, this distinction between the framing of labels is important, for immigration is handled through a series of varying policies and legislation implemented at the national level. However, in comparison, international or regional law is invoked by states when dealing with refugees. States within the European Union (EU) have an international as well as a regional responsibility for anyone seeking refuge in their country, due to having ratified the 1951 Refugees Convention. But, by using the label of migrant, as the UK prefers to do, the UK has been able to obscure, if not deny, specific legal protections to which refugees are entitled; what Zaharna (2004) would refer to as the coercive nature of linguistic propaganda. The labelling of the refugee other is a political act. It is a means of categorisation, stereotyping, as well as a means of establishing distinctions and differentiations between 'us' and 'them'. Through the politics of labelling there is a natural establishment of binarisms of 'us' versus 'them', or even 'them' versus 'another them' (Gupte and Mehta, 2007: 69). In this regard, labelling naturally confers 'another'. It is also a means of conferring various responsibilities, rights, and entitlements on the subject groups, and as such certain labels such as refugee can become prized categories that the state seeks to protect from perceived abuse. Hence, labelling is inherently political, and always intentional in its selection and application, and in this instance can be viewed as a technique of linguistic propaganda.

A refugee is an individual who has been forced to flee their country of origin and is seeking alternative state protection, thus it is a 'push factor' that has forced them to flee. The right to refuge is defined by the 1951 Refugee Convention, as well as the Universal Declaration of Human Rights (1948). Article 14 stipulates, '[E]veryone has the right to seek and to enjoy in other countries asylum from persecution', as such a refugee has an international right to protection; so, by engaging with refugees, a state is invoking international law. Yet, through the politics of labelling a hierarchy has emerged that situates the label of refugee at the pinnacle, followed then by the labels of asylum seeker, bogus asylum seeker, illegal immigrant, economic migrant, and so on. By failing to use the label of refugee in times of a global refugee crisis, UK governments have been able to successfully steer debates and create suspicion, tension, and reduced sympathy towards this group within society.

When it comes to the migrant label, it has become intertwined with the label of refugee and asylum seeker. Yet, there is no set international definition of migrant (IOM, n.d.). A migrant is commonly understood to be an individual who has left their country of origin for a variety of reasons, particularly economic factors. As such, a migrant can be understood to have left their country due to what can be termed, 'pull factors' such as economic and social-cultural attraction. A migrant has not fled their country of origin due to lack of state protection, and on their return they would still benefit from said protection, unlike a refugee (IOM, n.d.). But by using the label of migrant, as the UK prefers to do, the UK has been able to obscure, if not deny, specific legal protections to which refugees are entitled; for when engaging with migrants, national immigration law and processes are evoked. So, when the UK, through a process of linguistic manipulation (Zaharna, 2004), refers to the European refugee crisis as a migrant crisis, it is denying responsibility for refugees in states such as Italy and Greece that have been overwhelmed by the crisis – through a process of linguistic manipulation (Zaharna 2004). The outcome is that conflating the label of refugee and migrant 'can have serious consequences for the lives and safety of refugees. Blurring the two terms takes attention away from the specific legal protections refugees require' and, importantly, it can 'undermine public support for refugees and the institution of asylum' (UNHCR, 2019). As Zaharna (2004) states, this process is one of control and deception.

When utilising and addressing the myriad labels applied within the field of refugee policy, be it refugee, asylum seeker, migrant, bogus, or clandestine, it is important to remember that the application of specific labels is always intentional. As Zolberg et al. (1989: 4) remind us, defining refugees as other for the purpose of policy implementations requires a political choice and an ethical judgement. For it is important to highlight, as Tazreena Sjjad (2018: 56) stresses, that despite the vast array of labels that have emerged through the fractured refugee label:

> refugees, displaced, migrants, asylum seekers, expelled, stateless, repatriated, returned, illegal, unauthorised, undocumented, irregular – [they] have not indicated a broadening of the humanitarian safety-net to recognise drivers of displacement, but have, rather, reinforced the power of the state to create systems of hierarchy, making hyper-visible those who have transgressed a range of boundaries, and violated the natural order of the state-citizen relationship.

And it is important to reflect upon the real-world consequences of the politics of labelling 'with respect to the lives, rights and positions of the presented group in society'. For whether you are labelled as a migrant, a refugee, asylum seeker, or illegal does have real-world implications (Retzlaff, 2005: 620). Indeed, the discussion now is not on whether we label, 'but which, by whom, under what conditions, for what purpose, with what effects!' (Wood, 1985: 353). Indeed, in 2015, Barry Malone and the broadcaster Al Jazeera made the decision to stop using the word 'migrant' when reporting on the Mediterranean crisis. Malone (2015) argued that the umbrella term of 'migrant' was 'no longer fit for purpose when it comes to describing the horror unfolding in the Mediterranean. It has evolved from its dictionary definitions into a tool that dehumanises and distances, a blunt pejorative.'

Malone (2015) argued that the term 'migrant' had become a reductive term that was enabling dehumanisation, homogenisation, distancing, and racism towards refugee groups and argued that 'migrant is a word that strips suffering people of voice'. Malone continued that the use of the migrant label was politically motivated and the refusal to use the label of refugee gives 'weight to those who want only to see economic migrants', in what Zaharna (2004: 223) would term a process of deliberate manipulation of coercive misinformation. Now, this might appear as a semantic argument, stressing the various applications of labels within refugee politics. However, it highlights the unequal relationship between the labeller and the labelled that operates in the labellers' interests, and how labelling can be easily perceived as a technique of linguistic propaganda.

Government propaganda regarding refugees has focused on the labelling of those entering the European Union, framing individuals entering into the EU as (illegal) economic migrants, regardless of their origins, be they Syrian or otherwise, as (illegal) economic migrants. For the UK government, the genuine refugee resides in the region surrounding Syria, geographically framing the genuine refugee in need within that region alone, at the expense of the individuals entering Europe via the various routes from the South and the Eastern Mediterranean. Through what we can understand as the politics of labelling, the crisis is framed solely as a Syrian crisis, with those individuals entering into Europe transformed as (illegal) economic migrants. Thus, they are framed as of no concern for the UK. Indeed, British government propaganda since 2015 has increased tensions and fear regarding the refugee, migrant 'other', that has successfully led to reduced state responsibility within the crisis.

Within the UK government's framing of the refugee crisis, criminalisation as well as militaristic responses to humanitarian issues, as well the use of dehumanising language, particularly within the European setting, are central. For instance, when the Mediterranean crisis was unfolding, and following the Lampedusa mass tragedies in 2015, then UK Prime Minister David Cameron (cited in BBC News, 2015), asserted that we 'have got a swarm of people coming across the Mediterranean, seeking a better life, wanting to come to Britain because Britain has got jobs, it's got a growing economy, it's an incredible place to live'. As the crisis escalated in 2015, Cameron referred to the people entering the European Union using the language of 'swarms' to refer to them *en masse*, asserting that they were simply seeking a better way of life (cited in BBC News, 2015). Language and labelling have been central to the government framing of the European crisis, with the Prime Minister reaffirming that the crisis was not one of refugees, but rather of migrants: '[T]hey are economic migrants and they want to enter Britain illegally, and the British people and I want to make sure our borders are secure' (Khomami, 2015). In this respect it is, as O'Shaughnessy (2004: 74) notes, language and labelling being employed 'as a way of seeing but also not seeing ... veiling the reality of what is being done'. This is the technique of information control through language, labelling, and the power of emotional words. This is propaganda as a means to reframe the crisis as one of migration, rather than refuge.

THE CHRISTMAS DAY ARRIVALS

In examining the politics of labelling as a technique of government linguistic propaganda, the Christmas Day incident of 2018 is an excellent case study to draw upon. Over the course of 2018, the UK started to witness small, unregulated vessels crossing the English Channel, one of the busiest shipping lanes in the world. The vessels were carrying refugees, many of whom had survived war, conflict, and persecution in countries such as Syria, Iran, Afghanistan, and Eritrea (Refugee Council, 2019). The situation reached a peak on Christmas Day 2018, when 40 individuals travelling in five boats crossed the English Channel, arriving on the coast of Kent. On 27 December, 23 individuals reached the shores of Kent, and on 28 December, a further 12 arrived in two separate boats that were detained off the coast of Dover (BBC News, 2018). In responding to the English Channel crossings, then Home Secretary Sajid Javid declared the situation a 'major incident' (Home Office, 2019). The Home Office was quick to identify connections between the crossing and organised criminal gangs smuggling illegal immigrants, highlighting the criminality of such journeys (BBC News, 2018). Javid argued that 'these events are not something that I, as Home Secretary, will accept. Protecting the UK border and safeguarding lives is one of the Home Office's most important priorities.' But, in protecting lives, a contradiction appeared to emerge in the government's response to the Christmas arrivals. For Javid (Home Office, 2018) went on to argue that 'while we have obligations to genuine asylum seekers which we will uphold, we will not stand by and allow reckless criminals to take advantage of some of the most vulnerable people in our global society'. Indeed, Javid was focused on tackling the criminal gangs who were allowing 'illegal migration to flourish' (Javid, cited in House of Lords, 2019: 6). By utilising the label of 'illegal migration', with its inherent implications of secrecy, deviance, and criminality, and as the harbinger of security risks (Sjjad, 2018: 55), Javid was intentionally responding to the Christmas Day arrivals by emphasising the need for stronger deterrence against the dangerous crossings of the English Channel. Certainly, Christophe Castaner (cited in Rawlinson, 2019), French Interior Minister, stressed the need for deterrence to tackle the criminal crossings, asserting that, 'it is in our interest, as it is for the UK, to not allow new smugglers to operate which would attract new migrants'. In declaring a 'major incident', Javid was mocked for his perceived over-reaction to the Christmas Day arrivals. Gerry Simpson of Human Rights Watch (cited in Electronic Immigration Network, 2018) was quick to highlight comparisons, stating, 'at the height of the Syrian refugee crisis in 2015, Syria's neighbours took in 10,000 refugees per DAY. Yet the UK Home Secretary just called the arrival of 75 asylum seekers by boat in 3 days a "major incident".' Indeed, the government response to the Christmas Day arrivals focused on statistics, data, and analysis of the incident that reduced the arrivals merely to abstract figures and numbers. This language of data established a clinical, homogenous narrative (Malkki, 1996), whilst the 'messier vicissitudes of individualized experiences (pain, suffering, loss and also resourcefulness, ability etc) are left by the wayside' (Gupte and Mehta, 2007: 64). The individual stories and rationale of those undertaking the journeys are lost within the dominant state narrative of security, curtailment, and deterrence.

Yet Javid was also insistent on asserting that individuals 'genuinely' fearing persecution should claim asylum in the first safe country they reach, and that British 'officials are looking to strengthen our inadmissibility guidance for claims made by those who have travelled here through countries that are internationally recognised as being safe' (Javid, cited in House of Lords, 2019: 6). The British response to the landings saw humanitarian concerns marginalised, and the domination of state interests of security, prevention, and curtailment. The incident highlighted clearly the framing of migrants, regardless of their country of origin, as representing a perceived 'threat to the economic, cultural and political system of the state' (Jones, 2016: 167). Indeed, in response to the incident, Javid ordered two Border Force vessels to patrol the English Channel crossing, as a means to protect the UK border (Home Office, 2018). The emphasis was on stopping individuals from leaving France, a position that the government sought to maintain under Boris Johnson's premiership (cited in *Guardian*, 2019). Emphasising the illegality of the crossing in August 2019, the government asserted that 'we will send you back. The UK should not be regarded as a place where you could automatically come and break the law by seeking to arrive illegally. If you come illegally, you are an illegal migrant and I'm afraid the law will treat you as such.'

In framing the Christmas Day arrivals as engaging in a criminal crossing, government rhetoric and language was central. Javid was quick to question the motives of the individuals crossing the Channel, and questioned why individuals would make such a hazardous journey to Britain. Javid reiterated that 'the widely accepted international principle is that those seeking asylum should claim it in the first safe country that they reach – be that France or elsewhere'. The Home Secretary then went on to contest the genuineness of the individuals seeking refuge, attacking their integrity (BBC News, 2019). Javid pushed his argument further by claiming:

> People should not be taking this very dangerous journey and, if they do, we also need to send a very strong message that you won't succeed ... You are coming from France, which is a safe country. In almost every case you are claiming asylum in the UK but if you were a real, genuine asylum seeker then you could have done that in another safe country. (BBC News, 2019)

Through the politics of labelling and linguistic propaganda, the government is able to construct the genuine refugee as an individual who finds security in the first safe country, rather than attempting to reach the UK. By making the journey to the UK, the government perceives these individuals as not in genuine need of sanctuary. However, this reductionist approach to refuge overlooks the intersectional factors of history, colonialism, kinship, and family connections that spur individuals to seek refuge in specific states such as the UK (Refugee Council, 2018). Moreover, as Maurice Wren, Head of the Refugee Council (cited in Refugee Council, 2018) countered, 'the fact that people are boarding flimsy boats to cross one of the world's busiest and most dangerous shipping lanes highlights the sense of fear and hopelessness' that is affecting many individuals in 'safe countries' like France. Through relabelling the incident, the government allowed it to be deflected and, importantly, securitised.

However, the Christmas arrivals were not the first individuals to seek access to the UK by crossing the English Channel that month. Indeed, they were one of 539 'migrants' (Home Office, 2018) who attempted to cross the English Channel through November and December 2018 via a variety of boats, inflatables, and assorted craft, with over 40 per cent having been 'successfully' intercepted by the French coastguard (BBC News, 2018). The December Channel crossing is a prime example of the power of the politics of labelling. As refugees travel over the English Channel crossing with the intention to apply for asylum, they are instead relabelled by the UK government as illegal or economic migrants. They are transformed into something other, something dangerous, something unwanted that should be stopped and prevented. Furthermore, Javid applied a false logic, namely that if they were genuine refugees, they would not have travelled to Britain. A genuine refugee would have applied for asylum immediately in another country if they were truly in need of international protection. Importantly, in response to the December crossing, Javid stressed that UK refugee policy:

> clearly states that if an individual travels through a safe third country and fails to claim asylum, it will be taken into account in assessing the credibility of their claim. Following these recent events, I have instructed my officials to look at how we can tighten this further and ensure these provisions are working effectively. (Home Office, 2019)

Javid was projecting refuge beyond the shores of the UK, stressing firstly the hospitality of foreign states such as France, but also that the practice of refuge would not be offered at the British border either, a position entrenched by Theresa May, who stressed in 2015 that asylum would not be offered to 'those who have made it to Britain'. Through the politics of labelling, Javid was able to adopt a contrary position that altered the approach to the Channel crossing incident. He both upheld humanitarian concerns of individuals undertaking such a crossing, whilst relabelling the individuals as illegal immigrants, drawing simultaneously on the language of criminality, gangs, and smugglers, effectively undermining the credibility of those claiming asylum.

Indeed, this connects with the larger European refugee crisis where 'the dominant, but not uncontested, discursive construction of boat migrants crossing via the Central Mediterranean route as disguised economic migrants and therefore ' "illegal" ... is central to Europe's increasingly tougher response to crossings' (Sigona, 2018: 457). In making the connection with the politics of labelling, Zetter (2000: 353) argues that it highlights an 'increasingly pervasive tendency to constrain, restrict and redefine humanitarian responses which favour the providers not the recipients'. By fracturing the labelling and denying the use of refugee by Home Office authorities, those labelled 'illegal migrants' are othered and positioned with no rights at all, even denied the international right to refuge (Elgot and Walker, 2019). This is what Zolberg et al. (1989: 274) have argued to be an 'instrumental use of language to legitimize differential treatment' for specific client populations, even though the group may be entitled to it.

The reframing of the Christmas Day arrivals as criminal migrants removed the UK from responsibility, denying the incident a humanitarian foundation, and repositioned the arrivals as the threatening other. As Reece Jones (2016) argues, the exclusion of an external group, such as the refugee, from a state's territory and resources is founded upon the assumption that the 'in-group should be protected no matter what, with little regard for the effect it might have on the other and without questioning why there is a distinction between "us" and "them" in the first place'. Hannah Arendt ([1951] 1976: 296) referred to this as the fallacy of the 'right to have rights' and the assumed universality of human rights. The British position was that refugees could claim their right to asylum, just not in the UK.

CONCLUSION

The chapter has sought to highlight the centrality of labelling as a technique of linguistic propaganda within the UK refugee process, and the power that labelling can have in determining the course of action when it comes to state responses and responsibilities to refugees, be it the Mediterranean or the Channel crossing incidents. Labels are central, as they are intertwined and bound into the practice of welcome, allowing states to maintain control over the figure of the refugee. Wood (1985) argues that labelling is used in the ranking of people according to moral proximities. However, I would argue that in regard to the Mediterranean crisis and the Channel crossing incident we have witnessed the reversal of hierarchical labelling towards the refugee other, based on geographical closeness to Britain. Those who are geographically closer to the UK and situated within the EU are labelled as migrants, and thus not enacting UK state responsibility. The Christmas Day arrivals have been able to illustrate the full power of the labeller, with the politics of labelling on full show. The genuine refugee is not at the UK's border, but rather remains within the conflict region for assistance, being geographically externalised from the UK, and the EU. As such we are witnessing a process of miscommunication and deflection that operates in regards to those nearing or seeking refuge in the UK.

Niklaus Steiner (2001) argues that 'no one in Europe is arguing to have asylum abolished'. Yet continuous UK governments through the politics of labelling are doing all in their power to operate a policy of diminishing returns (McFadyen, 2016). The British state approach to refugees has been classed as 'paradoxical' (Gibney, 2014), depicting the refugees both as subjects of humanitarian aid and as threats to the economic security of the state. It is in this regard that the focus on the significance of the politics of labelling is instrumental for examining the UK refugee system and propaganda for, as Medina (2018: 52) argues, a 'key part of resisting propaganda is to unmask its self-hiding and self-protective mechanisms and to remove obstacles for the critical examination of the propagandistic message'. This chapter has sought to examine the British approach to refuge, through the lens of labelling, to highlight how it operates as a technique of linguistic propaganda. The politics of labelling, as well as the use of miscommunication to control and present a particular narrative of humanitarianism and security, has allowed the state to benefit from refugees. Such benefit takes the form of the state's affordances to masquerade its focus on curtailment, deterrence, and security, with the refugees marginalised, and preferably excluded.

REFERENCES

Ahmed, S. (2000), *Strange Encounters: Embodied Others in Post-coloniality*, London: Routledge.

Al Jazeera (2015), 'Dozens of refugees found dead in truck in Austria', accessed 16 June 2019 at https://www.aljazeera.com/news/2015/08/dozens-refugees-dead-truck-austria-150827094349613.html.

Arendt, H. [1951] (1976), *The Origins of Totatalitarianism*, London: Harvest Book.

BBC News (2015), 'David Cameron criticised over migrant "swarm" language', 30 July, accessed 3 October 2017 at http://www.bbc.co.uk/news/uk-politics-33716501.

BBC News (2018), 'Channel migrants: Home Secretary declares major incident', accessed 12 August 2019 at https://www.bbc.co.uk/news/uk-46705128.

BBC News (2019), 'Sajid Javid under fire over Channel migrant comments', 21 February, accessed 6 July 2019 at https://www.bbc.co.uk/news/uk-politics-46738126.

Berry, M., I. Garcia-Blanco, and K. Moore (2015), 'Press coverage of the refugee and migrant crisis in the EU: a content analysis of five European countries', accessed 30 September 2019 at www.unhcr.org/56bb369c9.html

Cameron, D. (2015), 'House of Commons Debate, Syria: refugees and counter-terrorism', *Hansard*, 7 September, Vol. 599, ccl. 24, accessed 10 January 2019 at http://www.publications.parliament.uk/pa/cm201516/cmhansrd/cm150907/debtext/150907-0001.htm#1509074000002.

Clemens, J. and D. Pettman (2004), *Avoiding the Subject: Media, Culture and the Object*, Amsterdam: Amsterdam University Press.

Cunningham, S. (2002), *The Idea of Propaganda: A Reconstruction*, London: Praeger.

Electronic Immigration Network (2018), 'Immigration minister: Government is keeping "compliant environment" policies despite Windrush', accessed 7 August 2019 at https://www.ein.org.uk/news/immigration-minister-government-keeping-compliant-environment-policies-despite-windrush.

Elgot, J. and P. Walker (2019), 'Javid under fire over "illegal" cross-Channel asylum seekers claim', *Guardian*, 2 January, accessed 21 February 2019 at https://www.theguardian.com/politics/2019/jan/02/people-crossing-channel-not-genuine-asylum-seekers-javid.

Gibney, M. (2014), 'Asylum: principled hypocrisy', in B. Anderson and M. Keith (eds), *Migration: A COMPAS Anthology*, Oxford: COMPAS, pp. 163–164.

Guardian (2019), 'Johnson warns against Channel crossings after dozens intercepted', accessed 29 August 2019 at https://www.theguardian.com/uk-news/2019/aug/23/channel-crossings-uk-and-france-to-meet-after-dozens-intercepted.

Gupte, J. and Mehta, L. (2007), 'Disjuncture in labelling refugees and oustees', in Joy Moncrieffe and Rosalind Eyben (eds), *The Power of Labelling: How People are Categorised and Why It Matters*, London: Earthscan, pp. 64–79.

Home Office (2018), 'Home Secretary sets out action on migrant crossings', accessed 12 August 2019 at https://homeofficemedia.blog.gov.uk/2018/12/31/home-secretary-sets-out-action-on-migrant-crossings/.

Home Office (2019), 'Statement by Sajid Javid: migrant crossing', accessed 21 June 2019 at https://www.gov.uk/government/speeches/statement-migrant-crossings.

House of Lords (2019), 'English Channel migrant boat crossing', Research Briefing, accessed 14 August 2019 at https://researchbriefings.parliament.uk/ResearchBriefing/Summary/LLN-2019-0029#fullreport.

International Organization for Migration (IOM) (n.d.), 'Who is a migrant?', accessed 25 August 2019 at https://www.iom.int/who-is-a-migrant.

Jackson, R. (2005), *Writing the War on Terrorism: Language, Politics and Counter Terrorism*, Manchester: Manchester University Press.

Jones, R. (2016), *Violent Borders: Refugees and the Right to Move*, London: Verso.

Jowett, G.S. and V. O'Donnell (2006), *Propaganda and Persuasion*, London: SAGE.

Khomami, N. (2015), 'David Cameron says migrants trying to "break in" to UK illegally', *Guardian*, accessed 8 August 2019 at https://www.theguardian.com/uk-news/2015/aug/15/david-cameron-says-migrants-trying-to-break-in-to-uk-illegally.

Malkki, L. (1996), 'Speechless emissaries: refugees, humanitarianism, and dehistoricization', *Cultural Anthropology*, 11(3), 377–404.

Malone, B. (2015), 'Why Al Jazeera will not say Mediterranean "migrants"', Al Jazeera, accessed 24 August 2019 at https://www.aljazeera.com/blogs/editors-blog/2015/08/al-jazeera-mediterranean-migrants-150820082226309.html.
Marlin, R. (2013), *Propaganda and Ethics of Persuasion*, London: Broadview Press.
Martin, R. (2013), *Propaganda and the Ethics of Persuasion*, London: Broadview Press.
McFadyen, G. (2016), 'The language of labelling and the politics of hospitality in the British asylum system', *British Journal of Politics and International Relations*, 18(3): 599–617.
Medina, J. (2018), 'Resisting racist propaganda: distorted communication and epistemic activism', *Southern Journal of Philosophy*, 56: 50–75.
Mediterranean Migration Research Project (n.d.), 'Research Brief 02: Understanding the dynamics of migration to Greece and the EU', accessed 25 August 2018 at http://www.medmig.info/research-brief-02-understanding-the-dynamics-of-migration-to-greece-and-the-eu/.
O'Shaughnessy, N. (2004), *Politics and Propaganda, Weapons of Mass Seduction*, Manchester: Manchester University Press.
Rawlinson, K. (2019), 'France steps up efforts to prevent Channel crossings', *Guardian*, accessed 29 August 2019 at https://www.theguardian.com/uk-news/2019/jan/04/france-steps-up-efforts-prevent-channel-crossings.
Refugee Council (2018), 'Refugee Council response to channel crossing news', accessed 12 August 2019 at https://www.refugeecouncil.org.uk/latest/news/5457_refugee_council_response_to_channel_crossing_news/.
Refugee Council (2019), 'Channel crossings – time to set the record straight', accessed 12 August 2019 at https://www.refugeecouncil.org.uk/latest/news/5459_channel_crossings_-_time_to_set_the_record_straight/.
Retzlaff, S. (2005), 'What's in a name? The politics of labelling and native identity constructions', *Canadian Journal of Native Studies*, 15(2), 609–626.
Sigona, N. (2018), 'The contested politics of naming in Europe's "refugee crisis"', *Ethnic and Racial Studies*, 41(3), 456–460.
Sjjad, T. (2018), 'What's in a name? "Refugees", "migrants" and the politics of labelling', *Race and Class*, 60(2), 40–62.
Spivak, G. (1994), 'Can the subaltern speak?', in P. Williams and K.L. Chrisman (eds), *Colonial Discourse and Post-colonial Theory: A Reader*, New York: Harvester, pp. 66–111.
Steiner, N. (2001), 'Arguing about asylum: the complexity of refugee debates in Europe', New Issues in Refugee Research, Working Paper No. 48, accessed 13 July 2019 at https://www.refworld.org/pdfid/4ff565292.pdf.
Turton, D. (2003), 'Conceptualising forced migration', Refugee Studies Centre Working Paper No. 12, accessed 8 August 2019 at http://www.rsc.ox.ac.uk/files/publications/working-paper-series/wp12-conceptualising-forced-migration-2003.pdf.
United Nations High Commissioner for Refugees (UNCHR) (1951), *Convention and Protocol Relating to the Status of Refugees*, UNHCR: Geneva.
United Nations High Commissioner for Refugees (UNHCR) (2019), 'Syrian emergency', accessed 7 August 2019 at https://www.unhcr.org/uk/syria-emergency.html.
Universal Declaration of Human Rights (1948), accessed at 30 August 2019 at https://www.un.org/en/universal-declaration-human-rights/.
Vigil, Y.N. and C.B. Abidi (2018), '"We" the refugees: reflections on refugee labels and identities', *Refuge: Canada's Journal on Refugees*, 34(2): 52–60.
Weber, J. (2015), *Language, Racism*, Basingstoke: Palgrave Pivot.
Welch, D. (2015), *Nazi Propaganda: The Power and the Limitation*, London: Routledge.
Wood, G. (1985), 'The politics of development policy labelling', *Development and Change*, 16(3): 347–373.
Zaharna, R.S. (2004), 'From propaganda to public diplomacy in the information age', in Y.R. Kamalipur and N. Snow (eds), *War, Media and Propaganda: A Global Perspective*, Oxford: Rowan & Littlefield, pp. 219–227.
Zetter, R. (1985), 'Refugees – access and labelling', *Development and Change*, 16(3): 429–450.
Zetter, R. (1991), 'Labelling refugees: forming and transforming a bureaucratic identity', *Journal of Refugee Studies*, 4(1): 39–62.

Zetter, R. (1998), 'Refugees and refugee studies – a label and an agenda', *Journal of Refugee Studies*, 1(1): 1–6.
Zetter, R. (2000), 'Refugees and refugee studies – a valedictory editorial', *Journal of Refugee Studies*, 13(4): 349–355.
Zetter, R. (2007), 'More labels, fewer refugees: remaking the refugee label in an era of globalization', *Journal of Refugee Studies*, 20(1): 172–192.
Zolberg, A., A. Suhrke, and S. Aguayo (1989), *Escape from Violence: Conflict and the Refugee Crisis in the Developing World*, Oxford: Oxford University Press.

15. Brexit uncertainties: political rhetoric versus British core values in the NHS

Georgia Spiliopoulos

INTRODUCTION

> We feel protected [from discriminatory incidents on the wards] in theory but there is still an attitude, you can feel there is something wrong in the air … After the Referendum the situation has changed. (Theodora, Greek nurse, January 2019, in Spiliopoulos and Timmons, 2019a: 7)

> How the [NHS] Trust will support the ward, it is all British and Filipinos here, all the Italians have left. (Martin, Filipino nurse, January 2019, in Spiliopoulos and Timmons, 2019a: 5)

The above quotations are taken from a study conducted in 2019 on the retention and recruitment of migrant nurses after Brexit (Spiliopoulos and Timmons, 2019a, 2019b). With fears being expressed over the large number of nurses from the European Union (EU) leaving the United Kingdom (UK) following the 2016 Referendum (Johnson, 2016; Matthews-King, 2017; Orr, 2017), and changes to the examination of the English language competence for EU nurses introduced by the Nursing and Midwifery Council (NMC) in 2017 (NMC, 2017), these events exposed chronic challenges faced by the National Health Service (NHS) in meeting safe staffing targets (King's Fund, 2018). The issues behind the retention and recruitment of migrant nurses are complex and symptomatic of the organisation's structural inequalities (Bloch et al., 2013; Kline, 2014; Solano and Rafferty, 2007; Spiliopoulos and Timmons, 2019a), but also more widely symptomatic of tensions over UK immigration controls and anxieties over British national identity (Solomos, 2003).

The image of the NHS as an 'inclusive' employer with a global reputation and as an emblematic institution of 'British core values' (Bivins, 2017) cannot be underestimated. Since its inception in 1948, the NHS has consistently relied on overseas recruitment (Buchan, 2009; Solano and Rafferty, 2007; Spiliopoulos and Timmons, 2019a). In 2019, it was estimated that one in eight members of NHS staff across occupations is international, with over 200 nationalities being represented (King's Fund, 2019). Moreover, in the opening ceremony of the London 2012 Olympic Games, the NHS figured prominently as a British 'national treasure' (Moreh et al., 2019).

The symbolic importance of the NHS and how it has been used in political propaganda to stir feelings of national belonging and Britishness, as exclusionary notions of those deemed non-British, can be seen in times of political and financial upheaval. The introduction of the NHS Immigrant Healthcare Surcharge for non-EU migrants (Gov.uk, 2015) is an illustrative example. Underlying crises in social welfare due to privatisation, asset-stripping by private equity firms, and cuts to local authority funding, and an overall 'shift from structural and institutional approaches to a focus on individual behaviour and responsibility' (Vickers, 2019: 107) were significant factors leading to a deterioration of welfare provision. However, the Conservative Party used immigrants as scapegoats and blamed 'health tourism', the abuse of NHS services by immigrants who do not contribute through taxation, as a reason for such deterioration (Campbell and O'Carroll, 2019). Following from the 2014 Immigration Act, migrants wanting to use NHS services need to have indefinite leave to remain (Vickers, 2019) or, since 2017, to pay £400 per year (Campbell and O'Carroll, 2019), otherwise they will be refused a visa automatically (Vickers, 2019). The impact of such measures is detrimental to the health and well-being of UK migrants whose data was shared with the Home Office in 2016 without their consent, and has led to those in need not seeking medical healthcare in fear of implications for their applications (Vickers, 2019). Days before the 2019 elections in the UK, the Conservative Party announced a possible increase of the surcharge up to £625 per person, which was criticised by a number of bodies, including the Royal College of Nursing (RCN), as 'immoral' for targeting non-EU migrants who are already paying contributions through taxes to use public services. They raised additional concerns over exacerbating even further the problems surrounding retention and recruitment of migrant nurses (Campbell and O'Carroll, 2019). Furthermore, this move was criticised as a way for the government to increase income by targeting non-EU migrants. Minnie Rahman, public affairs and campaigns manager for the Joint Council for the Welfare of Immigrants, stated the following: '[R]aising the NHS surcharge for the second time in two years is nothing more than a way to scapegoat migrants and distract everybody from the fact that it's austerity that is crippling our NHS' (Campbell and O'Carroll, 2019). In the midst of the 2020 Covid-19 pandemic and after pressure from bodies such as the Royal College of Nursing, the government announced a scrapping of the Immigrant Health Surcharge. However, at the time of writing (June 2020), the policy has not been terminated (Marsh and Gentleman, 2020).

The 'Leave' result of the 2016 Referendum, the December 2019 general election win for the Conservative Party, and the government's manifesto to lower immigration numbers through the 2020 Immigration and Social Security Co-ordination (EU Withdrawal) Bill and enable the UK '[F]or the first time in decades ... [to] have full control over who comes to this country' (Home Office, 2020: 4), are inextricably connected to a rising xenophobic sentiment, with significant implications for NHS overseas staff (Gye, 2020). I argue that these events are in fact the most recent manifestations of public anxiety over British national identity (Solomos, 2003), while stringent immigration controls which classify workers into 'skilled' and 'unskilled', and 'wanted' and 'unwanted', based on income threshold, despite great need in the healthcare sector, are part of what has been termed the 'dangerous politics of immigration control' (Anderson, 2013). I examine these indicators of political and racist propaganda and populist rhetoric against NHS nurses, initially from former colonies and in later years, European and non-European nurses, by using theoretical approaches of political propaganda (Bernays, 1955), racist propaganda (Durrheim et al., 2018), anti-immigrant propaganda (Jones et al., 2017), UK race relations (Solomos, 2003), right-wing xenophobia, and populism (Wodak, 2015). Furthermore, I offer some of the key findings of recent study on the retention and recruitment of migrant nurses following the 2016 EU Referendum (Spiliopoulos and Timmons, 2019a, 2019b) to scrutinise further the inherent contradictions within UK immigration policies, and serious implications for sectors such as healthcare which rely heavily on an immigrant labour force.

THE NHS'S DEPENDENCE ON MIGRANT NURSING STAFF: A 'TELLING' HISTORY

> What they didn't tell you to expect was the amount of prejudices and discrimination that you encountered. (Denzil Nurse, first generation of Caribbean NHS nurses, in Kramer, 2006: 23)

> Face the Facts: If you desire a coloured for your neighbour, vote Labour. If you are already burdened with one, vote Tory. The Conservatives, once in Office, will bring up to date the Ministry of Repatriation, to Speed up the return of home-going and expelled immigrants. (Poster from the 1964 British general election, in Kramer, 2006: 85)

These quotations reveal that in the mid-1960s the UK was struggling to come to terms with its growing multiracial and multi-ethnic society. The first quotation is indicative of the challenges the 'trailblazers' (Kramer, 2006), the first Caribbean nurses working for the NHS, faced in settling in the UK. The second quotation is indicative of the Conservative Party's racist propaganda, trying to gain support for their manifesto and creating a myth as an appealing and rational public opinion (Bernays, 1955). However, for Bernays (1955: 2), '[t]he instruments by which public opinion is organized and focused may be misused. But such organization and focusing are necessary to orderly life', while 'free competition' is an important element that 'society has consented to … be organized by leadership and propaganda' . Similarly, for others such as Durrheim et al. (2018), racist propaganda is influential because of the impact such messages have in scaremongering and inciting hatred and fear, but importantly they require an audience which is susceptible to such messages. I argue that political, financial, and social crises, such as Brexit and the Covid-19 pandemic, create fertile ground for the misuse of power, misinformation, and racist representations of the migrant labour force as being unwanted and unwelcome. In this section, I present NHS recruitment drives and ongoing reliance on migrant staff in a wider context of race relations and immigration controls in the UK. This sketching of a 'telling' history is necessary to provide an overview that shares parallels with the more recent Brexit uncertainties and contradictions over British national identity and immigration controls.

From the late 19th century to the mid-20th century, the main pattern of nurse mobility was from the UK to the colonies. However, the introduction of the Nurses' Act of 1949 permitted the registration of individual nurses through the General Nursing Council (GNC) and paved the way for hiring overseas nurses, but was 'framed in imperialist terms' (Solano and Rafferty, 2007: 1060), with the expectation that trainee nurses would eventually return to the colonies. Changes in demographics of the nursing workforce, with increased numbers of Caribbean and Asian nurses, sparked xenophobic reactions, for example in the *Nursing Times* in 1960, when race and ethnicity were equated with concerns over national identity (Solano and Rafferty, 2007).

The period between the late 1940s and late 1960s is crucial in understanding immigration policies post-World War II and their effects on the recruitment and settlement of overseas nurses in the UK. It is in this period that we can trace 'political and ideological racialisation of immigration policy' (Solomos, 2003: 52), as immigration policy and public debate were primarily focused on 'coloured' immigration, despite large numbers of Irish and Polish immigrants settling in the UK. The arrival of the *Empire Windrush* ship on 22 June 1948, which brought 494 West Indians and 65 Poles to Tilbury Docks, is hailed as a symbolic event in the framing of public debate and eventually policy responses to the anxieties over racial diversity (Bivins, 2017; Solomos, 2003).

As early as 1949 the NHS took an active role in recruiting from the colonies to meet staff shortages. According to Kramer (2006: 16), 'the Ministries of Health and Labour, together with the Colonial Office, the General Nursing Council (GNC) and the Royal College of Nursing (RCN), began a deliberate policy of recruiting from the British colonies, particularly the West Indies'. Deliberate policy manifested in advertisements in local newspapers and in senior British matrons travelling to the Caribbean to recruit. Staff needed from the Caribbean were nurses and trainee nurses, auxiliary staff, and domestic workers. The 1948 British Nationalities Act, which gave Commonwealth citizens automatic British citizenship, coupled with restrictions to migrate to the United States and pre-existing cultural ties with the UK, facilitated the movement of Caribbean immigrants to the UK. However, the 1962 Commonwealth Immigrants Act restricted free movement to the UK and required prerequisites for entry, such as holding employment vouchers issued by the Ministry of Labour, directly affecting the entrance of Caribbean nurses. The Labour opposition leader, Hugh Gaitskell, criticised this move as 'a plain anti-colour measure' (Kramer, 2006: 28). There are no exact numbers of Caribbean nurses and auxiliary staff entering the UK in 1948 to work for the NHS, but in '1954 more than 3,000 Caribbean women were training in British hospitals; by 1959 official statistics showed 6,365 colonial nursing students in Britain. In 1968, according to the trade union Unison, there were 6,450 West Indian trainees in British hospitals' (Kramer, 2006: 20). Caribbean nurses faced a number of restrictions and challenges: limited social mobility and obstacles in registering as advanced nurses in comparison to white, British nurses; working in wards unpopular with white nurses such as psychiatric or geriatric wards, and with little training in these fields; discrimination in and outside the hospitals and bias from senior staff (Kramer, 2006). While Norman Pannel MP stated in his correspondence with Minister of Health Enoch Powell, in 1961, that 'hospitals could not carry on with coloured immigrant nurses', the NHS has been 'slow' in recognising their significant contributions only since the 1990s (Kramer, 2006: 25).

Race became the visual marker for an outlet of anxiety and fear in a period of loss of Empire, with discussion in the public domain over the 'undeserving' migrant, portrayed often as and equated with 'coloured'. Photographic evidence dated from 1950s illustrates the rich ethnic and racial diversity within the NHS, mainly of black nurses, and fewer Asian nurses. Newspapers were very keen to portray a positive image of non-white nurses and, importantly, the inclusivity of the NHS and lack of racial prejudice. Additionally, cartoonists often used imagery to either condemn racism or celebrate racial diversity. However, such photographic evidence and imagery was used to depict the NHS, and more widely the British society, as predominately inclusive, devoid of racial bias and prejudice (Bivins, 2017).

Echoes of Enoch Powell's 'rivers of blood' speech in 1968,[1] which framed anxieties over 'Englishness' and British national identity within perceived threats emanating from multiracialism, targeting specifically black communities, reverberated within the 1970s and 1980s. His stance over 'Englishness or Britishness ... based on the notion of shared history, customs and kinship, which effectively excluded black and ethnic minorities from membership' (Solomos, 2003: 172), was repeated and defended in a political rhetoric which marked visibility of immigrant ethnic communities as clear division between those who belong and those who do not belong to the British nation. Moreover, race riots in the 1970s and 1980s were interpreted as direct results of unemployment and inner-city deterioration, and sparked local and national responses, hoping to deal with racial and ethnic discrimination by introducing 'equal opportunity strategies' (Solomos, 2003: 143). However, in the late 1970s and early 1980s, political rhetoric, and especially the new right and media outlets, continued to exacerbate the perceived 'threats' to white British citizens from black criminality, the 'enemies within', and hence general deterioration of the 'British way of life'. Established in the late 1960s, the far-right National Front group with explicit anti-immigration and racist propaganda was winning support from Labour and Conservative voters in the 1970s. Such a phenomenon can be partially explained by financial and social factors influencing local economies and also changes in inner cities, leading to support from white working classes for the National Front. In her speech in February 1978, the then leader of the Conservative Party, Margaret Thatcher, did not refute such stances but instead reiterated xenophobic sentiment, using an imagery of fear, of the British people being eventually 'swamped' by continuous immigration from the Commonwealth and Pakistan. This subtler stance led to this xenophobic rhetoric gaining a 'respectability' in the 'popular and political circles' (Solomos, 2003: 177), and in purely political advantage terms helped the Conservative Party to gain votes from the National Front.

Racialisation and othering practices targeted other minority ethnic groups, such as Irish immigrants. When considering the history of Irish nurses entering the NHS since the 1950s and their experiences of being othered, as 'white, European insiders, but cultural outsiders' (Ryan, 2007: 416), this illustrates the normalisation of such behaviours towards the Irish and subsequent 'racialization' (Walther, 2001, in Ryan, 2007), deeply rooted in colonial relations. Despite overt discrimination against Irish and black populations ('No Dogs, No Blacks, No Irish' signs were commonly seen outside lodgings) in the 1960s, British law has only recognised and sought to protect the Irish against discrimination and harassment towards the end of the 20th century (Ryan, 2007).

Trends for employing overseas nurses (and doctors) continued in the 1980s and increased in the following decades. Evidence of 'historical and continuing segregation of BME [black and minority ethnic] and migrant health workers employed in the NHS' (Bloch et al., 2013: 129) can be seen in limited social mobility, exploitation, deskilling, and discrimination practices. Despite numerous interventions to tackle discrimination and exploitation, the NHS 'has been very slow to implement equality policies' (Bloch et al., 2013: 130). Two noteworthy attempts in the 1990s were made by the Commission for Racial Equality (CRE), a non-departmental public body that promoted racial equality and addressed such issues of discrimination; and also by the Department of Health (DoH) following the Labour government series of announcements on these issues. However, very few district health authorities adopted the 1991 CRE 'NHS Contracts and Racial Equality' guide that sought to implement racial equality. The DoH five-year programme 'Vital Connections', launched in the late 1990s, promoted initiatives such as funding projects promoting racial equality and disseminating good practices. Moreover, the NHS was legally bound by the 2000 Race Relations Amendment Act 'to promote and implement race equality initiatives'. Any action to tackle these challenges was ultimately linked to 'the need to respond to [the health industry's] multiethnic constituency' (Bloch et al., 2013: 130).

The close link between political rhetoric and recruitment of overseas nurses is also evident through New Labour's 'modernization agenda', launched in 1997, which resulted in intensified international recruitment (Deeming, 2004) to improve the lowest nurse:patient ratio in the Organisation for Economic Co-operation and Development (OECD) countries (Buchan, 2004). Previous attempts to hire nursing staff from EU countries had been largely unsuccessful, which led to aggressive recruitment drives, targeting developing countries such as Zimbabwe, Kenya, and Zambia. The introduction of the NHS 'Code of Practice' on ethical recruitment in 2001 (Deeming, 2004) sought to tackle unethical recruitment by stipulating that NHS overseas recruitment would rely on pre-existing agreements with countries such as the Philippines and India (Buchan, 2006). However, regulating ethical recruitment proved to be a challenging task, with employers continuing to hire from Asia and Africa, especially from sub-Saharan Africa, in the early 2000s (Deeming, 2004).

With enlargement of the EU in 2004, more Eastern European nurses sought employment in the NHS, with Polish nurses being the most prominent example of newly non-UK registered nurses (Deeming, 2004). EU freedom of movement and NHS fiscal policies introduced in 2005/2006 influenced preference for EU nurses over non-EU nurses (Buchan, 2009). Following the global financial crisis, EU nurses from countries in Southern Europe, such as Spain and Italy, directly affected by the financial crisis, also sought employment in the NHS. The numbers of EU nurses thus increased significantly, from 7895 nurses and health visitors in September 2010 to 21 237 in September 2017 (NHS Digital, n.d.). Despite being a multi-ethnic and 'super-diverse' organisation, the NHS remains 'ethnically segregated', with its equality agenda being difficult to implement due to factors such as discriminatory and exclusionary practices at the micro level, and hesitancy from health authorities to embrace changes in practices with limited budgets, among others (Bloch et al., 2013: 128).

BREXIT ANXIETIES AND CONTRADICTIONS: POPULISM AND ITS IMPLICATIONS FOR MIGRANT NHS NURSES AND THOSE DEEMED 'NON-BRITISH'

> Ten thousand a week. Half a million a year. Five million economic migrants in 10 years coming to this country. Unprecedented. Never happened before. The effects are obvious in every part of our national life. The strain these numbers are putting on public services. Schools ... The NHS. The sheer weight of numbers that adds to the other problems. Demand pushes up prices. Wages are driven down by the massive over-supply of unskilled labour. (Farage, 2013, in Grierson, 2018)

> Hospital bosses told to get on a plane and find more foreign nurses to work in the NHS. (Bodkin, 2019)

Political propaganda and populist rhetoric played a significant role in vilifying immigrants, with a direct effect on the retention and recruitment of migrant NHS nurses. As seen in the 2016 EU Referendum, and then in the 2019 UK elections, and the introduction of the new Immigration and Social Security Co-ordination (EU Withdrawal) Bill (Home Office, 2020), populism has shaped political and policy responses, creating a more xenophobic rhetoric that has permeated societal relations and created divisions. The two quotations above showcase, firstly, how populism can impact upon and divert attention from complex issues, calling for simplistic interpretations and charismatic leaders to 'save' the population from threats to their nationhood (Wodak, 2015); and secondly, that controlling immigration, apart from belonging to populist discourse (Goodwin and Milazzo, 2017), is far more complex, considering that the NHS, among other UK employers and industries, relies on an immigrant labour force to fulfil its role and deliver, in this case, public healthcare (King's Fund, 2019).

The introduction of the 'hostile environment' policy in 2012 by the Home Secretary, Theresa May, provided fertile ground for vilifying immigrants and those deemed 'outsiders' prior to the 2016 EU Referendum. This cultivated 'hostility' towards (illegal) immigration, with echoes of fears and anxieties over uncontrolled immigration from Eastern European countries, first in 2004 (for example, Poland and Lithuania) and then in 2007 (Romania and Bulgaria) (Grierson, 2018), found visual expressions in the 'Go Home' vans which delivered the following message: 'In the UK illegally? GO HOME OR FACE ARREST. Text HOME to 78070 for free advice, and help with travel documents. We can help you return home voluntarily without fear of arrest or detention' (Jones et al., 2017: 11). Such imagery and xenophobic rhetoric can be traced to the National Front era of the 1970s, while New Labour's introduction of the points-based system in the late 2000s, that sought to regulate immigration from outside the European Economic Area (EEA), 'rooted in calculations of human capital, has the veneer of administrative governmentality, but it conceals a more violent sovereign logic focused on inclusion and exclusion' (Jones et al., 2017: 75). The 2010 UK elections were crucial in formulating heightened xenophobic rhetoric and racist propaganda (Durrheim et al., 2018) due to the growing popularity of the UK Independence Party (UKIP) with Nigel Farage as leader (Grierson, 2018). According to commentators, such as Grierson (2018):

> capitalising on disenchantment with austerity Britain and targeting traditional working class constituencies, UKIP experienced a spectacular shift in public support … In May 2013, the party put up a record number of candidates for the local elections and achieved its strongest ever result – polling an average of 23% in the wards where it stood and increasing its number of elected councillors from 4 to 147.

In his 2013 address at the UKIP party conference, Farage used populist rhetoric that targeted 'unskilled labour' and evoked feelings of fear over uncontrolled crime committed by Romanians in London, while simultaneously warning his followers about the loss of welfare and rights belonging to British citizens being abused by these 'criminal others'. The increasing popularity of UKIP provoked the introduction of the 'hostile environment' policy by the coalition government (Grierson, 2018). The ramifications of this policy and related xenophobic rhetoric could be seen in the pressures placed upon landlords and doctors to take on the role of immigration enforcement officers, and in the ensuing 'Windrush scandal' (Vickers, 2019), leading to the repatriation, homelessness, and even loss of life of those descended from the first generation of Caribbean workers who entered the UK after World War II (Gentleman, 2019).

Funding for the NHS and anxieties over staff shortages were used as bargaining chips leading up to the 2016 EU referendum and in the 2019 UK elections. One of the most enduring images of political propaganda used by the Leave campaign, headed by Boris Johnson, was the red 'NHS' bus, with the message: 'We send the EU £350 million a week – let's fund our NHS instead. Vote Leave. Let's take back control.' When questioned in 2018 on the accuracy of these Leave campaign figures on a live LBC radio show, Prime Minister Theresa May was reluctant to answer, replying that the NHS would be given '£394 million a year extra cash' (Drewett, 2018). Fears and anxieties over 'health tourists' and uncontrolled EU immigration had already set the scene for populist and racist propaganda; the 'use of increasingly hostile anti-migrant rhetoric in government and mainstream political debate seems to both authorise and fuel such hate filled outpourings, verbal and physical' (Jones et al., 2017: 3). Statistics released by the Home Office on the rise of hate crimes for the period between 2013 and 2018 (Quinn, 2019) showed that a spike in the rise of hate crimes was recorded in the immediate aftermath of the win for the Leave campaign, with discriminatory incidents taking place in public and in hospitals, targeting EU migrants.

In the aftermath of the 2016 EU referendum 'leave' result, significant numbers of EU nurses decided to leave the UK. In the period between 2016 and 2017, an estimated 4000 EU nurses left the UK (Matthews-King, 2017), while the NMC recorded a drop of 96 per cent in new applications made from EU nurses in 2017, in comparison to the previous year. Uncertainty over the rights of EU workers in the UK, coupled with the introduction of language requirements for EU nurses (NMC, 2017), previously in place for non-EU nurses but only recently required for EU nurses, impacted on retention and recruitment of EU nurses (King's Fund, 2018). NHS Trusts returned to practices of recruiting from overseas. In 2018, the government announced that it would recruit 5500 Jamaican nurses to work for the NHS for three years, 'under the slogan "earn, learn, return"' (Vickers, 2019: 111).

Qualitative research undertaken in 2019 showed that, from the perspective of nurses from the EU and from outside the EU, the 'Leave' result was interpreted and internalised as a clear message that migrants are 'unwanted' and 'unwelcomed' in the UK, while the majority of participants felt 'unsettled' following the referendum (Spiliopoulos and Timmons, 2019a, 2019b). The participants, nurses from the Philippines, Spain, Italy, and Greece, had been working for the NHS for under five years, had not yet progressed in their careers, and were considering alternative plans to a long-term stay in the UK. Filipino nurses working for over two years in the NHS considered taking nursing entrance examinations for the United States (NCLEX), while EU nurses considered either returning to their home countries or migrating elsewhere. Factors which would influence their decision to stay long term in the UK and continue to work for the NHS were: support with EU settlement status and renewal of visas for a three-year stay (instead of two-year visas being offered); opportunities for career progression and support against management bias; and support against discrimination and bullying by members of the public and other NHS staff. Other factors that would influence their long-term stay were connected to issues outside the remit of NHS Trusts, such as the strength of the British pound, following the UK exit from the EU (Spiliopoulos and Timmons, 2019a, 2019b). Finally, there was an increase in incidents of discrimination in the hospitals and in public after the 2016 Referendum. As mentioned by one of the participants, Theodora, NHS management had put in place policies to protect staff from discrimination, but these do not always translate into concrete action or bring change to deeply rooted bias and discrimination (Spiliopoulos and Timmons, 2019a).

In 2019, a number of contradictory media reports appeared, with messages such as 'Hospital bosses told to get on a plane and find more foreign nurses to work in the NHS' (Bodkin, 2019), and 'Plan to hire thousands of foreign nurses for NHS is axed (Target was politically difficult for a government committed to reducing net migration)' (Savage, 2019). While the first newspaper article conveys the urgency of hiring overseas nursing staff to combat staff shortages, the second conveys the message that the government is unable to meet recruitment targets for overseas nurses due to commitment to reducing immigration, a key point of the Brexit strategy (Goodwin and Milazzo, 2017). NHS funding and nursing staff shortages figured prominently in political pledges being made by all parties prior to the December 2019 UK election. Prime Minister Boris Johnson received harsh criticisms from NHS nurses, and was questioned as to whether he had a 'nurses tree' after promising to recruit 50 000 new nurses, when it was revealed that this included 18 500 nurses already working for the NHS who it hoped to retain (*Guardian*, 2019). Other parties promised funding for additional doctors, nurses, and a mental health workforce (Charlesworth, 2019). Furthermore, the 2020 Immigration Bill has been criticised by political figures such as the Shadow Home Secretary, Mr Thomas-Symonds, for its message to migrant staff earning less than the £26 500 threshold suggesting they are 'unskilled' and 'unwelcome' (Gye, 2020). Even though the 2020 Immigration Bill (Home Office, 2020) makes some allowances for those earning less than the threshold, the rhetoric used behind the anticipated points-based system, of attracting 'Global Talent' (p. 3), being 'fair and robust' (p. 10), and reviewing 'shortage occupation list', falls within broader populist rhetoric to 'fulfil our commitment to the British public and take back control of our borders' (p. 3).

POST-BREXIT CHALLENGES FOR MIGRANT NHS NURSE RETENTION AND RECRUITMENT: SOME CONCLUDING REMARKS

> [T]he most urgent challenge is the current shortage of nurses, who are critical to delivering the 21st century care set out in the NHS Long Term Plan. We must act now to support and retain our existing nurses, significantly increase the number of newly qualified nurses joining the NHS, bring in from abroad and ensure we make the most of the nurses we already have. (NHS England/Improvement, 2019: 5)

Future challenges for the NHS in meeting nursing and other shortages are further complicated due to ongoing Brexit uncertainties, the dangers of increasing xenophobia and 'normalisation of exclusion' (Wodak, 2015), and more recently, the Covid-19 pandemic crisis. The above quotation from the 'Interim People Plan' (NHS England/Improvement, 2019) clearly states that the ambitious NHS Long Term Plan cannot be sustained without sufficient numbers of nursing staff, and a continuing reliance on international nursing staff. The 'Interim People Plan' (NHS England/Improvement, 2019) has identified a significant shortfall of nursing staff, nearing 40 000 in 2019/2020, with the danger of reaching 70 000 by 2023/2024 if urgent action is not taken. International recruitment was only ever meant to be a 'quick fix' (Buchan, 2009). However, other ongoing issues such as the retirement and emigration of British nurses, low numbers of British nursing students, and nursing staff burnout (Spiliopoulos and Timmons, 2019a) all add to the pressures for safe nurse staffing on the wards. The Covid-19 pandemic has further exposed heightened risks and exploitation of migrant healthcare staff. Trade unions such as the GMB have criticised the Home Office's double standards, which under the 2020 bereavement scheme allows family members of NHS workers under the shortage occupation list to gain automatically indefinite leave to remain. Other NHS staff, such as porters and care workers who are exposed to the same dangers, are not qualified for this scheme, in the event that a family member dies due to Covid-19 (Courea, 2020). Other associations such as the Filipino UK Nurses Association (Williams, 2020) have reported increased number of deaths of Filipino nurses and healthcare workers in Wales, due to inadequate personal protection equipment (PPE) and lack of duty of care from employers. Finally, the 'clap for carers' practice, scheduled on Thursday evenings throughout the lockdown in 2020 and on the 72nd anniversary of the NHS, as symbolic appreciation of staff, has been criticised for being a token gesture embraced by the government, but undermined in practice by the Immigration Health Surcharge and the 2020 Immigration Bill (Anonymous, 2020).

Policy recommendations for the retention and recruitment of migrant nurses post-Brexit include tackling such issues as discrimination and discrepancies in support offered by different NHS Trusts, and focusing on management bias, increasing collaboration between NHS Trusts in sharing good practices, supporting career development, acknowledging migrant nurses' nursing experience, and using more effective mechanisms of checking nursing competences, amongst others (Spiliopoulos and Timmons, 2019b). As an international employer, the NHS needs to continue investing in the recognition of migrant and black and minority ethnic (BME) nursing staff, in order to eradicate racial inequality, and improving social mobility opportunities for migrant and BME staff in taking on leadership positions (Kline, 2014). The contributions made by Caribbean nurses, alongside other migrant healthcare staff, have only recently been recognised; for example, with the introduction of the NHS70 Windrush Awards in 2018, marking the 70th anniversary of the NHS and aimed at celebrating diversity in the NHS (Coghill, 2018).

In examining Brexit contradictions over immigration, and NHS challenges over retention and recruitment of migrant nurses, alongside a 'telling' history of nurse recruitment drives and heavy dependence on overseas staff, we can thus conclude that UK immigration policies and the realities of relying on an immigrant labour force are often at odds. The phenomenon of right-wing political propaganda and the appeal of populist political figures are not restricted to the UK, but are evident across Europe. A simplistic message and 'heroic' stance against social problems, but one which incites hatred, blames victims, and uses scapegoating of those considered non-citizens, such as migrants and BME populations, often goes against 'democratic traditions and values of many nations [sic] states [in Europe]' (Wodak, 2015: 178). Identity performances by right-wing propagandists, co-produced by followers and critics, carefully constructing racism in such a way as to create 'great political leverage' (Durrheim et al., 2018: 402), need further investigation in the current political post-Brexit climate. Such 'normalisation of exclusion' and instigated 'politics of fear' (Wodak, 2015), seen in the examples of the political and racist propaganda discussed here, should therefore be interrogated, and action taken by different factions of society, from employers and political figures to citizens, ascribing to anti-racist rhetoric which does not fuel anti-immigrant and racist propaganda but which unites under a common cause (Durrheim et al., 2018). The after-effects of Brexit and handling of anti-immigrant and racist propaganda will prove to be a major challenge in the coming years, in an effort to heal deep social divisions in British society.

NOTE

1. Enoch Powell's speech, delivered in Birmingham in 1968, focused on how to 'resolve' the 'race problem'. As quoted by the *Observer*, 21 April 1968: 'As I look ahead, I am filled with foreboding. Like the Roman, I seem to see the River Tiber foaming with much blood.' 'The tragic and intractable phenomenon which we watch with horror on the other side of the Atlantic, but which there is interwoven with the history and existence of the States itself, is coming upon us here by our own volition and our own neglect.' This imagined danger, conjured in political anti-immigrant propaganda, is also evident in warnings that white British citizens would become 'strangers' in their 'own country' (Solomos, 2003: 61), not able to find hospitals for their wives to give birth or places in schools for their children. Despite this speech leading to Powell's loss of his Cabinet position, his stance on controlling immigration and on repatriation of black immigrants residing in the UK eventually led to the 1969 Immigration Appeals Act, which 'institutionalised deportation for those breaking the conditions of entry' (Solomos, 2003: 62) and led to a number of controversial cases.

REFERENCES

Anderson, B. (2013), *US & Them? The Dangerous Politics of Immigration Control*, Oxford: Oxford University Press.

Anonymous (2020), 'I'm an NHS doctor – and I've had enough of people clapping for me', *Guardian*, 21 May, available at https://www.theguardian.com/society/2020/may/21/nhs-doctor-enough-people-clapping, accessed 23 May 2020.

Bernays, E. (1955) *Propaganda* (Kindle edition), New York: IG Publishing.

Bivins, R. (2017), 'Picturing race in the British National Health Service, 1948–1988', *Twentieth Century British History*, 28(1): 83–109.

Bloch, A., Neal, S. and J. Solomos (2013), *Race, Multiculture and Social Policy*, Basingstoke: Palgrave Macmillan.

Bodkin, H. (2019), 'Hospital bosses told to get on a plane and find more foreign nurses to work in the NHS', *Telegraph*, 23 March, available at https://www.telegraph.co.uk/news/2019/03/23/hospital-bosses-told-get-plane-find-foreign-nurses-work-nhs/, accessed 10 June 2019.

Buchan, J. (2004), 'International rescue? The dynamics and policy implications of the international recruitment of nurses to the UK', *Journal of Health Services Research and Policy*, 9 (Supplement 1): 10–16.

Buchan, J. (2006), 'Filipino nurses in the UK: a case study in active international recruitment', *Harvard Health Policy Review*, 7(1): 113–120.

Buchan, J. (2009), 'Achieving workforce growth in UK nursing: policy options and implications', *Collegian*, 16: 3–9.

Campbell, D. and L. O'Carroll (2019), 'Calls to scrap "immoral" NHS fee for foreign staff', *Guardian*, 20 November, available at https://www.theguardian.com/society/2019/nov/20/calls-scrap-plans-nhs-fee-foreign-staff-health-surcharge, accessed 30 November 2019.

Charlesworth, A. (2019), 'Politicians can't shake a magic people tree to staff the NHS: General Election 2019', *Health Foundation*, 20 November, available at https://www.healthfoundation.org.uk/news-and-comment/blogs/politicans-can%E2%80%99t-shake-a-magic-tree-to-staff-the-nhs, accessed 13 January 2020.

Coghill, Y. (2018), 'Windrush and the NHS at 70', *NHS* blog, 23 April, available at https://www.england.nhs.uk/blog/windrush-and-the-nhs-at-70/, accessed 14 January 2019.

Courea, E. (2020), 'NHS care workers left out of leave-to-remain scheme', *The Times*, 20 May, available at https://www.thetimes.co.uk/article/nhs-care-workers-left-out-of-leave-to-remain-scheme-jp8dzs9p0, accessed 10 July 2020.

Deeming, C. (2004), 'Policy targets and ethical tensions: UK nurse recruitment', *Social Policy and Administration*, 38(7): 775–792.

Drewett, Z. (2018), 'Boris's big red Brexit bus should have said £350,000,000 a year for NHS – not a week', *Metro.co.uk*, 16 November, available at https://metro.co.uk/2018/11/16/boriss-big-red-brexit-bus-might-have-been-accurate-after-all-8146322/, accessed 18 January 2020.

Durrheim, K., M. Okuyan, M. Sinayobye Twali, E. García-Sánchez, A. Pereira, J.S. Portice, et al. (2018), 'How racism discourse can mobilize right-wing populism: the construction of identity and alliance in reactions to UKIP's Brexit "Breaking Point" campaign', *Journal of Community and Applied Social Psychology*, 28: 385–405.

Gentleman, A. (2019), 'Three generations of Windrush family struggling to prove they are British', *Guardian*, 18 December, available at https://www.theguardian.com/uk-news/2019/dec/18/three-generations-of-windrush-family-struggling-to-prove-they-are-british, accessed 20 January 2020.

Goodwin, M. and C. Milazzo (2017), 'Taking back control? Investigating the role of immigration in the 2016 vote for Brexit', *British Journal of Politics and International Relations*, 19(3): 450–464.

Gov.uk (2015), 'News story: UK introduces Health Surcharge', available at https://www.gov.uk/government/news/uk-introduces-health-surcharge, accessed 14 January 2020.

Grierson, J. (2018), 'Hostile environment: anatomy of a policy disaster', *Guardian*, 27 August, available at https://www.theguardian.com/uk-news/2018/aug/27/hostile-environment-anatomy-of-a-policy-disaster, accessed 15 March 2019.

Guardian (2019), '"Do you have a nurses tree?" Johnson challenged over NHS pledges – video', 27 November, available at https://www.theguardian.com/politics/video/2019/nov/27/do-you-have-a-nurses-tree-johnson-challenged-over-nhs-pledges-video, accessed 10 January 2020.

Gye, H. (2020), 'Immigration system tells NHS frontline workers they are "unwelcome", ministers warned', *inews.co.uk*, 18 May, available at https://inews.co.uk/news/coronavirus-immigration-system-nhs-frontline-workers-unwelcome-warning-priti-patel-429026, accessed at 11 June 2020.

Home Office (2020), *The UK's Points-Based Immigration System: Policy Statement*, February, available at https://assets.publishing.service.gov.uk/government/uploads/system/uploads/attachment_data/file/866744/CCS0120013106-001_The_UKs_Points-Based_Immigration_System_WEB_ACCESSIBLE.pdf, accessed 9 July 2020.

Johnson, S. (2016), 'EU workers in the NHS: "I've faced racial abuse and will head home"', *Guardian*, 6 July, available at https://www.theguardian.com/healthcare-network/2016/jul/06/eu-workers-nhs-faced-racial-abuse-head-home, accessed 20 April 2019.

Jones, H., Y. Gunaratnam, G. Bhattacharyya, W. Davies, D. Sukhwant, et al. (2017), *Go Home? The Politics of Immigration Controversies*, Manchester: Manchester University Press.

King's Fund, (2018), 'The healthcare workforce in England: Make or break?', report, 15 November, available at https://www.kingsfund.org.uk/publications/health-care-workforce-england, accessed 5 April 2019.

King's Fund (2019), 'International recruitment in the NHS', report, 6 November, available at https://www.kingsfund.org.uk/projects/nhs-in-a-nutshell/nhs-international-recruitment, accessed 13 January 2020.

Kline, R. (2014), 'The "snowy white peaks" of the NHS: a survey of discrimination in governance and leadership and the potential impact on patient care in London and England', report, March, *Middlesex University's Research Repository*, available at https://www.england.nhs.uk/wp-content/uploads/2014/08/edc7-0514.pdf, accessed 17 April 2019.

Kramer, A. (2006), *Many Rivers to Cross: The History of the Caribbean Contribution to the NHS*, London: Stationery Office.

Marsh, S. and A. Gentleman (2020), 'Migrant healthcare staff still paying NHS fee despite Johnson U-turn', *Guardian*, 15 June, available at https://www.theguardian.com/society/2020/jun/15/migrant-healthcare-staff-still-paying-nhs-fee-despite-johnson-u-turn, accessed 16 June 2020.

Matthews-King, A. (2017), 'Brexit: numbers of EU and UK nurses leaving NHS since referendum surges', *Independent*, 2 November, available at https://www.independent.co.uk/news/health/brexit-nhs-nurse-numbers-fall-first-time-yearsa8032306.html, accessed 29 March 2019.

Moreh, C., A. Vlachantoni, and D. McGhee (2019), 'Britain's NHS is not that great, say EU migrants', Conversation, 21 March, available at https://www.theconversation.com/britains-nhs-not-that-great-say-eu-migrants-113147, accessed 20 June 2019.

NHS Digital (n.d.), 'Staff by nationality and staff group, September 2010 to 2017', available at https://digital.nhs.uk/data-and-information/find-data-and-publications/supplementary-information/2018-supplementary-information-files/staff-numbers/staff-by-nationality-and-staff-group-september-2010-to-2017, accessed 20 April 2019.

NHS England/Improvement (2019), 'Interim People Plan', report, 6 June, available at https://www.longtermplan.nhs.uk/publication/interim-nhs-people-plan/, accessed 5 October 2019.

Nursing and Midwifery Council (NMC) (2017), 'Changes to language testing requirements come into force', 1 November, available at https://www.nmc.org.uk/news/news-and-updates/changes-to-language-testing-requirements-come-in-force/, accessed 5 April 2019.

Orr, D. (2017), 'The latest Brexit shockwave – a 96% drop in EU nursing applications', *Guardian*, 13 June, available at https://www.theguardian.com/commentisfree/2017/jun/13/nursing-uk-crisis-brexit-worse-nhs, accessed 5 April 2019.

Quinn, B. (2019), 'Hate crimes double in five years in England and Wales', *Guardian*, 15 October, available at https://www.theguardian.com/society/2019/oct/15/hate-crimes-double-england-wales, accessed 28 October 2019.

Ryan, L. (2007), 'Who do you think you are? Irish nurses encountering ethnicity and constructing identity in Britain', *Ethnic and Racial Studies*, 30: 416–438.

Savage, M. (2019), 'Plan to hire thousands of foreign nurses for NHS is axed', *Observer*, 2 June, available at https://www.theguardian.com/society/2019/jun/02/foreign-nurses-target-cut-from-nhs-staffing-plan, accessed 10 August 2019.

Solano, D. and A.M. Rafferty (2007), 'Can lessons be learned from history? The origins of the British imperial nurse labour market: a discussion paper', *International Journal of Nursing Studies*, 44: 1055–1063.

Solomos, J. (2003), *Race and Racism in Britain* (3rd edn), Basingstoke: Palgrave Macmillan.

Spiliopoulos, G. and S. Timmons (2019a), 'How can the NHS recruit and retain migrant nurses after Brexit?', University of Nottingham Asia Research Institute, Policy Brief Background Report, June, available at https://www.nottingham.ac.uk/asiaresearch/documents/policy-briefs/policy-report-spiliopoulos.pdf.

Spiliopoulos, G. and S. Timmons (2019b), 'How can the NHS recruit and retain migrant nurses after Brexit?', University of Nottingham Asia Research Institute Policy Brief, June, available at https://www.nottingham.ac.uk/asiaresearch/documents/policy-briefs/policy-brief-spiliopoulos.pdf.

Vickers, T. (2019), *Borders, Migration and Class in an Age of Crisis*, Bristol: Bristol University Press.

Williams, R. (2020), 'Coronavirus: Filipino health workers "need extra protection"', BBC News, 24 June, available at https://www.bbc.co.uk/news/uk-wales-53149843, accessed 2 July 2020.

Wodak, R. (2015), *The Politics of Fear: What Right-Wing Populist Discourses Mean*, London: SAGE Publications.

16. The media, antisemitism, and political warfare in Jeremy Corbyn's Labour Party, 2015–2019
James R. Vaughan

INTRODUCTION

During his campaign to become Leader of the Labour Party in September 2015, Jeremy Corbyn presented himself as a new type of leader, promising a 'kinder' and 'more inclusive' brand of politics. The years that followed instead saw the Labour Party torn asunder by a series of vindictive conflicts. Among these, the allegation that Corbyn's leadership was responsible, directly or indirectly, for a rise in antisemitic discourse and behaviour among party members was among the most bitterly contested charges. This chapter explores media and propaganda aspects of Labour's antisemitism crisis. It charts the transformation of concerns about antisemitism within the Labour Party into a political battle waged in a public sphere defined by interaction between traditional and new forms of media. It analyses the general failure of the leadership group and its allies to develop an effective communications strategy capable of challenging the perception of widespread anti-Jewish prejudice within the Labour Party.

In treating the Labour Party's battles over perceptions and allegations of antisemitism as forms of political warfare, the chapter acknowledges the distinction between propaganda and mere advocacy, and draws on Nicholas Jackson O'Shaughnessy's use of the term 'bureaucratic propaganda'. In O'Shaughnessy's model, 'bureaucratic' propaganda functions as both a highly politicised and often neglected form:

> The official lies, evasions and bureaucratic fog often thrive beyond the radar of propaganda textbooks because they seem to be the antithesis of what is publicly imagined to be propaganda … Conventional propaganda is equated with lurid language but here is manifest the reverse … Bureaucratic propaganda delights in the language of obfuscation, obscurity, evasion and denial. (O'Shaughnessy, 2004: 34)

Therefore this chapter focuses on the Corbyn leadership's strategy of media management and press relations as an aspect of bureaucratic propaganda specifically geared towards managing public criticism and controversy over the question of antisemitism. This conception is well suited to an analysis of the Corbyn leadership's ultimately unsuccessful bid to deny, diminish, and distract from the charges of antisemitism levelled against them. The official spokesperson's line, repeated ad nauseam, that 'the Labour Party takes all complaints of antisemitism extremely seriously and we are committed to challenging and campaigning against it in all its forms', may also be regarded as a clear example of what O'Shaughnessy characterises as 'bureaucratic language [that] actively seeks to sedate' (O'Shaughnessy, 2004: 34).

CROSSMAN VERSUS MAYHEW: PROPAGANDA AND THE HISTORICAL ORIGINS OF LABOUR'S ARAB–ISRAELI WAR

That advocacy and lobbying are inextricably bound up with the business of propaganda is something of a truism. Nevertheless, it is still intriguing to note that the Labour Party figures who did most to establish conflicting advocacy groups seeking to influence the party's approach to the Arab–Israeli conflict had strong connections to the propaganda agencies of the British state. Much of the institutional and rhetorical terrain that characterised the Labour Party's 21st century battles over Israel, Zionism, and antisemitism, can be seen to have their origins in the work of Richard Crossman and Christopher Mayhew.

Crossman, the 'scintillating and unruly' (Marquand, 1991: 137) Winchester contemporary of Hugh Gaitskell (Labour Party Leader from 1955 to 1963), stands among the most fascinating figures in the history of the post-war Labour Party. Crossman's appointment, at the age of 23, to a fellowship in philosophy and history at New College Oxford was followed by a controversial series of broadcasts on the BBC and, in 1938, an assistant editorial role at the *New Statesman*. Upon the outbreak of war, he joined the Ministry of Information, before in the summer of 1940 he was recruited into the secret world of the Special Operations Executive (SOE) and, in 1941, its psychological warfare branch, the Political Warfare Executive (PWE). Working alongside Sefton Delmer, the creative genius behind Britain's wartime 'black' propaganda, Crossman directed the radio broadcasts of PWE's German Section. In 1943, after a posting to North Africa, he established a strong working relationship with C.D. Jackson (later Eisenhower's White House Special Advisor on Psychological Warfare), and accepted a role with the Psychological Warfare Division of Eisenhower's Supreme Headquarters Allied Expeditionary Force (SHAEF) in the last year of the war.[1]

Christopher Mayhew came from a similar educational background, though without emulating Crossman's intellectual brilliance. Having gone up to Balliol College, Oxford, from Haileybury in 1934, he joined the Oxford University Labour Club and embarked upon a trip to the Soviet Union alongside, among others, Anthony Blunt (famously revealed by Margaret Thatcher in 1979 to have been an agent of Soviet intelligence). It was, Mayhew wrote, 'an object-lesson in the dangers of the will-to-believe, of self-persuasion', and would ultimately inform the resolute anti-Communism that led Mayhew to play an important role in the propaganda battles of the early Cold War. 'Much of my later bitterness against western communists and fellow-travellers', he confessed, 'sprang, I am sure, from shame at my own obtuseness during that first trip to Russia' (Mayhew, 1987: 23–26).

During World War II, Mayhew accepted an invitation from Hugh Dalton (later to serve as Chancellor of the Exchequer in the post-war Labour government) to join the SOE, though he involved himself in special forces operations rather than the psychological warfare activities in which Crossman specialised. After the war, having won the seat of South Norfolk for Labour in the 1945 general election, he was appointed as a junior minister to Ernest Bevin at the Foreign Office and his contribution to the history of British Cold War propaganda began. His concerns about Britain's vulnerability to Soviet propaganda now resurfaced, not least in relation to some of Labour's more left-leaning backbenchers. Intriguingly, in his autobiography, Mayhew named just one MP in this context, the 'able and ambitious troublemaker' Richard Crossman (Mayhew, 1987: 98). Mayhew proposed the creation of the Information Research Department (IRD), a clandestine propaganda agency which, from 1948 until 1978, waged unrelenting psychological warfare upon Communism and the Soviet Union, while wielding increasingly what many have regarded as a controversial degree of influence within the United Kingdom's most important political, media, and academic institutions.

Mayhew's view of Crossman as a 'troublemaker' can be at least partly explained by the pair's profound disagreement about Palestine and the nature of Zionism. This personal antagonism, which would extend into a larger clash of factions within the Labour Party, began when Bevin, no doubt to his subsequent regret, appointed Crossman to the Anglo-American Committee of Inquiry into the Problems of European Jewry and Palestine. This decision, Crossman recalled with characteristic acidity, 'unwittingly forged my only intimate friendship with a great statesman. It was thanks to Ernest Bevin that I came to know Chaim Weizmann' (Crossman, 1960: 13–14).

That friendship with Weizmann, a chief architect of the Balfour Declaration and Israel's first President, created sympathy for Zionism and Israel that became a defining feature of Crossman's political identity. Michael Foot recalled how Crossman returned from the Anglo-American Committee's fact-finding trip to Palestine 'with a report which electrified the House of Commons and well-nigh electrocuted Ernest Bevin' (Foot, 1974). His belief that Prime Minister Clement Attlee and Bevin had betrayed the Jews of Palestine poisoned his relations with both, and he was not slow to ascribe the worst motives to them. As early as May 1946, Hugh Dalton received a complaint from Crossman about 'the presence of so many anti-Semites' (Pimlott, 1987: 372) within the government, and his judgement only hardened with the passing years. Interviewed by the Israeli newspaper *Yediot Ahronot* in 1971, he savaged Attlee as 'much worse than Bevin. That nasty, little man felt that the Jews had mounted a personal vendetta against him, and he really hated them. He believed that the Arabs would sweep over Palestine and that the Jews would capitulate immediately' (Bashan, 1971). 'I have never in my life met anything as wicked as what they did', he told Eric Silver for the *Jerusalem Post*. 'It was an attempted genocide' (Silver, 1971). Crossman's commitment to Zionism and Weizmann's memory never faltered. In 1957, he was instrumental in the establishment of the Labour Friends of Israel group and, though illness and death prevented him from fulfilling his role as Weizmann's official biographer, his research notes assisted Norman Rose in the completion of a much-lauded biography (Rose, 1986).

Christopher Mayhew, to put it mildly, maintained a rather different opinion of Jewish nationalism. 'I sympathized', he wrote in his memoirs, 'with [Bevin's] dislike of Zionist methods and, indeed, of the Zionist philosophy itself.' Bevin, he recalled, 'held that Zionism was basically racialist [and] inevitably wedded to violence and terror', and 'events have since proved him right – or so I would myself argue' (Mayhew, 1987: 118–119). If this loathing of Zionism had been forged alongside Bevin in the last years of the Palestine Mandate, it was only transformed into a practical commitment to the Palestinian Arab cause in the 1960s. Visiting Israel in 1963, he clashed with Foreign Minister Golda Meir, who he patronisingly dismissed as a 'superficial' and 'disappointing woman' (Mayhew, 1963). Mayhew later suggested that arguments with Israeli leaders on this trip explained Prime Minister Harold Wilson's decision to keep him away from the Foreign Office after Labour's 1964 general election victory (Mayhew, 1987: 159), a sign of a tendency towards conspiratorial thinking that would even persuade him to attribute the disappointing sales of his autobiography to the 'fact' that 'so many Jewish supporters of Israel are literary editors, reviewers, members of library committees and so on' (Mayhew, 1990).

In 1969, Mayhew founded the Labour Middle East Council (LMEC) as a vehicle for bringing pro-Arab opinion to bear upon the wider Labour movement (Vaughan, 2015). The new organisation immediately recruited nearly 30 MPs to its ranks and, by the mid-1970s, could exert significant influence within the parliamentary party, the National Executive Committee, and the trade unions. By 1972, its membership had grown to 160 (Mayhew, 1972), and in 1977, when the NEC established a Labour Party Sub-Committee on the Middle East, five LMEC members were appointed to it (Faulds, 1977). By the time that Mayhew, disturbed by the growing strength of the far left, abandoned Labour for the Liberal Party, he had laid the foundations for a cluster of pro-Palestinian organisations that provided a home to a new generation of left-wing anti-Zionists, including George Galloway, Ken Livingstone, and Jeremy Corbyn. Between them, two of Labour's most interesting political propagandists had established an order of battle that would later explode into a very public Labour Party civil war, intensely focused on the issues of Israel, the Palestinians, and antisemitism.

PATTERNS OF PREJUDICE: ANTISEMITIC TRADITIONS WITHIN THE UK LABOUR PARTY

It should be emphasised that the problem of antisemitism within the British Labour Party long pre-dates Jeremy Corbyn's election as Leader of the Labour Party in September 2015. One can point to the example of Beatrice Webb (a key figure in the Fabian Society, co-founder of the *New Statesman* and wife of the Colonial Secretary, Lord Passfield) and the rhetorical question she posed in a diary entry of 30 October 1930. 'Why is it,' she asked, 'that everyone who has dealings with Jewry ends up being prejudiced against the Jews?' (MacKenzie and MacKenzie, 1985: 231). Three years later, Labour's prospective parliamentary candidate for Tavistock informed the Assistant Secretary of the party, Jim Middleton, that 'the policy and methods associated with the Jews will be among the primary methods marked for destruction before Socialism will be realized' (Middleton, 1933). Ernest Bevin's anti-Jewish outbursts have been well documented, and led Harold Laski to the conclusion that the Foreign Secretary was both 'antisemitic in a brutal way' and implementing a policy that constituted 'an insult to the millions of Jewish dead'. 'I am not sure if EB hates Jews more than communists,' he wrote, but 'it must be a near thing' (Kramnick and Sheerman, 1993: 552–557). Clement Attlee was even reported to have rejected Ian Mikardo and Austen Albu for government positions on the grounds that 'they both belonged to the Chosen People, and he didn't think he wanted any more of *them*' (Andrew, 2009: 366).

Mayhew himself once described 'the Jews' as 'the world's best propagandists and pushers' (Mayhew, 1967), and in the aftermath of the 1973 Arab–Israeli War, his LMEC comrade, Andrew Faulds, was sacked from Harold Wilson's Shadow Cabinet after repeatedly 'impugning the patriotism of Jewish Members of Parliament' (Faulds, 1973), not least by claiming that a 'Zionist propaganda machine acts as a fifth column in every country in the world with a Jewish community' (*Hansard*, 1973). In the 1980s, the *Labour Herald* (a newspaper that linked members of Labour's far left to the Trotskyite Workers' Revolutionary Party), published a series of antisemitic reviews, articles, and cartoons that led to the Board of Deputies of British Jews referring the publication to the Attorney-General with a view to prosecution under race relations legislation (*Jewish Chronicle*, 1982). At that time, the co-editor of the *Labour Herald* was a rising star of the Labour left (and future London Mayor) called Ken Livingstone It is thus fitting that an older, if not necessarily wiser, Livingstone played the crucial role in ensuring that stirrings of discontent about antisemitism in Jeremy Corbyn's Labour Party were transformed into a major national news story.

FEAR AND LOATHING: LABOUR'S ANTISEMITISM CRISIS, 2015–2019

Livingstone's notorious appearance on BBC London radio on 28 April 2016 was ostensibly intended to defend the Labour MP Naz Shah against criticism for sharing a Facebook post that had suggested that Israeli Jews should be forcibly 'relocated' to the United States. However, he offered up the following comment during the interview: 'Let's remember when Hitler won his election in 1932, his policy then was that Jews should be moved to Israel. He was supporting Zionism – this before he went mad and ended up killing six million Jews' (Stone, 2016).

This statement, which recalled the *Labour Herald*'s old habit of promoting inflammatory material about Nazi–Zionist 'collaboration', led to a public confrontation with the Labour MP John Mann, who denounced Livingstone as a 'disgusting Nazi apologist'. The interview and its aftermath provided the lead story for almost every national newspaper on 29 April, with images of Mann's clash with Livingstone dominating the front pages of the *Daily Mirror*, *The Times*, and the *Daily Telegraph*.

The interview was instrumental in establishing the impression of a Labour Party riven by divisions over antisemitism and, at the same time, was influential in establishing the strategy of denial that characterised the initial response of the Corbyn leadership team and its supporters. Livingstone articulated the essential elements of this strategy in the following terms: 'There's been a very well-orchestrated campaign by the Israel lobby to smear anybody who criticizes Israeli policy as antisemitic' (Stone, 2016). Livingstone had used this argument many times before. In a *Labour Herald* article of July 1982, after making the dubious claim that Jewish MPs within the Labour Party formed part of 'a distortion running right through British politics', Livingstone warned his readers not to underestimate the 'forces' that would be mobilised against 'those of us who support the Palestinian people' (Livingstone, 1982). In 2006, following an incident in which he had likened a Jewish journalist to a 'German war criminal', Livingstone used the pages of the *Guardian* to defend himself against charges of antisemitism by launching the counter-accusation that, 'For far too long the accusation of anti-semitism has been used against anyone who is critical of the policies of the Israeli government' (Livingstone, 2006).

This argument has been subjected to a sustained critique by the sociologist David Hirsh. 'The Livingstone formulation', Hirsh observes, is a device enabling those who deploy it to deny concerns about antisemitism. It:

> does not simply accuse anyone who raises the issue of contemporary antisemitism of being wrong, but it also accuses them of bad faith … It is a mirror which bounces back an accusation, magnified, against anybody who makes it. It sends back a charge of dishonest Jewish conspiracy in answer to a concern about antisemitism. (Hirsh, 2008)

Livingstone was not the only close ally of Jeremy Corbyn to be well versed in this rhetorical technique. In 2002, 13 years before his appointment as Jeremy Corbyn's Executive Director of Strategy and Communications, Seamus Milne had developed his own version of the formulation. Milne found the charge that left-wing support for Palestinians was 'somehow connected to resurgent anti-Jewish racism' to be a 'smear' and 'an absurd slur'. If antisemitism could be demonstrated to be on the rise at all, then the threat came from the far right, and even this apparent concession was qualified with the observation that: 'anti-Arab racism and Islamophobia [were] both currently more violently represented on Europe's streets and more acceptable in its polite society than anti-semitism' (Milne, 2002).

The 'Livingstone formulation' thus acquired the status of an article of faith for a certain strand of the British anti-Zionist left, and it underpinned a series of statements by leading Labour figures responding to the burst of media interest in antisemitism provoked by Livingstone. On 1 May 2016, the Shadow Secretary of State for International Development, Diane Abbott, declared that: 'It's a smear to say that Labour has a problem with antisemitism … a smear against ordinary party members' (Syal, 2016). Abbott's subsequent promotion to Shadow Home Secretary, along with the near total failure of Shadow Minister for Diverse Communities, Dawn Butler, to engage with the British Jewish community (Dysch, 2017), were early signs of the breakdown in relations between Corbyn and the mainstream Jewish leadership that was to come. At the 2017 Party Conference, the General Secretary of Unite the Union, Len McCluskey, dismissed allegations about Labour antisemitism as 'mood music that was created by people who were trying to undermine Jeremy Corbyn' (Merrick, 2017). In one of the party's most notorious cases, Chris Williamson dismissed claims of antisemitism as 'proxy wars and bullshit' before denouncing 'the weaponization of antisemitism for political ends' as 'a really dirty, lowdown trick … smears and lies' (Mason, 2017). Williamson's outbursts eventually led to his suspension and removal as Labour's parliamentary candidate for Derby North, but it is all too readily apparent that his views were shared by at least some of Corbyn's closest allies. At a July 2018 meeting of the party's National Executive Committee, Peter Willsman denounced leaders of the Jewish community as 'Trump fanatics' who were 'making up' false allegations of antisemitism in order to damage the party. Despite a recording of these remarks leaking to the press, Labour members endorsed Willsman by re-electing him to the NEC, and it was only in May 2019, after Willsman claimed that the Israeli Embassy was 'almost certainly' responsible for engineering allegations of antisemitism against the Labour Party, that he was finally suspended (BBC News, 2019).

It was in this atmosphere that a number of fringe groups, dedicated to defending the Corbyn leadership and wider party membership against claims of antisemitism, emerged over the course of 2017. Jewish Voice for Labour (JVL) was established in July as a pro-Corbyn rival to the long-standing Jewish affiliate within the Labour Party, the Jewish Labour Movement (JLM). 'We have always claimed', wrote JVL secretary, Glyn Secker, 'that the campaign … of false allegations of antisemitism has a dual purpose: to attack the left and the rise of Corbyn, and to silence criticisms of Israel's human rights abuses' (Rich, 2018a: 309). JVL did not meet with universal approval, even from key figures in Corbyn's inner circle. Jon Lansman, founder of the grassroots Momentum organisation, launched a stinging attack, accusing the group of being 'part of the problem and not part of the solution to antisemitism in the Labour Party', and adding that 'neither the vast majority of individual members of JVL nor the organization itself can really be said to be part of the Jewish community' (Harpin, 2019a). However, perhaps more revealing of the leadership group's attitude was the decision of two of Corbyn's closest aides, Seamus Milne and Andrew Murray, to intervene in party disciplinary proceedings when Secker was suspended for an association with 'a Facebook group where members posted messages denying the Holocaust'. 'JC interested in this one', Murray announced in an email calling for Secker's suspension to be lifted (Shipman and Pogrund, 2019) and Secker was swiftly reinstated as a full party member. He rewarded his supporters with a speech at a Palestine solidarity rally in May 2019 in which he characterised Labour MPs with sympathies for Israel as 'a 'fifth column in the Labour Party', accused them of associating with the far right, and asked, 'What on earth are Jews doing in the gutter with these rats?' (*Jewish News*, 2019). A second group, Labour Against the Witch-Hunt, was formed in October by activists including Jackie Walker and Tony Greenstein, with the expressed aim of defending from disciplinary action party members accused of antisemitism. Despite attracting some high-profile supporters, including Noam Chomsky and Ken Loach, the fact that both Greenstein and Walker were expelled from the Labour Party does suggest that their group was not enormously successful (Dysch, 2018; Elgot, 2019).

An ultimately insurmountable problem for the 'Livingstone formulation' strategy of denial was the sheer quantity of evidence that testified to the scale of the party's antisemitism problem. The May 2016 Royall Report into the Oxford University Labour Club, whilst concluding that the Club was not institutionally antisemitic, declared that: 'It is clear ... from the weight of witnessed allegations received that there have been some incidents of antisemitic behaviour and that it is appropriate for the disciplinary procedures of our Party to be invoked' (Royall, 2016: 11). The prominent human rights lawyer Shami Chakrabarti's report of June 2016, whilst at pains to stress that the Labour Party was 'not overrun by antisemitism', acknowledged that 'there is too much clear evidence (going back some years) of minority hateful or ignorant attitudes and behaviours festering within a sometimes bitter incivility of discourse', and that 'too many Jewish voices express concern that antisemitism has not been taken seriously enough in the Labour Party and broader Left' (Chakrabarti, 2016: 1). While both reports disappointed those who had hoped for more critical findings and stronger recommendations (particularly Chakrabarti's, the credibility of which was undermined when its author was nominated by Jeremy Corbyn for a peerage shortly after her report's release), they did more than enough to discredit the idea that claims of antisemitism could be dismissed as a 'smear campaign'. The viability of the 'Livingstone formulation' suffered a decisive blow as a result, and the Equality and Human Rights Commission's (EHRC) report, *Investigation into Antisemitism in the Labour Party*, finally published in October 2020, concluded that suggestions that complaints of antisemitism were fake, or smears, served not only to undermine the Labour Party's commitment to anti-racism, but also ignored legitimate and genuine complaints of antisemitism within the party. Therefore they were an integral part of the unlawful acts of harassment and discrimination that had taken place (EHRC, 2020: 100).

In the years that followed, a damaging aspect of the media's coverage of Labour Party antisemitism concerned Corbyn's own historical associations and activities. Many of these stories were hardly new, especially to those familiar with Corbyn's career as a backbench campaigner, but they now began to make more of an impact on public opinion than had previously been the case. David Kogan has suggested that this was, at least in part, a consequence of Labour's unexpectedly strong general election performance in 2017. 'Prior to 2015', Kogan argues, Corbyn 'had no real public profile and indeed had not wanted one ... After 2017, when it appeared that Labour could win power with Jeremy Corbyn as prime minister, the attention fell on his beliefs' (Kogan, 2019: 334).

In 2015, a *Jewish Chronicle* report about Corbyn's support for an antisemitic mural by an artist known as Mear-One (Dysch, 2015) had been largely ignored. When the story re-emerged in March 2018, the response was very different. At this time Corbyn was under fire after the revelation that he had been an active member of a secret Facebook group, 'Palestine Live', which had propagated Holocaust denial as well as conspiracy theories about the Rothschilds, Israeli responsibility for the 9/11 and 7/7 terror attacks, and the creation of the Islamic State organisation. Corbyn acknowledged his membership of the group, while denying that he had seen any antisemitic content, and stressing that he had left it in 2015 (Elgot, 2018).

In the aftermath of this story, Corbyn's support for the Mear-One mural (which depicted wealthy, hook-nosed Jewish figures playing 'Monopoly' on the backs of oppressed workers) became national news, and Corbyn was forced into an embarrassing and unconvincing disavowal of his earlier support on the basis that he had not previously looked closely enough (BBC News, 2018a). On 26 March, after issuing a public statement which stated that Corbyn had 'again and again ... sided with antisemites rather than Jews' (Board of Deputies, 2018), the Board of Deputies and Jewish Leadership Council organised a rally in Parliament Square protesting against antisemitism in the Labour Party under the banner 'Enough is Enough' (Harpin, 2018a). There followed an unprecedented act of coordination by Britain's three main Jewish newspapers. On 27 July, the *Jewish Chronicle*, *Jewish News*, and *Jewish Telegraph* went to press with an identical front-page editorial claiming that a Jeremy Corbyn-led government would pose an 'existential threat to Jewish life in this country' (*Jewish Chronicle* et al., 2018).

July 2018 also saw the onset of a protracted dispute over the NEC's failure to adopt the International Holocaust Remembrance Alliance's (IHRA's) full definition of antisemitism with the party distancing itself from a series of examples that indicated how criticism of Israel could lapse into antisemitic discourse. Amid the rancour that followed, the Jewish Labour MP Margaret Hodge confronted Corbyn in Parliament, reportedly calling him 'antisemitic and a racist' to his face. Labour initially launched disciplinary proceedings, only to back down and drop any action, despite a public statement by Hodge rejecting any suggestion that she had apologised (Harpin, 2018b). The dispute over the IHRA definition of antisemitism rumbled on until September when, in another defeat for Corbyn, whose last-minute attempt to insert a qualifying statement was rejected, Labour's ruling body agreed to adopt the IHRA's definition of antisemitism in full (Sabbagh, 2018).

In the meantime, two more major stories had broken. The first was 'Wreathgate', based on Corbyn's participation at a 2014 memorial ceremony organised by the Palestine National Authority in Tunis. The story had made little impression when run by the *Sunday Times* during the 2017 general election campaign, but the *Daily Mail*'s account, published on 10 August, was far more damaging. Corbyn's claim only to have been paying respects to the victims of a 1985 Israeli airstrike was countered by photographs showing him at a wreath-laying ceremony at the graves of 'Black September' leaders believed to have been responsible for planning the 1972 Munich Olympic massacre. Corbyn's subsequent statement, 'I was present when [the wreath] was laid. I don't think I was actually involved in it', met with widespread ridicule, and the phrase 'present but not involved' entered the political lexicon as a symbol of both weakness and disingenuity. Attempts to defend Corbyn on the part of his most influential social media 'outriders' were similarly ineffective. Perhaps the most notorious example was Owen Jones's dismissal of the affair with a high-handed observation that 'No one [was] killed by a wreath' (Jones, 2018). In what was now becoming a pattern of bluster and retreat, the Labour Party lodged a formal complaint against *The Times*, *Sun*, *Daily Mail*, *Daily Telegraph*, *Daily Express*, and *Metro* with the Independent Press Standards Organization, only to quietly withdraw that complaint two months later (Tobitt, 2018).

The second story, perhaps more damaging to Corbyn's reputation as a 'lifelong anti-racist' than any other, appeared in the *Daily Mail* on 23 August (Simons, 2018). The news that Corbyn had appeared at a 2013 Palestine Return Centre conference alongside such controversial figures as Stephen Sizer and Alison Weir was not, by this stage, a startling revelation. A video of his speech, however, showed him recalling an earlier confrontation between a group of British Jews and the Palestinian representative to the United Kingdom, Manuel Hassassian. Corbyn recounted how Hassassian's speech:

> was dutifully recorded by the thankfully silent Zionists who were in the audience on that occasion, and then came up and berated him afterwards for what he'd said. They clearly have two problems. One is that they don't want to study history, and secondly, having lived in this country for a very long time, probably all their lives, they don't understand English irony either. (Stewart and Sparrow, 2018)

This statement proved to be a tipping point for many who had previously given Corbyn the benefit of the doubt. In the *New York Times*, Josh Glancy declared that:

> This was classic anti-Semitism. Here were a group of Jews with whom Mr Corbyn has a political disagreement. And he smeared them not on the basis of that disagreement but on the basis of their ethnicity. He accused them of failing to assimilate English values, of not fitting in, of still being a bit foreign. (Glancy, 2018)

In the *Guardian*, Jonathan Freedland asserted that:

> The implication of that remark is clear – and it has nothing to do with defending Palestinians. It's that Corbyn sees Jews as fundamentally alien, foreigners who might live here a long time, might even be born here, but are still essentially other. People who will never be truly English. There's nothing leftwing about that. On the contrary, it was the observation of a blue-blazered bigot at the 19th hole, the country house antisemite. (Freedland, 2018)

Simon Hattenstone, a *Guardian* journalist who had previously 'repeatedly defended Jeremy Corbyn against charges of antisemitism', now drew the conclusion that 'what the Labour leader said at a London conference convened by the Palestinian Return Centre in 2013 [was] unquestionably antisemitic' (Hattenstone, 2018).

Significant momentum was now building against the party leadership. In August 2018, Frank Field, Labour's MP for Birkenhead since 1979, resigned the party whip with the claim that the leadership had become 'a force for anti-Semitism in British politics' (BBC News, 2018b). February 2019 saw the resignation of nine more Labour MPs, with Luciana Berger announcing that she could no longer remain in a party that she regarded as 'institutionally anti-semitic'. That conclusion was lent additional weight when, on 28 May, the Equalities and Human Rights Commission (EHRC) announced that it had launched a full statutory investigation to determine whether Labour had 'unlawfully discriminated against, harassed or victimised people because they are Jewish' (*Jewish Chronicle*, 2019a). On 9 July, three Labour peers resigned the whip, with David Triesman stating that the party for which he had previously served as General Secretary was now 'plainly institutionally antisemitic' (Mason, 2019). The following day the BBC's flagship current affairs programme, *Panorama*, broadcast allegations based on the testimony of party whistleblowers about efforts by the Leader's Office to frustrate the work of the disputes and complaints department as it dealt with the mass of antisemitism cases that had arisen since 2015.

The responses of the leadership group and its media allies to all this proved inadequate and often counterproductive. The initial dismissal of antisemitism allegations as smears was no longer tenable and had actually fostered perceptions of complacency and complicity. Although an ill-advised (and ultimately costly) attempt was made to undermine the credibility of John Ware, the BBC journalist responsible for the *Panorama* documentary (Mendel, 2020), as well as the Labour Party 'whistleblowers' upon whose testimony much of the documentary was based, the leadership's approach was now becoming increasingly defensive in nature. The question was how to retreat from earlier positions of denial, which self-evidently necessitated acknowledging the reality of the problem, whilst minimising further reputational damage to the leadership group. The decision was taken to present documented examples of antisemitism within the party as the regrettable conduct of a tiny minority; a strategy of seeking to persuade the public that Labour was serious about tackling the problem, whilst simultaneously presenting that problem as one that had been exaggerated. Corbyn had already spoken of 'pockets of antisemitism' within the party before he articulated a clear example of this strategy of minimisation in April 2018. Writing in the *Evening Standard*, he now set out the (statistically unsubstantiated) claim that 'the number of cases over the past three years represents less than 0.1 per cent of Labour's membership of more than half a million' (Corbyn, 2018). On social media and in his *Guardian* column, Owen Jones proved to be an especially adept practitioner of this strategy of minimisation. Consistently denouncing antisemitism as an abstract presence in a 'fringe' of the left, Jones nevertheless found it peculiarly difficult to identify or condemn specific examples of it at the heart of the Labour Party. Furthermore, it was a short step from there to a strategy of deflection, which in Jones's case tended to combine an exaggerated assertion of his own credentials as a practitioner of 'all-out war' on antisemitism, with attacks on examples of racism found further away from home, particularly instances of Islamophobia in the Conservative Party (Jones, 2019).

Further examples of the failings of the party's communications strategy can be seen in the manner in which this recalibration of the public line on antisemitism was badly bungled by official spokespersons. Shadow Foreign Secretary Emily Thornberry was widely mocked for suggesting that Corbyn had been 'too upset' by allegations of antisemitism to be able to deal with the problem effectively (Zeffman, 2018). Shadow Home Secretary Diane Abbott (who, lest it be forgotten, was among those who had previously brushed off antisemitism allegations as 'smears') was now reduced to informing the BBC's *Today* programme that 'not every element of the Jewish community … believes Jeremy is an anti-Semite' (Steerpike, 2019).

Corbyn's own efforts to reach out to the British Jewish community were, on occasion, more eloquent. In the *Evening Standard* on 24 April 2018, he accepted that 'we have not done enough to get to grips with the problem', and acknowledged that 'the Jewish community and our Jewish members deserve an apology. My party and I are sorry for the hurt and distress caused.' The article pledged education for party members, better engagement with 'the full range and diversity of Jewish organizations', and an assurance that 'all complaints are dealt with swiftly and fairly' (Corbyn, 2018). As months passed with little in the way of meaningful action, however, these words came to ring hollow. When plans for antisemitism training were announced, it emerged that the leadership had sidelined the Jewish Labour Movement. 'For the Labour Party to institute training without the consultation of their Jewish affiliate', one JLM source responded, 'is an astonishing level of arrogance' (Harpin, 2019b).

This development did little to inspire confidence in Corbyn's promise to ensure better engagement with Jewish organisations, and this was compounded in July 2019 by the appointment of Heather Mendick as an official Labour Party liaison to the Jewish community. The Jewish Leadership Council described as 'beyond parody' the appointment of Mendick, who had campaigned against the adoption of the IHRA definition and in support of the suspended MP, Chris Williamson (Doherty, 2019). Promises about more robust disciplinary procedures were similarly exposed by a devastating series of leaks from party insiders that informed both the July 2019 edition of *Panorama* and a *Sunday Times* article of 8 December, revealing that even the 'most extreme complaints of incitement to racial hatred and calls for a second genocide against the Jews have remained unresolved for months or years' (Pogrund et al., 2019). Shadow Chancellor John McDonnell's claim, in an interview with the BBC's Andrew Marr, that 'we're doing everything we possibly can' was met with disbelief and anger, with the President of the Board of Deputies, Marie van der Zyl, describing the comment as one that 'stretches credulity' (*Jewish Chronicle*, 2019b).

On antisemitism, the leadership now suffered from a fundamental credibility problem that was exacerbated by its increasing reliance on marginal and alternative media outlets that actively contributed to the crisis that they sought to deny, minimize, or deflect attention from. In a June 2018 article (subsequently deleted from its website), the *Morning Star* appeared to suggest that a rise in antisemitism should be blamed on the complicity of British Jews in Israeli 'crimes' (Harpin, 2018c). Just three months later, the newspaper published a further article railing against the 'Jewish Establishment', and in a paragraph awash with antisemitic imagery, concluded that 'Labour's enemies, including its most embittered fifth column, have tasted blood and won't end their attacks until Corbyn is hung out to dry' (*Morning Star*, 2018). The *Skwawkbox* blog attracted widespread condemnation for a (subsequently deleted) tweet declaring that 'the Jewish "war against Corbyn" risks bringing real antisemitism to Britain'. Similarly, the *Canary*'s faltering reputation as a serious journalistic outlet was undermined by its editor, Kerry-Anne Mendoza's association with conspiracy theorists such as Richie Allen (Rich, 2018a: 266), and its employment of writers such as Steve Topple, whose Twitter feed contained a stream of invective against 'Rothschilds', as well as the observation that 'Maybe most Jews peaceful, but until they recognize and destroy their growing Zionist cancer they must be held responsible' (*Jewish Chronicle*, 2018). The *Canary* would claim that Topple was a reformed character, only to go on to blame its own financial difficulties on 'pressure from political Zionists' (*Jewish Chronicle*, 2019c). In the aftermath of Labour's 2019 general election defeat, Mendoza even took to Twitter to denounce the Jewish journalist Jonathan Freedland as a 'prick' who had 'manufactured' the election outcome (Mendoza, 2019). It was against this backdrop that John Mann, in a new role as the government's independent adviser on antisemitism, announced an investigation into the role of websites such as the *Canary* in fostering the spread of antisemitic discourse in the UK (*Jewish Chronicle*, 2019d).

This reliance on media outlets that demonstrated neither an understanding of 21st century antisemitism, nor the capacity to free themselves from the taint of it, was an enormous handicap to any public relations campaign aimed at distancing Corbyn and the wider Labour Party from politically damaging allegations. As Dave Rich has argued:

> An antisemitic political culture has taken root in the grassroots of the left-wing movement on which Mr Corbyn's project depends. This culture can be found in the Facebook groups that bear Mr Corbyn's name and the alt-left, new media blogs that count as news sources for his more devoted supporters … Websites like The Canary, Novara Media and Skwawkbox have a direct line to the party leadership and are more trusted by Mr Corbyn's supporters than most national newspapers … Whenever [Jews, Israel or antisemitism] are discussed in these forums, the dominant view is that Israel is an apartheid

or Nazi state, Zionists are deceitful, manipulative racists, and anyone who complains about antisemitism in Labour is, frankly, a liar and a political enemy. (Rich, 2018b)

DECLINE AND FALL: ANTISEMITISM AND THE GENERAL ELECTION OF 2019

On 12 December 2019, Jeremy Corbyn led the Labour Party to its worst general election defeat since 1935. Exactly how significant the issue of antisemitism had been in this outcome will require more substantial quantitative analysis than can be provided here. Ken Livingstone's immediate observation that 'the Jewish vote wasn't very helpful' (Kentish, 2019) may be regarded as typical of the man, and Colin Shindler is surely not alone in, firstly, wishing for 'other, saner voices' to shape the debate, and secondly, wondering 'what was gained by allowing anti-Semitism to fester and then attacking the Jewish Left, and more broadly the Jewish community, for having the temerity to call it out' (Shindler, 2019).

Peter Kellner, former President of the YouGov polling company, addressed the question in the following terms. 'In order to assess the impact of the antisemitism controversy on the election result, two questions must be answered', he wrote. 'First, did the issue matter? Second, did it directly affect the result? My answer is definitely yes to the first question but probably no to the second.' Kellner added that the controversy over antisemitism should not be considered in isolation from other issues. 'For millions of women and men, including a great many traditional Labour supporters,' he stated, 'it was one of a range of factors that, together, made the party and its leader unbearably toxic' (Kellner, 2019). Anshel Pfeffer, writing in *Haaretz*, reached a similar conclusion. Noting that 'the small Jewish community had an effect only on no more than three or four seats', Pfeffer suggested that antisemitism was indeed important in fostering the more general public perception that 'there's something wrong about Corbyn' (Pfeffer, 2019).

Such conclusions speak volumes about the collective failure of the Labour Party to deal with the perception of an organisation beset by antisemitism. At the heart of that failure was a communications strategy that veered from denial, through attempts at minimisation and deflection, to a grudging, half-hearted acceptance that the party's critics had a point. Even in the latter stages of this journey, Corbyn proved reluctant (strangely so, given the statement he had already directed to the Jewish community in April 2018) to offer an unqualified apology on behalf of the party during the election campaign. A catastrophic interview with the BBC's Andrew Neil on 26 November left many viewers with the impression of a man incapable of providing the leadership that might have drawn a line under the problem. That interview did much to justify Dave Rich's conclusion that the issue was not so much whether Corbyn had the power to bring about the change in the party's political culture that was necessary if the problem of antisemitism were to be tackled, as it was a question of 'whether, as a lifelong product and leader of that same political culture, he is even capable of recognizing that it is a choice he needs to make' (Rich, 2018a: 350).

The failure of Labour's communications strategists to address the public perception that there was 'something wrong about Corbyn' must also be considered in the light of Jowett and O'Donnell's astute observation that 'external propaganda may be created for internal purposes. Displays of aggression towards an enemy may not phase the enemy, but they can bolster morale at home' (Jowett and O'Donnell, 1999: 378). Examining the party leadership's approach to public perceptions of antisemitism using the bureaucratic propaganda model is instructive in this regard, particularly in the aftermath of the 2019 general election defeat and the recognition that Corbyn's term as Leader of the Opposition was drawing to a close. In this situation, the leadership group's parting shot was a ploy entirely in keeping with O'Shaughnessy's conception of bureaucratic propaganda as the manipulation of research, the massaging of information, the tactical use of internal enquiries and reports, and the selective withholding or leaking of information (O'Shaughnessy, 2004: 34).

In April 2020, an 850-page report, commissioned by General Secretary Jennie Formby and entitled 'The work of the Labour Party's Governance and Legal Unit in relation to antisemitism, 2014–2019', was leaked to, among others, the pro-Corbyn Novara media group. The report was clearly designed to shift the blame for a failure to tackle antisemitism in the party (the reality of which was acknowledged) away from the leadership. It was, among Corbyn's supporters at least, rapidly adopted as a 'stab-in-the-back' myth that purportedly revealed how a disloyal faction, which Emma Dent Coad, former MP for Kensington, ill-advisedly characterised as a 'powerful cabal' (Dent Coad, 2020), had aimed to 'weaponise' antisemitism and sabotage the leadership's genuine efforts to tackle it as part of a wider campaign to undermine Corbyn's electoral prospects. If the credibility of the report was subsequently undermined by the legal victory of the *Panorama* 'whistleblowers', to whom the Labour Party offered an unreserved High Court apology for previously made comments that it now accepted were 'false and defamatory' (BBC News, 2020a), it remained instrumental in establishing a narrative designed to shore up the longer-term legacy of the wider 'Corbyn project'.

The importance of this latter task can be gauged by Corbyn's own response to the publication of the EHRC report in October 2020. Labour's new Leader, Keir Starmer, offered an apology to the British Jewish community and a statement that:

> if, after all the pain, all the grief, and all the evidence in this report, there are still those who think there's no problem with anti-Semitism in the Labour Party, that it's all exaggerated, or a factional attack, then, frankly, you are part of the problem too and you should be nowhere near the Labour Party. (BBC News, 2020b)

Corbyn's contrasting response was that the issue of antisemitism under his leadership had been 'dramatically overstated for political reasons by our opponents inside and outside the party, as well as by much of the media' (Frot, 2020). His statement was a calculated risk that, while it led to his suspension from the party, was also a deliberate attempt to reinvigorate the narratives and arguments of the leaked 'Formby' report, as well as to protect his own reputation as 'a lifelong anti-racist' in the face of the EHRC's conclusion that 'serious failings of leadership' had led to 'unlawful acts of harassment and discrimination for which the Labour Party is responsible' (EHRC, 2020: 6).

By this stage, of course, the wider battle for public opinion had been comprehensively and deservedly lost. In the end, the much-vaunted 'Corbyn project' had been reduced to a series of questionable self-justifications and efforts to rally its remaining faithful. Insofar as it can lay claim to any kind of propaganda success in relation to antisemitism, it may well be in relation to the kind of ideas and prejudices that became normalised among the movement's grassroots supporters and, as David Hirsh has suggested, this possibility is a disconcerting one:

> Corbyn's movement has left behind many thousands of people who have been educated to believe that between 'us' and 'socialism' sits the formidable obstacle of Jewish power. The rage and shame

that they are feeling after their humiliating defeat should not be under-estimated. For many it will be a key formative experience. Political antisemitism has re-entered the British mainstream, and it is not going to just disappear. There is reason to believe that on the populist left people who have been learning to understand the world through antisemitism will find ways to actualise that in the development of antisemitic social movements. (Hirsh, 2019)

On the day of his election as Labour Party Leader, Keir Starmer sought to distance himself from the previous leadership with a letter addressed to the Board of Deputies, in which he apologised for the antisemitism that had been 'a stain on our party' and the 'grief [it had] brought to so many Jewish communities' (*Jewish Chronicle*, 2020). The manner in which several prominent Corbyn supporters responded to this shift in tone and direction, by denouncing it as an example of Starmer's 'capitulation to unaffiliated lobbies' (Harpin, 2020a) and the influence of 'Zionist money', was both depressingly predictable (Harpin, 2020b), and a disturbing reprisal of themes perpetuated by an openly antisemitic BNP campaign which had disseminated allegations that 'a wealthy circle of Zionist backers' had 'bought the Labour Party' (Macklin, 2020: 492). It is certainly clear that the new leadership has an unenviably difficult task in addressing an entrenched culture of antisemitic modes of thought, the dissemination and development of which may prove to be the defining and disturbing legacy of the Corbyn years.

NOTE

1. For an account of Crossman's wartime propaganda activities, see Chapter 8, 'Psychological Warrior' (pp. 83–107) in Anthony Howard's excellent biography of Crossman (Howard, 1990).

REFERENCES

Andrew, Christopher (2009), *The Defence of the Realm: The Authorized History of MI5*, London: Allen Lane.
Bashan, Raphael (1971), 'Richard Crossman: British MP and Editor of "The New Statesman"', translation from Hebrew of *Yediot Ahronot*', 23 April, Modern Record Centre, Warwick University, Richard Crossman Papers, MSS.154/3/LIT/14/44.
BBC News (2018a), 'Jeremy Corbyn regrets comments about "anti-Semitic" mural', 23 March, available at https://www.bbc.co.uk/news/uk-politics-43523445, accessed on 2 January 2020.
BBC News (2018b), 'Anti-Semitism row: Frank Field resigns Labour whip', 30 August, available at https://www.bbc.co.uk/news/uk-politics-45359009, accessed on 2 September 2018.
BBC News (2019), 'Peter Willsman: Labour suspends NEC member over anti-Semitism remarks', 31 May, available at https://www.bbc.co.uk/news/uk-politics-48472977, accessed on 2 June 2019.
BBC News (2020a), 'Anti-Semitism: Labour pays damages for "hurt" to whistleblowers', 22 July, available at https://www.bbc.co.uk/news/uk-politics-53489611, accessed on 22 July 2020.
BBC News (2020b), 'Labour broke equalities law over anti-Semitism', 29 October, available at https://www.bbc.co.uk/news/uk-politics-54730425, accessed on 29 October 2020.
Board of Deputies (2018), 'Enough is enough', 26 March, available at https://www.bod.org.uk/enough-is-enough-2/, accessed on 3 January 2020.
Chakrabarti, Shami (2016), 'The Shami Chakrabarti Enquiry', 30 June, available at https://labour.org.uk/wp-content/uploads/2017/10/Chakrabarti-Inquiry-Report-30June16.pdf, accessed on 16 December 2016.
Corbyn, Jeremy (2018), 'What I'm doing to banish anti-Semitism from the Labour Party', *Evening Standard*, 24 April, available at https://www.standard.co.uk/comment/comment/jeremy-corbyn-what

-i-m-doing-to-banish-antisemitism-from-the-labour-party-a3821961.html, accessed on 3 January 2020.

Crossman, Richard (1960), *A Nation Reborn: The Israel of Weizmann, Bevin and Ben-Gurion*, London: Hamish Hamilton.

Dent Coad, Emma (2020), '"I feel both furious and vindicated": the leaked report explains why Labour didn't help me after Grenfell', *Novara Media*, 14 April, available at https://novaramedia.com/2020/04/14/i-feel-both-furious-and-vindicated-the-leaked-report-explains-why-labour-didnt-help-me-after-grenfell/, accessed on 1 November 2020.

Doherty, Rosa (2019), 'Labour slammed for appointing "Jewish community liaison" who defended Chris Williamson', *Jewish Chronicle*, 18 July, available at https://www.thejc.com/news/uk-news/labour-slammed-for-appointing-activist-who-defended-williamson-as-liaison-to-the-jewish-community-1.486616, accessed on 18 July 2019.

Dysch, Marcus (2015), 'Did Jeremy Corbyn back artist whose mural was condemned as antisemitic?', *Jewish Chronicle*, 6 November, available at https://www.thejc.com/news/uk-news/did-jeremy-corbyn-back-artist-whose-mural-was-condemned-as-antisemitic-1.62106, accessed on 2 January 2020.

Dysch, Marcus (2017), 'A false dawn for Labour as Butler departs having made no mark at all', *Jewish Chronicle*, 8 February, available at https://www.thejc.com/comment/comment/dawn-butler-leaves-shadow-cabinet-analysis-1.432295, accessed on 10 February 2017.

Dysch, Marcus (2018), 'Tony Greenstein expelled from Labour Party over abusive behaviour', *Jewish Chronicle*, 18 February, available at https://www.thejc.com/news/uk-news/labour-expels-anti-zionist-activist-tony-greenstein-following-accusations-of-antisemitism-1.458908, accessed on 3 September 2019.

EHRC (2020), *Investigation into Antisemitism in the Labour Party. Report*, October, available at https://www.equalityhumanrights.com/en/publication-download/investigation-antisemitism-labour-party, accessed on 29 October 2020.

Elgot, Jessica (2018), 'Labour suspends party members in "antisemitic" Facebook group', *Guardian*, 8 March, available at https://www.theguardian.com/politics/2018/mar/08/labour-suspends-party-members-in-antisemitic-facebook-group, accessed on 4 May 2020.

Elgot, Jessica (2019), 'Labour expels Jackie Walker for leaked antisemitism remarks', *Guardian*, 27 March, available at https://www.theguardian.com/politics/2019/mar/27/labour-expels-jackie-walker-for-leaked-antisemitism-comments, accessed on 3 September 2019.

Faulds, Andrew (1973), 'Wilson to Faulds, 10 December 1973', British Library of Political and Economic Science, LSE, Andrew Faulds papers, Faulds 1/2.5.

Faulds, Andrew (1977), 'Labour Middle East Council newsletter, No. 1 (March 1977)', British Library of Political and Economic Science, LSE, Andrew Faulds papers, Faulds 3/2/15.

Foot, Michael (1974), 'Dick Crossman: the Left will not forget', *Tribune*, 12 April.

Freedland, Jonathan (2018), 'Jewish concern over Corbyn is not all about Israel. It's about antisemitism', *Guardian*, 5 September, available at https://www.theguardian.com/commentisfree/2018/sep/05/jewish-concern-corbyn-israel-palestine-antisemitism-ihra?CMP=Share_iOSApp_Other, accessed on 5 September 2018.

Frot, Mathilde (2020), 'Corbyn attacks media and political opponents over EHRC verdict', *Jewish Chronicle*, 29 October, available at https://www.thejc.com/news/uk/corbyn-attacks-media-and-political-opponents-over-ehrc-verdict-1.508022, accessed on 29 October 2020.

Glancy, Josh (2018), 'Getting off the fence about Jeremy Corbyn's anti-Semitism', *New York Times*, 27 August, at https://www.nytimes.com/2018/08/27/opinion/jeremy-corbyn-anti-semitism-labour-britain.html, accessed on 5 September 2018.

Hansard (1973), *Hansard, House of Commons Debates*, Vol. 861, Col. 498, 18 October.

Harpin, Lee (2018a), 'Huge crowds join Jewish community protest against antisemitism, in Westminster', *Jewish Chronicle*, 26 March, available at https://www.thejc.com/news/uk-news/jewish-community-protests-in-parliament-square-against-labour-antisemitism-enough-is-enough-1.461420, accessed on 2 January 2020.

Harpin, Lee (2018b), 'Labour drops action against Dame Margaret Hodge over Corbyn confrontation', *Jewish Chronicle*, 6 August, available at https://www.thejc.com/labour-drops-hodge-action-1.468085, accessed 10 August 2018.

Harpin, Lee (2018c), 'Morning Star newspaper deletes article that blamed "Israel's crimes" for rising antisemitism', *Jewish Chronicle*, 20 June, available at https://www.thejc.com/news/uk-news/morning-star-antisemitism-row-israels-crimes-1.465768, accessed on 21 June 2018.

Harpin, Lee (2019a), 'Lansman launches attack on Jewish Voice for Labour', *Jewish Chronicle*, 20 June, available at https://www.thejc.com/news/uk-news/lansman-launches-attack-on-jewish-voice-for-labour-1.485690, accessed on 24 June 2019.

Harpin, Lee (2019b), 'Labour ditches Jewish Labour Movement for antisemitism training, backs new university course instead', *Jewish Chronicle*, 11 March, available at https://www.thejc.com/news/uk-news/jewish-labour-movement-furious-as-labour-stops-using-them-for-antisemitism-training-1.481326, accessed on 3 January 2020.

Harpin, Lee (2020a), 'Labour left winger accuses Starmer of "capitulation to unaffiliated lobbies"', *Jewish Chronicle*, 5 May, available at https://www.thejc.com/news/uk-news/labour-left-winger-accuses-starmer-of-capitulation-to-unaffiliated-lobbies-1.499497, accessed on 6 May 2020.

Harpin, Lee (2020b), 'Bristol Professor attacks Starmer over "Zionist" money', *Jewish Chronicle*, 28 April, available at https://www.thejc.com/news/uk-news/bristol-professor-attacks-starmer-over-zionist-money-1.499258, accessed on 29 April 2020.

Hattenstone, Simon (2018), 'I gave Corbyn the benefit of the doubt on antisemitism. I can't any more', *Guardian*, 24 August, available at https://www.theguardian.com/commentisfree/2018/aug/24/jeremy-corbyn-antisemitism-labour-zionists-2013-speech?CMP=share_btn_tw, accessed on 28 August 2018.

Hirsh, David (2008), 'Anti-Zionism and antisemitism: decoding the relationship', *Z Word*, February, available at www.z-word.com/, accessed on 2 June 2011.

Hirsh, David (2019), 'Corbyn's legacy is that political antisemitism has reentered the British mainstream', *Fathom*, December, available at http://fathomjournal.org/the-uk-election-2019-corbyns-legacy-is-that-political-antisemitism-has-re-entered-the-british-mainstream/, accessed on 17 December 2019.

Howard, Anthony (1990), *Crossman: The Pursuit of Power*, London: Jonathan Cape.

Jewish Chronicle (1982), 'Board may sue paper', *Jewish Chronicle*, 2 July.

Jewish Chronicle (2018), 'BBC's The Mash Report hosts "left-wing journalist" who tweeted anti-Jewish conspiracy theories', *Jewish Chronicle*, 5 December, available at https://www.thejc.com/news/uk-news/bbc-the-mash-report-steve-topple-left-wing-rothschild-goldsmith-israel-conspiracy-theories-1.473498, accessed on 2 October 2019.

Jewish Chronicle (2019a), 'EHRC launches formal investigation into Labour antisemitism', *Jewish Chronicle*, 28 May, available at https://www.thejc.com/news/uk-news/ehrc-launches-formal-investigation-into-labour-antisemitism-1.484822, accessed on 28 May 2019.

Jewish Chronicle (2019b), 'Board & JLC slam John McDonnell claim that Labour is "doing everything to eliminate antisemitism"', *Jewish Chronicle*, 3 November, available at https://www.thejc.com/news/uk-news/labour-doing-everything-eliminate-antisemitism-john-mcdonnell-insists-bbc-andrew-marr-1.490990, accessed on 4 November 2019.

Jewish Chronicle (2019c), 'Pro-Corbyn website The Canary denies it is antisemitic, then blames "political Zionists" for forcing it to downsize', *Jewish Chronicle*, 2 August, available at https://www.thejc.com/news/uk-news/pro-corbyn-website-the-canary-blames-political-zionists-for-forcing-it-to-downsize-1.487095, accessed on 5 August 2019.

Jewish Chronicle (2019d), 'Government antisemitism adviser to launch hate probe into The Canary and other far-left websites', *Jewish Chronicle*, 13 December, available at https://www.thejc.com/news/uk-news/government-antisemitism-adviser-to-probe-canary-and-far-left-sites-1.494331, accessed on 13 December 2019.

Jewish Chronicle (2020), 'Apology to Jewish community is my "value statement", new Labour leader Keir Starmer says', *Jewish Chronicle*, 5 April, available at https://www.thejc.com/news/uk-news/apology-to-jewish-community-is-my-value-statement-new-labour-leader-keir-starmer-says-1.498793, accessed on 6 April 2020.

Jewish Chronicle, *Jewish News* and *Jewish Telegraph* (2018), 'United we stand', front page editorial published jointly by the *Jewish Chronicle*, *Jewish News* and *Jewish Telegraph*, 27 July, available at https://jewishnews.timesofisrael.com/voice-of-the-jewish-news-united-we-stand/, accessed on 27 July 2018.

Jewish News (2019), 'Speaker at anti-Israel London demo says Jewish organizations are "in the gutter"', *Jewish News*, 12 May, available at https://jewishnews.timesofisrael.com/speaker-at-anti-israel-london-demo-says-jewish-organizations-are-in-the-gutter/, accessed on 2 January 2020.

Jones, Owen (2018), @OwenJones84, Twitter, 13 August, https://twitter.com/OwenJones84/status/1029100205185159172.

Jones, Owen (2019), 'Where is the outrage about the Tory party's Islamophobia?', *Guardian*, 10 July, available at https://www.theguardian.com/commentisfree/2019/jul/10/islamophobia-tory-party-britain, accessed on 3 January 2020.

Jowett, Garth S. and O'Donnell, Victoria (1999), *Propaganda and Persuasion* (3rd edn), London: SAGE.

Kellner, Peter (2019), 'Antisemitism mattered but did it affect the general election result?', *Jewish Chronicle*, 18 December, available at https://www.thejc.com/comment/analysis/antisemitism-mattered-but-it-probably-didn-t-affect-the-general-election-result-1.494441, accessed on 19 December 2019.

Kentish, Benjamin (2019), 'Ken Livingstone claims Corbyn should have tackled antisemitism earlier and says "Jewish vote wasn't very helpful"', *Independent*, 13 December, available at https://www.independent.co.uk/news/uk/politics/general-election-ken-livingstone-jewish-vote-corbyn-resignation-a9244871.html, accessed on 3 January 2020.

Kogan, David (2019), *Protest and Power: The Battle for the Labour Party*, London: Bloomsbury Reader.

Kramnik, Isaac and Sheerman, Barry (1993), *Harold Laski: A Life on the Left*, London: Hamish Hamilton.

Livingstone, Ken (1982), 'Why Labour must back Palestinian rights', *Labour Herald*, 30 July.

Livingstone, Ken (2006), 'An attack on voters' rights', *Guardian*, 1 March, available at https://www.theguardian.com/politics/2006/mar/01/society.london, accessed on 2 January 2020.

MacKenzie, Norman and MacKenzie, Jeanne (1985), *The Diary of Beatrice Webb. Vol. Four 1924–1943. The Wheel of Life*, Cambridge, MA.: Belknap Press of Harvard University Press.

Macklin, Graham (2020), *Failed Führers: A History of Britain's Extreme Right*, London: Routledge.

Marquand, David (1991), *The Progressive Dilemma: from Lloyd George to Kinnock*, London: William Heinemann Ltd.

Mason, Rowena (2017), 'MPs should have no say over who leads Labour, argues shadow minister', *Guardian*, 28 August, available at https://www.theguardian.com/politics/2017/aug/28/make-labour-leadership-rules-more-democratic-urges-shadow-minister, accessed on 3 September 2019.

Mason, Rowena (2019), 'Three Labour peers quit over handling of antisemitism cases', *Guardian*, 9 July, available at https://www.theguardian.com/politics/2019/jul/09/labour-peers-resign-over-handling-of-antisemitism-complaints-triesman-darzi-turnberg, accessed on 10 July 2019.

Mayhew, Christopher (1963), 'Notes on Middle East tour – July 1963', Liddell Hart Centre, King's College London, Christopher Mayhew papers, Mayhew 9/1.

Mayhew, Christopher (1967), 'Christopher Mayhew to Norman Reddaway, 3 August 1967', Liddell Hart Centre, King's College London, Christopher Mayhew papers, Mayhew 9/1.

Mayhew, Christopher (1972), 'Minutes of a meeting of the LMEC Executive Committee, 16 July 1972', Liddell Hart Centre, King's College London, Christopher Mayhew papers, Mayhew 9/7.

Mayhew, Christopher (1987), *Time to Explain: An Autobiography*, London: Hutchinson.

Mayhew, Christopher (1990), 'Mayhew to Khazen, 5 April 1990', Liddell Hart Centre, King's College London, Christopher Mayhew papers, Mayhew 9/3.

Mendel, Jack (2020), 'Documentary-maker behind BBC Panorama on antisemitism is suing Labour', *Jewish News*, 20 January, available at https://jewishnews.timesofisrael.com/1-documentary-maker-behind-bbc-panorama-on-antisemitism-is-suing-labour/, accessed on 21 January 2020.

Mendoza, Kerry-Anne (2019), @TheMendozaWoman, *Twitter*, 13 December, https://twitter.com/TheMendozaWoman/status/1205284636001263622.

Merrick, Rob (2017), 'Len McCluskey dismisses Labour conference anti-Semitism claims as an attempt to "bring Jeremy Corbyn down"', *Independent*, 27 September, available at https://www.independent.co.uk/news/uk/politics/len-mcluskey-labour-anti-semitism-jeremy-corbyn-attempt-unite-chief-trade-union-friends-israel-a7969366.html, accessed on 3 September 2019.

Middleton, Jim (1933), 'Davies to Middleton, undated [May 1933]', Labour History Archive and Study Centre, Jim Middleton papers, LP/JSM/ZIO/103.

Milne, Seamus (2002), 'This slur of anti-semitism is used to defend repression', *Guardian*, 9 May, available at https://www.theguardian.com/world/2002/may/09/comment, accessed on 9 October 2010.

Morning Star (2018), 'Labour's fifth column won't end its attacks until Corbyn is hung out to dry', *Morning Star*, 5 September, available at https://morningstaronline.co.uk/article/labours-fifth-column-wont-end-its-attacks-until-corbyn-is-hung-out-to-dry, accessed on 6 September 2018.

O'Shaughnessy, Nicholas Jackson (2004), *Politics and Persuasion: Weapons of Mass Seduction*, Manchester: Manchester University Press.

Pfeffer, Anshel (2019), 'UK election: more than Johnson's Conservatives won, Corbyn's Labour lost Britain', *Haaretz*, 13 December, available at https://www.haaretz.com/world-news/europe/.premium-u-k-election-johnson-s-tories-didn-t-win-as-much-as-corbyn-s-labour-lost-britain-1.8264102, accessed on 17 December 2019.

Pimlott, Ben (1987), *The Political Diary of Hugh Dalton 1918–40, 1945–60*, London: Jonathan Cape.

Pogrund, Gabriel, Calvert, Jonathan, and Arbuthnott, George (2019), 'Revealed: the depth of Labour anti-semitism', *Sunday Times*, 8 December, available at https://www.thetimes.co.uk/article/revealed-the-depth-of-labour-anti-semitism-bb57h9pdz, accessed on 8 December 2019.

Rich, Dave (2018a), *The Left's Jewish Problem: Jeremy Corbyn, Israel and Antisemitism* (2nd edn), London: Biteback Publishing.

Rich, Dave (2018b), 'Jeremy Corbyn has lit a fire of Jew-hate that is now beyond his control', *Jewish Chronicle*, 3 October, available at https://www.thejc.com/comment/analysis/labour-dave-rich-on-corbyn-1.470453, accessed on 3 September 2019.

Rose, Norman (1986), *Chaim Weizmann: A Biography*, London: Weidenfeld & Nicolson.

Royall, Jan (2016), 'Allegations of anti-Semitism: Oxford University Labour Club', May, available at https://antisemitism.uk/wp-content/uploads/2016/08/Royall-Report.pdf, accessed on 16 December 2016.

Sabbagh, Dan (2018), 'Labour adopts IHRA antisemitism definition in full', *Guardian*, 4 September, available at https://www.theguardian.com/politics/2018/sep/04/labour-adopts-ihra-antisemitism-definition-in-full, accessed on 3 January 2020.

Shindler, Colin (2019), 'Corbyn, Labour's most "tragic" loser since the pacifist who met Hitler', *Haaretz*, 15 December, available at https://www.haaretz.com/world-news/.premium-corbyn-labour-s-most-tragic-loser-since-the-pacifist-who-met-hitler-1.8266688, accessed on 17 December 2019.

Shipman, Tim and Pogrund, Gabriel (2019), 'Seumas Milne and Corbyn aide blocked anti-semitism suspensions', *Sunday Times*, 10 March, available at https://www.thetimes.co.uk/article/seamus-milne-and-corbyn-aide-blocked-anti-semitism-suspensions-f7c3zjc0j, accessed on 2 January 2020.

Silver, Eric (1971), 'Crossman is named Weizmann biographer', *Jerusalem Post*, undated, Modern Record Centre, Warwick University, Richard Crossman Papers, MSS.154/3/LIT/14/62.

Simons, Jake Wallis (2018), 'Jeremy Corbyn said British "Zionists" have "no sense of English irony despite having lived here all their lives" and "need a lesson", while giving speech alongside Islamic extremists at a conference publicised by Hamas' military wing', *Daily Mail*, 23 August, available at https://www.dailymail.co.uk/news/article-6087783/Jeremy-Corbyn-said-British-Zionists-no-sense-English-irony.html, accessed on 24 August 2018.

Steerpike (2019), 'Diane Abbott not all Jews think Corbyn is an anti-Semite', *Spectator*, 6 November, available at https://blogs.spectator.co.uk/2019/11/diane-abbott-not-all-jews-think-corbyn-is-an-anti-semite/, accessed on 3 January 2019.

Stewart, Heather and Sparrow, Andrew (2018), 'Jeremy Corbyn: I used the term "Zionist" in accurate political sense', *Guardian*, 24 August, available at https://www.theguardian.com/politics/2018/aug/24/corbyn-english-irony-video-reignites-antisemitism-row-labour, accessed on 3 January 2020.

Stone, Jon (2016), 'Labour antisemitism row: read the Ken Livingstone interview transcripts in full', *Independent*, 28 April, available at https://www.independent.co.uk/news/uk/politics/labour-anti-semitism-row-full-transcript-of-ken-livingstones-interviews-a7005311.html, accessed 3 September 2019.

Syal, Rajeev (2016), 'Diane Abbott says claims of antisemitism within Labour are smears', *Guardian*, 1 May, available at https://www.theguardian.com/politics/2016/may/01/diane-abbott-smear-labour-antisemitism-problem-andrew-marr, accessed on 3 September 2019.

Tobitt, Charlotte (2018), 'Labour drops complaint against six newspapers over Corbyn wreath coverage after email leak "unacceptably compromised" IPSO process', *Press Gazette*, available at https://www.pressgazette.co.uk/labour-drops-complaint-against-six-newspapers-over-corbyn-wreath-coverage-after-email-leak-unacceptably-compromised-ipso-process/, accessed on 2 January 2020.

Vaughan, James R. (2015), 'Mayhew's outcasts: anti-Zionism and the Arab lobby in Harold Wilson's Labour Party', *Israel Affairs*, 21(1): 27–47.
Zeffman, Henry (2018), 'Jeremy Corbyn was "too upset" to tackle antisemitism', *The Times*, 28 December, available at https://www.thetimes.co.uk/article/jeremy-corbyn-was-too-upset-to-tackle-antisemitism-7wxmhz5qk, accessed on 3 January 2020.

17. Terrorist propaganda
Afzal Ashraf

INTRODUCTION

Despite causing a relatively small proportion of violent deaths, terrorism is currently the most high-profile aspect of political violence in public debate. A major reason for this is the intrinsic desire in terrorism to captivate public and political attention through acts of shocking violence, intended to communicate specific political messages. These messages often simultaneously attempt to appeal to several audiences. They can aim to coerce, deter, and attract, using both linguistic and behavioural rhetoric. Attraction is necessary for recruitment through radicalisation, which is an increasingly prominent issue. Radicalisation requires the propagation of a grievance narrative to excite the human desire for justice, the spreading of stories of success as motivation to confront otherwise formidable odds, and above all, it requires the conversion of a moral aversion to killing into a moral purpose of being. Understanding a terrorist group's propaganda can help to counter its appeal and reduce radicalisation to its cause.

It is no coincidence that terrorism has been described as the 'propaganda of the deed' as long ago as 1857, when the Italian anarchist Pisacane claimed that 'ideas result from deeds, not the latter from the former' (Hoffman, 2006: 5). Pisacane's comments came during the phase of anarchist political thinking that focused on overturning the perceived injustices of contemporary power structures. This phase assumed that an act of revolt would, in itself, produce a just system, as supposedly happened during the French Revolution. This assumption that anarchic deeds would result in ideas came before the widespread deployment of alternative political systems and ideologies such as Communism, Fascism, Zionism, Islamism, and so on. For decades after their authors articulated them, these ideologies remained just ideas. It was only after a militant group inspired by the ideology managed to achieve success through violently grabbing political power and influence that they suddenly attracted huge numbers of followers. Had Pisacane been writing today, he may have amended his thoughts thus: 'radicalisation results from deeds, not ideas'. However, he would have been only partially correct. It is the way ideas and deeds are blended, framed, and propagated that determines how terrorist movements grow and survive.

Why are the thoughts of somewhat obscure historical figures relevant to a discussion on the propaganda of contemporary terrorist groups such as Al Qaeda and ISIS? One reason is that many of the newer academic and journalist analysts looking at terrorism since the advent of ISIS have adopted an ahistorical approach. They have been mesmerised by the medium rather than by the message. Consequently, terrorist propaganda is incompletely understood as a feature of the Internet and social media, of Al Qaeda and ISIS ideology or, more inaccurately, as a feature of religion. A historical approach has the advantage of indicating continuities and discontinuities which can expose elements of thinking and actions that are either generic to politics, power, and terrorism or are specific to a group. A comparison with far-right terrorists, antithetical to these Islamist groups, can provide another filter to distil generic attributes from particular ones. That approach assumes that politics, power, and the art of rhetoric, which communicates both power and politics, are rooted in human character and beliefs. Time has only changed the means by which politics and power are exercised and the means by which they are communicated. Therefore, current terrorist propaganda is linked to changes in the nature of politics which has transitioned from elite or colonial rule to those advocating (but not necessarily delivering) representative rule and changes in power, particularly the advent of asymmetric warfare and digital communications, including the way news is produced and consumed. Exploring these continuities and discontinuities provides a more nuanced understanding of the role and impact of the propaganda of contemporary global terror groups.

This chapter considers terrorism as political violence and assumes that terrorist propaganda shares many attributes with political propaganda. Terrorism is a tactic used by virtually all forms of political movements throughout history, but for the purposes of this chapter terrorism is understood as the use of exemplary violence by non-state political groups.[1] The aim is to examine the messages underlying the deeds in a way that minimises superficial understanding and misinterpretation.

The chapter explores terrorist propaganda in terms of the radical nature of its political and psychological objectives, as well as the pragmatic options available to terrorist groups for communicating their message. According to Lasswell (1927: 627), 'Propaganda is the management of collective attitudes by the manipulation of significant symbols.' In this context 'attitude' means 'a tendency to act according to certain patterns of valuation'. This attitude involves a change of behaviour (or action), from those assimilated through lived experience to those influenced by symbolic messages contained in the propaganda. Therefore, terrorism as an action needs to be interpreted both through its symbolic message as well as through wider ideas associated with the worldview of its perpetrators. This combination of symbolic and ideological communication is the basis of terrorist propaganda. Collectively they attempt to communicate deterrence, defiance, and inspiration. They further publicise the group's political manifesto in a persuasive way. This last element is enshrined in the European Union's definition of terrorist propaganda: 'Propagation of a particular extremist worldview that brings individuals to consider and justify violence' (European Commission, 2018). In other words, radicalisation is one of the primary aims of terrorist propaganda. A major hurdle in inspiring political violence is the need to overcome what Reich (1998: 161) calls the psychological self-sanction against abhorrent conduct that exists in humans. Also discussed here is how terrorist propaganda addresses this challenge. Insights available through the writings of early terrorist ideologues will be used as analytical tools to expose the roles, style, and impact of contemporary terrorist propaganda. These will be mapped on to statements, actions, and justifications of contemporary terrorists to determine how terrorists use propaganda.

STATES' ACTIONS AS PRECEDENCE FOR NON-STATE TERRORISM PROPAGANDA

While this chapter deals with non-state terrorism, there is a link with perceived state terrorism that a study of propaganda cannot ignore. Modern terrorism started out as a positive instrument of state violence, mostly by regimes self-identifying as democratic. Revolutionaries in France guillotined publicly thousands of citizens suspected of being anti-revolutionaries, to strike terror into opponents. Its ideologues openly linked terrorism to their values of goodness and their political ideology: 'Terror is nothing other than justice, prompt, severe, inflexible; it is therefore an emanation of virtue; it is not so much a special principle as it is a consequence of the general principle of democracy applied to our country's most urgent needs' (Robespierre, 1794, quoted in Garrison, 2004: 260–261).

The appropriation of the religious concept of virtue for a political cause occurs in this case, and in many others, to give terrorism a spiritual dimension. This dimension is strongest when a crisis involves a perceived existential threat. It is counterintuitive for citizens of democracies to accept the apparent necessity of terror tactics to preserve democracy, yet this was how their leaders believed and acted. Towards the end of the Second World War Winston Churchill wrote to his chief military assistant, General Ismay, saying, 'It seems to me that the moment has come when the question of bombing of German cities simply for the sake of increasing the terror, though under other pretexts, should be reviewed' (Churchill, 1945).

The Allies had embarked on a policy of day and night terror bombing of the German civilian population in order to break their morale. This strategy was both necessary and justifiable in their minds because they, like the French revolutionaries, faced an existential threat. The difference between these two moments in history was that terrorism was no longer considered a 'virtue' by the time of the Second World War and so could only be practised 'under other pretexts'. Some 40 years later the pretexts became a precedent. Both Israeli prime ministers Menachem Begin and Shimon Peres manipulated the Allied bombing of Germany during the war to justify their bombing of civilians in 1982, claiming that 'the civilian casualties of 'air raids were no different from the civilians killed in Denmark in an RAF [Royal Air Force] raid' (Fisk, 2006). Similar comparisons were made by Israeli leaders with the British bombing of Dresden, to avert Western criticism of civilian casualties during their bombing of Lebanon in 2006. Both precedents were a misrepresentation of reality, but effective propaganda often necessitates reframing of facts.

Non-state actors use the perceived terrorism of states as a relativist argument to justify their own. In one of his speeches, Osama bin Laden, Al Qaeda's leader, justified his group's terrorism by referring to the American use of atomic weapons in Japan during the Second World War when many more civilians were deliberately killed than during all the attacks conducted by that terror movement: 'Nor should one forget the deliberate, premeditated dropping of the H Bombs [*sic*] on cities with their entire populations of children, elderly and women, as was the case with Hiroshima and Nagasaki' (Lawrence, 2005: 40).

That states use terror more extensively to repress and exploit helpless people, whereas non-state terror groups use it sparingly for the liberation of their particular people, is a major justification argument deployed by most terrorist groups. The sophistication and evidence necessary to back up such arguments cannot be conducted purely through symbolic acts of violence. Motivational speeches and the publication of polemical articles are needed to contextualise and justify terrorism's symbolic acts of violence. In this way, terrorist attacks become labels or memes, drawing attention to their arguments of political grievance and inspiring others to ignore the apparent power imbalance between the oppressors and the oppressed, so that they feel empowered to take individual action to either join or support the cause.

PROPAGATION OF IDEOLOGY AND INTERNATIONALISATION OF RESPONSE

Explaining the ideology and motivation behind a terror act, even if it may be obvious to most, is another continuity in terror propaganda. Robespierre felt he had to ensure that he labelled and described the actions of the French revolutionaries as a positive instrument in preserving the achievements of the revolution. Without a justification narrative, symbolic acts of terror become abstract and open to the interpretations by others, thus they can be more easily misrepresented as mindless actions of madmen. As Hanle says, 'Following nearly every terrorist attack, statesmen and journalists condemn the attack as being, "barbaric," "criminal," "mindless" ... such attacks are seldom, if ever, mindless' (Hanle and Alexander, 2007: 108). The allocation of an insanity label by states and journalists is facilitated by the very nature of terrorism. The emotion of terror necessitates an event so abnormally threatening that it defies logic or sanity, what the novelist Conrad refers to as any 'act of destructive ferocity so absurd as to be incomprehensible, inexplicable almost unthinkable; in fact, mad?' (Conrad, 1983: 31–32). There is consequently a dialogue between terrorists' propaganda and states' counterterrorist propaganda that influences both to adopt strategies to defend their own version of reality and to misrepresent the other's. This tactic is transparent to the targets of propaganda, and when successful can be frustrating, as indicated by this Al Qaeda spokesman:

> In all the reams of newspaper articles, stacks of video footage and radio interviews, has there been a single dedicated documentary into the 'hijackers' and their motives for the attack? No. Why? Because it is more convenient to label them as madmen, crazed, psychotic evil doers who either wallowed in the squalor of abject poverty and therefore had nothing to live for, or were psychotic fanatical killers easily brain-washed by power hungry religious nuts. (Quoted in Soriano, 2008: 7)

Similarly, British public opinion depicted 19th century anarchists 'as an unscrupulous movement as a conspiracy intent on unleashing revolutionary violence' (Shpayer-Makov, 1988: 487). Virtually nothing of their grievance narrative was represented to the public, despite many anarchists providing elaborate arguments for their grievances against the political elite and the church, as a case for violent action. The British and, to a greater extent, European governments were aware of the propaganda threat which they appeared to put on a par with the rampant security threat of anarchist assassinations of world leaders and bombings of public places. Their response was a pan-European conference held in Rome in 1898 (Jensen, 1981). Although most of the conference recommendations dealt with the expulsion and extradition of anarchists, the dangers of propaganda were recognised through laws passed at various times by 'France, Spain, Italy, Germany, Switzerland and several other countries ... aimed at controlling anarchist propaganda and the use of explosive' (Jensen, 1981: 325).

The outcomes of the Rome Conference indicated the beginning of a legal war to balance democratic states' liberal free speech rights with the need to restrict the impact of publicity motivating terrorism. More than a century later, European countries are debating laws to censor terrorist propaganda, with most people believing that this is a new challenge resulting from the increased use of social media. These debates build on several failed attempts by governments to 'fight' the propaganda war through legal instruments. One example of this is the famous battle cry by the United Kingdom (UK) Prime Minister, Margaret Thatcher, to deny terrorists the 'oxygen of publicity'. On 19 October 1988, the UK government issued a directive to the BBC and the Independent Broadcasting Authority (IBA) banning the spoken words of anyone representing any of 11 Republican or Loyalist paramilitary or political organisations (Edgerton, 1996). Even at the time of the announcement many articulated its likely failure, including a prominent parliamentary opposition politician, Paddy Ashdown, who warned that, 'you cannot defeat terrorism by destroying our liberties. This action is potentially dangerous, likely unworkable, and almost certainly ineffective' (quoted in Edgerton, 1996: 123).

Apart from a predominantly genuine desire to limit terrorists' access to the media, there is political advantage in introducing such measures under the guise of counterterrorism. Politicians instinctively identify the popular side of a debate, and will use Manichean tropes to support public opinion while discrediting the opposite view. Mrs Thatcher defended her government's censorship policy by stating: 'Either one is on the side of justice in these matters or on the side of the terrorists' (Edgerton, 1996: 126). President George W. Bush advanced a similar argument a decade later in relation to building a global coalition when he said that: 'Either you are with us, or you are with the terrorists.' Terrorist propaganda is therefore part of the counterterrorism war, and states and their leaders will act in ways that attempt not merely to censor it but also to maximise political advantage for them personally and for their wider political agendas.

TELEVISION AS A SHAPER OF PROPAGANDA

The construction and dissemination of terrorist propaganda was significantly affected by a shift in the media's traditional approach to 'integrative' ceremonial events towards a priority to disruptive events relating to conflict and crises (Katz and Liebes, 2007: 161). The relatively new medium of television was most effective in responding to and highlighting dramatic interruptions to normality, and was consequently an attractive conduit for both publicising terror attacks and communicating the associated message. In addition, while being disruptive and disturbing to the wider audience, these events were integrative to the minority audience who either supported or were susceptible to being supportive of the objectives of the perpetrators of such incidents. In this way, television coverage can unwittingly contribute to radicalisation.

These features partly inspired the wave of aircraft highjacks witnessed in the 1960s and 1970s. These were mostly reported after the event was under way or after it was over. The Munich Olympics massacre, on 5 September 1972, when the Black September group seized 11 Israeli athletes and coaches in the Olympic village, was one of the first terrorist events to be broadcast live on television. The attack ended with 11 Israelis killed, along with five of the eight terrorists. An estimated 500 million people watched the horror unfold on television, giving the terrorists unprecedented publicity. Notably, the cameras at the 'Munich Olympics did not dwell long on this aberration of the ceremonial media event which it interrupted – at least partly because it was considered "incorrect" to do so' (Katz and Liebes, 2007: 161). This partial self-censorship by the media has progressively given way to a 'full-time' coverage of terrorist attacks and their aftermath, with analysis of the individuals involved and their cause provided between news updates.

Intensification of coverage occurred because of the expansion of television and online news outlets all competing for exclusivity and speed of reporting. A byproduct of this increased reporting is that a relatively small or even a failed attack can gain a massive amount of publicity. Some believe that terrorist attacks are planned with news schedules in mind to maximise their propaganda value. These can present challenges to state authorities because persistent 'coverage of terror events puts pressure on governments to act more hastily, and more impulsively, than perhaps they might' (Couldry et al., 2009: 36). On the other hand, saturation coverage of attacks can also provide governments an opportunity 'to mobilize popular support for action against Evil', negating some of the terrorists' propaganda impact (Couldry et al., 2009: 37).

A symbiotic relationship exists between news media corporations and terrorist propaganda. It is a specific symptom of the wider relationship between the media, politics, and governance in contemporary society, and is increasingly explored by academics. Much of this work identifies the evaporation of previous limits to influence caused by geography, economic wealth, and political power. Instead they identify the impact on the news agenda by a mix of professional and citizen journalist and non-state actors as a challenge to the conventional 'hegemony' of state power (see, for example, Baker and Blaagaard, 2016: 16). McNair (2016: 1) deals specifically with the relationship between media and crisis, suggesting that power is exercised through communication within this space. Acts of terrorism are intended to create a crisis through which the terrorist group's power can be projected, knowing that modern media, with its tentacles in society, can magnify the messages communicated by the event. At the same time, governments, with their desire to maintain a monopoly of power, can make rash responses through which the intended impact of terrorists can be achieved (Couldry et al., 2009). Terrorist groups have not created the precarious interdependence between the media, politics, and governance that McNair describes. Instead, they have instinctively and largely successfully exploited the increasing opportunity for communication suffrage available to them. In this sense, they mediate both materially and spiritually between world events and their primary target audience; those on the fringes of their faith, or those who do or can be persuaded to support them.

Footage, analysis, and reports produced by news outlets, non-governmental organisations (NGOs), and governments have an 'integrative' effect on sympathisers to the terrorist cause, who selectively share these products on social media with like-minded contacts. These products are also recycled by the major terrorist propaganda organisations in their outputs. For example, *Inspire* and *Dabiq* magazines rely heavily on imagery and reports that they know their readership has already seen on television or the Internet, in order to illustrate their reframed version of events. This symbiosis can occasionally extend to academia in ways that unintentionally benefit the terrorists. Abu Mus'ab al-Suri is considered the foremost strategist of the global jihadist movement. His writings, amongst the most sophisticated strategic doctrines available to terrorist organisations, were not overly accessible to the average person, especially an English-speaking readership. Brynjar Lia, a Norwegian academic specialising in terrorism, wrote a book on al-Suri containing translations of his jihadist strategy (Lia, 2009). These were read by Smir Kahn, *Inspire*'s editor, who serialised the work in English, bringing al-Suri's writings to a wider and younger English-speaking readership than al-Suri could ever have done himself (Stalinsky, 2011).

RESPONSE TO THE INTERNET AS A MEDIUM OF PROPAGANDA

When ISIS and other terrorists have used social media for propagation, governments attempted initially to place responsibility for censorship onto Internet corporations through voluntary means. This had the political advantage of shifting the focus of responsibility or blame from the government to Internet service providers following an attack. While at the time of writing (spring 2021) the UK had yet to introduce legislation to force social networking sites to conform to set standards, other countries have already done so. For example, Australia has introduced 48-hour 'take down' notices. Russia has laws requiring this to be done in 24 hours, as well insisting that data on Russian citizens be hosted on servers within the country. China has also expressed concern over terrorism propaganda and claimed success with shutting down sites and removing apps deemed inappropriate (BBC, 2019b). These measures appear to be an extension of the country's existing strict political censorship measures, enforced by an army of trained state censors. Germany introduced a law in 2018 requiring content providers to have effective procedures to respond to complaints and to remove illegal material within 24 hours (BBC, 2019b).

All this was insufficient for the European Union's (EU) commissioner for security, who explained that the Internet is a 'vital tool for terrorists. It plays a central role in terrorism, whether through incitement, instruction or glorification.' Speed of propagation is a critical success factor in terrorist propaganda because once uploaded it 'spreads like a virus from platform to platform, infecting the minds of the vulnerable. Its potential for causing damage rising dramatically with every hour that it remains online' (Banks, 2019). Consequently, the EU is pushing for removal of content within an hour. Even if this requirement is met, in the words of Paddy Ashdown it will be 'almost certainly ineffective', as demonstrated by the New Zealand mosque shootings in 2019. A right-wing terrorist broadcast live as he killed 50 worshippers. Approximately 200 people are believed to have watched the event live, and the video was reported some 12 minutes after the shootings ended. Around 4000 people are believed to have watched the video before it was removed from Facebook. By that time, it had been uploaded on to alt-right websites, such as 8chan, from where many attempts were made to spread it. Facebook had to block 1.4 million attempts to upload the video and remove a further 300 000 successful uploads within just the first 24 hours alone. The New Zealand mosque attack was significant in many ways. It highlighted the relative futility of the measures taken by governments and companies to restrict the spread of terrorist propaganda, as it demonstrated that the broadcast of live events could not easily be stopped. Likewise, subsequent dispersal around the Internet via less well-controlled websites or websites sympathetic to the terrorists' cause could also not be stopped. New Zealand's Prime Minister, Jacinda Ardern, has attempted to transfer liability for terrorist material on the Internet by framing social networks providers as 'the publisher not just the postman' (BBC, 2019a). In this way, Ardern challenged the providers to either develop technical means for dealing with the real-time propaganda threat (currently an impractical option), or to stop providing a live broadcast service.

Even under current guidelines and laws, the technical challenge faced by Internet companies is immense. YouTube removed 7.8 million videos between July and September 2018, with 81 per cent automatically removed by machines and the remainder by its 10 000 employees dedicated to the role (BBC, 2019b). Facebook provides a graphic report of its efforts to remove terrorist content, indicating that in the first quarter of 2019 it removed 6.4 million postings, over 99.3 per cent of which were detected by the company before being reported by outsiders. Facebook has invested in a large global workforce, but the bulk of the work is done automatically by its own 'detection technology' (Transparency.facebook.com, 2019). Twitter and other social networks are making similar efforts. Nevertheless, these attempts to remove content are a tiny proportion of the overall content loaded on social media every second. A small but significant amount of material does get through, and sympathisers can then share it on smaller networks of encrypted messaging systems, such as Telegram and WhatsApp.

PREDOMINANCE OF TEXTUALITY

In the early days terrorist propaganda was almost exclusively in written text. Houen (2002) explains that terrorists have to address the 'interface of terrorist violence and textuality, negotiating the divide between the "visceral" reality of terrorism and discursive aspects of its representation' (Kolani, 2004: 213). There are few better examples of how this can be done well than through the writings of Karl Heinzen, a 19th century anarchist who Walter Laqueur described as modern terrorism's 'great visionary' (Bessner and Stauch, 2010: 143). His booklet, *Murder and Liberty*, published while in exile abroad and smuggled into Germany to taunt the Tsar and inspire rebellion through terror, can be described as the 'foundational text of modern terrorism in a similar way that *The Prince*' is for realism (Ashraf, 2012: 188).

Written text has remained the primary medium by which terror groups communicate their ideology and publicise their attacks. The digital age has made a significant difference to their capability, mainly in terms of dissemination of propaganda, bypassing banning policies or censorship and reaching specific groups or individuals. While there is an increasing use of imagery and videos, groups still publish digital news channels, magazines, and books, with an extensive proportion of textuality to provide the necessary 'discursive aspects' of the representation of terrorist actions. A study of propaganda material collected from 48 individuals convicted or killed as a result of terrorist action in the UK found that of nearly 2000 items reviewed, 41 per cent were written texts, 41 per cent were audio files, and only 18 per cent were videos (Holbrook, 2017: 90).

Al Qaeda's leader, Osama bin Laden, his deputy, Ayman Al-Zawahiri, and their lieutenants such as Abu Yahya Al-Libi and the American former Jewish convert, Adam Gadahn, all produced video or audio speeches throughout the group's decade of prominence, from before the 9/11 attacks to just after bin Laden's death. At first, these speeches were distributed via TV channels such as Al Jazeera. When that became difficult, the material was broadcast via Al Qaeda's own Internet channel, As-Sahab (The Cloud). These speeches served a similar purpose to those of any political movement, by identifying and reinforcing the group's aims and strategies. They went further to counter what was perceived to be Western-inspired counter-propaganda while highlighting the group's victories and eulogising its own losses as martyrdoms. In that role the speeches linked actions with ideology, most of which was articulated in books such as Sayyid Qutb's *Milestones* or Zawahiri's *Knights Under the Prophet's Banner*, the former being readily available in the West. The speeches did not dwell on these intellectual publications, focusing instead on invoking a selective misrepresentation of Islamic scripture, in the knowledge that these would better resonate with the identity of their primary audience who had little critical knowledge of their faith. This relationship between textuality, speech, and action is a constant feature of Al Qaeda's propaganda design, as it is of other terrorists including right-wing extremists.

Both Anders Breivik, the right wing-terrorist who murdered 77 people in Norway in 2011, and the New Zealand mosque shooter who killed 50 in 2019, left lengthy manifestos to be read after their attacks. These were meant to explain their actions and to inspire others to follow. Their writings were in turn inspired by older neo-Nazi writings such as the *Turner*

Diaries, a favourite book of Timothy McVeigh who in 1995 bombed a government building in Oklahoma, in the United States of America (USA), killing 168 people, including 19 children in a nursery. While Breivik and McVeigh relied on the news media to capture imagery of their attacks, and used the court and other opportunities to make statements, the New Zealand shooter took and broadcast a self-narrated video of his actions. All three demonstrated the importance of the link between textuality, action, and speech in being inspired by and in spreading the propaganda of the ideology to which they adhered. Martyrdom was celebrated in these three men's ideology. None of them were killed during their attacks, but McVeigh's request to have his execution broadcast was denied.

TEXTUALITY AND THE NEED FOR VISUALISATION

All successful terrorist propagandists instinctively shape their messages to overcome psychological and sociological taboos and self-sanction mechanisms against inhumane acts such as killing. Walter Reich explains how people attempt to overcome such scruples by 'reconstructing conduct as serving moral purposes, by obscuring personal agency in detrimental activities, by disregarding or misrepresenting the injurious consequences of one's actions, or by blaming and dehumanising the victims' (Reich, 1998: 161).

Of these five techniques the first, 'reconstructing conduct as serving moral purposes', is the most prevalent in propaganda. It is often implemented in a two-stage process. Firstly, there is a need to desensitise the reader to the gory sight of blood and death in order to prepare them to contemplate the act themselves. Heinzen does this by stressing to his 19th century readers that they live under tyranny and that theirs is a history written in blood. They have to draw blood to gain their freedom. He uses textual techniques to desensitise the readers' normal psychological aversion to the act of killing, with repeated emphasis on the word 'blood' in the context of the other (Ashraf, 2012: 192). The message is simply that blood, murder, killing, and so on, is the language of the tyrants, and it is only in that language that the ordinary aggrieved people can communicate with them: 'Blood is their alpha and blood is their omega, blood their end and blood their means, blood their desire and blood their life, blood their dream and blood their aspiration, blood is their principle and blood must be their end' (Bessner and Stauch, 2010: 160).

A senior Al Qaeda ideologue attempts to achieve a similar effect by asking his readers to visualise a video of his interpretation of a controversial incident occurring some 1400 years ago, involving the execution of male members of the Jewish Banu Quraidhah tribe. He writes:

> Imagine that the mass killing of the men of Banu Quraidhah was being broadcast to you live ... You see a Jewish man with a white beard, his braids hanging, who has descended from the fort, eyes widened, dragging his feet, as he is being driven to his death while he is watching. His hands are tied with a rope, and a Companion takes him by his arm, pulling him to the place where his neck will be struck. (Al-Libi, 2010)

Al-Libi explicitly invokes the impact of visualising history through the contemporary medium of a live broadcast. Visualisation is an important channel to cleave the emotions that preserve the scruples against drawing blood and killing another human. The author also recognises the psychological importance of visualising this event as opposed to reading about it when he says, 'you will find that you have uncovered feelings you would never have known nor felt if you merely read' (Al-Libi, 2010).

The second step is to convert moral aversion to killing into a moral purpose. Heinzen declares that it is his objective to 'annihilate the "moral" qualms, through which men' are 'frightened away from decisive action ... It was my object to bring honour to and make legitimate the goals of revolution, as well as the means of revolution' (Bessner and Stauch, 2010: 165). In his manifesto, Anders Breivik recommends listening to a number of music tracks during a suicide operation. That recommendation needs to be imagined for its horrific benefit to be emotionally absorbed, the importance of accepting the most difficult of all drawing of blood and murder, the killing of one's self:

> Imagine fighting for your life against a pursuing pack of system protectors (or as I like to call them: armed defenders of the multiculturalist system, also referred to as the police) ... You hear this song as you push forward to annihilate one of their flanks, head shotting [sic] two of your foes ... This angelic voice sings to you from the heavens, strengthening your resolve in a hopeless battle ...This voice is all you hear as your light turns to darkness and you enter into the Kingdom of Heaven. This must surely be the most glorious way to claim the honour of martyrdom in battle. (Breivik, 2011)

This glorification of suicide, understood by terrorists in spiritual terms as martyrdom, is popularly considered a peculiarly Muslim and recent manifestation of terrorism. In fact, it is a feature of nearly all terrorism in modern times. Heinzen described the most glorious killing as suicide; the ultimate act of violence and devotion to the cause by an individual, especially if it is in response to 'disgrace that would destroy his character' (Bessner and Stauch, 2010: 155). It is these very sentiments and language that bin Laden and Breivik repeat in their propaganda almost 150 years later. This style of propaganda reflects the need for reframing the past as an era of glory, reframing the present as a period of existential tyrannical repression, and visualising the future as one of heroic violence where the blood of both the terrorist and the victim must be sacrificed. This last point about visualisation indicates that the emergence of digital technology has not so much been an opportunity exploited by terrorist propagandists as it is a long-standing need fulfilled.

SLICK SALVATION

Discussion of speeches, promotion of imagery of attacks, and analysis of ideological texts are integrated and socialised in what have become known as jihadi lifestyle magazines. The genre began with Al Qaeda's *Jihad Reflections*. After a few issues this transformed into the *Inspire* magazine, described as an 'effort to be accessible, slick, and visually appealing, with pop graphics and colorful layouts' (Bamford, 2013). These qualities ensured that its message was exciting and inspiring to a young, mostly male, audience of radicals who were culturally attuned to the West. Unsurprisingly, the editor of these magazines was a young man of Pakistani origin, Samir Khan, who was brought up in the USA and started his publication activities in that country. He combined skilfully the discursive and presentational elements described above to give his readers the 'know why' of terrorism. Simple do-it-yourself instructions on surveillance techniques, bomb-making instructions, and so on, provided the 'know-how'. This was a highly successful formula judging by how, after Khan's death, ISIS copied the format for its *Dabiq* magazine.

ISIS inherited almost all of its ideological and theological fundamentals from its parent organisation, Al Qaeda. Its differences with Al Qaeda are mainly around issues of strategy, power, and leadership. Therefore, its propaganda challenges were simpler because it did not need to justify its cause, having – unusually for a terrorist group – achieved its objective of establishing the mythical Islamic State and restoring the Caliphate. Nevertheless, it spent a significant proportion of its budget on propaganda, the primary aim of which was to establish the authority of the new state, not just within its territory but also in the wider world of jihadist extremists. ISIS's chief propagandist, Adnani, issued orders that all Islamist terrorist groups should submit to the leadership of the self-appointed Caliph Al-Baghdadi. Another objective was to delegitimise its main rivals in Al Qaeda. The group issued several statements representing al-Zawahiri as inflexibly weak and inactive, contrasting this with the strength and achievements of Al-Baghdadi who was presented as a superhero (Gerges, 2017: 138).

ISIS is best known for its exploitation of social media and the impact it has had on the radicalisation of young people throughout Europe and the rest of the world. Postings on Facebook, YouTube, Instagram, and other social media outlets are 'high quality, slick, chatty and youth friendly' (Gerges, 2017: 299). They appeal to young people, 'especially unemployed, alienated, disfranchised, and religiously confused Muslims, [giving them] a higher cause to fight for and a more promising life under the self-proclaimed caliphate' (Gerges, 2017: 299). One ISIS innovation that stands in contrast to Al Qaeda and even right-wing terrorists is how they target young women. Mostly, this was to help even up the gender balance in what was to be a functioning state, but the messaging appealed directly to young women in a way that indicated that they too could contribute to the fight, as well as undertaking the more important roles of wife and mother. ISIS produced videos of attractive young fighters as 'eye candy' for prospective teenage brides. One young women explained, 'It was glamorous in the sense it was like "oh wow, I can get someone who practises the same religion as me, who's not necessarily from my ethnicity and that's exciting"' (BBC, 2015). Sex and the desire for marriage were therefore mobilised to radicalise and recruit young men and women to ISIS.

However, it would be simplistic to assume that the many thousands from across the world who have responded to ISIS's call did so purely or even mainly because of social media. Most people were drawn to the social media sites after they became aware of ISIS through news reports via conventional media. It was reports of the spectacular success of this hitherto obscure group in capturing huge swathes of territory in Syria and Iraq, its audacity in restoring the Caliphate, and its ability to create the mythical Islamic State, that were the most powerful radicalising influences. In that context, social media propaganda served mostly to reinforce these messages of success, and was a conduit for getting in touch with that mythical state.

STRATEGIC CONSEQUENCES OF UNDERSTANDING TERRORIST PROPAGANDA

At the strategic level, understanding a terrorist group's propaganda can help to counter its appeal and reduce radicalisation to its cause. States have done this by, for example, developing counternarratives to strengthen community resilience to prevent radicalisation, and to develop deradicalisation programmes. However, propaganda is a dynamic and interactive activity. Terrorist groups monitor the counternarratives being deployed against them and respond by developing counter-counternarratives. An example of this is Al Qaeda's 'battle of ideas', which it declares is 'one of the fierce fronts of the confrontation between us and our enemies' (Al-Libi, 2007). As part of this process the organisation provides counterpoints to attacks on its interpretation of jihad, on allegations that it kills and destroys the property of Muslims, and so on. In 2007, Abu Yahya Al-Libi outlined six fronts in the battle of ideas. He proposed confronting the issue through debate that matched the rhetorical quality of the attack: 'to meet argument with argument and eloquence with eloquence; to discuss treatises and rebut misconceptions; to remove misguidance, correct mistakes and rectify deviation; and deliver its speech with clarity and pureness' (Al-Libi, 2007).

Therefore, there is an interactive battle involving propaganda and counter-propaganda. A further advantage in understanding extremist propaganda is that it provides strategic insight into the intent, capability, and perceptions of the group. This can aid in forecasting likely outcomes. One such analysis based on the propaganda of Iraqi insurgent groups in 2006 concluded, 'there will be insurgency violence after coalition troops drawdown ... enough for the insurgents to claim a victory and continue to evolve to make Iraq ungovernable by a democratic system'. The evolution of ISIS in 2014 and the capture of large swathes of Iraq from a hapless Iraqi army and government supports the veracity of that prediction (Ashraf, 2006: 38).

CONCLUSIONS

Terrorist propaganda is intended to mesmerise its target audience with shock and horror. It aims to draw attention to the organisation's underlying cause and beliefs, to coerce its enemies, and to inspire courage, action, and support from its sympathisers. It represents a revolutionary and insurgent form of politics, which is increasingly international, with global aspirations. As such, it presents a direct security threat to all states and regimes. Most analysts and commentators have tended to be mesmerised by the slick content and methods (the means and not the message) of the propaganda, and have consequently been unable to identify its distinctive style within the broader genre of political propaganda. In order to do this, it is necessary to identify continuities and discontinuities in the way propaganda was used during the century or so history of modern terrorism.

A critical relationship exists between the terror deed and the terrorists' ideology. This places a priority on the need to link visual imagery with the textuality of the treatise. A study of modern terrorist ideology indicates that these needs have been increasingly met by, rather than being created by, developments in technology. Current trends indicate that propagandists will quickly and effectively exploit future technological developments, forcing states to respond ineffectively. Governments and NGOs have perceived terrorist attacks and their supporting messages as security threats. Attempts to introduce counternarratives to fight the terrorists' messages have had little impact. The reason for this has been partly because they have attempted to exploit the fight against terrorism to further wider political agendas, and have chosen to misrepresent the terrorists' message rather than confront it. Ever since the Rome Conference of 1898, states have cooperated and shared instruments to block the means by which terrorist propaganda is disseminated. Their efforts have tended to be reactive rather than proactive, and consequently have had relatively little success. Understanding terrorist propaganda enables identification of counter-propaganda in what is an interactive battle of ideas. It also enables an improved capability for political analysis and prediction of outcomes.

NOTE

1. That is to say, groups that are not elements of a nation state structure such as an army or intelligence service. This description can include groups that may be sponsored or supported by a state.

REFERENCES

Al-Libi, A.Y. (2007), 'Dots on the Letters', as-Sahab's 2nd Interview with Sheikh Abu Yahya Al-Libi, Two Years After His Deliverance from Bagram Prison.
Al-Libi, A.Y. (2010), 'Quraidhah and America', available at https://www.cia.gov/library/abbottabad-compound/3D/3D542432CD7712D763C44921C52CE78C_E_2.pdf.
Ashraf, A. (2006), 'Iraqi Insurgency: Using the Internet to Exploit Asymmetry and Balance the Battlefield', Paper presented at the Cooperating Against Terrorism EU-US Relations Post September 11 conference, Sweden.
Ashraf, A. (2012), 'Al Qaeda's Ideology Through Political Myth and Rhetoric', PhD thesis, University of St Andrews.
Baker, M. and B.B. Blaagaard (2016), *Citizen Media and Public Spaces*, London: Routledge.
Bamford, J. (2013), 'Inspire Magazine: The Most Dangerous Download on Earth', *GQ.com*, December 9, available at https://www.gq.com/story/inspire-magazine-al-qaeda-boston-bombing.
Banks, M. (2019), 'EU Security Tsar Criticises Member States for Being "Slow" to Counter Terrorist Threats', *Parliament Magazine*, 26 August, available at https://www.theparliamentmagazine.eu/articles/news/eu-security-tsar-criticises-member-states-being-%E2%80%9Cslow%E2%80%9D-counter-terrorist-threats.
BBC (2015), 'Attractive Jihadists can Lure UK Girls to Extremism', 3 March, available at https://www.bbc.co.uk/news/uk-31704408.
BBC (2019a), 'Facebook: NZ Attack Video Viewed 4,000 Times', 19 March, available at https://www.bbc.co.uk/news/business-47620519.
BBC (2019b), 'Governments v Social Media', available at https://www.bbc.co.uk/news/technology-4713.
Bessner, D. and M. Stauch (2010), 'Karl Heinzen and the Intellectual Origins of Modern Terror', *Terrorism and Political Violence*, 22(2): 143–176.
Breivik, A.B. (2011), '2083 – A European Declaration of Independence', *Public Intelligence*, 28 July, available at https://publicintelligence.net/anders-behring-breiviks-complete-manifesto-2083-a-european-declaration-of-independence/.
Churchill, W. (1945), *General Ismay For COS Committee*, Whitehall: London
Conrad, J. (1983), *The Secret Agent*, Oxford: Oxford University Press.
Couldry, N., A. Hepp, and F. Krotz (2009), *Media Events in a Global Age*, London: Routledge.
Edgerton, G. (1996), 'Quelling the "Oxygen of Publicity": British Broadcasting and "the Troubles" during the Thatcher Years', *Journal of Popular Culture*, 30(1): 115–131.
European Commission (2018), 'Migration and Home Affairs', *European Commission*, 12 June, available at https://ec.europa.eu/home-affairs/e-library/glossary/terrorist-propaganda_en.
Fisk, R. (2006), 'Slaughter in Qana', *Independent*, 30 July, available at https://www.independent.co.uk/voices/commentators/fisk/robert-fisk-slaughter-in-qana-6232087.html.
Garrison, A.H. (2004), 'Defining Terrorism: Philosophy of the Bomb, Propaganda by Deed and Change through Fear and Violence', *Criminal Justice Studies*, 17(3): 259–279.
Gerges, F.A. (2017), *Isis: A History*, Princeton, NJ: Princeton University Press.
Hanle, D.J. and Y. Alexander (2007), *Terrorism: The Newest Face of Warfare*, Washington, DC: Potomac Books.
Hoffman, B. (2006), *Inside Terrorism*, New York: Columbia University Press.
Holbrook, D. (2017), 'The Spread of its Message – Studying the Prominence of al-Qaida Materials in UK Terrorism Investigations', *Perspectives on Terrorism*, 11(6): 89–100.
Houen, A. (2002), *Terrorism and Modern Literature: From Joseph Conrad to Ciaran Carson*, Oxford: Oxford University Press.

Jensen, R.B. (1981), 'The International Anti-Anarchist Conference of 1898 and the Origins of Interpol', *Journal of Contemporary History*, 16(2): 323–347.

Katz, E. and T. Liebes (2007), '"No More Peace!": How Disaster, Terror and War Have Upstaged Media Events', *International Journal of Communication*, 1(1): 157–166.

Kolani, R. (2004), 'Terrorism and Modern Literature, From Joseph Conrad to Ciaran Carson', *Partial Answers: Journal of Literature and the History of Ideas*, 2(2): 213–218.

Lasswell, H. (1927), 'The Theory of Political Propaganda', *American Political Science Review*, 21(3): 627–631.

Lawrence, B. (2005), *Messages to the World: The Statements of Osama bin Laden*, London: Verso.

Lia, B. (2009), *Architect of Global Jihad: The Life of Al Qaeda Strategist Abu Mus' ab al-Suri*, New York: Columbia University Press.

McNair, B. (2016), *Communication and Political Crisis: Media, Politics and Governance in a Globalized Public Sphere* (Global Crises and the Media, Vol. 16), New York: Peter Lang Publishing.

Reich, W. (1998), 'Origins of Terrorism: Psychologies', *Ideologies, Theologies, State of Mind*, Washington, DC: Woodrow Wilson International Center for Scholars.

Shpayer-Makov, H. (1988), 'Anarchism in British Public Opinion 1880–1914', *Victorian Studies*, 31(4): 487–516.

Soriano, M.R.T. (2008), 'Terrorism and the Mass Media after Al Qaeda: A Change of Course?', *Athena Intelligence Journal*, 3(1): 1–20.

Stalinsky, S. (2011), 'Al-Qaeda Military Strategist Abu Mus' ab Al-Suri's Teachings on Fourth-Generation Warfare (4GW), Individual Jihad and the Future of Al-Qaeda', Inquiry & Analysis Series (698).

Transparency.facebook.com. (2019), Facebook Transparency Report | Community Standards, available at https://transparency.facebook.com/community-standards-enforcement#terrorist-propaganda.

18. Propaganda through participation: counterterrorism narratives in China
Chi Zhang

INTRODUCTION

The idea that the masses are the foundation of the survival of the Communist Party is an important part of communist rhetoric. The Chinese Communist Party (CCP) pledges to 'serve the people wholeheartedly' (*quanxin quanyi wei renmin fuwu*), which has become the motto that is considered 'a great work of communist education … for revolutionary people [to remould] their ideology and [establish] the proletarian world outlook' (*Liberation Army Daily*, 1967). This motto contrasts with the top-down, centralised, and bureaucratic style of security governance that prioritises state security and social stability over civil liberties. China's heavy-handed projects to counter violent extremism (CVE) are a case in point. While foreign media bombarded China's treatment of the Uyghurs in the Xinjiang Uyghur Autonomous Region (XUAR), some Chinese seem to be bewildered by the human rights criticism coming from the West. Beyond the official discourse, local-level cadres, 'cultural workers' (*wenyi gongzuozhe*), and peasant artists demonstrate a high level of homogeneity with the state's narratives in publicly available information from Chinese sources. As a continuum of the Down to Grassroots (*xia jiceng*) programme, the Visit, Benefit, and Gather (*fang, hui, ju*) programme, started in 2014, involved sending 200 000 cadres down to communities and remote villages in Xinjiang. Cadres were sent down to live with the local communities, improve their access to public goods, and ultimately win their hearts and minds. A significant volume of reports by Visit, Benefit, and Gather working teams have been produced in response to Western criticism, providing rich resources to investigate contemporary communication tactics employed by the CCP. Examining these reports, this chapter argues that participatory propaganda remains crucial in mobilising support in order to temper the more coercive approach in countering violent extremism in China.

This chapter begins by situating China's contemporary local approach to propaganda within the broader discussion around participatory propaganda, before briefly discussing the application of the Mass Line ethos in the counter-terrorism discourse and practice. Then the chapter focuses on how local cadres, cultural workers, and peasant artists are transformed from receivers of propaganda to active producers, a process whereby propaganda materials are internalised and further disseminated. This chapter concludes with some remarks on reception and similar efforts in other countries in the broader context of countering violent extremism.

PARTICIPATORY PROPAGANDA

Building on Jowett and O'Donnell's (2019: 6) definition, Wanless and Berk define participatory propaganda as 'the deliberate, and systematic attempt to shape perceptions, manipulate cognitions and direct behaviour of a target audience while seeking to co-opt its members to actively engage in the spread of persuasive communications, to achieve a response that furthers the desired intent of the propagandist' (Wanless and Berk, 2017: 92).

The Internet has fundamentally changed how propaganda works, by blurring the boundary between the receiver and producer or disseminator of propaganda (Garrett and Weeks, 2013; Wanless and Berk, 2017). Empowered to generate information, citizens became the 'co-producers' who work with regimes to spread propaganda (Mejias and Vokuev, 2017). Through state-sponsored trolls and computational propaganda, states can now rely on citizens to do the work for them (Asmolov, 2019). The increasingly participatory nature of state-led communication in the Internet age gave rise to what Repnikova and Fang (2018: 765) refer to as 'Participatory Persuasion 2.0'. Compared to 'Participatory Persuasion 1.0', that involves community engagement tactics in the pre-Internet age when citizens were called upon to act as propagandists to 'produce propaganda content for the state in the form of art, posters and literature, among other genres' (Repnikova and Fang, 2018: 771–772), the Internet has given more space for individuals to use their creative ideas. For Wanless and Berk (2019), this shift gives rise to a qualitatively new phenomenon that was first identified during the 2016 United States (US) presidential election, and online political activities in the United Kingdom and Canada. Ostensibly 'democratising' communication by empowering the grassroots, 'Participatory Persuasion 2.0' creates the impression that people genuinely think in the ways in which they have been manipulated to think, so that more will be inspired to follow. This kind of propaganda could potentially be more influential depending on who is participating in spreading it.

As observed in China, the control of information is by no means carried out online alone. While research has been done on participatory propaganda on the internet (for example, see Farkas et al., 2018; Helmus et al., 2018; Repnikova and Fang, 2018; Woolley and Howard, 2018; Wanless and Berk, 2019), less attention has been paid to offline 'hearts and minds' campaigns in the Internet age. The counter-terrorism propaganda campaign in the XUAR demonstrates the continuities in China's rationale for propaganda. At the grassroots level, local governments rely heavily on pre-Internet, offline mass mobilisation techniques, as they tend to provide visible outcomes that can be measured and used for career advancement. In poverty-stricken regions where sources of information are often limited, the CCP pours resources into various cultural activities to ensure that the official narratives of counter-terrorism remain dominant in relation to separatist or extremist ideologies, at least in terms of their pervasiveness.

However, the government's reliance on offline activities for mass mobilisation is not a return to 'Participatory Persuasion 1.0'. As this chapter will show, some of the activities involve training participants to use social media to extend their role as propagandists online. While online propaganda to promote counter-terrorist narratives is an interesting topic that deserves its own research, this chapter highlights the unusual fact that even in the Internet age, the Chinese state relies heavily on pre-Internet experience and techniques to forge loyalty through physical commitment in order to 'manually' blur the 'sender–receiver' boundaries by embedding counter-radicalisation messages in various aspects of life.

MASS LINE IN COUNTER-TERRORISM

Counter-terrorism in China is more widely known for its 'hard' approaches, such as the Strike Hard campaign in the XUAR.[1] Observers outside China tend to assume that China's counter-terrorism is predominantly top-down, oppressive, and characterised by unbridled force. However, aside from these measures, China's counter-terrorism strategy involves a range of 'hard' and 'soft' policies that work interactively to curb terrorism. The softer 'hearts and minds' projects in the XUAR are an important but overlooked part of the overall counter-terrorism strategy to rally support and temper the more coercive approaches that are likely to exacerbate tensions and 'otherise' the Uyghur population (Newman and Zhang, 2020).

The Mass Line has been embedded in China's counter-terrorism strategy for this purpose. The initial idea, derived from Lenin's 'democratic centralism', seeks to improve the accountability and responsiveness of the government by encouraging people to participate voluntarily in politics (Zhang, 2019). The Mass Line reflects the CCP's emphasis, at least rhetorically, on the consent and political participation of the people. Under the leadership of Mao Zedong, the idea manifested itself in the form of the 'people's democratic dictatorship'. The revival of this concept under the current leadership indicates that the government is aware of the legitimacy crisis in which the party became increasingly disconnected from the people, and that its centralised governance must be tempered by a high degree of popular support to ensure the survival of the regime. Traditionally, the CCP has sought to obtain popular support by launching mass propaganda campaigns, such as the Patriotic Health Campaign and the Iron Girl campaign in the Mao era. Beginning in the 1950s, Mao's power grab took the form of political campaigns in various aspects of life. These campaigns played an important role in mobilising the masses towards a particular policy goal, be it eliminating epidemics or turning women into the labour force.

With its long tradition of launching mass 'movement-style' (*yundongshi*) political campaigns, the CCP is able to build on its past experience in mobilising the grassroots and coordinating various sectors of society towards a particular policy objective. Two slogans in the Anti-Terrorism Law and counter-radicalisation regulations capture the importance of the Mass Line: 'Combining Specialized Efforts with the Mass Line' and 'Mass Prevention and Mass Governance'.

In China's counter-terrorism discourse, 'culture' is reified into a 'battlefield' that is 'occupied' by one or another. In the Xinjiang conference in 2014, Xi Jinping stressed the need to 'use Socialist Core Values to construct the spiritual home of all ethnic groups in Xinjiang and resolutely occupy the battlefield of propaganda, culture and education' (Xinhua, 2014). The term 'cultural construction' appeared in two Xinjiang conferences in 2010 and 2014, leading to a boost in the study of 'cultural counter-terrorism' in China.

In contrast to actual terrorist attacks, in the eyes of Chinese officials and scholars, violent extremism must be dealt with in the realm of culture. Hu Yifeng, a member of the China Federation of Literary and Art Circles, believes that 'terrorism' is a kind of 'ideology; an act and a cultural form that sabotages social development'. He refers to terrorism as a 'cancer of the society' and an 'evil culture' that must be fought by translating the idea of 'harmony' in the Chinese culture into counter-terrorism policies and 'increasing the dose of culture' in existing policies (Hu, 2014). According to the official narratives, 'three forces' – terrorism, separatism, and extremism – encourage believers to resist public services provided by the government, 'modern' or ethnic traditional garments, music, dancing, and poems. In response, the government must occupy the 'cultural battlefield' by improving media's ability to self-censor to counteract this kind of terrorist propaganda (*Xinjiang Daily*, 2017).

In research commissioned by the Ministry of Justice, Feng Weiguo (Feng, 2016), a professor of law at the Northwest University of Political Science and Law, advocates 'cultural counter-terrorism', as opposed to surveillance and detention, to promote the 'soft means' of counter-terrorism, and create the environment in which extremist ideologies cannot survive. 'Cultural counter-terrorism' ranges from ritualistic displays of loyalty such as flag-raising events and singing the national anthem or 'red songs' (*hongge*), to academic fieldwork among locals to understand their real-life concerns.[2] It is interesting to note that while some scholars and officials recognise the pitfalls of mass movements, given how the politics is structured in China, policies inevitably degenerate into another round of mass movement. For example, Feng (2016) has explicitly warned against the tendency towards the 'movement-style' campaign and asked for the government's respect for the independence of academic and artistic production. However, the implementation of the Mass Line project Visit, Benefit, and Gather in the following years demonstrates how the movement-style governance reinvents and replicates itself at the grassroots level. While the initial time frame for Visit, Benefit, and Gather was three years from 2014 to 2017, activities under its banner became routinised, as they can be used to demonstrate political achievement (*zhengji*) of local working teams.

The fight against radicalisation in the cultural realm depends on support from the public. To promote the credibility of the official narratives of counter-terrorism, the CCP employs a range of tactics to transform various local actors – including cadres at the local level of government, cultural workers, peasant artists, senior party members retired from their positions, and college and university students – into grassroots propagandists. They form the basis of the CCP's sprawling network for deep-reaching community engagement efforts.

PERFORMING COUNTER-RADICALISATION

Local governments and 'cultural workers' – referring to singers, dancers, performers, and in a broad sense, including writers – embedded counter-radicalisation narratives into the cultural products they produce. Maidina Abudurusuli, Director of the Singing and Dancing and Drama Troupes of Ili Prefecture, uses musicals to reflect the benefit and changes brought by the Visit, Benefit, and Gather and the Ethnic Groups Unite as a Family (*minzu tuanjie yijiaqin*) campaigns (Abudurusuli, 2018). Abudurusuli (2018) is blunt about the purpose of their performance: they regard the stage as a 'battlefield', using their performance as a weapon to transform and educate people, to guide the masses to 'feel the Party's kindness and obey and follow the Party'.

The Visit, Benefit, and Gather working teams played an important role in leading, organising, and supporting such cultural activities, including providing infrastructural facilities. According to a government brief on Visit, Benefit, and Gather in Korla city, working groups in villages and communities in the city helped them build a 'Big Cultural Stage' and paid for the props, musical instruments, audio equipment, and costumes. They made use of almost all forms of entertainment that locals enjoy. They help local governments and communities organise 'grassroots performing arts propaganda teams' (*caogen wenyidui*), 'grassroots celebrities' (*caogen yiren*), and peasants and shepherds to carry out theatrical performances, a silk fashion show, a 'beautiful long hair model show', Naqareh drum show, 'counter-radicalisation' sketches, and fun sports games. The Municipal Cultural Centre organised a contest of sitcoms on the theme 'Countering Radicalism and Building a Beautiful Home', seeking to use 'down-to-earth' (*jie diqi*) and 'localised' (*bentu hua*) styles of discourse to rehabilitate (*ganhua*) the locals.

Local governments support this mass mobilisation initiative by organising training for grassroots propagandists to communicate with online audiences. The local government in Yanqi county provided training for cultural workers to use smartphone apps to create and edit videos (Gou et al., 2019). Senior media experts from NetEase, Bayingolin Daily, and County Broadcasting station were invited to teach local propagandists communication techniques, including, among others, using social media platforms such as WeChat public accounts and Douyin (Xue, 2020).

The method of performing counter-radicalisation soon gained traction at the grassroots. A report in 2018 indicates how intensive such activities became. In one month from 21 May to 22 June, a Visit, Benefit, and Gather performance team composed of members of the Drama Troupe, Traditional Chinese Musical Instruments Troupe, and Orchestra of the Xinjiang Art Theatre, as well as the Xinyu Song and Dance Troupe in Khotan, reportedly gave 206 performances in over 100 places in Kashgar, Khotan, and the Kizilsu Kyrgyz Autonomous Prefecture, reaching over 60 000 audiences. Interestingly, although they targeted Uyghur audiences, the performances did not always use the Uyghur language. A staged play entitled *Sincere Care*, praising the party for its caring character, was performed in Mandarin Chinese. In an attempt to achieve the intended effect of persuasion, the Drama Troupe had to hire two ethnic minorities to join the play so that performers could use Mandarin and Uyghur in turn (*Xinjiang Daily*, 2018).

The Visit, Benefit, and Gather went beyond its three-year time frame as initially planned. In the following years, working teams remained stationed in local communities. In 2019, a gala held at the Karamay Stadium drew on stories and experience of the Visit, Benefit, and Gather working team to create sketches and sitcoms to show the kindness of the working team and local cadres (Propaganda Department of Karamay Municipal Party Committee, 2020). The gala started with a song and dance entitled 'Servants of the People' to reflect the life of the working team in the past three years (Karamay Government, 2020.

WRITING STATEMENTS AND PLEDGING LOYALTY

The act of writing statements to pledge loyalty is often seen in the aftermath of a terror attack in support of an immediate crackdown. On 30 April 2014, a group of individuals attacked passengers and detonated bombs at the exit of Urumqi South Station. On 1 May, an open letter by 11 Uyghur university students was published. The reporters, including journalists of the *China Youth Daily*, devoted much ink to describe how these students, aged from 24 to 29, thought spontaneously of the idea of writing the open letter. The letter highlights that Uyghurs themselves fell victim to terrorist attacks, because of which the entire Uyghur community has been stigmatised. Instead of focusing on systemic discrimination against the Uyghur population, media reports celebrated the Uyghurs' support for counter-terrorism measures. According to a report in Guanchazhe (2014), most readers of this letter sympathised with the writers and condemned terrorists in their comments. On 8 May, a commentator in the *People's Daily* praised the letter for reflecting the 'common aspirations' (*gongtong xinsheng*) of all ethnic groups in Xinjiang (*People's Daily Commentator*, 2014).

Soon, others followed. In June, 15 Uyghur writers, poets, critics, and translators reached out to 200 colleagues to sign an open letter entitled 'It is our responsibility and mission to never remain silent – an open letter to Uyghur compatriots' (Dai, 2014). The letter serves as a call for Uyghur cultural workers and intellectuals to 'utter the correct voice', 'to tell those who respect you how to live in order to attain true happiness'. The letter emphasises their inescapable responsibility to speak up, because of the credibility attached to their identities: 'others can be silent, but you must utter your voice, because you are national elites, and many people admire you as the incarnation of truth' (Dai, 2014). On 7 July, the Xinjiang Science and Technology Press published the Mandarin edition of *We Will Not Remain Silent*, followed on 15 July by the publication of its Uyghur and Kazakh editions. The book contains over 40 articles, including, in addition to the above-mentioned two open letters, a joint letter by Xinjiang students studying abroad, 15 Xinjiang youth in Beijing, five assistants for political and ideological work (*fudao yuan*) at the Xinjiang Agricultural University, joint letters from social organisations (*shehui tuanti*) and relevant departments, speeches and articles by XUAR leaders, and published articles by religious figures (Y. Zhang, 2014).

Following this momentum, it became clear that making statements to 'speak up and brandish the swords' (*fasheng liangjian*) against terrorism has become a trend for local governments, the Xinjiang Production and Construction Corps (XPCC), enterprises, schools, and universities.[3] Although no officials explicitly said 'You are either with us, or with the terrorists', using the language of the former US President George W. Bush, such a trend highlights the good–evil dualism in the counter-terrorism discourse that forces Uyghurs not only to choose the 'correct' side, but also to denounce loud and clear the terrorists who happen to be Uyghurs.

The grassroots level soon began to replicate the 'speak up and brandish the swords' event. The party branch and residents committee of the Bageqi Village and the Visit, Benefit, and Gather team organised 14 students who came back for holidays from where they attended colleges and universities to sing the national anthem, denounce the 'three forces' and discuss the change brought by people-benefiting policies (*huimin zhengce*) and their understandings and thoughts on ethnic unity and poverty alleviation, and to express their gratitude to the motherland in the 'speak up and brandish the swords' ritual (Bageqi village working team of the Xinjiang Branch of the Chinese Academy of Sciences, 2018).

Corroborating evidence comes from a huge volume of speech samples available on various essay-writing websites (for example, see Xi, 2020). It is often assumed that the speaker is a Uyghur, and sample essays considerately include Uyghur proverbs and Uyghurs' personal experience into the formula to condemn extremism and express their deep gratitude to the good policies of the party. While some of these speech samples might be crafted entirely for the user, others might have been presented at a real event. They include detailed information, such as the time and date of the event, and even the speaker's name (Hengdengshijiuduan, 2020; Wunaiwoye, 2020; Xi, 2020). These details suggest that the uploader did not make any changes to the original content, not even to anonymise it. The details also suggest that 'speak up and brandish the swords' events and the accompanying pledging rituals have taken place at numerous party-organised events, meetings, youth symposia, street speeches, and heart-to-heart talks (*tanxin hui*). The (imagined) authorship suggests that Uyghur party members and teachers, whose own loyalty may have a great impact on other community members, are most likely to be asked to pledge loyalty publicly. With such a huge volume of ready-to-use speeches written up for Uyghurs, it does not take too much effort to draft one's own speech that sounds exactly like the official narratives, even for those who are not proficient in Mandarin Chinese.

TURNING COUNTER-RADICALISATION INTO ART

The CCP has a long tradition of using propaganda posters in various political campaigns. In line with Mao's 'Talks at the Yan'an Forum on Literature and Art', the CCP considers art a 'powerful weapon' (*Xinjiang Daily Commentator*, 2014) to 'declare a war against extremism' (Wu and Li, 2014). Wang Chunxing, Kashgar Prefectural Party Committee and Head of Propaganda Department, refers to peasant artists as 'both artists and warriors' who use brushes as spears and daggers to stab the 'three forces' and religious extremism (S. Zhang, 2014).

Building on past experience of producing and disseminating propaganda posters, the grassroots level invested heavily into a series of 'counter-radicalisation' peasant art contests. It was hoped that art works produced by peasants would resonate more effectively with locals (Wu and Li, 2014). Initially organised by the Propaganda Department of the Xinjiang Committee of the CCP, the Cultural Department of the XUAR, and the Federation of Literary and Art Circles of the XUAR, the peasant art contest gained great media coverage and inspired the grassroots governments to follow.

Mobilising peasants to create art requires more than providing the venue for exhibitions. From August to November, the contest went through six stages, including creation, organisation, tutorial, initial screening, second evaluation, and final evaluation. The local governments were involved in the entire process of the art creation, organising local artists to provide tutorials. In the process of creating art, the peasants not only produced a mass amount of propaganda material, but also educated themselves to learn about the government's attitude towards ethnic unity. As summarised in a report: 'the process of holding the contest is also a process for the masses to self-educate, self-inspire, self-purify, to take the initiative to oppose religious extremist ideology and three forces' (Lin, 2015). It is interesting to note the use of the word 'purify', to indicate the process of deradicalisation, as if extremist ideas are stains that can be removed by washing with propaganda.

The grassroots governments played an important role in disseminating peasants' art. The paintings were displayed across Xinjiang, both offline and online, and turned into posters or calendars which were then disseminated in counties, villages, and communities; the paintings were written into a DVD which was sent down to local units of government; 'excellent' works were to be published as pamphlets, displayed on local noticeboards, billboards, or displayed as spray-painting on the 'cultural wall' (Tianshanwang, 2015). Sometimes the propaganda materials were repackaged at the grassroots level. In Baicheng county, a 'cultural products dispatch station' (*wenhua chanpin peisong zhan*) was established to localise propaganda so that it could be better received by the local masses (Wang, 2014).

The messages conveyed by the peasants' art contests have compressed complex realities into simple dualist oppositions of good and evil, the masses and the enemies, educated and obscurantist, and pure and impure, 'reducing every issue in a complicated life to a single set of slogans that are said to embody the truth as a totality' (Lifton, 1981 [1996]). While 'purity' is not a dominating idea in the discourse of counter-terrorism, local officials' references to it indicate the continuities of the good/evil and us/them dichotomy that plagued the Mao era. As Robert J. Lifton (1996) puts it, 'The demand for purity is a call for radical separation of good and evil within the environment and within oneself'. Therefore the process of turning counter-radicalisation policies into art involves more than political artistic creation, but more specifically requires a confession that enforces conformity through denouncing old, backward, ignorant ways of life, and declaring one's rebirth through 'big propaganda and education' (*da xuanjiang*), 'big lambasting' (*da jiepi*), 'big reflection' (*da fansi*), and 'big reprimand' (*da shengtao*). By reproducing the propagandists' worldviews, peasant artists share their power of being the ultimate judges of good and evil.

Despite warnings against 'movement-style' political campaigns, the case of peasant art contests demonstrates that when counter-radicalisation measures deemed 'successful' are replicated and rolled out on a large scale at the grassroots level, the kind of language used in state–society communication starts to acquire cult-like characteristics often seen in the Mao era: 'repetitiously centred on all-encompassing jargon, prematurely abstract, highly categorical, relentlessly judging, and … deadly dull' (Lifton, 1989: 429).

FORMING KINSHIP

'Becoming a family' is not only part of the rhetoric that imagines 'the people of all ethnic groups closely united like pomegranate seeds' within the big family of the Chinese nation (*zhonghua minzu*). Also, in a literal sense, individuals of the Visit, Benefit, and Gather working teams are required to pair up with designated families, referring to them and treating them as their own relatives. Gao and Tyson (2020) highlight this unusual practice of legitimation through an invasive process of kinship-claiming. Kinship-forming events aim to bring officials and the masses closely together, requiring regular visits; living, studying, and working together; and learning each other's languages.

In October 2017, the XUAR Party Committee mobilised all cadres in Xinjiang to form kinship with grassroots masses. It is clear from the 2018 Xinjiang Yearbook (Statistic Bureau of Xinjiang Uyghur Autonomous Region, 2019) that the government sought to institutionalise (*zhiduhua*) and normalise (*changtaihua*) and extend the duration (*changxiaohua*) of the kinship-forming practice. Mainstream media, including *Xinjiang Daily*, *Xinjiang Economy*, Xinjiang People's Broadcasting Station, and Xinjiang Television, set up special columns for Ethnic Groups Unite as a Family (*minzu tuanjie yijiaqi*), using different ethnic languages to produce a massive amount of propaganda material. Grassroots units encouraged those who participated in the kinship-forming activities to tell their stories through public speeches, in-home propaganda talks, virtual talks via loudspeakers installed in rural villages, an interactive question-and-answer, quiz, and Aken songs. The Office of the XUAR Ethnic Groups Unite as a Family Leading Group, together with the Office of the Cyberspace Administration, launched an online campaign entitled I Am a Pomegranate Seed. Such a title reproduces the official narrative on ethnic unity that envisions ethnic groups hugging each other tightly as if they were pomegranate seeds. This campaign attracted 10 200 entries, some of which were published by mainstream platforms such as Tianshanwang and WeChat, and reposted by Xinhua, CCTV, Phoenix, and Sina, among others.

To institutionalise Ethnic Groups Unite as a Family, the grassroots units, such as local governments, enterprises, schools, and XPCC divisions, turned the loosely defined term 'ethnic unity' into a quantitively measurable quota (*zhibiao*). For example, Tarim University stipulates that from 11 September to the end of December 2019, each of its departments must carry out at least three inter-ethnic networking events (Office of the Party Committee, 2019). When the Seventh Division of the XPCC organised its sixth Ethnic Groups Unite as a Family networking week, it required cadres to visit designated households at least three times, spend at least three days living in their homes, and hold themed events at least twice. After the visits, cadres will be required to submit reports and photos. Cadres' attendance will be checked through a designated data management platform which shows how many times cadres have befriended their adopted families on WeChat and registered their attendance (United Front Department, 2020).

Such events seek to impress the masses by materialising the 'kindness' of the party. In addition to assistance on issues such as accessing medical care, schooling, and employment, those who joined the scheme enjoy some other privileges. For example, the Urumqi Railway Bureau set up a special train named 'Ethnic Groups Unite as a Family', with a dedicated waiting room for cadres and their adopted families (Statistic Bureau of Xinjiang Uyghur Autonomous Region, 2019).

Required networking activities turned faceless propaganda into individuals who might empathise and care for the locals. However, replicating the same model within every community does not always achieve the intended target of uniting the locals. Cadres have found creative ways to circumvent regulations, such as verbally asking adopted families for positive comments about their work (Gao and Tyson, 2020). As cadres mainly answer to their superiors, the initiative aiming at easing ethnic tensions often degenerates into formalism at the grassroots level.

CONCLUSION

This chapter has highlighted the fact that while the world seems to have moved entirely onto the Internet, the CCP poured a huge amount of resources into mobilising the grassroots to participate physically in propaganda in the form of various cultural events, public statements and loyalty-pledging rituals, and kinship-forming network activities. As such, the pre-Internet persuasion tactics in China's counter-terrorism efforts reveal striking continuities with Maoist-style propaganda techniques. Imposed physical participation changes people's behaviour so dramatically that they become part of the propaganda apparatus. The Maoist doctrine on the political function of art and culture remains prominent in open letters, musicals, dances, sketches, and paintings. They evoke the memories of Model Operas (*yangbanxi*), propaganda posters, and the 'loyalty dance' (*zhongzi wu*) of Mao's China that fundamentally reconfigure art and culture for political purposes. Meetings to 'speak up and brandish the swords' remind us of those that 'recall bitterness and reflect on sweetness' (*yiku sitian*) during the Socialist Education Movement, in which individuals were asked to think of the past hardships and appreciate the present good life through comparison (Anagnost and Comaroff, 1997).

Both were almost routinised into a form of religious ritual that educates the people to see truth within the framework provided by the official narratives. The practices of self-purification through confession, criticism, and self-criticism are characteristic of the tradition of thought reform built on the Soviet model. These propaganda techniques reveal an underlying inconsistency about governance in China. While the state has been in power for over half a century, it still relies heavily on revolutionary modes of mass mobilisation. In its transition from a revolutionary party to a ruling party, the CCP struggles to maintain legitimacy from alternative sources. Participatory propaganda gradually limits people's ability to think in alternative ways, as they learn to speak, live, and create in a way rigidly prescribed by the CCP through the repetition of revolutionary songs, observing the patriotic rituals, retelling the same stories of cadres' kindness, and lambasting the evilness of the 'three forces'.

Although this chapter does not seek to address the reception of counter-radicalisation propaganda, research on the 'vocational training camps' in the XUAR (Zenz, 2019; Zenz and Leibold, 2019; Roberts, 2020) suggests that coercive persuasion, in combination with a number of other coercive measures, might have produced a negative image of the state that it wished to avoid.[4] Although some research shows a surprising degree of public support for the presence of the government in propaganda production and dissemination in China (Esarey et al., 2017), the attitudes of the Uyghurs – the target audience of counter-radicalisation narratives – remain difficult to grasp, because the expression of alternative interpretations of history and ethnic relations risks violating the very purpose of the 'propaganda and education' (*xuanjiao*), which is to establish 'correct outlooks' on these issues. In this context, the 'success' in translating the Mass Line into actual support among the Uyghur population is questionable, as the 'support' can only be measured by a high level of political conformity, which can be induced by the fear of penalties as much as by genuine approval.

Words can be used as a weapon that must be handled carefully with reasonable knowledge about what the weapon can and cannot achieve. Similar efforts are found in other countries. The Think Again, Turn Away initiative under the US Department of State facilitated the sharing of stories, images, and arguments to challenge the extremist ideology, which were ridiculed by ISIS sympathisers (Braddock, 2020: 6). A cross-country study of educational initiatives in counter-extremism reveals that despite the prevalence of some preventative initiatives, such as cognitive behavioural initiatives or mentoring initiatives, it is difficult to evaluate whether they have achieved the intended outcomes (Davies, 2018: 15). Unlike other programmes, such as the Building Resilience against Violent Extremism Initiative in Kenya that used stories of returning fighters to counteract terrorist narratives, the Chinese state's strict control over the information about terrorist cases has minimised the exposure of stories of returning fighters. China's approach to countering violent extremism indicates that the Chinese state is in a similar dilemma whereby efforts to co-opt community members might result in further erosion of the credibility of its narratives. While 'grassroots celebrities', opinion leaders, teachers, and intellectuals were encouraged to speak up because of their influence within the Uyghur community, their endorsement faded into a haze of propaganda in the absence of alternative voices that broaden the narrowly defined 'correct outlooks' on ethnic history, culture, and inter-ethnic relations. The CCP's ability to ensure implementation through 'movement-style' governance allows the state propaganda apparatus to reach deep into communities and penetrate various spheres of life, while its efforts to evaluate the effectiveness in winning hearts and minds, as evidenced by the reports from Visit, Benefit, and Gather teams, remain largely superficial.

NOTES

1. China has a tradition of launching 'strike hard' campaigns against perceived security threats, such as crime, drugs, drug trafficking, and prostitution. Strike Hard against Violent Terrorism was launched in 2014 following several high-profile terrorist incidents in 2013 and 2014.

2. 'Red songs' are also known as revolutionary songs that praise the CCP, the People's Liberation Army, and People's Republic of China and socialism. Revolutionary songs 'became instruments of socialization, political control, and ideological persuasion in Communist China during the Cultural Revolution' (Lu, 2004: 120).
3. The XPCC is a semi-military organisation in Xinjiang that performs administrative duties, promotes economic development, and ensures social stability.
4. According to Ajit Singh and Max Blumenthal (2019), the general understanding of the 'vocational training camps' in the West is largely based on the dubious studies by the US government-backed network of Chinese Human Rights Defenders and Adrian Zenz, a far-right fundamentalist Christian who 'believes he is "led by God" on a "mission" against China' (Chin, 2019).

REFERENCES

Abudurusuli, M. (2018), 'Guiding and inspiring people with advanced culture', available at http://wap.xjdaily.com/xjrb/20180206/98555.html, accessed 3 October 2020.

Anagnost, A. and J.L. Comaroff (1997), *National Past-Times: Narrative, Representation, and Power in Modern China*, Durham, NC: Duke University Press.

Asmolov, G. (2019), 'The effects of participatory propaganda: from socialization to internalization of conflicts', *Journal of Design and Science*, 6: 1–25, available at https://jods.mitpress.mit.edu/pub/jyzg7j6x/release/2.

Bageqi village working team of the Xinjiang Branch of the Chinese Academy of Sciences (2018), 'Bageqi village organised returning college and university students to carry out "speak up and brandish the swords" themed activity', available at http://www.xjb.ac.cn/ztlm/fhjzt/201807/t20180727_5051146.html, accessed 6 October 2020.

Braddock, K. (2020), *Weaponized Words: The Strategic Role of Persuasion in Violent Radicalization and Counter-Radicalization*, Cambridge: Cambridge University Press.

Chin, J. (2019), 'The German data diver who exposed China's Muslim crackdown', *Wall Street Journal*, available at https://www.wsj.com/articles/the-german-data-diver-who-exposed-chinas-muslim-crackdown-11558431005, accessed 1 March 2021.

Dai, L. (2014), 'It is our responsibility and mission to never remain silent: over 200 Uyghur writers, poets and scholars signed an open letter', available at http://xj.people.com.cn/n/2014/0625/c188514-21512620.html, accessed 4 October 2020.

Davies, L. (2018), *Review of Educational Initiatives in Counter-Extremism Internationally: What Works?* Gothenburg: Segerstedt Institute, University of Gothenburg.

Esarey, A., D. Stockmann, and J. Zhang (2017), 'Support for propaganda: Chinese perceptions of public service advertising', *Journal of Contemporary China*, 26(103): 101–17.

Farkas, J., J. Schou, and C. Neumayer (2018), 'Cloaked Facebook pages: exploring fake Islamist propaganda in social media', *New Media and Society*, 20(5): 1850–1867.

Feng, W. (2016) 'On cultural counter-terrorism and counter-radicalisation', *Journal of Rule of Law*, 1: 96–103, available at https://cati.nwupl.edu.cn/bgpl/rdsp/681.htm, accessed 4 October 2020.

Gao, H. and A. Tyson (2020), 'Poverty relief in China: a comparative analysis of kinship contracts in four provinces', *Journal of Contemporary China*, 29(126): 901–915.

Garrett, R.K. and B.E. Weeks (2013), 'The promise and peril of real-time corrections to political misperceptions', *Proceedings of the 2013 Conference on Computer Supported Cooperative Work*, 23–27 February, San Antonio, TX.

Gou F., J. Xi, and B. Yang (2019), 'Xinjiang Yanqi County held a thoughts and culture propaganda cadres training class', available at https://ishare.ifeng.com/c/s/7kgnAVQ2NHF, accessed 8 October 2020.

Guanchazhe (2014), 'Behind the 11 Uyghur students' open letter condemning violent terrorist attacks: we will not remain silent', available at http://www.guancha.cn/society/2014_05_04_226367.shtml, accessed 31 December 2017.

Helmus, T.C., E. Bodine-Baron, A. Radin, M. Magnuson, J. Mendelsohn, et al. (2018), 'Russian social media influence: understanding Russian propaganda in Eastern Europe', Santa Monica, CA: Rand

Corporation, available at https://www.rand.org/pubs/testimonies/CT496.html, accessed 1 March 2021.
Hengdengshijiuduan (2020), 'Returning students' "speak up and brandish the swords" speeches', available at https://m.dawendou.com/jianghuagao/biaotaifayan/103768.html, accessed 24 October 2020.
Hu, Y. (2014), 'Cultural counter-terrorism: a theoretical reflection based on practical issues', available at http://theory.people.com.cn/n/2014/0917/c168825-25676056.html, accessed 3 October 2020.
Jowett, G.S. and V. O'Donnell (2019), *Propaganda and Persuasion* (7th edn), London: SAGE.
Karamay Government (2020), '"Visit, Benefit and Gather" themed performance held in Karamay', available at https://www.klmy.gov.cn/002/002003/20200119/2a945ecf-f00f-4d1d-bda2-062f532844db.html, accessed 6 October 2020.
Liberation Army Daily (1967), 'Study "Serve the People"', *Peking Review*, 10(2): 9–13, available at https://www.marxists.org/subject/china/peking-review/1967/PR1967-02e.htm, accessed 2 October 2020.
Lifton, Robert J. (1981 [1996]), 'Cult formation', The Harvard Mental Health Letter, 7(8), February 1981, reprinted in *AFF News* 2(5), 1996.
Lifton, R.J. (1989), *Thought Reform and the Psychology of Totalism: A Study of 'Brainwashing' in China*, Chapel Hill, NC: University of North Carolina Press.
Lin, W. (2015), 'De-radicalisation peasants' art contest in Xinjiang amplifies positive energy', *People's Daily Online*, 1 January, available at http://xj.people.com.cn/n/2015/0101/c368617-23413939.html, accessed 3 February 2018.
Lu, X. (2004), *Rhetoric of the Chinese Cultural Revolution: The Impact on Chinese Thought, Culture, and Communication*, Columbia, SC: University of South Carolina Press.
Mejias, U.A. and N.E. Vokuev (2017), 'Disinformation and the media: the case of Russia and Ukraine media', *Culture and Society*, 39(7): 1027–1042.
Newman, E. and C. Zhang (2020), 'The Mass Line approach to countering violence extremism: the road from propaganda to hearts and minds', *Asian Security*, 12 October, advance online publication, available at https://www.tandfonline.com/doi/full/10.1080/14799855.2020.1825379.
Office of the Party Committee (2019), 'Notice on further deepening the "Ethnic Groups Unite as a Family" and ethnic unity networking events', available at https://www.taru.edu.cn/news/nry1.jsp?urltype=news.NewsContentUrl&wbtreeid=10533&wbnewsid=280306, accessed 7 October 2020.
People's Daily Commentator (2014), 'Resolutely oppose religious extremist ideologies', 8 May, available at http://opinion.people.com.cn/n/2014/0508/c1003-24989168.html, accessed 6 October 2020.
Propaganda Department of Karamay Municipal Party Committee (2020), '"Visit, Benefit and Gather" themed performance held in Karamay', available at http://www.xj.xinhuanet.com/zt/2020-01/17/c_1125473483.htm, accessed 14 October 2020.
Repnikova, M. and K. Fang (2018), 'Authoritarian participatory persuasion 2.0: netizens as thought work collaborators in China', *Journal of Contemporary China*, 27(113): 763–779.
Roberts, S.R. (2020), *The War on the Uyghurs*, Princeton, NJ: Princeton University Press.
Singh, A. and M. Blumenthal (2019), 'China detaining millions of Uyghurs? Serious problems with claims by US-backed NGO and far-right researcher "led by God" against Beijing', *Grayzone*, 21 December, available at https://thegrayzone.com/2019/12/21/china-detaining-millions-uyghurs-problems-claims-us-ngo-researcher/, accessed 5 November 2020.
Statistic Bureau of Xinjiang Uyghur Autonomous Region (2019), '"Ethnic Groups Unite as a Family" and ethnic unity networking events', available at http://www.xjtonglan.com/xjxd/xjmc/4613.shtml, accessed 7 October 2020.
Tianshanwang (2015), '"Counter-radicalisation" Peasant Art Contest: use art to speak up and brandish the swords', available at http://www.guanhaihk.com/home/index/article/id/1436/p/2.html, accessed 3 October 2020.
United Front Department (2020), 'The Seventh Division of the XPCC organised the six round of "kinship-forming" activities', available at http://www.nqs.gov.cn/nqs/pmain/420/20200116/112521625140763.html, accessed 17 October 2020.
Wang, S. (2014), 'Let cultural propaganda be everyone's duty and task', *Guangming Daily*, 26 October, available at http://epaper.gmw.cn/gmrb/html/2014-10/26/nw.D110000gmrb_20141026_6-02.htm?div=-1, accessed 14 August 2020.

Wanless, A. and M. Berk (2017), 'Participatory propaganda: the engagement of audiences in the spread of persuasive communications', *Social Media and Social Order, Culture Conflict 2.0 Conference*, Oslo, 30 November–2 December.

Wanless, A. and M. Berk (2019), 'The audience is the amplifier: participatory propaganda', in P. Baines, N. O'Shaughnessy, and N. Snow (eds), *The SAGE Handbook of Propaganda*, London: SAGE, pp. 85–104.

Woolley, S.C. and P.N. Howard (2018), *Computational Propaganda: Political Parties, Politicians, and Political Manipulation on Social Media*, Oxford: Oxford University Press.

Wu, M. and X. Li (2014), 'Counter-radicalisation peasant arts inspire the masses', 24 November, available at http://www.xjdaily.com/sfhh/005/1152594.shtml, accessed 5 October 2020.

Wunaiwoye (2020), 'Personal statements for "speak up and brandish the swords" events', available at https://m.dawendou.com/jianghuagao/biaotaifayan/1597.html, accessed 24 October 2020.

Xi, T. (2020), 'Students' speeches countering terrorism, speaking up and brandishing the swords', available at https://m.dawendou.com/jianghuagao/biaotaifayan/16514.html, accessed 5 October 2020.

Xinhua (2014), 'Xi Jinping presided over the Politburo meeting to study further promoting social stability and long-term stability in Xinjiang', 26 May, available at: http://cpc.people.com.cn/n/2014/0526/c64094-25067153.html, accessed 3 October 2020.

Xinjiang Daily (2017), 'Extremist speech and conduct disrupt the order of normal social and cultural life', 14 July, available at http://www.zytzb.gov.cn/mzzj/112814.jhtml, accessed 3 October 2020.

Xinjiang Daily (2018), '"Visit, Benefit and Gather" performances are on the go', 28 June, available at http://xj.people.com.cn/n2/2018/0628/c186332-31754153.html, accessed 6 October 2020.

Xinjiang Daily Commentator (2014), 'Let brush become a powerful weapon of "counter-radicalisation"', 7 November, available at http://cpc.people.com.cn/pinglun/n/2014/1107/c78779-25993317.html, accessed 1 March 2020.

Xue, L. (2020), 'How to transform correspondents in the era of media convergence: Yanqi county carried out focused training for grassroots correspondents', available at https://www.hotbak.net/key/%E8%9E%8D%E5%AA%92%E4%BD%93%E6%97%B6%E4%BB%A3%E9%80%9A%E8%AE%AF%E5%91%98%E5%A6%82%E4%BD%95%E5%8F%98%E8%BA%AB%E6%96%B0%E7%96%86%E7%84%89%E8%80%86%E5%8E%BF%E5%BC%80%E5%B1%95%E5%9F%BA.html, accessed 8 October 2020.

Zenz, A. (2019), '"Thoroughly reforming them towards a healthy heart attitude": China's political re-education campaign in Xinjiang', *Central Asian Survey*, 38(1): 102–128.

Zenz, A. and J. Leibold (2019) 'Securitizing Xinjiang: police recruitment, informal policing and ethnic minority co-optation', *China Quarterly*, 242: 1–25.

Zhang, C. (2019), 'Community engagement under the mass line for counterterrorism in China', *Studies in Conflict and Terrorism*, 44(10): 1–19.

Zhang, S. (2014), 'Tour exhibition of excellent works from counter-radicalisation Xinjiang peasant art contest arrives in Kashgar', *Tianshanwang*, 5 December, available at http://news.sina.com.cn/c/2014-12-05/181831251730.shtml, accessed 5 October 2020.

Zhang, Y. (2014), '*We Will Not Remain Silent* is published to enhance ethnic unity', *Xinjiang Daily*, 11 July, available at http://www.chinanews.com/gn/2014/07-11/6376540.shtml, accessed 4 October 2020.

19. Countermeasures to extremist propaganda: a strategy for countering absolutist religious beliefs in northeast Nigeria

Jacob Udo-Udo Jacob

INTRODUCTION

This chapter is drawn from a Countering Violent Extremism (CVE) programme developed and implemented in the author's Fall 2016 class at the American University of Nigeria (AUN) Yola, for the Peer-to-Peer (P2P) Challenging Extremism Global University competition – an Obama White House initiative, jointly sponsored by the United States (US) State Department and Facebook.

Yola is less than 250 miles from Maiduguri, the birthplace of Boko Haram and the epicentre of the Boko Haram insurgency. In the autumn of 2014, at the height of the insurgency, Boko Haram insurgents captured Mubi, about 120 miles north of Yola. More than half of the city's estimated 400 000 residents fled to Yola, forcing a humanitarian crisis. As the Nigerian government, local and international humanitarian aid agencies were still figuring out how to feed and keep engaged the several thousands of displaced youth, tensions were rising between Christian and Muslim youth in the internally displacement persons (IDP) camps and communities. With limited access to education and livelihood opportunities, the mélange of displaced angry Muslim and Christian youths at the IDP camps presented a new threat to an already fragile society. Named #IAmABeliever, this CVE campaign was developed to build tolerance and create a converged space for divergent religious beliefs and identities to coexist in harmony.

THE P2P CHALLENGING EXTREMISM COMPETITION: PROGRAMME OVERVIEW

In response to the increasing global threats posed by violent extremist organisations (VEOs), in 2014 the US government hired EdVenture Partners (EVP), a California-based strategic communications firm, to engage college students globally in the fight against extremism (Moffett and Sgro, 2016). This approach was novel in one significant way: it involved students. Students were to conceptualise, plan, and implement an authentic campaign that resonated with their peers and communities. EVP had a history of previous collaborations with the US Department of State, the Central Intelligence Agency (CIA), and the Federal Bureau of Investigation (FBI), but this was different. With funding from the White House National Security Council, the US Department of Homeland Security, US Department of State, and the National Counterterrorism Centre, EVP launched the first global campaign in early 2015 with an initial cohort of 23. Facebook later joined as the technology partner in the autumn of 2015, and built a more globalised collaboration between a government agency, a tech giant, and education institutions in countering violent extremism. It was the first collaboration of its kind.

THE APPEALS OF EXTREMIST PROPAGANDA IN NORTHEAST NIGERIA

Since the Maitatsine Islamic revivalist movements of the 1980s, various Islamist groups have emerged in northern Nigeria and the broader West African Sahel (Isichei, 1987). However, they were swiftly subdued militarily. Boko Haram and its Islamic State West Africa (ISWA) splinter has endured despite relentless military pressure not only from Nigeria, but also from a regional Multinational Joint Task Force (MJTF), comprising the militaries of Nigeria and regional neighbours Niger, Chad, Benin, and Cameroon. Boko Haram presents two fundamental challenges to Nigeria and the MJTF that previous violent sects did not: (1) a well-defined ideology; and (2) a strong community that provides a place for belonging and, more importantly, a sense of group identity for members. Its ideology has its roots in Salafi jihadism, driven by Takfirism (Jacob and Akpan, 2015). Salafists believe that they alone incarnate the original practices and beliefs of the Prophet Muhammed and early Islamic clerics (Thurston, 2016). In Salafist-Takfirism, violence is legitimised against other Muslims who do not follow the prescribed absolutist beliefs (Barrett, 2014). Moderate Muslims and other Islamic denominations such as Shi'ites and Sufis are seen as kafirs or infidels, or even worse as kufars or disbelievers, thus deserving of execution.

Moreover, a strong sense of group membership extends to their spouses. As Hilary Matfess has argued, women have willingly followed their husbands and sons into Boko Haram because of the sense of community, respect, and protection that membership confers (Matfess, 2017). A robust religious identity blends with a strong ideology to create a community of like-minded believers. This can be very forceful in a context where notions of citizenship and national identity are both meaningless and dubious. Furthermore, the rising inequality caused by the brazen corruption and the ostentatious lifestyle of Nigeria's political elite has driven large segments of the country's youth, particularly in the northern part of the country, to seek alternative spaces for hope and transcendental meaning. Although Nigeria is ostensibly a secular democracy, abstract notions of secularism, the rule of law, the freedom of the press, and the judiciary have not translated into concrete economic dividends for the poor masses. Rising social discontent, mainly exacerbated by the increasing concentration of wealth in much fewer hands at the top of the political-economic chain, at the expense of the uneducated and the poor, have intensified a sense of resentment against the state and its various representations and constructs (Hansen, 2020). These range from law enforcement agencies and courts, to notions of Western education as the only licence to jobs and the good life.

Unfortunately, most of the Muslim youth in Nigeria lack education. According to a Pew Research global demographic study on differences in educational attainment, 61 per cent of Muslim adults have no formal schooling, compared with 26 per cent of Christian adults, with each making up about half of Nigeria's population (Pew Research Center, 2016). Young Muslims have seen their status and dignity degraded since Nigeria's return to democratic rule in 1999. The subsequent privatisation and commercialisation of previously state-owned parastatals by the Olusegun Obasanjo administration gave birth to a more knowledge-driven economy. The mostly uneducated northern Muslim youths were simply unprepared for the new economy that required a more educated and technically agile workforce.

Twenty years later, the conditions are far worse. There is a collective sense of hopelessness that now pervades disadvantaged communities in northern Nigeria. Although Nigeria's economy has been growing fairly steadily over the past two decades, resulting in rising urbanisation, it has been a much different story for most of the populations in the rural north of the country, where millions of young men have been dispossessed of economic opportunities and the dignity that comes with earning a living. These, left behind by the society and driven to the margins, are attracted to the appeals of extremist propaganda: a sense of purpose among a community of similar others that confers an identity woven around absolute religious beliefs; and a religious Hero who symbolises those beliefs.

THE PROPAGANDA OF ABSOLUTIST RELIGIOUS BELIEFS

Absolutist religious beliefs have been at the root of religious propaganda and the many atrocities that have been committed in the name of religion throughout history, from the Crusades of the medieval period to the more recent Salafi jihadism which broke into the global limelight with Al-Qaeda's attacks against the US on 9/11. At the core of absolutist religious beliefs is propaganda of idealised sacrosanctity and the vilified 'Other', often labelled as heretic, infidel, or blasphemer. All propaganda labels for the non-believer are laden with notions not just of wrongness, but also and, most importantly, of judgement and condemnation, punishable by at least excommunication and at most execution. Absolutism demands absolute loyalty and submission to identified beliefs, which can provide the justification and legitimacy for extremist violence. The role of extremist propaganda is to create extra-state legitimising structures for absolutism.

Legitimised absolutisms provide the justification for acts in the name of religious beliefs or a religious Hero. The essence of religious absolutism is that the believer is not subject to reason or the regular checks external to the dictates of the beliefs. Legitimacy is embedded in the belief. The believer is essentially the authority, and their beliefs are the creed and bond that bind fellow believers together. These provide the networked power that beliefs need to endure and to thrive. State authorities must increasingly contest for legitimacy with absolutist religious beliefs. Just having the title of a state or military is not enough to guarantee legitimacy. As Hoskins and O'Loughlin have aptly noted, legitimacy requires lots of representational work (Hoskins and O'Loughlin, 2010).

When religious beliefs challenge the absolutism of state authority, the state is weakened and vulnerable to civil unrest. Anarchy becomes inevitable. The Hobbesian view of absolutism, though tied to political authority, applies here: it is the justification of absolute obedience to a power structure, which can be justified based on presumed total ownership of that which is supremely true and righteous and worth defending. Essentially, the owned absolute truth is not just a means but also a form of power without limits or responsibility. Beliefs thus become more than mere expressions of religious or transcendental devotion. They become an organising principle and a reference point for regularising and rationalising behaviours with the Other, and with the social self. When this is the collective reality in society, as it is in northern Nigeria, a patrimony of religious beliefs emerges. Radicalised power and social rewards flow directly from the belief to the believer, and vice versa. A society of believers emerges, quite distinct from the social and political structures and systems in society. There is fundamentally no distinction between the believer and the belief, with both being swallowed up by the other to form one indistinguishable mesh. The believer's identity, networks, and concepts of self, the Other, and reality are tied to the belief.

THE PROPAGANDA OF THE RELIGIOUS HERO

One of the fundamental findings that emerged from our formative survey was the role of the religious Hero, defined here as the person who symbolises the absoluteness of religious text and through whom believers establish a vicarious primordial relationship with their religious beliefs. I use Hero here in a similar way as Martin Heidegger does in his exposition on the choosing of a hero: a deliberate, intentional decision to make one's life a replication of an original authentic life (Heidegger, 1980). The life of Jesus Christ, for example, is the quintessentially authentic life after which Christians seek to pattern their lives. The Heideggerian Hero, as used here, inspires devotion and propels believers into a mechanical, amorphous, collective abnegation of personal will and agency in favour of a collective unified faith that modulates personal and collective behaviour. In modelling the Hero's devotion to the letter, the believer models scriptural living.

Heroes are not just faith leaders. They wield enormous personal and social influence and domination, as they are associated with scriptural texts and, by extension, religious beliefs. The propaganda of the religious Hero is contained in the human face and form that they give to scripture through their absolute devotion to doctrinal beliefs. This bestows enormous powers and influence on them, as they become the standard and authority for the right form of religious behaviour. The Hero's authority is derived from the absoluteness of his beliefs. The more absolutist the belief, the greater the patrimonial authority that the Hero enjoys among believers. Indeed, the legitimacy of patrimonial authority is tied to the absolutism of the Hero's beliefs, with the Hero seen as a champion of the believer. The Hero may not necessarily be the traditionally recognised religious leader. Rather, the Hero may be obscure, but his patrimonial influence is not, so long as he represents the most extremist expressions of doctrinal beliefs. The Hero commends absolute devotion to equally absolute beliefs, for devotion to the absolute beliefs is an extended devotion to the Hero. Extremist leaders such as Osama bin Laden, Abu Bakr al-Baghdadi, and Abubakar Shekau, do not have any of the conventional religious credentials that Islamic clerics have. They do not have any special spiritual powers like the ancient or modern saints and sages of their faith. However, what they do have in common, like all other religious Heroes, is the absolutism of their beliefs and their ability to command devotion based on that absolutism.

The misstep of working with 'moderate' religious leaders in countering violent extremism is that the moderate leader, though he may be the Emir, Sultan, or an established cleric, lacks the patrimonial authority that true believers look up to for standards and patterns for the manifest expression of their beliefs. The Hero is not just a metaphor for absolute beliefs; the Hero is the believer's alter ego, everything the believer wants to be. Devotion to the Hero is seen as devotion to scripture.

Extremist individuals see their Heroes as templates for their beliefs. The Hero does not just model and project unto believers who they are and what they stand for, but also who they are not and what they are against. As in Heidegger's Hero, the heroic template that extremist individuals and societies choose provides a sense of what is and is not important, and in many ways shapes the cause and battles they choose to take on. Understanding to whom a religious community looks to as their Hero for patterns and standards of sacredness is critical to developing a compelling intervention strategy.

In its patrimonial form, absolute religious beliefs mutate into systems of social control, domination, and rewards. Scriptural injunctions, symbolised and signified by the most religious Heroes, penetrate the society not through mainstream or conventional pipelines such as mosques or churches, mainstream media, family units, and so on, but through diffused repetitions of behaviours, codes, and mores which eventually become standards of religious behaviour. In this extended form, absolutist beliefs go beyond the regular religious systems, personalities, or institutions that modulate religious practices and performances in society. They define the forms and patterns of internal and external relationships.

The influence of religious beliefs and the Heroes who represent them can be sublime, but hugely influential and hegemonic. Gramsci's thesis on hegemony (see Bates, 1975) suggests that groups accept the ideas, values, and leadership of other groups or persons, not necessarily because they are physically or mentally induced, or because they are ideologically indoctrinated, but because they have a reason of their own to do so. It is this 'spontaneous consent', be it moral, superstitious, spiritual, or conceptual, that creates a fundamentally powerful role-set for religious beliefs and the Heroes who symbolise their most absolute doctrinal versions. Believers have their own reasons to believe. By modelling absolute devotion to religious texts, and ascribing piety to similar absolute adherence, Heroes exert normative influence and social control. For example, Boko Haram's Abubakar Shekau constantly criticises and derides the Emirs and other traditional religious leaders as *kafirs* or disbelievers, so the religious Hero advocates a hard-line stance. It is not long before the hard-line posture of the Hero, who in most cases is socially embedded in the community, becomes the social norm.

Absolutists or followers of the Hero apply the standards of absolute beliefs across situations. Situations and people become invariant, and behaviours are not determined by the situation's variables but by the rigidly formed and held religious beliefs about appropriate actions and behaviours. Thus, in any given circumstance, the right form of behaviour is predetermined by existing beliefs. Through repetitions of similar behaviours and devotion, a social norm is created. Built into its core is a predetermined notion of the right form of religious behaviour. Thus the influence of the Hero is diffused across religious society.

#IAMABELIEVER: THE CAMPAIGN STRATEGY

Countering diffused absolutist religious beliefs is difficult, if not impossible, for they are sacrosanct and radicalised extensions of the believer. They determine standards of normative behaviour. Instead of seeking to counter them, the #IAmABeliever campaign sought to respect and validate all beliefs as beliefs, but distinct from the believer. However, before I discuss the campaign strategy, I will briefly provide a taxonomy of the absolutist beliefs we encountered during our formative research.

Table 19.1   Categories of absolutist beliefs

Category of absolutist beliefs	Description	Example of statements of belief
Legitimating beliefs	Legitimating beliefs exceptionalise and justify one's faith or ideology as superior to other beliefs and above the laws of the state.	Our God is the only true God; therefore, it is more important for us to obey the laws of God than the laws of the state (which are made by unbelievers).
Unifying beliefs	Unifying beliefs construct, mobilise, and deploy hatred into an emotionally unifying resource.	The Other group is opposed to everything we stand for. We must stick together to resist them.
Othering beliefs	Othering beliefs create an all-encompassing damned conceptual category for non-believers.	Those who do not believe what we believe are condemned or will go to hell or deserve whatever evil befalls them.
Blaming beliefs	Blaming beliefs create a unifying, universalised, and justified object of blame or guilt.	The problems in our society and in the world are caused by other people who do not share what our group believes.
Threatened body beliefs	Threatened body beliefs consider one's social identity as under existential threat, hence worthy of active defence. This gives mobilising power to the believers' collective body.	Our (religious/ethnic/racial) group is under threat. If we do not do something to defend our group now, then our children and future generations will not grow to meet this group in existence.

Taxonomy of Absolutist Beliefs

From a formative survey of 192 religious individuals in northeast Nigeria and follow-up focus group discussions we identified five categories of absolutist religious beliefs (see Table 19.1). It is noteworthy that these are not representative of the dominant beliefs in Nigeria, considering that we used a very small sample. However, they do indicate the extremist religious beliefs that the campaign sought to challenge, and which informed the campaign strategy. Moreover, they cover core characteristics or facets of the beliefs and ideologies upon which extremist groups, including nativist, neo-Nazi, and other alt-right movements, build their collective identity. They also provide essential signposts and a basis for anchoring counternarrative campaigns in societies where members of extremist groups hold similar beliefs or in contexts where dogmatic beliefs have taken over faith.

The campaign described in this chapter was built on the assumption that support for absolute beliefs, as Eric Hoffer aptly observed in his 1951 classic *The True Believer*, does not necessarily provide a transcendental spiritual meaning, but a radicalised substitute for the loss of faith in oneself (Hoffer, 1951).

The #IAmABeliever campaign sought to disidentify the absolute believer from the above beliefs as the first step towards deradicalisation. The campaign revolved around the concept of: I am a believer, but I am also human, a brother, a sister, an artisan, a father, a mother, a student, and so on.

The success of the campaign depended on how well we inspired target audiences to see themselves as individuals distinct from their absolute religious beliefs. Rather than seek to challenge the absolutist beliefs, we decided that the campaign should:

1. Focus on relatedness and interdependence of all believers.
2. Emphasise the validity of all religious beliefs, without putting any down.
3. Integrate each belief into the larger context of other beliefs.
4. Focus not on persuasion but on understanding, mutual agreement, and collective action.

5. Focus less on trying to change the opinion or behaviours of individuals but more on transforming relationships.

THEORETICAL FRAMEWORK: THE CONVERGENCE MODEL OF COMMUNICATION

A vast majority of counternarrative messaging can be grouped into two broad categories, namely campaigns that seek to counter extremist narratives, and those that promote pro-tolerant attitudes and behaviours. The former assumes that counter-messaging campaigns, like bullets or hypodermic needles, can achieve desired impacts when they hit the target. In contrast, the latter assumes that messages, like vaccines, can be deployed to inoculate minds against extremist appeals. The two are based on two different approaches, but they do share a common linear causal-determinist model. They both privilege the message or the narrative, and much less the context within which meanings of phenomena are made, or behaviours are formed and performed.

However, since the 1970s, starting from the influential work of Everett Rogers and D. Lawrence Kincaid, communication scholars have criticised this linear model of communication (Rogers and Kincaid, 1981). Rogers and Kincaid's convergence/network model of communication provides an interesting conceptual framework for the approach that was used in the campaign. Essential to the convergence model is Rogers and Kincaid's argument that communication is a dynamic process of knowledge or information-sharing through an ongoing process of dialogue or mutual interaction between or among active participants. Rogers and Kincaid's convergence model addresses the intersection between shared information, mutual understanding, and (collective) action. A key element in the model is that information-sharing occurs horizontally among participants in a social ecosystem. The outcome at the individual level is perception, interpretation, and understanding, which can lead to belief and, subsequently, mutual agreement. Another critical element in the model is that it implies an ongoing dialogue between participants until a mutual agreement is reached to enable (collective) action. It is important to note that within the convergence model, differing groups do not always converge: they can diverge. There could be misperceptions, misinterpretations, misunderstandings, and disbeliefs, which can ultimately lead to disagreements and conflicts. The model envisions a cyclical process of dialogue between two contending psychological realities, where the feedback gleaned can lead to more exchanges and potentially lead to mutual understanding, mutual agreement, and collective action. Convergence does not necessarily imply perfect agreement, but rather beliefs diffusing across two opposing realities to create a mutual understanding and a more balanced social reality (Rogers and Kincaid, 1981).

The convergence model provides an interesting conceptual framework for a campaign that seeks not necessarily to persuade, but to create a multidimensional space for dialogue to happen between groups, and within oneself, and with the Other. It is built on the assumption that the more people communicate and interact with each other, the more similar their views of the world can become. The mission of the campaign then was to create multiple spaces and opportunities for communicative interaction and for shared beliefs to coexist and interact within a setting where each belief is respected, valued, and validated as a belief distinct from the believer. This was articulated in the emphasis of 'I am' in the concept of 'I am a believer'.

The 'I am' part of the campaign sought to honour and value the individual believer, not just create aggregates of 'believers'.

APPLICATION OF THE CONVERGENCE MODEL TO THE CAMPAIGN

The physical reality originates from the religious Hero's model of piety and devotion. So, the campaign's mission was to create a social reality drawn from the believer's new perception, interpretation, and understanding of their religious beliefs, but in relation to who they are.

The campaign followed a six-step plan to move our target audiences from the divergent psychological realities of their beliefs to mutual understanding, and thus a new social reality. Here are the steps:

1. Emphasise personal identities.
2. Emphasise beliefs as beliefs.
3. Use credible religious voices to support the campaign.
4. Use songs/local music to reach the youth.
5. Inspire personal, collective, and legacy action.
6. Build a shared digital religious space.

Emphasise Personal Identities

We worked with a local youth NGO in Mubi, a neighbouring town that was captured, occupied, and mutilated by Boko Haram in November 2014, to develop a programme on a local radio station. The programme featured interviews and in-depth personal stories of a range of absolute believers from Muslim and Christian faith groups. The personal interviews emphasised the interviewees' personal identities: their family background, their occupation or vocation, their favorite meals, and various aspects of their identities other than their religious beliefs. Unmistakably, the campaign's intention was to create an opening for the personal (non-religious) identities of absolute believers to emerge so that both the interviewees and their listeners can value those other aspects of their identities. Due to its popularity, this programme continued on the youth radio station even after the campaign had come to an end. More interestingly, the youth that participated in the radio programme went on to create a non-governmental organisation, Inganta Rayuwa Peace Network, and took the campaign further in their own way.

Emphasise Beliefs as Beliefs

A crucial part of the strategy was emphasising beliefs and showing them for what they are. By discussing beliefs and describing the distinctiveness of each belief (not morally or judgmentally), it was possible to highlight the variety and differences in beliefs. There was no attempt to analyse any of the beliefs based on how true or false they were, but the campaign placed emphasis on their beingness in a descriptive manner. By describing, rather than explaining, the different Islamic and Christian beliefs, it was possible to treat each belief with respect, showing the distinctiveness of each, and how different they all are. Even within each tradition, it was possible to show the intricate nuances of beliefs within the religious groups. We aimed to show that the value of beliefs is not in whether they are true or false, but in the respect they receive by both believers and non-believers. This was diffused principally through the youth radio programme and through various short video clips on YouTube and other social media platforms.

Use Credible Religious Voices to Support the Campaign

One of the most critical aspects of our work was identifying credible religious voices to support the campaign. We worked with a Catholic Bishop and a respected Muslim Imam, who was also a professor. His mosque was mainly attended by college students and young adults in the Yola community, so he had credibility among the relevant population. However, because he was also a university professor, he was seen as too moderate and too academic, if not elitist, by several of the at-risk Muslims, particularly the uneducated. We were successful in finding a religious Hero in the neighbouring Mubi who attended a story-telling event with our team. The story-telling event brought Muslim and Christian security groups together to share their experience of the Boko Haram invasion of Mubi. Just the presence of the Imam, who is highly revered among the absolute believers, was a massive boost to the event. The stories from the event showed that Christians as well as Muslims lost both property and loved ones from the invasion.

Use Songs/Local Music to Attract the Youth

Music is a vital part of the local culture in northeastern Nigeria, particularly among the youth. We used music to popularise the slogan 'I am a believer'. A local musician, who was also a part of the class project, created a song with lyrics drawn from the core message of the campaign. In addition to adding much-needed fun and entertainment to the campaign, the song gave an identity to the campaign, as it soon turned into an anthem among young followers, keen to show both their religiosity and their 'coolness'.

Inspire Personal, Collective, and Legacy Action

A critical aspect of any campaign is to inspire personal action, collective action, and legacy action, as follows.

Personal action
It was critical to get individuals to take a form of action to show their support of the campaign, particularly in the early stages. We called for personal action on social media, mainly Facebook and Twitter. We first held a Tweetathon, encouraging people to tweet what they believed in for a chance to win a prize of free pizza and a T-shirt in a raffle draw. Within a few hours, #ChallengeExtremism became the No. 4 trending topic on Nigerian Twitter, reaching more than 1 million people. On Facebook, we invited our followers to post pictures and videos of themselves with posters showing different aspects of their identities.

Collective action

A key threshold of the campaign was having people come together outside of social media to mobilise and show their support. Our initial workshops with youth groups went well, but we wanted to expand the platform for people to come together to take action in support of the campaign. We held what we called the I-Believe football tournament. The football event served two purposes: first, to use sport as a means to popularise the campaign; and second, to construct new identity groups outside of the existing dominant religious identities. With the several thousands of jobless youth at the time (made up mainly of Boko Haram displaced persons), we received more applications for participation among our targeted population than we had space for. To participate in the football tournament, local youths created teams that had to be inter-religious. The four teams finally selected to participate involved youths from both Muslim and Christian communities. Before the commencement of the tournament, we held a seminar with participants to explain the campaign objectives and mission.

Football typically has red cards and yellow cards to punish deviant behaviour, but we introduced a 'green card' policy to encourage pro-social behaviours: if an opponent falls or is accidentally brought down, anyone from the other team who reaches out and pulls him up from the ground earns a green card for the team. There was a prize at the end of the tournament for the team with the highest number of green cards. With this, it was possible not only to get the teams to be less combative, but also to model the behaviours that we expected from the spectators who showed up for every game. The games provided opportunities to spread the message of the campaign further.

A leading Imam and a Catholic Bishop attended the tournament's finals and addressed the spectators on the importance of religious unity and interdependence. The tournament provided an excellent opportunity for each team to build a support base in the community, and a new identity for players and supporters that was different from their religious identities.

Legacy action

In our legacy action, we inspired other universities and local community-based organisations to join the campaign. Students at two neighbouring universities started a branch of the project on their campuses. As previously mentioned, youths in Mubi came together to create a non-governmental organisation.

Build a Shared Digital Religious Space

Since it was not possible to get Christians and Muslims to worship together at the same place, we built a digital space for believers from the two faiths to come together to talk about their faith in a respectful way. In addition to social media, we felt the need to build a tool that can provide a shared space for respectful debate and contemplation on our collective human condition, using the prism of religious beliefs. Thus we created Beliepedia for conversations between Islam and Christianity on common topics of interest. We also created the Bible and Qur'an in Conversation series to compare texts from the two holy books on core topics such as forgiveness, mercy, oneness of God, and so on. Beliepedia allowed approved religious influencers (both clerics and Heroes) to register as contributors and post content, while everyone can comment, like, and share. Editors review content from the contributors to prevent publication of hateful or inflammatory materials. The overall site content was fully moderated to ensure it was not offensive to any faith.

THEORETICAL IMPLICATIONS

There is no consensus on why individuals become radicalised and join VEOs, nor about the perfect pathway to deradicalisation. However, there are some important theoretical pointers, which this work helps to frame.

Social identity theory (SIT) provides some interesting insights into the dynamics of in-group and out-group identities, and how conceptual categorisations affect behaviours toward members of both. It proposes that a person does not have one identity, but multiple identities or selves, and that a person might act differently in different contexts, depending on the group they belong to in that context, which may include for example a sports team, an ethnic or language group, a family, or a religious group (Tajfel, 1974). SIT further proposes that when acting in groups, individuals define themselves in terms of their group membership and seek to have their group valued positively relative to other groups. We observed this phenomenon first-hand in this project. We built a multidimensional space around religious identities by constructing and highlighting other aspects of the believer's identity. We observed that individuals acted out patterns that were consistent with the new identities. For example, in the football tournament, the religious groups that individuals belonged to became slightly less important when the individuals were split into multi-faith football teams. From the moment they were in their football team, which included mixtures of various Christian and Muslim denominations, they sought the success of their football team. If multiple opportunities are built into the lived experience of radicalised individuals within which they describe and socialise themselves more in terms of identities other than religious (perhaps a sports team and a tournament), they would want their team to do better than other teams, irrespective of the religious composition of team members. The outcome would be a slightly less absolute religious identity. This is what we observed.

Extremist propaganda relies on the social categorisation of beliefs and believers as a necessary condition for sacrosanctity. This is even more significant when there are competing groups seeking similar objectives. The minimal group experiments that led to the development of SIT showed that the mere idea or knowledge of being in a different category or group is sufficient to provoke antagonism against the other group (Tajfel, 1970). For example, being categorised as a Muslim constitutes an important part of the believers' self-concept, as it distinguishes them from Christians and non-believers. When a particular group is the individual's dominant ideologically and emotionally committed identity, it becomes a significant organising structure of social reality and must therefore be the main target of any countermeasure campaign.

Because religious beliefs are derived from transcendental stories and regimes of meaning, they constitute even more powerful mechanisms of identification and categorisation. Essentially, as long as absolute believers derive their sense of 'I am' or self from their beliefs, they will remain committed to their absolute beliefs. However, when the 'I am' or sense of self is expanded to include other elements of one's identity, the tyranny of absolute beliefs is weakened. This also applies to nativist and alt-right movements in contemporary society. Members of such groups seek to mobilise the conceptualised group against the conceptualised Other; which, more often than not, is the foreigner.

Religious absolutism is produced by an avowed identity derived from strong religious beliefs and a strong in-group membership that stigmatises and dehumanises other groups and beliefs. At the core of radicalisation is identification with religious beliefs (Jacob,

2017). Current interventions mainly deploy counternarratives to challenge religious beliefs. However, in challenging absolute beliefs, the believer is also challenged, thus foreclosing the only pathway to redemption: the believer's identity. Challenging the believer's Hero is equivalent to questioning the believer's beliefs, which comes back to the same cul-de-sac. Such counternarrative campaigns can even end up having boomerang effects. This is one of the reasons that counternarratives fail, because they appeal to reason and scripture, and seek to discredit a Hero. The Hero is scripture and everything the believer wants to be, so cannot be discredited. Reason has already been taken over by a radicalised identity, so is out of reach.

There are important implications on theory, policy, and practice in real-world settings which must not be missed. It can be counterproductive to deploy a counternarrative messaging campaign as a countermeasure against the Heroes and any of the five previously described categories of absolutist beliefs (legitimating, unifying, othering, blaming, and threatened body beliefs). While messaging has its place as part of propaganda countermeasure, messages are not magic bullets. Actually, they can backfire if recklessly deployed. The way target audiences respond to messages is determined by where the messaging appeal is located on what Muzafer Sherif and Carl Hovland (1961) have termed the 'latitude of attitude'. In their social judgement theory (SJT), Sherif and Hovland argue that attitude is made up of three zones or latitudes: the 'latitude of acceptance' (behavioural appeals that are acceptable and sit well with one's absolute beliefs), 'latitude of non-commitment' (behavioural appeals that are neither objectionable nor acceptable), and 'latitude of rejection' (behavioural appeals that are objectionable to one's absolute beliefs). Radicalised individuals use their anchored ideology or absolutist beliefs as a comparison point to weigh any incoming appeal. They first judge how far the appeal is from their anchored position, which is located deep within their 'latitude of acceptance'. The target audience's reflex response to a message is determined by the distance of the message's appeal from their anchored position. SJT therefore posits that instead of changing attitudes, messages that fall deep into a target audience's 'latitude of rejection' can achieve the direct opposite of their intended purpose and can drive target audiences to hold on more firmly to their anchored ideology.

In cases where there is 'ego involvement' or a high emotional attachment to an ideology, as is the case with radicalised individuals to extremist ideologies, the 'latitude of rejection' is wider. In such cases, absolutist beliefs are part of the radicalised individual's sense of identity and community, hence always protected. Seeking to influence audiences with high ego involvement or wide latitudes of rejection will produce a boomerang effect where the targets are driven deeper into their anchored positions. Such messages fall at the extreme of the 'latitude of rejection'. This can explain why many counternarrative campaigns are ineffective. Some do indeed trigger the boomerang effect when their appeals are diametrically at variance with the target audience's latitude of acceptance. Interestingly, messages that target extremists' latitude of non-commitment are much more likely to achieve the desired impact than messages that explicitly seek to counter deeply held ideologies or beliefs.

Most counternarrative messages fall within the target audience's wide 'latitude of rejection' and are thus fundamentally at variance with their anchored beliefs. Instead of changing minds, such messages only serve the purpose of reinforcing extremists' absolute ideological anchors. On the other hand, messages that target the latitude of non-commitment are less likely to be forthrightly rejected, as they do not necessarily propose a path or action opposed to the believer's anchored positions. Besides, they do not risk the boomerang effect. Such messages, that should typically be part of a broader countermeasure campaign, may seem vague and ambiguous, but they are more effective than they appear. By anchoring our message on the personhood of the believer, the #IAmABeliever campaign aimed at the target audience's latitude of non-commitment. This approach was intended not to directly challenge extremist beliefs, but to enable the emergence of a multidimensional space for different beliefs and multiple identities to coexist.

CONCLUSION: IDENTITY AND THE POWER OF 'I AM'

Our campaign sought to popularise the notion that one's beliefs, however absolute, are merely beliefs distinct from the believer. This process of separation of one's identity from one's belief was central to the campaign and was our conceptual point of mutual agreement. The campaign created a multidimensional space through various events and platforms for the convergence of divergent beliefs and identities. In this converged space, multiple beliefs and identities were recognised, and the believer's humanity and personal identity were celebrated. A range of activities was created for new social identities to emerge within new converged spaces and communities of belonging, so that the believer is seen as more than his beliefs.

A post-intervention survey of 138 respondents showed significant differences after less than two months of exposure. We observed some significant variances between baseline and endline attitudes that indicated shifts in notions of the self and the Other. We recorded a 21 per cent increase in the number of respondents who said they were willing to live with people of other religious faiths, and a 15 per cent decrease in the number of respondents who agreed with the absolutist statement: 'anyone who doesn't worship my God deserves evil', vis-à-vis baseline responses. While the outcomes are very encouraging, they must be taken with some scepticism. Many other reasons could have contributed to the change. The project and the research was developed and implemented in an undergraduate class within a semester. Therefore, many of the usual checks and institutional review processes were not followed due to time constraints and funding limitations. Nevertheless, they are worthy of note and further studies.

Moreover, the work points in an important direction: a multidimensional space for different beliefs and believers to coexist and explore questions that traverse religious fault lines can help build opportunities for convergence. Beliepedia provided a converged religious space where Christians and Muslims could go to contemplate existential questions such as 'What is the purpose of life?', 'Why does God allow good people to suffer?', and 'What is evil?', among others. Functioning almost as a Bible–Qur'an concordance, verses from the holy books of both faiths enabled believers from both groups to expand the centre of their religious inquiry. Many users from both faiths said they realised that the two books were not so different after all on some of the most important questions of life. Many were seeing the religious Other's scriptural texts for the first time. The Bible and Qur'an in Conversation series was born from the need to build more opportunities for adherents of both faiths to expand their value for the Other's beliefs.

We found that the more opportunities for communication, interaction, and collective action there were between believers, the more ideological configurations declined. To further situate this communicative interaction and collective action within practical contexts, we sought to work with schools, colleges, and universities to have similar multi-faith spaces for prayer and quiet meditation. Finally, although this was a class project for a global university competition, there are important lessons that need further reflection. Countermeasures to extremist propaganda are much more than messaging and counternarratives. They involve the creation of new multidimensional communities and spaces for new and multiple identities to emerge, and for beliefs, however absolute, to be emphasised as merely so and as separate from the believer.

POSTSCRIPT

The #IAmABeliever campaign won first place at the maiden edition of the Africa Regional Finals of the P2P Challenging Extremism Competition (Fall 2016). The campaign morphed into a new class project, Women Against Violent Extremism (WAVE), which won second place at the global finals of the Facebook Global Digital Challenge in Spring 2017.

ACKNOWLEDGEMENTS

The author acknowledges the efforts of his students in the Public Diplomacy and Strategic Media Intervention class of Fall 2016 at the American University of Nigeria; and the support of EdVenture Partners (EVP).

REFERENCES

Barrett, R. (2014), 'Objectives and ideology: political and religious in Soufan Group, the Islamic State', available at www.jstor.org/stable/resrep10786.8, accessed 29 September 2020.

Bates, T. (1975), 'Gramsci and the theory of hegemony', *Journal of the History of Ideas*, 36(2), 351–366. doi:10.2307/2708933.

Hansen, W. (2020), 'The ugly face of the state: Nigerian security forces, human rights and the search for Boko Haram', *Canadian Journal of African Studies/Revue Canadienne des études Africaines*, 54(2), 299–317.

Heidegger, M. (1980), *Being and Time*, trans. John Macquirre and Edward Robinson, Oxford: Basil Blackwell.

Hoffer, E. (1951), *The True Believer: Thoughts on the Nature of Mass Movements*, New York: Harper & Row.

Hoskins, A. and B. O'Loughlin (2010), *War and Media the Emergence of Diffused War*, Cambridge: Polity.

Isichei, E. (1987), 'The Maitatsine Risings in Nigeria 1980–85: a revolt of the disinherited', *Journal of Religion in Africa*, 17(3), 194–208.

Jacob, J.U. (2017), 'Owning God: an identity-based view of violent extremism', *Global Peace Operations Review*, available at https://peaceoperationsreview.org/commentary/owning-god-an-identity-based-view-of-violent-extremism/, accessed 31 July 2017.

Jacob, J.U. and I. Akpan (2015), 'Silencing Boko Haram: mobile phone blackout and counterinsurgency in Nigeria's Northeast Region', *Stability: International Journal of Security & Development*, 4(1), Art. 8.

Matfess, H. (2017), *Women and the War on Boko Haram: Wives, Weapons, Witnesses*, London: Zed Books.

Moffett, K. and T. Sgro (2016), 'School-based CVE strategies', *Annals of the American Academy of Political and Social Science*, 668(1), 145–164.

Pew Research Center (2016), 'Religion and education around the world', available at https://www.pewforum.org/2016/12/13/religion-and-education-around-the-world, accessed 15 April 2020.

Rogers, E.M. and D.L Kincaid (1981), *Communication Networks: Toward a New Paradigm for Research*, New York: Free Press.
Sherif, M. and C.I. Hovland (1961), *Social Judgment: Assimilation and Contrast Effects in Communication and Attitude Change*, New Haven, CT: Yale University Press.
Tajfel, H. (1970), 'Experiments in intergroup discrimination', *Scientific American*, 223, 96–102.
Tajfel, H. (1974), 'Social identity and intergroup behaviour', *Social Science Information*, 13(2), 65–93.
Thurston, A. (2016), *Salafism in Nigeria: Islam, Preaching and Politics*, Cambridge: Cambridge University Press.

20. Imagined minorities: making 'real' images of ethnic harmony in Chinese tourism

Melissa Shani Brown and David O'Brien

INTRODUCTION

In this chapter, we explore the representation of ethnic minorities within China as a form of propaganda, arguing that the ways in which they are depicted serve political ends. Other scholars have studied the official depictions of ethnic minorities in China and the extent to which such imagery depicts minority groups as tied to the past and in need of the Chinese Communist Party (CCP), or more generally the majority Han, in order to modernise (for example, Gladney, 1994; Oakes, 1998; Zhang et al., 2018). Our analysis expands this by exploring a particular case study: the widespread practice of renting 'ethnic costumes' at tourist sites for the purpose of self-photography. The practice of dressing up in costume at tourist sites is common within mainland China and has been present for decades, and these rented costumes are predominantly those of Chinese ethnic minorities. Such ethnic costumes are also easily available online (complete with props and backdrops). Rather than delimiting such playful practices as mere entertainment, we seek to analyse the ways in which this both reveals and reiterates particular stereotypes about ethnic minority groups, tropes which ultimately serve political purposes.

We take an interdisciplinary approach to explore the interweaving of political propaganda and tourism, arguing that the latter is a key site for the spread of the former, precisely because it is a site of entertainment and pleasure, and because tourists project an authenticity onto their experiences and the images they create. We begin with the representation of ethnic minority groups; though documented by other scholars, here we explore the ways in which this constitutes propaganda. We then move to the main focus of our analysis, the aforementioned self-photography. Drawing on four years of ethnographic research at a variety of tourist sites within mainland China, and interviews with Han[1] tourists who had engaged in the practice, we consider the significance of the images, and of tourists' perspectives. Tourists duplicated the tropes common in propaganda, and there was little or no attempt to disrupt or challenge these tropes. The interviews revealed the extent to which many of the tourists implicitly believed in the tropes they performed. This illustrates the extent to which the state's control over the depiction of ethnic minorities has been effective in creating a fairly homogenous shared meaning around ethnic identities in China. We also reflect upon the significance of considering tourist photography through the lens of propaganda: as 'real photographs', such images carry with them an aura of authenticity and come to function as if they were photographs of 'real' ethnic minorities. The playful elements of such dressing up draws the participants into the enactment of the tropes, a focus on the fun of make-believe that largely allowed for participants to believe that they were genuinely getting an insight into what it is really like to be one of an ethnic minority. That is, rather than explore the efficacy of propaganda by directly talking to participants about what they think about ethnic minorities, we are able to explore these questions in a 'non-serious' context. As entertainment, it was implicitly rendered innocent rather than ideological. Finally, the widespread diffusion of these images on social media is itself a proliferation of these tropes, making the tourists as ordinary citizens producers, not just audiences, of such discourses.

PROPAGANDA AND TECHNOLOGIES OF WORLD-MAKING

As Edney (2014) observes, the definition of 'propaganda' differs somewhat between Anglophone contexts and China, with the terms *xuanchuan* or *sixiang gongzuo* carrying neutral or positive connotations rather than negative ones. The negative connotations of 'propaganda' are clear if we consider the recurring theme of manipulation in many definitions: 'Propaganda is a major form of manipulation by symbols' (Goldhamer and Shils, 1994: 103); 'the deliberate manipulation of representations (including text, pictures, video, speech etc.) with the intention of producing any effect in the audience' (Briant, 2015: 9). This is also implicit in definitions which focus on propaganda as persuasion, shifting the question of whether or not representations are manipulated to the intended social repercussions: 'Propaganda is the deliberate, systematic attempt to shape perceptions, manipulate cognitions, and direct behaviour to achieve a response that furthers the desired intent of the propagandist' (Jowett and O'Donnell, 2015: 7). Such definitions highlight that propaganda as a form of communication is predicated upon the desire for such media to have particular effects.

Exploring the terms in the Chinese context, Edney (2014) recognises that it is largely the use of *xuanchuan* and *sixiang gongzuo* within official discourses dating back to the founding of the People's Republic of China (PRC) which gives the terms their positive meanings, as being forms of 'educating' or 'informing the masses' (Edney, 2014: 22), something 'seen as both necessary and desirable' (ibid.: 23). Edney also notes that in contemporary Chinese definitions of *xuanchuan*, the term is sometimes explicitly contrasted with the meaning of 'propaganda' in the West:

> [dictionary definitions state] the original meaning of the term in the West refers to the spreading of a philosophical argument or opinion … in the West the term is now commonly used in the context of supporting a particular government or political group. It then offers the following three definitions of *xuanchuan* in the Chinese context: to announce or convey information (*xuanbu chuanda*); to explain something to someone, or to conduct education (*xiang ren jiangjie shuoming, jinxing jiaoyu*); and to disseminate or publicize (*chuanbo, xuanyang*). (Ibid.: p. 22)

While this illustrates different connotations, it also confuses translation and definition. Given its connotations, and indeed that *xuanchuan* is usually a verb and not a noun, one could translate it in a variety of ways. This is what the CCP has done; for example the *Zhongyang xuanchuan bu* (Central Propaganda Department) has in recent years been officially translated into English as the Publicity Department (Edney, 2014: 23). However, what this dictionary explanation does instead is presume a direct equivalence between *xuanchuan* and 'propaganda', which implies that the term has different meanings: that in the West 'propaganda' is subjective (opinion) whereas in China it is objective (to convey information, to educate), and, implicitly, that the Western concept might not be applicable to the Chinese context. Significantly, none of the definitions found by Edney (2014: 23) mention censorship, despite this being a key component of the CCP's propaganda work. It is important that linking 'propaganda' to *xuanchuan* politicises all public dissemination of information. This is an idea tacitly taken for granted by the CCP if we consider the extent to which the Great Firewall is justified as a protective measure to ensure that Chinese citizens are not exposed to particular forms or content of information. What is useful here is that public discourses become situated as a site in which 'truths' are staked.

Edney's (2014) work focuses upon news media, but his definition of propaganda within China is useful for this chapter. It is 'a collection of practices through which the Party-state exercises power ... [this includes] the Party-state's use of *power practices to control what is articulated publicly* and the *power of discourse itself to produce shared meanings that shape political life*' (Edney, 2014: 8). That is, within China as elsewhere, propaganda involves a variety of means of exerting power over, and through, public discourses and shared meanings. The breadth of 'public discourses' implies that virtually anything might be situated as a potential site of propaganda. Edney's (2014) definition of propaganda is not described as indebted to Foucault, though there are points of similarity with Foucault's notion of 'power' as a means of determining shared meanings: 'In fact, power produces; it produces reality; it produces ... truth' (Foucault, 1977: 194). Thus, various forms of media become important as forms of representation which at least in part construct and delimit our ideas about the world. Here we are looking at the ways in which official imagery is reproduced and reinforced by tourists' own photographs, which means we are ultimately exploring the ways in which the 'tourist gaze' is informed by and reiterates representations, rendering tourist snapshots political.

The notion of the tourist gaze is not solely about the importance of photography within tourist practices, but photography is a crucial site to explore how other places and people are visually presented to and then represented by tourists. In exploring the practice of self-photography in costume we highlight that imaginative play has an analytic role: the 'what if' of 'being another person' reveals preconceptions of what it means to be 'a person like them'. This is the realm of identity and ideology, and therefore the political stakes are high. Such practices cease to be merely playful tourist pastimes because they segue into wider representations of ethnic minorities and also perpetuate them, constituting an extension and diffusion of propaganda. The idea of the tourist gaze is indebted to Edward Said's (1978) 'imaginative geography', discussed in his work on orientalism. Imaginative geography is the 'fictional reality' of another place (Said, 1978: 52), not necessarily grounded in reality, but assumed as general knowledge. We might translate this into stereotypes of another culture. As Said's critique emphasises, the imaginative geography of 'the Orient' was the product of a colonial imagination, particular stereotypes were not only practices of othering but part of a justification for domination. We argue here that the self-photography in costume that is widespread at tourist sites in China creates 'imagined minorities'. The photographs recreate the predominant images of minority groups, but in so doing 'make them real' and disseminate them further. These photographs become part of wider depictions of these ethnic groups. We are not simply focusing on the fictionality of the images, but on the importance of the effects of taking them to be 'true': 'Instead of seeing photographs as reflections or distortions of a pre-existing world, they can be understood as a technology of world-making ... Rather than mirroring or representing geographies, photographs partly create them, culturally, socially and materially' (Urry and Larsen, 2011: 67). This means that tourist photographs are not only souvenirs, but they also function indexically both by depicting something and in claiming to be evidence of it. That is, these photographs both represent 'ethnicity' and claim to be true representations, because they are photographic. In this, Urry and Larsen's (2011) understanding of the role of photography in creating imagined geographies is aligned to propaganda because it functions as a means not of simply presenting 'the truth' but of actively creating 'shared meanings that shape political life' (Edney, 2014: 8). Being digital enables them to be distributed far more widely than their material predecessors. Urry and Larsen (2011) do not situate such photographs as innocent, since they are very much tied to the wider context of imaginative geographies: that is, the stereotypes, judgements, and power relations of given societies. Here we argue that this practice and these photographs 'make real' particular depictions of ethnicity in China, and do so through a clear circumnavigation of actually photographing 'real' ethnic minorities, because they depict the tourists themselves play-acting as though they were members of other groups. This is what we denote through the term 'imagined minorities', with 'imagined' meaning not only an abstract idea, but one simultaneously made real through particular images.

ANALYSIS

In this section we explore the ways in which ethnic minorities are depicted within public discourses in China. To gesture back to Edney, we aim to trace 'what is articulated publicly' in order to identify the ways that 'discourse itself ... produce[s] shared meanings that shape political life' (Edney, 2014: 8). This serves as the basis of comparison for our subsequent analysis of tourists' self-photography. It is worth noting that while couples and families do dress up, it is predominantly younger women – occasionally alone, but also in small groups – who are the most common participants and who formed the majority of those who volunteered to be interviewed (we discuss the significance of gender later). For many of our interviewees, dressing up in costume was a key part of the tourist experience that allowed them to 'experience ethnic culture'. Although from our own observations as well as from the interviews, this experience was not the main motivating factor; rather, it was primarily an opportunity to share these photographs with family and friends. Dressing up was a demonstration of touristic experiences generally, of the financial ability to travel and thus middle-class-ness, curating a particular persona on social media, rather than being conceptually oriented towards engagement with people from the areas being visited. Despite the focus on this practice as being playful or entertaining, the purpose of our analysis is to consider the significance of the tropes which were 'played at'.

OFFICIALLY FRAMING ETHNICITY IN CHINA

Ethnicity is an official classification within China, appearing on ID cards and disclosed on various official documents such as doctors' notes. Although the identification of ethnic minority groups in the early years of the PRC was carried out by ethnographers in dialogue with various groups, ethnicity is not a category one chooses, nor can one officially identify with multiple groups (for example, if one's parents or grandparents are from different ethnicities). In this section, we explore the ways that being an ethnic minority has been framed; that is, not merely how ethnicity is defined, but how ethnic difference has been represented.

Historically, what are now classified as ethnic groups were differentiated as 'barbarian' peoples on the peripheries of the 'civilized' centre of the Chinese empire (Fiskesjö, 2012; Harrell, 1996). Denton's description of this is typical:

> In ancient China, a variety of terms meaning 'barbarian' were used to refer to non-Han ethnic groups. The Han understanding of these peoples was generally cultural rather than racial, that is, they were barbarian not because they looked different, but because they were 'uncivilized'. By bestowing on them the civilizing effects of the Chinese cultural tradition (that is, Confucian ethics), these barbarians could be redeemed and brought into the realm of the humane (ren). (Denton, 2013: 201)

However, of the 'variety of terms meaning "barbarian"', the most common classifiers referred to animals (Dikötter, 1992; Wilkinson, 2000; Fiskesjö, 2012). For Dikötter (1992) and Fiskesjö (2012), the focus on the historical conception of difference as merely cultural (rather than racial) sidesteps what is at stake in equating 'civilisation' with 'being fully human': 'This was not simply a derogatory description: it was part of a mentality that integrated the concept of civilization with the idea of humanity' (Dikötter, 1992: 3). As Fiskesjö (2012) emphasises, this is hardly unique to China. It is a key feature of Western racism, but what is more particular to the Chinese context is that these monikers were not ethnic slurs, but official nomenclature: 'This was no unorthodox or secret practice but the standardized and authoritative system for writing the names of the barbarians, lasting for more than two millennia' (Fiskesjö, 2012: 61). Although there were attempts to ban or censor 'anti-barbarian sentiments' by dynasties such as the Qing (Wilkinson, 2000: 712), the Nationalist government was the first to alter systematically pejorative ethnonyms, tasking an ethnologist, Ruey Yih-fu (Rui Yifu), in 1939 with finding ways to remove the animal radicals and construct new ways of writing ethnonyms that indicated that they were 'people' (Fiskesjö, 2012: 20). The changes were issued as a government order in January 1940, though formal widespread implementation was hampered by the war. Many of Ruey Yih-fu's new ethnonyms were subsequently adopted by the CCP (ibid.).

The CCP adopted Stalin's definition of ethnic groups as 'a historically evolved, stable community of people, based upon the common possession of four principal attributes, namely: a common language, a common territory, a common economic life, and a common psychological make-up manifesting itself in common special features of national culture', scaled upon the Marxist universal progression of history (the primitive, slave, feudal, capitalist, and finally socialist modes of production) they had reached at the time of classification (McKhann, 1996: 47). In the early years of the PRC the emphasis was on nation-building and bringing ethnic minority groups from the border regions 'into the nation'. As noted by Harrell (1996), this was a fundamental change, since it situated all the ethnic groups, including Han, on a path of historical progress upon which they were legally and morally equal. Though rendered alike in their struggle to escape a feudal past and develop into a socialist modernity, Mao drew attention to social as well as economic disparities. In one of his most famous speeches, 'On the 10 Major Relationships' (Mao, 1956), he spoke of the need to promote equality and respect:

> The minority nationalities have all contributed to the making of China's history ... All through the ages, the reactionary rulers, chiefly from the Han nationality, sowed feelings of estrangement among our various nationalities and bullied the minority peoples. Even among the working people it is not easy to eliminate the resultant influences in a short time. So we have to make extensive and sustained efforts to educate both the cadres and the masses in our proletarian nationality policy and make a point of frequently reviewing the relationship between the Han nationality and the minority nationalities. (Mao, 1956)

Despite the tone of this speech, iconic depictions of ethnic minorities during this time period establish a far more simplistic picture.

In official posters, as well as photographs curated in museums such as the Cultural Palace of the Minorities in Beijing, there is an emphasis on depicting the 'liberation' of ethnic minorities, and an illustration of 'ethnic harmony' which iconographically appears the same, namely depictions of minority groups as generically jubilant. However, unlike Mao's more reflexive point above, such imagery depicts a narrative of a 'civilizing mission' (Harrell, 1996). As with significantly older discourses of 'sinicization' in which Chinese history was largely depicted as a one-way process of ethnic groups assimilating into 'Chinese' (Confucian) culture (see Denton's (2013) point previously), here too the process is depicted as unidirectional. Harrell also notes three recurring metaphors within Communist imagery of ethnic minorities, all of which symbolize a scale or hierarchy: 'the metaphor of sex', the widespread tendency to represent minorities as women; 'the metaphor of education', which represents them as children; and 'the metaphor of history', which represents them as tied to the past (Harrell, 1996: 13). Such depictions, despite the Communist assertion of equality, do not divest themselves of a hierarchical scaling of ethnic difference. As we have shown elsewhere (Zhang et al., 2018), the representation of ethnic minorities as childlike is still a common trope in propaganda posters, but within our focus here on tourism it is femininity and traditionality which are most relevant.

Depiction of ethnic minority groups has varied somewhat. During the earlier years of the CCP, there was more focus on poverty and backwardness; this has gradually been more sidelined as tourism has commodified and idealised rural traditionality as an antidote to Han urban modernity (O'Brien and Brown, 2020). Since the 1980s, Beijing's policy towards its minority regions has focused on economic development. Any ethnic conflict was framed as the result of economic disparities, circumnavigating a variety of other factors. Therefore, propaganda revolved around the notion that economic development of the minority areas would solve any such problems (Becquelin, 1997). However, ethnic tensions in China have escalated in recent years, with both Xinjiang and Tibet witnessing outbreaks of violence. The 2009 riots in Urumqi were the worst outbreak of social unrest in China since the Tiananmen Square protests in 1989, and have had wide-ranging repercussions for local and national governments (O'Brien, 2015). Restrictions on movement, hugely invasive surveillance, and a campaign to prevent – according to the Chinese government – the 'radicalisation' of Uyghurs that has seen upwards of 1 million people interned in prison camps (Zenz, 2019), has become the reality of life for the citizens of Xinjiang. There have also been parallel changes in how Uyghurs have been represented, with media depictions of Uyghurs performing Han traditional culture (for example, Beijing Opera) becoming increasingly foregrounded. Anderson and Byler (2019) position this as an emphasis on cultural assimilation, something increasingly promoted as Uyghur traditional culture becomes positioned as suspect due to its Islamic heritage. Uyghurs performing Han traditions for a Han audience thus becomes a symbolic form both of 'ethnic harmony' and of 'sinicisation' (Anderson and Byler, 2019). Despite these broader tensions, China continues to emphasise the notion of ethnic harmony, asserting such harmony as the natural historical norm for all ethnic relations within China. The assertion that ethnic groups have only ever existed in harmony implicitly renders any tensions or violence unnatural, rather than part of far more complicated histories and social relations (Zhang et al., 2018). It is taboo to discuss ethnic tension in China, and any problems are blamed on terrorists and foreign forces, rather than being contributed to by policy, inequality, or a wider context of prejudice.

A government White Paper on Xinjiang released in the wake of mounting international criticisms of internment makes this clear in its preamble:

> China is a unified multiethnic country, and the various ethnic groups in Xinjiang have long been part of the Chinese nation. Throughout its long history, Xinjiang's development has been closely related to that of China. However, in more recent times, hostile forces in and outside China, especially separatists, religious extremists and terrorists, have tried to split China and break it apart by distorting history and facts. (White Paper, 2019)

The significance of such statements is manifold. History is mobilised both as the reason why ethnic minority regions are part of China, but also as that which is being 'distorted' by others.

Numerous other scholars have identified that that the contemporary representation of the Han as modern, urban, normal, and minority groups as culturally traditional, pastoral, and different, continues to be widespread both in official propaganda posters and government statements, as well as in museums, films, and other media (Gladney, 1994; Zhang, 1997; Brown and O'Brien, 2019). For example, in the Cultural Palace of the Minorities in Beijing, a touchscreen represents the 56 ethnic groups. The Han are represented by a man in a white lab-coat, examining an industrial chrome cylinder. In contrast, the other ethnic groups are represented mostly by young women in rural settings, tending to livestock, dancing beneath grape vines, or engaging in activities such as plaiting one another's hair. As Gladney puts it: 'The Han are frequently represented as somewhere near the modern end of a Marxist historical trajectory upon which China's minorities must journey. Much of this derives from a continued commitment in Chinese social science to the study of minorities as "living fossils"' (Gladney, 1994: 99). Oakes (1998) argues that the minorities play a twofold symbolic role: simultaneously being a romanticised 'other' to Han modernity, and depicting the minorities as implicitly impoverished and in need of development also serves to reinforce the image of the CCP as a benevolent nation state. Such depictions of ethnic minorities thus function with a particular political aim. The widespread depiction of ethnic minorities largely as regards their historical cultural heritages also circumnavigates visualising ethnic minorities' stakes in the present and imagined future of the nation (Brown and O'Brien, 2021).

The official representations of ethnic groups fall into a narrow range of tropes, some of which have clear positive and negative binaries. As reiterated previously, ethnic minorities are almost exclusively represented through the over-arching trope of 'traditionality'. See Table 20.1, which lists the signifiers. These may vary in terms of the themes signified, most of which have different valences depending on context (Table 20.2).

The positive themes are those most often represented, largely because too much focus on the negative would belie the assertion of 'ethnic harmony'. The positive themes are also those which lend themselves to commodification, such as within tourism; as we have argued elsewhere, ethnic minorities are simultaneously 'othered' and 'idyllized' (O'Brien and Brown, 2020). Idealisation obscures even as it represents. Though a vast amount of research on stereotyping and power dynamics exists within studies of tourism, with the exception of museums, these are not often framed as a form of propaganda (something particularly important when considering internal tourism within China, where tourism is precisely a mediation of histories, peoples, places, often for an internal audience). Here, we focus on several interrelated aspects of our case study: the way in which the creation and diffusion of such images is rendered 'trivial' (implicitly apolitical), and the extent to which the images reiterate and proliferate dominant tropes found in other media.

Table 20.1 Visual signifiers of 'traditionality'

Signifiers of 'traditionality'	
Costume	These indicate specific ethnic groups, but also can involve amalgamations of 'traditional dress'. More elaborate, 'formal' wear depicted as though worn all of the time.
Objects	Hand-made objects, jugs of water, bushels of fruit.
Acts	Tending to animals, craft work such as weaving, bathing in streams, communal hair-braiding.
Cultural activities	Singing and dancing, generic spiritual gestures such as praying.
Locations	Natural landscapes, small villages, religious sites (e.g., shrines with prayer flags in Tibet).

Table 20.2 Positive and negative valences: implicit meanings of signifiers of 'traditionality'

Themes	
Positive connotations	*Negative connotations*
Spiritual	Religious, superstitious
Sensual, emotive	Irrational, violent
Pastoral, 'traditional ways of life'	Poverty, ignorance, uneducated
Idyllic natural locations, 'living closer to nature'	Rural, undeveloped

IMAGINED MINORITIES: MAKING 'REAL' IMAGES OF ETHNIC HARMONY

As noted, within China the practice of dressing up in costume at tourist sites is widespread, but there has been little research on this practice (see, however, Brown 2021 for an exploration of its cultural politics). This practice does, however, receive brief mention in Varutti's (2011) article focusing on museums of ethnic minority cultures:

> The idealized image of 'exotic' communities living in a distant, undefined place and time, 'peacefully' and 'in harmony with nature' resonates the nostalgic desire for an ideal world 'unspoilt' and 'uncorrupted' by modernization … . Also, the widespread practice of having one's photo taken in ethnic garments, is quite telling of the degree to which ethnic identity can be appropriated and, literally, worn and divested. 'Being ethnic' is here a game, it's a safe estrangement, a close encounter with the Other within the non-threatening realm of the *mise-en-scene*. (Varutti, 2011: 8)

Our research corroborates this. As covered in our previous sections, ethnic minorities tend to be represented singing or dancing, in pastoral settings, engaged in 'traditional' activities. This was precisely the role play enacted by the tourists, but as Varutti (2011) observes, they also situated this as playful, fun, and trivial. As noted earlier, it is predominantly younger women who engage in this activity, for several reasons. Most interviewees proffered that women were more 'used to dressing up', and conversely men would be more likely to feel awkward. However, it is worth noting that the prevalence of official imagery of ethnic minorities as young and female means that the referent images for such role play is offered more readily to young women.

Unlike other forms of propaganda, the offerings of costumes at these tourist sites are 'invitations to play'. As prompts, the costumes are there to be played with (for a price). In this, the tourists are invited to take part in a playful proliferation of propaganda images, to create 'participatory propaganda', to reframe Jenkins's (2013), 'participatory culture'. This is not unique; we might consider similar techniques in marketing where consumers become key participants in publicising a product: 'they talk of two-way communications with consumers, which sounds very egalitarian. But what it really means is that consumers are now circulating entertaining viral adverts on Facebook' (Jowett and O'Donnell, 2006, p. 6). Such participatory propaganda implicates the various individuals and groups who become complicit in the diffusion of the message or image; in being 'ordinary citizens' they provide an aura of authenticity, even as they remain conduits in their creation of reiterated stock images. This is particularly clear in these examples: tourists perform preformed tropes, and though the photographs are technically real, they do not actually represent 'real' ethnic minority individuals, but the tourists themselves enacting their imagination of such an identity.

At the tourist sites promotional photographs (ostensibly representing other tourists) also provided referent images, setting out the same tropes already described and enacted in the particular location. This encourages tourists to engage with the tourist sites as sets; that is, backdrops and props. For example, at the Beijing Ethnic Cultures Park, a museum and a theme park spread over around 350 hectares, there are various stores renting costumes surrounded by promotional photographs showing tourists in costume posing around the nearby buildings. The promotional images in other locations, such as at the Forbidden Cityin Beijing, also offer a fixed scene that tourists are invited to mimic. What is significant here is that such 'invitations' actively interpellate tourists to 'act out' the images, to become participants, rather than passive observers.

As noted by interviewees, most had preformed images in mind when they took photographs:

> It is a fantasy, you feel like this is what it would be like to be born with a different nationality [*minzu*], experiencing what it is like to be an ethnic person. I followed the images on social media posts to teach people how to pose.

> You pose like the pictures. A lot of the minorities show off their beautiful clothes, like dancing.

This was also confirmed in our observations. The images recreated poses and shots, so that tourist photographs resembled the promotional photographs, which resembled various other propaganda images. As noted by Urry and Larsen (2011: 169), 'Once fixed in the imagination, even when they encountered different realities, [tourists] photographed the imagination.' The photographs make real the imagined image, an experience that is understood as 'authentic', but also clearly a pretence oriented towards the final photographs: 'It is fun to imagine how you would look if you were a minority. I like those [costumes] that are authentic with the bright colours which look good on camera.'

This 'authenticity' was often asserted without being fully explained. Here authenticity is linked to looking good, meaning looking like images which have been previously seen: authenticity as familiarity. Tourists often asserted some kind of authenticity even when it was clear that the costumes were held on by Velcro, made of polyester, or were pinafores to be tied on over the tourists' clothes. There was a link with the presumed reality of 'feeling what it is like to be an ethnic person' because a costume has been donned. Though asked if there was any comparability, similarities to cosplay were denied by the interviewees. Cosplay involves investment and identification with a character. Conversely, what was being enacted was a trope (being 'Manchu' or 'Tibetan') rather than a character with a story, and interviewees pointed out that cosplay characters are fictitious: 'Cosplay represents characters from the 2-D world. I mean, they're not real.' While obviously true, this circumnavigates the fact that the tropes in the tourist photographs were also derived from media, as interviewees stated they already knew how to pose from other pictures they had seen. Of importance here is that the tropes of ethnic minorities were situated as 'more real' than fiction. That is, there was a general acceptance that what was represented was basically accurate, much as the clothing was presumed to be 'authentic'.

The tourists' photographs tended to represent recurring themes. The sites already delimited the 'traditional' settings and 'traditional' costumes, emplacing the representation of 'being ethnic' within this frame. Little or no attempts appeared to be made to disrupt this trope; for example, through 'ironic' shots in costume next to vending machines or holding Canon cameras or soft drinks. Though in some photographs it was evident that there were other non-costumed tourists as well as evidence of modernity in the background, the framing of the photographs usually attempted to exclude such signs as much as possible, trying to maintain rather than disrupt 'traditionality'. For example, in several cases participants took off their sneakers, since such shoes were seen as being out of place; but also, as one participant stated, 'it would be normal for minorities to be barefoot'. Of significance in this statement was both its inaccuracy, given that the rest of the costume was 'Tibetan', but also that such bare feet could represent alternately poverty, sensuality, or a closeness to nature (in the photographs the tourist was dangling her feet over water). In the images, and in some of the interviews, the 'traditionality' of ethnic minorities was taken to be how they 'really' are: 'Other people live easier lives and are closer to the past. It is fun to pretend like I can feel the way they do and don't have to worry about the normal stress.'

Alongside this, most interviewees asserted particular stereotypes about ethnic minorities despite the fact that they were themselves enacting such identities in the photographs they were taking. They also identified that their engagement with actual ethnic minorities was very limited as part of this experience:

> The costume sellers were Han. But they showed us how to put the clothes on. [My grandfather] didn't understand why we would dress as backward people. But he said I looked pretty.

> [In the Beijing Ethnic Cultures Park] I talked a little to the women [at the photo stall], but I wouldn't try to speak to most of them [at the site], many of the minorities cannot talk a lot due to their illiteracy [i.e. lack of proficiency in Mandarin] and they are so different from me as a Han person. And I would never try to speak to the boys, they might grab a knife and stab me! (laughter) ... Maybe that is an exaggeration, but I did feel like that.

These statements emphasise the extent to which feelings of 'authenticity' or 'feeling the way they do' was largely about the creation of pictures which look the part, not necessarily predicated upon direct contact with actual ethnic minority people. They also evidence tacit acceptance of stereotypes of ethnic minorities as impoverished, backwards, or irrationally violent.

The tropes that were enacted largely fell into a handful of overlapping categories: joyful, spiritual, romantic, sensual, sexual. These are the same as official representations. The 'joyful' poses were some of the most common, with tourists often posing as though dancing. The 'spiritual' poses were those in which participants were photographed as though they were engaging in particular religious acts, like spinning prayer wheels at the Tibetan area of the Beijing Ethnic Cultures Park, or posing as though praying (hands pressed together, often with eyes closed). These are 'pretences' because the purpose of the acts was the photographs; actions were repeated for better shots, or uncompleted (for example, pausing while walking around prayer wheels so as not to blur, but still poised as though walking). The 'romantic' poses were contemplative: participants gazed into the distance, gazed upon flowers, fruit, touched or attended to details of their clothing (for example, adjusting a skirt hem or stroking a collar), or else were photographed with their eyes closed as though listening to something in the surrounding environment. Some of these overlap with the 'spiritual' in implying a 'deeper appreciation' of the contemplated object or experience. But such contemplation – particularly of flowers, fruit, as well as attentiveness to clothing – could also signify sensuality, linked to the more sexualised depictions, a counterpoint to the innocence generally implied here.

In the tourist photographs the eroticisation of ethnic minorities was implicit in some cases, more explicit in others. It was implicit at the Kazakh village tourist site at Tianshan in Xinjiang, where participants could be photographed in costume 'marrying a Kazakh girl' in front of a yurt. It was also implicit in some poses, such as where tourists stood or sat with long skirts lifted or held aside to purposefully reveal legs or thighs. More explicit eroticisation was evident in photographs taken in studios (rather than at tourist sites themselves), and in particular some of the online sites selling ethnic costumes in which models pose provocatively. In some cases, the models were partially disrobed, despite the fact that it is the clothing that is being sold. In these, clothing was pulled aside to reveal shoulders, cleavage, or thighs, or participants were lying on the ground, or in iconic 'pinup' poses. Adapting Varutti (2011), these images imply the costumes to be literally 'worn and divested'. The props are also of interest here, including opium pipes and small but ornate knives. These are striking in introducing elements of danger to the images, enfolding signifiers of addiction and ethnic violence into otherwise 'alluring' photographs.

Sensuality/sexuality is a recurring trope in representations of ethnic minorities within China, as noted by others (Gladney, 1994; Harrell, 1996; Hyde, 2001), but also evident within our wider ethnography. For example, a massive mural in Lhasa airport depicts a Tibetan woman naked to the waist, braiding her hair, while other women dance nearby. In an Urumqi hotel a long mosaic depicts Uyghur women dancing in an orchard, their breasts and nipples visible through their shirts. The sound-and-light performance *Impression Sanjie Liu* (directed by Zhang Yimou) includes a dance sequence where young minority women strip down to flesh-coloured bodysuits to frolic by the water. Varutti (2011) identifies a miniature diorama at the Yunnan Nationalities Museum labelled 'topographical conditions' which includes small figurines of bare-breasted Dai women in a stream (Varutti, 2011: 7). For Harrell (1996), this representation of ethnic minorities as 'female/sexual' functions as a metaphor of cultural hierarchy (not knowing how to behave 'properly', something simultaneously dangerous but desirable), but also a male gaze through which subordination is implied because rendered sexually female, implicitly passive. Harrell (1996) also notes a further feature of tending to represent ethnic minorities as women: they become a twofold figure of those who the CCP have 'liberated' from the oppression of tradition. This becomes contradictory when they metonymically represent tradition. There is a temporal displacement here. Whereas Han women are represented as liberated from traditional clothes and culture 'now', minority women are figured still 'awaiting' it, because, conversely, the traditionality of minority cultures is given a positive valence within tourism. However, in wider social discourses this also positions minorities as perpetually in need of development, despite having been liberated more than half a century ago, the same as everyone else in China (Brown and O'Brien, 2021).

The spiritual, the sensual, and the sexual are telling as performances of minority others, here very much a 'playing at being other' that emplaces them as conceptual counterpoints to the 'normal' self. As Said notes of imaginative geographies, they 'help the mind to intensify its own sense of itself by dramatizing the distance and difference between what is close and what is far away' (Said, 1978: 55). Certainly, the tropes set out here would be familiar within Orientalism, but the enjoyment of this playful practice is one of the reasons why it is 'trivialised' by the interviewees: 'Travelling is not a serious thing. It should not be. I did not try to connect it to exploration [of culture]. That is kind of heavy. Instead, travel should be entertaining.'

The 'entertainment' of such role play obscures the seriousness of such images, and the ambiguous extent to which at least some participants believe what they enact:

> Other people live easier lives and are closer to the past. It is fun to pretend like I can feel the way they do and don't have to worry about the normal stress.

> I kind of felt I engaged with that group of people ... It was so different from how we live. They sing and dance regardless of locations and time.

Implicit in such images was thus a belief in what is being depicted, an acceptance that ethnic minorities really do sing and dance 'all the time' (not just as a performance for tourists, or particular cultural contexts such as celebrations), that they really are somehow 'closer' to the past despite living in the present, and don't have 'normal stress'. Such photographs represent an idyllic depiction, creating the same images widespread in propaganda, but at least in part because the tourists themselves make the images, they project a 'reality' onto what is depicted. This is perhaps more striking since the images are self-portraits.

SHARED MEANINGS THAT SHAPE POLITICAL LIFE

Our interviewees confirmed the widespread diffusion of the photographs on various social networking sites, often within minutes of being taken. The discussion of these images leads to an interesting blurring of what was depicted. While clearly identifying the photographs as being of themselves, or friends, many interviewees situated the images as 'what it is really like'. That is, because they were real photographs, and recreated familiar tropes, they were situated as real representations of ethnic minorities. In this, the practice of pretending, though clearly an act of make-believe, ends up embodying belief: 'Can it not be said that the purpose and power of make-believe is, at least in certain cases, precisely that – to make us believe, and so accept its representation as believably "the real thing"?' (Lockyer and Pickering, 2005: 13). Propaganda involves a complex circuit of communication, one that can be a 'co-production in which we are willing participants' (O'Shaughnessy, in Jowett and O'Donnell, 2006: 7); this is what we refer to as 'participatory propaganda'. Here the tourists play a central role in re-presenting such depictions, but also in asserting their reality.

What do such tropes achieve if understood as propaganda, that is, a form of purposeful representation, an exertion of power over and through discourses which establish shared meanings? As Edney (2014) identifies, much of Chinese propaganda revolves around an assertion of the cohesion of the nation, and the representation of ethnic minorities – even in times of ethnic violence – segues into this. As Edney recognises regarding the news coverage around the Tibetan riots in 2008:

> The coverage focused on the violence of Tibetan rioters. It largely ignored any Tibetan victims, the peaceful protests that also took place, and the underlying reasons behind the unrest ... The Party-state also attempted to reassure the public that Tibetans were in fact happy with official policies and had a good relationship with the mainstream Chinese population by blaming outside agitators for causing the riots and announcing that the responsibility for masterminding the violence lay with the Dalai Lama ... They linked these claims to the Party-state's broader historical narrative of Tibetan liberation at the hands of the CCP, which the Party-state had continually articulated over a period of many decades. (Edney, 2014: 171)

The depictions we have examined are part of this broader narrative. The tropes enacted in these photographs are ones which represent this assertion of general happiness, even when touching on evidence of poverty (the supposed normality of being barefoot) or violence (the presence of knives). It mobilises imagery originally utilised decades ago to show jubilation at the coming of the CCP, but decontextualises it, makes it timeless; a timelessness which is dissociated from clear emplacement in the present (is this meant to be a Miao woman now? A century ago?). The 'traditionality' and pastoral imagery has multiple valences, as we have already noted. The depiction of implicit poverty legitimises CCP leadership when they situate themselves as harbingers of modernisation, as liberators from historical oppression, and those upon whom economic development relies. However, particularly within tourism such 'pastoral scenes' are simultaneously commodifiable, valuable as an 'antidote' to modernity (they do not have 'normal stress'), but in being rendered desirable, in depicting the minorities as happy in their idyll, this also diverts any criticisms of failures to deal with the economic and social inequalities which the CCP both foregrounds and denies as the basis of ethnic tension. The lack of 'contemporaneity' also enables the circumnavigation of other contemporary questions: how the ethnic minorities navigate modernity in a context where their cultures are depicted as historical rather than lived; how they navigate the massive social changes that have transformed much of China in the past few decades. These tourist photographs normalise and diffuse the official discourse that the minority groups live somewhat idyllic, pastoral lives, and are without exception happy with their ways of life, be it pastoral or the modernity furnished courtesy of the CCP. This ties into wider discourses in which discord or tension is not in any conceivable way home-grown, but rather has been caused solely by the instigation of malign foreign powers.

CONCLUSION

Our framing of tourist photography as propaganda sought to highlight the political implications behind stereotypical representations, and to emphasize that the 'participatory propaganda' of everyday citizens has a key role in normalizing these ideas through their ability to make and disseminate images that directly parallel 'official propaganda', but being 'grassroots' is less subject to identification or critique in such terms. Our use of ethnography aimed to explore how tourists were active participants in the creation of such images, and the extent to which the widespread representation of ethnic minorities has been largely effective at creating a homogenous 'shared meaning' around ethnic groups that the tourists were not only aware of, but took to be true. The tourists' self-photography is here part of a much larger circuit of images of ethnicity within China. Such official imagery precedes the images the tourists create; tourists are aware of and perform to these pre-existing images. These include promotional images at the tourist sites, general tropes (such as posing as though dancing, or sexual provocation) drawn from posters and other media, as well as images of other tourists on social media. However, as images of leisure tourism, these photographs are both distributed widely, and with a presumed innocence of being propagandistic. Thus, such images made by citizens themselves become part of the wider propagation of such discourses, and part of a more general assertion of the 'reality' they depict. For the tourists, this was a playful part of being on holiday which is presumed to be 'unserious'. It is important to consider the ways in which such playful participation readily obscures the extent to which this reinforces particular stereotypes or offers little in the way of deeper engagement. Such photographs are part of an ongoing lack of engagement with the basis of ethnic tensions within China, for the tourists offered little or no reflection upon stereotypes of poverty, backwardness, sexuality, or violence. They also function as interesting embodiments of these discourses of 'ethnic harmony'. In such photographs an abstraction of ethnicity is represented, while actual ethnic minority people are rendered invisible.

NOTE

1. There are several reasons for this. Methodologically, the majority of those who responded were Han, therefore our research focuses upon them. This does, however, reflect other social factors: for economic reasons, and the fact that they constitute over 90 per cent of the population, the vast majority of tourists to these sites are Han.

REFERENCES

Anderson, A. and D. Byler (2019), '"Eating Hanness": Uyghur Musical Tradition in a Time of Re-education', *China Perspectives*, 2019 (3): 17–26.

Becquelin, N. 1997. 'Trouble on the Margins: Interethnic Tensions and Endemic Poverty in the National Minority Areas', *China Perspectives*, 10: 19–28.

Briant, E.L. (2015), *Propaganda and Counter-Terrorism: Strategies for Global Change*, Manchester: Manchester University Press.

Brown, M.S. (2021), 'Heterophotographies: Play, Power, Privilege, and Spaces of Otherness in Chinese Tourist Photography', in M.S. Brown and C. Lam (eds), *Special Issue: Playces – Spaces of Play in Culture, Theory and Critique*, Taylor & Francis. DOI:10.1080/14735784.2021.1943698.

Brown, M.S. and D. O'Brien (2019), 'Defining the Right Path: Aligning Islam with Chinese Socialist Core Values at Ningbo's Moon Lake Mosque', *Asian Ethnicity*, 21 (2): 269–291.

Brown, M.S. and D. O'Brien (2021), '"Whose Chinese Dream is it Anyway?" Temporalities of "Ethnicity" in Inner Mongolia and Xinjiang', in J. Farley and M.D. Johnson (eds), *Redefining 'Propaganda' in Modern China: The Mao Era and its Legacies*, London: Routledge, pp. 266–294.

Denton, K.L. (2013), *Exhibiting the Past: Historical Memory and the Politics of Museums in Postsocialist China*, Honolulu: University of Hawai'i Press.

Dikötter, F. (1992), *The Discourse of Race in Modern China*, San Francisco, CA: Stanford University Press.

Edney, K. (2014), *The Globalization of Chinese Propaganda*, New York: Palgrave Macmillan.

Fiskesjö, M. (2012), 'The Animal Other: China's Barbarians and Their Renaming in the Twentieth Century', *Social Text*, 29 (4): 57–79.

Foucault, M. (1977), *Discipline and Punish: The Birth of the Prison*, London: Penguin.

Gladney, D. (1994), 'Nationality in China: Refiguring Majority/Minority Identities', *Journal of Asiatic Studies*, 53 (1): 92–123.

Goldhamer, H. and E.A. Shils (1994), 'Types of Power and Status', in John Scott (ed.), *Power: Critical Concepts*, London: Routledge, pp. 103–111.
Harrell, S. (ed.) (1996), *Cultural Encounters on China's Ethnic Frontiers*, Seattle, WA: University of Washington Press.
Hyde, S.T. (2001), 'Sex Tourism Practices on the Periphery: Eroticizing Ethnicity and Pathologizing Sex on Lancang', in N. Chen, C. Clark, S. Gottschang, and L. Jeffery (eds), *China Urban: Ethnographies of Contemporary Culture*, Durham, NC: Duke University Press, pp. 143–164.
Jenkins, H. (2013), *Textual Poachers: Television Fans and Participatory Culture*, London: Routledge.
Jowett, G.S. and V. O'Donnell (2006), *Propaganda and Persuasion* (4th edn), London: SAGE.
Jowett, G.S. and V. O'Donnell (2015), *Propaganda and Persuasion* (6th edn), London: SAGE.
Lockyer, S. and M. Pickering (eds) (2005), *Beyond a Joke: The Limits of Humour*, Basingstoke: Palgrave Macmillan.
Mao, Z. (1956), 'On the Ten Major Relationships', *Marxists Internet Archive*, available at https://www.marxists.org/reference/archive/mao/selected-works/volume-5/mswv5_51.htm.
McKhann, C. (1996), 'The Naxi and the Nationalities Question', in S. Harrell (ed.), *Cultural Encounters on China's Ethnic Frontiers*, Seattle, WA: University of Washington Press, pp. 39–62.
Oakes, T. (1998), *Tourism and Modernity in China*, London: Routledge.
O'Brien, D. (2015), '"If there is Harmony in the House there will be Order in the Nation": An Exploration of the Han Chinese as Political Actors in Xinjiang', in A. Hayes and M. Clarke (eds), *Inside Xinjiang: Space, Place and Power in China's Muslim Far Northwest*, London: Routledge, pp. 32–52.
O'Brien, D. and M.S. Brown (2020), '"Ethnic Heritage" on the New Frontier: The Idealisation and Commodification of Ethnic "Otherness" in Xinjiang', in C.Y. Ludwig Wang and L. Walton (eds), *The Heritage Turn in China: The Reinvention, Dissemination and Consumption of Heritage*, Amsterdam: Amsterdam University Press, pp. 277–296.
Said, E. (1978), *Orientalism*, New York: Pantheon Books.
Urry, J. and J. Larsen (2011), *The Tourist Gaze 3.0*, London: SAGE.
Varutti, M. (2011), 'Miniature of the Nation: Ethnic Minority Figurines, Mannequins and Dioramas in Chinese Museums', *Museum and Society*, 9 (1): 1–16.
White Paper (2019), *Historical Matters Concerning Xinjiang*. Government White Paper. Beijing: The Information Office of the State Council, July, http://english.www.gov.cn/archive/whitepaper/201907/21/content_WS5d33fed5c6d00d362f668a0a.html.
Wilkinson, E. (2000), *Chinese History: A Manual, Revised and Enlarged*, Cambridge, MA: Harvard University Asia Center.
Zenz, A. (2019), '"Thoroughly Reforming Them Towards a Healthy Heart Attitude": China's Political Re-education Campaign in Xinjiang', *Central Asian Survey*, 38 (1): 102–128.
Zhang, X., M.S. Brown, and D. O'Brien (2018), '"No CCP, No New China": Discourses of Pastoral Power in China', *China Quarterly*, 235: 784–803.
Zhang, Y. (1997), 'From "Minority Film" to "Minority Discourse": Questions of Nationhood and Ethnicity in Chinese Cinema', *Cinema Journal*, 36 (3): 73–90.

21. The language of protest: slogans and the construction of tourism contestation in Barcelona

Neil Hughes

INTRODUCTION

Tourism contestation is increasingly prevalent in major city tourism destinations across the world (see Colomb and Novy, 2016). In Europe, from Venice to Valencia and from Barcelona to Berlin, new and more established activist groups are mounting high-profile campaigns against the negative economic, social, cultural, and environmental effects of mass tourism. Evidence of the increasing importance of these campaigns and the issues they raise can be found in the in-depth treatment they receive in major international newspapers and other media outlets such as the *New Yorker* (Mead, 2019), *Time* (Abend, 2018), the *Conversation* (Milano et al., 2018) and the BBC (Campoamor, 2017), to name just a few. While still understudied in the academic literature, scholars are gradually turning their attention to these events as they seek to understand the contexts within which they emerge, the language they use to articulate grievances, the social and political actors involved, the action repertoires they mobilise, the changes they espouse, and the effects of their action (Hughes, 2018; Milano et al., 2019). Much of the media attention has focused on events in Barcelona and Catalunya (Catalonia) more widely. For example, as Mead (2019) writing in the *New Yorker* reports, since 2014 this region of Spain has been the epicentre of some of the most high-profile anti-tourism activism witnessed anywhere in the world.

An aspect of the events mentioned frequently in journalistic treatments of the issues, but that has so far eluded academic scholarship, is a focus on the rich linguistic repertoires used by the social actors engaged in contestation against mass tourism's excesses. A cursory glance at coverage in the print, broadcast, and online media (see, for example, Burgen, 2018) reveals the variety of semiotic resources employed by anti-tourism protestors to vent their concerns and demand reform of an economic model based on mass tourism and unrestricted commercial growth across neighbourhoods until recently untouched by its worst effects. Such an omission is surprising in Barcelona's case, given that one of the abiding memories for anyone visiting the city in recent years are the ubiquitous slogans daubed on walls across the city articulating popular anger against tourism and the negative impact it is having on the city. In neighbourhoods such as Barceloneta, Poblenou and El Gòtic, and on or near important attractions such as Gaudi's Parque Guell or Sagrada Familia, slogans claiming that 'tourism is killing the city' or 'tourist you are the terrorist' divert visitors' attention from the gothic, modernist, and contemporary notes that constitute the city's unique architectural identity. As well as appearing on publicly accessible surfaces, still and video images of the slogans have been widely disseminated by activists and the media on their websites and across social media sites such as Facebook and Instagram. Such images have been particularly important in spreading awareness of the anti-tourism movement in Catalonia, and its emergence as one of the most potent causes of mobilisation in the region in recent years, second only to Catalan nationalism itself.

Given the slogans' prominence during the protests and resonance beyond the confines of the city, this chapter proposes a more theoretically grounded analysis of this dimension of tourism contestation in Barcelona. To do so, it pursues the following lines of enquiry. It begins by briefly setting out some of the most important properties of political slogans and provides examples of their use in both mainstream politics and contexts of political contestation. Drawing on the work of Gasaway Hill (2018) and political discourse analysis (PDA), primarily in the work of van Dijk (1997), the chapter then sets out a theoretical framework that conceptualises slogans as protest speech acts that contain powerful illocutionary force and provoke far-reaching perlocutionary effects. In applying the framework to the Catalan case, consistent with PDA, it delineates the context within which the slogans are deployed, focuses attention on how they work linguistically to construct contestation and build protester collective identity, and sets out the actions the slogans inspire amongst a range of audiences including tourism activists.

SLOGANS AS POLITICAL COMMUNICATION

Slogans made up of short and memorable phrases are an important political communication genre that, according to Lu (1999: 493), 'unify public thought and agitate public actions and reactions'. While on the surface they may appear superficial or simplistic, they have been important in forming political and social identities and agitating for change during some of the most important political events in history, from revolutions in France, China, and Russia to the protests for civil rights in the United States (US). In 2008, they played a pivotal role in Barack Obama's campaign to become the first black American president, in which the message of hope contained in 'Yes We Can' helped to mobilise widespread support for the hitherto little-known politician (Hodges, 2014). They were also a key feature of the Arab Spring, the Indignados protests in Spain, anti-austerity protests in Greece, and in Hong Kong, where they were prominent in both the Umbrella Revolution (see Kuo, 2014) and the pro-democracy demonstrations that have wracked Hong Kong since June 2019.

The presence of slogans in political action ranging from campaigning through to protesting, both throughout history and across cultures, means that they have received academic attention, in the work of Al-Sowaidi et al. (2017), Hodges (2014), Gasaway Hill (2018), and Serafis et al. (2018), to name just a few. Such interest is also a testament to the centrality of slogans in the communication strategies of a host of actors ranging from governments, political parties and their candidates, to social and protest movement groups and actors. While they have been around for hundreds of years, they appear to be even more pervasive in an era in which the Internet has created reliance on superficial, rapid, and uncomplicated messages, and spawned new political communication genres such as memes that combine pithy language and humorous images to important rhetorical effect.

Much of the power of slogans comes from their ability to simplify complex issues into memorable phrases that trigger deeper reflection and persuade people to participate in political action. To achieve such effects, slogan writers employ a range of linguistic tools and devices. For example, they regularly employ non-finite verb forms such as imperatives to raise awareness of issues and to persuade audiences to action, as in 'Save the Whale', or 'Vote

Leave' used by pro-Brexit supporters during the United Kingdom's 2016 European Union referendum campaign. Imperatives were also in evidence in pro-democracy uprisings in Egypt in which 'leave' was also a common protest refrain, urging Hosni Mubarak to step down from the presidency, as well as in the 2019 *Gilets Jaunes* (Yellow Vest) protests in France where '*Macron demission*' or 'Macron resign' has been a common call.

As Bussmann (1996: 1086) explains, slogans are 'precise and impressively formulated expression(s) with a persuasive function, frequently formed as an elliptic sentence and equipped with figures of speech such as repetition, alliteration, rhythm and rhyme'. In their work on the Arab Spring, Al-Sowaidi et al. (2017: 629) address the elliptical and phonetic dimensions of slogans and their importance in triggering memorability. These authors set out a range of criteria against which political slogans can be assessed, such as lexical economy (the use of a single word or phrase), clarity, 'eye-catchiness' and 'special sound patterns' that mean they 'easily stick to minds'.

According to Hodges (2014), the rhetorical power of political slogans often comes from the use of linguistic devices such as irony, metaphor, the 'rule of three', and synecdoche. The rule of three, for example, was used to powerful effect in 'Yes We Can' to call Barack Obama's supporters and the wider US electorate to action during the 2008 presidential election campaign. The slogan first came to prominence at the beginning of the campaign amongst committed supporters, for whom it became a 'rallying cry for Obama … in much the way it had for the United Farm Workers in a previous generation' (Hodges, 2014: 350). As the campaign's momentum grew, 'Yes We Can' became more widely diffused and began to play a significant role not just with the committed, but also amongst the wider US public. By encapsulating a complex electoral message for change into a simple three-word message, it provided an uncomplicated and memorable way of reminding voters of Obama's central campaign themes of hope, change, and unity.

Much of the work on slogans in political science has emphasised the textual form and the psychological and practical effects of slogans in more mainstream political contexts such as during elections. Less attention has been paid to their study in contexts of contestation and dissent, such as rallies, protests, demonstrations, and episodes of anti-hegemonic conflict or outright rebellion. While of course there are some notable exceptions to this, such as the study cited above looking at the role of protest slogans during the Arab Spring (Al-Sowaidi et al., 2017), work on the Gazi Park protests in Istanbul (Gasaway Hill, 2018), or studies of anti-austerity protests in Greece (Serafis et al., 2018), it remains an under-analysed field. One of the main obstacles to the development of work in this area has been the absence of an overarching conceptual framework linking elements of theory, practice, and outcomes to help guide the enquiry of protest language and its use by anti-hegemonic actors across time, space, and communication genres, as well as linguistic and cultural boundaries. Recently, Gasaway Hill (2018) has sought to fill this gap in the literature by providing a theoretical account of protest language and its deployment across a range of communicative genres including songs, poetry, chants, and slogans. The next section sets out the main assumptions of Gasaway Hill's framework and explores its implications, as a prelude to applying its insights to the analysis of data drawn from the anti-tourism case in Barcelona and Catalonia more widely.

SLOGANS: A THEORETICAL FRAMEWORK

Protest texts, of which slogans are one of several genres, are conceptualised by Gasaway Hill (2018) as performative speech acts that critique hegemonic discourses, build counter-narratives, and develop strategies to actualise protesters' vision for a better world. Gasaway Hill explores the power of protest texts to represent reality and construct an alternative future through the Austinian concepts of locution, illocution, and perlocution, which according to Gasaway Hill are present in every protest utterance. While locution refers to the act of producing an utterance, illocution relates to its functional dimension. As she explains (Gasaway Hill, 2018: 40), 'the illocutionary act is the interactional function and intention of the work done by the utterance and occurs when the saying is the doing, like a request, demand or invitation'. On the other hand, perlocutionary acts refer to the changes in behaviour brought about by speech acts. As Austin (1962: 101) himself points out, 'saying something will often, or even normally, produce certain consequential effects upon the feelings, thoughts, or actions of an audience, or of the speaker, or of other persons'. Drawing on Judith Butler (1997), Gasaway Hill (2018: 41) considers the temporal dimension of perlocution, pointing to the possible time-lag between the illocutionary function of performative speech acts and their perlocutionary consequences. She highlights this with the example of anti-war protest. Thus, while protestors chanting 'Not in my Name' are clearly performing an illocutionary act of protest, their perlocutionary goal of 'building solidarity' amongst protest actors or 'publicising the protest' or persuading the government to stop 'sending troops into another country', is often delayed (ibid.).

Gasaway Hill utilises a range of analytical concepts to explore the language of protest. Most notably these include the Althusser (1971) idea of 'interpellation' (when ideology 'hails' individuals to take subject positions in society), what she refers to as 'vocative address' relating to the audiences the speech act is directed towards, and 'convocativity'. Convocativity is what happens when protesters articulate a counter-version of reality that compromises dominant discourse and 'undermines public consent to hegemonic power' (Gasaway Hill, 2018: 63). This leads to an 'Us and Them' split between two opposed collective identities, described by Serafis et al. (2018) as 'an inclusive, positively characterised, in-group of "we", made up of those that align themselves to the protests and a negatively characterised out-group of "others" that resist the counter-hegemonic call'.

CONTEXT

According to Gasaway Hill (2018), the way in which instances of protest language are understood and the inferences actors draw from them is contingent on the context within which they are produced and operate. This position is shared by Serafis et al. (2018), who also argue that it is only by looking through the lens of both language and context that it is possible to reveal 'protesters' efforts to place themselves against the dominant values and institutions and highlight 'the emergence of a collective identity'.

To provide an account of the interplay between context and language, Gasaway Hill draws on work in the fields of critical discourse analysis (CDA) and political discourse analysis (PDA) by the likes of Fairclough (1995) and van Dijk (1997, 2005). Coming at this from a PDA perspective, van Dijk (2005) is at pains to explain that understanding the political function and effects of discourse requires an approach that relates it to prevailing 'attitudes, norms, values and ideologies' as well as to relevant features of the wider socio-political context within which it is produced, such as a country's political or legal system, or the role and influence of its mass media.

RENOVATED FELICITY CONDITIONS

To assess the extent to which protest speech acts achieve their illocutionary and perlocutionary effects, Gasaway Hill (2018) integrates an emphasis on Austin's 'felicity conditions' into her theoretical framework. These are best thought of as a set of social conventions and conditions that must be satisfied for any performative speech act to be considered successful, or 'felicitous' in Austin's terms (Austin, 1962). The postulation of a set of conditions, or 'renovated protest felicity conditions' (Gasaway Hill, 2018: 41–44), specific to the context of protest, in addition to acting as a tool for exploring the meaning, impact, and wider context for protest performatives, also aids comparison between different protest genres such as chants, slogans, songs, and poems. As Gasaway Hill (2018: 42) states, 'the felicity conditions take on a life as a proscenium arch that is movable to compare one protest genre with another, from chants in Gezi Park, to songs at the Berlin Wall, from poems at the Somme, to condemnations on *Cuatro Caminos*'.

Gasaway Hill (2018) outlines four renovated protest felicity conditions to be met if protest utterances are to achieve their intended effects. Renovated protest felicity conditions 1 and 2 encompass a wide range of 'presuppositions' that must prevail for protest speech to be effective. In the case of condition 1, for example, she argues that, 'it must be a commonly accepted convention that the uttering for, on or in a public space, of words that challenge social, political or cultural hegemonic power(s) … will lead to a margin-centre convocativity on said challenge' (Gasaway Hill, 2018: 55). On the other hand, renovated protest felicity condition 2 focuses on the anti-hegemonic nature of the act that automatically places protesters, 'on the margin in tension with the power centre for that issue' (Gasaway Hill, 2018: 56). One of the key contextual presuppositions discussed by Gasaway Hill (2018: 58) is the presence of 'circumstances appropriate to a protest'. These come about as the result of conflict rooted in patterns of oppression and/or discontent between the 'powers that be' and at least one other person or group. Such conflict is often illuminated or triggered by flashpoint events such as the introduction of a new policy or a repressive act carried out by the political authorities. Through their public response to injustice, protestors display critical awareness of both its causes and potential solutions, which stand in stark and emphatic contrast to the dominant ideological discourse surrounding the issue. Another key aspect of renovated protest felicity condition 1 discussed by Gasaway Hill relates to the use of language. Thus, the lexical, grammatical, and syntactical choices made by protest actors constitute a 'semantics of opposition' (Gasaway Hill, 2018: 59) that highlights disagreements and, either directly or indirectly, articulates the requirement for change.

Whereas renovated protest felicity conditions 1 and 2 emphasise presuppositional dimensions of protest language, renovated protest felicity conditions 3 and 4 interrogate issues related to protest actors' attitudes, feelings, and aspirations, and their willingness to participate in social action consistent with their views (Gasaway Hill, 2018: 66). Through the performance of political speech acts, particularly in high-risk contexts, protestors demonstrate commitment to the cause they seek to advance (condition 3). Protest speech act performance is also an indication of protesters' willingness to sustain action in pursuit of their demands (condition 4). As in the case of condition 3, the extent to which this is possible or sustainable depends on the type of action contemplated and the level of risk entailed. The latter is an important indicator of the depth of commitment to the cause, as are the number of speech acts performed, and the extent to which they connect to other expressions of protest (Gasaway Hill, 2018: 67). The level of risk is a key contextual factor shaped by the nature of the political regime within which the protest takes place, and the type of action contemplated by protesters.

In the section that follows, the theoretical framework outlined above is applied to the analysis of three of the innumerable slogans that have appeared in Barcelona and more widely across Catalonia: '*El Turisme Mata Els Barris*' (Tourism Is Killing the Neighbourhoods), '*Fem Plaça*' (Let's Make the Square), and 'Tourist You Are the Terrorist' in recent times. As in Gasaway Hill's (2018: 79–121) own empirical exploration of the use of protest speech by activists in the US and during the Gezi Park occupation in Turkey, the analysis is prefaced by an attempt to situate the slogans in their broader historical context. They are then subject to particular scrutiny under 'the proscenium arch of the renovated felicity conditions' (Gasaway Hill, 2018). This provides the means for exploration of key questions including the linguistic form and illocutionary function of the slogans, contextual factors important to their meaning and their role in constructing anti-tourism contestation, as well as a collective protester identity within the city.

THE DEEP STORY OF ANTI-TOURISM SLOGANS IN CATALONIA

The slogans discussed are part of an anti-tourism protest cycle in Barcelona dating back to at least 2014 (Hughes, 2018: 471). The main driver for the acts of contestation carried out during the cycle is opposition to a process of over-tourism that has transformed residential areas into tourist accommodation zones shared by locals and sometimes poorly behaved foreign tourists. According to Milano et al. (2019), over-tourism occurs in the context of an 'excessive growth of visitors leading to overcrowding in areas where residents suffer the consequences of temporary and seasonal tourism peaks, which have caused permanent changes to their lifestyles, denied access to amenities and damaged their general well-being'.

In Barcelona's case, over-tourism is fuelled by the popularity of short-term holiday rentals booked online through peer-to-peer platforms such as Airbnb, and low-cost air travel provided by the likes of Ryanair. This combination of factors has led to a significant increase in the numbers of international travellers and tourists looking to spend time in one of Europe's most popular tourist destinations. Residents in neighbourhoods such as Barceloneta and El Gòtic have been particularly critical of the deterioration in their quality of life due to the anti-social practices of some young people staying in Airbnb-type accommodation (see, for example, Hughes, 2018; Lambea Llop 2017; and Sans and Quaglieri Domínguez, 2016, for wider discussion).

Anti-social behaviour is a key factor in a process of population displacement, as residents have sold their properties to escape the nuisance caused by the influx of young people into the city (Gravari-Barbas and Jacquot, 2017). Displacement is also being driven by the upward pressure that demand for properties from Airbnb speculators is having on both house prices and rents. This is primarily an issue for neighbourhoods near the city centre or beach areas, where demand for space has increased and prices have risen accordingly. Many residents see this as particularly problematic for young people, who are forced to either live at home with their parents or move out of areas they have lived in all their lives due to their inability to pay the high market rents demanded by property owners.

Other concerns raised locally include the impact of tourism on both popular local businesses and public services such as transport. While the former have been replaced by tourist-facing services such as bike hire and souvenir shops, the latter are becoming difficult to access or overcrowded. Another factor contributing to these aspects of over-tourism is the weight of traffic from cruise ships. With its nine terminals, Barcelona is home to the Mediterranean's largest port. Prior to Covid-19, around 3 million cruise passengers descended on the city each year, and there could be as many as 25 000 cruise passengers in the city on any one day (Escalante, 2019). Barcelona has also experienced a threefold increase in hotel demand – from 3 million to 9 million overnight stays – in the last 20 years (Hughes, 2018: 476). Given Barcelona's relatively small population of 1.6 million, this is placing considerable pressure on the local community, and according to some observers, has only limited benefits. Regarding employment, for example, the overall impact has been surprisingly weak, with only a 0.63 per cent increase during the 2008–2016 period that witnessed a 20 per cent increase in the number of visitors to the city. The quality of the jobs created is also a concern, with the Candidatura d'Unitat Popular (Popular Unity Candidacy) political party describing most of them as, 'seasonal, precarious, and part-time' (Candidatura d'Unitat Popular, 2017).

THE TRIGGER EVENT

Flashpoint events play a key role in illuminating disagreements in the life of any conflict. For example, during the Umbrella Revolution in Hong Kong, China's attempt to parachute its chosen candidates into local government elections in 2014 was considered an important flashpoint in the conflict between the pro-democracy movement and the Chinese government (Gasaway Hill, 2018: 58). Similarly, in the case of tourism activism in Barcelona, popular anger has been especially intense since the summer of 2014, when a group of young tourists was seen to be wandering naked around the streets of the traditionally working class Barceloneta whilst uploading videos of their exploits to YouTube. In response, hundreds of locals took to the streets in spontaneous protest against the tourists whose uncivilised behaviour, they argued, was blighting their neighbourhood (Hughes, 2018).

Since 2014, Barcelona has witnessed continued anti-tourism activism, with the only pause coming in the wake of the August 2017 Islamist terror attacks that targeted pedestrians in Barcelona's central tourist avenue, Las Ramblas, and the nearby seaside resort of Cambrils, that left 16 dead and over 100 injured. The months prior to the attack saw an apparent shift in the protest repertoire of anti-tourism activists away from the peaceful demonstrations, gatherings, and marches that had characterised their activities up to that point, towards more violent forms of action targeted at both tourism businesses and foreign tourists themselves, in which slogans featured prominently.

PRESUPPOSITIONAL RENOVATED FELICITY CONDITIONS 1 AND 2

As already discussed, to be effectively realised such performative acts of protest must fulfil certain conditions relating to the context within which they are uttered (public space), the people protesting (people interpolated as protesters), the language they use (vocatives), and the effects of the protest (convocative split). As I will demonstrate, these conditions are clearly satisfied in the case of the three protest slogans chosen for more detailed analysis in this chapter, '*El Turisme Mata Els Barris*' (Tourism Is Killing the Neighbourhoods), '*Fem Plaça*' (Let's Make the Square) and 'Tourist you are the Terrorist' (see Table 21.1).

The slogans are part of a highly visible public campaign, uniting neighbourhoods across the city and provoked by the deep feelings of frustration and anger felt at the pernicious effects that tourism is having on their neighbourhoods. Popular dissatisfaction has fuelled calls from an increasingly vociferous coalition of social groups and activist organisations for city authorities to ensure that their neighbourhoods remain accessible and liveable for local people. In recent years, according to Hughes (2018), at least 30 local neighbourhood groups have joined together with more traditional organisations such as trade unions to mobilise support and demand action. One of the key actors that has been at the heart of the mobilisation is the La Barceloneta Diu Prou (Barceloneta Says Enough) collective, which was set up in 2014 to coordinate action against the tourist apartment phenomenon and related uncivilised tourist behaviour (see Hughes, 2018 for wider discussion). La Barceloneta Diu Prou has also participated in attempts to unite the disparate anti-tourism struggles that have broken out in neighbourhoods across Barcelona, into a common front against the economic, social, and environmental costs of a process of city redevelopment that has transformed Barcelona from an ageing industrial

Table 21.1   *Terrorist slogans*

Slogans	Authors	Language	Illocution	Perlocution
El Turisme Mata Els Barris	Arran	Catalan	Counter dominant narratives Call activists to arms Unify neighbourhood opposition Construct an existential threat narrative	Convoked 'us and them' split Mobilised activists to take direct action including acts of vandalism and violence Created tension within the movement Prompted claims of tourismphobia
Tourist You Are the Terrorist	Tal Tal Crew	English	Counter dominant narratives Call activists to arms Other tourists	Convoked 'us and them' split Mobilised activists to take direct action including acts of vandalism and violence Created tension within the movement Prompted claims of tourismphobia
Fem Plaça	Fem Plaça Collective	Catalan	Community mobilisation Build solidarity	Strengthened neighbourhood unity Mobilised community-based activism Reappropriated public space United neighbourhood-based opposition

port city into a not to be missed destination for many discerning travellers. It organised, for example, the '*Barcelona no Está en Venda*' (Barcelona is not for sale) demonstration that saw some 2000 protestors representing more than 40 residents' and community groups stage an occupation of Las Ramblas in January 2017. It was also involved in the setting up the Assemblea de Barris per un Tursime Sostenible, or Neighbourhood Assembly for Sustainable Tourism, that organises coordinated action against the negative impact of mass tourism in the city (Hughes, 2018: 472).

Many of those involved in the collectives and neighbourhood assemblies that took part in the campaigns are activists in left-wing parties and groupings such as Barcelona En Comú (Barcelona in Common) and the more explicitly anti-capitalist Candidatura d'Unitat Popular (Popular Unity Candidacy). The Candidatura d'Unitat Popular, which was formed in the mid-1980s, is distinguished from other Spanish political parties by its horizontal structure and lack of recognisable leadership. For most of its existence it has been a peripheral figure in Catalan politics, limiting its involvement to the municipal level where its members espouse a radical agenda that combines anti-capitalism, Catalan nationalism, and libertarian localism. Its position on mass tourism is set out in *Els Mites del Turisme* (Candidatura d'Unitat Popular, 2017). In it, the Candidatura d'Unitat Popular identifies the 1992 Olympics as the point at which Barcelona became a brand and the city was 'put up for sale' as part of a far-reaching economic redevelopment programme. According to the report, while tourism-inspired regeneration has been successful in attracting visitors and foreign investment, it has also been the catalyst for a process of gentrification that is pricing locals out of their homes and changing the character of local neighbourhoods. This claim acts as a powerful antidote to the official narrative extolling the virtues of tourism and its positive impact on Barcelona. According to *Els Mites del Turisme* (Candidatura d'Unitat Popular, 2017), the 'triumphalist' discourse used by public authorities about the success of Barcelona's redevelopment programme is coming under increasing scrutiny given the negative 'externalities' it generates for locals.

One of the main sources of such discourse is Turisme de Barcelona, a public–private partnership set up in the wake of the 1992 Barcelona Olympics with representation from Barcelona Municipal Council, the Barcelona Official Chamber of Commerce, Industry and Shipping, and the Barcelona Promotion Foundation. It describes tourism as 'one of our crown jewels' that creates wealth and employment in the city (Turisme de Barcelona, 2007). The report goes on to claim that the industry 'contributes to the preservation of our culture and the cultural spaces that make us different from others' (Turisme de Barcelona, 2007). According to the consortium (Zerva et al., 2019), it is incumbent on the citizenry to behave appropriately towards tourists if the city is to retain its attractiveness as one of Europe's most important city destinations: 'Barcelona is and must remain an attractive destination internationally for its quality and conviviality. It is a city where tourism supports the daily life of its inhabitants and we are proud to be people of Barcelona.'

Organisationally, the Candidatura d'Unitat Popular (Popular Unity Candidacy) is best understood as a coalition that integrates several grass-roots assemblies that meet in towns and cities across Catalonia and several semi-autonomous factions. These include Poble Lliure (Free People) and the two groups claiming responsibility for many of the acts of vandalism and violence targeting both tourism businesses and tourists that have come to international attention in recent years: Arran (Level With) and Endavant-Organització d'Alliberament Nacional (Forward-Socialist Organisation of National Liberation). Arran, whose members have played a central role in many of the high-profile anti-tourism actions, is a militant youth organisation with approximately 500 members distributed across Catalonia, Valencia, and the Balearic Islands. Formed in 2012, it sees itself as the socialist and feminist youth organisation of the pro-independence left. In addition to its campaign against mass tourism, its members have carried out high-profile action against political parties that oppose the right to Catalan self-determination such as the centre-left Socialist Party of Catalonia (PSC) and the centre-right Popular Party (PP), whose Catalan headquarters they attempted to occupy in March 2017. On 1 June 2017, several members were arrested after they chained themselves to the Barcelona Stock Exchange in action against capitalism and the iniquities of high finance (Brunat, 2017).

In particular, Arran has been associated with use of slogans critical of tourism's impact on the city. For example, in July 2019 *El Pais* reported the appearance of a banner (in English) containing the slogan 'Tourism Kills the City' flying prominently from the roof of one of Barcelona's iconic tourist attractions, Gaudi's modernist La Pedrera, located on one of the Catalan capital's busiest thoroughfares, Passeig de Gràcia. Arran is aided and abetted in the anti-tourism campaign by activists from Forward: The Socialist Organisation of National Liberation. Endavant, the most radically anti-capitalist faction within the Candidatura d'Unitat Popular, characterises itself as an 'assembly-based political organisation that works for an independent, socialist, ecologically sustainable, territorially balanced Catalunya free from all forms of patriarchal domination' (Endavant, 2019).

'*EL TURISME MATA ELS BARRIS*' (TOURISM IS KILLING THE NEIGHBOURHOODS), AND 'TOURIST YOU ARE THE TERRORIST'

As part of the campaign, activists have employed many of the linguistic conventions of writing protest slogans set out earlier in the chapter, such as the use of non-finite verb forms and figures of speech to deconstruct the view that tourism contributes positively to people's lives, thereby placing them in clear opposition to the hegemonic centre. In the case of '*El Turisme Mata Els Barris*' (Tourism Kills the Neighbourhoods), for example, personification rhetoric is used to both counter the discourse that interpellates Catalans as passive agents of 'conviviality' and represent the city's neighbourhoods as a unified group (us) threatened by the pernicious role that tourism plays in their lives. Linguistically, it is distinguished by its use of a present continuous aspect to create a temporal sense of events beginning in the past that are inexorably moving towards a dystopic future. In this way, it serves as a warning to Catalans of what will happen if action to 'reclaim' the city from those that threaten it fails to materialise. By embedding into the public consciousness the idea that tourism constitutes an existential threat to the city, the slogan acts as a call to arms for activists to take action to protect Barcelona from the danger posed to it.

The use of existential threat rhetoric is also evident in other slogans that have graced the city since 2014. 'Tourist You Are the Terrorist', for example, is clearly more directly confrontational, and provides evidence of the extent of local opposition to the tourism boom, and anger at the behaviour of many tourists. In it, tourists are effectively 'othered' as an outsider group based on their identity as visitors to the city. This externally facing vocative uses English alliteration, consonance, and assonance, both to grab the audience's attention and to ensure that what in some circles might be considered hate speech lingers long in the memory.

'FEM PLAÇA' (LET'S MAKE THE SQUARE)

Some of the most aggressive anti-tourism sloganeering has appeared in neighbourhoods with little history of tourism prior to 1992 such as Ciutat Vella, Barceloneta, El Gòtic, El Raval, Poblenou, Poble Sec, and Eixample. Their location, near the city centre and/or the beach, means they have been particularly affected by the tourism apartment phenomenon. For example, more than half the buildings in the El Gòtic area contain tourist flats for rent online (Moll, 2016). The main reason is the level of rental income that property owners can derive from tourist flats, which according to one estimate is at least four times higher than from conventional tenancy arrangements (Sanz, 2018). The letting of apartments in residential blocks has caused considerable tension between tourists and locals, as is clear in the 'us and them' rhetoric apparent in tourist-facing vocatives such as 'Tourist You Are the Terrorist'.

There is a growing consensus that issues such as property speculation and tourism-fuelled gentrification is threatening neighbourhoods' authenticity and integrity embodied in public spaces. In Ciutat Vella, the urban collective *Fem Plaça* (Let's Make the Square) has been particularly vociferous in its condemnation of the impact of over-tourism on the neighbourhood's squares and plazas. As an alternative to the current model, the Fem Plaça Collective calls for greater regulation by the city and regional authorities, and an approach based on communitarian principles that reclaims privately appropriated public space. This view is reflected in the slogans that adorn the Fem Plaça Collective's posters and banners in the streets and squares of Ciutat Vella. These make wide use of the Catalan imperative form to call for citizen-generated urban interventions, including the taking over and repurposing of public space lost to commercial activity, as in the case of '*Recuper l'espai public com a lloc de convivencia*' (Take back public space as a place of co-existence) (Bruttomesso, 2018). The combination of imperatives and the use of first-person plural forms apparent in the collective's name and in slogans such as, '*Fem Plaça, Fem Platja*' (Let's Make the Square, Let's Make the Beach) act as an internally oriented vocative that challenges the commodification of space and helps build solidarity within Ciutat Vella and with other neighbourhoods involved in tourism contestation. Such language use, much in the way described by Serafis et al. (2018), contributes to the construction of wider social movement identity and helps build cohesion across the diverse network of actors involved in the protests. The 'us/them' dichotomy is clearly at play here. Thus, the 'us' group of protesters is explicitly invoked in the Catalan imperative form *fem* ('let's') that both implores locals to act in defence of their neighbourhood, and also inscribes the protests into a wider network of city districts struggling against tourism and its effects.

The slogans, the messages they convey, and the wider action of which they are a part have clearly contributed to the forging of a convocative split on the issue of tourism, with many locals aligning with the anti-hegemonic view embodied in slogans such as '*El Turisme Mata Els Barris*' (Tourism is Killing the Neighbourhoods). This is substantiated by polling data that shows 48.9 per cent of the population seeing tourism as a greater threat to Barcelona than economic problems, climate change, or criminality (Candidatura d'Unitat Popular, 2017). There is also some evidence suggesting that tourists themselves, at least in 2017, have acted in accordance with some of the more threatening anti-tourism vocatives such as 'tourist, leave or die'. According to the General Secretary of the United Nations World Tourism Organization (UNWTO), Zurab Pololikashvili, Catalonia suffered a 15 to 20 per cent fall in tourism during the final third of 2017 (Hosteltur, 2018). Although other factors such as a jihadist-inspired terrorist attack on Las Ramblas and outbreaks of regional nationalist political violence on Barcelona's streets are also important factors here, there can be no denying the part anti-tourism activism played in the reported decline.

RENOVATED FELICITY CONDITIONS 3 AND 4

There have been many actions consistent with the anti-tourism stance since the protest cycle began. Chief amongst these are acts of violence and vandalism carried out by Arran activists in Barcelona and other important Catalan tourist destinations such as Palma. In such cases, the slogans appear to have functioned as a call to arms, urging protesters to take action to protect the city and return it to its people. In the most high-profile action, in August 2017 a group of masked members of Arran stopped a sightseeing bus full of British tourists close to the Camp Nou home of Barcelona Football Club. As the stunned holidaymakers watched on, the bus was daubed with the slogan 'tourism kills neighbourhoods' and had its tyres slashed. A video of the attack in which the anti-tourism slogans figure prominently was uploaded to YouTube shortly after the events accompanied by the caption, 'mass tourism kills neighbourhoods, destroys the territory and condemns the working class to misery'. In other incidents, for-hire bicycles also had their tyres punctured, and several hotels and restaurants were paint-bombed. Again, the video's accompanying slogans appear to legitimise the vandalism, as do subsequent justifications for the attacks issued by Arran activists in which they describe their action as acts of 'self-defence' against the tourism invasion. While nobody was hurt in the actions, the willingness of the activists to risk punishment, including heavy fines and incarceration, is clear evidence of their commitment to the cause (see Hughes, 2018 for wider discussion).

The most important effects of '*Fem Plaça*' (Let's Make the Square) are embodied in the frequent neighbourhood-based action and events that take place in the likes of Sant Antoni and Ciutat Vella aimed at reappropriating public space. The Fem Plaça Collective, for example, organises regular 'community gatherings' which, they argue, 'act as some form of prosthesis for the lost street life and casual encounters, which had been amputated and disappeared from the neighbourhood', The location, times, and days of the events are designed to meet local community needs. In Sant Antoni, for, example, family-based activities take place after school on Fridays, and locals are invited to meet to chat and drink vermouth at lunchtime on Sundays.

The fact that the slogans continue to appear in public places more than five years after the initial triggering event is evidence of the sustained nature of the conflict, and that despite attempts by city officials to address local concerns, the grievances remain. While 2017 was undoubtedly the high point of action in Catalonia, articles still appear in the national and regional press attesting to the ongoing tensions aroused by the issue. In August 2019, for example, the Catalan regional newspaper, *La Vanguardia* (2019), reported on attacks being carried out by anti-tourism activists on car-rental companies in Mallorca, and as already mentioned, banners containing anti-tourism sentiment were unfurled by Arran activists on the roof of Gaudi's La Pedrera during the same month (*El Pais*, 2019).

Although, as these events demonstrate, the illocutionary call to arms present in many of the protest slogans has been faithfully obeyed by young activists, their actions have not gone without criticism. As might be expected, amongst those in support of the redevelopment model based on mass tourism there has been an attempt to delegitimise the protests by accusing the perpetrators of 'tourismphobia'. Criticism of Arran's actions has also come from within the ranks of the wider anti-tourism movement itself, with many baulking at the scapegoating of tourists, and the acts of violence and vandalism directed at foreign visitors to the city and tourism businesses such as hotels, restaurants, and vehicle hire companies. For some, such acts constitute an act of opportunism by the Candidatura d'Unitat Popular (Popular Unity Candidacy) as it jockeys to be seen as the main protagonist in the struggle against mass tourism. For others, by focusing on innocent tourists it shifts attention away from the real structural and agential causes of overtourism in Barcelona: namely, a redevelopment model that prioritises profits over the people (see discussion in Hughes, 2018). In so doing, it plays into the hands of elite actors such as Turisme de Barcelona, who rather than seeing the action as an expression of legitimate concern, are given licence to dismiss it as evidence of the 'tourismphobic' attitudes of which the activists stand accused.

CONCLUSIONS

This chapter has looked at the way in which slogans are used by activists to construct tourism contestation in Barcelona through the lens of an analytical framework that draws on work in the fields of speech act theory (SAT) and political discourse analysis (PDA). By subjecting the slogans to scrutiny under the 'proscenium arch' of Gasaway Hill's (2018) renovated felicity conditions, it has revealed insights that might otherwise have remained hidden from view. Chief among these are the ways in which the movement actors use language to deconstruct dominant narratives, build contestation, and promote movement identity by fostering an 'us and them' split between those they target in their campaigns and the neighbourhoods worst affected by over-tourism.

Through their use of 'differentiating discursive options' (Serafis et al., 2018: 5) in slogans such as '*El Turisme Mata Els Barris*' (Tourism is Killing the Neighbourhoods), movement actors organised in La CUP, Arran, and the Fem Plaça Collective have managed to fashion a convocative split between themselves and the neighbourhoods they purport to represent, and those more accepting of the official line on tourism. This is most clearly seen in the accusatory vocative used to 'other' tourists as in some of the less agreeable slogans, such as 'Tourist You Are the Terrorist', that have appeared on Barcelona's streets since the cycle of tourism contestation began. It is also present in '*Fem Plaça*' (Let's Make the Square). This vocative calls on local people to oppose the commodification of space by reappropriating for the community public squares, one of the sites most closely associated with tourism-related commercial activity. The split is intensified by official attempts to discredit the protestors by accusing them of 'tourismphobia', and by raising the threat of draconian sentences if they fail to desist in their activism.

The study has also shown that, as Gasaway Hill and advocates of the PDA approach such as van Dijk (1997, 2005) claim, the meaning of the slogans can only really be understood in their wider socio-economic, cultural, and/or political context. The most salient contextual factor for deciphering the meaning of these texts is a model of economic development that has seen Barcelona transformed from the rather dilapidated port it was in the early 1990s, to the global city it is today. While exploitation of the city's cultural heritage may have been successful in attracting foreign investment, knowledge workers, and international visitors to the city, it has also been responsible for a process of over-tourism that has benefited elites, not society in general. The levels of both popular anger and critical awareness of the causes of discontent are characterised by negative surveys of public opinion identifying tourism as one of the biggest problems facing the city, regular bouts of activism directed at tourists and tourism-related business interests. Examples presented in the chapter range from the ongoing Sant Antoni gatherings in which neighbours reappropriate public space on Sunday afternoons over a glass of vermouth, to the hijacking of a tourism bus near the Camp Nou football stadium in 2017.

Finally, one of the most striking conclusions to be drawn from this study relates to space and the way in which the slogans work to anchor the contestation within particular sites of protest such as the city, the neighbourhood, and the square. By doing so, the slogan authors inscribe the protests in similar action (see Debras, 2019 for a discussion of how such anchoring operates in both time and space) taking place beyond their own locales, in other squares and neighbourhoods in cities both elsewhere in Spain and beyond. This centrifugal trajectory of the protests is aided and abetted by the translation of many of the slogans into multiple languages. This serves to carry the protests beyond their own context of origin, to places where protestors are also engaged in mobilisations against the urban tourism phenomenon.

REFERENCES

Abend, L. (2018), 'Europe Made Billions from Tourists. Now It's Turning Them Away', available at https://time.com/5349533/europe-against-tourists/, accessed 26 July 2019.

Al-Sowaidi, B., F. Banda, and A. Mansour, A. (2017), 'Doing Politics in the Recent Arab Uprisings: Towards a Political Discourse Analysis of the Arab Spring Slogans', *Journal of Asian and African Studies*, 52(5): 621–645.

Althusser, L. (1971), *Lenin and Philosophy and Other Essays*, London: New Left Books.

Austin, J.L. (1962), *How to Do Things with Words (The William James Lectures)*, Oxford: Clarendon Press.

Brunat, B. (2017), 'Así es Arran, las juventudes antisistema que han tomado las calles de Barcelona', available at https://www.elconfidencial.com/espana/2017-08-02/arran-cup-referendum-cataluna-violencia-callejera_1423992/, accessed 2 August 2019.

Bruttomesso, E. (2018), 'Making Sense of the Square: Facing the Touristification of Public Space through Playful Protest in Barcelona', *Tourist Studies*, 18(4): 467–485.

Burgen, S. (2018), '"Tourists Go Home, Refugees Welcome": Why Barcelona Chose Migrants over Visitors', available at https://www.theguardian.com/cities/2018/jun/25/tourists-go-home-refugees-welcome-why-barcelona-chose-migrants-over-visitors, accessed 25 June 2020.

Bussmann, H. (1996), *Routledge. Dictionary of Language and Linguistics*, London, UK and New York, USA: Routledge.

Butler, J. (1997), *Excitable Speech: A Politics of Performance*, London, UK and New York, USA: Routledge.

Campoamor, J. (2017), 'Turismofobia: Barcelona y otras ciudades en pie de guerra contra el turismo de masas', available at https://www.bbc.com/mundo/noticias-40107507, accessed 1 June 2019.

Candidatura d'Unitat Popular (2017), 'Els mites del turisme', available at http://turisme.capgirembcn.cat/, accessed 31 August 2019.

Colomb, C., and J. Novy (2016), *Protest and Resistance in the Tourist City*, London: Routledge.

Debras, C. (2019), 'Political Graffiti in May 2018 at Nanterre University: A Linguistic Ethnographic Analysis', *Discourse and Society*, 30(5), 441–464.

El Pais (2019), 'Arran cuelga una pancarta en La Pedrera: "El turismo mata la ciudad"', available at https://elpais.com/ccaa/2019/07/02/catalunya/1562065191_682813.html, accessed 2 July 2019.

Endavant (2019), *Endavant*, available at https://www.endavant.org/, accessed 31 August 2019.

Escalante, J.L. (2019), 'La llegada de cruceristas a Barcelona se desinfla y cae un 10% en lo que va de 2019', available at https://cronicaglobal.elespanol.com/business/cruceristas-barcelona-turismo_245508_102.html, accessed 31 August 2019.

Fairclough, N. (1995), *Critical Discourse Analysis*, Boston, MA: Addison Wesley.

Gasaway Hill, M.L. (2018), *The Language of Protest: Acts of Performance, Identity, and Legitimacy*, New York: Springer International Publishing.
Gravari-Barbas, M. and S. Jacquot (2017), 'No conflict? Discourses and management of tourism-related tensions in Paris', in C. Colomb and J. Novy (eds), *Protest and Resistance in the Tourist City*, New York: Routledge, pp. 31–51.
Hodges, A. (2014), '"Yes, We Can": The Social Life of a Political Slogan', in C. Hart (ed.), *Contemporary Critical Discourse Studies*, London: Bloomsbury Academic, pp. 347–365.
Hosteltur (2018), 'La OMT señala que la caída del turismo en Cataluña roza el 20%', available at https://www.hosteltur.com/125992_omt-senala-caida-turismo-cataluna-roza-20.html, accessed 31 August 2019.
Hughes, N. (2018), '"Tourists go Home": Anti-Tourism Industry Protest in Barcelona', *Social Movement Studies*, 17(4): 471–477.
Kuo, L. (2014), 'The Backstory to Seven of the Most Popular Protest Slogans in Hong Kong's Umbrella Movement', *Quartz*, available at https://qz.com/285990/the-backstory-to-seven-of-the-most-popular-protest-slogans-in-hong-kongs-umbrella-movement/, accessed 28 October 2019.
La Vanguardia (2019), 'Arran publica un vídeo en el que vandalizan vehículos para criticar el alquiler de coches a turistas en Mallorca', available at https://www.elmundo.es/economia/2019/08/05/5d4815b8fc6c83992f8b46a8.html, accessed 31 August 2019.
Lambea Llop, N. (2017), 'A Policy Approach to the Impact of Tourist Dwellings in Condominiums and Neighbourhoods in Barcelona', *Urban Research and Practice*, 10(1): 120–129.
Lu, X. (1999), 'An Ideological/Cultural Analysis of Political Slogans in Communist China', *Discourse and Society*, 10(4): 487–508.
Mead, R. (2019), 'The AirnBnB Invasion of Barcelona', *New Yorker*, available at https://www.newyorker.com/magazine/2019/04/29/the-airbnb-invasion-of-barcelona, accessed 20 August 2019.
Milano, C., J. Cheer, and M. Novelli (2018), 'Overtourism: A Growing Problem', *Conversation*, available at https://theconversation.com/overtourism-a-growing-global-problem-100029, accessed 18 July 2019.
Milano, C., M. Novelli, and J. Cheer (2019), 'Overtourism and Tourismphobia: A Journey Through Four Decades of Tourism Development, Planning and Local Concerns', *Tourism Planning and Development*, 16(4): 353–357.
Moll, I. (2016), 'Más de la mitad de los edificios del Barrio Gótico de Barcelona albergan pisos turísticos', available at https://www.tourinews.es/resumen-de-prensa/notas-de-prensa-espana-turismo/mitad-edificios-barrio-gotico-barcelona-albergan-pisos-turisticos_327345_102.html, accessed 20 August 2019.
Sans, A., and A. Quaglieri Domínguez (2016), 'Unravelling Airbnb: Urban Perspectives from Barcelona', in P. Russo and G. Richards (eds), *Reinventing the Local in Tourism. Travel Communities and Peer-Produced Place Experiences*, London: Channel View, pp. 209–228.
Sanz, E. (2018), '¿Alquiler turístico vs tradicional? Solo es más rentable a partir del 60% de ocupación', available at https://www.elconfidencial.com/vivienda/2018-06-27/alquiler-turistico-rentabilidad-alquiler-tradicional-precios_1584220/, accessed 10 August 2019.
Serafis, D., E. Dimitris Kitris, and A. Archakis (2018), 'Graffiti Slogans and the Construction of Collective Identity: Evidence from the Anti-Austerity Protests in Greece', *Text and Talk*, 38(6): 775–797.
Turisme de Barcelona (2007), *Annual Report 2006*, Barcelona: Tourisme de Barcelona.
van Dijk, T.A. (1997), 'What is Political Discourse Analysis?', *Belgian Journal of Linguistics*, 11(1): 11–52.
van Dijk, T.A. (2005), 'War Rhetoric of a Little Ally. Political Implicatures of Aznar's Legitimization of the War in Iraq', *Journal of Language and Politics*, 4(1): 65–92.
Zerva, K., S. Palou, D. Blasco, and J.A.B. Donaire (2019), 'Tourism-Philia Versus Tourism-Phobia: Residents and Destination Management Organization's Publicly Expressed Tourism Perceptions in Barcelona', *Tourism Geographies*, 21(2): 306–329.

22. The Mexican 2018 presidential election in the media landscape: newspaper coverage, TV spots, and Twitter interaction

Rubén Arnoldo González

INTRODUCTION

With over 3400 candidates running for federal, state, or municipal posts, the 2018 election was Mexico's largest electoral process. It was also the first time that a left-wing candidate won the presidential race. Disturbingly, these historic events derived from violence and polarised campaigns. At least 100 candidates were killed or injured during the process, although there were neither official reports nor investigations into these casualties. On the other hand, polarisation was the hallmark of the messages between competitors and their supporters.

Andrés Manuel López Obrador, leader of the Juntos Haremos Historia coalition, won the election with 53.19 per cent of the votes. The coalition integrated the National Regeneration Movement, Labour Party, and Social Encounter Party. Following in second place was Ricardo Anaya with 22.27 per cent, representing the Por México al Frente coalition, supported by the National Action Party, Democratic Revolution Party, and Citizen Movement. Third place went to José Antonio Meade of the Todos por México coalition (Institutional Revolutionary Party, Green Party, and New Alliance), who obtained 16.4 per cent. Jaime Rodríguez, the independent candidate, got 5.23 per cent (INE, 2018).

This chapter presents an overview of the 2018 electoral process from three different vantage points of traditional and social media platforms, namely newspapers, television, and Twitter. It draws on secondary data from three independent studies on press coverage, campaign spots, and candidates' Twitter activity after the debates. The core argument is that propaganda determined the competitors' communication strategies. That is, whilst news stories were devoted to reproduce candidates and political elites' discourses, TV spots emphasised contenders' image to the detriment of their proposals, and candidates did not promote deliberation on Twitter, because they merely used it as another way to reproduce their positions.

PROPAGANDA: AN OVERVIEW

Traditionally propaganda has been associated with pejorative notions of mind control, distortion of reality, and mass manipulation, with the ultimate goal of getting people to support an idea, but not to think about it (see, e.g., Silverstein, 1987; Herman and Chomsky, 1988; Chomsky, 1992). Nonetheless, recent studies advocate for a more neutral approach to the concept (e.g., Taylor, 2003; Auerbach and Castronovo, 2013; Rawnsley, 2013), considering it as an instrument of governance. That is, in order to strengthen their legitimacy, contemporary governments – and other institutions such as political parties – seek to communicate better with their constituencies. Thus, authorities are constantly publicising their levels of performance and delivery, because that may promote popular support (Rawnsley, 2013; Baines, 2014; Zollman, 2019).

Therefore, propaganda is the process of production and dissemination of ideas (Taylor, 2003). In this regard, it seeks to shape receivers' beliefs and/or actions by sending them a wide array of messages. In order to encourage people's participation, these kinds of content are coherent and consistent images aimed to appeal to specific target audiences (Baines, 2014). Consequently, the content includes information that is framed according to ideals shared by senders and receivers. As a mass phenomenon, these messages must reach large numbers of individuals. Thus, mass media play an important role in this process (Auerbach and Castronovo, 2013).

In this regard, journalism is frequently associated with the notion of propaganda (e.g., Herman and Chomsky, 1988; Hearns-Branaman, 2018; Zollman, 2019). In democratic countries, wealthy businessmen who belong to the powerful elites own commercial news outlets and, hence, defend the values of capitalism (Herman and Chomsky, 1988). On the other hand, in authoritarian regimes media are extensions of the state apparatus, thus they function as communication organs of the government (Taylor, 2003). In both cases, the content of the news tends to emphasise the dominant groups' side of the story. That is to say, official powerful agents and groups are the most recurrent sources of information, to the detriment of critical or alternative voices (Hearns-Branaman, 2018; Zollman, 2019).

Besides press coverage, TV spots are another format to convey propagandistic messages, especially during elections (see, e.g., García and D'Adamo, 2006; Cwalina et al., 2015). Therefore, despite the arrival of social media and other digital platforms, the spot is still relevant for electoral campaigns in both consolidated and transitional democracies (Cwalina et al., 2015). Contrary to the news-making process in which diverse actors intervene (reporter, photographer, editor, anchor, and so on), the production of a spot is solely controlled by the candidates' teams. For that reason, the content of this kind of message is framed according to the competitors' interests and needs. As a result, the target audience only receives the information that favours the runner and/or attacks the rest of the opponents (García and D'Adamo, 2006).

In addition, thanks to their inherent capabilities to spread information, new communication technologies have facilitated the expansion of propaganda (Rawnsley, 2005; Bastos and Farkas, 2019; Woolley and Howard, 2019; Lock and Ludolph, 2020). Unlike the traditional media, digital channels foster the massive diffusion of messages not only by political elites, but by citizens as well. In other words, the decentralised structure of social media platforms allows every user to receive, produce, and share content (Bastos and Farkas, 2019; Lock and Ludolph, 2020). In propaganda terms, this is particularly useful for powerful agents, because if they can engage with a robust group of supporters, the latter may help to propagate the formers' messages. In doing so, governments, political parties, and other institutions may increase their legitimacy by relying on public support (Lock and Ludolph, 2020). Nonetheless, this may also be problematic because there is an increasing use of automated software that artificially inflates online support, promotes polarisation, or spreads hate speech or fake news (Woolley and Howard, 2019).

POLITICAL AND ELECTORAL COVERAGE IN MEXICO

Journalism and politics are interdependent concepts. The origins of the former are associated with the development of the latter. Therefore, directly or indirectly, media have links with certain political parties. The ideological convergence between both actors determines newsrooms' editorial profile. That is, tacitly or explicitly, any given news outlet's agenda responds to the ideological alignment of its owners and chief editors. In other words, the media–politics relationship shapes the content and framing of news stories (Pineda and Del Palacio, 2003; González, 2018).

Mexico is an illustrative example because here journalism has been historically linked to either a political party or a group within it. Since the 19th century, media have been used, willingly or unwillingly, as mouthpieces of governments and other political actors. Thus, the information that the Mexican audience gets from newspapers, news sites, TV or radio stations reflects that kind of relationship (Lawson, 2002; Pineda and Del Palacio, 2003; Hughes, 2006; González, 2013, 2018). In other words, propaganda is evident when journalists tend to depend on official sources, neglecting contradictory – or, at least, alternative – voices, thereby presenting only one side of the story.

During much of the last century (1929–2000), the Institutional Revolutionary Party (PRI) exerted a nearly complete hegemony over most of public matters. As a result, the diversity of ideological expressions was significantly limited. The state apparatus achieved this by different means of coercion, such as controlling the newsprint supply, radio and TV concessions, or access to information. In addition, the government spent a lot of public money on advertising and bribes. For that reason, most of the Mexican news organisations uncritically reproduced the PRI propagandistic discourse (Lawson, 2002; Hughes, 2006; González, 2013, 2018).

In doing so, the PRI regime shaped political coverage in at least three ways: controlling the public agenda, demanding selective silence on crucial issues, and fostering a biased coverage of elections (Lawson, 2002). Regarding the first aspect, government authorities and party leaders were the main sources of information and therefore news stories were framed according to the PRI's interests. In practice, the state was largely the primary definer of news content (Lawson, 2002; González, 2018).

In relation to the second aspect, the selective silence meant that compromising information about the president and his closest circle was banned from mainstream media. News stories on government corruption or wrongdoing were practically absent. Furthermore, reporters were expected to only diffuse the authorities' official version, without any context or follow-up (Lawson, 2002; Hughes, 2006; González, 2018).

Finally, during elections the Mexican press adopted a role as cheerleader of the PRI candidate. Coverage of campaigns was openly biased to favour the future successor of the president or governor, neglecting the opposition candidates' activities and rallies (Lawson, 2002; Adler-Lomnitz et al., 2004). Despite the reduced citizen mobilisation, the regime invested large amounts of money in media because they were instrumental to the overall campaign ritual, which would transform the official candidate into 'the emperor of the Republic' (Adler-Lomnitz et al., 2004: 254). That is to say, the PRI contender was expected to become the next president and, hence, media presented him as such.

Therefore, the historical features of the mainstream media in Mexico are: dependence on press releases, a dominance of the agenda by political authorities, officialdom, and a lack of investigative reporting. In short, due to their own professional limitations, most of the news outlets tend to be lapdogs instead of watchdogs (Reyna, 2014; Espino, 2016; González, 2018).

However, it is important to stress that not all media organisations have reacted to this situation in the same way. Certain newspapers and, more recently, news sites have shown more sensitivity and assertiveness than radio and television. These outlets have understood the increasing democratic aspirations of a large number of Mexican citizens, who constantly demand that the authorities build a more modern political system, in which journalists have freedom of expression and access to crucial information. In doing so, media can strengthen people's right to know (Lawson, 2002; Hughes, 2006; González and Echeverría, 2018).

Although this transformation has not involved the Mexican media system as a whole, there are some signs of professionalisation, particularly in the more developed cities such as Mexico City, Guadalajara, Monterrey, and Tijuana. Quality press in those places is known for being independent, critical, politically detached, and civic-oriented; that is, close to the so-called liberal journalistic model (Lawson, 2002; Hughes, 2006; González and Echeverría, 2018; Salazar, 2018). On the contrary, news outlets in the rest of the country lag behind their more progressive counterparts. This is because journalism practice in those regions struggles to survive within an authoritarian and clientelist environment (Guerrero and Márquez, 2014; González and Echeverría, 2018; Salazar, 2018). These tensions between change and continuity appeared in the press coverage of the 2018 presidential elections.

MEDIATISATION, PERSONALISATION, AND TV SPOTS

Mediatisation is the outcome of a long process of social disappointment towards politicians and governments, which has led to the weakening of political parties and the rise of charismatic leaders. As a result, the political discourse has moved from ideological debates to current social issues. That is, the monolithic ideas of left and right that used to define the identity of diverse groups and institutions have been replaced by the discussion of citizens' specific worries and aspirations. Therefore, rather than seeking agreement regarding abstract concepts such as democracy or development, parties – and particularly candidates – aim to persuade voters through propaganda messages focused on individual politicians' image, rather than concrete proposals (Blumler and Kavanagh, 1999; Strömbäck, 2008).

In this context, mediatisation means the adoption of media formats and content by politicians. That is, in their constant search for attention, political actors have adopted diverse aspects of message production. For that reason, they have learnt to choose certain themes, framings, and narratives that may appeal to journalists' interest and hence to larger audiences. In doing so, media logic has permeated political logic (Blumler and Kavanagh, 1999; Strömbäck, 2008; Landerer, 2013).

The implementation of media parameters in the political arena involves the strategic planning and execution of party and/or government activities according to the news-making process. In other words, mediatisation refers to the diffusion of a political message that is produced following mainstream media standards: simple, brief, highly emotional, little informative, visually attractive, repetitive, spectacular, and focused on conflict, amongst other features (García and D'Adamo, 2006; Landerer, 2013).

Under these circumstances, the image of political actors has become a central aspect of the transition from political logic to media logic. Because of the aforementioned increasing disillusionment with the performance of both parties and governments, most people do not trust politicians any more. Therefore, political messages in general, and electoral campaigns in particular, present politicians and candidates as individuals. That is, instead of members of a party or institution, they are framed as citizens who share the same problems and aspirations as the rest of society. This strategy is known as personalisation, and its aim is to attract support from wide segments of voters, especially those who do not feel represented by traditional politics (Blumler and Kavanagh, 1999; Rahat and Sheafer, 2007; Holtz-Bacha et al., 2014).

In this regard, the ultimate channel for political propaganda is the television spot. This is because the aforementioned factors naturally converge in this format. In other words, the production of those kinds of messages is based upon personalisation and persuasion. In very concrete terms, a political spot is an audio-visual message, which aims to offer its audience information and/or points of view about a specific issue. One of its main characteristics is its brevity (20 or 30 seconds), and hence, its content tends to be superficial or at least less informative. Contrary to press coverage or users' comments on social media, candidates have complete control over the content. That is, the politician and their team decide what kind of information, framing, images, and even music will be included. This is possible because it is a paid message and, thus, media organisations do not have any involvement in the production. Finally, spots still offer a wide audience to candidates, especially those with limited access to other sources of information (García and D'Adamo, 2006; Cwalina et al., 2015).

In spite of these advantages, the spot has also a set of disadvantages as a vehicle for political messages. The most evident limitation is related to the content quality that, as observed, is determined by the length of the message. In other words, there is a lack of substantial information due to the short duration of the spot. Therefore, this kind of audio-visual production prioritises emotional images that do not contribute to deliberation on public issues. The content is limited to the self-promotion of the candidate as the leader who will solve all of the country's problems, and in doing so, he criticises and even insults his opponents without any solid argument (García and D'Adamo, 2006; Cwalina et al., 2015).

This is a problematic situation, particularly in transitional democracies such as Mexico, because the average citizen utilises TV as their main source of information. Therefore, they cannot be easily informed about relevant issues related to electoral campaigns, because on the one hand spots are not informative messages, and on the other hand political coverage pays more attention to candidates than to their proposals (Juárez and Echeverría, 2013; Echeverría and Meyer, 2018). In addition, the cost–benefit relationship of the spot as an electoral communication vehicle is negative. This is because its production and diffusion are highly expensive, but its significance in terms of social impact is most of the time reduced. This means that the correlation between watching a TV spot and casting a vote for a specific candidate is not necessarily direct, because the latter involves other aspects such as homophily, family ties, self-interests, and so on (Juárez and Echeverría, 2013; Echeverría and Meyer, 2018).

SOCIAL MEDIA, POLITICS, AND DELIBERATION

Besides traditional media, contemporary political communication and marketing utilise digital platforms for sharing messages. An increasing number of voters, especially the young, get information and interact with one another via social media. Furthermore, users are not only mere consumers, but also can produce and share their own content. This is a challenging situation for politicians, because they do not always promote a bidirectional and horizontal communication with citizens.

According to Jenkins's seminal work (Jenkins, 2009), new communication technologies have fostered a 'participatory culture'. That is, thanks to the development of Web 2.0 and other associated electronic devices such as smartphones, people have developed a more active role in terms of communication. This is because they can easily establish, maintain, and strengthen social ties. In addition, online platforms allow them to freely (re)create and share different kinds of messages. Therefore, this participatory culture may minimise the barriers to political engagement, because political elites and mainstream media no longer have the monopoly over political information (Stieglitz and Dang-Xuan, 2012; Leetoy and Figueroa, 2016). As a result, there is discussion of a new global online public sphere in which there is free interaction amongst citizens around the world (Jenkins, 2009; Curran and Witschge, 2010).

Due to its rapid penetration and expansion, the arrival of the Internet represents a communicational revolution. Thus, it has had an evident impact on different aspects of public life such as journalism and electoral campaigns. However, the extent and direction of this impact is still being debated. Whilst some hold over-optimistic, and even celebratory, positions, others express critical and sceptical points of view regarding the so-called power of digital technologies (Rawnsley, 2005; Curran and Witschge, 2010; Torres, 2014; Larrosa-Fuentes, 2016; Flaxman et al., 2016; Echeverría and Meyer, 2017).

In political communication terms, the first position suggests that Web 2.0 technologies facilitate the creation of networks of active citizens who constantly participate in the public sphere, suggesting and discussing relevant issues (Jenkins, 2009; Curran and Witschge, 2010). Online space is supposed to be a place for communication, in which participants may simultaneously be authors, editors, and receivers of information and opinions (Larrosa-Fuentes, 2016). Especially in authoritarian regimes, digital platforms can also offer an alternative source of information for the state propaganda (Gómez and Treré, 2014; Harlow et al., 2017). As a result, most democratic governments are now using online communication strategies, and making public their processes and decisions (Rawnsley, 2005).

Notwithstanding, the second position argues that the majority of the advantages associated with Web 2.0 tend mainly to be taken for granted. In other words, as a mere possibility, new communication technologies may contribute to the creation of a more democratic society. Nonetheless, there is not enough empirical evidence that in practice technology per se fosters the structural changes that are associated with social media (Curran and Witschge, 2010; Stieglitz and Dang-Xuan, 2012; Torres, 2014; Larrosa-Fuentes, 2016; Flaxman et al., 2016; Echeverría and Meyer, 2017). Therefore, the idea of Web 2.0 as a facilitator of civic transformation is based upon three assumptions (Rawnsley, 2005): society as a whole wants to participate in politics, traditional communication channels are not enough, and online spaces – especially social media – represent the solution.

However, taking for granted these assumptions is highly problematic for several reasons. Firstly, although one of the main criticisms of mainstream media is their lack of plurality and political bias, blogs and social media do not offer an alternative either. This is because these kinds of content tend to marginalise opposite points of view, the origins of information cannot always be verified, and sometimes it is fake (Rawnsley, 2005; Torres, 2014). Secondly, the Internet confirms the fact that instead of changing opinions, media reinforce ideas, habits, and political attitudes. That is, in spite of the wide array of sources of information, its regular user is inclined to mainly seek the content that does not challenge their previously accepted thoughts (Flaxman et al., 2016; Echeverría and Meyer, 2017). In addition, rather than political or social issues, high consumption of online content is mostly related to entertainment or banal messages (Curran and Witschge, 2010; Goriunova, 2012). Finally, Internet access is a barrier in most of the Global South countries such as Mexico, where the digital divide impedes the dissemination of online political messages. Furthermore, the technological gap is also a reflection of other endemic problems such as the access to health and education (Larrosa-Fuentes, 2016).

Under these circumstances, Twitter represents a paradigmatic example of this discussion. This is because, in the collective imaginary, this platform promotes the democratic and civic values of the participatory culture; but in practice it does not always function that way. In other words, there are indeed some signs in specific cases when, for example, its use facilitates the interaction between a candidate and voters (Leetoy and Figueroa, 2016), amongst supporters of a social movement (Gómez and Treré, 2014), or between certain trending topics and their coverage by journalists (Rúas-Araújo et al., 2016).

Nevertheless, the academic literature consistently highlights that in political terms the most influential users are not average citizens, but the traditional opinion leaders instead (politicians, journalists, scholars, intellectuals, and so on) (Stieglitz and Dang-Xuan, 2012; Torres, 2014; Rúas-Araújo et al., 2016). This situation suggests that, despite some particular exceptions, online political communication is not significantly different from the offline environment. That is, more than a bidirectional flux of information between participants, Twitter is mostly used as another channel for propaganda from the same political actors who are reluctant to directly interact with citizens, just as the results of the 2018 Mexican presidential election case will show.

THE 2018 PRESIDENTIAL ELECTIONS IN THE MEDIA LANDSCAPE

This section aims to describe the 2018 presidential elections in Mexico from three different angles related to media: press coverage, TV spots, and candidates' interaction on Twitter. It is important to clarify that the data analysed in the following pages come from three independent studies. Therefore, rather than a comparative approach as such, this chapter proposes an integrated reading of those findings under the concept of propaganda. That is, the raw material selected from those datasets will be reinterpreted and discussed from a propagandistic point of view. Thus, the central argument is that the messages that circulated on these platforms during the campaign emphasised the image of candidates, as well as their discourses, neglecting alternative voices and deliberation.

PRESS COVERAGE: IMPARTIALITY AND SUPERFICIALITY

The previously discussed context of the aspirations and historic limitations of the Mexican press is necessary in order to evaluate the newspaper coverage of the 2018 presidential election.[1] The findings show a relatively impartial coverage for every candidate (see Table 22.1),[2] but slightly higher for Andrés Manuel López Obrador (AMLO), who became the winner. Considering the mere amount of news stories, he obtained 29.9 per cent of the content,

Table 22.1 Press coverage of candidates and coalitions

Actor	Coverage	Positive	Negative
Candidates (%)			
Andrés Manuel López	29.9	27.6	31.3
José Antonio Meade	22.8	27.8	16.3
Ricardo Anaya	21.1	22.4	19.4
Jaime Rodríguez	26.2	22.2	33.1
Coalitions (%)			
Juntos Haremos Historia	30.4	29.1	30.8
Todos por México	23.2	27.9	17.8
Por México al Frente	22.2	22.5	20.9
Independent	24.1	20.5	30.5

followed by the independent Jaime Rodríguez, JR (26.2 per cent), José Antonio Meade, JAM (22.8 per cent), and Ricardo Anaya, RA (21.1 per cent).

Valence was another relatively balanced indicator, because there was practically no difference in positive content between AMLO and JAM (27.6 per cent and 27.8 per cent, respectively), followed by the other two candidates with 22.4 per cent and 22.2 per cent (RA and JR, respectively). However, there was certain disparity related to negative news: AMLO and JR received more negative coverage (31.3 per cent and 33.1 per cent, respectively) than RA and JAM (19.4 per cent and 16.3 per cent, in that order).

The printed press covered coalitions in a similar way to their candidates. That is, AMLO's Juntos Haremos Historia received more positive news (29.1 per cent) than JAM's Todos por México (27.9 per cent), RA's Por México al Frente (22.5 per cent), and the independent candidate (20.5 per cent). On the other hand, considering the negative stories, there was a different order: Juntos Haremos Historia and the independent obtained 30.8 per cent and 30.5 per cent, followed by Por México al Frente (20.9 per cent), and Todos por México (17.8 per cent).

The overall results indicate that there were no relevant differences related to visibility and treatment, which would have suggested a significant bias. Notwithstanding, there are two details worth noting. First, being the PRI candidate – the then ruling party – JAM got more positive coverage than negative, whilst AMLO represented just the opposite case. Second, as a whole, the coverage does not represent parties' economic resources or institutionalisation levels. That is, it is unusual that a new party, such as AMLO's MORENA, and an independent candidate received more media attention than the older and more traditional parties (PAN, PRD, and PRI).

In addition, there was a sense of plurality regarding the issues reported by media during campaigns (see Table 22.2). However, the coverage of the topics was uneven, and mainly focused on the daily events of the race (52.2 per cent) – conflicts, scandals, and debates – rather than on aspects related to public policies proposals. To a lesser extent, there were two sets of issues that journalists reported on during the electoral process. The first included aspects such as internal party politics (10.8 per cent), public security (7.5 per cent), and corruption (6.2 per cent). The second set was more homogeneous in terms of coverage, but the topics received less attention: the economy (3.9 per cent), education (3.3 per cent), and infrastructure (3 per cent). Despite their relevance for society, the rest of the topics were largely neglected by news workers and, hence, integrated here under the label of 'Other'. A couple of illustrative examples were health and gender, which were only mentioned in 0.7 per cent and 0.4 per cent of the content.

Table 22.2   Issues covered by the newspapers during the campaign

Issue	Coverage (%)
Campaign and debates	52.2
Political parties	10.8
Security	7.5
Corruption	6.2
Economy	3.9
Education	3.3
Infrastructure	3.0
Citizen participation	2.4
Transparency and accountability	1.7
Childhood and youth	1.3
Public administration	1.3
Jobs	1.1
Other	5.2

Table 22.3   Actors included in the coverage of the campaigns

Issue	Coverage (%)
Candidate	74.1
Member of a political party	5.8
Electoral authority	6.9
Businessmen	1.4
President of Mexico	1.7
Government authority	1.3
Citizens	1.2
Congressmen	2.0
Scholars and intellectuals	1.2
Journalists	1.2
NGOs	1.1
Other	2.1

Diversity of sources and, thus, voices is another indicator of quality journalism (Hughes, 2006; González, 2013; Reyna, 2014). Nonetheless, candidates nearly monopolised the coverage of the 2018 Mexican presidential election (see Table 22.3), because they represented 74.1 per cent of the main actors of the stories, and appeared in 88 per cent of the news about the campaign. Electoral authorities and party members received significantly less attention as main actors of the content (6.9 per cent and 5.8 per cent, respectively). The rest of the social actors – for instance, business people, scholars, non-governmental organisations (NGOs), and citizens – had a marginal presence in the coverage.

Finally, public policy proposals are supposed to be the core argument of the electoral campaigns, but in this case a little more than one-third of the content (36.1 per cent) included a specific proposal (see Table 22.4). It means that roughly one out of three stories reported what the candidates planned to do if they were elected, whereas the rest focused on the campaign daily activities (where they went, who they met with, and so on). Consequently, only 34.9 per cent of the stories contained rational arguments provided by the candidates related to their points of view. That is, only one-third of the news included factual information about competitors' proposals (deadlines, budgets, specific actions, and so on). Regarding the framing of the news, less than a third (29.1 per cent) discussed political issues (candidates' proposals, evaluations

Table 22.4 Proposals, rational arguments, and framing of the coverage

Indicator	Average
Candidates' proposals (%)	
Yes	36.1
No	34.1
N/A	29.8
Rational arguments (%)	
Yes	34.9
No	41.9
N/A	23.1
Framing (%)	
Political	29.1
Strategic	41.4
N/A	29.6

of social problems, parties' ideologies, and so on), whereas 41.4 per cent presented a strategic content focused on the horse-race logic (predictions of who the winner may be, according to surveys), personalisation (candidates presented as individuals), and infotainment (scandals, candidates' mistakes, funny anecdotes, and so on) (see Chapter 23 by Franco Estrada and Rawnsley in this volume).

TV SPOTS: PERSONALISATION WITHOUT INFORMATION

Despite the arrival of social media, TV spots are still important vehicles for political messages, especially during campaigns. The 2018 presidential election in Mexico is an illustrative example, because the four runners utilised this format as a conveyor of their proposals. Nonetheless, the National Electoral Institute is the only actor that controls the number of spots that a candidate can have, which directly depends on the political parties' past performance. For that reason, the parties that obtained more votes in the previous election will have more spots for the next one. This is problematic for the new parties and independent candidates, because they can only have a significantly limited number of spots (Echeverría and Meyer, 2018).

This section will analyse the content of the spots broadcast during the 2018 campaigns for the Mexican presidency, specifically in terms of personalisation.[3] As discussed before, this term refers to the increasing emphasis on candidates as individuals, rather than on the political parties they represent. In doing so, instead of ideologies, messages tend to highlight specific themes. Additionally, the content gives prominence to emotional aspects, but not to rational arguments. Thus, thanks to its inherent characteristics, a TV spot represents the ideal vehicle for these types of propaganda messages. Table 22.5 summarises the findings regarding the case under inquiry.

The results indicate that rather than political parties, candidates were the central actors of campaign spots (see Table 22.5). This is because, most of the time, they were present either during the whole message or in part of it. Andrés Manuel López Obrador (AMLO) appeared in nine out of ten of his spots (71.43 per cent during the whole spot, and 19.05 per cent in part of it), José Antonio Meade (JAM) did so in eight out of ten (31.82 per cent, and 50 per cent), and

Table 22.5 Indicators of personalisation in the 2018 Mexican presidential election TV spots

Indicator	AMLO N = 21	JAM N = 22	JR N = 3	RA N = 22
Presence of the candidate (%)				
Whole spot	71.43	31.82	100	59.09
Part of the spot	19.05	50.00		9.09
Absent	9.52	18.18		31.82
Presenter (%)				
Candidate	66.67	45.45	100	50.00
Someone else	33.33	45.45		40.91
Voice-over		9.09		9.09
Company (%)*				
Alone	84.21	72.22	66.67	66.67
With people	15.79	27.78	33.33	33.33

Note: * These figures are related to those spots in which the candidates appeared during the whole spot or, at least, in part of it.

Ricardo Anaya (RA) in seven out of ten (59.09 per cent, and 9.09 per cent). Jaime Rodríguez (JR), the independent candidate, appeared during the whole duration of his three spots.

Closely connected with this situation, candidates themselves tended to present their own messages on camera during the spots, instead of letting someone else do it (see Table 22.5). This is a relevant finding because it underlines that the candidates are the central figure of contemporary campaigns and, hence, their personal image tends to be the focus of the content. In that sense, AMLO delivered his messages in two-thirds of his spots, whereas in the remaining third another person did it. In exactly half of his spots, RA presented his proposals, but in the rest someone else did it (40.91 per cent on camera, and 9.09 per cent using voice-over). JAM had nearly the same performance. He presented his arguments in 45.45 per cent of the times, with the same frequency another person spoke on his behalf, and in 9.09 per cent there was a voice-over. Once again, JR personally shared his ideas in his three spots.

In order to emphasise their own image and reinforce their status as the main character of the campaigns, candidates preferred to be the only person on camera (see Table 22.5). That is, when they personally appeared in either part or the whole spot, they did it alone most of the times: AMLO (84.21 per cent), JAM (72.22 per cent), and both JR and RA (66.67 per cent).

Finally, as Figure 22.1 illustrates, the vast majority of the spots did not deliver rational arguments supported by facts. On the contrary, the candidates mainly shared their assumptions and opinions without any supporting evidence. That is, emotional messages filled air-time on TV. In such a way, JR only presented subjective content, whilst JAM did so in 95.45 per cent of the time, AMLO in 90.48 per cent, and RA in 81.82 per cent.

CANDIDATES ON TWITTER: INTERACTION WITHOUT DELIBERATION

Debates between candidates are supposed to be one of the hallmarks of campaigns in a democratic political system. Within a more or less controlled environment, competitors have the chance to present their proposals, challenge their opponents, and even criticise one another in

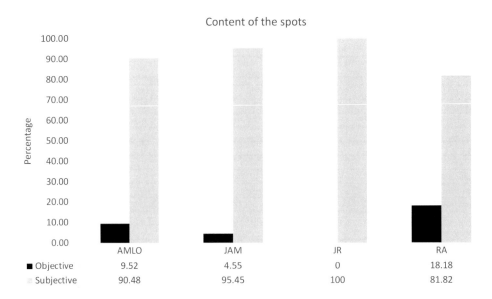

Figure 22.1   Content of the spots

front of the cameras and microphones of a large number of news outlets. In terms of deliberation, this is supposed to be a key moment during the electoral process, because voters can have a wide vision of each candidate's ideas and, thus, use that information to vote rationally. In addition, as commented before, social media have the potential to promote a direct flux of communication between candidates and citizens.

Therefore, this section will describe the interaction on Twitter between users and competitors in the 2018 Mexican presidential election.[4] The analysis considered the tweets that every candidate wrote right after each one of the three debates organised by the National Electoral Institute,[5] and the interaction that they fostered. Interaction here is understood as the extent that candidates established a two-way communication process with the users of the platform, and also between the users themselves (Lee and Shin, 2012). According to Alvídrez (2017), this can be measured by the level of replies, retweets, and favourites. Depending on the response rate, the level of interaction that a tweet generates may be classified as high (more than 1000 actions), medium (between 501 and 999 actions), or low (from 0 to 500 actions).

After the first debate, Ricardo Anaya (RA) and Andrés Manuel López Obrador (AMLO) only had one tweet, whereas José Antonio Meade (JAM) wrote two, and Jaime Rodríguez (JR) wrote 11. As Figure 22.2 shows,[6] AMLO and JAM had high levels of replies (1750 and 1400, respectively), RA medium (747), and JR low (221). Regarding retweets, JAM was the only one with a high level (2300), RA and AMLO medium (877 and 600, respectively), and JR low with 374. Finally, the four candidates had high levels of favourites: AMLO (16 000), JAM (5350), RA (2500), and JR (1803). These results indicate that the only competitor who consistently had high levels of interaction on this platform was JAM, because he exceeded the barrier of 1000 actions in each indicator. Nonetheless, AMLO surpassed him in replies and favourites, but not in retweets.

For the second debate, RA wrote two tweets, AMLO one, and JR wrote 17. Surprisingly, JAM did not tweet at all. In that sense, Figure 22.3 shows[7] that RA had high level of replies

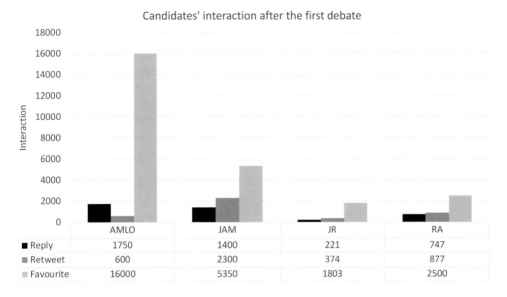

Figure 22.2 Candidates' interaction after the first debate

(1600), AMLO medium (834), and JR low (77). Related to retweets, AMLO and RA had high levels (2900 and 1300, respectively), but JR low with 147. The same trend resulted for the favourites, because AMLO and RA scored high (10 000 and 4400, respectively), and JR barely reached medium (516). This time, RA was the only candidate with high levels of interaction in every aspect, even though his competitor AMLO had higher levels of retweets and favourites than him.

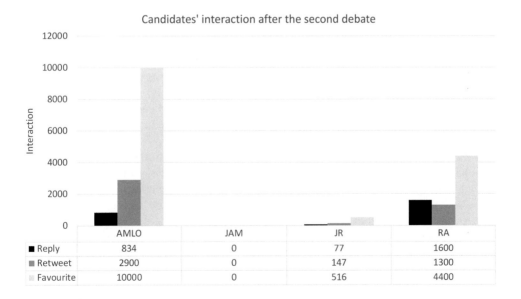

Figure 22.3 Candidates' interaction after the second debate

As the campaigns approached election day, the candidates participated in the third debate. After the event, AMLO tweeted once, JAM twice, RA three times, and JR 11 times.[8] Figure 22.4 shows that, in terms of replies, AMLO and RA had high levels (1500 and 2425, respectively), whilst JAM and JR had low levels (485 and 59, respectively). With the exception of JR, who scored low (182), the rest of the candidates reached high levels of retweets: AMLO (6800), RA (3207), and JAM (1550). Regarding favourites, the trend was similar: AMLO (19 000), RA (8600), and JAM (2850) had high levels, but JR barely reached medium (558). Once more, RA's interaction levels were consistently high, and for the first time that was AMLO's case too.

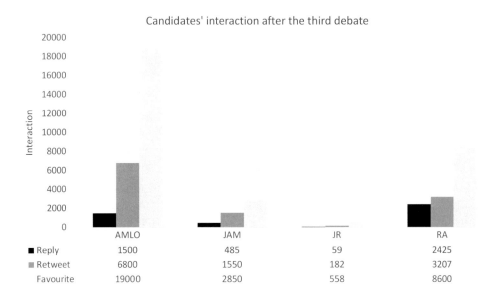

Figure 22.4   Candidates' interaction after the third debate

Although none of the candidates obtained high nor low levels in every single indicator during the three debates, there were indeed certain consistencies. Firstly, every time that AMLO scored high, he widely surpassed his opponents in almost everything, especially in terms of favourites. On the contrary, JR consistently got the poorest results. In fact, he was actually the competitor that promoted the lowest levels of interaction. Therefore, despite that he tweeted many more times, he could not engage with the users of this platform. A viable explanation is that he was never perceived as a possible winner, because he persistently appeared in every survey as the least favourite runner. Thus, contrary to his competitors, voters may not have taken JR seriously. This situation is particularly interesting because, as the only independent candidate, JR emphasised from the beginning of the electoral process that, due to his limited economic resources, his campaign was going to rely mainly on social media. Secondly, although JR did actually reply to some of the users' comments on his tweets, none of the other candidates directly communicated with the people. For that reason, the amount of replies reported here represents the interaction between citizens themselves, but not between them and the candidates. It is precisely this indicator that may promote online deliberation, but at least in this case it seemed that politicians were unwilling to do so.

PROPAGANDA AND THE MEXICAN 2018 PRESIDENTIAL ELECTIONS

Politics in general, and electoral campaigns in particular, are about communication. Rather than face-to-face, mainstream media and digital platforms facilitate the dissemination of current political messages. Therefore, analysing the media landscape is relevant for understanding elections. In doing so, this last section offers a discussion on the relation between the findings and the concept of propaganda as communication strategy.

Regarding press coverage, the results presented indicate that, contrary to old inertias, newspapers tended to report on the campaigns in a balanced way. That is, every candidate received a rather homogeneous coverage in terms of quantity and quality. It means that, unlike previous elections (especially prior to the political transition in 2000) there was not an open bias to favour someone to the detriment of his competitors. Nevertheless, the content of the news stories did not include important information on crucial issues, or candidates' public policies proposals. This is because journalists paid greater attention to the horse-race elements, but neglected other relevant aspects. In addition, news stories were mainly based upon the political elites' discourse. Subsequently, newspapers finally achieved impartiality, but failed to provide better content. As commented in a previous section, the reliance on official sources of information, and the absence of crucial issues such as specific government plans, indicate that the campaign coverage adopted a form of propaganda (see Herman and Chomsky, 1988; Hearns-Branaman, 2018; Zollman, 2019).

On the other hand, campaign TV spots presented high levels of personalisation and poor content in terms of information. That is, candidates' presence on the majority of the spots became the most important part of their messages. In doing so, factual information was neglected because the content was built upon competitors' perceptions and points of view. Thus, candidates sought voters' support by appealing to emotional messages, rather than specific proposals, so TV spots functioned as conveyors of propaganda (García and D'Adamo, 2006; Cwalina et al., 2015; Echeverría and Meyer, 2018).

Press coverage and TV spots coincide in two aspects: personalisation and lack of information. The increasing focus on the candidates' image to the detriment of their proposals suggests that, rather than political logic, media logic determined much of the content that audiences received. In other words, the messages were not framed according to the citizens' needs, but to politicians' interests instead. Consequently, both media platforms diffused consistent propaganda messages that emphasised the image and voice of competitors over substantial content. In other words, candidates themselves, and not their policy proposals, were the most important feature of their communication strategies (see also Franco Estrada and Rawnsley, Chapter 23 in this volume).

The data on candidates' Twitter activity showed that they did not promote direct communication with the users, despite the potential of the platform to do so. Although some had high levels of interaction (replies, retweets, and favourites), it does not mean that they actually interacted with the people. In other words, they merely sent content of up to 280 characters and then waited for a reaction. That is, since the candidates only used this platform as another vehicle for propagating their messages, interaction could not evolve into deliberation. This finding suggests that competitors were reluctant to discuss their ideas with the Twitter users. Thus, they merely reinforced their campaign messages without further explanation of their proposals. As an echo chamber (Larrosa-Fuentes, 2016; Flaxman et al., 2016; Echeverría and Meyer, 2017; Woolley and Howard, 2019), this social medium served as another form of propaganda, because it fostered emotional support and polarisation amongst users.

In this regard, the Mexican 2018 presidential campaigns illustrate the concept of propaganda as a tool to disseminate a consistent and repetitive message. Considering the press coverage, TV spots, and Twitter activity as part of their communication strategy, candidates imposed their agenda and framing of the contents related to their activities. Therefore, the electorate did not get enough factual information in order to cast a rational vote. Conversely, as these three independent studies suggest, the citizens received unidirectional messages highlighting candidates' persona, and little more than that.

NOTES

1. Dr Martín Echeverría (Benemérita Universidad Autónoma de Puebla), who coordinated the project Evaluation of the Political Communication Model during the 2018 Federal Elections, generously shared the dataset analysed in this section of the chapter.
2. The sample size was 2095 news stories published by 22 quality newspapers from Mexico City, Jalisco, Nuevo León, Guerrero, Coahuila, Baja California, and Veracruz. The stories were collected during 17 dates within the official period of the campaigns (30 March – 27 June 2018), following a random systematic jump logic.
3. The information presented here is courtesy of Ana Martha Luna, whose MA thesis focused on the persuasive elements of the 2012 and 2018 Mexican presidential elections TV spots.
4. The data presented here was kindly shared by Ana Karen Reyes, whose MA thesis analysed candidates' Twitter activity after the debates.
5. This was the first time that the Mexican electoral authority had organised three debates, because previous presidential campaigns had only one. The dates of the 2018 debates were: 23 April, 21 May, and 13 June.
6. JAM and JR's number of actions displayed in Figure 22.2 are averages because they both had more than one tweet after the first debate.
7. Since RA and JR wrote more than one tweet, the results included in Figure 22.3 represent averages.
8. Regarding JAM, RA, and JR's results, Figure 22.4 displays averages because they all tweeted more than once.

REFERENCES

Adler-Lomnitz, L., R. Salazar, and I. Adler (2004), *Simbolismo y ritual en la política mexicana*, Mexico City: UNAM/Siglo XXI Editores.
Alvídrez, S. (2017), 'Interactividad en Twitter: el efecto de la identidad partidista sobre la evaluación de candidatos políticos y sobre sus intenciones de voto', *Comunicación y Sociedad*, (29): 117–137.
Auerbach J. and R. Castronovo (2013), 'Introduction: Thirteen propositions about propaganda', in J. Auerbach and R. Castronovo (eds), *The Oxford Handbook of Propaganda Studies*, Oxford: Oxford University Press, pp. 1–16.
Baines, P.R. (2014), 'Al-Qaeda messaging evolution and positioning, 1998–2008: Propaganda analysis revisited', *Public Relations Inquiry*, 3(2): 163–191.
Bastos, M. and J. Farkas (2019), '"Donald Trump Is my President!": The Internet research agency propaganda machine', *Social Media + Society*, 5(3): 1–13.

Blumler, J.G. and D. Kavanagh (1999), 'The third age of political communication: Influences and features', *Political Communication*, 16(3): 209–230.
Chomsky, N. (1992), *Media Control: The Spectacular Achievements of Propaganda*, New York: Seven Stories Press.
Curran, J. and T. Witschge (2010), 'Liberal dreams and the internet', in N. Fenton (ed.), *New Media, Old News: Journalism and Democracy in the Digital Age*, London: SAGE, pp. 102–118
Cwalina, W., A. Falkowski, and B. Newman (2015), *Political Marketing: Theoretical and Strategic Foundations*, London: Routledge.
Echeverría, M. and J. Meyer (2017), 'Internet y socialización política. Consecuencias en la participación juvenil', *Anagramas*, 15(30): 29–50.
Echeverría, M. and J. Meyer (2018), 'El Estado contra la deliberación: El modelo de comunicación política en la reforma electoral 2014', *Argumentos*, 30(85): 197–214.
Espino, G. (2016), 'Periodistas precarios en el interior de la República mexicana: atrapados entre las fuerzas del mercado y las presiones de los gobiernos estatales', *Revista Mexicana de Ciencias Políticas y Sociales*, 61(228): 1–30.
Flaxman, S., S. Goel, and J.M. Rao (2016), 'Filter bubbles, echo chambers, and online news consumption', *Public Opinion Quarterly*, 80(S1), 298–320.
García, V. and O. D'Adamo (2006), 'Comunicación política y campañas electorales. Análisis de una herramienta comunicacional: el spot televisivo', *Polis: Investigación y Análisis Sociopolítico y Psicosocial*, 2(2): 81–111.
Gómez, R. and E. Treré (2014), 'The #YoSoy132 movement and the struggle for media democratization in Mexico', *Convergence: The International Journal of Research into New Media Technologies*, 20(4): 496–510
Gonzalez, R. (2013), 'Economically-driven partisanship – Official advertising and political coverage in Mexico: The case of Morelia', *Journalism and Mass Communication*, 3(1): 14–33.
González, R. (2018), 'Silence or alignment: Organized crime and government as primary definers of news in Mexico', *Observatorio (OBS*) Journal*, 12(4): 125–139.
González, R. and M. Echeverría (2018), 'A medio camino. El sistema mediático mexicano y su irregular proceso de modernización', *Revista Mexicana de Opinión Pública*, 13(24): 35–51.
Goriunova, O. (2012), 'New media idiocy', *Convergence: The International Journal of Research into New Media Technologies*, 19(2): 223–235.
Guerrero, M. and M. Márquez (2014), 'El modelo "liberal capturado" de sistemas mediáticos, periodismo y comunicación en América Latina', *Temas de Comunicación*, 29: 135–170.
Harlow, S., R. Salaverría, D.K. Kilgo, and V. García (2017), 'Protest Paradigm in multimedia: Social media sharing of coverage about the crime of Ayotzinapa, Mexico', *Journal of Communication*, 67(3), 328–349.
Hearns-Branaman, J.O. (2018), 'What the propaganda model can learn from the sociology of journalism', in J.P. Carañana, D. Broudy, and J. Klaehn (eds), *The Propaganda Model Today. Filtering Perception and Awareness*, London: University of Westminster Press, pp. 25–36.
Herman, E. and N. Chomsky (1988), *Manufacturing Consent: The Political Economy of Mass Media*, New York: Pantheon Books.
Holtz-Bacha, C., A. Langer, and S. Merkle (2014), 'The personalization of politics in comparative perspective: Campaign coverage in Germany and the United Kingdom', *European Journal of Communication*, 29(2): 153–170.
Hughes, S. (2006), *Newsrooms in Conflict: Journalism and the Democratization of Mexico*, Pittsburgh, PA: University of Pittsburgh Press.
Instituto Nacional Electoral (INE) (2018), 'Da a conocer INE resultados del cómputo de la elección presidencial 2018', available at https://centralelectoral.ine.mx/2018/07/06/da-conocer-ine-resultados-del-computo-de-la-eleccion-presidencial-2018/.
Jenkins, H. (2009), *Confronting the Challenges of Participatory Culture: Media Education for the 21st Century*, Cambridge, MA: MacArthur Foundation.
Juárez, J. and M. Echeverría (2013), *Cuando el spot llega a lo local: publicidad política en los estados de la República*, Mexico City: Universidad Nacional Autónoma de México.
Landerer, N. (2013), 'Rethinking the logics: A conceptual framework for the mediatization of politics', *Communication Theory*, 23(3), 239–258.

Larrosa-Fuentes, J.S. (2016), 'Ni todos pueden ni todos quieren participar: Usos y explotación de la infraestructura material del sistema de comunicación política en la Internet durante el proceso electoral Guadalajara 2015', in M.S. Paláu (ed.), *Medios de comunicación y derecho a la información en Jalisco, 2015*, Guadalajara: ITESO, pp. 139–162.

Lawson, C. (2002), *Building the Fourth Estate: Democratization and the Rise of a Free Press in Mexico*, Berkeley, CA: University of California Press.

Lee, E.J. and S.Y. Shin (2012), 'Are they talking to me? Cognitive and affective effects of interactivity in politicians' Twitter communication', *Cyberpsychology, Behavior, and Social Networking*, 15(10): 515–520.

Leetoy, S. and J.E. Figueroa (2016), '#Losmurossícaen: Wikipolítica y la ciudadanización de la política en México', *Perspectivas de la Comunicación*, 9(1): 43–64.

Lock, I. and R. Ludolph (2020), 'Organizational propaganda on the Internet: A systematic review', *Public Relations Inquiry*, 9(1): 103–127.

Pineda, A. and C. Del Palacio (eds) (2003), *Prensa decimonónica en México*, Guadalajara: Universidad de Guadalajara/UMSNH/CONACYT.

Rahat, G. and T. Sheafer (2007), 'The personalization of politics', *Political Communication*, 24(1): 65–80.

Rawnsley, G. (2005), *Political Communication and Democracy*, London: Palgrave Macmillan.

Rawnsley, G. (2013), '"Thought-work" and propaganda: Chinese public diplomacy and public relations after Tiananmen Square', in J. Auerbach J. and R. Castronovo (eds), *The Oxford Handbook of Propaganda Studies*, Oxford: Oxford University Press, pp. 147–159.

Reyna, V.H. (2014), *Nuevos riesgos, viejos encuadres: la escenificación de la inseguridad pública en Sonora*, Hermosillo: El Colegio de Sonora.

Rúas-Araújo, J., I. Puentes-Rivera, and M.I. Míguez-González (2016), 'Capacidad predictiva de Twitter, el impacto electoral y actividad en las elecciones del parlamento de Galicia: un análisis con la herramienta LIWC', *Observatorio (OBS*) Journal*, 10(2): 55–87.

Salazar, M.G. (2018), '¿Cuarto poder? Mercados, audiencias y contenidos en la prensa estatal mexicana', *Política y Gobierno*, 25(1): 125–152.

Silverstein, B. (1987), 'Toward a science of propaganda', *Political Psychology*, 8(1): 49–59.

Stieglitz, S. and L. Dang-Xuan (2012), 'Social media and political communication: A social media analytics framework', *Social Network Analysis and Mining*, 3(4): 1277–1291.

Strömbäck, J. (2008), 'Four phases of mediatization: An analysis of the mediatization of politics', *International Journal of Press/Politics*, 13(3): 228–246.

Taylor, P. (2003), *Munitions of the Mind: A History of Propaganda from the Ancient World to the Present Era*, Manchester: Manchester University Press.

Torres, L.C. (2014), 'El poder de las redes sociales: La "mano invisible" del framing noticioso. El caso de #LadyProfeco', *Icono 14*, 12(2): 318–337.

Woolley, S. and P. Howard (2019), *Computational Propaganda: Political Parties, Politicians, and Political Manipulation on Social Media*, Oxford: Oxford University Press.

Zollman, F. (2019), 'Bringing propaganda back into news media studies', *Critical Sociology*, 45(3): 329–345.

23. Political propaganda and memes in Mexico: the 2018 presidential election

Penélope Franco Estrada and Gary D. Rawnsley

INTRODUCTION

In his study of his homeland's identity, the poet Octavio Paz said of his fellow Mexicans: 'Each time we try to express ourselves we have to break with ourselves' (Paz, 1985: 53). Mexico is a land of rupture, and earthquakes have defined Mexicans. Two major earthquakes have hit Mexico, the first on 19 September 1985, and the second on the very same day in 2017. Both tragedies marked symbolic moments that brought Mexicans together. It did not matter if one was rich or poor, a leftist or a rightist, a fan of the football team 'America' or their rival '*Las chivas*', or if one thought the northern states are superior to the south; what mattered most was pulling together to face the catastrophe and helping to rebuild the country.

In 2018, Mexico experienced a political earthquake, an event just as life-changing, when for the first time a representative of the political left won the presidency. But this time Mexico was torn apart and the country has not 'pulled together' in the aftermath. The elections on 1 July were the largest in history: Mexicans were going to the polls to choose not only a president, but also 128 members of the Senate and 500 members of the Chamber of Deputies. Moreover, most states held their own local elections, including nine governorships. In all, over 3000 positions were up for grabs. The 2018 election is also historic for another reason: it was the most violent on record, with 130 political figures killed since September 2017.

Andrés Manuel López Obrador, known as AMLO, secured his electoral victory with 53.17 per cent of the vote, the largest win in Mexico's history, on an extraordinary high turnout (63.44 per cent). The 2018 election campaign is important not just because of the result, but because of the methods of political propaganda the candidates used to mobilise voters and disparage their opponents. In the 2006 presidential election candidates had already demonstrated their growing familiarity with online platforms and digital technologies. The Partido Accion Nacional (PAN) hired Antonio Solá, the self-styled 'Creator of Presidents',[1] to direct its propaganda against the frontrunner, López Obrador, through social networks, and using the bots and trolls that have since become so familiar in election campaigns around the world.

By the 2012 election the parties were using social media not only to blacken their opponents, but also to encourage popular participation and interaction with political elites (Camp, 2013). Suddenly the newsfeeds on social media, once used only for accessing news and entertainment and networking with friends, were populated by the political opinions of ordinary voters. All Mexicans with an Internet connection could express their ideas and opinions, and convey their judgements of both the candidates and the country's volatile political landscape. There was no 'pulling together': the two main political parties, the PAN and the Partido Revolucionario Institucional (PRI), used new communication technologies to spread their propaganda, and to target journalists and activists (Bradshaw and Howard, 2017). Online propaganda spread conspiracies and polarised voters even further, with campaign communications ridiculing candidates, exaggerating their physical appearance, and reproducing rumours and lies about their personal lives. These campaigns fitted the traditional descriptions of propaganda (Shabo, 2008).

Very quickly Facebook – along with WhatsApp, the most popular social media platform in Mexico – became a virtual no-man's land, with images, infographics, memes, and videos 'going viral' seconds after being posted (sometimes by bots; Camp, 2013), and reproduced and shared without verification, analysis, or reflection (though television remained the primary source of information about politics; Camp, 2013). Two years into the presidency he won in 2012, Enrique Peña Nieto, the former 'golden boy' with the good looks and the telenovela star wife, was subject of a viral meme campaign that focused on his wife's finances, his failure to find the 43 students who disappeared in 2014 (known as the Ayotzinapa 43), and which ridiculed his broken English. Like all other PRI presidents before him, he turned to censorship as a way of fighting back. The Internet can destroy as well as create images and reputations. When the Attorney General said he was tired (*'ya me cansé'*) of popular demands to investigate the Ayotzinapa 43, the hashtag #YaMeCansé circulated online to indicate the people's exhaustion with the lack of government action. This was followed by calls for Peña Nieto's resignation – #DemandoTuRenunciaEPN (I Demand Your Resignation, EPN) – and #TodosSomosAyotzinapa (We Are All Ayotzinapa). News and images of the missing spread throughout Latin America and reached the United States (US). In documenting the story of these memetic activities, Mina observes how:

> In the story of Ayotzinapa ... the response rippled forth from a small town, out to Mexico City, from there to the Spanish-speaking world, and then to the world at large. Their portraits [of the missing], riding on hashtags and online actions, went viral in a way that is rare even today, drawing attention to a rural community overlooked by the global community. (Mina, 2018: 146–147)

Such is the power of memes.

By the time of the 2018 election, both sides of the political spectrum had weaponised social platforms. Campaign teams and their supporters used Twitter, Facebook, and WhatsApp to spread misinformation and disinformation, including doctored photographs of candidates and provocative statements falsely attributed to the candidates (Verificado, 2018; Dwoskin, 2018; Glowacki et al., 2018). Now memes emerged as a potent and central campaign weapon in Mexican elections to oppose as well as to support candidates. The PRI would use again the very same themes Antonio Solá introduced in the 2006 election to attack López Obrador, once more the frontrunner. Memes demonised AMLO as a Latin American *caudillo* like Hugo Chavez who would bring to Mexico Venezuela-type chaos, and as a Mexican version of the despised American president, Donald Trump. The humble meme, available to anyone with access to MS Paint and an Internet connection, has become the centrepiece of propaganda and disinformation campaigns. They have targeted undecided voters and attacked radical political groups, vulnerable minorities, and organisations in Mexico that actively defend human rights, gender politics, and environmental causes.

In this chapter we discuss the use and value of memes as instruments of propaganda in Mexico's political culture, with particular focus on the 2018 presidential election. Data that reveals how Mexicans consumed news during the election provides the context to understand the propaganda power of social platforms and memes. In a survey conducted and reported by the Reuters Institute in 2018:

- 49 per cent of respondents said they trusted the media.
- 63 per cent responded that they were 'very' or 'extremely' concerned about the reliability of online news.
- 90 per cent received their news from online sources, including social platforms.
- 45 per cent received their news from print media.
- 74 per cent said their primary device for accessing the news is their smartphone.
- 61 per cent get their news from Facebook.
- 37 per cent get their news from YouTube.
- 35 per cent get their news from WhatsApp.
- 23 per cent get their news from Twitter (Newman et al., 2018).

In 2012, the year of the previous presidential election, there were c. 33 million Facebook users in Mexico, and c. 10.5 million Twitter accounts; by 2018, the number of Facebook users increased to c. 77 million, and Twitter accounts remained more or less the same. WhatsApp remains a popular platform, with c. 84 million users at the time of the election.

However, before we examine Mexico specifically, first it is important to establish what memes are and why they are important.

MEMES

'… small expressions with big implications.'
(Milner, 2016: 14, definition of memes)

The Internet and social media have transformed the design and performance of political propaganda by state and non-state actors across the world. As many chapters in this volume confirm, much of the research on modern propaganda directed through the social media has focused on (allegedly) dialogical platforms such as Twitter and Facebook. These platforms have contributed to new political cultures and discourses largely since the so-called Arab Spring in 2011 crystallised attention around their capacity to mobilise popular resistance against unpopular regimes, and since Evgeny Morozov (2011) explored what he called the 'dark side of Internet freedom'. Use of social media to participate in politics has been described as 'armchair activism' and 'hashtag activism', suggesting a political ecology where involvement in politics has moved into a virtual space (Manderlink, 2015). While suggesting the creation of new landscapes for popular participation in politics that amplifies previously neglected or marginalised voices, this evolutionary process is not without its critics. Some commentators have disparaged the 'slacktivism' that encourages users to 'like' and 'share' without having to commit or serve (Rawnsley and Voltmer, 2009; Howard et al., 2017; Rawnsley and Ma, 2017). The so-called 'slacktivism hypothesis' suggests that 'if Internet or social media use increase, civic engagement declines' (Howard et al., 2017). However, far from being apathetic, millennials have mobilised around a range of causes and have discovered new forms of political participation via the social media (ibid.). They also recognise that to be successful they must combine online and offline engagement; online engagement alone is insufficient (Rawnsley and Ma, 2017).

Memes are just one more innovative way of expanding political voices. While they may be judged as no more than a collection of humorous ideas, images, and slogans that draw inspiration from popular culture (Heiskanen, 2017), memes have political power. Anastasia Denisova (2016) described memes as 'fast food media', and warned that 'politicians are ignoring them at their own peril'. Heiskanen (2017) concluded that what is termed 'meme-ing' occurs 'outside the control of political and media gatekeepers, enabling challenges of status quo representations'. Denisova (2019) agrees, noting that memes have thrived in 'restrictive environments' where digital platforms 'empower … dissidents with the layer of anonymity or curated digital identity' (Denisova, 2019: 16). However, while the temptation is to focus on how political opposition movements and civil society groups use memes (Mina, 2018), Mexico draws our attention to their appropriation by political elites for their own propaganda.

Memes are valuable as instruments of political propaganda for three reasons. First, memes confirm the significance of networks in modern political communications and propaganda, forging horizontal connections between creators and consumers, activists and elites (as demonstrated by the YoSoy132 – 'I am 132' – network of student activists in Mexico). Memes are 'best understood as groups of digital items or texts created and shared separately by many individuals but in awareness of one another and having common characteristics' (Huntington, 2016). In the age of social media, networked politics are more visible and more powerful than at any time in the past, bringing into conversations a range of voices that were once marginalised or excluded entirely (for example, Mexico's Ayotzinapa43 movement, see below). Hence 'memetic processes' – the methods by which information, news, and culture are communicated and spread – are as important, if not more so, than the content itself.

Second, memes drive us to consider the intersection of culture and politics. For Limar Shifman, memes are 'multi-participant creative expressions through which cultural and political identities are communicated and negotiated' (Shifman, 2014: 15). Ryan Milner describes memes as 'multimodel artefacts remixed by countless participants, employing popular culture for public commentary', and notes that 'Image memes … house potential for populist expression and conversation' (Milner, 2013: Locations 2357, 2360). So by mixing and remixing images and texts 'to create new layers of meaning' (Huntington, 2016), memes can draw users' attention to political ideas, critiques, and commentaries in ways that will resonate with consumers; and then these critiques are spread even further along the networks of like-minded users. Zac Moffat, chief executive officer of the Targeted Victory marketing agency, has described memes as 'a shortcut to a larger point'. Memes, Moffat said, 'are successful when they repackage information in a lighthearted, shareable way' (Flynn, 2019). Hence memes are similar to other propaganda tools that use shortcuts – stereotypes, for example – to convey a single message to a specific audience that will find it most appealing.

Third, memes build and sustain the inside/outside groups that are so crucial to political propaganda, especially in the social media ecology. Propaganda rarely changes minds, but rather reinforces existing opinions and prejudices. This is why memes are so useful: Heiskanen (2017) notes that 'the basic assumption behind meme-making is that recipients need to "get" the meme in order to be in on the joke; if not, the meme loses its potential. For this reason, Internet memes are more powerful when distributed within a peer group of already likeminded users.' Memes reflect the shortening attention spans of social media users, the need to express opinions in no more than 140 characters, and provide simple solutions to complex problems (Rawnsley on Trump, Chapter 4 in this volume):

The nonchalance of a police officer pepper-spraying college students and the genuine frustration, sadness, and despair animating #BlackLivesMatter and #HandsUpDontShoot resonated deeply enough to inspire an outpouring of memetic media. Even in the most harrowing cases, memetic engagement follows familiar patterns; hefty conversations can resonate right alongside cute cats and "Sad Batman." Memetic media do not follow a specific template; they circulate when they connect with the participants who circulate them.

And individual resonance spirals into collective participation. (Milner, 2016: 217)

It is useful to reference An Xiao Mina's observation that memes – if understood as symbols, images, and slogans that are spread to advance a political thought – have a long history that predates the Internet, and that they are enabled by technology. This is the core argument of Mina's book: 'people have been generating the media, slogans, and performances for their movements for all of recorded history', writes Mina, 'and they've frequently been borrowing from, co-opting, and challenging opposition groups at the same time' (Mina, 2018: 183).

Memes have emerged as a central component of modern propaganda, such that it is now possible to reference 'meme wars': the use of slogans, images, and videos that are spread via online social networks for explicitly political or military purposes, and often containing (at best) misinformation or (at worst) disinformation. Well documented are the ways right-wing 'populist' governments and political movements use memes to influence and disrupt political processes, including democratic elections, throughout the world (Moore, 2018; Pomerantsev, 2019). Where once social activists created memes anonymously to spread political ideas in a humorous way, sinister groups have since appropriated them for sinister purposes, often using classic propaganda techniques. Writing about the far-right anti-immigration group Infokrieg, Pomeranstev says: 'what caught my eye … was the language used by some of its participants. Don't use any National Socialist memes. Focus on lowest common-denominator themes: mass migration, Islamification, Identity, Freedom, Tradition' that will appeal most to target audiences (Pomerantsev, 2019: Location 1201). Martin Moore describes how in September 2017 the German far-right group Alternative für Deutschland (AfD) 'announced publicly that it was "opening the meme war against the half-breeds in parliament". "Blitzkrieg Against the Old Parties!" one of the members screamed online' (Moore, 2018: 16). An Xiao Mina notes the appearance of swastikas in the US after Donald Trump became president in 2016, 'emerging in the context of a sharp increase in hate crimes and hate speech, both online and offline' (Mina, 2019: 179).

Some critics have connected memetic processes to the more discredited theories of how propaganda works. These processes, the critics claim, overstate the way propaganda is disseminated and value less the agency involved in both the creation and reception of memes (Jenkins et al., 2013; Shifman, 2014). In this way, memetic processes echo the 'hypodermic needle' model that defined so much of the official understanding of propaganda during the Cold War: 'We speak, you listen, you are persuaded.' Shifman notes that memes have been used 'in a problematic way, conceptualizing people as helpless and passive creatures, susceptible to the domination of meaningless media "snacks" that infect their minds' (Shifman, 2014: 11). However, this misses the participatory way memes are created, spread, and consumed by users who wish to communicate in inclusive ways specific political ideas, and challenge political elites. There is agency involved, and we modulate the power of memes as propaganda if we discount how they are produced and circulated and by whom.

In this chapter we use as a framework Heiskanen's 'reflections' to reinforce our narrative around the value of memes in the political propaganda of election campaigns generally, and in Mexico specifically. Memes, Heiskanen says:

1. speak to the intersection of electoral activism and cultural representation
2. enable users to rapidly take a stand on and react to developing political events in real time
3. provide alternative parallel discourses to mainstream media viewpoints
4. enable mobilization of voters outside of official political discourses, including the potential to influence voting practices. (Heiskanen, 2017)

THE PERSONALISATION OF POLITICS

Four candidates contested the 2018 election,[2] three of whom represented Mexico's biggest and most powerful political forces: Partido Revolucionario Institucional (Institutional Revolutionary Party, PRI), Partido Acción Nacional (National Action Party, PAN), and Movimento Regeneración Nacional (the National Regeneration Movement, MORENA), albeit as part of coalitions with other parties and movements: Andrés Manuel López Obrador, founder of MORENA, represented an alliance of left-wing movements, Juntos Haremos Historia (Together We Will Make History); Ricardo Anaya Cortés of the PAN represented Por México al Frente (For Mexico to the Front), a coalition of centre-right and centre-left movements; and José Antonio Meade of the PRI represented Todos por México (Everyone for Mexico), which included Mexico's Green Party.

The fourth candidate in the election was an independent, Jaime Heliodoro Rodríguez Calderón. Known as 'El Bronco' (Wild Horse), Calderón was a former member of the PRI and Governor of Nuevo León. His candidacy provides a valuable snapshot of the power of social media and memes in Mexican politics, but also their limitations. Howard et al. (2017) describe how Calderón used Facebook and Twitter to build his base for governor in 2015, with two conclusions: his campaign, they write, 'highlights the notable outcome of an independent candidate winning an election through dedicated social media engagement with voters'; and it is 'one of the first clear cases of a political candidate successfully using social media to win political office and sustain public conversation' (Howard et al., 2017).

Famous for advocating hard-line responses to organised crime and corruption, including the return of the death penalty to Mexico, Calderón stunned viewers and the moderator in the first presidential debate in April 2018 when he declared: 'We have to cut off the hands of those who rob. It's that simple.' Instantly he soared ahead of his rivals in terms of trending on Twitter, and his words provoked a series of memes. One superimposed his face on a picture of what appeared to be an Islamist terrorist chopping off a man's hand. During the debate, Calderón also announced his phone number so viewers could contact him on WhatsApp, proposed militarising schools, and answered questions on same-sex marriage by saying he believes so strongly in marriage he has had three wives. While his views were judged eccentric, he nevertheless used the debate to position himself as a prominent outsider, acquire free media coverage, and appeal to his base, thus growing his profile substantially among voters nationally. Calderón had built his political career via Facebook, winning the 2015 election for Governor of Nuevo León through social platforms while disparaging 'mainstream media'. In 2018, he again used social media, and the social media – via memes – used him.

The memes had discovered Calderón's politics and his personality: reactionary, controversial, provocative. While the memes deriding his position were satirical, those that targeted the other candidates rounded on their personality. They were less satirical and more vicious, and few focused on campaign promises or the record of candidates in political office. Perhaps it is fair to say that Ricardo Anaya Cortés was attacked fairly lightly compared to the others. Referring to him as 'Little Chicken', memes emphasised Anaya Cortés's youth (just 39 years old at the time of the election), thus suggesting his inexperience for high office; his 'intellectual' appearance and white skin; and his middle-class background. His class, representative of the PAN, appeared as the target in several memes, including one that described 'PANsplaining':

> When your boyfriend – the one whose parents paid for him to attend the most expensive schools, gave him his first car, got his first job through his dad's contacts, and started a business with money his family gave him – explains to you that people are poor because they don't want to achieve things through their own efforts.

Another noted that the 2018 football World Cup competition in Russia coincided with the election. Around 30 000 Mexicans went to Moscow to watch the national team beat Germany in the opening round. One meme showed Anaya Cortés seated in a sporting event, tight-lipped and showing no emotion while those around him cheered. The accompanying text read: 'When you realise that Mexico's upper middle class went to Russia and won't be able to vote for you.'

Other memes focused on allegations of corruption. One titled Rickly Riquín Canallín (Richie Rich Little Swine) depicted a cartoon version of Anaya Cortés in a laundrette removing wet cash from a washing machine. Through humour and images the memes immediately positioned the candidate and his party: middle class, privileged, out of touch with ordinary Mexicans, and guilty of corruption.

In contrast, memes about José Antonio Meade were more aggressive. Meade suffered from vitiligo, a condition in which the skin loses its pigment cells which causes discolouration. Memes compared him to the leader of the cartoon *ThunderCats*, Lion-O, who appears to have discoloured skin around his eyes and mouth. In December 2017, Meade created his own video on the satirical digital site *El Deforma*. Asked, 'Do you think you will soon become president?' Meade replies, 'Of course, if I have the Sword of Omens', the most powerful weapon wielded by the leader of the ThunderCats. Meade's face is then superimposed on the body of Lion-O. This is a classic technique of political propaganda: candidates defuse popular ridicule by ridiculing themselves first, thus showing they can take a joke.

At 65 years old, AMLO was the oldest candidate. Memes mocked both his age and his southern accent as symbolising his *chairos* appeal, the left-leaning working classes who were demonised as ignorant and poor. However, these memes overlooked the strength of AMLO's support among his base, the very population they derided; and more importantly they also ignored how AMLO's appeal extended beyond his traditional constituency and was reaching younger, educated, middle-class voters who hungered for change. One video meme showed a sexy young woman in a church standing with a robed priest and several altar boys. She is a *fresa*, an 'upper-middle-class entitled brat' from Guadalajara who confesses she will vote for AMLO. This is a rejection of her upbringing as a *niña bien* (rich girl) from a traditional, conservative, Catholic family who always vote for the PAN. She sings that Mexico needs a change and that 'you know who' is the man for the job.[3]

ATTACKING AMLO

AMLO had long been the focus of condemnation in the public sphere, and throughout his political career Mexicans have been mobilised to both support and condemn him. In the March of Silence on 24 April 2005, a mass demonstration passed through the streets of Mexico City to protest the withdrawal of immunity from AMLO, the city's governor, by President Vicente Fox. This decision was criticised so heavily because Fox was the first president in history to represent Mexico's opposition, yet he was using the same tactics as the dictatorship to silence his own opponents. Carlos Monsiváis described the march as representing 'the most rational performance by the Mexican left in a very long time' (Monsiváis, 2009: 407). Estimates of the number who marched vary from 120 000 to over 1 million, drawn from all backgrounds (Andrade and Zarza, 2013). Supporters called AMLO 'Peje', a nickname because of his southern origins, and because *pejelagarto* is a species of fish found in the south. It also referenced the way AMLO talked, mispronouncing some consonants. Participants in the march proclaimed '*Peje el Toro es innocente*' ('Peje the bull is innocent'), a reference to the famous Mexican film *Nosotros los pobres* (*We, the Poor*) (dir. Ismael Rodríguez), in which its main character, Pepe el Toro (played by Pedro Infante), is sent to jail for a crime he did not commit. In this way, we see the kind of wordplay and cultural references that would later become familiar in political memes. The movement defined AMLO as the leader of a new crusade, the 'Fourth Transformation', and positioned him as a candidate in the 2006 presidential election, carrying with him no indictments from this time. The March of Silence was a turning point in the way the news media reported Mexican politics (Andrade and Zarza, 2013), as well as in increasing the visibility of a style of humour that would become common in the era of Internet memes.

In the 2018 presidential election, opinion polls organised by newspapers and television stations indicated that AMLO enjoyed a large margin of support. This meant he had a distinct advantage over his competitors: being seen as the frontrunner gave him more prominent space in the media landscape, and it helped him gain support from Mexico's biggest media companies, including Televisa, the second-largest in Latin America and well known for its political ties, its own controversial reporting, and accusations of disinformation (Noel, 2017). However, being the frontrunner also brought its disadvantages. AMLO was now the target of an information war fought through the social media. The fact-checking organisation Verificado18 found that around 80 per cent of the fake stories, memes, and videos that circulated during the campaign were themed around AMLO. In particular, propaganda predicted that if he became president, Mexico would become 'socialist' and another Venezuela. The social media space was flooded with messages that 'AMLO is a danger to Mexico', a theme first used by Antonio Solá for the PAN campaign in the 2006 election. The PRI president, Enrique Ochoa Reza, said that 'if the people from MORENA like Venezuela so much, they should just go and live there'. Venezuela, he said, is 'a country with unemployment, with a shortage of food, medicine for children, a country without social peace' (*Periodismo Negro*, 2017). The PRI was thought to have hired the Venezuelan right-wing strategist J.J. Rendón to lead its campaign. His commitment to defeating AMLO was clear. In January 2018 he promised to do 'everything within the law to prevent López Obrador from being President'. In the same month, former President Felipe Calderón shared a video on social media showing a Venezuelan citizen living in Mexico urging voters not to elect AMLO, as he would put Mexico on the same 'path to ruin' as Hugo Chavez in Venezuela. The actress in the video was Carmen Martinez, who in a previous video had expressed her opinion that all street vendors should be 'exterminated'. The PRI also suggested repeatedly that 'Venezuelan and Russian interests' supported AMLO, again a theme first used by Solá. The candidate dismissed these claims and made light of them, jokingly calling himself 'Andrés Manuelovich' (Reuters, 2018). It is interesting that Venezuela is used so prominently in Mexico's political propaganda. It is the demonised 'other' in the same way that Mexico is judged in Donald Trump's 2016 election campaign (see Rawnsley, Chapter 4 in this volume), although as in American elections, perceptions of 'the other' are not constant. Rather, they oscillate according to internal electoral need and domestic political strategy. This is why Mexicans' position on Venezuela changes constantly from engagement to hostility and fear (Lozano, 2019).

With AMLO as the clear frontrunner in the days leading up to the election, political propaganda that was both supportive and hostile intensified. Both sides participated in a hashtag campaign – #AMLOFest – to promote and smear the candidate. The DRFLab, on behalf of the Atlantic Council, has made a deep study of Mexico's digital campaign. Writing on #AMLOFest in particular, Ben Nimmo has noted that '80 percent of all hashtag mentions were retweets, indicating that only a small number of accounts generated unique content, while the remaining users simply amplified it. The high level of amplification indicates automation or – at the very least – a small number of hyperactive users purposefully boosting the campaign' (Nimmo, 2018). The same conclusions are drawn from close examination of Facebook pages that criticised AMLO and attracted thousands of likes but no other comments or reactions, suggesting automation or bots. Many were found to originate in Brazil. Others were possibly the creation of the self-proclaimed 'King of Fake News', Mexican businessman Carlos Merlo, who bragged in interviews about how he had invented news sites and networks of users to spread inauthentic information and stories.

Other memes that circulated included a doctored image claiming AMLO's wife was the granddaughter of a Nazi. Posted originally on *Amor a México* (Love for Mexico), a site run by a Calderón supporter that changed its name three times during the campaign, the meme was shared *c.* 8000 times on Facebook and WhatsApp before it was refuted. Another video that circulated on WhatsApp showed a crowd burning a man alive in Mexico's Tabasco region. The accompanying text blamed AMLO supporters for this atrocity. Again, the claim was debunked, but only after several weeks. Memes, like all content on social media, circulate so quickly that any delay in verifying the source or the content is too late. Verificado18, Mexico's first independent fact-checking organisation, was established in March 2018 (Linthicum, 2018), but could not keep pace with the volume or speed of the fake stories that characterised the campaigns.

CONCLUSIONS

> 'In politics, you want to define yourself, your opponent, and what's at stake. If you look at memes through that lens, it's just another way to help candidates do that.'
> (Rob Shepardson, SS+K marketing agency, in Flynn, 2019)

Electoral democracy is a relatively recent addition to Mexico's political culture; and the descriptions of elections there suggest that Mexicans have embraced the vibrancy of election campaigns that we can witness in other junior democracies, including the less appealing aspects of campaigns such as the personalisation of politics, negative campaigning, and extreme voter polarisation (Rawnsley, 2006; Voltmer and Splicahl, 2006). Campaigns are so important in Mexico that R.A. Camp concluded that they 'do change outcomes ... in presidential races' (Camp, 2013: 453), but we have reason to infer that this was less the case in 2018 than in previous elections.

Of course negative campaigning is unique neither to Mexico nor to the age of social media. However, the significance of the social media in Mexico, where Facebook and WhatsApp have overtaken television and newspapers as the dominant source of information about politics, has amplified the more negative character of campaigns; and memes represent the latest way that voters and parties express their opinions of candidates, but rarely their policies and platforms. Mexico's electoral laws specify a news blackout for 72 hours before the voting begins, but this applies only to what are termed the mainstream media: newspapers, television, and radio. It does not apply to the social media space. This means that the campaigns continue to persuade, attack, disparage, and ridicule as the voters go to the polls. Does this matter? Not in the 2018 presidential election, when the polls showed a clear lead for AMLO long before the ballot boxes were sealed. What happens offline will always exert far more influence than what occurs online (Rawnsley and Ma, 2017).

While the 2012 presidential election was fought partly on Facebook and Twitter, it is only when we look beyond the mediascape that we can truly understand the outcome. The changes in Mexico's electoral culture and demographics explain the decline of the dominant PRI and the outcome of elections since 2000 (Camp, 2013). In 2018 it is possible that the official investigation by the Attorney General of the Republic (PRG) into accusations against candidate Ricardo Anaya of money laundering affected his popularity; and that corruption involving local governors from the PRI hit that party and its candidate, José Antonio Meade, particularly hard. Responsible for the Secretariat of Social Development, Meade was linked to the so-called *La Estafa Maestra*, the 'Master Robbery' through corrupt practices of around 435 million pesos from the government purse, though there was no evidence of his direct involvement. PRI legislators angered Mexicans by stopping investigations into illicit campaign donations from a Brazilian conglomerate to the 2012 presidential campaign. A further 22 ex-state governors, all members of the PRI, were accused of misusing public money while Meade was in charge of the Secretariat of Social Development. All in all, the credibility of the PRI – a party that held uninterrupted power in Mexico for 71 years from 1929 to 2000, and then regained the presidency in 2012 – was damaged by accusations of corruption and its failure to deal with soaring crime. Moreover, we should not discount the impact of the Ayotzinapa43 movement and its many hasthtag campaigns that kept visible (and continue to keep visible) the names and faces of the missing students, as well as condemning the lack of government success in finding them. These problems and issues, more than memes and political propaganda, secured AMLO his victory in 2018. In addition, the candidate who valued and appropriated the social media more than any other, the independent Jaime Heliodoro Rodríguez Calderón, who became a state governor in 2015 because of his use of Facebook and Twitter, attained only 5.23 per cent of the vote in 2018, the lowest of the four candidates.

Evidence suggests that AMLO was the most able to appeal to the educated young who decided the election: around half of all voters were under 39 years of age, and one in five was a first-time voter. While these voters confess they still had their doubts about AMLO, it seems he did best of all the candidates to attract their support on the issues they most cared about and which affected them directly: corruption, crime, drug violence, and stagnant wages (Villegas, 2018). Thus there is a fundamental flaw in the argument that image is politically decisive, for it underestimates the political sophistication and preferences of voters. It is a fact of political life that parties do lose elections despite their aggressive or creative and well-funded campaign techniques.

However, while politics offline determined the outcome in 2018, there is no doubt that what happened online shaped the political culture, the discourses of electoral politics, and the popular perception of Mexico's democratic processes and institutions.

Presidential campaigns are by their very nature personal, and the social media – and memes in particular – have amplified the focus on candidates and their personal attributes. In other words, Mexico is as much an image-based political culture as any other modern democracy. This is understandable, since candidates running for national office, and especially the presidency, tend to be experienced national celebrities, prominent in the media through their years of political service. These candidates are not under any serious pressure to invest excessive amounts of precious campaign funds or time in ensuring that they are easily identified and associated with a particular platform. However, it is common for such candidates to engage in brutal personalised negative campaigning, since their celebrity makes them more vulnerable to exposures of character blemishes and flaws in their political and personal lives. Memes provide visual, humorous, and easily accessible frameworks of interpretation – propaganda 'shortcuts' – for audiences who respond to politics within a context of references to popular culture. They speak clearly to Mexico's culture. In his landmark study of Mexican humour, Samuel Schmidt notes:

> In general, Mexico's humoristic culture transgresses norms, traditional values, and established symbols. Mexicans, like all people of course, laugh and make fun of taboos and moral restrictions, but there is much literature on Mexicans' humor in particular; some say their psyche is saturated with humor even in the most desperate of circumstances. (Schmidt, 2014: 62)

Schmidt describes how Mexicans laugh at themselves as a self-defence mechanism, to show they do not take life too seriously and can overcome all manner of problems, whether it is corrupt politicians or defeats in football matches. In Mexico, as in other countries, 'humor is perhaps the instrument to relieve political frustration; it is an escape valve that society uses to take revenge on politicians without risking political stability' (ibid.: 8). Moreover, it is possible to argue that memes are particularly popular in Mexican politics because of their anonymity and the absence of accountability. Mexicans tend to distrust institutions, whether they be media or political (González, Chapter 22 in this volume). Therefore memes provide a space for users to bypass such institutions and participate in their country's political life without having to engage in open political debate.

At the same time, Mexico is also a victim of its own culture of 'fake news' and political disinformation, a situation that is exaggerated by the velocity and reach of the social media, and by the corresponding lack of trust in 'mainstream media' and journalism. The 2018 election campaign was no doubt one of the most personal and vicious in Mexico's short history of democracy, with spurious sources creating and circulating questionable information, often through memes. While this situation prompted fact-checking through the creation of Verificado18 (Linthicum, 2018), it was difficult to keep pace with the flow of 'fake news', which had reached its target audience by the time its authenticity is checked and pronounced.

Returning to Heiskanen's (2017) framework, the creation and circulation of memes in Mexico's 2018 election certainly speaks 'to the intersection of electoral activism and cultural representation'. The humour in memes about all the candidates included references to popular culture – the American cartoons *ThunderCats* and *Richie Rich*, for example – but also to local contexts that will be instantly recognisable to voters (references to Mexico's middle class, the *niña bien* from Guadalajara, the *chairos*). This connects with Heiskanen's understanding that memes allow voters to 'provide alternative parallel discourses to mainstream media viewpoints'. This is especially important in Mexico's election propaganda, as Facebook and WhatsApp in particular have overtaken television and newspapers as the primary sources of political news and engagement. Memes have opened new spaces for mobilisation: their anonymity, humour, local references, and the speed at which they can react to developments offline (Heiskanen's second principle) make them valuable instruments of political propaganda, while their transmission through established networks appealed to the voters who decided the 2018 election: the young, the educated, the first-time voters who challenged the status quo and were most familiar with the protocols of social media:

> The Mexican, whether young or old, criollo or mestizo, general or laborer or lawyer, seems to me to be a person who shuts himself away to protect himself: his face is a mask and so is his smile. In his harsh solitude, which is both barbed and courteous, everything serves him as a defense: silence and words, politeness and disdain, irony and resignation. (Paz, 1985: 29)

NOTES

1. See Solá's website, https://antoniosola.com/trayectoria/#campanas, for further details.
2. A second independent candidate, Margarita Zavala, dropped out of the race on 16 May 2018.
3. The authors acknowledge the work of Peter W. Davies whose website, Latin America Focus, posts some of the memes described in this chapter (https://peterwdavies.com/).

REFERENCES

Andrade, Eva Sagado and Frida Villavicencio Zarza (2013), 'Journalistic reconstruction of new ways of democratic life (the "March of Silence", April 2005)', *Descartos*, 43: 45–66, available at http://www.scielo.org.mx/scielo.php?script=sci_arttext&pid=S1607-050X2013000300004&lng=es&nrm=iso&tlng=es.

Bradshaw, S. and P.N. Howard (2017), 'Troops, trolls, and troublemakers: a global inventory of organized social media manipulation', working paper 2017.12, Oxford: Oxford Internet Institute.

Camp, R.A. (2013), 'The 2012 presidential election and what it reveals about Mexican voters', *Journal of Latin American Studies*, 45: 451–481.

Denisova, Anastasia (2016), 'Memes, not her health, could cost Hillary Clinton the US presidential election', *Independent*, 12 September, available at https://www.independent.co.uk/voices/hillary-clinton-health-pneumonia-political-memes-a7238581.html.

Denisova, Anastasia (2019), *Internet Memes and Society: Social, Cultural, and Political Contexts*, London: Routledge.

Dwoskin, E. (2018), 'Facebook's fight against fake news has gone global. In Mexico, just a handful of vetters are on the front lines', *Washington Post*, 22 June.

Flynn, Kerry (2019), 'The 2020 meme election: how memes became a mainstream tool in politics', *Digiday*, 5 June, available at https://digiday.com/marketing/meme-election-memes-became-mainstream-tool-politics/.

Glowacki, Monika, Vidya Narayanan, Sam Maynard, Gustavo Hirsch, Bence Kollanyi, et al. (2018), 'News and political information consumption in Mexico: mapping the 2018 Mexican presidential election on Twitter and Facebook', COMPROP Data Memo 2018.2/June 29, 2018, available at https://comprop.oii.ox.ac.uk/research/mexico2018/.

Heiskanen, Benita (2017), 'Meme-ing Electoral Participation', *European Journal of American Studies*, 12(2), available at https://doi.org/10.4000/ejas.12158.
Howard, P.N., S. Savage, C.F. Saviaga, C. Toxtli, and A. Monroy-Hernandez (2017), 'Social media, civic engagement, and the slacktivism hypothesis: lessons from Mexico's "El Bronco"', *Columbia SIPA Journal of International Affairs*, 29 January, available at https://jia.sipa.columbia.edu/social-media-civic-engagement-and-slacktivism.
Huntington, H.E. (2016), 'Pepper spray cop and the American Dream: using synedoche and metaphor to unlock internet memes' visual political rhetoric', *Communication Studies*, 67(1): 77–93.
Jenkins, Henry, Sam Ford, and Joshua Green (2013), *Spreadable Media: Creating Value and Meaning in a Networked Culture*, New York: New York University Press.
Linthicum, Kate (2018), 'Mexico has its own fake news crisis. These journalists are fighting back', *Los Angeles Times*, 15 April, available at https://www.latimes.com/world/la-fg-mexico-fake-news-20180415-story.html.
Lozano, Genaro (2019), 'How to understand Mexico's lonely stance on Venezuela', *Americas Quarterly*, 13 December, available at https://www.americasquarterly.org/article/how-to-understand-mexicos-lonely-stance-on-venezuela/.
Manderlink, D. (2015), 'Armchair activism and why it's problematic', *Twenty Something Living*, available at http://twentysomethingliving.com/armchair-activism-and-why-its-problematic.
Milner, Ryan (2013), 'Pop polyvocality: internet memes, public participation, and the Occupy Wall Street movement', *International Journal of Communication*, 7: 2357–2390.
Milner, Ryan M. (2016), *The World Made Meme: Public Conversations and Participatory Media*, Cambridge, MA: MIT Press.
Mina, An Xiao (2018), *Memes to Movements: How the World's Most Viral Media is Changing Social Protest and Power* (Kindle edn), Boston, MA: Beacon Press.
Mina, An Xiao (2019), *Memes to Movements: How the world's most viral media is Changing Social Protest and Power*, Boston, MA: Beacon Press.
Monsiváis, Carlos (2009), *Apocalipstick*, México, D.F.: Debate.
Moore, Martin (2018), *Democracy Hacked: Political Turmoil and Information Warfare in the Digital Age*, London: Oneworld
Morozov, Evgeny (2011), *The Net Delusion: The Dark Side of Internet Freedom*, New York: PublicAffairs.
Newman, N., R. Fletcher, A. Kalogeropoulos, D.A. Levy, and R.K. Nielsen (2018), *Reuters Institute Digital News Report 2018*, Oxford: Reuters Institute.
Nimmo, Ben (2018), '#ElectionWatch: Bot Battlefield at #AMLOFest', DRFLab, 30 June, available at http://medium.com/drflab/botspot-amlofest-turns-into-a-bot-battlefield-796d8d048389.
Noel, Andrea (2017), 'Mexicans outraged after praying for fake "trapped child"', *Daily Beast*, 22 September, available at https://www.thedailybeast.com/mexicans-outraged-after-praying-for-fake-trapped-child.
Paz, Octavio (1985), *The Labyrinth of Solitude*, New York: Grove Press.
Periodismo Negro (2017), 'Si a los de Morena les gusta Venezuela, que se vayan a vivir allá: Ochoa', 15 November, available at https://www.periodismonegro.mx/2018/01/19/la-campana-del-miedo-contra-amlo/.
Pomerantsev, Peter (2019), *This is Not Propaganda: Adventures in the War Against Reality* (Kindle edn), London: Faber & Faber.
Rawnsley, Gary (2006), 'Democratisation and election campaigning in Taiwan: professionalizing the professionals', in Katrin Voltmer (ed.), *Mass Media and Political Communication in New Democracies*, London: Routledge, pp. 114–129.
Rawnsley, Gary and Yiben Ma (2017), 'The Rise of New Media in East Asia', in Tun-jen Cheng and Yun-han Chu (eds), *The Routledge Handbook of Democratisation in East Asia*, London: Routledge, Chapter 18.
Rawnsley, Gary and Katrin Voltmer (2009), 'The Media', in Christian Haerpfer, Ronald Inglehart, Chris Welzel, and Patrick Bernhagen (eds), *Democratization in a Globalized World*, Oxford: Oxford University Press.

Reuters (2018), '"Andres Manuelovich": Mexican leftist laughs off Russian election jabs', 19 January, available at https://www.reuters.com/article/us-mexico-politics/andres-manuelovich-mexican-leftist-laughs-off-russia-election-jabs-idUSKBN1F735X.

Schmidt, Samuel (2014), *Seriously Funny: Mexican Political Jokes as Social Resistance*, Tucson, AZ: University of Arizona Press.

Shabo, Magedah E. (2008), *Techniques of Propaganda and Persuasion*, Smyrna, DE: Prestwick House.

Shifman, Limar (2014), *Memes in Digital Culture*, Cambridge, MA: MIT Press.

Verificado (2018), available at https://verificado.mx/categoria/noticias-falsas/.

Villegas, Paulina (2018), 'Disenchanted youth may tip Mexican election to López Obrador', *New York Times*, 25 June, available at https://www.nytimes.com/2018/06/25/world/americas/mexico-election-youth.html.

Voltmer, Katrin and Slavko Splicahl (eds) (2006), *Political Communication, the Mass Media and Transitions to Democracy*, London: Routledge.

24. Political parties, rallies, and propaganda in India

Andrew Wyatt

INTRODUCTION

Propaganda is integral to the conduct of party politics in India. In parts of India, it seems there is an election in progress all the time. Politics is constantly in view with large numbers of posters pasted on walls and synthetic flex banners vying with other commercial billboards for attention. The posters are refreshed weekly and party logos are daubed on walls. Important meetings or visits by party leaders require additional effort and the number of posters and banners multiply on routes leading to the venue. Neighbourhood units of political parties claim public space for themselves by erecting a statue and/or flying their flag (Gorringe, 2017: 182–186). Some propaganda is also public art, especially the colourful wall paintings used to praise the virtues of party leaders past and present.

The purposes of propaganda in India are myriad. This chapter concentrates on the uses of propaganda to win elections, but the Indian state also promotes itself and shapes public discourse (Gould, 2017; Roy, 2007). Social and political movements, which have a broader agenda than winning office, use propaganda to promote social change and transform the country. The Hindu nationalist movement that generated the party currently governing India, the Bharatiya Janata Party (BJP), has been active since the late 19th century, promoting its religion's nationalism though education, pamphleteering, development work, and social action (Zavos, 2000). Philip Taylor (2003: 6) defines propaganda as a 'deliberate attempt to persuade people to think and behave in a desired way'. Attempts by elites to set the agenda are complicated by changes in media operations and democratic political processes, meaning propagandists become more creative in developing political narratives. Taylor also notes that propaganda is directed at committed supporters as well as those who are uncertain; effort is expended to make sure partisan supporters remain persuaded (ibid.: 4).

Most of this chapter focuses on propaganda used in election campaigning. However, this is not how propaganda originated in India. Before 1947, propaganda battles were fought over more profound political questions pertaining to the legitimacy of the colonial regime, and involved very basic 'sowing, germination and cultivation of ideas' (Taylor, 2003: 2). Guha (1992) argues that, at heart, nationalist politics were a battle for ideological hegemony. The colonial regime engaged in propaganda campaigns, seeking to discredit its opponents, and in some cases censoring them. The nationalist movement sought to undermine the colonial regime while advocating a moderate ideology that would not weaken bourgeois interests within India. This ideological contest continued after India's independence in 1947 (Guha, 1982: 6–7), with the ruling Congress Party using the organs of the state to promote its vision of nationalist developmentalism. The rise to power of the BJP, accompanied by vigorous propaganda in favour of its nationalist ideas, has once again brought the question of hegemony to the forefront of discussions (Sinha, 2017; Palshikar, 2019).

This chapter connects the propaganda techniques developed during colonial-era politics with contemporary electioneering. The intensified use of propaganda was very apparent in the national parliamentary elections in 2019. The dataset for this chapter includes a review of numerous rallies organised by leading political parties in 2019 (Wyatt, 2021) and personal observation of populist politics in south India since 2000 (Wyatt, 2013). The approach taken is qualitative and investigates attempts by political elites to persuade voters to support their parties.

THE CONTEXT: PARTY POLITICS IN INDIA

Beginning in the late 19th century the Indian National Congress (INC) battled for control of the political agenda (Gould, 2011). In the anti-colonial struggle, Indian politicians adapted and adopted propaganda techniques used elsewhere including party newspapers, leaflets, public meetings, and protests, which would be reported by other media. Distinctively Indian methods were used as well, such as infusing religious ceremonies, festivals, and rituals with new political content (Gould, 2017: 84). The nationalist movement expanded in the 1920s under the leadership of M.K. Gandhi. He planned a variety of mass protests and proved adept at gaining media coverage. Gandhi promoted the making and wearing of homespun textiles, known as *khadi*. He argued that Indians should wear clothes made from *khadi* as a nationalist uniform to publicise their cause (Trivedi, 2007). *Khadi* remains in use among male politicians who want to communicate their authenticity and signal a patriotic connection to Gandhi.

The INC movement was the basis for the centre-left Congress Party which dominated Indian politics from the time of independence in 1947 until the late 1980s. In spite of Congress dominance, many other parties emerged to contest elections. Initially Congress faced the strongest opposition from leftist parties, but over time the challenge from the right became stronger. The Hindu nationalist BJP campaigned vigorously against Congress in the late 1980s and has since emerged as India's largest party, winning the last two national elections in 2014 and 2019. A 'third force' in Indian politics are the regional parties that capitalise on the linguistic and cultural diversity of the country.

For a long time, Congress succeeded in pulling together a coalition of supporters from the many different regions. India's federal system includes 28 states that have significant devolved powers. Within each state there are cleavages based on religion and the social hierarchy of caste. Congress was relatively successful at bridging these differences and promoting a message of composite nationalism, reflected in the phrase 'unity in diversity' (Chiriyankandath, 1997). However, over time opposition parties worked to undermine the credibility of Congress, exposing inconsistences in its approach to government. For example, the BJP raised the charge of 'pseudo-secularism', arguing that Congress did not treat all religious groups equally and favoured religious minorities over Hindus. Other political entrepreneurs tried to open cleavages of region and caste, focusing their propaganda efforts on building up sectional identities. Often, they were very successful in resetting the pattern of political competition, articulating new narratives of politics that made possible the rise of new small and regional parties (Wyatt, 2015, 2019). Competition between the multitude of parties encourages innovation in propaganda and different ways of appealing for support.

ELECTIONS: RALLYING SUPPORT

The end of colonial rule in 1947, and the prompt move towards universal suffrage, changed the style and content of political communication. Protest politics and street-level demonstrations were still used to persuade, but the object and purposes of protest were less 'national'. Elections had to be won from 1952 onwards. Congress used its network of volunteers, professional party workers, and control of office to communicate its message. In mid-20th century India high levels of illiteracy shaped propaganda styles. Parties contesting elections in the colonial period were allocated colours, and campaigners informed voters which coloured box should receive the ballot on polling day. After independence the new Election Commission allocated parties a logo or visual symbol to identify them on the ballot paper (Vittorini, 2014), and parties took up the task of promoting their unique sign among voters. This remains the case, and so all contemporary Congress Party posters and wall paintings reference the 'hand' symbol, for example. India is much closer to full literacy now, but a significant minority of the electorate (about 20 per cent) still cannot read, and party symbols are placed on electronic voting machines to guide voters.

Political rallies were used by Congress as part of the anti-colonial struggle before 1947, and taken up again in election campaigns. Holding a well-attended rally demonstrates the vitality of a party and its potential as an election winner. Congress had a starter's advantage in the 1950s, but other parties and movements also organised rallies to show their support. Rallies are often associated with special locations. In the state of Bihar, the Gandhi Maidan in Patna has been used repeatedly for mass gatherings by state and national leaders (M.K. Gandhi used the location before 1947, when it was known as Patna Lawns). Shivaji Park in Mumbai has a similar history. The rally creates a special atmosphere, and entertainment value, as a local event (Spencer, 2007). The rally is not just a local event, however, as media coverage advertises the party and its message to a state-wide or national audience (Roy, 2021). To guarantee success, parties bus in volunteers, as well as paying and feeding other people to attend. Poorly attended rallies will be mocked by political opponents. Large rallies are expensive to organise and can be used by larger parties to intimidate smaller parties (*Indian Express*, 2019). Novelty is added by recruiting entertainers, including singers and comedians.

Politicians include humour or sarcasm in their speeches to catch attention. They articulate strong propaganda, claiming artistic licence when stretching facts and joking about other parties. Navjot Singh Sidhu, a well-known cricketer turned television personality, joined the Congress Party in 2017 (after over a decade with the BJP) and has spoken at rallies and events across north India. Sidhu sings, jokes, and seeks controversy, which generates further publicity (he was banned from speaking at events for 72 hours by the Election Commission for breaking the election code in April 2019).

In the 1970s, Prime Minister Indira Gandhi made effective use of rallies to project her image and appeal directly to crowds of voters. Travelling by helicopter she was able to speak at locations across India in the run-up to the 1971 election campaign. Indira was presented as a national, almost presidential leader who towered above her opponents. The current Prime Minister, Narendra Modi, appears at numerous rallies making similar claims to eminence.

As the governing party after 1947, Congress had several advantages. All India Radio was a state-run enterprise and privately owned newspapers were cautious when criticising the government (with which they also had to register). Cinema advertising was dominated by government-produced newsreels and short films (Roy, 2007). Congress found it relatively easy to raise funds to pay for propaganda and expensive rallies. Opposition parties were obliged to innovate. They set up their own newspapers and magazines which party members were expected to buy. Political education classes and travelling theatre groups promoted alternative ideas. Some parties established reading rooms where people could read newspapers and discuss politics (Subramanian, 1999). An innovation used in south India was infiltration of the film industry to produce films with political content. The official censor was alert to this and would demand cuts, or occasionally ban films where the propaganda was too overt. Song lyrics, the showing of party flags, and the social issues raised in the plotlines were very successful ways of promoting party messages (Pandian, 2000). The songs, a popular element of most Indian films, took on a life of their own after the films were released, providing their sponsors with free and memorable publicity for years (or even decades) afterwards.

A long-standing propaganda technique favoured by opposition parties and movements is the *padayatra* or long-distance walk. M.K. Gandhi popularised the protest walk with his famous 'salt march' in 1930, when he took 24 days to walk to the Gujarat coast, make salt, and break the colonial tax laws. The *padayatra* was already familiar among Hindus as a form of pilgrimage (Kumar, 2017: 33). The format has been used by numerous politicians and social campaigners since. It costs little and attracts media attention over a period of weeks or months if performed well. Political leaders enhance their image as earnest, disciplined, and close to the people.

THE HINDU NATIONALIST MOVEMENT

The Hindu nationalist movement became active in the late 19th century as various movements and individuals argued that the Hindu religion should be fundamental to the ethos and politics of Indian society. The movement came to maturity under the guidance of the Rashtriya Swayamsevak Sangh (RSS), formed in 1925, which has developed dozens of associated institutions and front organisations. The movement, and its party-political wing, the BJP, became the leading rival to Congress Party in the late 1980s. Miscalculations by Congress governments aided the BJP, but the movement also escalated its propaganda efforts in the 1980s. The BJP, which is India's largest party, spends a vast amount of money on political communication. Also significant is the ground-level propaganda work of the wider Hindu nationalist movement, coordinated by full-time workers who guide millions of volunteers. Many of these volunteers would not recognise the political nature of their work, preferring to describe their work as 'service', but they want to create a social environment receptive to Hindu nationalist ideas (Alder, 2018: 423).

The Hindu nationalist movement began to promote itself with renewed vigour in the late 1980s. It picked up causes which it could popularise, and so undermine the more secular-minded politicians holding office. Most notable was the campaign to build a temple in the north Indian town of Ayodhya, at a location said to be the birthplace of the god Ram. The project had added piquancy because campaigners wanted to demolish a mosque built on that very location.

This controversial demand and the energy with which the campaign was promoted attracted public interest. Members of the public were urged in roadside meetings to buy bricks for the construction of the temple. The message was declaimed in fiery speeches that circulated on inexpensive audio cassette tapes. Propaganda films were shown to neighbourhood audiences using video vans. The campaign was guaranteed national attention in September 1990 when the BJP president L.K. Advani commenced a *yatra* or pilgrimage to Ayodhya. He travelled across northern India on a truck decorated to appear as Ram's chariot. The campaign created civil disorder and riots in which several hundred people died (Panikkar, 1993: 71–72). The *yatra* did not reach Ayodhya, as Advani was arrested in late October, but it raised the profile of the BJP and pushed religious issues up the political agenda. The electoral popularity of the BJP increased, and it was able to win enough seats in parliament to form a coalition government in 1998. One of the organisers of Advani's 1990 *yatra* was Narendra Modi, who went on to become chief minister of the state of Gujarat in 2001. He relied heavily on rallies and television coverage to shape his image and win elections for his party (Jaffrelot, 2015). As he sought a place in national politics, Modi fashioned an image as a hard-working and development-oriented leader. His administration concentrated on projects that would be visible, such as roads, electricity supply, large industrial projects, and tourist promotion (Mukhopadhyay, 2013: 381). Overseas investors were hosted at high-profile events. As well as associating himself with development, Modi took care to promote himself in areas far beyond his home state, making personal visits and placing advertisements in regional newspapers (Sinha, 2014). In doing so he deflected attention from his strong nationalist beliefs and uncompromising attitude towards religious minorities. After winning the general election in 2014, Narendra Modi formed a government with a majoritarian character (Adeney, 2015). The new administration continued to promote the Hindu nationalist ideas that inspired the formation of the BJP. Some of this propaganda was intended to pull less committed voters into the orbit of the movement. Patriotism was promoted with reference to the flag and the national anthem. Conflict with Pakistan has been used to strengthen ideas of Indianness, as the BJP has sprung to the defence of India using aggressive rhetoric. The overall objective has been to conflate Hindu nationalism with mainstream nationalism and everyday patriotism. Some argue that this is an attempt to establish the hegemony of Hindu nationalist ideas (Palshikar, 2019: 104–106). Some of the initiatives are more obviously ideological and help generate propaganda that is well received by activists within the movement. Targeting left-wing student activists with verbal and physical assaults falls in this category (Martelli and Parkar, 2018: 3597).

Narendra Modi's entry into national politics was accompanied by intensified propaganda efforts. He has fashioned his image, taking meticulous care to dress appropriately (Vittorini, 2022), and to stage his appearance at national events. Modi uses the rally format both to promote government projects and for party events. State assembly elections are staggered, so several occur each year, and Modi canvasses for the BJP during these campaigns. Again, he addresses mass rallies in these state election campaigns and generates soundbites for wider consumption. Modi travels ceaselessly in India and abroad, creating spectacles the media will cover. He participated in over 200 events in the lead-up to the 2019 general election (Wyatt, 2021). Most of these events were large-scale rallies during which Modi attacked his enemies and promoted the achievements of his government. The events were covered by professional media and by supporters of the Prime Minister on social media. Before the event, partisans would herald his arrival in a state on Twitter, and afterwards talking points from his speeches would be highlighted. Excerpts from Modi's speeches are available for sharing via his website. A full-length video of the speeches themselves would be made available by the party via social media.

PROPAGANDA AND THE EXPANSION OF THE INDIAN MEDIA SINCE THE 1980S

The messaging work of parties and movements has adapted to changes in India's media. Television came late to India, introduced by the state-owned broadcaster Doordarshan, which achieved national coverage only in the early 1980s. Since then, the television industry has been transformed, and by 2014 a majority of households (65 per cent) owned a television. Private satellite broadcasting expanded in the early 1990s, adding several 24-hour news channels and a host of other regional channels that carry news output (Mehta, 2015a: 54). In 2019, no less than 902 private satellite channels had registered with the Telecom Regulatory Authority of India (TRAI, 2019: 6). The large number of channels is partly the result of India's linguistic diversity, which creates a segmented market, and also an outcome of the commercial logic of the broadcasters, which promote a bundle of channels catering to different interests including films, music, and news (Mehta, 2015a: 56–57).

The changing broadcast environment has three implications for the use of propaganda in India. Firstly, the ubiquity of television gives political parties another medium in which to seek support. Larger parties can buy airtime for political advertising, with the caveat that the broadcasts are vetted by the Election Commission before they are shown. This advertising can be used on social media as well. Secondly, the expansion of television changes the way in which politics is seen. Voters have much more information to process, and political parties struggle to control their message, having to adapt to an omnipresent media hungry for interesting content. In a fragmented market there is intense competition for viewers, which encourages sensationalist reporting and angry panel debates among commentators. This in turn shapes the behaviour of politicians, who realise they can get coverage by performing visual stunts and by making outrageous claims (Sardesai, 2014: 194). Thirdly, the loose rules on media ownership mean that some politicians get extraordinary benefits. Initially, the national governing party had a monopoly on sympathetic coverage from state-run broadcasters. This included special access, allowing the Prime Minister to broadcast to the nation on important topics and senior officials to manipulate coverage (Baru, 2014: 119). However, many parties now have privileged access to broadcasters. Regional politicians, or businesses close to them, often set up their own satellite channels. Some of these 'channels' are fairly obscure or run for just a few hours a week. Other politically connected media firms are established broadcasters that run multiple channels with full schedules which include soaps, films, and news programmes. News television is often a loss-making business, opening opportunities for those with political ambitions and corporate interests seeking influence (Gundimeda, 2017; Mehta, 2015a: 59–60). The options for propaganda are multifarious. News items can be heavily biased; negative stories on those friendly to the channel are likely to be overlooked; reports that show the opponents in a poor light can be highlighted and endlessly repeated.

While India has a vibrant media, it also has an ambiguous relationship with the state. Politicians in power at the national and state levels take a view of what constitutes 'balanced' coverage and put pressure on media outlets. This is not unique to India, but it does have some unusual features, including heavy spending by government departments on newspaper advertising (*New Indian Express*, 2019). In the background is the threat of withdrawing advertisements, with some politicians being more willing than others to use this leverage.

The broadcasting environment shifted as Narendra Modi became a national political figure from 2013 onwards. Modi is a newsworthy individual, drawing viewers while he campaigned for office, and then working hard to create news once he became Prime Minister. Astute media management has helped the BJP get favourable coverage since 2014, which includes supplying high-quality video coverage of party events to television channels (Mehta, 2015b). Modi's public appearances are carefully staged, and he gave only one press conference between 2014 and 2019 (in which he watched a colleague answer all of the questions). Ownership patterns are also a factor. Set up in 2017, Republic-TV is a news channel founded, fronted, and partly owned by the media personality Arnab Goswami, who is an avowedly nationalist broadcaster. In 2014, Network 18 was taken over by Reliance Industries, India's largest company, which has to work with numerous state regulators to run its businesses, including its mobile telephone operations. The founder of Zee-TV, Subhash Chandra, was elected to the upper house of India's national parliament with support from the governing BJP in June 2016 (Kumar, 2019). Zee News is very supportive of the ruling party (Ninan, 2019).

Broadcasters and newspaper publishers have become more cautious since 2014, often giving attentive coverage of the Prime Minister's work. Media reports are monitored by state officials, and channels are offered advice about how coverage of the government could be improved (Kumar, 2019: 512–515). Conversations with owners of media outlets also take place, and since 2017 two editors of national newspapers have abruptly left their jobs after running stories that upset senior members of the government (Inamdar, 2019). Journalists and news anchors have been put under pressure from a combination of quiet interventions from senior politicians and activists issuing threats on social media (Kumar, 2019: 510–511).

The expansion and changes to conventional media have to be connected to new technology and media forms. The expansion of mobile communication increases the demand for content. The growing consumption of news and propaganda online includes video material recycled from traditional media sources (Mehta, 2015a) and new content produced for online use only. Social media has a new dynamic, allowing individuals and politicians to generate their own material. This 'hybrid media system' is used by India's political parties (Neyazi, 2019).

DIGITAL PROPAGANDA

Election propaganda in India is increasingly influenced by new technology and the work of professional consultants. Political parties have well-established ways of connecting with voters, but using new methods is attractive because it might give a candidate or party that marginal advantage of a few thousand votes to win a competitive election (Singh, 2019). Some platforms, such as Twitter, are extremely cheap to use (Pal et al., 2019). Even so, the expansion of television advertising and social media calls for new skills that are supplied by consultants. Parties also have their own employees, including the members of information technology (IT) 'cells' that create and circulate content. The IT cells link up with volunteers who promote party messages on social media and in their own personal networks (Sharma, 2019). Some of these volunteers are very aggressive, advocating hard-line nationalist views, and troll opponents online (Chaturvedi, 2016: 67–68).

Social media are used to manipulate public opinion, cultivating narratives that favour one party over another. The sentiment that the governing Congress Party was corrupt and inept was encouraged through social media in the lead-up to the 2013 election (Singh, 2019: 79–80). Some of this work is done by volunteers and sympathisers, but bots are also used to generate Twitter trends and inflate particular points of view. In the case of the 'surgical strike' against militants based in Pakistan that took place in September 2016, a couple of dozen accounts were revealed to be putting out thousands of tweets calling for aggressive action (Neyazi, 2019: 8). Opinions on social media are taken by other media outlets as a proxy for public opinion, ignoring the fact that vested interests cultivate or manufacture Twitter trends (ibid: 4; Kumar, 2019: 507). Narendra Modi makes full use of social media, with a presence on almost every available platform (Pal et al., 2019). Hindu nationalists use social media to promote Modi vigorously. A snapshot of their impact is given by Sinha (2017: 4172): 'Twitter became an arena for circulating and endorsing official information on Modi, but also a vast reservoir of half-truths and untruths, fake news, rumors, and slander against Modi's opponents.'

Political parties are learning how to use propaganda more efficiently, communicating different messages to different audiences. Facebook advertisements are used for this purpose, but this can be done even more precisely by circulating messages via WhatsApp. To segment the audience further, political parties, and especially the BJP, are trying to streamline WhatsApp groups, making them socially homogenous so that propaganda can be micro-targeted, with different messages being sent to different demographic groups (Singh, 2019: 81–84).

Technology has enabled parties to broaden the range and variety of propaganda they use. In the 2000s, short pieces of propaganda were sent to mobile phone users via cheap SMS text messages, and if done well they might catch attention. Well-crafted jokes might go viral and damage the reputation of an opponent. Smartphones widened the creative possibilities. The Congress leader Rahul Gandhi featured in numerous memes during the 2014 election that denigrated his stature and maturity. Other material that circulates easily includes campaign songs and videos. In 2019, the most popular campaign song, 'Ravali Jagan', produced by the regional party YSRCP and its political consultants, was viewed over 20 million times on YouTube. The song was accompanied by a watchable and sharply edited video which used footage of a 3648-kilometre *padayatra* tour undertaken in 2018 by the party leader, Jagan Mohan Reddy (*News Minute*, 2019).

CELEBRITY POLITICS

Since the 1950s, actors in India have had mixed film and political careers. The south Indian film star MGR was put to work in the 1960s addressing rallies for his regional party, the DMK. His party leader is reputed to have said: 'When we show his face, we get 40 000 votes; when he speaks a few words, we get 4 lakhs [400 000]' (Hardgrave, 1973: 302). Parties hope that associating with famous individuals will make it easier to persuade voters to support them. They also know that they will get free publicity and perhaps access to an extensive network of fan clubs to boost party membership. Celebrities are a propaganda resource increasingly used by political parties in recent elections. Some celebrities have been persuaded to stand as candidates and are revealed to the media at special news conferences shortly before the polls. As well as film stars, athletes, cricketers, singers, and retired military officers have been nominated for election. The retired cricketer Gautam Gambhir joined the BJP in March 2019 and was nominated to contest a seat in the 2019 general elections on 22 April. The party undoubtedly valued his link with over 9 million Twitter followers, as well as popularity in his own parliamentary constituency. Other parties have made similar moves. The Samajwadi Party persuaded the actor Poonam Sinha to fight the Lucknow seat in 2019. Sinha's social media presence is evolving, but her daughter (and actor) Sonakshi joined the campaign and retweeted photographs to her 14 million Twitter followers. The TMC, a regional party from West Bengal, included five film stars in its list of 42 candidates for the 2019 parliamentary election (Pramanik, 2019). Newspapers and websites respond enthusiastically to photo-ops with celebrity candidates. Celebrity candidates absorb attention during elections, and if elected generate free publicity over a much longer period.

THE SIGNIFICANCE OF PROPAGANDA IN CONTEMPORARY INDIA

The content and type of propaganda used has wider implications for Indian politics. Parties can open discussions of sensitive or controversial issues that otherwise would not be generally mentioned. A common theme that is raised in propaganda is corruption, which at times has been a very successful way of attacking incumbent parties. Ironically, the expanding range of propaganda tools is intimately linked to the problem of systemic corruption. Parties routinely exceed official limits on campaign spending while drawing on funds without clear provenance.

There are certain topics in Indian politics that cannot be mentioned by broadcasters and newspapers in ordinary circumstances. Politicians attempt to coerce media outlets by denying interviews, withdrawing advertising, filing defamation cases, or in extreme cases threatening journalists. Business houses can also exert pressure, so corporate corruption is under-reported by commercial media outlets. Yet, political parties in campaign mode are relatively free to strike against this informal censorship, and resorting to sensational claims attracts publicity. The anti-corruption candidate Arvind Kejriwal used this tactic in 2014, and Rahul Gandhi took a similar approach prior to the 2019 election. Once the story is in the public domain, the media have more freedom to report allegations made during campaign speeches. Propaganda can expand the range of topics and issues open for public discussion.

Corruption has been a recurrent theme in Indian politics since the 1940s, with ambitious politicians accusing their opponents of malfeasance. Ingenious ways of presenting the issue and some plausible evidence might make it a live topic. This happened between 2012 and 2014 when an anti-corruption movement centred on Delhi staged a series of demonstrations, hunger strikes, and vigils to press claims for stronger anti-corruption institutions. Part of this movement split away to form a political party, the Aam Aadmi Party, to press for legal and administrative changes (Wyatt, 2015: 168–169). Narendra Modi picked up the theme in 2014 and joined this to the idea of Congress being a dynastic party. With favourable media coverage the BJP shaped a narrative of crisis which needed correction by a strong leader.

Not all propaganda is effective. The issue of corruption can become salient in Indian politics, but at other times voters may not take allegations of corruption seriously (Singh, 1997). Voters decide, with incomplete and contradictory evidence, which story to believe. A striking feature of (Indian) politics is that even when the evidence is compelling, so much so that the authorities charge and convict a politician, it may not sway the judgement of voters. Rahul Gandhi's repeated allegations in the 2019 national election campaign against the government had little impact, in spite of their prima facie credibility. How voters process and receive propaganda has to be kept in view (Taylor, 2003: 15). Voters may not find corruption allegations plausible, or they may prefer to overlook awkward evidence and give their favoured leader or party the benefit of the doubt.

The pattern of political competition in recent elections in India has raised concerns about the polarisation of public opinion (Neyazi, 2019). Propaganda battles have been fierce, and political pluralism has been under pressure since 2014, as the BJP advances a strong nationalist agenda. Institutions, intellectuals, the press, and critics have been confronted by ruling party propaganda that promotes a particular idea of patriotism and demonises 'anti-national' activity. In some case propaganda raises social tensions or cultivates hatred between different groups. Religious minorities have been the target of some of this propaganda, with false stories and crude stereotypes invoked (Jha, 2017).

Yet, the attempts by large political parties to dominate the agenda have to be balanced against the pluralist tendencies of Indian politics. Social diversity confronts any political party with national ambitions, and the federal segmentation of the country gives regional movements and parties spaces in which to work. The formal media, in spite of its ownership structure, is still a diverse field with multiple newspapers, satellite channels, and magazines on offer. India's linguistic diversity encourages 'vernacular' politics that speak to the concerns of individual states, and localities in those states (Tanabe, 2007). Alternative propaganda circulates in leaflets, songs, social media, and protest events. Several notable political entrepreneurs mobilised against the Modi-led government that was elected in 2014. Determined and well-organised movements have so far been able to spread their preferred messages. In various ways, attempts to achieve nationalist hegemony have been resisted.

REFERENCES

Adeney, Katharine (2015), 'A move to majoritarian nationalism? Challenges of representation in South Asia', *Representation*, 51(1): 7–21.

Alder, Ketan (2018), 'Authority, ethics and service (seva) amongst Hindu nationalists in India's assertive margins', *Contemporary South Asia*, 26(4): 421–438.

Baru, Sanjaya (2014), *The Accidental Prime Minister: The Making and Unmaking of Manmohan Singh*, New Delhi: Viking.

Chaturvedi, S. (2016), *I am a Troll: Inside the Secret World of the BJP's Digital Army*, New Delhi: Juggernaut Books.

Chiriyankandath, James (1997), '"Unity in diversity"? Coalition politics in India (with special reference to Kerala)', *Democratization*, 4(4): 16–39.

Gorringe, Hugo (2017), *Panthers in Parliament: Dalits, Caste, and Political Power in South India*, New Delhi: Oxford University Press.

Gould, William W. (2011), *Religion and Conflict in Modern South Asia*, Cambridge: Cambridge University Press.

Gould, William W. (2017), 'From Gandhi to Modi institutions and technologies of speech and symbolism in India', in Monroe Price and Nicole Stremlau (eds), *Speech and Society in Turbulent Times: Freedom of Expression in Comparative Perspective*, Cambridge: Cambridge University Press, pp. 79–95.

Guha, Ranajit (1982), 'On some aspects of the historiography of colonial India', *Subaltern Studies*, 1: 1–7.

Guha, Ranajit (1992), 'Discipline and mobilize', *Subaltern Studies*, 7: 69–120.

Gundimeda, S. (2017), 'Caste, media and political power in Andhra Pradesh: the case of Eenadu', *History and Sociology of South Asia*, 11(2): 192–203.

Hardgrave, Robert (1973), 'Politics and the film in Tamilnadu: the stars and the DMK', *Asian Survey*, 13(3): 288–305.

Inamdar, Nikhil (2019), 'How Narendra Modi has almost killed the Indian media', *Quartz*, March 12, available at https://qz.com/india/1570899/how-narendra-modi-has-almost-killed-indian-media/.

Indian Express (2019), 'As BJP, Cong bring out big guns, Kejriwal rallies at a halt, focus on road shows', 2 May, available at https://indianexpress.com/elections/as-bjp-cong-bring-out-big-guns-kejriwal-rallies-at-a-halt-focus-on-road-shows-5701673/.

Jaffrelot, Christophe (2015), 'Narendra Modi and the power of television in Gujarat', *Television and New Media*, 16(4): 346–353.

Jha, Prashant (2017), *How the BJP Wins: Inside India's Greatest Election Machine*, New Delhi: Juggernaut.

Kumar, Radhika (2017), 'Padayatras and the changing nature of political communication in India', *Studies in Indian Politics*, 5(1): 32–41.

Kumar, Ravish (2019), 'Bad news', in Niraja Gopal Jayal (ed.), *Re-forming India: The Nation Today*, Gurgaon: Penguin.

Martelli, Jean-Thomas and Khaliq Parkar (2018), 'Diversity, democracy, and dissent: a study on student politics in JNU', *Economic and Political Weekly*, 53(11): 3597–3606.

Mehta, Nalin (2015a), 'India and its television: ownership, democracy, and the media business', *Emerging Economy Studies*, 1(1): 50–63.

Mehta, Nalin (2015b), 'Modi's media', *Social Text*, 27 February, available at https://socialtextjournal.org/periscope_article/modis-media/.

Mukhopadhyay, Nilanjan (2013), *Narendra Modi The Man, The Times*, Chennai: Westland.

New Indian Express (2019), 'Narendra Modi government spending more on ads in Hindi newspaper: RTI', 8 September, available at http://www.newindianexpress.com/nation/2019/sep/08/narendra-modi-government-spending-more-on-ads-in-hindi-newspapers-rti-2030684.html.

News Minute (2019), 'From "Ravali Jagan" to "Nayakuda Nayakuda", AP politicians are setting the tempo for polls', 8 April, available at https://www.thenewsminute.com/article/ravali-jagan-nayakuda-nayakuda-ap-politicians-are-setting-tempo-polls-99690.

Neyazi, Taberez (2019), 'Digital propaganda, political bots and polarized politics in India', *Asian Journal of Communication*, 30(1): 1–19.

Ninan, Sevanti (2019), 'How India's media landscape changed over five years', *India Forum*, 7 June, available at https://www.theindiaforum.in/article/how-indias-media-landscape-changed-over-five-years.

Pal, Joyojeet, Azhagu Meena, Drupa Dinnie Charles, and Anmol Panda (2019), 'The use of social media', *India Seminar*, available at https://www.india-seminar.com/2019/720/720_joyojeet_pal_et_al.htm.

Palshikar, Suhas (2019), 'Toward hegemony: the BJP beyond electoral dominance', in Angana P. Chatterji, Thomas Blom Hansen, and Christophe Jaffrelot (eds), *Majoritarian State: How Hindu Nationalism is Changing India*, London: Hurst, pp. 101–116.

Pandian, M.S.S. (2000), 'Parasakthi: life and times of a DMK film', in R.S. Vasudevan (ed.), *Making Meaning in Indian Cinema*, New Delhi: Oxford University Press.

Panikkar, K.N. (1993), 'Religious symbols and political mobilization: the agitation for a mandir at Ayodhya', *Social Scientist*, 21(7–8): 63–78.

Pramanik, Probir (2019), 'Glamour in Trinamool list: why Mamata Banerjee prefers film stars over politicians', *Outlook India*, 12 March, available at https://www.outlookindia.com/website/story/india-news-glamour-in-trinamool-list-why-mamata-banerjee-prefers-film-stars-over-politicians/326956.

Roy, Indrajit (2021), 'Dignified development: democratic deepening in an Indian state', *Commonwealth and Comparative Politics*, 59(1): 47–73.

Roy, Srirupa (2007), *Beyond Belief: India and the Politics of Postcolonial Nationalism*, Durham, NC: Duke University Press.

Sardesai, Rajdeep (2014), *The Election that Changed India*, New Delhi: Viking.

Sharma, Amogh Dhar (2019), 'How far can political parties in India be made accountable for their digital propaganda?', *Scroll*, 11 May, available at https://scroll.in/article/921340/how-far-can-political-parties-in-india-be-made-accountable-for-their-digital-propaganda.

Singh, Gurharpal (1997), 'Understanding political corruption in contemporary Indian politics', *Political Studies*, 45(3): 626–638.

Singh, Shivam Shankar (2019), *How to Win an Indian Election: What Political Parties Don't Want You to Know*, Gurgaon: Penguin.

Sinha, Aseema (2014), 'The making of Narendra Modi', *Ballots and Bullets*, School of Politics & International Relations, University of Nottingham, 8 April, available at https://nottspolitics.org/2014/04/08/the-making-of-narendra-modi/.

Sinha, Subir (2017), 'Fragile hegemony: Modisocial media and competitive electoral populism in India', *International Journal of Communication*, 11: 4158–4180.

Spencer, Jonathan (2007), *Anthropology, Politics and the State: Democracy and Violence in South Asia*, Cambridge: Cambridge University Press.

Subramanian, Narendra (1999), *Ethnicity and Populist Mobilization: Political Parties, Citizens and Democracy in South India*, New Delhi: Oxford University Press.

Tanabe, Akio (2007), 'Toward vernacular democracy: moral society and post-postcolonial transformation in rural Orissa, India', *American Ethnologist*, 34(3): 558–574.

Taylor, Philip M. (2003), *Munitions of the Mind: A History of Propaganda*, Manchester: Manchester University Press.

Telecom Regulatory Authority of India (TRAI) (2019), 'Consultation paper on issues related to interconnection regulation, 2017', 25 September, Consultation Paper No. 16/2019, New Delhi.

Trivedi, Lisa (2007), *Clothing Gandhi's Nation: Homespun and Modern India*, Bloomington, IN: Indiana University Press.

Vittorini, Simona (2014), 'The two yoked bullocks, the ladder and the lamp: India's electoral symbols as vehicles of national identity', *Nations and Nationalism*, 20(2): 297–316.

Vittorini, Simona (2022), 'Modi à la Mode. Narendra Modi's fashion and the performance of populist leadership', mimeo, SOAS, forthcoming.

Wyatt, Andrew (2013), 'Populism and politics in contemporary Tamil Nadu', *Contemporary South Asia*, 21(4): 365–381.

Wyatt, Andrew (2015), 'Arvind Kejriwal's leadership of the Aam Aadmi Party', *Contemporary South Asia*, 23(2): 167–180.

Wyatt, Andrew (2019), 'Small parties and the federal structure of the Indian state', *Contemporary South Asia*, 27(1): 66–72.

Wyatt, Andrew (2021), 'Clientelist politics and material appeals: the BJP under Modi', mimeo, University of Bristol.

Zavos, John (2000), *The Emergence of Hindu Nationalism in India*, New Delhi: Oxford University Press.

25. Media and majoritarianism in India: eroding soft power?
Daya Thussu

INTRODUCTION

The election of Narendra Modi as the Prime Minister of India in 2014 is seen by many commentators as the advent of a majoritarian turn in a hitherto secular country. Modi's considerable communication skills and formidable party apparatus have created a media ecosystem where majoritarianism is thriving (Price, 2015; Ullekh, 2015). With the revolution in media production and distribution, as well as in mobile and online communications, such messages and concepts are now reaching a wide audience within the country as well as around the globe. Before the coronavirus pandemic hit India, the country had risen to be the world's third-largest economy after China and the United States (US) (on the basis of purchasing power parity) and, in overall gross domestic product (GDP) terms, had surpassed the United Kingdom in 2019 to become the fifth-largest economy globally, according to data from the International Monetary Fund (IMF, 2019).

The concept of soft power – arguably a more acceptable form of political propaganda – is associated with the work of the Harvard political scientist Joseph Nye, who coined the term in an article he wrote for the journal *Foreign Policy* in 1991. This was a significant time in international relations, with the fracturing of the Cold War framework that had defined multilateral relations since 1945. In his 2004 book *Soft Power: The Means to Success in World Politics*, Nye suggested that soft power was an integral part of foreign policy, especially for states seeking to 'incorporate the soft dimensions into their strategies for wielding power' (Nye, 2004: 1). Its role in foreign policy is important precisely because, 'in behavioural terms, simply put, soft power is attractive power' (ibid.: 6), pursued to influence the behaviour of other states. Although Nye's formulation of soft power was developed primarily in relation to the US, it is an indication of the intellectual and informational power of US academia and elite mass media that the term has been rapidly globalised, entering the lexicon of foreign policy mandarins across the world and promoted by the 'nation-branding' industry that has emerged in the past three decades to help countries be attractive to foreign investment.

The thin line between propaganda and soft power is often ignored in Western discourses. It is important to remember that the word 'propaganda' itself has its roots in Europe, from the Latin *propagation*, 'the breeding of specimens of a plant or animal by natural processes from the parent stock'. The *Oxford Dictionary of Media and Communication* defines propaganda as: 'Persuasive mass communication that filters and frames the issues of the day in a way that strongly favours particular interests, usually those of a government or corporation' (Chandler and Munday, 2011: 326). Any standard text on propaganda would also note that the concept has strong religious connotations: the Catholic Church formalised the use of propaganda when Pope Urban II (1035–1099) used it to generate support for the Crusades, while printing presses disseminated propaganda to a much wider audience and, in 1622, Pope Gregory XV established the *Congregatio de Propaganda Fide* (Congregation for Propagating the Faith) for promoting the faith in non-Catholic countries. From legitimising colonialism and sponsoring capitalism, to using information during (hot and cold) conflicts, the Western imprint on propaganda discourse is well established. Indeed, until the 1930s, propaganda was used as a positive concept in political science and international relations departments, particularly in the US universities. However, in more recent decades, a sophisticated and persuasive version of propaganda, disseminated through mass media and global public relations networks, has come to dominate the discourse within democracies, while crude propaganda is associated with authoritarian states. Their soft power initiatives are summarily dismissed as propaganda, and countries such as China and Russia have been characterised as exercising 'sharp' power which 'pierces, penetrates, or perforates the political and information environments in the targeted countries' (Walker and Ludwig, 2017: 13). In the case of a large and diverse democracy such as India, a distinction between soft power and propaganda can be made in that unlike the authoritarian states, the Indian government has no systematic approach towards propagating its ideas and has deployed limited resources for such purposes. Instead, as noted below, the government has collaborated with private corporations, media and entertainment companies, and civil society groups – both diasporic and domestic – to frame the country's global narrative within a civilisational framework, one which goes back to draw inspiration from India's Hindu traditions, part of a project of majoritarianism which has come to represent Modi's India.

India's public-diplomacy strategy under the Hindu-nationalist Bharatiya Janata Party (BJP) government of Prime Minister Modi elected in 2014, and re-elected with an even bigger mandate in 2019, has emphasised India's intellectual, religious, and cultural wealth, using the country's considerable media and creative industries, and the global Indian diaspora (Tandon, 2016; Lahiri, 2017; Mazumdar, 2018; Gautam and Droogan, 2018). As outlined in a 2017 documentary, *India Boundless – A Place in the Heart of the World*, produced for the Public Diplomacy Division of India's Ministry of External Affairs, India's global presence and influence (artistic, spiritual, and intellectual) are rooted in its civilisational power (*India Boundless*, 2017). In this chapter, I discuss how India has deployed its soft power assets, including mass media, diaspora, religion, and culture, to create awareness and appreciation of India globally (Tharoor, 2012; Thussu, 2013; Kugiel, 2017). After examining the role of mass media in this process, the chapter explores how the trend towards majoritarianism has dented India's global image.

SOFT POWER PROJECTION IN A CIVILISATIONAL FRAMEWORK

One major and visible change in India under Modi has been the attempt by the state and the government to hark back to India's civilisational attributes. Although India came into being as a modern nation state only in 1947 after it gained independence from British colonialism, Indic civilisation dates back more than 5000 years as one of the most ancient and continuous cultural formations in the world, with wide-ranging influences in areas from religion and philosophy, to arts and sciences, language and literature, trade and travel (Thussu, 2013). As the origin of four of the world's major religions – Hinduism, Buddhism, Jainism, and Sikhism – and as the place where many faiths have coexisted for millennia, India offers a unique and syncretised religious discourse. Buddhism was founded in India and remains the most enduring and powerful idea associated with India today, and connects Indian culture with countries across Asia. In addition, both Christianity and Islam have long associations with India. Some of the earliest Christian communities were established in India. St Thomas, who is believed to have visited southern India in the first century, is supposed to be buried in Chennai; while one of the world's oldest mosques, Cheraman Juma Mosque, is located in Kerala, where Jewish communities have also lived for millennia.

The majoritarian mindset which has become increasingly visible within media space is keen to emphasise India's ancient past, suggesting for example that the dissemination of Hindu and Buddhist ideas across Asia, evident in examples such as Garuda, the name of the official airline of Indonesia, the world's largest Muslim country, and a Sanskrit word for the eagle on which the Hindu god Vishnu rides. The dispersion of ideas associated with Hinduism and Buddhism across East and Southeast Asia from the third century BC onwards created a strong cultural and communication dimension to the millennia-old relationship between India and the rest of Asia (Mookerji, 1947; Sen, 2005). Stories of the Buddha's life and teachings remain a cultural referent in much of Asia, while traces of Indic languages, religious rituals, cuisine, dance, and other art forms survive in parts of Southeast Asia, notably in Thailand, Cambodia, and Indonesia (Sen, 2003; Sen, 2005; Thussu, 2013).

Buddhism was also a central link between India and China, indicating a very long historical association between the two great civilisational powers of Asia (Sen, 2017). Centres of higher education such as Nalanda, an international Buddhist university based in eastern India between the fifth and twelfth centuries, existed for 500 years before universities were established in Europe (and has been recently revived as part of a pan-Asian project linking China and India, as well as some other Asian nations). Even today, when Buddhism is a minority religion in India and China is the largest Buddhist country in the world (notwithstanding the relatively insignificant role that religion plays in a supposedly communist country), Buddhism remains a powerful link between the two civilisations.

Under Modi's stewardship, this civilisational link has been invoked in policy formulations, if not in their implementation (Karnad, 2018). The government has propounded the idea of 'sanskriti evam sabhyata' (culture and civilisation) as one of the key principles for promoting India's image globally. In 2018, a prominent pro-government think tank, the India Foundation, organised its first soft power conference, with an emphasis on India's past glories (India Foundation, 2018). The majoritarian discourse has received approval at the highest level. Perceiving and presenting India as a civilisational power is articulated by India's Minister of External Affairs in a recent book simply called *The India Way*, which draws on Indian civilisational traditions to reclaim the country's place in the new world order (Jaishankar, 2020). Others, representing the new generation of intellectuals, have argued that 'India is a civilization which is transforming into a "nation" through the instrumentality of a sovereign democratic State' (Madhusudan and Mantri, 2020: xxix).

Invoking India's past, which the Modi government has been keen to emphasise, makes sense in an age in which cultural revivalism is occurring across the globe. Modi's promotion of Buddhism is one visible sign of India's cultural diplomacy. With its focus on peace and non-violence, 'faith-based' diplomacy, with Buddhism at its core, is seen as a useful soft power tool for India, which has traditionally projected itself as a peace-loving nation. However, at the same time, a muscular and not particularly subtle Hindu nationalism is also being promoted within official and media discourses (Mazumdar, 2018).

Another theme of soft power promotes yoga and Ayurveda (the traditional Indian medicine and well-being system), a process which started in earnest soon after Modi took office. He engaged in intense lobbying within the United Nations (UN) General Assembly to pass the resolution for an international day of yoga, which has been celebrated annually on 21 June by the UN since 2015 as International Yoga Day. Drawing on an ancient Hindu spiritual tradition to promote an Indian 'alternative' lifestyle fits in well with a Hindu nationalist leader, who is himself a devoted yoga enthusiast and a very public practitioner (Mazumdar, 2018; Gautam and Droogan, 2018). 'The Modi government has raised the bar on the relationship between India's soft power potential and its foreign policy', noted one commentator. 'For the first time', he wrote, 'the Indian state is beginning to make systematic use of the rich cultural and human resources that have previously developed quite independently of its policies' (Martin, 2015).

THE RISE OF MAJORITARIANISM

The coming to power of Modi in 2014 triggered much commentary and criticism, nationally and internationally, about the rise of the right and associated majoritarianism in a country that has always celebrated its pluralist tradition. 'India found itself divided between one segment of people who felt that Modi's victory signified the glorious consolidation of their own economic and social ascendancy', noted one commentator associated with the previous regime, 'and another segment who felt devastated by the result, seeing in it a crushing of their dreams for themselves, their communities and their country' (Mandar, 2015: xxxvi).

The BJP's 2014 victory under Modi's leadership, the first comfortable parliamentary majority achieved by a single party for 30 years, put an end to the coalition politics that had restrained the majoritarian agenda of the previous BJP governments between 1998 and 2004. In many ways, the rise of Modi from a regional leader to the national limelight reflected similar trends in global politics, where those leaders projected to be 'strongmen' have come to set the national agenda. Among the notable cases of this new kind of muscular nationalism one may include Donald Trump in the United States, Xi Jinping in China, Vladimir Putin in Russia, Recep Erdoğan in Turkey, and Jair Bolsonaro in Brazil, to name the leaders representing the major countries across the globe. Though each leader has his distinct approach towards articulating a nationalist agenda, they share some common attributes: namely, populism and ruthless pragmatism.

Modi's well-known commitment to *Hindutva* (Sanskrit for Hinduness), sometimes interpreted as 'Hindu nationalism', was considered as being at the heart of the majoritarian project. Modi has a very close association with the BJP-affiliated Rashtriya Swayamsevak Sangh (RSS) (National Volunteer Service), a radical right-wing Hindu nationalist organisation founded in 1925. Though for decades he was one of RSS *pracharaks* (active preachers), his focus during his first term in office was the mantra of *vikas* (development) rather than promoting Hindutva. '*Sabka Saath, Sabka Vikas*' (Collective Efforts, Inclusive Growth) was the catchy slogan that contributed to his victory in 2014. Supporters point out Modi's achievements as the long-serving (2001 to 2014) and effective Chief Minister of Gujarat, one of the country's most industrialised states. Under his stewardship, the GDP growth rate of Gujarat averaged 10 per cent, constantly above that of the national figure. However, Modi's critics blamed his administration's role during the 2002 violent Hindu–Muslim riots in his state that claimed hundreds of lives, although in 2012 a special body appointed by India's Supreme Court stated that investigations found no evidence to prosecute Modi for what happened during one of the worst riots in India.

However, also in this narrative Modi constantly drew on Indian civilisational and cultural repertoires, making references to ancient Hindu texts as well as works of more recent Hindu nationalist intellectuals such as Vivekananda (real name Narendranath Datta) (1863–1902) and right-wing ideologues, notably Vinayak Damodar Savarkar (1883–1966) and Madhav Sadashiv Golwalkar (1906–1973). The core of this ideology is that India's identity is essentially Hindu. The Hindus, who constitute more than 80 per cent of India's 1.3 billion people, can claim India to be their *pitribhumi* (Sanskrit for 'fatherland'), and *punyabhumi* (Sanskrit for the 'land of pious faith'). In such formulations, minorities such as Muslims and Christians, whose religions originated outside India, have to prove their Indian credentials.

The RSS, which claims to be the world's largest social and cultural organisation with more than 5 million members, is the BJP's ideological parent organisation. Its majoritarian and exclusivist ideology champions the transformation of India into a '*Hindu Rashtra*' (Hindu nation). Many of its critics highlight the narrow vision that the RSS promotes, undermining the secular and inclusive India guaranteed under its constitution to every citizen, irrespective of creed, caste, or ethnicity. For its critics among the liberal intelligentsia in India and the diaspora, the organisation is viewed as extremist, even racist, with its inspiration from Fascist Europe, especially in its early decades (Noorani, 2019; also see essays in Chatterji et al., 2019). A recent study has highlighted the functioning of this organisation, which has 6000 full-time workers and more than 36 affiliates and 100 subsidiaries active in such diverse sectors as education, health, and rural development, among others. It notes: 'Amidst the diversity of India – with its dozens of languages and associated cultures, countless permutations of the hierarchical Hindu caste system and vast economic gulfs – the proliferation of affiliates provides many different avenues by which to mobilize support for the Hindutva message of unity' (Andersen and Damle, 2019: xvi).

DIASPORA AND MAJORITARIANISM

Another dimension of India's growing global soft power profile is its extensive and increasingly visible diaspora, scattered around the globe and estimated, according to figures from India's Ministry for External Affairs, at nearly 30 million. Sections of this diaspora, especially in the US, where an estimated 4.6 million people of Indian origin live, have excelled in many spheres of life and enriched US cultural and economic life (Chakravorty et al., 2017). There is a strong Indian presence in senior positions in Ivy League universities (for example, Srikant Datar, Dean of Harvard Business School), international media (such as Fareed Zakaria, a leading CNN commentator and *Washington Post* columnist, and Ravi Agrawal, managing editor of *Foreign Policy*), and multilateral organisations (Gita Gopinath, the first woman to become chief economic advisor to the International Monetary Fund), as well as transnational corporations (notably Satya Nadella, the chief executive officer of Microsoft; and Sundar Pichai, chief executive of Google). In US politics too, the Indian presence is growing: Vice President Kamala Harris's mother was Indian.

In a globalised and interconnected world, diasporas can be a vital strategic instrument and channel of communication to further foreign policy goals, depending on their economic and political influence within the centres of global power (Chakravorty et al., 2017). Such 'soft power resources' have become an important component in foreign policy priorities for Modi. He has underlined the need to further strengthen the linkages between India and its diaspora, as indicated in his various stage-managed 'town hall' events in the US, full of razzmatazz, notably the 2014 mega-show in New York's Madison Square Garden and the 'Howdy Modi' event in Houston with US President Trump in September 2019 (Yee, 2014; Paul, 2019). These carefully choreographed shows were very well attended and received wide media coverage. Such media-friendly strategies are being deployed by India's government, in collaboration with increasingly globalising Indian industries, to project India as an investment-friendly, pro-market democracy. Indian corporations are keen to engage with the diasporic elites to further their own interests.

As India's international profile has grown in recent decades, members of its diaspora are reconnecting with the homeland. Although Modi has prioritised engagement with the diaspora, he is benefiting from steps taken by his predecessors, especially Prime Minister Atal Behari Vajpayee, who headed the BJP-led coalition government in 1998. A certain affinity with this majoritarian project can be detected in sections of the diaspora which has been created and sustained by BJP and its various affiliates. Such organisations as the Overseas Friends of the BJP as well as Vishwa Hindu Parishad (World Hindu Council) are effective in tapping into the diasporic resources – including fund-raising – to mobilise Hindus to realise the majoritarian project. However, they have had to contend with the numerous critics of majoritarianism among the Indian diaspora based in the US, particularly those sections active in academia, the non-governmental sector, and social movements (about gender and caste equality, religious tolerance, and Islamophobia). However, in the past decade or so, and particularly since the ascent of Modi to the national and international scene, the Hindu-nationalist groups have become more visible, especially on social media.

MEDIATISING MAJORITARIANISM

In the age of instantaneous communication, 'political life is ever more thoroughly infused with symbolic practices and communicative dynamics; the idea and practice of politics is endlessly *narrated*, *mediated*, *affected*, *imagined* and *technologized*' (Davis et al., 2020: 2). Media, and especially visual media, have played a crucial role in contributing to the majoritarian discourse in India where, it has been suggested, the media mobilisation is taking place with both legacy and digital media working together (Neyazi, 2018). To understand this process, it is important to provide a brief background to the transformation of news media in the world's largest democracy in the era of globalisation.

The rapid liberalisation, deregulation, and privatisation of media and cultural industries in India during the 1990s transformed the media sector. The Indian media space was reconfigured by what has been described as the 'triumph of the liberal model' (Hallin and Mancini, 2004: 251) of media, partly 'because its global influence has been so great and because neo-liberalism and globalization continue to diffuse liberal media structures and ideas' (ibid.: 305). The increasing availability of digital delivery and distribution mechanisms in the past three decades has created a new market for 24/7 news. This is evident in the exponential growth in television channels: from Doordarshan – a notoriously monotonous and unimaginative state monopoly until 1991 – to in excess of 800 channels, including more than 400 dedicated news networks, making India home to the world's most competitive news arena, catering to a huge domestic audience as well as the large diaspora.

In a liberalised and privatised economy, while the proliferation of media outlets continued apace, the competition for audiences and, crucially, advertising revenue, intensified as the audiences fragmented in a multi-channel environment. This structural change, paralleling the growing commercialisation of news, forced broadcast journalists and television producers to make news entertaining, borrowing and adapting ideas from the world of entertainment. As I have documented elsewhere, the global popularity of such infotainment-driven programming indicates the success of this formula (Thussu, 2007). Another structural change was that many news networks were receiving investments from conglomerates which made profits in the entertainment industry and thus directly or indirectly influenced editorial content: for example, greater coverage of sports and lifestyle stories about celebrities from the world of entertainment, drawing on Bollywood or Bollywoodised content. A symbiotic relationship between the news and new forms of current affairs and factual entertainment genres such as reality TV developed, blurring the boundaries between news and entertainment. In a fiercely competitive and crowded market, such hybrid programming fed into and benefited from the 24/7 news cycle, providing a feast of entertainment-driven compelling content which sustained ratings and kept production costs low. Two seasoned commentators lamented the fact that mainstream media in India can now be marked as 'celebratory media dominated by breathless gossip about cricketers, billionaires and Bollywood stars and point-scoring among the political elite' (Drèze and Sen, 2013: 263).

This excessive marketisation also led to marketing executives influencing the politics of television news. News became increasingly shrill and partisan as well as regional in its orientation, reflecting the growing importance of regional parties in national politics. In such an altered polity, many more media groups – distinct in terms of language, region, political orientation, and economic interests – invested in television news, making it multi-vocal and multilayered in terms of audiences and production values. Zee TV, India's pioneering television conglomerate, was the first network to launch a 24-hour Hindi news channel in India, Zee News. This gave the channel an important voice in the politically crucial Hindi heartland of India, where it had to compete in later years with Aaj Tak, part of the India Today Group and the most successful news channel, since its inception in 2000 (Ninan, 2007; Neyazi, 2018). In southern India, the relationship between television news and politics was well established. In Tamil Nadu, two main regional parties, All India Anna Dravida Munnetra Kazhagam (AIDMK) and Dravida Munnetra Kazhagam (DMK), had their sympathetic Tamil-language networks. Jaya TV was unabashedly pro-AIDMK, while Sun TV supported the DMK party. In other southern states too, many round-the-clock news channels had clearly defined political affiliations. For example, Eenadu TV, part of the largest circulated Telugu daily group, extended strong support to the Telugu Desam party, while in Kerala, Kairali TV had a pro-communist news agenda.

These channels became an integral part of political communication in their respective states, increasingly being sought after by politicians and their image managers. Scholars have contextualised this expansion of media within the discourse of deepening democracy in India, with the process of what has been termed 'local democratization' (Sadanandan, 2017). Nationally, although English-language news channels have disproportionate influence given their relatively small but elitist viewership, news in Hindi and in other major languages in India has a much wider audience base (Ninan, 2007). The BJP politicians and spin doctors were quick to make use of this powerful medium for ideological proselytisation. They saw the exponential growth of regional media in the past two decades, and especially the Hindi-language television, as a useful ally in promoting their majoritarian political agenda (Neyazi, 2018).

Before Modi's ascent to power, much of the media in India operated within what might be termed as a largely liberal centrist cultural space, though there existed small but vocal sections of right-wing outlets as well as radical left-leaning media. Majoritarianism was not the main concern of much of the media, and politicians such as Modi faced a critical, if not hostile media, especially from those media houses belonging to the English-language elite networks. To break this hold, media strategists of the BJP steadily cultivated certain media houses to support the cause of majoritarianism. One early supporter was Zee network, one of India's largest media conglomerates whose owner was elevated to be a nominated member of the upper house of India's parliament. As a quid pro quo, the network began to support the Hindu nationalist cause, especially promoting Modi and his muscular version of majoritarianism.

An even more far-reaching change was the acquisition, just before the 2014 election, of News 18 (India's largest television network with dozens of regional-language channels as well as collaboration with CNN) by Reliance group, India's largest conglomerate, with investments in vital sectors of the country's economy, including energy, retail, and telecommunications. Reliance's entry into the media arena, building on its ownership of Jio, India's most prominent mobile and internet provider, raised concerns about the concentration of communication power within a small circle of hugely influential corporates with close connections to Modi and his majoritarian agenda. A recent study about this ownership issue noted: 'Ownership concentration is likely to intensify as content media companies identify synergies with wireless telephony companies for distribution. The advent of vernacular language-enabled smartphones is likely to play an important role in the convergence scenario and the ensuing concentration of ownership' (Bhattacharjee and Agrawal, 2018: 56).

Another major shift of the mainstream TV news towards the majoritarian project was the launch in 2017 of Republic TV, with its very overt nationalist agenda, and changing the contours of national conversation on how Indian identity should be defined. The network closely identified with its owner-anchor Arnab Goswami, who unabashedly adopted what has been termed as 'campaigning frame', which 'declares the news outlet's stance on a particular issue or cause and typically seeks to galvanize sympathies and support for its intervention, political or otherwise, beyond the world of journalism' (Cottle and Rai, 2008: 83).

DIGITAL MAJORITARIANISM

The majoritarian media agenda reflects the growing polarisation of politics in India and, as one study showed, 'social media has facilitated the expression of polarized views online' (Neyazi, 2020: 49). Against this changed media ecology, the extraordinary growth of internet and social media in India (the country is home to nearly 700 million internet users; both Facebook and WhatsApp have their largest audiences in India) contributed significantly to promoting the majoritarian agenda which Basu sees as the quest for a Hindu 'political monotheism' as an advertised and informational Indian experience of urban normativity that some have called 'Hindutva 2.0' (Basu, 2020: 4). Labelling this 'Hindutva 2.0 as Advertised Monotheism', Basu writes: 'In recent decades, with the ushering-in of an informational world and networks of electronic urbanization, the literary-cultural project of Hindu nationalism has undergone fundamental transformations' (ibid.: 8).

One key element of this nationalism project is anti-Islamic rhetoric, which is particularly toxic on social media. For example, the notion of 'love jihad' is a narrative which accuses young Muslim men of luring Hindu women into a fake marriage, with the aim of forcefully converting them to Islam and discarding them afterwards. Another relates to the Muslims violating the so-called 'beef ban'. In the majoritarian discourses the claim is made that, before Modi took office, the previous governments had been 'appeasing' the Muslim population as a 'vote bank' and the mainstream liberal media was implicitly supporting this.

Challenging the mainstream liberal media discourses, such pro-majoritarian online media platforms as Swarajamag.com (launched September 2014) and OpIndia.com (launched December 2014) have gained a steady following among the so-called 'Internet Hindus' (Chadha and Bhat, 2019: 119). A study termed such sites as crucial building blocks of 'the effort to establish a right-wing ecosystem'. These sites, the study found, 'are coming to constitute a parallel discursive arena where conservative activists are not only able to articulate their core principles, but can also define their own identity, highlight perceived misrepresentations, and develop oppositional discourses challenging what they consider to be a biased mainstream media narrative' (ibid.: 132).

Despite having acquired large sections of sympathetic television news outlets as indicated above, Modi avoided interactions with mainstream news media, for example never addressing a press conference during his six years in power. Instead, he created a direct connection with people by having a monthly radio programme in Hindi called *Mann Ki Baat* ('Inner Thoughts'), which has been broadcast every month on the national broadcaster All India Radio since October 2014, dubbed in various Indian languages, and also broadcast live on Doordarshan, as well as the main social media platforms (for a compilation of Modi's monthly thoughts, see BlueKraft Digital Foundation, 2017). Not only have such communicative strategies popularised Modi's agenda among the majority of India's population, but also the cash-strapped public broadcaster has gained advertising revenue, as these 'thoughts' have big nationwide audiences. By adopting an old media technology such as radio, Modi was aiming to reach the semi-urban and rural areas where radio remains a major source of information, despite expansion of television and, more recently, social media. As one commentator noted: 'Modi is an unusual communicator in that while he uses the media as an intermediary to propagate his message, he takes away the media's gatekeeper role, and curbs its ability to edit or censor him' (quoted in ibid.: 24). Even more effective is Modi's clever use of social media platforms to promote his agenda. In 2020, he had the second-largest Twitter following of any head of state after President Trump. 'Social media, its culture, and its communication practices,' a recent study found, 'enabled Modi's rise from local leader to prime minister' (Sinha, 2017: 4163).

The BJP's so-called IT Cell, or the public relations machinery, is extremely active on social media, formulating and disseminating a majoritarian agenda, if not always in a particularly subtle fashion. The BJP, which now claims to be the world's largest political party, has professionally managed campaigning for elections, both nationally and for the states. Apart from the diasporic sympathisers of the majoritarian cause, the IT Cell is increasingly influencing news agendas by providing newsworthy tips and stories at a time when news networks have been facing financial strain. Apart from slashing news-gathering costs, and resorting to opinionated 'news' content that is cheap and easy to produce, and whose feisty quality may even attract advertising, many media houses have resorted to sharp practices in order to squeeze revenue out of 'news'. The phenomenon of 'paid news', when advertisements, whether political or corporate, are presented as real news, further undermines the credibility of news media. One veteran commentator described Modi's media strategy as 'of disdaining any form of direct interaction with the media, leaving that to chosen functionaries who could set a suitable tone of truculence on the airwaves, and otherwise fielding a vast army of internet operatives to colonise that space' (Muralidharan, 2018: 441).

Given the so-called 'demographic dividend' – more than 70 per cent of Indians are below the age of 30 – a sizeable segment of young India is also connecting to these narratives. According to industry estimates, by 2019, digital news readership had grown to more than 300 million (FICCI/EY, 2020). Indians are increasingly going online, producing, distributing, and consuming news, especially using their skills in the English language, the vehicle for global communication and commerce. Both the telecommunications sector and the media and entertainment sector are part of the current government's Make in India plan, and therefore have been given special attention. In 2018, the government released the National Digital Communications Policy catered towards the establishment of 'ubiquitous, resilient and affordable digital communications infrastructure and services'. Among its key objectives is to attract investments of $100 billion in the digital communications sector to facilitate 'India's effective participation in the global digital economy' (FICCI/EY, 2020: 20).

COMMUNICATING MAJORITARIANISM

A politically polarised, domestic-oriented and hyper-commercial media has not contributed to India's voice being heard in the international arena. Unlike India's commercial film industry, which has had a global presence for many decades and arguably a soft power role, especially among many developing countries, Indian news and current affairs continue to be largely absent in the global news arena, and in an era when news media are a key instrument of public diplomacy. A report about global Doordarshan noted, 'Foreign policy is important, and the world wants to know what the Indian government has to say on a wide range of issues. So far, India's foreign policy and its communication have been reticent' (Lakshman, 2014: 5). The capacity to communicate Indian perspectives on international affairs to a globalised audience is extremely limited, despite having a vibrant media and a well-established tradition of English language media. The *Times of India*, one of the country's oldest daily newspapers, was set up in 1838, indicating that generations of educated Indians have worked within an English-language and democratic media environment. Yet, despite ambitions for a global role for India as a civilisational power, it is the only major country whose national broadcaster is not available in the major capitals of the world. The external service of Doordarshan, DD World, launched in 1995 and now called DD India, has very limited international viewership.

This is unfortunate, given that India is one of the world's largest English-language news markets, and when English-language 24/7 news networks emanating from many non-English speaking countries such as China (CGTN), Russia (RT), Qatar (Al Jazeera English), Iran (Press TV), and Turkey (TRT-News) are widely distributed around the world, not only in English but in a range of languages. All these are state broadcasters and are perceived as such by international viewers, providing their own perspectives on and narratives of global affairs, while the Indian state broadcaster – the second-largest in the world after CCTV in China –

remains notably absent in global news space. Although such private English-language news networks as NDTV 24x7, CNN-News 18, India Today TV, Republic TV, Times Now, and WION (World is One News) are available globally, their focus has remained on diasporic audiences.

However, their web presence is growing both nationally and internationally, and apart from the oldest among these (the left-liberal-leaning NDTV 24x7) the others listed above have generally been following, to varying degrees, the majoritarian agenda, with Republic TV being the most closely associated with such editorial positioning.

Modi's government so far has not taken the international aspects of its message that seriously, despite being a formidable communicator himself and in command of a substantial and sophisticated political public relations expertise and resources in his party. Outside the party structures, India's Ministry of External Affairs (MEA), one of the early adopters of social media platforms to connect with diasporic communities, had its Twitter account @IndianDiplomacy created in 2010, and its MEA India Facebook page set up in 2012. The ministry also maintains two YouTube channels (MEA India and Indian Diplomacy) and has official accounts on various platforms, including Instagram, Soundcloud, Flickr, LinkedIn, as well as a Google+ channel. However, under Modi's stewardship these digital handles have been deployed to promote the civilisational agenda. Under the government's Digital India project, these are likely to be accelerated as India adopts 5G-based technology: the economic impact of introducing 5G technology is estimated by the government to reach $1 trillion by 2035 (FICCI/EY, 2020: 20).

IS MAJORITARIANISM ERODING INDIA'S SOFT POWER?

Despite the Modi government's active and effective use of social media and other forms of communication, India's soft power initiatives are not centrally managed by the government, which has traditionally taken a back seat (Mukherjee, 2014; Sinha-Palit, 2017). The country's creative and cultural industry, its religions and spirituality, as well as its active diaspora and commercial corporations, have been more visible symbols of Indian global presence.

One key aspect of India which distinguishes it from other developing countries is the fact that it is the 'world's largest democracy'. One indication of this is the fact that, despite his very humble background as the son of a *chaiwala* (tea seller, a fact which the media-savvy politician is never shy of publicly extolling), Modi was elected twice to the highest office in the land. However, this largely successful experience of democratic governance can also be an easy route towards legitimising majoritarianism, which appears to be the case in India, as outlined above. 'India's assets are countered by its considerable liabilities', notes one recent study (Kugiel, 2017: 157). A majoritarian mindset inevitably alarms minority communities, and moves to curtail their rights and privileges dent India's secular and democratic credentials. In its history as a new democracy, India has demonstrated that a unified nation state can function as a socially and culturally diverse, multilingual and multi-faith country. Such 'unity in diversity' was considered India's major strength in a globalised world. This polity is being increasingly challenged by growing majoritarian nationalism, undermining efforts to promote India's global image.

The anti-Muslim sentiment driven by a populist Hindu nationalism is likely to undermine India's soft power efforts, especially among the 50 Muslim-majority nations in the world with which India has deep cultural and commercial ties, as well as diasporic connections (Ahmed, 2019). In addition, among its Western allies the majoritarian tendencies have evoked bad press as well as trenchant criticism from human rights groups. The contribution of India's 200 million Muslims, the world's largest minority, to the national culture (in terms of music, cuisine, language, arts, and architecture) has been largely ignored, while the emphasis has been on promoting India's Buddhist and Hindu legacy. This has been at the heart of the Modi government's cultural agenda, though primarily aimed at domestic consumption and skilfully exploited for electoral gains. As for reaching the global audience beyond the diaspora, the government's initiatives have been limited and ineffective, partly because of the extremely scarce resources earmarked for overseas soft propaganda. Unlike other major democracies, Indian soft power, as the preceding discussion has demonstrated, has largely been promoted by private initiatives: its voluble diaspora, celebratory religiosity, popular cinema, and information technology industries creating a narrative in which the state apparatus has a very limited role, namely organising 'Festivals of India' in various capitals around the world. Indeed, it can be argued that precisely because the state intervention is so insignificant, India's soft power narrative is not perceived as a propaganda project. However, as the majoritarian propaganda takes hold in India's domestic communication space for reasons outlined above, the soft power discourse is likely to be undermined. Whatever the ideological imperatives for privileging and promoting a majoritarian narrative, it is important to emphasise that India cannot afford to ignore, let alone antagonise, its largest minority, a huge proportion of whom are poor and marginalised. Beyond majoritarianism, Modi should recognise that India's soft power will only be effective when the country is able to eliminate extreme poverty, as China, the only comparable country in terms of scale and scope of social inequality, has done. If India could achieve this within a multicultural and multilingual democracy, then it would offer a new model and its status as a major civilisational and economic power could be realised.

REFERENCES

Ahmed, Hilal (2019), *Siyasi Muslims – A Story of Political Islams in India*, New Delhi: Viking.
Andersen, Walter and Shridhar Damle (2019), *Messengers of Hindu Nationalism: How the RSS Reshaped India*, London: Hurst.
Basu, Anustup (2020), *Hindutva as Political Monotheism*, Durham, NC: Duke University Press.
Bhattacharjee, Anuradha and Anushi Agrawal (2018), 'Mapping the power of major media companies in India', *Economic & Political Weekly*, 21 July, 53(29): 48–57.
BlueKraft Digital Foundation (2017), *Mann Ki Baat: A Social Revolution on Radio*, New Delhi: BlueKraft Digital Foundation in collaboration with LexisNexis.
Chadha, Kalyani and Prashanth Bhat (2019), 'The media are biased: exploring online right-wing responses to mainstream news in India', in Shakuntala Rao (ed.), *Indian Journalism in a New Era: Changes, Challenges, and Perspectives*, New Delhi: Oxford University Press, pp. 113–139.
Chakravorty, Sanjoy, Devesh Kapur, and Nirvikar Singh (2017), *The Other One Percent: Indians in America*, New York: Oxford University Press.
Chandler, Daniel and Rod Munday (2011), *Oxford Dictionary of Media and Communication*, Oxford: Oxford University Press.
Chatterji, Angana, Blom Thomas Hansen, and Christophe Jaffrelot (eds) (2019), *Majoritarian State: How Hindu Nationalism is Changing India*, London: Hurst.
Cottle, Simon and Mugdha Rai (2008), 'Television news in India: mediating democracy and difference', *International Communication Gazette*, 70(1): 76–96.
Davis, Aeron, Natalie Fenton, Des Freedman, and Gholam Khiabany (2020), *Media, Democracy and Social Change: Re-imagining Political Communications*, London: SAGE.

Drèze, Jean and Amartya Sen (2013), *An Uncertain Glory: India and its Contradictions*, Princeton, NJ: Princeton University Press.
FICCI/EY (2020), *The Era of Consumer A.R.T. (Acquisition, Retention, Transaction): India's Media & Entertainment Sector*, Mumbai: Federation of Indian Chambers of Commerce and Industry and London: Ernst & Young, February.
Gautam, Aavriti and Julian Droogan (2018), 'Yoga soft power: how flexible is the posture?' *Journal of International Communication*, 24(1): 18–36.
Hallin, Daniel and Paolo Mancini (2004), *Comparing Media Systems: Three Models of Media and Politics*, Cambridge: Cambridge University Press.
India Boundless (2017), *India Boundless – A Place in the Heart of the World*, New Delhi: Public Diplomacy Division, Ministry of External Affairs, produced by Wide Angle Films, 15 August, available at https://www.youtube.com/watch?v=hj60g06VQCk.
India Foundation (2018), 'Focus: soft power', *India Foundation Journal*, 7(2): 2–34.
IMF (2019), *World Economic Outlook*, April, Washington, DC: International Monetary Fund.
Jaishankar, Subrahmanyam (2020), *The India Way: Strategies for an Uncertain World*, New Delhi: HarperCollins.
Karnad, Bharat (2018), *Staggering Forward: Narendra Modi and India's Global Ambition*, New Delhi: Penguin.
Kugiel, Patryk (2017), *India's Soft Power: Foreign Policy Strategy*, London: Routledge.
Lahiri, Swaroopa (2017), 'Soft power – a major tool in Modi's foreign policy kit', *Journal of South Asian Studies*, 5(1): 39–47.
Lakshman, Nandini (2014), *Doordarshan Diplomacy*, Mumbai: Gateway House – Indian Council on Global Relations, Report No. 11, September.
Madhusudan, Harsh and Rajeev Mantri (2020), *A New Idea of India: Individual Rights in a Civilisational State*, New Delhi: Westland.
Mandar, Harsh (2015), *Looking Away*, New Delhi: Speaking Tiger.
Martin, Peter (2015), 'Yoga diplomacy: Narendra Modi's soft power strategy', *Foreign Affairs*, 25 January, available at https://www.foreignaffairs.com/articles/india/2015-01-25/yoga-diplomacy.
Mazumdar, Arijit (2018), 'India's soft power diplomacy under the Modi administration: Buddhism, diaspora and yoga', *Asian Affairs*, 49(3): 468–491.
Mookerji, Radha Kumud (1947), *Ancient Indian Education (Brahminical and Buddhist)*, London: Macmillan.
Mukherjee, Rohan (2014), 'The false promise of India's soft power', *Geopolitics, History, and International Relations*, 6(1): 46–62.
Muralidharan, Sukumar (2018), *Freedom, Civility, Commerce: Contemporary Media and the Public*, New Delhi: Three Essays Collective.
Neyazi, Taberez (2018), *Political Communication and Mobilisation: The Hindi Media in India*, Cambridge: Cambridge University Press.
Neyazi, Taberez (2020), 'Digital propaganda, political bots and polarized politics in India', *Asian Journal of Communication*, 30(1): 39–57.
Ninan, Sevanti (2007), *Headlines from the Heartland: Reinventing the Hindi Public Sphere*, New Delhi: SAGE.
Noorani, Abdul Ghafoor (2019), *The RSS: A Menace to India*, New Delhi: LeftWord Books.
Nye, Joseph (2004), *Soft Power: The Means to Success in World Politics*, New York: Public Affairs.
Paul, Sonia (2019), '"Howdy, Modi!" was a display of Indian Americans' political power', *Atlantic*, September 23, available at https://www.theatlantic.com/politics/archive/2019/09/howdy-modi-rally-trump-divides-indian-diaspora/598600/.
Price, Lance (2015), *The Modi Effect: Inside Narendra Modi's Campaign to Transform India*, London: Hodder & Stoughton.
Sadanandan, Anoop (2017), *Why Democracy Deepens: Political Information and Decentralization in India*, Cambridge: Cambridge University Press.
Sen, Amartya (2005), *The Argumentative Indian*, London: Penguin.
Sen, Tansen (2003), *Buddhism, Diplomacy, and Trade: The Realignment of Sino-Indian Relations, 600–1400*, Honolulu: Association for Asian Studies and University of Hawai'i Press.

Sen, Tansen (2017), *India, China, and the World: A Connected History*, Lanham, MD: Rowman & Littlefield.
Sinha, Subir (2017), 'Fragile hegemony: Modi, social media and competitive electoral populism in India', *International Journal of Communication*, 11: 4158–4180.
Sinha-Palit, Parama (2017), *Analyzing China's Soft Power Strategy and Comparative Indian Initiatives*, New Delhi: SAGE.
Tandon, Aakriti (2016), 'Transforming the unbound elephant to the lovable Asian hulk: why is Modi leveraging India's soft power?', *Round Table: The Commonwealth Journal of International Affairs*, 105(1): 57–65.
Tharoor, Shashi (2012), *Pax Indica: India and the World of the Twenty-first Century*, New Delhi: Penguin.
Thussu, Daya Kishan (2007), *News as Entertainment: The Rise of Global Infotainment*, London: SAGE.
Thussu, Daya Kishan (2013), *Communicating India's Soft Power: Buddha to Bollywood*, New York: Palgrave Macmillan.
Ullekh, N.P. (2015), *War Room: The People, Tactics and Technology Behind Narendra Modi's 2014 Win*, New Delhi: Roli Books.
Walker, Christopher and Jessica Ludwig (2017), 'From "Soft Power" to "Sharp Power": Rising Authoritarian Influence in the Democratic World', in *Sharp Power: Rising Authoritarian Influence*, Washington, DC: National Endowment for Democracy, pp. 8–25, available at https://www.ned.org/wp-content/uploads/2017/12/Sharp-Power-Rising-Authoritarian-Influence-Full-Report.pdf.
Yee, Vivian (2014), 'At Madison Square Garden, chants, cheers and roars for Modi, *New York Times*, 29 September, available at: https://www.nytimes.com/2014/09/29/nyregion/at-madison-square-garden-chants-cheers-and-roars-for-modi.html.

26. Korean cultural diplomacy in Laos: soft power, propaganda, and exploitation

Mary J. Ainslie

INTRODUCTION

The increasing export of South Korean (henceforth: Korean) popular culture into neighbouring East Asian countries – known as the 'Korean Wave' or 'Hallyu' – since the mid-2000s, has received academic and popular attention both within and outside this region. Associated primarily with pop music and TV dramas after the significant overseas success of programmes such as *Dae Jum Geum* and *Winter Sonata*, as well as later K-pop bands such as Girls Generation and Big Bang, this widespread phenomenon also encompasses food, movies, and other prominent cultural signifiers of Korea. Today the Korean Wave still remains the dominant incarnation of East Asian popular culture and Hallyu is credited with creating enthusiasm for all things Korean across the world. Indeed, the effects of the Korean Wave can be found across Asia in the many remakes, parodies, adoptions, and other forms of cultural adaptation in products from societies as diverse and wide-reaching as Thailand, Indonesia, Japan, Kazakhstan, Vietnam, Argentina, and Hong Kong.

These cultural products are part of a very adept form of political propaganda, one regularly supported and openly referenced by Korean political actors. This is largely in service of economic interests and, as explored in this chapter, overseas investment opportunities for Korean companies. This began in the late 1990s, when the Korean government switched to view the cultural industries as a central means of supporting economic growth, and so began to aggressively promote digitisation and the proliferation of cultural products abroad (Kwon and Kim, 2014). Korea's economy and society had developed rapidly over a relatively short period in the 1990s, yet such accelerated internal development left the country without a corresponding strong national image and brand to project abroad. As a means to grow such an image quickly amidst the democratised and globalised communication system of the modern world, authorities placed strong emphasis upon winning the 'hearts and minds' of foreign publics through popular culture, which then became a key part of broadening the nation's economic prosperity.

This chapter addresses Korean interests and corresponding propaganda in the Laos People's Democratic Republic (henceforth: Laos), one of the poorest countries in Southeast Asia. It first outlines how Hallyu functions as a recognised and effective form of propaganda for Korean interests around the world, and how Southeast Asia has been a key area of economic significance since the 2000s. Outlining Korean economic interest and investment in Laos in particular, the chapter illustrates how such products are part of a political discourse constructing Korea as desirable and beneficial to Laos, as well as an equal partner in this relationship. Yet this discourse functions not only to construct a favourable image of Korea, but also to deflect from growing critique of Hallyu as an industry and its wider consequences. This includes the exploitation that has resulted from unchecked Korean international investment, some of which has had disastrous consequences.

HALLYU AND KOREAN DIPLOMACY

More than just persuasion, soft power constitutes the ability to entice and attract (Nye, 2008: 95) and if we judge such power by the outcome of its resources (as per Nye's definition), then Hallyu has been a very effective asset. Among East Asian countries which lack the resources of the United States (US) and China, Korea stands out as a particularly effective case of propaganda through popular culture (Lee and Melissen, 2011). Compared to China's investments in New Year celebrations and Mandarin schools, and Japan's lack of a concise worldview upon which to model its overseas image, Hallyu has become a model example of propaganda through cultural products, with these 'solid gains' evident through Korea's ranking as seventh globally in terms of cultural exports (Hall, 2017). Indeed, Hallyu has since formed a 'cool' cultural brand to promote Korean exports (such as consumer electronics and cosmetics) and disseminate general positive constructions of Korea internationally (Nye and Kim, 2013).

Scholars have long explored the links between Hallyu promotion and the Korean economic agenda, identifying various internal initiatives supporting such global expansion (see, for example, Hong, 2014; Shim, 2011, 2013; Suh et al., 2013; Chung, 2013; Vial and Hanoteau, 2019). The export and promotion of Hallyu is heavily supported and subsidised by Korean authorities and artificially sustained to maintain the otherwise itinerant nature of such cultural 'waves'. Indeed, while the Hallyu phenomenon initially appeared as merely an itinerant wave of popular culture akin to that of 'Cool Japan' or 'Cool Britannia', Hallyu's substantial contribution and support to the export-orientated Korean economy ensured its impressive longevity.

Political support is crucial to continuing this process of cultural industries as propaganda, and direct institutional and financial support from the government continues to increase. The Ministry of Culture directly assists domestic firms exporting into global markets by supporting activities such as expos, concerts, and festivals (Kwon and Kim, 2014). The Korean Foundation for International Cultural Exchange (KOFICE), a division of the Korean Ministry of Culture, Sports and Tourism, continues to support and fund regular academic and pop culture events. It also supports global Hallyu fan communities, producing regular reports on such activities and the status of the Korean cultural industries internationally (see http://eng.kofice.or.kr). The ministry even launched the K-Culture Road website in 2019, designed to provide better information about the many international Korean culture events that the ministry organises and supports. Academia also became an important resource within this agenda. Research funded by institutions such as the Ministry of Education and the National Research Foundation of Korea produced a host of celebratory and positive projects, many of which seek to generate data that can contribute towards ensuring the longevity and profitability of Hallyu. In a reverse case, more recent research highlights Hallyu as an important 'pull' factor for Korean tourism, an industry that is becoming increasingly important to the export-orientated Korean economy, given the potential negative impact from countries introducing protectionism in the form of tariffs and quotas (Lim and Giouvris, 2020).

Through the high-quality aesthetics and pan-Asian image of modernity embedded in Hallyu products, this political propaganda supports a carefully constructed international image embedded within an experience of rapid and successful modernisation and democratisation (Geun, 2009). This promoted narrative of 'exceptionalism' references the 'economic miracle' of Korea in order to lend legitimacy to its position as 'a development partner and norm creator' (Schwak, 2019: 4), all of which contributes towards presenting Korea as a benevolent assistant to developing nations in particular. Propaganda assets such as Hallyu are therefore designed to cultivate appeal and trust (Enna Park, 2020: 332). Likewise, throughout Asia products such as TV dramas tend to place emphasis upon the 'traditional values' and sentiments from this region, aiming to construct both cultural proximity and relevance to these societies (Shim, 2008; Chon, 2001; Heo, 2002; Shim, 2013; Suh et al., 2013; Chung, 2013).

KOREAN INTERESTS IN SOUTHEAST ASIA

Southeast Asia is of significant interest to Korean overseas investment and is a key site for Hallyu products. Known for its rich natural resources (of tin, rubber, rice, timber, and many more), its rapidly growing economies, and its strategic position between Chinese and American economic domination, the region has been gradually increasing in economic and political prominence since 2000 since its amalgamation under the Association of Southeast Asian Nations (ASEAN) rubric. East Asian countries have been careful to retain prominence within the region as ASEAN integrates and the ASEAN Economic Community (AEC) solidifies (with such initiatives as ASEAN+3[1]). In the mid-2000s, initiatives from Korea focused upon strengthening the Korea–ASEAN relationship, noted as crucial to improving Korea's overseas interests and investments (Conference on Strengthening the Korea–ASEAN Relationship, 2005). Since then South Korea has signed free trade agreements with all ASEAN nations and the area has become an important production base for Korean companies that are attracted by both economic growth potential and cheap labour. South Korean firms then invested up to US$5.26 billion in the region in 2017, a 17 per cent growth from 2016 (Workman, 2021).

The area is also a significant export market for South Korea. ASEAN as a whole is the country's second-largest trading partner, third-largest investment partner, and second-largest overseas construction market (in 2016) (ASEAN–Korea Centre, 2017). Since coming to power in 2017, Korean President Moon Jae-in sought to increase the South Korean focus upon Southeast Asia, with Korea introducing the New Southern Policy (NSP) in 2018, an initiative aiming to increase Korean strategic ties with ASEAN members and India, and elevate these up to the more major ties with the US, China, Japan, and Russia (Kwak, 2018, 2020). One goal of the NSP is to establish a 'people community', achieved through human resource capacity-building (a crucial part of enabling that information and communication technologies in particular are sustainable) and, notably, 'cultural exchange' (Kwak, 2020). In 2018 and 2019, President Moon Jae-in visited all ten Southeast Asian nations as a means of fulfilling this goal, also holding numerous bilateral summits and signing memorandums of understanding (MOUs).

In Southeast Asia, Hallyu products became a primary form of East Asian pop culture at a moment when Southeast Asian economies grew rapidly, had greater access to international media, and no longer looked towards the US and Europe for aspirational models of globality. The image of South Korea is also very different to that of the historically dominant powers. Japan carries the stigma of a brutal wartime past, Beijing's funding of educational projects cannot counteract China's overall coercive and aggressive economic power, while Donald Trump's nationalist rhetoric undermined decades of US soft power. Without a problematic background of historical domination in the region, Korea does not elicit the same concerns and suspicions towards its activities (Hoa, 2002; Ainslie and Lim, 2015: 7).

The urban-based *mise en scène* and professional characters depicted in so many Hallyu dramas, songs, and movies also resonated with the economic growth and urbanisation experienced across this region since the 2000s. Southeast Asian consumers seem keen to construct such cultural similarity and are drawn to the Asian cultural traits represented in Korean TV dramas and pop music (Ainslie, 2015; Chung, 2013; Young, 2014; Tae-Sik Kim, 2020). Such success also grew as digital technology improved and increased the circulation of Korean products, which became increasingly accessible to both consumers and producers (Lee, 2009). Hallyu's widespread popularity coalesces with the high number of social media users in countries such as Indonesia, the Philippines, Vietnam, Thailand, and Malaysia, echoing how Korean products were often originally circulated through local informal fan networks in a 'bottom-up, audience-centered approach' (Chung, 2013: 199). Likewise, the content and style of local pop culture products in countries such as Thailand, Indonesia, Malaysia, Singapore, Vietnam, and the Philippines demonstrate the adoption and integration of Hallyu influences.

LAOS AND THE CLMV COUNTRIES

While the Southeast Asian region as a whole remains an area of significant strategic importance to foreign investors, what are known as the 'CLMV countries' (an acronym referring to Cambodia, Laos, Myanmar, and Vietnam) retain key importance in overseas investment and production. Referred to as Southeast Asia's 'last frontier market', there is a dramatic increase of trade between East Asian countries and these ASEAN nations (Singapore Institution of International Affairs, 2018). These relatively less developed countries in ASEAN recently emerged as a very promising new developing market and attracted significant economic interest. These younger member states all became part of ASEAN in the late 1990s after transitioning from centrally planned to open market economies, a process in which domestic controls upon foreign investment were gradually relaxed.

There is a significant development gap between the CLMV countries and the other ASEAN nations. In 2011, these four countries counted for less than 10 per cent of ASEAN's nominal gross domestic product (GDP), and closing this gap was considered to be crucial to the final integration of both ASEAN and the wider East Asian community. However, Laos and Myanmar still remain far behind in terms of real per capita GDP and income gap (Furuoka, 2019). There is also dramatic difference between wider Southeast Asian Internet access and usage in these two poorest CLMV countries. In 2014 in Malaysia almost 78 per cent of citizens were Internet users, with the Philippines at 71 per cent and Thailand at 74 per cent (Moore, 2021). However, only 39 per cent of the populations of Laos and Myanmar are Internet users (ibid.).

CLMV leaders place strong emphasis upon the need to attract foreign investment as a means to sustain their gradual economic growth in the 21st century. Due to the opening up of these countries and their encouragement of foreign direct investment, all CLMV countries have recently emerged as attractive locations for export bases for foreign direct investment (FDI) and multinational companies. Such openness has been labelled as 'one of the defining characteristics of the CLMV economies since the mid-1990s' (OECD, 2013: 296), particularly since in the same time period such FDI has declined in the other economically more prosperous ASEAN nations. Therefore, despite their small market size, and as a result of positive FDI policies, the CLMV countries have emerged as 'dynamic open economies' following around two decades of integration and transition (ibid.: 292) and remain very attractive locations for foreign investors.

Laos in particular has enjoyed very heavy foreign investment, overwhelmingly from China, Thailand, and Vietnam. Most of this investment focuses upon hydropower, mining, and agriculture (including rubber plantations and cash crops). This significant investment can be explained through the country's abundant natural resources, cheap workforce, and burgeoning market economy. The Laos government has strongly promoted the country as an attractive location for foreign investment, touting itself through the slogan 'Land of Ample Opportunities and Successes' as a safe investment climate with relative political stability within the region. An examination of figures indicates huge investment at an extremely rapid rate.[2] After drops and fluctuation in the late 2010s, the government even amended investment laws in 2016 and 2017, aimed at making the process easier and more attractive for foreigners by eliminating minimum capital requirements.

KOREAN INTEREST IN LAOS

Diplomatic relations between Laos and South Korea were severed in 1975 due to the establishment of Laos's Communist government and affiliation with the Soviet Union, but were re-established in 1995. This was exactly the period when the CLMV countries were transitioning rapidly to market economies favouring foreign investment, and Laos was beginning to enjoy both increased overseas tourism and political stability. Korean overseas direct investment in the country increased dramatically to a cumulative FDI of US$740 million from 1989 to 2012. After China, Thailand, and Vietnam, Korea is the joint fourth-largest foreign investor in Laos (tying with Malaysia), accounting for 4 per cent of Laos's FDI stock in 2017 (OECD, 2017).[3] Laos also receives grant aid from the Korea International Cooperation Agency and loans from the Economic Development Cooperation Fund (EDCF). Indeed, Korean overseas development grants worth US$18 million were extended to Laos for nine projects across 2010 and 2011, and in 2019 EDCF loans including US$44 million for water supply development projects in Southern Laos were agreed.

Such investment shows no sign of slowing down. Laotian President Choummaly Sayasone's three-day visit to South Korea in 2013 was the first state Korea–Laos visit since the re-establishment of diplomatic ties, and included summit talks with then South Korea President Park Geun-hye, in which a memorandum of understanding was reached involving more EDCF loans. President Moon Jae-in then visited Laos in 2019, the first state visit to the country by a Korean president, unveiling the Republic of Korea-Mekong Vision, an initiative in which Korean companies will continue to build infrastructure across the Mekong region.

Korean companies also have a heavy presence in Laos and are present across diverse economic sectors, including manufacture, hydropower, service industries, and telecommunications. The South Korean companies SK Engineering & Construction (SK E&C) and Korean Western Power Company were the primary financers of the 410 megawatt Xe Pian Xe Namnoy hydroelectric power station, holding 51 per cent equity in the project. This aimed to construct a series of dams across the Bolaven Plateau in the Mekong River in southern Laos, using the flow of water to generate electricity, 90 per cent of which was to be sent to Thailand. The car company Kolao Holdings (later changed to LVMC Holdings) that made and distributed cars and other vehicles in Laos was (until the late 2010s) the biggest non-state company and private enterprise in the country. Registered as a Laotian company (though also operating in Cambodia, Singapore, and Myanmar) it was founded by a Korean and was listed upon

Korea's stock market (Kospi) from 2010. Likewise, the export of Korean products to Laos has increased and goods such as electronics, cosmetics, and mobile phones are of particular prominence (Yohan and Somsamone, 2011: 118). In 2011, the new stock market Laos Securities Exchange opened, trading in two countries. This was very much aimed at foreign investors and, notably, 'the funding for the set-up of the exchange has come from South Korea, which has invested $9.8m, or 49% of the capital, for the venture. The Bank of Laos, the country's central bank, has invested the rest' (BBC News, 2011). Together with its financing of the Cambodian Stock Exchange, such radical commitment indicates Korea's desire to position itself as a significant power in control of the CLMV financial centres.

Adding to such expensive projects, Korea has also engaged in major investment in Laos's universities, and there has been a heavy concentration upon the development of Korean Studies in Laos. In 2019, the South Korean Ministry of Education signed a memorandum of understanding with Laos to begin trials teaching Korean language at Lao secondary schools, while the smaller Laos Korean College was founded in 2012, growing rapidly after receiving regular donations from Korean companies (Kang, 2019). The National University of Laos, the leading university in the country, also has a number of Korean-supported and -linked projects throughout its departments. Souphanouvong University in Luang Prabang also experienced heavy Korean investment. A new campus was built in 2007 that was financed by a loan from the Economic Development Cooperation Fund of Korea, an arrangement set up by the Korean contractor POSDATA consortium through the Korean government, which together would oversee the management of the university for the next 30 years. In 2008, the Korean Cooperation Centre opened and the Lao–Korea Science and Technology Centre (LKSTC) officially opened at the university in 2015. Aimed at developing profitable agricultural technology, the centre is largely staffed by Korean researchers. After 2015, authorities then established a Korean Studies Institute in the university, hosting the 1st International Conference On Korean Studies soon after.

The Korean embassy in Laos also promotes Korean language and culture through education, while the Korean government financially supports a small number of Lao students to study in Korean universities. Korean tourism to Laos also increased significantly. In 2012, the number of South Korean tourists increased by 46 per cent from 2011, and totalled 170 000 in 2018, with Laos Airlines and budget Korean airlines operating direct flights between Seoul, Busan, and the Laotian city Luang Prabang and the capital Vientiane.

HALLYU IN LAOS

Such initiatives are indicative not only of Korea's heavy interest in Laos, but also of the country's strategic plan to invest in projects that require long-term presence and commitment. Operating as propaganda for such political-economic interests, the heavily subsidised promotion of Hallyu in Laos seeks to reinforce and sustain Korean influence in this country, constructing this as an enticing and attractive phenomenon that is both desirable and beneficial to Laos and its people (Nye, 2008: 95).

The function of Hallyu as a means to further Korean economic interests is now common knowledge and explored by journalists, critics, and consumers themselves. In Laos the lack of broadcasting infrastructure and heavy reliance upon overseas investment means that the function of and agenda behind Hallyu as propaganda is both blatant and explicit. In their overview of Hallyu in Laos, Yohan and Somsamone (2011: 117) openly state that 'The Korean Wave has contributed to a more positive perception of Korea and has strengthened the nation's "Soft Power".' The popular Korean website Arirang also observes Korean support for the Laos broadcasting industries that 'continued exposure to Korean culture through collaborations like these have led to better business in Laos for Korean companies' (Haejoo, 2008).[4] Likewise, the Korean Foundation for International Cultural Exchange (KOFICE) explains how the funding of 'multimedia rooms' in the National University of Laos and the National Institute of Fine Arts is designed 'to build infrastructure for experiencing Hallyu in Laos' as a means for 'constructing positive images of Korea and carrying out "Good Hallyu" activities in cooperation with our country's private enterprises expanded abroad' (Korean Foundation for International Cultural Exchange, 2016a).

The arrival of the Korean Wave in Laos was slightly later than in other countries, though Hallyu was already established long before it 'officially' arrived in Laos in 2007–2008, due to prior exposure through both Thai TV channels and the extensive cheap pirate VCD networks across Southeast Asia (Yohan and Somsamone, 2011: 116). Since then, Korean popular culture has been both influential and prolific. In 2007, the Korea Broadcasting Commission donated almost US$100 000 worth of broadcasting facilities to Laos's state-run television network and its cultural ministry, after an MOU was signed between the broadcasting companies from the two countries. In November of that year three Korean hit drama series were launched on Laos TV: the historical dramas *Hwang Jini* and *Dae Jang Geum*, and the modern-set Cinderella story *Stairway to Heaven*, all broadcasting a year after the incredibly successful 2005–2006 transmission of *Dae Jang Geum* in neighbouring Thailand (Visit Korea, 2008).

This broadcast was then quickly followed by a number of concerts from very prominent K-pop groups. For the 2008 New Year, female K-pop band Baby V.O.X. Re.V gave a New Year concert at the Lao international Trade Exhibition and Convention Center, the largest venue in Laos at the time. Mobile phone company Millicom Lao Co. Ltd (known as Tigo) hosted the concert, and tickets were available free with a mobile phone top-up and lucky draw (Thevongsa, 2007). In April that year Tigo again brought a K-pop band to Laos. Paran gave a concert to an audience of 10 000 at the national football stadium in Vientiene, a record for a pop concert in Laos, to celebrate Tigo's anniversary, and the event was also televised on local channel Lao Star TV (Pimmata, 2008). Again, tickets could be purchased through Tigo's phone service.

In June 2008 a Korean B-Boy break dancing troupe, singers, and beatbox performers travelled to give a performance at the Laos national culture hall in Vientiene, organised and sponsored by the Korea Foundation, the Korean Embassy in Laos, and the Lao Ministry of Information and Culture. All the performances were reportedly free and attended by diplomats, while performers also visited local schools to 'present scholarship aid and school supplies to students' (Korea Foundation, 2008). Writing in 2011, Yohan and Somsamone report that over 50 per cent of all music programming on Lao Star TV channel was Korean pop songs. Laotian viewers can also receive Korean dramas through both Thai TV and Lao Star TV, which has now shown Korean dramas continually throughout the year since 2009 (Yohan and Somsamone, 2011).

Despite Laos's small consumption base and rural-based population, this presence continued into the 2010s with the K-POP World Festival. This annual event, supported by Korean government agencies, brings contestants from various countries to Korea in order to compete by performing K-pop songs and dances. In 2013, 2014, and 2019, the festival included performers from Laos. Most notably, in 2016, Feel Korea, a cultural festival held annually around the world since 2012 in countries which are either on the periphery of the Hallyu experience and/or are significant developing overseas markets for Korea, was held in Vientiane as Feel Korea in Laos, and included a concert with performances from prominent K-pop artists such as BTOB, Halo, CLC, and KNK. Hosted and organised by KOFICE and sponsored by the Korean embassy and a number of Korean companies in Laos, the event included booths offering 'experiences' of Korean food, photography, and traditional clothing, with many activities aimed at school children.

Such heavy cultural investment is indicative of Moon Jae-in's newly introduced Republic of Korea–Mekong Vision, one to be achieved through 'cultural and tourism collaboration' (Moon, 2019b). These comments indicate how Hallyu is and will remain a key part of supporting Korean interests in Laos, and is integral to Korea's political interests in the country. When leaving Laos after his first visit, President Moon Jae-in's final speech remarked specifically upon the importance and responsibility of continuing to promote Hallyu: 'I was able to see for myself the potential of the Hallyu culture, which is loved in ASEAN. I'd like to express my heartfelt appreciation to all the Koreans who have helped raise the Republic of Korea's standing' (Moon, 2019a).

A DISCOURSE OF MUTUALITY

Despite the very obvious differences between these two nations, a discourse of mutuality remains an integral part of Korean political propaganda in this nation. Describing the growth of Hallyu in Laos as a mutual exchange, a benevolent force, and an organic process instigated by consumers is designed to omit the significant economic benefits to Korea, knowledge of which could threaten this positive image. As Nye states, 'Policies that appear as narrowly self-serving or arrogantly presented are likely to prohibit rather than produce soft power' (Nye, 2008: 102). Presenting Korea as a generous and benevolent nation that is culturally similar (and therefore equal) to Laos can counter the unappealing 'self-serving' and 'arrogant' nature of Korean economic gain and superiority in this much poorer nation.

This discourse of mutuality is evident in President Moon Jae-in's speech at the unveiling of the Korea–Mekong Vision during his visit to Laos. The speech significantly deploys the 'economic miracle' discourse of Korea (Schwak, 2019) and also continues the theme of mutuality, referring to 'common prosperity', 'an equal footing', and 'mutual understanding'. Likewise, similarity is also constructed through a supposedly 'similar path' in which both Korea and the Mekong nations 'rose above the pain of colonial rule and achieved growth, preserving our own survival and dignity while stuck between major powers during the Cold War' (Moon, 2019b).

This emphasis is also evident in business relations. For instance, Mr Bae Chang-Heon, the Vice-President of the Korea Trade-Investment Promotion Agency (KOTRA), an organisation involved in promoting Korea's export-led economic development and which opened up an office in Vientiene in 2011, describes Korean investment in Laos as akin to an 'exchange', stating:

> Laos has targeted R. Korea as source of investments. In July 2012, the Prime Minister of Laos and accompany with over 60 officials and business leaders joined Lao Investment seminar in at KOTRA Headquarter in Seoul. In return in this December, KOTRA has brought over 18 Korean firms to

Vientiane capital for seeking the business opportunity and expand their business operation. (Ministry of Planning and Investment, 2014)

The suggestion that Korean firms were brought to Laos for expansion in return for the Laos Prime Minister's visit to Korea is highly dubious, as is the construction of the much poorer Laos 'targeting' Korea.

In keeping with this tone, the growth in Korean products, language courses, food, and other signifiers continues to be presented as a grassroots and mutually beneficial organic arrangement by Korean organisations and political actors. Purportedly, the popularity of Hallyu in Laos is based upon notions of cultural proximity and a supposed shared set of Asian values that exist between these radically different and unequal countries. The emphasis is therefore upon language that implies mutual benefit and cooperation. For instance, funded by the Academy of Korean Studies, the first academic study examining the growth of Hallyu in Laos argues that it 'makes sense' for Hallyu to 'catch on' in the country, and attributes the success of the Korean Wave to what is termed 'Asian cultural affinity' (Yohan and Somsamone, 2011: 117).

This construction of mutuality is also evident in a statement by Khamla Xayachack, the Laotian ambassador to South Korea, who refers to the current 'deepening and broadening exchange' between Laos and Korea (which is exclusively Korean investment) that has been 'underpinned by the hallyu phenomenon rippling across Southeast Asia' (Iglauer, 2014). There is very little evidence of 'exchange' in this relationship, while the use of the word 'rippling' also suggests a natural and harmless phenomenon rather than a deliberate (and at times aggressive) promotion. Likewise, in a newsletter from the Korea Foundation, the Korean B-Boy performance in the Laos national culture hall was described as 'cultural diplomacy', a phrase that suggests a negotiated mutually beneficial arrangement that will 'enrich the life of the Lao people and develop more cooperative relations between our two countries' (Korea Foundation, 2008).

The reports from KOFICE are also extremely eager to portray Hallyu events as a mutual form of exchange. The 2016 Feel Korea in Laos event is described as a 'Cultural Exchange Festival' and 'a genuine two-way culture festival', with such mutuality largely hinging upon the fact that the K-pop groups attempt to sing some local Laos pop songs during the performance (Korean Foundation for International Cultural Exchange, 2016b). KOFICE also describes a K-pop performance to high school students in Laos as enabling them 'to communicate and sympathize with each other through culture' (ibid.). However, there is no real explanation of what is meant by the term 'sympathize' or how any 'communication' takes place exactly.

Such language feeds into a discourse that not only constructs such relations as mutual, but also positions Hallyu, and by extension Korea, as a benevolent force that is generously assisting Laos and offering Laos people more opportunities. The Korea Foundation states that the Hallyu cultural events it organises and financially supports, including festival performances in Vientiane and Laos, are designed to 'introduce the diversity and richness of Korean culture to international communities and also to provide local audiences with increased opportunities for direct contact with Korean culture and arts' (Korea Foundation, 2011: 28).

CRITIQUING HALLYU

Obscuring Korean gains, and pushing celebratory discourses of cultural proximity, mutuality, and benevolence, is a strategy designed to counter growing critique of Korean overseas activities and Hallyu as an industry. Within Korea there is debate about the effect on the Korean creative industries of cultivating so many cultural products to serve as international propaganda. The production of Hallyu is part of a neoliberal oligopoly dominated by a small number of elitist companies, under which cultural products become both predictable and nationalistic (Kim et al., 2017: 317). There is growing awareness of the potential damage the manufactured Hallyu 'machine' is enacting upon local Korean creative industries, when non-Hallyu cultural products and artists that do not fall under the rubric of propaganda are marginalised and remain peripheral, and with the alternative Korean voices and diversity they represent both denied and underexplored (ibid.: 316). This lack of diversity also affects Hallyu's overseas appeal. My research with Lim and Lipura (Ainslie et al., 2017) identified a growing backlash against Hallyu in Thailand, Malaysia, and the Philippines. Consumers express fatigue at the sheer volume of Hallyu and the similarity of these products, and instead turn to more adept and appropriate locally based versions of these products, regarding the heavily manufactured Hallyu songs, performers, and dramas as 'trashy'.

This lack of diversity and alternative 'voices' could also result in an inability to adapt products to new situations and contexts. Korean cultural products are critiqued as being badly designed in terms of outlook, instead displaying an obsession with promoting cultural products regardless of how inappropriate and unwanted these may be (Suweon Kim, 2020: 145). For instance, the introduction of Hallyu in some African countries (a continent of current interest for East Asia due to its rapidly developing economies) is significantly problematised for approaching this continent as a 'monolithic entity', rather than recognising the complexity of each nation (Suweon Kim, 2020: 145).

There are also many examples of the way in which the 'values' represented in Hallyu products that are designed to project a positive image of Korea can actually clash with existing cultural norms. In Southeast Asia alone the reception of Hallyu is highly complex and warrants much closer inspection as to the ways in which it intersects with local discourses. For instance, Tambunan's (2015) and my own research (Ainslie, 2017) highlights how the metrosexual constructions of masculinity in Korean dramas and pop music can clash with these dominant discourses in Malaysia and Indonesia, and so complicate the reception of Hallyu in these countries. Likewise, Lim (2015) argues that Malaysian youth's engagement with Hallyu does not replicate or imitate such aesthetics, but actually transcends and reshapes these notions of Asianness. Liew (2015) argues that Thai cinema uses Hallyu representations to project its own imaginaries back to Korea and speak back against (while also critiquing) this dominant cultural flow.

Finally, there is also a growing critique of the agenda that Hallyu as political propaganda supports, in particular, the exploitation that accompanies investment in poorer countries. Korean overseas economic interests are part of a neoliberal development agenda that rests upon inequality, repression, and exploitive labour regimes being exported to developing nations, and one that is becoming increasingly apparent to researchers, journalists, and consumers themselves (Schwak, 2019). Participants in my own research question the construction of Korea as a non-aggressive and non-imperialistic world power, expressing resentment at the imperialistic overtones of the sheer volume of Hallyu products arriving unsolicited in their nations (Ainslie et al., 2017).

Hallyu in Laos deserves such critique. Indeed, close examination of Laos reveals a situation in which the Korean presence has not necessarily been of benefit to many Lao citizens, with little possibility of the implied mutual exchange or cooperation. The Lao government's open-door policy towards overseas investment and interests has left the country easily exploitable and heavily dependent upon foreign aid and investment. The United Nations (UN) describes Laos as an LLDC, a 'landlocked and least developed country', that has yet to reach the status of a developing nation. It is considered to be the poorest country in Southeast Asia, and the most rural and agricultural based, in which around 80 per cent of citizens are farmers and the majority practice subsistence farming.

While the economic reforms in Laos since the late 1980s were designed to turn the country from socialism to a market-orientated economy, there have been no accompanying democratic reforms, and the country has remained a one-party state with no opposition party and corruption rife amongst officials (Hutt, 2019). Economists note that the successful economic growth through FDI in the CLMV countries must be followed by corresponding social and political developments in which the benefits of such growth are shared across society (OECD, 2013), yet in Laos very little dissent is allowed, and human rights violations, disappearances, and detention without trial are still common. There is also significant suppression of political dissent. European diplomats who raise concerns are expelled and the country is difficult to access by international bodies such as the UN, meaning that, unlike other CLMV countries, there is no international support for potential dissenters and opposition parties.

Peasants are often forced to sell their land to make way for foreign companies; and in 2013, an article in *The Economist* notes that 'More land is now in the hands of foreigners than is used to grow rice', and cautions against 'the emergence of a landless poor' (*The Economist*, 2013). Such developments have disproportionally affected ethnic minorities, who make up 70 per cent of the Laos population and farm resource-rich upland areas that are often seized without compensation. Non-governmental organisations warn that large-scale land leases to overseas private companies by the Laos government have left such citizens displaced and impoverished due to 'land grabs', leading to increased mortality rates, conflict, and reduced access to health and education (MacLean, 2014).

While the economy has grown and Laos is noted as a 'top mover' in terms of human development, the country is still severely impoverished, and even became the most impoverished in Southeast Asia in the mid-2010s, with 44 per cent of children classified as malnourished (see Rural Poverty Portal, 2013; International Fund for Agricultural Development, 2014) and maternal health significantly below that of Cambodia (*The Economist*, 2013). The significantly low wages make Laos an attractive export base and, indeed, many foreign companies such as Yamaki Co. have moved their factories from Thailand to Laos to take advantage of this cheaper workforce.

The Chinese Kunming–Vientiene high-speed rail connection is an example of such concerns. The US$7 billion cost of the project is entirely funded by Laos itself, with the money borrowed from Beijing in exchange for future raw materials. This initiative will make Laos one of the most indebted countries in the world, and the World Bank ultimately calls it 'unaffordable' as a loan, with no real compensation plan for the affected people and villages displaced by the scheme.

KOREAN EXPLOITATION IN LAOS

Korea is deeply involved in such exploitation, to the extent that the communications processes that project Hallyu as propaganda and use this as an instrument to support investment must tackle increasing awareness around the reality of Korean actions in Laos. Indeed, such actions are significantly out of sync with the 'political values' and 'foreign policies' communicated through Hallyu, two of Nye's three resources that make up a country's soft power. As Nye observes, 'cultural soft power can be undercut by policies that are seen as illegitimate' (Nye, 2008: 96), and the controversies over the damage caused by Korean companies in Laos would seem to undercut claims of benevolence and mutuality that seek to imbue the culture, values, and policies communicated through Hallyu.

In 2013, a number of governments and organisations (including the European Union, the US, Australia, New Zealand, the World Bank and the Asian Development Bank) expressed their concern around the building of the primarily Korean-funded Xe Pian Xe Namnoy hydroelectric power station and its series of dams across the Mekong River. Part of an ambitious strategy by the Laos government to turn the country into the 'Battery of Asia' by exporting electricity from hydropower, dams have been constructed across the country at breakneck speed, with little consideration for the financial, environmental, and social costs. The Mekong River Commission (MRC) Council stated that 'building dams on the mainstream of the Mekong may irrevocably change the river and hence constitute a challenge for food security, sustainable development and biodiversity conservation', arguing that the potential environmental and social impacts of the project have not been adequately assessed (Hydro World, 2013). Then, despite agreeing to a Vietnamese proposal of a ten-year moratorium on dam construction in the Mekong, the US-based advocacy group International Rivers found that the Laotian government had been continuing secretly with the project, and even awarding more contracts to overseas construction companies (ibid.). Finally, in 2018, the Xe Pian Xe Namnoy dam collapsed, affecting up to 16 000 people, displacing around 6000 from their homes, and leaving around 1000 missing. The collapse was attributed to substandard construction by the Korean company SK E&C (the main stakeholders) in particular, which initially denied the collapse, claiming the dam had merely overflowed due to heavy rain (Jee Hee, 2019; Flintrop, 2019).

The Korean government expressed concern about the disaster's potential damage to the positive image of Korea in Laos, one cultivated through over a decade of expensive propaganda. As part of managing this image, Korea struggled against accepting responsibility for the dam's collapse. The Korean government disagreed with the International Expert Panel that eventually found the collapse was entirely preventable and blamed poor construction by the Korean company SK E&C, which allegedly filled the foundations with soil rather than more expensive concrete (Yeon-soo, 2019). Teams sent from the Korean government disputed criticism of poor construction, an issue that is ongoing. Then, despite disputing responsibility, the Korean government sent a large packet of aid relief, with a number of initiatives designed to assist the area following later. An article in the *Korea Times* highlights the Korean president's decision to send government aid to assist in a foreign rescue as unusual, directly connecting this to how 'the disaster could adversely affect Korea's image' in the significant markets of Southeast Asia (*Korea Times*, 2018).

Korean rights organisations were deeply critical of the Korean government's public–private partnership projects, an initiative introduced after the Asian financial crisis in which the government partnered with private entities (such as SK E&C) in order to develop sustainable infrastructure. Using the example of SK E&C, environmental and left-wing Korean organisations claimed that the development cooperation projects seek only profit, rather than the stated desire to improve quality of life, and that the companies involved do not have to comply with any code of responsibilities or ethics, with the implementation of human rights and safety guidelines not enforced by the Korean government (Korean Civil Societies for the Xe Pian-Xe Nam Noy Dam Collapse, 2018). However, rather than focus upon practical steps to prevent such disasters from happening again, the Korean government instead continues to push the discourse of mutuality and affiliation through funding strategies such as Hallyu products and events, so seeking to remove attention from this continuing exploitation.

CONCLUSION

A case study of Hallyu in Laos highlights the very explicit use of Korean popular culture as a key form of political propaganda in this nation. Constructed as part of an overarching discourse of mutual exchange and benevolence, Hallyu and its ongoing presence is supported and referenced by high-level political actors, demonstrating the continued significance of the Korean creative industries to the nation's overseas interests.

However, in Laos, few of the benefits from current foreign investments actually reach ordinary Laos consumers, while the fast and huge opening up of the Laos economy to foreign investment is problematic and worrying in many respects. Hallyu products instead become part of an exploitive agenda that rests upon the huge disparity and inequality between Laos and Korea, a situation that ended tragically in the badly planned and poorly executed Xe Pian Xe Namnoy dam.

Given the levels of current economic exploitation in Laos and the vast inequality between these two nations, it is difficult to envision any form of mutual exchange between Laos and Korea. Yet Korean political discourse continues to construct Hallyu as a mutually beneficial and benevolent force based upon cultural affinity. Such discourses of mutuality continue even after the 2018 Xe Pian Xe Namnoy dam collapse, when the Korean government is refuting responsibility for the disaster and withholding compensation. A growing body of emerging research is beginning to critique Korean overseas actions and Hallyu as an industry. If the image of Korea becomes attached to dubious, corrupt, and unethical practices and activities, then it remains to be seen whether music concerts and cultural festivals can distract from this reality and remain an effective tool of political propaganda.

NOTES

1. This initiative was formed between the Southeast Asian nations and the three East Asian nations of Japan, China, and South Korea. It was a means to counter the strength and influence of the US dollar after the 1997 crisis.
2. Laos's strategic geographical position between China and Thailand makes it a gateway to Southeast Asia for Chinese interests, and the country is a key part of the Belt and Road Initiative. The multi-billion dollar Kunming–Vientiene high-speed rail connection is aimed for completion in 2021, while Chinese authorities are responsible for building hospitals in Luang Prabang and funding the airport. The railway will offer a means through which to send raw materials directly from Laos to China, and in doing so, to draw Southeast Asia closer to China economically. This deepening

relationship has been noted by the US, which has kept a close eye upon such developments. In 2012, US Secretary of State Hillary Clinton visited Laos, the first visit of a senior US politician to the country since 1955; Secretary of State John Kerry visited Laos twice in 2016, and finally President Obama in late 2016.
3. It is also perhaps a measure of South Korean's commitment to such schemes that very little commotion was raised about the 2013 decision by Laos authorities to send nine escaped young North Korean refugees back to Pyongyang, instead of allowing them passage to Thailand and eventually South Korea. Despite significant outrage from South Korean and other international agencies, there have been no repercussions toward the Laotian authorities.
4. This support of the Laos broadcasting industries as a means of maintaining influence follows similar moves by other nations. Broadcasting has been used extensively by China as a means to influence and invest in Laos. Various Chinese companies financed the improvement of Laos's telecommunications infrastructure during the 1990s and into the 2000s, of which the most notable outcome was the development and launch of Laos's first satellite, LaoSat-1, in 2015. Coordinating with other Asian satellite networks from the Asia region, this was designed to allow Chinese companies to become the major operator and provider for this sub-region Mekong area. In 2013, Lao National Television (LNTV), the national television station which runs two channels, signed an MOU with Yunnan Radio and Television (YRT) from China, while in 2014 it joined with Guangxi People's Broadcasting Station of China to produce and broadcast Chinese theatre productions.

REFERENCES

Ainslie, Mary J. (2015), 'National Hierarchies and Hallyu Fans: Perceptions of Korea and Korean-ness by K-drama Fans across Thailand', in M. Ainslie and J. Lim (eds), *The Korean Wave in Southeast Asia: Consumption and Cultural Production*, Kuala Lumpur: SIRD, pp. 95–114.
Ainslie, Mary J. (2017), 'Korean Soft Masculinity vs. Malay Hegemony: Malaysian Masculinity and Hallyu Fandom', *Korea Observer*, 48(3): 609–638.
Ainslie, Mary J. and Joanne B.Y. Lim (2015), 'Introduction', in M. Ainslie and J. Lim (eds), *The Korean Wave in Southeast Asia: Consumption and Cultural Production*, Kuala Lumpur: SIRD, pp. 1–14.
Ainslie, Mary J., Joanne B.Y. Lim, and Sarah Domingo Lipura (2017), 'Understanding the Potential for a Hallyu "Backlash" in Southeast Asia: A Case Study of Consumers in Thailand, Malaysia and Philippines', *Kritika Kultura*, 28: 63–91.
ASEAN–Korea Centre (2017) 'ASEAN–Korea Relations', available at https://www.aseankorea.org/eng/ASEAN/ak_overview.asp.
BBC News (2011), 'Laos Stock Market Opens to Boost Economy', BBC News Business, 11 January, available at http://www.bbc.com/news/business-12160402.
Chon, G. (2001), 'Golden Summer', *Asiaweek*, 26 October: 46–49.
Chung, Peichi (2013), 'Co-Creating Korean Wave in Southeast Asia Digital Convergence and Asia's Media Regionalization', *Journal of Creative Communications*, 8 (2–3): 193–208.
Conference on Strengthening the Korea–ASEAN Relationship (2005), *Trends in Southeast Asia 10*, Singapore: Institute of Southeast Asian Studies.
The Economist (2013), 'The Future of Laos: A Bleak Landscape', 26 October, available at http://www.economist.com/news/asia/21588421-secretive-ruling-clique-and-murky-land-grabs-spell-trouble-poor-country-bleak-landscape.
Flintrop, Piet (2019), 'Laos' Investment Outlook for 2019', *ASEAN Briefing*, February 8, available at https://www.aseanbriefing.com/news/laos-investment-outlook-2019/.
Furuoka, Fumitaka (2019), 'Do CLMV Countries Catch Up with the Older ASEAN Members in Terms of Income Level?', *Applied Economics Letters*, 26(8): 690–697.
Geun, Lee (2009), 'A Theory of Soft Power and Korea's Soft Power Strategy', *Korean Journal of Defense Analysis*, 21(2): 205–218.
Haejoo, Shin (2008), 'Korean Hit Dramas Shown in Laos', *Arirang News*, available at http://www.arirang.co.kr/News/News_View.asp?nseq=80590&code=Ne6&category=7.

Hall, Kenji (2017), 'Monocle's Ranking of Soft Power in Asia', *Nikkei Asia*, 23 November, available at https://asia.nikkei.com/Life-Arts/Monocle-s-ranking-of-soft-power-in-Asia.
Heo, J. (2002), 'The "Hanryu" Phenomenon and the Acceptability of Korean TV Dramas in China', *Korean Journal of Broadcasting*, 16(1): 496–529.
Hoa, Tran Van (2002), 'Korea, China and Japan: Their Trade with the World and its Impact on New Asian Regionalism ASEAN+3', University of Wollongong Department of Economics Working Paper Series 2002, available at https://citeseerx.ist.psu.edu/viewdoc/download?doi=10.1.1.959.6011&rep=rep1&type=pdf.
Hong, Euny (2014), *The Birth of Korean Cool: How One Nation Is Conquering the World Through Pop Culture*, New York: Picador.
Hutt, David (2019), 'Laos Democrats Fight a Lonely Losing Struggle', *Asia Times*, 27 November, available at https://asiatimes.com/2019/11/laos-democrats-fight-a-lonely-losing-struggle/.
Hydro World (2013), 'Laos' Neighbors Unhappy with Xayaburi Dam Construction', *Hydro World*, available at http://www.hydroworld.com/articles/2013/january/laos--neighbors-unhappy-with-xayaburi-dam-construction.html.
Iglauer, Philip (2014), 'Profile of Laos on the rise', *Korea Herald*, available at http://www.koreaherald.com/view.php?ud=20140223000410.
International Fund for Agricultural Development (2014), *Investing in Rural People in the Lao People's Democratic Republic*, Vientiene: IFAD.
Jee Hee, Kim (2019), 'SK E&C Blamed for Dam Collapse, Rebuffs Result', *Korea Joong Ang Daily*, 29 May, available at https://koreajoongangdaily.joins.com/news/article/article.aspx?aid=3063688.
Kang, Taejun (2019), 'Laos to Teach Korean Language at Secondary School Next Year', *Laotian Times*, November 27, available at https://laotiantimes.com/2019/11/27/laos-to-teach-korean-language-at-secondary-school-next-year/.
Kim, Jeongmee, Michael A. Unger, and Keith B. Wagner (2017), 'The Significance of Beyond Hallyu Film and Television Content in South Korea's Mediasphere', *Quarterly Review of Film and Video*, 34(4): 315–320.
Kim, Suweon (2020), 'Dynamics of Korea–Africa Cultural Engagements', in Yongku Chang (ed.), *South Korea's Engagement with Africa: A History of the Relationship in Multiple Aspects*, Singapore: Palgrave Macmillan, pp. 133–158.
Kim, Tae-Sik (2020), 'Young Migrant Vietnamese in the Czech Republic Reflect Diasporic Contexts in Their Identification of Cultural Proximity with Korean Media', *Journal of Intercultural Studies*, 41(4): 524–539.
Korea Foundation (2008), 'Korea's B-Boy Performers Thrill Audiences in Laos', *Korea Foundation Newsletter*, available at http://newsletter.kf.or.kr/english/contents.asp?vol=96&lang=English&no=1147.
Korea Foundation (2011), *2011 Annual Report*, Seoul: Korea Foundation.
Korea Times (2018), 'President Orders Rescue Team for Flood Victims', *Korea Times*, 26 July, available at https://www.koreatimes.co.kr/www/opinion/2018/07/202_252883.html.
Korean Civil Societies for the Xe Pian-Xe Nam Noy Dam Collapse (2018), 'The Xe Pian-Xe Nam Noy Dam Project which Takes the Whole Life of the People of Laos: For Whom was the Development Designed?', *People's Solidarity for Participatory Democracy*, 9 August, available at http://www.peoplepower21.org/index.php?mid=English&document_srl=1577704&listStyle=list.
Korean Foundation for International Cultural Exchange (2016a), *2016 Cultural ODA Project in Laos*, 25 November, available at http://eng.kofice.or.kr/d00_MainActivitie/d3010_cultural_exchange_view.asp?seq=617&g_mno=239&gubun=D.
Korean Foundation for International Cultural Exchange (2016b), '2016 Feel Korea in Laos', *Cultural Exchange Projects*, 25 November, available at http://eng.kofice.or.kr/d00_MainActivitie/d3010_cultural_exchange_view.asp?seq=521&g_mno=240&gubun=C.
Kwak, Sungil (2018), 'Korea's New Southern Policy: Vision and Challenges', *Korea Institute for International Economic Policy*, 12 November, available at https://think-asia.org/bitstream/handle/11540/9407/KIEPopinions_no146.pdf?sequence=1.
Kwak, Sungil (2020), 'A View from South Korea', *ASAN Forum*, 7 January, available at http://www.theasanforum.org/a-view-from-south-korea-3/.

Kwon, Seung-Ho and Joseph Kim (2014), 'The Cultural Industry Policies of the Korean Government and the Korean Wave', *International Journal of Cultural Policy*, 20(4): 422–439.

Lee, J. (2009), 'Contesting the Digital Economy and Culture: Digital Technologies and the Transformation of Popular Music in Korea', *Journal of Inter-Asia Cultural Studies*, 10(4): 489–506.

Lee, S.J. and J. Melissen (eds) (2011), *Public Diplomacy and Soft Power in East Asia*, New York: Palgrave Macmillan.

Liew, Kai Khiun (2015), 'Into the Heart of the Korean Wave in Banjong Pisanthanakun's *Hello Stranger* and Poj Arnon's *Sorry, Sarangheyo*', in M. Ainslie and J. Lim (eds), *The Korean Wave in Southeast Asia: Consumption and Cultural Production*, Kuala Lumpur: SIRD, pp. 115–132.

Lim, Joanne B.Y. (2015), 'Engaging Participation: Youth Culture and the Korean Wave in Malaysia', in M. Ainslie and J. Lim (eds), *The Korean Wave in Southeast Asia: Consumption and Cultural Production*, Kuala Lumpur: SIRD, pp. 155–174.

Lim, SungKyu and Evangelos Giouvris (2020), 'Tourist Arrivals in Korea: Hallyu as a Pull Factor', *Current Issues in Tourism*, 23(1): 99–130.

MacLean, Dana (2014), 'Laos "Land Grabs" Drive Subsistence Farmers Into Deeper Poverty', *IRIN*, available at http://www.irinnews.org/report/100116/laos-land-grabs-drive-subsistence-farmers-into-deeper-poverty.

Ministry of Planning and Investment (2014), 'Elevating Level of Laos–Korea Investment Cooperation', Investment Promotion Department (Laos PDR), available at http://www.investlaos.gov.la/index.php/news-and-events/item/4-elevating-level-of-laos-korea-investment-cooperation.

Moon, Jae-in (2019a), 'Message from President Moon Jae-in upon "Leaving Laos"', Office of the President, 6 September, available at https://english1.president.go.kr/BriefingSpeeches/Speeches/656.

Moon, Jae-in (2019b), 'Remarks by President Moon Jae-in at Ceremony in Laos to Unveil "Republic of Korea-Mekong Vision"', Office of the President, 5 September, available at https://english1.president.go.kr/BriefingSpeeches/Speeches/655.

Moore, Molly (2021), 'Social Media Penetration SEA 2021 by Country', January, available at https://www.statista.com/statistics/487981/social-penetration-in-southeast-asian-countries/.

Nye, J. (2008), 'Public Diplomacy and Soft Power', *ANNALS of the American Academy of Political and Social Science*, 616(1): 94–109.

Nye, J. and Y.N. Kim (2013), 'Soft Power and the Korean Wave', in Y.N. Kim (ed.), *The Korean Wave: Korean Media Goes Global*, London: Routledge, pp. 31–42.

OECD (2013), 'Integrating CLMV Countries through Trade and Investment', in *OECD, Southeast Asian Economic Outlook 2013: With Perspectives on China and India*, Paris: OECD Publishing, pp. 291–327.

OECD (2017), *OECD Investment Policy Reviews: Lao PDR*, Paris: OECD Publishing.

Park, Enna (2020), 'Korea's Public Diplomacy', in Nancy Snow and Nicholas J. Cull (eds), *Routledge Handbook of Public Diplomacy* (2nd edn), New York, USA and London, UK: Routledge, pp. 323–330.

Pimmata, Ounkham (2008), 'Paran, Famous Korean pop will perform in Laos', *Samakomlao*, March, available at http://samakomlao.blogspot.com/2008/03/paran-famous-korean-pop-will-perform-in.html.

Rural Poverty Portal (2013), 'Rural Poverty in Lao People's Democratic Republic', *Rural Poverty Portal*, available at http://www.ruralpovertyportal.org/country/home/tags/laos.

Schwak, Juliette (2019), 'Nothing New Under the Sun: South Korea's Developmental Promises and Neoliberal Illusions', *Third World Quarterly*, 41(2): 1–19.

Shim, Doobo (2008), 'The Growth of Korean Cultural Industries and the Korean Wave', in Doobo Shim and Koichi Iwabuchi (eds), *East Asian Popular Culture: Analyzing the Korean Wave*, Hong Kong: Hong Kong University Press, pp. 15–32.

Shim, Doobo (2011), 'Waxing the Korean Wave', ARI Working Paper, No. 158, June, available at www.nus.ari.edu.sg/pub/wps.htm.

Shim, Doobo (2013), 'The Korean Wave in Southeast Asia: The Case of Singapore', *Journal of Southeast Asian Studies*, 23(1): 277–311.

Singapore Institution of International Affairs (2018), 'CLMV Countries Must Go Beyond Regional Integration', *Economic Research Institute for ASEAN and East Asia*, 1 February, available at https://www.eria.org/news-and-views/clmv-countries-must-go-beyond-regional-integration/.

Suh, C., Y. Cho, and S. Kwon (2013), 'The Korean Wave in Southeast Asia: An Analysis of Cultural Proximity and the Globalization of the Korean Cultural Products', available at http://congress.aks.ac.kr/korean/files/2_1358476377.pdf.

Tambunan, Shuri Mariasih Gietty (2015), 'Imaginary "Asia": Indonesian Audience's Reflexivity on K-dramas', in M. Ainslie and J. Lim (eds), *The Korean Wave in Southeast Asia: Consumption and Cultural Production*, Kuala Lumpur: SIRD, pp. 75–94.

Thevongsa, Phoonsab (2007), 'Popular Korean Band "Baby Vox" to Take the Stage in Vientiane, Laos', *Samakomlao*, December, http://samakomlao.blogspot.com/2007/12/popular-korean-band-baby-vox-to-take.html.

Vial, Virginie and Julien Hanoteau (2019), 'The Sustained Incremental Multi-Actor Multi-Action Building of South Korean Soft Power in Indonesia', *Pacific Review*, 32(1): 56–75.

Visit Korea (2008), 'Korean Hit Dramas Shown in Laos', *Visit Korea*, available at http://english.visitkorea.or.kr/enu/CU/content/cms_view_556528.jsp.

Workman, Daniel (2021), 'South Korea's Top Trading Partners', *World's Top Exports*, available at http://www.worldstopexports.com/south-koreas-top-import-partners/.

Yeon-soo, Kwak (2019), 'Laos Blames SK E&C for Dam Collapse', *Korea Times*, 29 May, available at https://www.koreatimes.co.kr/www/tech/2019/06/693_269690.html.

Yohan, Lee and Vilayphone Somsamone (2011), 'The Korean Wave and Lao People's Perception of Korea', *Review of Korean Studies*, 14(1): 115–143.

Young, Seaon Park (2014), 'Trade in Cultural Goods: A Case of the Korean Wave in Asia', *Journal of East Asian Economic Integration*, 18(1): 83–107.

27. Fact-checking false claims and propaganda in the age of post-truth politics: the Brexit referendum

Jen Birks

INTRODUCTION

The notion of an age of 'post-truth politics' exploded into public consciousness in 2016, following the United States (US) presidential election and the United Kingdom's (UK) referendum on membership of the European Union (EU) that year. In much of the handwringing about the state of contemporary democracy that followed the Brexit vote, there was a sense that the Leave campaigners did not so much win the EU referendum as the Remain camp lost it. This is partly because the polls indicated that Remain started out ahead, but often also seems to assume that the Remain case was objectively stronger because it had more official, authoritative, and expert voices lined up behind it, and so the outcome was intrinsically problematic.

Much like the 2016 US presidential election, the Brexit vote reflected a wider resurgence in nationalist populism in Western democracies, which is in turn attributed to dissatisfaction with globalisation, especially in terms of the mobility of labour. Like US President Trump's totemic pledge to build a border wall, claims about immigration by the Leave campaign and their tabloid press supporters were highly propagandistic, but in very familiar ways (for example, see Briant et al., 2013). News coverage featured sweeping, unsubstantiated claims about the social and economic impact of immigration, associating migrants with crime, and using apocalyptic metaphors such as swarming, flooding, invading (Moore and Ramsay, 2017: 78). This rhetoric goes beyond mere stylistic sophistry; by playing to negative, divisive emotions of fear of 'the other' and dehumanising migrants, the Leave propagandists aimed to manipulate people into a defensive position against international cooperation. However, 'post-truth' anxiety centred on the perception that the Leave campaign had illegitimately undermined the more rational case to remain in the EU, despite the availability of news reporting and fact-checking conveying the 'facts' about the economic cost of leaving. This interpretation blames both the political campaigners and the voters for the rancorous and uninformative debate, but it does not recognise any lessons for journalists.

Therefore this chapter examines whether the Brexit campaigns and the response of referendum voters support these popular assertions about post-truth politics, and in particular, examines the role of journalism in parsing the former to inform the latter. The next section examines the emergence of concern over the truthfulness of political communication, and voters being swayed by instinctive beliefs, values, and emotions rather than 'facts'. The following section explores challenges to journalists' distinction of 'objective' news-work from these subjective and emotional discourses that they claim to eschew as propagandistic. The EU referendum debate is then examined via a secondary analysis of research on the campaigns, news reporting, and corresponding shifts in public opinion in order to evaluate the characterisation of

British political culture as 'post-truth'. Here, I consider the extent to which mainstream media reporting did effectively convey all the relevant claims and counterclaims in the debate on leaving or remaining in the EU, with a focus on two opposing economic claims that are used to exemplify post-truth politics in the UK. Finally, I assess the contribution of fact-checking journalism to the debate, and the implications for the future of journalism.

FROM TRUTH TO TRUTHINESS?

Although 'post-truth' was 'word of the year' in 2016, the associated concerns about the 'truth' as a neglected and even maligned concept had been bubbling under the surface for at least a decade. Michael Schudson (2009) identifies the 2003 invasion of Iraq on false premises as the key moment when politicians embraced a relativist conception of truth and gave academics pause, in an essay that is one of three in Barbie Zelizer's collection *The Changing Faces of Journalism* under the section heading 'On Truthiness'. The term 'truthiness' itself dates back to 2005, when it was coined by satirist Stephen Colbert (Schudson, 2009) to capture the Bush administration's perceived lack of concern with interpretations of reality. However, others (Miller, 2003; Stauber and Rampton, 2003) understood this as a return to propaganda in American foreign policy after a period of post-Cold War uncertainty in which the media became briefly influential in what was dubbed 'the CNN effect' (Robinson, 2005), rather than a novel political embrace of postmodern relativism.

Trump brought a new meaning to 'truthiness', asserting claims that he *felt* to be true and that some supporters apparently also instinctively believed, regardless of whether the checkable, 'factual' support he offered was disputed or proven false. There is evidence that Trump's loyal supporters tended to believe his claims, but they were no less supportive of him after accepting that the claim was untrue (Nyhan et al., 2019; Swire et al., 2017). Swire et al. (2017: 1) conclude that people 'do not necessarily insist on veracity as a prerequisite for supporting political candidates', but the data only supports the conclusion that Trump supporters do not. Moreover, if voters are given the impression from news reporting of political campaigning that all candidates are economical with the truth in some way, or in a (falsely) equivalent way (Birks, 2019b), then they may conclude that they are not in a position to demand veracity via the choice they have been given.

Misleading or erroneous truth claims are not a new phenomenon in political communication, and nor is negative campaigning and political journalism that focuses disproportionately on politicians' gaffes and untruths (Blumler and Gurevitch, 1995). However, what is distinctive about Trump is not only that he lies so prolifically, but that, as psychologist Bella DePaulo (2017) observed, 'he doesn't seem to be thinking about how he can lie in ways that can be defended as truthful'. Perhaps this kind of lying – not slyly twisting the statistics, not engaging in sophistry, but just straight-up having a disregard for the truth – is regarded as less hypocritical.

Discussing fact-checkers being driven 'to distraction' by Trump's erroneous claims, Selena Zito argued that, 'When he makes claims like this, the press takes him literally, but not seriously; his supporters take him seriously, but not literally' (Zito, 2016). In other words, supporters perceive that Trump sees the world the way that they do, rather than fixating on the specific claims he uses to elaborate on that worldview as journalists do.

This is the nub of what is meant by 'post-truth politics', and it suggests that journalists cannot tackle political disinformation of this kind, either through the traditional conventions of objective journalism or through the more recent genre of fact-checking journalism (Ball, 2017; d'Ancona, 2017; Davis, 2017). Vos and Thomas (2018) argue that following the 2016 US presidential election, journalists used the discourse of post-truth 'to diffuse the blame – this was not a crisis of journalistic authority, but authority in general', since 'journalists had done their democratic duty and yet the public did not act as expected' (Vos and Thomas, 2018: 2007).

The fact-checking movement emerged in parallel with the development of concerns that political communication was become detached from objective reality. However, unlike those who identify the problem as a 'post-truth' culture and society, fact-checking was substantially inspired by journalists' perception of their own profession's failings in the wake of 9/11; in particular, their credulity at the case for the invasion of Iraq (Dobbs, 2012).

The movement began in 2003 with the Annenberg Public Policy Center of the University of Pennsylvania launching Factcheck.org as 'a nonpartisan, non-profit "consumer advocate" for voters that aims to reduce the level of deception and confusion in US politics' through 'the best practices of both journalism and scholarship' (Factcheck.org, 2020). In the UK, Channel 4 News piloted its FactCheck service for the 2005 general election, and brought it back permanently in the run-up to the following election in 2010. Other well-known fact-checking organisations in the US include the *Washington Post* Fact Checker and the *Tampa Bay Times*'s widely syndicated Politifacts, both of which launched in 2007; and in the UK the *BBC News* service Reality Check and independent non-profit Full Fact have both operated since 2010.

In the US, fact-checkers have diligently recorded Trump not only stating falsehoods extravagantly often, but repeating the same factually untrue statements despite fact-checkers' corrections: in July 2020 when he breached the 20 000 mark in the *Washington Post* Fact Checker database, there were almost 500 untruths that he had repeated at least three times, and 40 false claims that he had repeated at least 20 times (Kessler et al., 2020), and this only escalated during the US presidential election campaign five months later (Kessler, 2020). That Trump lost that election is no more a repudiation of the post-truth thesis than his victory in 2016 was a repudiation of fact-checking, given that in both cases there were many other factors at work (including wild conspiracy theories and 'fake news' on the one hand, and very visible mishandling of the Covid-19 pandemic on the other). The Trump era did mark a departure from politics as usual. However, it is not clear that it represented a wider shift in the political climate in and beyond the US, and in particular, to the EU referendum debate in the UK.

BREXIT: PROPAGANDA IN A POST-TRUTH POLITICAL CLIMATE?

The campaign for Brexit is frequently mentioned alongside Trump's presidency as evidence of post-truth political communication based on emotional appeals and misinformation. Prominent Leave campaigners have fed this narrative. The second most prominent pro-Brexit group after the official Vote Leave campaign, Leave.EU, acknowledged aspiring to Trump-style tactics. Co-founder Arron Banks, otherwise best known at the time as the main donor to the UK Independence Party (UKIP), was reported to have said, after the vote, 'The Remain campaign featured fact, fact, fact, fact, fact. It doesn't work. You've got to connect with people emotionally. It's the Trump success' (Deacon, 2016). However, at the same time, the official pro-Brexit campaign, Vote Leave, characterised the Remain campaign's central messaging – warnings of dire economic consequences of leaving the EU – as 'Project Fear', and not as factual but based on forecasting methods with a poor track record of accuracy.

Both sides, then, were accused of propagandistic disinformation and emotional manipulation. Nonetheless, the following section will argue that there were no mainstream British politicians on either side of the debate who displayed anything like Trump's disregard for empirical facts in their campaigning, and that voters were not demonstrably misinformed by the problematic claims. The emotional narratives were more problematic, but here the tabloid press were more culpable than the political campaigns.

A notable contrast with the US is that the UK has a very highly partisan press, which has long peddled a Eurosceptic framing of the EU. This was established and reinforced by decades of Euro-myths peddled in jokey stories about 'bonkers' EU regulations on how bendy a banana could be or placing size limits on condoms (Wring, 2016). These entirely false stories were promoted by anti-EU newspapers, including many written by chief Brexiteer, and now Prime Minister, Boris Johnson whilst EU correspondent for the *Telegraph*. Unsurprisingly, then, the most problematically propagandistic campaign claims were not attenuated but exacerbated by sensationalist reporting that drowned out the more sober and nuanced arguments.

In the following sections I will explore the more dubious, misleading, and manipulative claims made in the referendum campaigns, the ways in which they were reported and fact-checked, and the evidence for audience reception of these claims extrapolated from polling. Finally, I will discuss the overall role of the news media in the EU referendum debate, whether it is another authoritative voice that has been rejected by a post-truth public, or is more complicit in amplifying the more problematic aspects of political communication.

THE CAMPAIGNS' CONTESTED AND MISLEADING EMPIRICAL CLAIMS

Whilst not on the same scale as Trump's presidential bid and term in office, the EU referendum debate was not entirely untainted by false claims. An investigation by Channel 4 News (2019) found that a video produced by Leave.EU that had gone viral on social media had been faked. It purported to show how easy it was to smuggle migrants into the UK, but satellite data obtained by Channel 4 News showed that the shots of the 'migrants' – actually British soldiers – disembarking in Folkestone unopposed were actually shot first, before the boat had left British waters. The boat then went from Dover to France and back again, without making the drop-offs that the video presenter suggested should arouse suspicion.

Nonetheless, this was not the kind of self-aggrandising, belittling, or blatant lies that Trump made throughout his political career. The video sought to makes its claims defensible with reference to 'evidence' that people could see with their own eyes. It was an old-fashioned propaganda stunt, albeit more clumsily executed than we are accustomed to seeing from professional public relations (PR) and spin, more comparable perhaps with a sensationalist tabloid 'investigation'.

Then there was the notorious claim on the side of the Vote Leave bus that has become a synecdoche for post-truth politics in the UK (Ball, 2017; d'Ancona, 2017; Davis, 2017; Rose, 2017). All three of the main British fact-checkers pointed out that it was misleading to claim that the UK sends £350 million to the EU every week, much less to suggest this amount of money would be available to the National Health Service (NHS) on departure from the EU. Apart from the rebate granted to the UK, the country benefited from farming subsidies, research grants for universities, and funding for infrastructure projects. The Remain campaign decided that it was not worth feeding the story by criticising the figure, since there was no one figure all could agree was the most correct or representative, but mostly because the alternatives also sounded like a lot of money.[1] FactCheck (Worrall, 2016) chose to present it as a per annum cost per person, which arguably gives the difference in numbers that are more comprehensible – from £252 to £89 – but could also be interpreted as making it sound more reasonable.

Therefore it is important to note that Vote Leave's claim was defensible – it was transparently based in credible published data – and that the selection of the most relevant figures and their most appropriately contextualised presentation is by no means self-evident, but rather contestable. Moreover, the alternative ways of expressing the same statistic in fact-checking journalism need to be justified as more representative and relevant to the overall argument (see Birks, 2019a for a more detailed discussion of this point) to inform the audience's own subjective judgement of whether the cost is reasonable or not, rather than to direct them toward a particular assessment.

On the other side of the debate, the official Remain campaign, Britain Stronger in Europe, despite the choice of name, focused on the weaknesses of the UK alone. The central argument was the projected economic cost of leaving, rather than the benefits of remaining in the EU. Furthermore, the Remainers' attempt to bring this cost closer to home was also somewhat misleading. The key claim, published in a Treasury report launched by Chancellor of the Exchequer George Osborne, was that leaving the EU would cost UK households £4300 per annum by 2030. The calculation appears to be an attempt to contextualise the forecast damage to gross domestic product (GDP), and to suggest that this was not just a cost borne by big business and wealthy individuals who had benefited economically from globalisation, but would be felt by everyone in the country. However, there are many flaws to that argument, as laid out in the fact-checks on the claim (for example, Reuben, 2016). Average GDP per household is not the same as household income, which is what is inferred here. The comparator is also not made clear in the claim, leaving people to assume that they would be worse off than they are now, rather than worse off than they would have been with the higher economic growth the country would have enjoyed in the EU. The difference between slower growth and recession is significant: voters might be more prepared to give up a notional gain in the future in return for national pride or defence of traditional culture, than to lose what they have.

So, there were misleading claims on both sides, but all of the most prominent claims (other than the staged 'evidence' of how easy it is for migrants to cross the channel undetected) were based on legitimate statistics. The selective presentation of statistics is as commonplace in political PR and spin as it is in corporate PR and marketing. The problem with these claims is not that they are 'untrue', but that they are used as premises in bad arguments and manipulative strategic communication.

THE CAMPAIGNS' WIDER ARGUMENTS

The Remain campaign's economic claims appealed to instrumental interests that had apparently proven successful in the 'No' campaign in the run-up to the Scottish independence referendum. In both cases their opponents were nationalists, but of very different kinds. In Scotland, independence is a civic nationalist cause that seeks sovereignty to make more progressive laws; it is not exceptionalist or isolationist, and indeed the Scottish Nationalist Party (SNP) campaigned passionately to remain in the EU, and Scots voted 62 per cent Remain. In contrast, the Vote Leave campaign sought sovereignty principally to limit immigration, implicitly invoking divisive ethnic nationalism. Whilst the official campaign framed this in various pragmatic ways, in terms of pressure on schools, housing, and the health service, the Leave.EU campaign used a photograph of largely non-white migrants and refugees queuing to cross a border to illustrate their urge to 'take back control of our borders'. Whilst Vote Leave campaigners criticised the poster, it arguably simply makes explicit the dog-whistle politics of the official slogan 'Take Back Control': that is, to signal recognition to nationalist and even racist supporters in a way that was also publicly deniable.

Bryant (1995) argues that civic nationalism is based on civility, which is a cool and detached sentiment in contrast with the warm 'fraternity' of communal association that characterises ethnic nationalism. The Leave campaigns embraced the latter by promoting a sense of Britishness that was not dissimilar to the Trump presidential campaign: a vision of recapturing past glories, a sense of grandeur based in competitiveness, and a desire to 'win' rather than to cooperate for mutual gain. The arguments that countered the Remainers' dire economic warnings were arguably based more in this instinctive nationalistic self-importance than in cold hard fact, given that, contrary to the aggrandising boasts of Leave campaigners, the UK has not struck the 'easiest deal in human history' with the EU as Brexiteer Liam Fox claimed (Sommerlad, 2019), nor with other countries. It was this note of optimism, the hope that can motivate people to risk change, that allowed the Leave campaigns to label the Remain campaign 'Project Fear', despite their own ethnic nationalism being based substantially in fear of the 'other' in our midst.

Unsurprisingly, the Remain campaigners did not risk challenging inflated national pride, nor point out the vulnerabilities or weaknesses of the UK, but rather pointed to the bottom line, namely the economic losses that were likely to result, without any sense of why the economy would lose out. This was an argument that had to be taken on trust. It was based in the cognitive authority granted to economists in prominent national think tanks such as the Institute for Fiscal Studies (IFS), business lobby group the Confederation of British Industry (CBI), and powerful international organisations in finance and trade such as the International Monetary Fund (IMF) and the Organisation for Economic Co-operation and Development (OECD). Critics' disproportionate focus on Vote Leave's battle bus slogan is perhaps because the message was so straightforward, namely the literal cost of EU membership. By contrast, the cost of leaving was abstract and theoretical, and no one in the Remain campaign troubled the voters with an explanation as to how it had been arrived at, or the contributory factors that fed into the forecasting models.

However, the emotional charge of ethnic nationalism is based more in the negative feelings that motivate exclusion of the 'other', than in love of the country or the fellow national. This, too, was expressed with erroneous and dubious claims, such as the claim of pressure on public services and wages from immigration from the EU. However, these assertions were only occasionally backed up by research, in particular selective and erroneous use of a Bank of England report that found a small impact on wages of unskilled workers, only where there was a very high proportion of foreign-born labour in the workplace (Birks, 2019b). The problem for fact-checking journalists was that the most problematic arguments left the discretely checkable empirical premises unspoken. However, the greater problem was that those arguments appeared more in the tabloid press than in the campaigns themselves.

NEWS REPORTING

The most contested assertion from the Leave campaign, that the UK sent the EU £350 million a week, was only the eighth most commonly raised economic argument in the news during the campaign – appearing in just 147 of the sampled 14 779 articles – according to Moore and Ramsay's (2017) research. They found that it received considerably less attention than the combined coverage of forecasts and reports (437 articles) from what Leave campaigner Michael Gove dismissed as 'organisations with acronyms saying that they know what is best and getting it consistently wrong': the IMF (which alone appeared in 214 articles), IFS (184), OECD and CBI, albeit much less critically (Zelizer, 2018).

The same study found that the most commonly reported economic argument from the Leave campaign was, in fact, the claim that migration placed pressure on public services (234 articles), which 'was frequently repeated in the editorials of some news outlets without being subject to the skeptical or forensic analysis applied to Remain's economic arguments across the whole range of publications'. Far from acknowledging the limitations of the Leave campaign's arguments, the tabloid press sought out their own, including connecting immigration with the other long-established tabloid folk devil of the 'benefit cheat', taking welfare payments to which they are not entitled (Gavin, 2018).

Zelizer (2018) argues that broadcast news was still less critical, despite broadcasters' adherence to the dominant conventions of due impartiality, in contrast to the openly partisan press. The 'balancing' of conflicting truth claims was at best conveyed as 'statistical tit-for-tats' (Cushion and Lewis, 2017) that illuminated nothing beyond presenting both sides as contested, and 'facts' as scarce.

This is where fact-checkers should step in, but the two broadcaster-run services were marginalised online and their findings did not make it into their parent organisations' news bulletins. Here they functioned as little-read footnotes to the news, which journalists could point to as proof of their public service without risking flak for deigning to take sides between information and disinformation (Dobbs, 2012), or boring the audience with detail (Chadwick, 2017).

Another challenge for journalists was that Leave claims were less specific and 'costed', so less criticised or fact-checked than the economic forecasts that formed the central planks of the Remain campaign (Moore and Ramsay, 2017: 55). The 2017 snap general election also demonstrated the limitations of fact-checkers' focus on politicians' overt claims, and especially those that are in some way quantified (Birks, 2019a). This allows the more implicit or vague claims to go unchallenged, even if they are a key premise in the overall argument being advanced. One such omission was the implied premise that the UK is in a stronger negotiating position with non-EU countries alone than as part of the EU trading bloc. This means that politicians are able to leave premises unstated specifically and strategically to avoid being held to account for them.

Conversely, the economic forecasting behind Remain's main argument was heavily contested in the pro-Brexit press. Moore and Ramsay (2017: 57) found that it was described as 'scaremongering' 737 times, and characterised as 'Project Fear' in 38 headlines, 30 of which appeared in the *Daily Express* and the *Sun*. Those two newspapers were also identified in the research as frequently pressing 'the fury button': 'A prominent and persistent characteristic of this Leave approach was to focus on the "outrage" or "fury" that greeted a Remain claim, or on the "attack" or "backlash" it was said to have provoked' (Moore and Ramsay, 2017: 51).

This is a form of ventriloquising often employed by journalists to attribute the newspaper's editorial position and associated subjective judgements to a source, and in doing so to assert for the reader the appropriate emotional response. Zelizer (2018: 148) argued that broadcast news also 'normalized a sense of outrage and then capitulated as it intensified'.

It is absurd, therefore, for journalists to suggest that they did their best to hold dissembling politicians to account, but were disregarded by voters who are culturally resistant to facts (Davis, 2017: loc. 1833). Ball acknowledges that mainstream media reporting did not pick up fact-checkers' findings because they rely on details that are too dry and 'wonkish' to be newsworthy, other than to 'make it a fight' in which the original claim gets repeated (Ball, 2017: loc. 662). However, Ball sees this as a failure of the audience, rather than of journalists' low assessments of them. Zelizer (2018: 152) accordingly recommends to journalists 'getting rid of condescension or understanding that anger at elites includes them'.

Nonetheless, we cannot assume that Brexit voters accepted the Leave campaign and tabloid claims on the cost of EU membership, or disbelieved Stronger in Europe campaign claims about the costs to the economy of leaving. It could be that they accepted the risk of economic costs but voted on other priorities, not least on migration, which was reported in a universally negative manner across the press, and in a highly alarmist and fearmongering tone in the pro-Brexit press.

AUDIENCE/VOTERS

A huge quantity of public opinion polling on the EU and the referendum has been collated on the website whatukthinks.org/eu by the National Centre for Social Research. Surveys from various sources found that more people expected leaving the EU to damage the economy than thought the country would be better off, but because a substantial proportion thought it would make no difference, the Remainers' case was still a minority position. Furthermore, those who voted to remain in the EU were far more convinced that leaving would damage the economy, whilst those who voted to leave were more confident that it would benefit the economy. The UK's most prominent psephologist, John Curtice (2016), argued that this high correspondence was peculiar to the economic argument and indicated that the economy was an important factor determining the direction of votes. But of course, correlation does not mean causation, and this could be post-facto rationalisation of a choice made on other grounds.

If the campaign was decisive in persuading voters that leaving the EU would not be economically damaging, we would expect to see a trend in longitudinal polling toward that belief. According to YouGov polling (What UK Thinks: EU, 2016), in late 2015, following the launch of Vote Leave and its report that concluded the EU had a net cost, there was a slight decline in the proportion of people who believed that the UK would be economically worse off if it left the EU. This reached a low of 31 per cent in early 2016, but actually grew slightly to 40 per cent between the launch in May 2016 of the bus and its contentious £350 million per week slogan, and the time of the vote (see Figure 27.1).

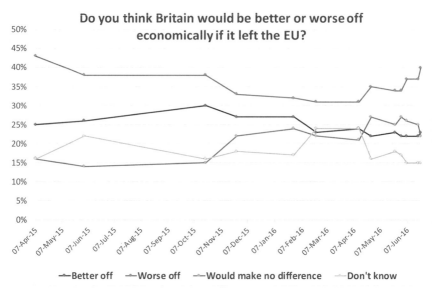

Source: What UK Thinks: EU (2016).

Figure 27.1 Polling from April 2015 to June 2016 (from the Referendum Act passing to the referendum poll date)

So, there is little evidence in the polling to support the supposition that the controversial bus slogan in itself was decisive, or even persuasive. Additionally, slightly fewer people thought that they *themselves* would be worse off than thought the economy would be badly affected (see Figure 27.2), which could reflect the 'left behind' voters thinking that they were kicking big business who were the ones benefiting from globalisation. Finally, even though there was a striking correspondence between views on the economy and direction of vote, that does not necessarily prove that this was the primary issue on which people decided how to vote.

In 2015, the year before the referendum, some people did tell pollsters (What UK Thinks: EU, 2015a) that saving the UK money would be the strongest argument to vote Leave (12 per cent in July 2015, 18 per cent in December 2015), but twice as many chose border or immigration control as the most persuasive (24 per cent in July, rising to 38 per cent in December). In contrast, respondents were split on the most persuasive argument to remain in the EU (What UK Thinks: EU, 2015b): there was no one killer argument, and though the potential loss of 3 million jobs was the most popular, it was only chosen by fewer than one in five people (17 per cent, rising to 18 per cent).

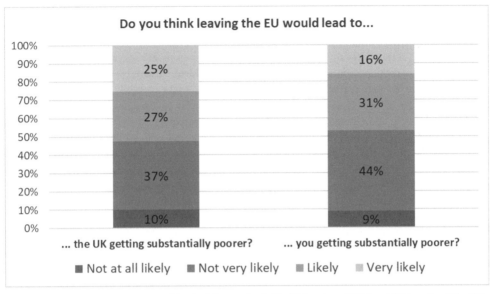

Source: Polling from YouGov/Future of England Survey, funded by University of Edinburgh/University of Cardiff, October 2019 (England only), https://d25d2506sfb94s.cloudfront.net/cumulus_uploads/document/5gl2yxhbzn/England%2016%20Oct%20AH.pdf.

Figure 27.2   Polling indicating that voters were less worried about the impact of Brexit on their own wealth or income than that of the country

A POST-TRUTH CAMPAIGN?

It is not tenable to conclude from the evidence reviewed above that the slim majority in favour of leaving the EU is, in itself, evidence of post-truth politics, simply because there were some questionable tactics and statistical manipulations on the side that won, and somewhat less so on the side that lost. The picture is much more complex than that. Furthermore, we must also recognise that the emotive narrative that connects the issue to voters' personal political values is not established overnight by a clever but transparent lie or two, but over a much longer period of incidental messaging from stories whose persuasive intent is much less apparent.

It is fair to say that elements of the pro-Brexit campaigns attempted to import the 'culture wars' from the US, but their nationalist populist propaganda was more conventional and recognisable as 'spin' than is contended in the 'post-truth politics' thesis. Indeed the most baseless fabrications date back decades and were created by the tabloid press, who are still responsible for most fake news circulating in the UK (Chadwick et al., 2018). Imke Henkel (2018) argues that the reason Euro-myths endured for years and decades after being debunked was that they appealed to a wider narrative, or myth of the 'irreverent, laughing Briton' who battled ludicrous bureaucracy with ridicule.

It is equally likely that, to the extent that the more dubious claims of the campaigns were accepted by the audience, it was because they supported a worldview they already held, namely that it is easy for migrants to reach the UK undetected; that the EU spends our money without being accountable to citizens – a notion promoted without irony by UKIP Members of the European Parliament (MEPs), whose own jobs were to represent the country in the European Parliament; that 'Eurocrats' are obsessed with creating new regulations or 'red tape'. Similarly, a majority of people already thought that immigration was too high and that leaving the EU was the only way that immigration could be reduced, so it is likely that the campaign raised the salience of immigration as an issue, and potentially gave social licence to anti-immigrant sentiment, with an increase in hostility and racist incidents after the result.

On the economy, the Leave campaigns were on the defensive (Moore and Ramsay, 2017), and there is little evidence in the exhaustive polling on the issue to support the assertion that Leave's emphasis on the high cost of membership of the EU was persuasive. However, the 'Project Fear' soundbite may well have been their strongest counter-attack line, not because it undermined the credibility of the economic warnings, but because it reflected a negative valence to the Remain campaign that has also been observed in content analysis of the way it was reported (Levy et al., 2016).

It is impossible to say whether the EU referendum campaigns were any more or less manipulative or deceptive than past campaigns for either referenda or elections, but Moore and Ramsay (2017: 130) argued that there was an unusual number of accusations of lying, compared to the previous referenda on Scottish independence (in 2015) and adopting an Alternative Voting system (in 2011). Negative campaigning and reporting can lead voters to curse both their houses and disengage altogether; but the turnout (78 per cent) was higher than for any general election in the 21st century. However, in the overbearing atmosphere of negativity that clouded the referendum campaigns, the comparatively hopeful and optimistic messaging of the Leave campaign and its tabloid cheerleaders, coupled with dissatisfaction with the status quo, may have swung it for the Brexiteers.

Referendum campaigning was fought not on the basis of narrow factual (or counterfactual) truth claims, but on the wider argument in which those claims were not the only premises. It is not true to say that the Remain campaign appealed to voters' reason. The Leave characterisation of the economic warnings as 'Project Fear' was not unfounded, but ironic, given that the Leave campaign was fought primarily on the ground of immigration, and was based on fear of the 'other'. However, Leave could at least leaven this with a sense of hope for something better, which may have had more appeal than a sense of threat to the status quo for those who felt they had nothing to lose.

Proponents of the post-truth characterisation of the contemporary political landscape see this as evidence of irrationality, but in fact it simply reflects the fact that voting preference has never been based on a cost–benefit analysis but on a wider set of personal and political values (Enke, 2020; Schwartz et al., 2010). These values are not irrelevant to political decision-making, nor evidence of an irrational electorate. They are legitimate premises in political argumentation (Fairclough and Fairclough, 2012; Van Eemeren and Houtlosser, 2003; Walton, 2006).

Emotion too is politically relevant, as it animates those values, such as outrage at injustice and hope for change (Castells, 2015; Wahl-Jorgensen, 2019). However, emotional appeals can be persuasive in problematic ways that we might recognise as propagandistic (Welch, 2013). There is a fine line, perhaps, between anger at injustice and more popular resentment towards those perceived as being unfairly favoured. Theories that explain Trump's success in terms of emotional populism, and especially 'angry populism', contend that Trump voters were either (or perhaps both) those left behind by globalised capitalism or those who had lost social and cultural privilege through socially progressive shifts (Wahl-Jorgensen, 2019). This would seem to characterise the success of Brexiteers' appeal to the northern post-industrial towns.

Most of all, however, the discourses of angry populism were articulated in the right-wing tabloid press. Moore and Ramsay (2017) found fury at immigration and at the claims made by the Remain campaign.

FACT-CHECKING IN ARGUMENTATIVE CONTEXT

To some extent it is fair to say that the discourse of post-truth politics was used by journalists to pass the blame for audiences' credulity and acceptance of misleadingly propagandistic claims, though it also overstates that credulity. If journalists have lost credibility with their audience, it is more likely to be for their own role in amplifying the narrow and unilluminating shouting match of contemporary campaigning, rather than because the audience have lost interest in knowing what is true.

So, what can journalists do to earn back the cognitive authority they and other institutional sources have lost in recent years and decades?

- Step outside the political campaign agenda: there were positive arguments to be made for the benefits of EU membership, and even immigration, that would have been informative, even if the campaign strategists neglected them as insufficiently persuasive.
- Point out weak argumentation: although massaged statistics can be defended as technically true, they are used in selective and misrepresentative ways. However, it can be counterproductive to 'press the fury button' without explaining how and why the argument is flawed.
- Show, don't tell: journalists can avoid expecting the audience to take a claim on trust on the basis of authority, expertise, or other heuristics of credibility. Under-estimating the intelligence of the audience, or their interest in the details, only risks giving the impression that something is being suppressed, and sending them looking for answers down the rabbit hole of conspiracy theory pattern-finding.
- Acknowledge caveats more routinely: especially on forecasts and predictions. Gove's notorious 'had enough of experts' line was actually a specific attack on economists' poor record on modelling economic outcomes. This can be a reasonable critical question, but when ambiguity is avoided in fear of confusing the audience, credibility too easily becomes a binary judgement.

Of course, there are some newspapers that have cornered a market in reactionary outrage and will continue to plough that profitable furrow, but fact-checking journalism could indicate a more proactively anti-propagandistic direction for mainstream news.

NOTE

1. For example, Channel 4 FactCheck (Worrall, 2016) reported calculations from the Institute for Fiscal Studies that put it at £14.4 billion per annum, or £277 million per week net after the rebate; £9.8 billion or £188 million per week after subsidies distributed via government; and £5.7 billion or £110 million per week after other funding grants. The lowest figure is most representative of what membership costs the UK – though of course there are trade advantages in return that are more difficult to quantify – but the net figure is arguably the most relevant if talking about having control

over how the money was spent; yet by proposing to spend it all on the NHS they should make clear that farmers, universities, business, and so on, would necessarily lose out.

REFERENCES

Ball, J. (2017), *Post-Truth: How Bullshit Conquered the World*, London: Biteback Publishing.
Birks, J. (2019a), *Fact-Checking Journalism: A British Perspective*, Basingstoke: Palgrave Pivot.
Birks, J. (2019b), 'Fact-checking, False Balance, and "Fake News": The Discourse and Practice of Verification in Political Communication', in S. Price (ed.), *Journalism, Power and Investigation: Global and Activist Perspectives*, London: Routledge, pp. 245–264.
Blumler, J., and M. Gurevitch (1995), *The Crisis of Public Communication*, London: Psychology Press.
Briant, E., G. Philo, and P. Donald (2013), *Bad News for Refugees*, London: Pluto Press.
Bryant, C.G.A. (1995), 'Civic nation, civil society, civil religion', in J.A. Hall (ed.), *Civil Society: Theory, History, Comparison*, Cambridge: Polity Press, pp. 136–157.
Castells, M. (2015), *Networks of Outrage and Hope: Social Movements in the Internet Age*, Hoboken, NJ: John Wiley & Sons.
Chadwick, A. (2017), *The Hybrid Media System: Politics and Power*, Oxford: Oxford University Press.
Chadwick, A., C. Vaccari, and B. O'Loughlin (2018), 'Do tabloids poison the well of social media? Explaining democratically dysfunctional news sharing', *New Media and Society*, 20(11), 4255–4574.
Channel 4 News (2019), 'Revealed: How Leave.EU faked migrant footage', available at https://www.channel4.com/news/revealed-how-leave-eu-faked-migrant-footage, accessed 12 December 2020.
Curtice, J. (2016), 'The economics of Brexit in voters' eyes. Or, why the Remain campaign failed', whatuthinks.org, available at https://whatukthinks.org/eu/wp-content/uploads/2016/11/The-Economics-of-Brexit-in-voters-eyes.pdf, accessed 12 December 2020.
Cushion, S., and J. Lewis (2017), 'Impartiality, statistical tit-for-tats and the construction of balance: UK television news reporting of the 2016 EU referendum campaign', *European Journal of Communication*, 32(3): 208–223.
d'Ancona, M. (2017), *Post-Truth: The New War on Truth and How to Fight Back*, New York: Random House.
Davis, E. (2017), *Post-Truth: Why We Have Reached Peak Bullshit and What We Can Do About It*, London: Little, Brown.
Deacon, M. (2016), 'In a world of post-truth politics, Andrea Leadsom will make the perfect PM', *Daily Telegraph*, 9 July, available at https://www.telegraph.co.uk/news/2016/07/09/in-a-world-of-post-truth-politics-andrea-leadsom-will-make-the-p/, accessed 12 December 2020.
DePaulo, B. (2017), 'How President Trump's lies are different from other people's: Trump is a liar, but so are you. Here's the more interesting way he stands out', *Psychology Today*, available at https://www.psychologytoday.com/us/blog/living-single/201712/how-president-trumps-lies-are-different-other-peoples, accessed 12 December 2020.
Dobbs, M. (2012), 'The rise of political fact-checking, how Reagan inspired a journalistic movement', New America Foundation, available at https://www.issuelab.org/resources/15318/15318.pdf, accessed 12 December 2020.
Enke, B. (2020), 'Moral values and voting', *Journal of Political Economy*, 128(10): 3679–3629.
Factcheck.org (2020), 'Our mission', available at https://www.factcheck.org/about/our-mission/, accessed 12 December 2020.
Fairclough, I., and N. Fairclough (2012), *Political Discourse Analysis*, Abingdon: Routledge.
Gavin, N.T. (2018), 'Media definitely do matter: Brexit, immigration, climate change and beyond', *British Journal of Politics and International Relations*, 20(4): 827–845.
Henkel, I. (2018), 'How the laughing, irreverent Briton trumped fact-checking: a textual analysis of fake news in British newspaper stories about the EU', *Journalism Education*, 6(3): 87-97.
Kessler, G. (2020), 'Trump is averaging more than 50 false or misleading claims a day', *Washington Post* FactChecker, 22 October 2020, available at https://www.washingtonpost.com/politics/2020/10/22/president-trump-is-averaging-more-than-50-false-or-misleading-claims-day/, accessed 12 December 2020.

Kessler, G., S. Rizzo, and M. Kelly (2020), 'Fact-Checker: President Trump has made more than 20,000 false or misleading claims', *Washington Post*, 13 July, available at https://www.washingtonpost.com/politics/2020/07/13/president-trump-has-made-more-than-20000-false-or-misleading-claims/, accessed 12 December 2020.

Levy, D.A.L., B. Aslan, and D. Bironzo (2016), 'UK press coverage of the EU Referendum', Reuters Institute, available at https://reutersinstitute.politics.ox.ac.uk/sites/default/files/2018-11/UK_Press_Coverage_of_the_per cent20EU_Referendum.pdf, accessed 12 December 2020, accessed 12 December 2020.

Miller, D. (2003), *Tell Me Lies: Propaganda and Media Distortion in the Attack on Iraq*, London: Pluto Press.

Moore, M., and G. Ramsay (2017), 'UK media coverage of the 2016 EU Referendum campaign', Centre for the Study of Media, Communication and Power, KCL, available at https://www.the7eye.org.il/wp-content/uploads/2017/05/UK-media-coverage-of-the-2016-EU-Referendum-campaign-1.pdf, accessed 12 December 2020.

Nyhan, B., E. Porter, J. Reifler, and T.J. Wood (2019), 'Taking fact-checks literally but not seriously? The effects of journalistic fact-checking on factual beliefs and candidate favorability', *Political Behavior*, 42: 939–960.

Reuben, A. (2016), 'Reality check: would Brexit cost your family £4,300?', BBC Reality Check, available at https://www.bbc.co.uk/news/uk-politics-eu-referendum-36073201, accessed 12 December 2020.

Robinson, P. (2005), 'The CNN effect revisited', *Critical Studies in Media Communication*, 22(4): 344–349.

Rose, J. (2017), 'Brexit, Trump, and post-truth politics', *Public Integrity*, 19(6): 555–558.

Schudson, M. (2009), 'Factual knowledge in the age of truthiness', in B. Zelizer (ed.), *The Changing Faces of Journalism: Tabloidisation, Technology and Truthiness*, Abingdon: Routledge, pp. 104–113.

Schwartz, S.H., G.V. Caprara, and M. Vecchione (2010), 'Basic personal values, core political values, and voting: a longitudinal analysis', *Political Psychology*, 31(3), 421–452.

Sommerlad, J. (2019), 'Ten politicians who claimed Brexit negotiations were going to be easy', *Independent*, available at https://www.indy100.com/news/brexit-easy-nigel-farage-theresa-may-david-davis-boris-johnson-8846041, accessed 12 December 2020.

Stauber, J.C., and S. Rampton (2003), *Weapons of Mass Deception: The Uses of Propaganda in Bush's War on Iraq*, London: Robinson.

Swire, B., A. Berinsky, S. Lewandowsky, and U. Ecker (2017), 'Processing political misinformation: comprehending the Trump phenomenon', *Royal Society Open Science*, 4(3): 1–21.

Van Eemeren, F.H., and P. Houtlosser (2003), 'The development of the pragma-dialectical approach to argumentation', *Argumentation*, 17(4): 387–403.

Vos, T.P., and R.J. Thomas (2018), 'The discursive construction of journalistic authority in a post-truth age', *Journalism Studies*, 19(13): 2001–2010.

Wahl-Jorgensen, K. (2019), *Emotions, Media and Politics*, Cambridge: Polity.

Walton, D. (2006), *Fundamentals of Critical Argumentation*, Cambridge: Cambridge University Press.

Welch, D. (2013), *Propaganda: Power and Persuasion*, London: British Library.

What UK Thinks: EU (2015a), 'Which argument is most likely to make you want to vote to leave the EU?', available at https://whatukthinks.org/eu/questions/please-rank-the-following-argument-most-likely-to-make-you-want-to-vote-to-leave-the-eu-at-the-top-to-the-argument-least-likely/, accessed 12 December 2020.

What UK Thinks: EU (2015b), 'Which argument is most likely to make you want to vote to stay in the EU?', available at https://whatukthinks.org/eu/questions/which-argument-is-most-likely-to-make-you-want-to-vote-to-stay-in-the-eu/, accessed 12 December 2020.

What UK Thinks: EU (2016), 'Do you think Britain would be better or worse off economically if it left the EU? (YouGov)', available at https://whatukthinks.org/eu/questions/do-you-think-britain-would-be-better-or-worse-off-economically-if-it-left-the-eu/, accessed 12 December 2020.

Worrall, P. (2016), 'Do we really send £350m a week to Brussels?', Channel 4 FactCheck, available at https://www.channel4.com/news/factcheck/factcheck-send-350m-week-brussels, accessed 12 December 2020.

Wring, D. (2016), 'From super-market to Orwellian super-state: the origins and growth of newspaper scepticism', EU Referendum, Analysis, available at https://www.referendumanalysis.eu/, accessed 12 December 2020.

Zelizer, B. (2018), 'Resetting journalism in the aftermath of Brexit and Trump', *European Journal of Communication*, 33(2): 140–156.

Zito, S. (2016), 'Taking Trump seriously, not literally', *Atlantic*, 23 September, available at https://www.theatlantic.com/politics/archive/2016/09/trump-makes-his-case-in-pittsburgh/501335/, accessed 12 December 2020.

28. Beyond the smear word: media literacy educators tackle contemporary propaganda
Renee Hobbs

INTRODUCTION

The term 'fake news' brought public attention and interest to the disinformation and misinformation that is spread by politicians, bad actors, bots, and trolls. Widespread concerns have mounted about the dangers of our polluted and poisoned information ecosystem. It is a common refrain of politicians and thought leaders alike: the digital landscape is now a treacherous place that has been damaged by Silicon Valley's technologies, as people now spread poison through social media, moving it up the chain to infect mainstream media and make bad ideas seem believable. Moreover, political demagogues have exploited the digital media ecosystem to inspire their followers to incite violence against governments (Russonello, 2021).

Academics from many fields and disciplines have raced to examine this dangerous new world. Intentionally choosing not to use the word 'propaganda', Claire Wardle and Hossein Derakshan coined a new term, 'malinformation', to describe information that is not false or inaccurate, but that is shared specifically to cause harm, as when someone uses a picture of a dead child refugee in an effort to ignite hatred of a particular ethnic group. Phillips and Milner (2021) use the term 'polluted information' to describe how lies and falsehoods exert substantial damage to the information ecosystem. They claim that, with the convergence of technological and economic efficiencies, poison spews from digital platforms that aim to maximise user engagement. Even traditional mainstream news publications contribute to the pollution by their increasingly partisan stance, structuring content in pursuit of the clicks, likes, and shares that are their primary source of revenue. Plus, users themselves are not merely victims of this poison: they create it themselves. Dramatic language is often used to frame the severity of this problem, as in this sample sentence: 'The crash and thunder of attack after attack, hoax after hoax, manipulation after manipulation has wrought a media landscape so inundated that it can be difficult to distinguish what's true from what's trash' (Phillips and Milner, 2021: 1).

Such hyperbolic language might seem justified by both the volume and diversity of online misinformation and manipulation. While the public is free to tune out the madness of Trump tweets, journalists and academics cannot, and for some the barrage has been emotionally exhausting. Many politicians, journalists, and academics who followed the President's Twitter account experienced feelings of anger, rage, hopelessness, and despair as Trump and his enablers peddled false narratives about Special Counsel Robert S. Mueller III's investigation, the tariffs on China, legislative gridlock, and much more (Lithwick, 2019). The range and diversity of harmful propaganda included: organised disinformation campaigns waged through decentralised and distributed networks (Benkler et al., 2018); right-wing nationalists and white supremacists eager to bring their ideas into the mainstream (Marantz, 2019); disguised information that appeared to derive from within a target population, who were actually unaware of the manipulation (US District Court, 2018); bots and trolls that amplified nationalist extremism (Woolley and Howard, 2018); and authoritarian governments around the world who ramped up censorship, removing critical voices and using surveillance to monitor the actions of political dissidents (Bastos and Farkas, 2019). Under these circumstances, it is not surprising that academics and journalists took up the metaphor of the poisoned information ecosystem with such enthusiasm. It captured a sense of the ubiquitous phenomenon they were trying to understand.

However, the discourse norms of contemporary journalism, with its own need to generate clicks through likes and shares, may not serve the needs of educators who are faced with the challenge of preparing students to thrive in a time of increased political polarisation, where distrust and apathy form a toxic stew, and where the adolescent pleasures of transgressive trolling, the 'allure of the lulz' (Mina, 2019), lead many young people to act like Josh Hall, a 21-year-old food delivery driver. Over the course of a single year, he impersonated members of the Trump family on Twitter and gained a large following of supporters by hosting fake fundraising events, mixing raunchy political commentary with wild conspiracy theories. Hall claims he was 'just trying to rally up MAGA [Make America Great Again] supporters and have fun' (Nicas, 2020: 5). As educators in the United States and around the world explore strategies that may help young people understand both the power and the social responsibilities of life online, the concept of propaganda proves to be supremely useful in examining the emotional power of digital media as a strategic tool of social influence.

In this chapter, I first examine some primary reasons why propaganda education is not a more substantive part of elementary and secondary education, by looking closely at the rise of the Common Core State Standards for English language arts and the impact of growing political polarisation on the work of social studies educators. Then I report on a global initiative in which I participated, working with educators in both the United States and Europe with initial support from the United States Holocaust Memorial Museum and later from the Evens Foundation and the European Commission. Working with a group of international media literacy educators, we took up the challenge of integrating the study of contemporary propaganda into the practice of media literacy education, targeting high school students and their teachers. The most significant benefit of this work helped to demonstrate the value of contemporary propaganda in the classroom as it cultivates appreciation for nuance and multi-perspectival thinking in the process of activating intellectual curiosity.

As I will show, the dialectic between protection and empowerment stances, which is a long-standing feature of media literacy education, propels educators to teach about propaganda in ways that emphasises benefits as well as its harms. Although media literacy educators fear the unpredictability of teaching about harmful propaganda in an increasingly polarised world, they also recognise the value of conceptualising propaganda more broadly to acknowledge it as 'one means by which large numbers of people are induced to act together' (Smith and Lasswell, 1945: 2). The study of propaganda provides opportunities to reflect on how the meaning-making process is situational and contextual, how the ancient Greek philosophers' ideas of persuading with *logos*, *ethos*, *pathos*, and *kairos* is still relevant today, even when applied to memes, sponsored content, partisan news, and eyewitness protest videos posted to YouTube.

THE EDUCATIONAL RESPONSE TO FAKE NEWS AND PROPAGANDA

How did educators respond to the rise of the so-called fake news crisis? In general, if they tackled it at all, librarians and educators placed their efforts on activating cognition and critical thinking to help learners recognise and evaluate problematic news and information (Burkhardt, 2017). With the blessing and support of journalists and with support from journalism philanthropies, some educators and librarians began to teach students to evaluate credible information sources, explaining how journalists verify information to determine its truth value, with the goal of increasing trust in mainstream media (Ashley, 2019). Others engaged students in creating school news media, to better understand how journalism is constructed (Hall et al., 2015). Still other educators emphasised to their students the value of civic action, using an approach called youth participatory politics, where students were engaged in social change initiatives by making creative work that explicitly responds to the needs of a community and addresses civic and political goals (Kahne et al., 2015). In helping students to create positive propaganda in the form of public service announcements and social issue advocacy documentaries, some classroom teachers have emphasised that such forms of expression are essential to the practice of democratic self-governance (Selfe and Selfe, 2008).

At the college level, some media literacy educators adopted an approach that examines the relationship between the Internet and democracy in the age of fake news, filter bubbles, and Facebook security breaches, explaining to students how the democratising potential of the Internet has been radically compromised by the logic of capitalism and the unaccountable power of a handful of telecom and tech monopolies (Jhally, 2018). In helping college students to analyse news, the function of news as propaganda is sometimes examined. For a generation of college students, the work of Herman and Chomsky (1988) supported the careful examination of news by showing how the political economy of journalism and the routines and norms of the press uphold the power of big business and big government. Unlike the traditional story that gets told in American public schools (that is, the idea that mass media upholds the practice of self-governance in a democratic society), Herman and Chomsky offered an alternative view, claiming that the function of the mass media is to deeply inculcate people into social roles that support the existing institutional power structures of the society.

However, for those working in K-12 (kindergarten to 12th grade) public education it was not so easy to explore ideologically rich topics in the school classroom. It is often difficult for teachers (who, after all, are agents of the state) to interrogate news, current events, political campaigns, and contemporary propaganda in the classroom (Mason et al., 2018).

Well-meaning efforts to label the diverse forms of expression students experience each day with terms such as 'malinformation' or 'pollution' does little to advance learning goals. In a society less trustworthy of media institutions (Bowyer and Kahne, 2016) media literacy educators have long recognised the dangers of inadvertent indoctrination, where the teacher offers activities strategically designed to inculcate the teacher's own world view and values. They know that teaching students how to critically read media does not automatically increase trust in news. Research by Mihailidis (2009) found that by focusing media literacy on critical skills alone, college students were prone to be more cynical, less willing to engage in dialogue, and less trustful of media and institutions in the first place. Learning to use labels such as 'malinformation' and 'information pollution' may promote cynicism or even actively interfere with critical thinking if learners merely use such labels to call out content they dislike as a means to buttress pre-existing views.

Moreover, young people may feel the increased need to join in what Mihailidis and Viotty (2017: 443) call the 'spreadable spectacle'. Today propaganda is spread more by viral sharing than by its one-way transmission by governments or corporations. Growing up in a partisan age, students may feel that keeping up with current events is mostly a matter of finding and sharing news that aligns with existing beliefs and values. News content can be easily judged from an egocentric approach where content that supports existing beliefs is prioritised. Such a practice has the added benefit of conveying aspects of personal identity to one's peer group. For this reason, Mihailidis and Viotty (2017: 450) wonder: 'Perhaps the US electorate is not "ill-informed" so much as they would rather find information that fits their world view. If finding truth is not as large a priority as finding personally relevant information, then what good is knowing how to critique a message in the first place?'

Another challenge to teaching about propaganda in the K-12 classroom is people's general repugnance when encountering the word itself. In a 1979 essay, Neil Postman once noticed that because propaganda is a 'smear word', educators may feel little need to examine it. Some academic experts like to restrict the use of the term 'propaganda' to refer only to efforts by state actors such as the Russian or Chinese governments. Gentler terms such as 'strategic communication', 'public diplomacy' (Cull, 2013), 'public relations' (Bernays, 1928), or 'activism' (Gelders and Ihlen, 2010) are used to describe propaganda that is close to home. In analysing the historical trajectory of public diplomacy, Cull (2013: 143) explained:

> It was certainly convenient for US information work to be able to reserve the term propaganda for the works of the enemy and to embrace a new benign term for its own democratic practice. Yet the extent to which public diplomacy was different from propaganda was seldom emphasized on Capitol Hill.

While state-supported propaganda has continued to be a substantial feature of contemporary propaganda, it is also produced by a variety of actors, not just states or would-be states. Now anyone, from anywhere, can influence public opinion by leveraging social media in ways that compel attention from television networks, newspapers of record, and leading online news sources. Sponsored content, memes, videos, vlogs, and social media posts may all function as propaganda. One scholar puts it this way: 'One person's activism – or education, or journalism, for that matter – is another person's propaganda' (Jack, 2017: 1).

Perhaps the most important reason why a more neutral, less negative definition of propaganda is valuable is because it expresses the strategic practice of communication as a form of social influence, as a means to achieve social power (Ellul, 1973). Definitions of propaganda are situational and contextual, responding to changes in society and culture (Hobbs, 2020). Educators and scholars often call upon history to defend a more neutral framing of the term. When propaganda is understood 'as a central means of organizing and shaping thought and perception', it is typical to call upon the modern origins of the term, which go back at least to the spread of religious doctrine during the European Counter Reformation (Auerbach and Castronovo, 2013: 2). Seen this way, propaganda functions a form of social glue that binds people to each other.

Because we are attracted to propaganda that aligns with our pre-existing beliefs and values, we might not recognise unifying propaganda that takes the form of aphorisms or truisms about democracy. When propaganda takes the form of inspirational, patriotic ditties or even protest songs, it may go unnoticed. Today, public service announcements may proclaim 'Love has no labels' to advance social values of equality and freedom, or warn you to wear a mask and wash your hands to avoid coronavirus infection. By activating strong emotion, simplifying information, and appealing to the audience's hopes, fears, and dreams, propaganda helps influence the public mind.

However, when the term is only used as a smear word to criticise messages we dislike, people may develop a blind spot in recognising and respecting forms of propaganda designed to build consensus. Because propaganda activates both negative emotions (such as hatred, fear, and envy) and more positive feelings (such as pleasure, joy, belonging, and pride), it may offer comfort from the chaos of information overload (Lippmann, 1922 [1997]). For educators, there is also practical value to conceptualising propaganda as potentially either beneficial or harmful. It not only aligns with teachers' mandate to bring quality information sources into the classroom, but also it may sensitise learners to the use of propaganda by activists and change agents, who take epistemic responsibility for their responsible use of language, images and symbols in adopting an identity as a 'positive propagandist'.

THE STUDY OF PROPAGANDA GENRES IN AMERICAN PUBLIC SCHOOLS

The analysis and production of propaganda is part of public education in the United States and around the world, but it is not a common or well-recognised practice (Hobbs, 2020). There are at least two primary reasons why propaganda education is not a more substantive part of elementary and secondary education. The study of propaganda has been largely abandoned by English teachers as the Common Core State Standards placed exclusive emphasis on informational texts, and social studies teachers, who have long struggled with teaching controversial issues, have found that the increased political polarisation in the community makes teaching propaganda genres risky. Because the term by some is used as a synonym for 'bad', many teachers hear the word 'propaganda' and have a knee-jerk reaction to it, believing that it should have little or no role in the classroom.

A short history of teaching about propaganda reveals that although the topic makes some teachers uncomfortable, at times it has also inspired them to action. In the 1930s, teachers who were concerned about the rise of anti-Semitism and the increasing role of radio and movies found a champion in Clyde Miller, a journalist who worked at Columbia University. With philanthropic funding from Boston business leader Edward Filene, Miller launched the Institute for Propaganda Analysis (IPA), a short-lived but influential initiative in propaganda education. Its monthly publication was distributed to thousands of high schools and public libraries, and the list of rhetorical devices it developed is still used in American public schools today to analyse propaganda. If American students get any opportunity at all to examine propaganda in schools, it is most likely that they will be encouraged to use labels to identify propaganda techniques, with terms such as 'glittering generalities', 'bandwagon', and 'card stacking' (Hobbs and McGee, 2014).

Miller's team explicitly framed propaganda education as an antidote to being victimised by a presumably powerful and manipulative persuader (Miller, 1941). Teachers were encouraged to use examples of contemporary propaganda in the classroom, leading students through a process of critical thinking about the messages used to shape and influence public opinion.

IPA documents argue that awareness of these devices 'keeps us from having our thought processes blocked by a trick', keeping people from being fooled or manipulated (Miller and Edwards, 1936).

However, repeated use of the word 'trick' in IPA publications does not align with the wisdom of the ancient rhetoricians. Suggesting that the rhetorical tools themselves are somehow inherently immoral or unethical practices of communication is itself a propaganda ploy (Hobbs and McGee, 2014). Given the dangerous rise of fascism in Europe, the use of this strategy was to be expected. However, it does not seem consistent with classic articulations of propaganda as rhetoric, where strategies used may be beneficial or harmful depending on the context and motives of the communicator (Cunningham, 2002).

Propaganda education continued in the 1970s as media literacy educators developed a new paradigm for the critical analysis of popular culture. At that time, rising levels of concern about the influence of television on children led to the creation of 'critical viewing skills education', a term used to define media literacy education by focusing exclusively on analysing media. The publication of *Media&Values* magazine by the Los Angeles-based Center for Media Literacy accelerated interest in media literacy across the country (RobbGrieco, 2018). By the 1990s, there was some considerable enthusiasm for integrating critical analysis of contemporary mass media and popular culture into the curriculum, as a national membership organisation formed to support it. During the 1980s and into the 1990s, this grass-roots group accelerated its focus on integrating media literacy education into the curriculum, and it began to be included in state education standards in Maryland, Massachusetts, Minnesota, Texas, and many other states. Public interest in '21st century skills' was also instrumental in furthering the placement of media literacy training on state standards (Thoman and Jolls, 2004).

Among educational leaders in states such as Texas, media literacy was seen as a new and technologically relevant set of competencies that are essential to keeping abreast of media and technological developments (Ward-Barnes, 2010). Instructional practices include examining how meaning is conveyed through visual representations by interpreting maps, charts, and even video segments. Students were also required to create and produce visual images to convey meaning using technology and media. Students compared and contrasted visual, print, electronic media, and written stories in books, graphic art, illustration, and photojournalism.

By 1994, widespread support for education reform intensified and the US Congress passed legislation entitled the Goals 2000: Educate America Act, which allowed the federal government to financially contribute to the states' curriculum and standards planning processes. In Texas, this effort resulted in the Texas Essential Knowledge and Skills (TEKS) in 1995, a set of standards that was created with significant input from Texas educators, scholars, experts, and members of the public. Texas educators adapted, with modifications, the media literacy concepts that other states had created, and emphasised the importance of making education relevant to contemporary society by articulating what each student should know and be able to do in the digital age (Ward-Barnes, 2010).

By 2009, however, the work of educators in the states gave sway to a much more centralised effort by state leaders to shape the American curriculum. Governors and state commissioners of education coordinated this effort through the National Governors Association Center for Best Practices and the Council of Chief State School Officers. Known as the Common Core State Standards (CCSS), this work had a transformational impact on American public education. In English language arts, media literacy (which had been called 'viewing and representing' in some states) virtually disappeared from the education standards and in its place was a strong emphasis on 'the special place of argument'. Although the architect of the CCSS state standards has stated that students must learn to read complicated texts of all sorts, English teachers shifted their focus towards informational texts and omitted persuasive forms completely (Redmond, 2015).

Thus, the study of propaganda in American secondary schools fell off the map. In a compelling historical and critical analysis which traces the 'fear of persuasion' in English language arts education, Fleming (2019) explains that the CCSS near-exclusive focus on argumentation led writing and composition scholars to ignore persuasive genres, creating an 'explicit bias' against persuasive genres (Fleming, 2019: 522). Functioning as a de facto national curriculum, the CCSS set forward a binary opposition between persuasion and argumentation, substantially misrepresenting the 2000-year-old history of rhetorical scholarship.

In analysing examples of lesson plans and typical K-12 classroom practices in English language arts, Fleming shows how the rhetorical triangle of *logos*, *ethos*, and *pathos* was turned into a simple hierarchy. He offers evidence to show the many substantial ways in which English language arts educators have privileged *logos* over *pathos* and *ethos*, claiming that a generation of educators has been taught to position argumentation as uniquely 'truth seeking' and thus superior to persuasion, which uses 'mere emotion' and appeals to character as a (presumably unethical) form of influence. As a result, persuasive genres have been nearly banished from K-12 schools in English language arts (Fleming, 2019: 522).

Fear of persuasion has had a deadly impact on American public education beyond the English classroom. There is a long and well-established scholarly literature showing how American social studies teachers lack confidence to, or choose not to, teach about controversial issues on topics including gun control, abortion, immigration, systemic racism, climate change, and more (Hess, 2004). Though schools have long been understood as important sites of civic learning, the relationship between students, teachers, public schools, and their communities is inherently political. When there is heightened political polarisation, the challenge of engaging young people in controversial issues becomes even more precarious (Hess and McAvoy, 2015).

When educators feel like their own political views differ from those of the community and parents, they may be less likely to engage in learning activities about controversial issues. In some communities, talking about elections in school can create tension between parents and school leaders. Teachers may get clear signals from their school leaders, who may suggest that students have their political discussions at home. During the presidential election of 2016, a study published in the *American Educational Research Journal* found that many teachers wanted to talk with students about the election and related issues but were also afraid of backlash. Many felt they should not, or could not, share their political affiliations or feelings due to the idea of maintaining political neutrality in the classroom (Dunn et al., 2019).

In Geller's (2020) study of social studies teachers, the vast majority described making efforts to not reveal their personal political beliefs and opinions, a stance they viewed as politically balanced. For teachers, this often meant ensuring representation of both sides of issues by playing devil's advocate or articulating the views of the 'other side'. Sometimes it meant providing materials or multiple sources that would be seen as representing a variety of viewpoints. But even innocuous practice can be controversial in some communities. One teacher described how, in his conservative area of Tennessee, a school librarian put up a sticker that used symbols from world religions to spell out 'COEXIST' and that some students complained that it was discriminatory toward their Christian beliefs.

In a 2016 survey by the Southern Poverty Law Center of more than 10 000 teachers, counsellors, and school administrators, 90 per cent reported that school climate was negatively affected by heightened anxiety immediately after the election of President Donald Trump, especially from marginalised students, including immigrants, Muslims, African Americans, and lesbian, gay, bisexual, and transgender (LGBT) students. Participants reported derogatory language directed at these students, and students were targeting each other based on which candidate they had supported. Thousands of educators described specific incidents of bigotry and harassment that were inspired by election rhetoric, with swastika graffiti, assaults on students and teachers, property damage, fights, and threats of violence, among the most commonly reported (Southern Poverty Law Center, 2016). While some educators felt helpless and hopeless, others were fully aware that they simply lacked a solid understanding of what should be taught or learned.

The coronavirus pandemic, with its accompanying array of misinformation, malinformation, conspiracy theories, and propaganda, created new stresses with the shift to remote emergency instruction. In making the transition to online learning, teachers recognised that some of their students were experiencing trauma. It could take the form of arguing, refusing to work, communicating in verbally aggressive ways, or bickering with parents in the background during Zoom class meetings when students learned at home. The absence of students as they withdrew from schoolwork was another unhealthy coping pattern (Pickens, 2020). As election season approached, teachers voiced concerns that learning about the presidential election campaign could be challenging for both students and teachers. Some teachers made the decision to avoid the topic, because they experienced events both at home and at school that led them to believe that talk about the elections would simply be unproductive. Many felt they should not, or could not, share their political affiliations or feelings, due to the idea of maintaining political neutrality in the classroom (Hobbs, 2020).

As my sympathy for secondary educators who struggled with these challenges increased, I was fortunate to have an opportunity work with American social studies and English teachers with an interest in teaching propaganda as part of a consultancy with the United States Memorial Holocaust Museum beginning in 2007. In the next section, I describe how the experience of working with media literacy educators led to a deeper appreciation of the importance of teaching about propaganda in ways that acknowledge its variety of forms, including news and journalism, advertising and public relations, government and politics, activism, entertainment, and education. Eventually the fruits of this work functioned to reshape my understanding of the value of a truly global propaganda education, framed as both empowerment and protection, as a means to cultivate multi-perspectival thinking and respect for diverse interpretations.

IN THE EYE OF THE BEHOLDER: PROPAGANDA EDUCATION GOES GLOBAL

In 2007, the museum exhibition 'The State of Deception', curated by Stephen Luckert of the United States Holocaust Memorial Museum, examined propaganda in the Third Reich, demonstrating the variety of sophisticated techniques used by the Nazi Party to sway millions of Germans and other Europeans 'with appealing ideas of a utopian world along with frightful images of enemies it deemed threats to those dreams' (USHMM, 2007). The exhibit showed the use of propaganda as an essential part of the political process in Germany's young democracy. Then it illustrated how propaganda was used to implement radical programmes under the Third Reich dictatorship, with examples of propaganda in education, entertainment, news and journalism, and all aspects of cultural life. Filled with original artefacts, short videos, and compelling interactive multimedia exhibits, museum patrons also learned how propaganda was used to justify war and mass murder by dehumanising Jews and other people, and by representing territorial expansion as a form of self-defence (Luckert and Bachrach, 2009).

I was engaged to work as a consultant for the initiative to help the museum build connections between past and present in its education outreach initiative. Museum educators realised that, in helping people to recognise and understand propaganda, their efforts were a form of media literacy education (Wasserman, 2017). In collaboration with the education staff, we developed and implemented a variety of outreach programmes for teachers, students, journalists, and public policy leaders. As part of this work, there were many opportunities to talk about historical and contemporary propaganda with many people across the country. The deep negative connotations of the word 'propaganda' in relation to the Third Reich clearly seemed to limit people's thinking about forms of contemporary propaganda that people encounter every day. As we met with journalists as well as high school and college educators in Philadelphia, St Louis, Washington, DC, and Chicago, I gained a deeper appreciation of the many challenges of examining connections between historical and contemporary propaganda.

When the Brussels-based organisation Media and Learning asked me to offer a two-day masterclass on teaching propaganda in March 2016, I got the chance to engage with some of the leading media literacy experts in Europe. In discussing and debating various strategies for teaching about the new forms of media that people encounter as part of daily media use, we considered the importance of critically analysing memes, sponsored content, clickbait, pseudoscience, hoaxes, satire, partisan news, viral videos, and more. But the rise of public apathy, disengagement, and political polarisation were recognised as substantial challenges to the future of democracy in Europe and around the world. We wondered: could an approach to media literacy focused on propaganda education address concerns about terrorism, migration and immigration, Islamophobia, radicalisation, and populist and extremist forms of nationalism? What ideas, lesson plans, and digital education resources and tools could help support the development of learners' critical thinking skills in ways that promote tolerance, increase intellectual curiosity, and build appreciation of diverse perspectives and interpretations?

At the same time as our discussions were under way, concerns about so-called 'fake news' emerged after the inauguration of President Donald Trump, when White House officials presented 'alternative facts' about the size of the inauguration crowd. Thanks to support from public affairs professionals in the United States (US) State Department, I gave workshops and interacted with international journalists and educators in Brazil, Germany, and Italy. Working in collaboration with Professor Silke Grafe at the University of Wurzberg, and with support from the US State Department, we offered workshops to German high school teachers in four cities that focused on contemporary propaganda. We also used a virtual exchange programme to connect students from Germany and the United States to actively construct knowledge about contemporary propaganda. Students watched and annotated digital videos, and engaged in synchronous and asynchronous learning experiences, which helped them analyse and evaluate the emotional appeals of propaganda and the accuracy of the information contained in it. Through cross-cultural interaction, students gained sensitivity to the idea that people interpret media messages differently, using their prior knowledge and cultural context as a guide.

Researchers found that in evaluating the potential benefits and/or harms of contemporary propaganda, students use information outside the text to inform their judgement (Hobbs et al., 2018).

In more than 40 meetings with media literacy educators in Romania, Croatia, Belgium, Italy, Poland, Germany, Japan, Finland, and Brazil over four years, much was learned about how to teach today's students about propaganda, advertising, public relations, social media, and activism as forms of contemporary propaganda that shape public discourse and public life (Hobbs, 2020). With support from the Evens Foundation and a grant from the European Commission, a team of European and American educators took up the challenge of integrating the study of contemporary propaganda into the practice of media literacy education, targeting middle school and high school students and their teachers. The Mind Over Media educational website was adapted with support and collaboration from educators in France, Finland, Belgium, Romania, Croatia, and Poland. We expanded the educational platform (www.propaganda.mediaeducationlab.com) that uses crowdsourcing to provide a continually fresh gallery of new examples of global propaganda that are part of our global culture today. In interacting on the website, learners review and upload examples of propaganda and discuss the potential benefits and harms. In this work, we developed a unified and coherent approach to cultural adaptation of curriculum materials; mapped learning outcomes to national standards; developed teacher education training protocols to support the use of the Mind Over Media propaganda gallery; and documented our local outreach work on a blog.

Educators in each country do not all share the exact same values and priorities about how to teach about propaganda. Digital and media literacy competencies are needed not only to strengthen people's capacity to use information for personal and social empowerment, but also for addressing potential risks associated with mass media and digital media. Different countries address the themes of protection and empowerment at particular time periods based on ongoing national dialogues. For example, media literacy was conceptualised with the frame of empowerment in 2011 after the Arab Spring led to enthusiasm among educators and academics about the democratic potential of social media (Mihailidis, 2011). In Belgium, protectionist concerns about radicalisation increased dramatically in the months following the terrorist attacks in Paris and Brussels in 2015 and 2106, which led to competing opinions about the problem of radicalisation in Belgium (Figoureux and Van Gorp, 2020). In Germany, a protectionist frame was evident in the months leading up to the passage of the General Data Protection Regulation (GDPR) in 2018, the toughest privacy and security law in the world, which offers a firm stance on data privacy and security that shifts decisively away from a focus on vulnerable audiences towards a broader conceptualisation of information rights (Savirimuthu, 2020).

For these reasons, the Mind Over Media team recognised the value of adding country-specific lesson plans that enabled educators to explore topics of particular relevance to their national context. Comparing the lessons from Finland and Romania elucidates some important differences in priorities regarding how protection and empowerment are understood, with different ways of considering issues of social responsibility. In Finland, educators wanted students to understand that there are Finnish laws that limit some online marketing practices that take advantage of people's vulnerability to propaganda. In Finland, with WhatsApp, Facebook, and YouTube being used daily by 70 per cent of the population (Statista, 2020), many high school students are quite familiar with social media influencers, and some have strong positive opinions about them. There, a number of young YouTubers have created personal brands, and media literacy educators have introduced the subject of influence marketing to their students.

As part of the Mind Over Media project, Sonja Hernesniemi of the Finnish Society on Media Education developed a workshop for teens where students explore the commercial side of YouTube content production and influence marketing. In her workshop with teens, Sonja uses a Walk the Line warm-up activity where students indicate their opinions on several statements about influence marketers. Students who agree with the statement stand on an imaginary line in the classroom, with 'strongly agree' at one end of the line and 'strongly disagree' at the other end. They volunteer to share their opinions by agreeing or disagreeing to a variety of statements, including such examples as: 'Influencers on YouTube are more trustworthy than people who don't promote products on their channel' (Media Education Lab, 2016).

This activity gives students a playful way to share their ideas about a topic, while helping the teacher increase knowledge of students' existing attitudes and beliefs. In other activities, students learn key marketing and advertising terminology, and discuss the ethical and legal boundaries of advertising. Working in small groups, students analyse a marketing case in which the Council of Ethics in Advertising in Finland received a complaint about the lack of fiscal transparency of an online content provider. In a simulation activity, small groups learn more about influence marketing by playing one of three roles: a business or company that wants to promote products using influence marketing, a YouTube content provider, or a multichannel network organisation of YouTube content providers. During this activity, the groups research and evaluate the marketing process from the perspective of their assigned role. After gathering information online, they share their insights with the whole group (Media Education Lab, 2016). The study of influence marketing inevitably leads to deeper ethical questions about the practice of monetising relationships and selling authenticity, a topic with substantial relevance to propaganda.

The Romanian curriculum offers a special lesson on nationalist propaganda. Media literacy educator Nicoleta Fotiade, the founder of Mediawise Society, developed this activity after reading a quote from a historian who commented on Romanian culture: 'Due to tradition and custom, but also to insistent propaganda, the Romanians seem to be more attracted by symbols specific to national cohesion and authority than to those characteristic of democratic life' (Boia, 2001). Nationalist propaganda frames social problems by appealing to simple narratives and myths, which bypass reasonable deliberation and critical thinking. It often finds an 'other' to blame as justification for present or future actions.

In the lesson, students learn how propaganda techniques are used to stir both positive feelings towards one's country and negative emotions towards various social, cultural, or ethnic groups. Students reflect on the possible effects of nationalist propaganda upon socio-cultural groups, including exclusion, segregation, superiority, and even violence. In the activity, students first look at 6–8 different visual representations of liberty and unity from Romanian media across history, and discuss how people's needs and values can be given different meanings depending on their context, framing, and producer's political or ideological ideas. Students are asked to identify which examples might be labelled as nationalist propaganda. How could the propaganda have a negative impact on other social or cultural groups?

Then they view two different propaganda videos on the Mind Over Media Romania site. Each student uses a two-column notation system. In the left column, students write down all the emotions they believe were activated by each video. In the right column, students write down the specific groups of people or countries represented in each example. Students use lines to connect the names of the emotions in the left column with the associated people, groups of people, or countries on the right column. They discuss how positive emotions are often used in relation to one's country, such as pride, unity, and safety, while negative emotions are activated towards other groups. Which are the possible consequences of such persuasive strategies? What are the downsides of blaming a cultural, national, or mysterious other? (Media Education Lab, 2016).

The lesson helps students reflect on nationalist propaganda that activates strong emotions of national pride, doubled by emotions of hatred, fear, or anger towards others considered 'outside' the national group. When media messages tap into audience needs for belonging, safety, unity, hope, and historical justice, they can be compelling. Students learn to be wary of media messages that attack cultural groups, foreigners, or mysterious others. They see how simple explanations of national identity with familiar historical or cultural narratives can substitute for examining the complex realities of social problems.

Propaganda education must be deeply situational and contextual in order to help students understand the carefully constructed nature of the media environments they inhabit. Instructional practices should centre not on the transmission of information, but on the development of dialogue and discussion skills that support the practice of strong-sense critical thinking, where intellectual humility is encouraged by increasing people's awareness of the partial and incomplete nature of knowledge (Paul, 1981). To illustrate the alignment between media literacy education and propaganda education, Table 28.1 offers some key concepts of media literacy as they apply to seven lesson plans from the American version of the Mind Over Media curriculum for high school students.

As is evident in the table, media literacy education pedagogy requires active inquiry and critical thinking about the messages we receive and create. By expanding the concept of literacy to include all forms of media, media literacy education builds and reinforces skills for learners of all ages. Like print literacy, those skills necessitate integrated, interactive, and repeated practice. Media literacy education develops informed, reflective, and engaged participants essential for a democratic society, recognising that media are a part of culture and function as agents of socialisation. Finally, media literacy educators affirm that people use their individual skills, beliefs, and experiences to construct their own meanings from media messages (NAMLE, 2008).

Among the many insights that resulted from this four-year initiative, new questions about the pedagogy of propaganda education arise. In emphasising the value of learning to analyse both the potential benefits and harms of contemporary propaganda, researchers and teachers should continue to explore the value of the concept of *kairos* in helping learners understand the forms of propaganda they are likely to encounter on social media. *Kairos*, a concept that is often left out of rhetorical education at the high school level, conveys the idea that persuasive genres make adaptations and accommodations to convention even as they are 'uniquely timely, spontaneous, and radically particular' (Paul, 2014: 43). Conveying the importance of directing a persuasive message in the 'right way' at the 'right time', the concept of *kairos* has linked to the problem of moral relativism. Ancient Greeks believed that an exploration of *kairos* could help people determine whether expression was 'good or bad, honorable or dishonorable, based on its accordance with that particular moment' (Paul, 2014: 46). As a theory of both political speech and political action, the concept of *kairos* may offer some useful structure for exploring how context shapes both the construction of contemporary propaganda and its interpretation. Virtual encounters with the global 'other' may be transformative pedagogies to help students

Table 28.1 *Media literacy theory aligned with high school lessons in contemporary propaganda*

	Media literacy theory	Mind Over Media: lessons in contemporary propaganda
1	Media messages impact people's attitudes and behaviours.	What is Propaganda? Review different definitions of propaganda from multiples time periods and contexts. Identify some common themes and then create a personal definition that reflects the way you experience contemporary propaganda.
2	Production techniques are used to construct media messages.	Recognising Propaganda Techniques. Review diverse examples of contemporary propaganda to identify four persuasive techniques, including activating strong emotions, simplifying ideas, responding to audience needs, and attacking opponents.
3	The content of media messages contains values, ideology, and specific points of view.	To Share or Not to Share. Select 1 example of contemporary propaganda you would share to your social network, and 1 you would never share. Reflect on the potential benefits and harms that may result from the viral spread of propaganda.
4	Media messages are selective representations of reality.	Where Propaganda Can be Found. Find examples of contemporary propaganda in news and public relations, advertising and marketing, government and politics, activism, entertainment, and education.
5	People judge the credibility of media messages using features like authority and authenticity.	Analyse Propaganda with Critical Questions. Analyse examples of contemporary propaganda by asking critical questions about the message that identify its author, purpose, and point of view. Consider how different features of propaganda can make it seem credible.
6	Authors create media for different purposes, shaping content to appeal to particular target audiences.	Talking Back to Propaganda. Create a video response to an example of propaganda after analysing it. By creating a short video response, you are using the power of image, language, and sound to convey your own important ideas.
7	Both authors and audiences add value to media messages as part of an economic and political system.	Keep Learning. Explore additional information resources to learn more about propaganda. Deepening your own knowledge of contemporary propaganda is excellent preparation for work, life, and citizenship.
8	Media messages use stereotypes to express ideas and information.	Reflect on Propaganda. Consider the stereotypes that people have about the term 'propaganda' and reflect on how your beliefs and attitudes about propaganda have changed as a result of your learning experience.

Sources: Adapted from Hobbs (2020) and Media Education Lab (2016).

gain metacognitive awareness about the limitations of their own interpretations of contemporary propaganda, helping to build respect for diverse perspectives (Hobbs et al., 2018).

Faced with the substantial challenges of reconciling the values of 'do no harm' in teaching with the rise of fake news in a polarised 'post-truth' landscape, media literacy educators naturally place a high value on logical reasoning and critical analysis. They recognise the value of identifying filter bubbles and confirmation biases. However, they also intuitively understand the limits of logical appeals and 'true facts' because they understand that social influence is created through feelings as well as facts. Focusing on contemporary propaganda provides plentiful opportunities to bring *logos*, *pathos*, *ethos*, and *kairos* into the classroom in ways that do not exacerbate perceptions of educational indoctrination or deepen political rifts within communities. Because the study of contemporary global propaganda provides opportunities to reflect on how the meaning-making process is situational and contextual, educators can comfortably use empowerment and protection strategies to cultivate multi-perspectival thinking and activate intellectual curiosity.

REFERENCES

Ashley, S. (2019), *News literacy and democracy*, New York: Routledge.
Auerbach, J., and R. Castronovo (2013), 'Introduction: Thirteen propositions about propaganda', in J. Auerbach and R. Castronovo (eds), *The Oxford handbook of propaganda studies*, New York: Oxford University Press, pp. 1–16.
Bastos, M., and J. Farkas (2019), '"Donald Trump is my President!": The internet research agency propaganda machine', *Social Media + Society* 5(3): 1–13.
Benkler, Y., R. Faris, and H. Roberts (2018), *Network propaganda: Manipulation, disinformation and radicalization in American politics*, New York: Oxford University Press.
Bernays, E. (1928), *Propaganda*, New York: Ig Publishing.
Boia, L. (2001), *History and myth in Romanian consciousness*, Budapest: Central European University Press,
Bowyer, B., and Kahne, J. (2016), 'When young people get involved in online communities it leads them towards politics', Monkey Cage, *Washington Post*, 21.
Burkhardt, J.M. (2017), 'Combating fake news in the digital age', *Library Technology Reports*, 53(8): 4–37.
Cull, N. (2013), 'Roof for a house divided: How US propaganda evolved into public diplomacy', in J. Auerbach and R. Castronovo (eds), *The Oxford handbook of propaganda studies*, New York: Oxford University Press, pp. 131–146.
Cunningham, S. (2002), *The idea of propaganda: A reconstruction*, Westport, CT: Greenwood.
Dunn, A.H., B. Sondel, and H.C. Baggett (2019), '"I don't want to come off as pushing an agenda": How contexts shaped teachers' pedagogy in the days after the 2016 US presidential election', *American Educational Research Journal*, 56(2): 444–476.
Ellul, J. (1973), *Propaganda: The formation of men's attitudes* (trans. K. Kellen), New York: Vintage Books.
Fleming, D. (2019), 'Fear of persuasion in the English Language Arts', *College English*, 81(6): 508–541.
Figoureux. M. and B. Van Gorp (2020), 'The framing of radicalisation in the Belgian societal debate: a contagious threat or youthful naivety?', *Critical Studies on Terrorism*, 13(2): 237–257.
Gelders, D., and Ø. Ihlen (2010), 'Government communication about potential policies: Public relations, propaganda or both?', *Public Relations Review*, 36(1): 59–62.
Geller, R.C. (2020), 'Teacher political disclosure in contentious times: A "responsibility to speak up" or "fair and balanced"?', *Theory and Research in Social Education*, 48(2): 182–210.
Hall, H.L., M. Fromm, and A. Manfull (2015), *Student journalism and media literacy*, New York: Rosen Publishing Group.
Herman, Edward S., and Noam Chomsky (1988), *Manufacturing consent: The political economy of the mass media*, New York: Pantheon.
Hess, D.E. (2004), 'Controversies about controversial issues in democratic education', *PS: Political Science and Politics*, 37(2): 257–261.
Hess, D.E., and P. McAvoy (2015), *The political classroom: Evidence and ethics in democratic education*, New York: Routledge.
Hobbs, R. (2020), *Mind over media: Propaganda education in a digital age*, New York: W.W. Norton.
Hobbs, R., and S. McGee (2014), 'Teaching about propaganda: An examination of the historical roots of media literacy', *Journal of Media Literacy Education*, 6(2): 56–67.
Hobbs, R., C. Seyferth-Zapf, and S. Grafe (2018), 'Using virtual exchange to advance media literacy competencies through analysis of contemporary propaganda', *Journal of Media Literacy Education*, 10(2): 152–168.
Jack, C. (2017), 'What's propaganda got to do with it?', *Data and Society*, 5 January, available at https://points.datasociety.net/whats-propaganda-got-to-do-with-it-5b88d78c3282.
Jhally, S. (2018), Executive producer. *Digital disconnect: How capitalism is turning the Internet against democracy*. Motion picture. Northampton, MA: Media Education Foundation.
Kahne, J., E. Middaugh, and D. Allen (2015), 'Youth, new media, and the rise of participatory politics', in D. Allen and J.S. Light (eds), *From voice to influence*, Chicago, IL: University of Chicago Press, pp. 35–56.
Lippmann, W. (1922 [1997]), *Public opinion*, Boston, MA: Free Press.

Lithwick, D. (2019), 'The demoralizing reality of life under Trump', *Slate*, August 21, available at https://slate.com/news-and-politics/2019/08/demoralizing-reality-of-life-under-trump.html.
Luckert, S., and S. Bachrach (2009), *The state of deception: The power of Nazi propaganda*, New York: Norton.
Marantz, A. (2019), *Antisocial: Online extremists, techno-utopians, and the hijacking of the American conversation*, New York: Viking.
Mason, L.E., D. Krutka, and J. Stoddard (2018), 'Media literacy, democracy, and the challenge of fake news', *Journal of Media Literacy Education*, 10(2): 1–10.
Media Education Lab (2016), 'Mind over media: Analyzing contemporary propaganda', available at https://propaganda.mediaeducationlab.com.
Mihailidis, P. (2009), 'The first step is the hardest: Finding connections in media literacy education', *Journal of Media Literacy Education*, 1(1): 5.
Mihailidis, P. (2011), 'New civic voices and the emerging media literacy landscape', *Journal of Media Literacy Education*, 3(1): 3.
Mihailidis, P., and S. Viotty (2017), 'Spreadable spectacle in digital culture: Civic expression, fake news, and the role of media literacies in "post-fact" society', *American Behavioral Scientist*, 61(4): 441–454.
Miller, C.R. (1941), 'Some comments on propaganda analysis and the science of democracy', *Public Opinion Quarterly*, 5(4): 657–655.
Miller, C.R., and V. Edwards (1936), 'The intelligent teacher's guide through campaign propaganda', *Clearing House*, 11(2): 69–77.
Mina, A.X. (2019), *Memes to movements*, Boston, MA: Beacon.
NAMLE (2008), 'Core principles of media literacy education in the United States', National Association for Media Literacy Education, available at https://namle.net/wp-content/uploads/2020/09/Namle-Core-Principles-of-MLE-in-the-United-States.pdf.
Nicas, J. (2020), 'He passed as Trump, even with Trump', *New York Times*, 13 December, Y1, p. 5.
Paul, J. (2014), 'The use of Kairos in renaissance political philosophy', *Renaissance Quarterly*, 67(1): 43–78.
Paul, R. (1981), 'Teaching critical thinking in the "strong" sense: A focus on self-deception, world views, and a dialectical mode of analysis, *Informal Logic*, 4(2): 2–7.
Phillips, W., and R.M. Milner (2021), *You are here: A field guide for navigating polarized speech, conspiracy theories, and our polluted media landscape*, Cambridge, MA: MIT Press.
Pickens, I. (2020), 'Virtual signs of serious mental health problems: A teacher's guide to protecting students', *EdSurge*, 7 October, available at https://www.edsurge.com/news/2020-10-07-virtual-signs-of-serious-mental-health-problems-a-teacher-s-guide-to-protecting-students.
Postman, N. (1979), 'Propaganda', *ETC: A Review of General Semantics*, 36(2): 128–133.
Redmond, T (2015), 'Media literacy is common sense: Bridging Common Core Standards with the media experiences of digital learners', *Middle School Journal*, 46(3): 10–17.
RobbGrieco, M. (2018), *Making media literacy in America*, Lanham, MD: Rowman & Littlefield.
Russonello, G. (2021), 'An ugly day in America', *New York Times*, 7 January, available at https://www.nytimes.com/2021/01/07/us/politics/protests-trump.html.
Savirimuthu, J. (2020), 'Datafication as parenthesis: Reconceptualising the best interests of the child principle in data protection law', *International Review of Law, Computers and Technology*, 34(3): 310–341.
Selfe, R.J., and C.L. Selfe (2008), '"Convince me!" Valuing multimodal literacies and composing public service announcements', *Theory into Practice*, 47(2): 83–92.
Smith, B.L., and H.D. Lasswell (1945), *Propaganda, communication and public opinion*, Princeton, NJ: Princeton University Press.
Southern Poverty Law Center (2016), 'The Trump effect. Teaching tolerance', available at https://www.tolerance.org/magazine/publications/after-election-day-the-trump-effect.
Statista (2020), 'Statistics about technology and telecommunications in Finland', available at https://www.statista.com/map/europe/finland/technology-telecommunications.
Thoman, E., and T. Jolls (2004), 'Media literacy – A national priority for a changing world', *American Behavioral Scientist*, 48(1): 18–29.
United States Holocaust Memorial Museum (USHMM) (2007), 'Propaganda: The state of deception', available at https://www.ushmm.org/information/exhibitions/traveling-exhibitions/state-of-deception.

US District Court (2018), *United States of America versus internet research agency LLC*, Case 1:18-cr-00032-DLFFiled C.F.R., 16 February, Washington, DC: United States District Court for the District of Columbia, pp. 1–37.
Ward-Barnes, A. (2010), 'Media literacy in the United States: A close look at Texas', MA Thesis, 16 April, Georgia State University, available at https://scholarworks.gsu.edu/communication_theses/58.
Wasserman, J. (2017), Personal communication with the author, 10 June.
Woolley, S.C., and P.N. Howard (eds) (2018), *Computational propaganda: Political parties, politicians, and political manipulation on social media*, New York: Oxford University Press.

Index

9/11 terrorist attacks 17
24-hour news channel 365

Aaj Tak 365
Aam Aadmi Party 355
Abbott, D. 229, 233
absolutist religious beliefs
 taxonomy of 276
Abudurusuli, M 260, 267
acceptance, latitude of 281
Acosta, J. 58
Adnani, A.M. Al- 253
Advani, L.K. 351
advertising 352
 Russian ads during the 2016 US presidential election campaign 95
Africa 382
Africa Bureau 185
African American issues 81
Ahmed, S. 198
Al Qaeda 16, 17
Albu, A. 227
Alibaba 122
Allcott, H. 32, 33, 36
Allen, R. 234
alternative facts 51, 54, 60, 63
Alternative für Deutschland (AfD) 337
Amandla Festival 193
America Online 112
American International Exhibition, Moscow 14
Anaya Cortés, R. 339, 338, 342
anime 152
Anna Dravida Munnetra Kazhagam (AIDMK) 365
Anti-Apartheid Movement (AAM) 188, 190, 191
Anti-Apartheid News 188
anti-Islamic rhetoric and sentiment 367
Arab Spring 335

Ardern, J. 249
Arendt, H. 63, 207
Ashdown, P. 247, 249
Ashmanov, I. 68, 72
Association of Southeast Asian Nations (ASEAN) 375, 376, 380
Astor, D. 185
AT&T 112
atomic weapons 245
attention economy 2, 33
Attlee, C. 226, 227
Austin, J.L. 303
Australia 249
availability cascades 34
Ayotzinapa 43 missing students 336
Ayurveda 362

Baby V.O.X. Re.V 379
Bageqi Village 262
Baghdadi, A.B. Al- 253
Bakshy, E. 83
Baldwin, T. 53, 54
bandwagoning 56, 58–59
Banks, A. 47, 393
Bannon, S.K. 32, 36
Banu Quraidhah tribe 251
'barbarians' 289
Barcelona 4
Barnard, C. 186
Begin, M. 245
Beijing
 Cultural Palace of the Minoritiies 290
 Ethnic Cultures Park 293
 Forbidden City 293
Belgium 414
Beliepedia 279, 282
Belt and Road Initiative (BRI) 19, 98, 102, 103, 106
Benkler, Y. 29
Berger, L. 232
Berger, T. 8

421

Berk, M. 258
Bernays, E.L. 23, 213
Berry, M. 163
Bevin, E. 225, 226, 227
Bharatiya Janata Party (BJP) 347, 348, 349, 350, 351, 353, 354, 355, 356
  IT Cell 367
  majoritarian 362
  majoritarianism 360, 362, 364
big data
  Cambridge Analytica 1, 137
big tent propaganda 7
'Billy Bush affair' 60–61
Bin Laden, O. 245, 250, 252
Blumler, J. 6
Blunt, A. 225
BNP 237
Boesak, A. 190
Boko Haram 270, 271, 274, 277, 278, 279
Bolton, J. 44
Border Force patrols 205
Bormann, E.G. 80, 84, 85
bots 59
Boyd-Barrett, O. 17
Breivik, A. 252
Brexit
  referendum campaign 1
BRICS 19
Buddhism 361
Building Resilience against Violent Extremism Initiative 266
bureaucratic propaganda 224, 236
Bush, G.W. 247
Bussmann, H. 302
Butler, D. 229

Cadwalladr, C. 47
Calderón, F. 340
Cambridge Analytica 1, 137
Cameron, D. 204
Campaign for Nuclear Disarmament 185
Campaign Legal Center 44
Canary 234
Candidatura d'Unitat Popular (Popular Unity Candidacy) 312
Caplan, R. 36

cardstacking 56, 57, 58, 61, 62
Caribbean immigrant nurses 214, 220
Carow, H. 159, 160, 161, 164
Carter, J. 168
cartoons 117
Cathay Pacific 148
celebrating Black individuals and culture 87, 89
censorship
  China
    social media 249
  terrorist propaganda 249
Centennial Goals 106, 108
Center for Media Literacy 410
Central China Television (CCTV) News 116
Central Leading Group for Cyber Security and Informatization (CLGCSI) 131
Chakrabarti, S. 230
Chancellor, J. 43, 46
Chan, J. 148
Chandra, S. 353
Channel 4 47
  News FactCheck service 392
charity 169, 177
Chen, D. 107
Cherry, C. 15
Chiang, H. 163
Chiang, Kai-shek 107
China 4, 18, 24, 178, 249, 306, 361
  2014 Guiding Opinion 132
  2014 Interim Regulations 133
  Account Names Regulations 134
  blamed by Trump for Covid-19 62
  CCP Central Leading Group for Cyber Security and Informatization (CLGCSI) 133
  censorship 127, 128, 129, 131, 134, 135, 137, 138, 247, 249
  Central Leading Group for Comprehensively Deepening Reform (CLGCDR) 130
  Central National Security Commission (CNSC) 130
  Cultural Revolution 104
  False News Notice 134
  Interrogation Regulations 134

media convergence 127
politicisation of the social media market 137
queer film *Lan Yu* 165
scientific development 99
Socialist Education Movement 265
State Internet Information Office (SIIO) 133
China and representation of ethnic minorities
  photographs in ethnic costume 285
China Dream 98, 101, 103, 106, 108
Chomsky, N. 407
Christianity 361
Churchill, W.S. 245
Citizen, The 189
Civil Human Rights Front 146
'clap for carers' 219
climate change 61
Clinton, B. 61
Clinton, H. 44, 46, 53, 55, 58, 60, 61, 82
CLMV countries 383
Cobb, R.W. 144
cognitive biases 58
Cohen, S. 177
Cold War 11
Coleman, S. 35
collective action 275, 276, 278, 279, 282
Collins, J. 185, 193
'colour revolution' 152
Come Back, Africa 185, 195
Coming Out 159
commercial Internet companies 122
Commission for Racial Equality (CRE) 215
community gatherings 311
computational propaganda 120
conglomeration 113, 116, 123
Congregation for Propagating the Faith 3, 11, 360
Congress Party 347, 348, 353, 355
Connelly, M. 5
Conrad, J. 246
Convention and Protocol Relating to the Status of Refugees 197, 202
convocativity 303, 304, 307, 310, 312
Corbyn, J. 227, 228

antisemitism in the Labour Party under 224
corruption 339, 342, 355
cosplay 293
Couldry, N. 248
counter-counternarratives 253
counternarratives 253, 254
Covid-19 pandemic 4, 62, 120, 212, 213, 219, 412
creative industries 382, 385
credible religious voices 277, 278
crisis 248
critical international relations theory 9
critical viewing skills education 410
cruise ships 306
Cry the Beloved Country 191
Cry Freedom 191
cryptic cues 84, 85
Cull, N. 408
cultural imperialism 15
Cultural Palace of the Minorities, Beijing 290, 291
culture
  anti-Apartheid struggle 185, 189
  memes and the intersection of politics and 336
  participatory 113, 118, 119, 320
  Russian ads celebrating Black individuals 87, 89
Cunningham, S. 4
Curry, A. 63
Curtice, J. 397
cyber-security 131

Dabiq 248, 252
Daily Express 397
Dalton, H. 225, 226
Dammers, J. 190
data exploitation 43
data harvesting 44
Davies, H. 47
DDB 188
Defiance Campaign 184
definitions of propaganda 3, 408, 417
DeKlerk, F.W. 192
Delmer, S. 225

democracy 360, 364, 365, 369, 370, 407, 408, 413
Deng, L. 105
Deng, X. 105, 113
Denham, E. 44, 45
Denisova, A. 336
Dennis, D. 161, 162
Dent Coad, E. 236
Denton, K.L. 289, 290
Denzau, A. 32, 33, 34
DePaulo, B. 391
Derakshan, H. 28, 405
deregulation 112
deterrence of Black voters 46
dialogic communication 8, 10
Diba 148
digital religious space 277, 279, 280
Dikötter, F. 289
Ding, G. 99
Dipple-Johnstone, J. 45
Dirlik, A. 157
discrimination 86, 87, 88, 92, 94
disinformation 28, 29, 30, 31, 32, 33, 36
  echo chambers 80, 81, 82, 83, 95
dissidents 101, 108
Donetsk 72, 75
Donetsk People's Republic (DPR) 75
Doordarshan 352, 364, 367, 368
Douyin (known as TikTok outside China) 116, 118, 121, 123
Dravida Munnetra Kazhagam (DMK) 354, 365
Du Bois, W.E.B. 183
Duggan, L. 158
Dunn, A.H. 411

Eastern Europe 192, 193
echo chambers 55
economic development
  China 290, 297
Edney, K. 288
education 378, 383
  propaganda education 5
EdVenture Partners (EVP) 270
Eenadu TV 365
ego 171, 172, 173, 174, 175, 180

Eikenberry, A. 175
Elder, C.D. 144
election campaigns
  Mexican presidential election 315
  UK general election 2019 237
  US presidential campaign 2008 302
  US presidential campaigns 2016
    Russian ads 81
  US presidential election 2008 301
  US presidential election 2016 29, 30, 390, 392
elections
  US presidential election 2016 32
elites 7, 19, 100
Ellul, J. 10, 52
'*El Turisme Mata Els Barris*' (Tourism Is Killing the Neighbourhoods)' 305, 307, 309, 310, 312
Emerson, K. 193
empowerment 406, 412, 414, 417
Endavant-Organitzaci d'Alliberament Nacional (Forward-Socialist Organisation of National Liberation) 308, 309
'end of history' 16
Eng, D. 163
Engels, F. 175
Equality and Human Rights Commission (EHRC) 230, 232, 236
eroticisation of ethnic minorities 295
Escobar A. 176
ethnic costume, tourists' photographs in 285, 288
Ethnic Cultures Park 294
Ethnic Groups Unite as a Family 260
European Union (EU) 197, 202, 203, 204, 207, 244, 249
  Brexit referendum 1
  definition of terrorist propaganda 244
  nurses in the UK 211, 216, 218
existential threat rhetoric 309

Facebook 249, 253, 270, 278, 283
  Cambridge Analytica scandal 42, 45
  Mexico 335, 341, 342, 344
fact-checking 404

Factcheck.org 392
fake news 405, 407, 413, 417
   Mexico 343
fandom girls 148
Fang, K. 118, 119, 258
fantasy themes 81, 84, 85, 86
Farage, N. 216, 217
Faris, R. 29
fascism 161
fatal shootings of young black males 87, 89, 94
Faulds, A. 227
Feel Korea 380, 381
'Fem Plaça' (Lets Make the Square)' 305, 307, 308, 312
Feng, W. 260
Ferrara, E. 59
Field, F. 232
Filipino nurses and healthcare workers 219
filter bubbles 95
First, R. 190
Fisher, M. 159
Fiskesjö, M. 289
Flaxman, S. 83
Fleming, D. 411
Fletcher, R. 35
football tournament 279, 280
Foot, M. 226
Forbidden City, Beijing 293
'Formby' report 236
Fotiade, N. 415
Foucault, M. 287
Fox News 53
Fox, V. 340
fractured globalisation 11
Freedland, J. 232, 234
French Revolution 246
Freud, S. 172, 181
friendly nations 102
Fromm, E. 171
Fugard, A. 189
Fujian Triad 151
Fukuyama, F. 16

Gadahn, A. 250
Gaitskell, H. 214
Galloway, G. 227
Gambhir, G. 354
Gandhi, I. 349
Gandhi, M.K. 348, 349, 350
Gandhi, R. 354, 355
Garrett, R.K. 83
GDR Complex, The 157
Geller, R.C. 411
General Data Protection Regulation (GDPR) 414
Geng, S. 145
genocide 92
Gentzkow, M. 30, 32, 33, 36, 83
Geoghegan, P. 53
Gerasimova, T. 73, 74
German Democratic Republic (GDR) 156, 157, 159, 160, 161, 162, 164
Germany 245, 246, 249, 250
   Nazism 3, 52, 156, 161
   World War II bombing of cities in 245
Glancy, J. 232
Glassner, M. 55
glittering generalities 56–58
global warming 61
globalisation 11, 18
   fractured 11
Gluck, M. 188
'Go Home' vans 217
Golwalkar, M.S. 363
Gordimer, N. 189
Goswami, A. 353, 366
Gove, M. 396, 401
Gramsci, A. 274
Grandi, F. 197
'Grand Propaganda' 130
Grassenger, H. 47
Greenstein, T. 230
Gregory, D. 193
Grierson, J. 216, 217
group consciousness 95
Guha, R. 347

Hall, J. 406
Hallyu (Korean Wave) 389
Hanle, D.J. 246
Happer, C. 51, 52

Harrell, S. 289, 290, 295
#AMLOFest 341
#IAmABeliever (CVE) campaign 270
Hassassian, M. 232
Hattenstone, S. 232
hegemony 274
Heidegger, M. 273
Heinzen, K. 250, 251, 252
Heiskanen, B. 336, 338
Hellman, J. 178
Henkel, I. 399
Herman, E.S. 407
Hernesniemi, S. 415
heroes, religious 272, 281
Herrera, O.T. 178
Hindu nationalism 347, 351, 354, 356, 361
Hindu Vedas 7
Hirsh, D. 228
history
  'end of history' 16
Hitler, A. 228
Ho Kwan-yiu, J. 146
Hodge, M. 231
Hoffer, E. 275
homonationalism 156
Hong Kong
  police 146, 147, 148, 149, 150, 151, 152, 153
  Umbrella Revolution 301, 306
Hopkins, R. 9, 13
Houston, W. 193
Hovland, C. 281
Howard, P.N. 333, 335, 338
'How Leaders are Made' cartoon video 117
Hu, J. 99, 100, 101, 103, 106, 107, 109, 110
Hu, Q. 99
Hu, Y. 259
Huddleston, T. 185, 193

I Am a Pomegranate Seed campaign 264
I-Believe football tournament 279, 280
identity 278
ideological convergence 21
ideological faiths 20
ideology 7, 8, 9, 16, 17
ideotainment 118

illocution 303, 308
immigration 400
  Brexit referendum campaigns 393, 398
Impression Sanjie Liu 295
incipient hegemon's public diplomacy plexus (IHPDP) 19
India
  Digital India project 369
  Ministry of External Affairs (MEA) 360, 363, 369
  National Digital Communications Policy 368
India Boundless – A Place in the Heart of the World 360
India Foundation 361
Indian National Congress (INC) 348
Industrial Revolution 169, 176
Infokrieg 337
information war
  Ukraine 67
Inkatha 190
Inspire 248, 252
Institute of Propaganda Analysis (IPA) 51, 55, 56
Institutional Revolutionary Party (PRI) 315, 317, 333, 334, 342
intention 4, 5, 10
international regimes 9
international relations theory 9, 18
  levels of analysis 12, 13
international system 9, 12, 13, 18
Internet
  and democracy 407
  fake news 32
  participatory propaganda 258
Internet sovereignty 68
investigative journalism 122
Ipi Tombi 189
Iraq war of 2003 54, 391, 392
Irish immigrants 215
Islam 11, 17, 361, 367
  anti-Islam rhetoric and sentiment 367
Islamic State (IS or ISIS) 1, 3, 243, 253, 254
Islamic State West Africa (ISWA) 271
Israel 156, 245, 247

Jaishankar, S. 361
Jaya TV 365
Jenkins, C. 91
Jenkins, H. 111, 113, 320
Jenkins, M. 169
Jewish Board of Deputies 227, 231, 234, 237
Jewish Labour Movement (JLM) 229, 233
Jewish Leadership Council 231, 234
Jewish Voice for Labour (JVL) 229
jihadi lifestyle magazines 252
Jihad Reflections 252
Johnson, B. 217, 218, 393
Jones, J. 45
Jones, O. 231, 233
Jones, R. 205, 207
Jordan, H. 178
Jordan, P. 192
journalism
  investigative, in China 122
  Mexico 315, 318
Jowett, G.S. 100, 235
Juntos Haremos Historia 315, 322

K-Culture Road website 374
K-pop bands 373, 379
Kairali TV 365
Kaiser, B. 44, 45, 47
Kakutani, M. 54
Kang, Y. 107
Kautsky, J. 22
Kazanzhy, Z. 74
Kejriwal, A. 355
Kellner, P. 235
Kenya 266
khadi 348
Khamla, X. 381
Khan, S. 248, 252
Khruschev, N. 14
Kincaid, D.L. 276
King, D. 191
Kakutani, M. 54
Kogan, A. 43, 46, 47
Kogan, D. 230
Korea Foundation 379, 381
Korean cultural diplomacy 374
Korean Foundation for International Cultural Exchange (KOFICE) 374, 379, 381
Kosinski, M. 43
Kristof, N. 52, 54, 55, 63
Krogerus, M. 47
Kunming–Vientiene high-speed rail connection 383
Kurtz, H. 52, 53
Kwan, S. 159, 162

Labour Against the Witch-Hunt 230
Labour Herald 227, 228
Labour Party
  New Labour 217
Lakoff, G. 69
Lam, C. 150, 153
Lan Yu 165
Lang, G.E. 144
Lang, K. 144
Lansman, J. 229
Laos 373
Laos Securities Exchange 378
Laski, H. 227
Lasswell, H. 7, 8, 12, 24, 80, 244
Last Grave at Dimbaza 188
latitude of acceptance 281
latitude of rejection 281
Lazer, D.M.J. 29, 31, 37
leadership and compassion 168
Leave campaigns (Brexit) 390
  battle bus claims 395
legacy action 277, 278, 279
Lerner, D. 12
Lethal Weapon 2, 191
'Let's Make the Square' (*Fem Plaça*) 305, 307, 312
Lewis, S. 51
Lia, B. 248
Liang, Q. 107
Libi, A.Y. Al- 250, 254
Lim, Z.W. 29, 31
Lincoln, A. 20
Ling, R. 29, 31
links to external websites/social media profiles 87, 90, 94
Linowitz, S. 179
Liu, Q. 120, 132

Liu, X. 109
Liu, Y. 99
Live Aid concerts 177
Livingstone, K. 227, 228, 229, 230, 235
Lobachevo 77, 78
locution 303
López Obrador, A.M. (AMLO) 315, 321, 322, 324, 325, 326, 327, 328, 333, 334, 339, 340, 341, 342
loss aversion 33
Luckmann, P. 8
Ludendorff, E. 3
Ludwig, J. 22
Luhansk 70, 72, 76, 77
Luthuli, A. 186

M López Obrador, A.M. (AMLO)
memes 334
Machiavelli, N. 20
mainstream news media
  US and the Trump presidential election campaign 54–55, 55
Make America Great Again 53, 56
Make America Number 1 (MAN1) PAC 44
Makeba, M. 185
Malan, D.F. 184
Malaysia 376, 377, 382
malinformation 405, 407, 412
Malone, B. 203, 209
Mandela, N. 186, 188, 190, 191, 192, 193, 194, 195
Mandela, W. 190, 192
Mann, J. 228, 234
Mann Ki Baat ('Inner Thoughts') 367
Mao, Z.
  mass propaganda campaigns 259, 265
March of Silence 340
marketisation 115, 144, 154
Marley, B. 193
Martin, R. 199
Martin, T. 87, 89, 92
Marxism 101
Mass Line 266
master analogues 84
May, T. 206, 216, 217
McCluskey, L. 229

McDonnell, J. 234
McNair, B. 248
McVeigh, T. 251
Meade, J.A. 315, 322, 338, 339, 342
Media and Learning 413
Meir, G. 226
meme wars 337
Mendick, H. 234
Mendoza, K.-A. 234
Mercer, R. 43, 44, 46
Merlo, C. 341
Mexico
  immigration to the US from 60
  presidential election 2018 315
MGR 354
middle class 100, 101, 108
migration
  Brexit referendum campaigns 399, 400
Mikardo, I. 227
Millicom Lao Co. Ltd (known as Tigo) 379
Milner, R.M. 335, 336, 337, 345, 405
Mina, A.X. 334, 336, 337
minimisation strategy 233, 235
Ministry of External Affairs (MEA) 369
Mirabella, R. 175
misinformation 28
modern literacy education 5
Modi, N. 349, 351, 352, 353, 354, 355, 356, 359, 360, 361, 362, 363, 364, 366, 367, 368, 369, 370
  majoritarianism 359, 364, 369
  media management 353
  social media 354, 367
Moeketsi, S. 190
Moffat, Z. 336
Moffitt, B. 29
Moon, J-i. 375, 377, 380
Moonves, L. 55
Moore, M. 4, 5, 337, 390, 396, 397, 400, 401
Moore, S. 170
moral relativism 416
Morning Star 234
Morton, J. 160
Motion Picture Association 10
Mubi, Nigeria 270, 277, 278, 279
Mueller, R. 42

Muldergate Scandal 189
Multinational Joint Task Force (MJTF) 271
Munich Olympics massacre 247
Murray, A. 229
Murtfeld, R. 45
muscular nationalism 362, 366
music 277, 278
Mutz, D.C. 83
Myanmar 2, 4

Nalanda, Buddhist university 361
name-calling 56, 59–61, 197, 199
National Front 215, 217
National Health Service (NHS)
  Code of Practice on ethical recruitment 216
  Interim People Plan 219
  NHS70 Windrush Awards 220
nationalism
  China 107, 118, 143
  India
    Hindu nationalism 347, 354, 356, 361
    muscular 362
    nationalism 361
national key labs 121
National University of Laos 378, 379
nation branding 186
Nazi Party 3, 52, 156, 161
neoliberalism
  nature of 174
New Labour 217
New Zealand 4
  mosque shootings 249
Newman, N. 35, 335
News18 (Network 18) 353, 366
news from within the Black community 87, 94
newspapers
  UK tabloids 390, 397, 399, 401
Nimmo, B. 341
Nix, A.A. 42, 43, 44, 46
Nixon, R. 14, 57
Non-Aligned Movement 14
North, D. 32, 33, 34
Northern Ireland 4
Nowell-Smith, P. 171
Nye, J. 359, 374, 378, 380, 384

Nzima, S. 188

Obama, B. 87, 301
Obama, M. 44
O'Donnell, V. 100, 235
Okasha, S. 172
Onuf, N. 7
OpIndia.com 367
opponent countries 102
Orwell, G. 51
O'Shaughnessy, N. 198, 224
othering 200, 303
outrage 397
Overseas Friends of the BJP 364
Oxford University Labour Club 225

padayatra (long-distance walk) 350
Pakistan 102
Palestine 226
'Palestine Live' Facebook group 230
Palestine Return Centre conference 232
Palmieri, J. 55
Pan Africanist Congress (PAC) 185
Pannel, N. 214
Panorama
  'whistleblowers' 232
Paran 379
Park Geun-hye 377
Parscale, B. 45
participation persuasion 2.0 119
participatory culture 113, 119
participatory persuasion 2.0 258
participatory propaganda
  counterterrorism narratives in China 258
  tourist photography in China 293
Partido Accion Nacional (PAN) 333
Partido Revolucionario Institucional (PRI) 315, 317, 334
Paton, A. 185
patriotism 147
Paul, R. 416
Paz, O. 333
Peña Nieto, E. 334

People's Daily
  Hong Kong anti-extradition bill

movement 144
  media convergance 120
People's Liberation Army (PLA) interactive program 118
Peres, S. 245
perlocution 303
personal identities, emphasising 277
personalisation
  personification rhetoric 309
persuasion
  participatory 258
Pfeffer, A. 235
Phelandaba/End of the Dialogue 188
Phillips, W. 405
Pieterson, H. 188
pink washing 156
Pisacane, C. 243
plainfolks device 61
Plummer, K. 159
police
  Hong Kong 147
Political Warfare Executive (PWE) 225
polluted information 405
Pololikashvili, Z. 310
Pomeranstev, P. 337
Pool, I. de S. 111
populism 29
  angry 400
Por México al Frente 315
poses, in tourist photographs 293
positive propaganda 127
postcolonial theory 15
post-truths (alternative truths) 54
poverty 383
Powell, E. 214
power 287
  sharp 10, 360
  soft 360
pragmatic nations 102
privately owned social media platforms 122
'Project Fear' 393
Pronay, N. 6
propaganda education 5
propaganda society 169
prosumers 113
protection 406

psychosocial strain 94
public opinion
  China 129
public policy proposals 323
public-private partnership projects 384
Puchala, D. 9
Putin, V. 68

Quad (Quadrilateral Security Dialogue) 19
queer films
  Coming Out 159
  Lan Yu 159
Quinn, S. 111

Raddon, M. 175
Rahman, M. 212
Ramsay, G. 390
Rashtriya Swayamsevak Sangh (RSS) 350
Ravali Jagan 354
Reagan, R. 168
Reddy, E.S. 187
Reddy, J.M. 354
Redfield, R. 62
Reich, W. 244
rejection, latitude of 281
rejuvenation 98
Reliance Industries 353
religious absolutism 272
religious Heroes 273, 274
Remain campaign 392, 394, 395, 396, 400, 401, 402
renaissance 98, 103, 109
Rendón, J.J. 340
renovated felicity conditions 305, 312
rented ethnic costumes, photographs in 285
Repnikova, M. 117, 118, 119, 125, 258, 268
Republic of Korea-Mekong Vision 377, 388
Republic TV 366, 369
Republic-TV 353
Revolution of Dignity 70
Reza, E.O. 340
rhetorical vision 81, 84, 85, 86, 87, 94, 95
rhetorical visions
  Russian ads dealing with African American issues 86
Roberts, H. 29, 38
Robespierre, M. 245, 246

Rodríguez Calderón, J.H. 315, 322, 325, 326, 338, 342
Rogers, E. 276, 284
Röllig, M. 157
Romania 414, 415
Rome Conference 246
Royall Report 230
Ruey Yih-fu 289
Runciman, D. 52, 54, 58, 59, 65
Russell, B. 185
Russia 156
Russian Spring 72
Ryan, M. 62

Said, E. 287
Salafist-Takfirism 271
Samajwadi Party 354
Sanders, B. 53
'sanskriti evam sabhyata' (culture and civilisation) 361
satellite TV channels 352
satire 29, 31, 36, 37, 191
Savarkar, V.D. 363
Sayasone, C. 377
Schieffer, B. 63
Schnellenbach, J. 33
Schopenhauer, A. 168
Schudson, M. 391
Schwartz, M. 47
scientific development 99
scientific expert opinion 62
SCL Elections Ltd (SCL-E) 43
Scott, M. 185
Scottish independence referendum 395
Secker, G. 229
Second World War 245
self-photographs in Chinese ethnic costume 285
self-photography 285, 287, 288, 297
sensuality 294
seven propaganda devices 51–56
Shah, N. 228
Shapiro, J.M. 83
shared digital religious space 277
shared meanings 285, 297
shared mental models 32

Sharpe, T. 191
Sharpeville massacre 186
sharp power 4, 10, 80
Shekau, A. 273
Sherif, M. 281
Shindler, C. 235
Sichuan Province earthquake 118
Sidhu, N.S. 349
Sieg, K. 161
'Silent Majority' 57
Silverman, C. 28
Simon, B. 189
Simon, P. 193
Simpson, G. 205
Sincere Care 261
Sinha, P. 347
Sjjad, T. 203
SK E&C 377
Skwawkbox blog 234
social identity theory (SIT) 280
social injustices 175
social judgement theory (SJT) 281
social media 1, 2, 4, 20, 51, 315
  and fake news 36
  bandwagoning 58
  India 351
  politics and deliberation 315
  terrorist propaganda 243
social newsnews 34
Socialist Education Movement 265
sociological propaganda 8, 10, 21, 22, 24
soft power 10, 11, 12, 18, 19, 22, 24, 26, 374
Solá 333, 334, 340, 344
Somsamone, V. 378
Souphanouvong University 378
South Africa
  Suppression of Communism Act 1950 184
Southern Poverty Law Center 412
South Korea
  interests and propaganda in Laos 373
  New Southern Policy (NSP) 375
Soviet Union
  Cold War 12, 14, 15, 18, 22, 67
Sowaidi, B. Al- 301
'speak up and brandish the swords' 262
Special Economic Zones 105

Special Operations Executive (SOE) 225
'spectacle' 168, 170
   spreadable 408
Spitting Image 191
sporting boycott 187
Sproule, M.J. 55
Starmer, K. 236
statement writing 261
'State of Deception, The' 412
state-supported propaganda 408
state terrorism 244
Statue of Liberty 93
Stillwell, D. 43
Strategic Communications Laboratories
      (SCL) 42
suicide 252
Sullivan, M. 28
Sun, the 397
Sun TV 365
Sun Yatsen 107
Sunstein, C. 81
Suri, A.M. Al- 248, 256
Sussman, G. 169
Swarajamag.com 367
Swire, B. 391
Sykes, C. 54
symbolic cues 85, 86, 94, 95
symbolic fantasies 80
Syrian refugee crisis 205

tabloid press 390, 393, 396
Tajfel, H. 280
'Take Back Control' 395
Tambo, O. 188, 192, 193, 195
Tandoc, E.C. 29
target audience analysis (TAA) 41
tax havens 179
Taylor, P.M. 6, 347
Tchenguiz, V. 42
technocrats 99
television
   Laos 379
television spots
   Mexico 2018 presidential election 319
Tencent 121
terrorism 3
   ANC branded as terrorists 187
   counterterrorism narratives in China 259
   globalisation, propaganda and 16
   Islamist terrorirst attacks in Barcelona 306
testimonials 56
Texas Essential Knowledge and Skills
      (TEKS) 410
Thailand 2
Thatcher, M.H. 177, 190, 215, 246, 247, 255
them/us dichotomy 310
Think Again, Turn Away initiative 266
Third Reich 412, 413
Thomas, R.J. 392
Thomas-Symonds, N. 219
Thornberry, E. 233
Tian'anmen Square incident 162, 163
Tibetan riots 2008 296
Tigo (Millicom Lao Co. Ltd) 379
Time magazine 1
Times of India, The 368
Time Warner 112
TMC 355
Todos por México 315
Topple, S. 234
tourism
   Korean tourism to Laos 378
'Tourism Is Killing the Neighbourhoods' (*El
      Turisme Mata Els Barris*) 305, 307
tourismphobia 308, 311, 312
'Tourist You Are the Terrorist' 305, 309, 310,
      312
traditional media 4
traditionality, signifiers of 292
transfer 56
Triesman, D. 232
trolling 80
Trump, D. 1, 51, 390
   political propaganda in the age of 51–56
   presidential campaign 28
   use of propaganda techniques 56, 62
trust 30, 56
truthiness 391
Tsai Ing-wen 148
Tucker, J.A. 81
Tufekci, Z. 55
Turisme de Barcelona 308, 312, 314

Tutu, D. 190
Twitter 278, 315
  India 351
  Mexican presidential election 2018 315, 321, 326, 329, 330, 332
  Trump 52, 405

UK Independence Party (UKIP) 217
  MEPs 400
Ukraine 67, 70, 72, 73, 76, 77, 78
uMkhonto we Sizwe (MK) 186
underblocking 37
UNESCO New World Information and Communication Order 15, 16
unifying propaganda 408
unintended influence 7
United Democratic Front 190
United Kindom (UK)
  and Apartheid 183
United Kingdom (UK) 1
  British Nationalities Act 1948 214
  Christmas Day arrivals 204
  Commonwealth Immigrants Act 1962 214
  Department of Health (DoH) 215
  General Election 2019 212
  Immigrant Healthcare Surcharge for non-EU migrants 211
  Immigration Bill 2020 219
  Information Commissioners Office (ICO) 41
  Insolvency Service 42
  labelling and refugees 201
  Labour Party antisemitism and political welfare 230
  migrant nurses in the NHS 211
  Nurses' Act 1949 213
  Race Relations Amendment Act 2000 215
  trust in news 32
United Nations High Commissioner for Refugees (UNHCR) 197
United Nations (UN) 13, 310
  struggle against Apartheid 183, 192, 193, 194
United States (US) 11, 334
  9/11 terrorist attacks 17
  and Apartheid 189
  China–US relationship 102
  Cold War 11, 68, 69, 72
  Commission on United States–Latin American Relations 179
  Fairness Doctrine overturned 54
  fractured globalisation 12
  Goals 2000
    Educate America Act 410
  Holocaust Memorial Museum 406, 412, 419
  homonationalism 156
  hypocrisy 69
  Indian diaspora 360, 364
  political polarisation 34
  political propaganda in the age of Trump 55
  presidential election 2008 302
  presidential election 2016 29, 390, 411
  propaganda education 406
  Senate Select Committee on Intelligence (SSCI) 42
  Think Again, Turn Away initiative 266
Universal Declaration of Human Rights 202
university
  Laos 378
Urry, J. 288
Urumqi riots 2009 290
Urumqi South Station terrorist attack 261
us/them dichotomy 310
Uyghurs 257, 261, 262, 266, 268, 290
Uys, P.-D. (Eva Bezuidenhout) 191, 192, 195

Vajpayee, A.B. 364
values 390
  clashing 382
van der Zyl, M. 234
Van Zandt, S. 190
Varutti, M. 292
Verificado18 340, 341, 343
Victoria Harbour protest 147
Vietnam 188, 189, 373, 376, 377
Vietnam War 188
Viotty, S. 408
virtue 10, 245
virtuosity 23
Vishwa Hindu Parishad (World Hindu Council) 364
Visit, Benefit, and Gather programme 257,

260, 261, 262, 264, 266
visualisation 251
Vivekananda (N. Datta) 363
Vorster, J. 186
Vos, T.P. 392

Walker, C. 22
Walker, J. 230
Wallerstein, I. 15
Waltz, K. 12
Wang Chunxing 263
Wang, H. 163
Wanless, A. 257
Wardle, C. 28, 405
Ware, J. 233
Washington Post 1
Washington Star 189
We Will Not Remain Silent 262
'weaponisation' of information 51
Web 2.0 technologies 320
Webb, B. 227
Weinberger, S. 42
Weizmann, C. 226
Welch, D. 3, 52, 199
WhatsApp
  India 354
  Mexico 354
Wikileaks 42
Wilby Conspiracy, The 191
Williamson, C. 229
Willsman, P. 229
Wilson, H. 226
Windrush scandal 217
Windrush ship 213
'with Chinese characteristics' 105
Witt, W. 161
Wojcieszak, M.E. 83
Wolff, M. 54
women
  representation of ethnic minorities in China 285
  young women 253
Women Against Violent Extremism (WAVE) 283
'Work of the Labour Party's Governance and Legal Unit in relation to antisemitism, 2014-2019' ('Formby' report) 236
world system theory 15
World Trade Organization (WTO) 16, 105
Woza Albert! 189
'Wreathgate' 231
Wren, M. 206
writing loyalty-pledging statements 265
Wylie, C. 43

Xe Pian Xe Namnoy hydroelectric power station 377, 384
Xi Jinping 117, 127, 259
  media convergence as national strategy 119
  narratives promoted by 98
  strategy for digital propaganda 127
Xinjiang Uyghur Autonomous Region (XUAR) 257
Xinwen Lianbo 146, 147, 148, 155
Xu Lin 135
Xuexi Qiangguo ('Study to Make China Strong') 122

Yalvaç, F. 9
Yanukovych, V. 70
'Yes We Can' slogan 301, 302
yoga 362
Yohan, L. 379
young women 253
youth participatory politics 407
YouTube 249, 354
  propaganda education in Finland 415

Zaharna, R. 197, 198, 199, 202, 203, 209
Zawahiri, A. Al- 250
Zee network 366
Zee TV 365
Zetter, R. 200
Zhang, X. 113
Zheng Bijian 109
Zimbardo, P. 173
Zionism 225
Zito, S. 391
Zuboff, S. 42, 169